Business Logistics Management

A Supply Chain Perspective

THIRD EDITION

WESSEL J. PIENAAR
and **JOHN J. VOGT**

OXFORD
UNIVERSITY PRESS

SOUTHERN AFRICA

Oxford University Press Southern Africa (Pty) Ltd

Vasco Boulevard, Goodwood, Cape Town, Republic of South Africa
P O Box 12119, N1 City, 7463, Cape Town, Republic of South Africa

Oxford University Press Southern Africa (Pty) Ltd is a subsidiary of
Oxford University Press, Great Clarendon Street, Oxford OX2 6DP.

The Press, a department of the University of Oxford, furthers the University's objective of
excellence in research, scholarship, and education by publishing worldwide in

Oxford New York

Auckland Cape Town Dar es Salaam Hong Kong Karachi
Kuala Lumpur Madrid Melbourne Mexico City Nairobi
New Delhi Shanghai Taipei Toronto

With offices in

Argentina Austria Brazil Chile Czech Republic France Greece
Guatemala Hungary Italy Japan Poland Portugal Singapore South Korea
Switzerland Turkey Ukraine Vietnam

Oxford is a registered trade mark of Oxford University Press
in the UK and in certain other countries

Published in South Africa
by Oxford University Press Southern Africa (Pty) Ltd, Cape Town

Business Logistics Management: A Supply Chain Perspective
Third edition
ISBN 978 0 19 598652 5

© Oxford University Press Southern Africa (Pty) Ltd 2009

The moral rights of the author have been asserted
Database right Oxford University Press Southern Africa (Pty) Ltd (maker)

Third edition published 2009

All rights reserved. No part of this publication may be reproduced,
stored in a retrieval system, or transmitted, in any form or by any means,
without the prior permission in writing of Oxford University Press Southern Africa (Pty) Ltd,
or as expressly permitted by law, or under terms agreed with the appropriate
designated reprographics rights organization. Enquiries concerning reproduction
outside the scope of the above should be sent to the Rights Department,
Oxford University Press Southern Africa (Pty) Ltd, at the address above.

You must not circulate this book in any other binding or cover
and you must impose this same condition on any acquirer.

Publishing manager: Alida Terblanche
Assistant commissioning editor: Marisa Montemarano
Managing editor: Lisa Andrews
Editor: Mark Ronan
Indexer: Adrienne Pretorius
Designer: Samantha Rowles
Ilustrator: Richard Commin
Cover design: Judith Cross
Indexer: Adrienne Pretorius
Cover photo: iStockphoto

Set in Electra LT Std 9 pt on 12 pt by Barbara Hirsch
Printed and bound by ABC Press, Cape Town
111252

Acknowledgements
The authors and publisher gratefully acknowledge permission to reproduce copyright material
in this book. Every effort has been made to trace copyright holders, but if any copyright
infringements have been made, the publisher would be grateful for information that would
enable any omissions or errors to be corrected in subsequent impressions.

Contents

Contributors vi

Preface vii

1 Introduction to business logistics
(W.J. Pienaar) 1
Introduction 1
Business logistics in a macroeconomic perspective 2
Evolution of the concept of logistics 5
Emergence of logistics in a business context 5
The concepts of logistics and supply chain management 8
Business logistics activities 11
Conclusion 15

2 Competitive advantage created by logistics
(W.J. Pienaar) 19
Introduction 19
Logistics linkages with the value chain 19
The value-added role of logistics 22
Customer service 25
Aspects of competitive advantage 29
Wealth creation through logistics 30
Conclusion 31

3 Logistics and supply chain strategy planning
(J. Louw) 34
Introduction 34
What do strategy and strategic management mean? 35
Organisational strategy 36
The strategy formulation process 37
Developing a logistics and supply chain strategy 39
Implementing a logistics and supply chain strategy 48
Conclusion 50

4 Tactical logistics management and supply chain integration
(W.J. Pienaar) 56
Introduction 56
Tactical logistics activities 56
Managing the goods flow 57
Product supply chain processes 59
Time management in supply chains 66
Conclusion 73

5 Financial aspects of logistics and supply chain management
(W.J. Pienaar) 76
Introduction 76
Shareholder value 76
Cost of equity 77
Free cash flow 78
Economic value added 78
Value drivers 79
Return on investment 82
Logistics costing and activity-based costing 84
Marginal costing 86
Cost-volume-profit analysis 90
Worked examples 94

6 Forecasting supply chain requirements
(W.J. Pienaar) 104
Introduction 104
Features of forecasting 105
Types of forecasting 106
Long-term and short-term forecasting 107
The forecasting process 107
Selecting appropriate forecasting techniques 108
Validating forecasting models 111
Techniques for stationary time series data 112
Techniques for forecasting time series data with a trend 120
Forecasting seasonality 125
Example of the forecasting process 128
Conclusion 134
Appendix 138

7 Network integration
(J. Louw) 144
Introduction 144
Network integration and supply chain design 145
Supply chain configuration and functional requirements 147

The stages of supply chain design and
implementation ... 149
Factors to take into account in supply
chain design ... 157
Modelling approaches ... 159
Conclusion ... 163

8 Production and operations management
(J. van Eeden) **167**
Introduction ... 167
Strategic and planning concepts ... 170
Quality management ... 178
Inventory management ... 182
Operations management: current approaches
and philosophies ... 184
Operations management in the service sector ... 188
Conclusion ... 189

9 Procurement management
(W.J. Pienaar) **193**
Introduction ... 193
The objectives of procurement management ... 193
The strategic role of procurement within a
business ... 195
Tiers of procurement management ... 196
The nature and classification of purchased
products ... 197
Selecting and developing suppliers ... 200
Procurement-related activities that enhance
supply chain success ... 204
Procurement cost management ... 205
Electronic procurement ... 207
Conclusion ... 209

10 Inventory management
(J.N. Cronjé) **213**
Introduction ... 213
The purpose of inventory ... 214
Types of inventories ... 216
Important inventory concepts ... 218
Inventory costs ... 220
Inventory planning ... 223
Inventory control ... 240
Conclusion ... 244

11 The design of storage and handling facilities
(J. Vogt) **250**
Introduction ... 250
Initial requirements ... 251
Sizing the warehouse ... 252
Operations and warehouse management
systems ... 253
The design process ... 253
Fire ... 262
Security ... 263
Lighting ... 264
Conclusion ... 264

12 Packaging and containerisation
(U. Kussing and P. Kilbourn) **267**
Introduction ... 267
Definition and functions of packaging ... 267
The role of packaging in logistics ... 269
Marketing ... 271
Development of packaging solutions ... 272
Containerisation ... 276
Integrating technology with packaging and
containerisation ... 279
Packaging: a supply chain perspective ... 281
Conclusion ... 282

13 Equipment used in facilities
(J. Vogt) **285**
Introduction ... 285
Selection of equipment ... 285
Risks involved in purchasing equipment ... 286
Storage methods for small items ... 286
Pallets and their storage ... 289
Hanging rail systems ... 293
Moving loads ... 294
Moving and sorting ... 296
Containers ... 298
Conclusion ... 300

14 The operation of a warehouse
(J. Vogt) **302**
Introduction ... 302
Warehouse processes ... 302
Errors in operation ... 304
Stock management ... 304
Types of warehouses and facilities ... 305
Cross-dock operations ... 305

Efficiency in a warehouse ... 308
Processes and operations ... 309
Delivery-transport operations ... 317
Bar coding, scanning and radio frequency identification technology ... 317
The challenge of managing continuous change ... 319
Lean and six sigma operations ... 320
Safety ... 321
Conclusion ... 321

15 The transport system
(W.J. Pienaar) **323**
Introduction ... 323
Operational characteristics of the various modes of freight transport ... 324
Terminals ... 330
Goods carried in the transport system ... 331
Freight transport service providers ... 333
The freight transport user ... 335
Government as stakeholder in the transport system ... 336
Conclusion ... 337

16 Transport cost structures and pricing principles
(W.J. Pienaar) **341**
Introduction ... 341
Efficiency in transport ... 341
Economies of scale ... 341
Competition within modes of transport ... 344
Cost structures of the different transport modes ... 347
Cost trade-offs in transport ... 352
Profit planning and control ... 355
Tariff quoting ... 356
Conclusion ... 358

17 Transport management
(W.J. Pienaar) **362**
Introduction ... 362
Strategic transport management ... 363
Tactical transport management ... 368
Principles of efficient operational transport management ... 373
Conclusion ... 379

18 Managing international supply chains
(W.J. Pienaar and J. Vogt) **383**
Introduction ... 383
Distribution channels ... 383
Transporting goods internationally ... 386
International trade ... 392
Customs departments ... 394
Security issues ... 394
Free-trade agreements and free-trade zones ... 396
International trade information requirements ... 397
International trade documentation ... 398
Data to be submitted for international movement ... 403
International commercial terms ... 404
Conclusion ... 414
Incoterms 2000: a visual guide ... 418
Appendix ... 420

19 Product returns and reverse logistics management
(U. Kussing and W.J. Pienaar) **421**
Introduction ... 421
The role of reverse logistics within the product returns management process ... 421
Product returns management: scope and activities ... 422
The impacts of reverse logistics ... 426
Product returns and reverse logistics processes ... 429
Logistics and the environment ... 431
Closed-loop supply chains ... 433
Conclusion ... 434

20 Controlling logistics performance
(U. Kussing) **438**
Introduction ... 438
The process of control ... 439
The concept of quality ... 442
Performance measurement ... 444
Benchmarking ... 450
The SCOR model ... 453
Business intelligence ... 455
Conclusion ... 456

Index ... **460**

Contributors

Wessel Pienaar is Professor and Head of the Department of Logistics at Stellenbosch University. He has obtained the following advanced degrees: MEcon in Transport Economics (Stellenbosch University); MS (Eng) (University of California, Berkeley); DComm in Transport Economics (Unisa); PhD (Eng) in Civil Engineering (Stellenbosch University). In 2000, he received the Rector's Award for Outstanding Research at Stellenbosch University. He is a rated researcher at the National Research Foundation. He serves on the board of the South African Academy for Science and Art. He has also published in German, French and Russian.

John Vogt holds a PhD in Logistics (Stellenbosch University), an MBL (Unisa) and a BSc (Eng) (University of the Witwatersrand). He has a wide range of international experience and industry knowledge. He is currently the global logistics director for an international oil and gas services company. He has consulted in the supply chain field with his own consulting company. Prior to that, he was a senior executive for a major forwarding company, leading its logistics division and supplying third- and fourth-party services to the paper, aluminium, automotive, apparel and chemical industries.

Kobus Cronjé is Associate Professor in Transport Economics and Logistics Management at the North-West University. He has more than 20 years' experience in curriculum development and teaching both undergraduate and postgraduate courses. Professor Cronjé has developed practical logistics courses for the industry nationally and internationally, delivered a number of conference papers and been involved in numerous transport and logistics reports.

Peter Kilbourn obtained his BCom, BCom (Hons) and MCom degrees from the Rand Afrikaans University. He is a senior lecturer and logistics management subject head at the University of Johannesburg. He teaches logistics management at undergraduate and postgraduate levels and has been involved in various extracurricular and industry training programmes in logistics management.

Ulrike Kussing is a supply chain strategist at UTi. Her work involves strategic value assessments, supply chain modelling, redesign and optimisation. She is an expert in supply chain modelling software and has worked on projects in several industries, including the automotive, FMCG and consumer electronics sectors. Before joining UTi, she lectured in Quantitative Management and Logistics Management at Stellenbosch University.

Johan Louw holds a BEng (Industrial) (University of Pretoria), an MBA (Potchefstroom University) and a PhD in Logistics (Stellenbosch University). He is the Subject Head of Logistics Management at the Department of Logistics, Stellenbosch University. He teaches in the Logistics and Supply Chain Management programme, and supervises postgraduate students. His research interests are supply chain strategy, planning, design and competency development.

Joubert van Eeden holds BEng (Elec), MSc (Eng) (Industrial) and MBA degrees and teaches Project Management and Operations Management at Stellenbosch University. He is involved in research with several large institutions in South Africa. His research interests are transportation demand modelling, operations management and the effective use of enterprise resource planning systems.

Preface

How does one ensure that the goods demanded by the client are at the designated place, at the right time, in the required condition and quantity and at the right price? Why has coordination of the supply chain become so crucial in logistics management? How does consistent order fulfilment enable competitive advantage? How do recent advances in logistics technology and the freer exchange of information impact on business? These are the tenets of this new edition of Business Logistics Management – A Supply Chain Perspective.

In most countries economic life from the late 1970s to the early 1990s was marked by rapid change. First, the economic deregulation of freight transport and agricultural produce marketing, combined with the liberalisation of international trade and the end of trade sanctions against South Africa made transport decision making more market-driven. Second, the development of effective information technology, widespread electronic communications, the ability to perform comprehensive and complicated analyses through the use of computer technology and new holistic management approaches have made it possible to manage logistics channels and other complicated processes in an integrated and coordinated fashion, almost in real time.

Increasing business competition and more sophisticated consumer service requirements led to the realisation that product competitiveness would henceforth be determined more through logistically arranged product supply chains, rather than through individual firms operating in isolation. Successful supply chain management requires that decisions reached on strategic, tactical and operational levels must be founded quantitatively, mainly because of the various cost trade-offs and process coordination involved in the logistics decision-making process.

These trends convinced the University of Stellenbosch to introduce Logistics Management as an undergraduate and postgraduate field of study with effect from 1992. Subsequently other tertiary institutions followed suit from the mid-1990s onwards. Today, Logistics/Supply Chain Management is taught at several tertiary teaching institutions in South Africa.

The public sector and private business management alike are currently benefiting from developments in logistics. In addition, modern computer systems make it possible for organisations to continuously improve all their logistics activities. Organisations can now hold smaller inventories, and transport systems are effectively linked to their operations. Modern computerised warehouses and handling equipment are increasingly used and improved procurement systems developed to enhance the flow of materials from the raw-material stage through the logistics chain to the end-user. Advanced logistics activities make it possible for organisations to manage their incoming and outgoing goods and service flows more efficiently. This has a positive effect on customer service and ultimately on maximising revenue and wealth. The same contemporary logistics principles apply equally to public and non-governmental organisations and private trading enterprises.

To some extent, logistics/supply chain management is still an emerging field of study – there are not many second-generation logistics and supply chain managers in practice; the majority are of the first generation trained in the field, while some have moved into this field from other functional areas, namely procurement and supply management, inventory and warehouse management, production and operations management, transport and distribution management and marketing management.

For this reason this book has been structured so that it can be used at universities, universities of technology, business schools and vocational training providers in the tertiary sector. It is believed that the lecturer/instructor can select and combine the assessment material in the instructor's manual in such a way that the book will meet the teaching objectives and outcomes at junior undergraduate, senior undergraduate and postgraduate levels. The following course outlines are suggested:

Comprehensive year course in supply chain management: the whole book.

Junior undergraduate year course in logistics management: the whole book, excluding Chapters 5; 6 and 8.

Senior undergraduate and postgraduate year course in logistics management: the whole book, excluding Chapter 8.

Procurement/materials management: Chapters 1–10; 14; 17; 20.

Distribution management: Chapters 1–7; 10; 12 and 14–20.

Operations and production management: Chapters 1; 4 and 5–13.

Storage and inventory management: Chapters 1; 4; 6 and 10–14.

Ancillary material – including an Instructor's Manual containing a case study chapter and a brand-new set of PowerPoint slides – is available to lecturers prescribing the book (on CD and the Oxford University Press website: www.oxford.co.za).

A special word of appreciation goes to Marisa Montemarano, Lisa Andrews and Mark Ronan, our Oxford University Press team, who are highly professional – and three very effective 'logisticians'. Special thanks are due to Professor Leon Loxton for technical input with Chapter 5 to ensure that the chapter conforms to the latest international financial reporting standards, and to Professor Hannelie Nel for technical input with Chapter 6 to ensure that the chapter can be applied using Microsoft Excel 2007.

Wessel Pienaar
John Vogt

1 Introduction to business logistics

W.J. Pienaar

> **Learning outcomes**
>
> After you have studied this chapter, you should be able to:
> - describe why there is a need for logistics as a business system;
> - explain the need for logistics management as a teaching discipline;
> - describe the evolution of the concept of logistics;
> - explain how logistics emerged in the context of business;
> - describe the concepts of supply chain management, logistics management, the systems – or total-cost approach – and systems analysis;
> - understand the difference between a logistics approach and a logistics system;
> - describe what is meant by strategic, tactical and operational logistics management; and
> - give a brief account of the various activities of business logistics.

1.1 Introduction

No region on earth is singly capable of providing all the products to satisfy everybody's material needs. There is invariably a spatial and temporal separation between where the natural resources for production occur and where most people live. Similarly, there is a time gap between when production is feasible and when people need or desire to consume certain products. Adequate quantities of desired goods can either be collected wherever and whenever they are available, or alternatively, they can be stored and delivered to people where and when they demand them.

Sustained economic growth and development are dependent on the continued improvement of production efficiencies and the profitable exchange, or trade, of goods, services and information. Profitable trade presupposes local surplus production of those goods that might be more efficiently produced in a region in exchange for goods produced more efficiently elsewhere. This prerequisite level of comparatively or relatively advantageous efficiency stems from the economies of scale achievable from productive regional specialisation, division of labour, development of skills and large-scale production.

> To maximise a region's net gain in wealth created through local economies of scale and comparative efficiency requires effectively integrated and co-ordinated transport and storage systems, known as business logistics systems.

Product supply chains need not only to be planned, organised and controlled with a reasoned, scientific logistics approach, but must also be supported by efficient, effective physical logistics systems.

The application of a reasoned, systematic logistics approach within product supply chains and the management of business logistics systems so that customers are provided consistently with the desired quality and required quantity of products, where and when they are needed, at an acceptable cost, are the topics of this book.

By the early 1970s, all the industrialised nations had well-developed road networks, providing access to property and enabling commercial road transport to offer a fair degree of market coverage. Compared to rail, road transport offers more logistics-friendly attributes. These include shorter door-to-door transit times; greater flexibility; better accessibility; superior reliability; greater frequency of collection and delivery; better goods security; lower barriers to market entry and the opportunity of being better in control of goods during transit. Such factors led to less dependency of shippers on government-protected rail transport and, at the same time, gave rise to an increase in demand for road transport. Furthermore, the use of standard-size intermodal freight containers first came into widespread use in the 1970s and has remained in widespread use internationally ever since. This enabled the swift transhipment, or changing the means of transport, of containerised consignments between container vessels, road-freight vehicles and rail wagons.

During the early 1970s, the general view prevailed that because of i) economies of scale, ii) the need to protect rail carriers, and iii) the potential for serious market failure, it was in the public interest to regulate freight transport through economic control. However, the operational business requirements of industrialised and trading nations called for liberalisation and reform. These came about from the late 1970s onwards. The new viewpoint that was taking root was that regulatory failures are often more damaging than market failures.

Economic life in most countries from the late 1970s to the early 1990s was marked by rapid change. This was facilitated and fuelled by two main driving forces: the emergence of freer competition both within domestic borders and internationally, and swift advances in technology.

First, the emergence of more open market conditions was made possible mainly by the economic deregulation of both freight transport and the marketing of agricultural produce; the privatisation of many utility industries; the globalisation of business activities and the liberalisation of international trade. South Africa also benefited by the lifting of trade sanctions. The effect was to make transport decision making and the distribution of goods more market-driven.

Next, the introduction of specialised bulk-cargo ships, container vessels and high-capacity cargo aircraft; the development of effective information technology and easy electronic communications; the ability to perform comprehensive, complex numerical analyses through the use of information technology and new holistic management approaches have all made it possible to manage logistically arranged supply channels in an integrated, coordinated fashion – almost in real time.

In the 1980s, increasing business competition and more sophisticated consumer service requirements led to the realisation that product competitiveness would henceforth be determined more through logistically arranged product supply chains, rather than through individual firms operating in isolation. These trends led to the introduction of logistics management as a major field of study at tertiary educational institutions internationally since the 1980s.[1]

1.2 Business logistics in a macroeconomic perspective

The physical components of South Africa's gross domestic product (GDP), namely, the outputs of primary-sector production and secondary-sector manufacturing, require the carriage and storage of approximately 803 million tons of goods annually.[2] These are divided as shown in Table 1.1.

Table 1.1 Physical components of South Africa's GDP, 2006

Sector	Tonnage (million)	
Mining	500	62%
Agriculture	40	5%
Subtotal primary	540	67%
Manufacturing	263	33%
Total	803	100%

During 2006, the total logistics cost for South Africa that relates to these outputs amounted to R274 billion, or 15,7 per cent of the country's GDP. The various elements of these costs are transport; storage; ports; management; administration; profits; and inventory carrying (i.e. opportunity cost of inventory). The primary sector incurs 48 per cent of these costs and the secondary (i.e. manufacturing) sector 52 per cent.

Table 1.2 Logistics costs associated with the physical components of South Africa's GDP

Logistics cost elements	Primary (R billion)	Secondary (R billion)	Total (R billion)
Transport	78	79	157
Storage and ports	21	18	39
Management, administration and profits	23	25	48
Inventory-carrying costs	10	20	30
Total	132	142	274

Table 1.3 South Africa's logistics cost as a percentage of GDP (compared to the USA)

Year	USA (% of GDP)	South Africa (% of GDP)
2003	8,6	16,7
2004	8,8	16,5
2005	9,4	16,2
2006	9,9	15,7

South Africa's logistics cost compared to that of the USA (which was 9,9 per cent of GDP in 2006) and compared to other OECD countries (9,0 per cent of GDP in 2006) is high, but it has been possible to reduce it over the last few years.

The biggest driver of logistics costs in South Africa, i.e. transport costs (57 per cent of logistics costs), compares poorly with the global figure (38 per cent) and the USA's proportion of transport costs to logistics costs, i.e. 49 per cent. The US figure is also high, but this is supported by a highly densified economy, although current and future energy and environmental challenges could also be expected for the USA. South Africa's spatial challenges are exceptional for such a relatively small economy and derive from the fact that the industrial heartland is far from the coast.

Figures 1.1 and 1.2 illustrate the distribution of the 329 billion ton-kilometres that are required to keep South Africa's economy going and the relative challenges compared to transport inputs of global competitors.

Corridor transport refers to long-distance movement between industrial centres; primary

Figure 1.1 Typologies of freight transport in South Africa

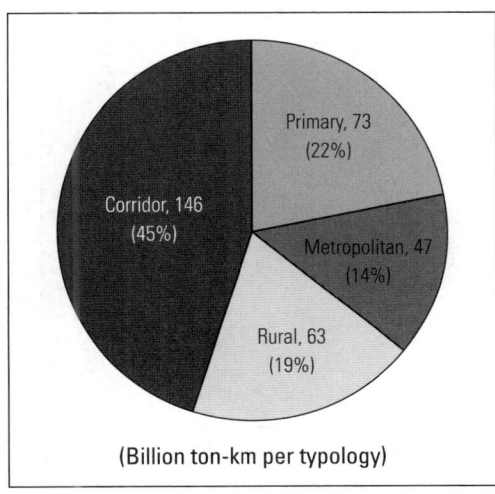

(Billion ton-km per typology)

Figure 1.2 South Africa as a percentage of the world

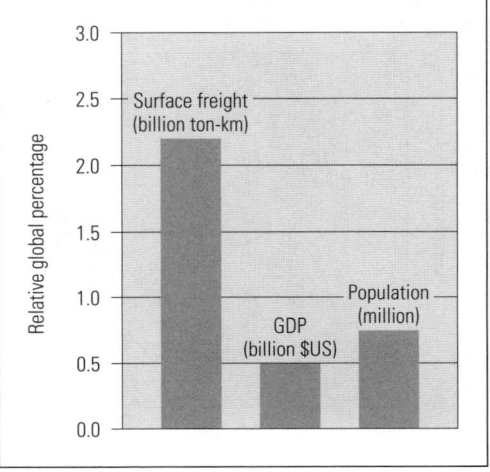

transport is the export of mining commodities through specialised export systems (unfortunately, also far from the ports of export); rural transport is low-density movement in rural areas; and metropolitan transport represents urban movement in the major industrial areas. The long-haul corridors in South Africa, especially between Cape Town, Gauteng and Durban, make distribution inordinately difficult in all sectors. This means that relatively low-value primary mining and agricultural commodities have to be transported over long distances to points of beneficiation, thereby attracting logistics charges that increase the cost of these commodities by much more than would be expected. In the secondary sector of the economy manufactured products require an extensive network of intermediary and final distribution centres, which are difficult to manage because these centres were not created around specific logistics hubs, and they are not served by efficient long-haul transport. Even highly densified long-haul corridors are mostly served by road transport, and in urban areas deliveries face congestion. In rural areas the government has the objective of developing 30 per cent of the approximately 3 million subsistence farmers into commercial farmers. However, these targeted agricultural development areas are also far removed from points of consumption, with little supporting logistics infrastructure to support this drive.

A mere 1 per cent reduction in logistics costs would save South Africa approximately R2,74 billion per annum in 2008 terms. If effective logistics education and training could contribute, say, 10 per cent of such an efficiency improvement, the value of offering the discipline of logistics management could be said to be worth at least R274 million per annum for the country's economy.

The Supplychainforesight report for 2008 demonstrated that there is a significant correlation between supply chain reform and business success.[3] The report is the result of a countrywide survey that obtained more than 400 responses from major South African industrial companies. From the survey results, companies were grouped into four quadrants (illustrated in Figures 1.3 and 1.4) by considering measures of the complexity of their value chains and their capability of dealing with that complexity.

On the complexity axis, companies were rated in terms of their involvement in the product supply activities of procurement; manufacturing operations; sales; and extent of global marketing. On the capability axis, companies were rated in terms of their relative competitiveness, based on factors such as product innovation; time to market; manufacturing flexibility; logistics effectiveness; and supply chain reliability. The business success indicators used related to profitability; revenue growth; market share growth; and customer retention.

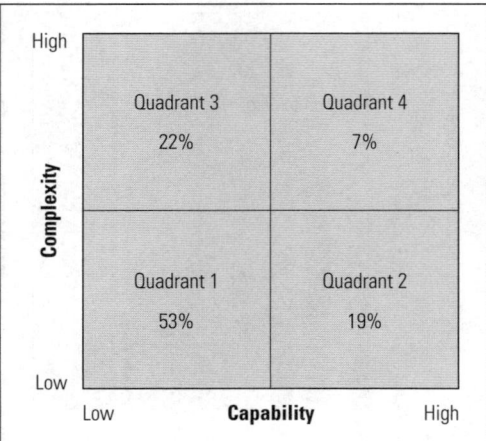

Figure 1.3 Distribution of companies according to the complexity and capability indices

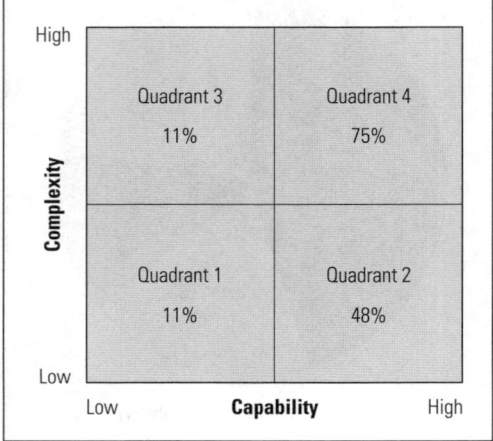

Figure 1.4 Percentage of companies per quadrant reporting greater success than competitors

The study showed that 75 per cent of all companies that fall in the high complexity-high capability quadrant (quadrant 4) rate themselves as more successful than their competitors. Quadrant 4 represents only 7 per cent of companies surveyed. On the opposite end of the scale, quadrant 1 (low complexity supply chains with companies of low capability) represents 53 per cent of the sample, but only 11 per cent view themselves as more successful than their competitors. For quadrant one companies an immediate objective should be to improve efficiencies in their supply chains in order to improve their level of competitiveness. It is, therefore, clear that there is, firstly, a great need for effective logistics education and training in South Africa and, secondly, a desperate need for more advanced and successful management of logistics and product supply chain processes in the country.

Not only focusing on the traditional supply chain objectives of cost reduction and service enhancement, quadrant 4 companies place a strong focus on improving information visibility and integrating their logistics functions. The major challenges to meet the stated objectives (as faced by the quadrant 4 companies) relate to the diverse needs of customers, planning and forecasting capabilities and integrating their logistics functions. In the quadrant 4 category, the logistics and supply chain management capabilities of companies are appropriate for dealing with the complexities they face in their value chains.

1.3 Evolution of the concept of logistics

The word 'logistics' is derived from the Greek adjective, *logistikos*, which means 'skilled in calculating', relating to arithmetic or 'concerned with reason'. The adjective is derived from the verb, *logizomai*, meaning 'to calculate, to reason' or 'to think'. The verb is based on the word *logos*, which is translated as 'reason', 'word' or 'discourse', depending on the context.

The Greek *logistikos* entered the main European languages via the Low Latin *logisticus*, which became *logistique* in French. In 1611, the noun *logistique* was used with reference to the four basic processes of arithmetic and algebra (adding, subtracting, multiplying and dividing). In 1765, the adjective, *logistique*, meaning 'with reference to calculation', was derived from this noun.[4]

The introduction of the word *logistique* – recognised by the French Academy in 1840[5] – to describe the art of combining and coordinating the quartering, means of transport, supplying and supporting of troops through reasoning by calculation during a military campaign is attributed to Antoine Henri, Baron of Jomini. Jomini served as a brigadier general in Napoleon's army. He first used the word in 1836 in this context in his seminal work *Précis de l'art de la guerre* (Summary of the art of war).[6, 7]

In line with the meaning that Jomini attached to the word logistics, Plowman[8] comments as follows:

'Logistics, a plural word derived from logistic, means, in military science, the planning and handling and implementation of personnel, also the related material, facilities, and other factors. Thus logistics means the application of reasoning, especially mathematical analysis and synthesis, to the complex and inter-related problems of coordinating manpower and supplies and barracks. Military logistics is a major factor in making it possible for an army to march and fight and win its battles. Defined thus, military logistics includes the interrelated and largely mathematical procedures, and the resulting coordinating decisions.'

1.4 Emergence of logistics in a business context

After the devastation caused in western Europe during the World War II, Jomini's legacy of military logistics gave birth to what later became known as business logistics. The war crippled much of western Europe's infrastructure and capital stock. Furthermore, huge areas of farmland that became battlefields during the war were not readily available for agricultural activities. Similarly, large industrial centres were demolished by ruinous bombardments from the air and the impact of artillery fire.

Once the hostilities ended in 1945, the economic reconstruction of western Europe began. Experts specialising in different fields of logistics, systems analysis and operations research, who were no longer needed for warfare, were employed in this reconstruction and revitalisation. The countries involved in this regional effort were Belgium, France, West Germany, Italy, Luxembourg and the Netherlands.

The efforts to revive this region were intense and concerted. It was deemed imperative that primary production, secondary manufacturing and tertiary service delivery had to be redeveloped swiftly in order for western Europe to regain economic self-sufficiency. The restoration – and even improvement on previous standards – of local and intra-regional accessibility and mobility was afforded precedence, as it was clear that western Europe's recovery would best be served through cooperation, regional specialisation, intra-regional sourcing and the creation of a common market. The catalyst to achieve this was putting into operation an effective logistics system derived from the military model. Within the region logistics chains emerged as if no international borders existed.

The abovementioned six countries established the European Community (EC) as a regional organisation in 1958 through the Treaty of Rome. The treaty provided for the gradual elimination of intra-regional customs duties and other trade barriers; the establishment of a common external tariff against other countries; the gradual integration of a common agricultural policy and guarantees of free movement of labour, capital and physical resources.[9] By this time, coordinated logistics practice had taken root in western Europe. The strategy of constructing and coordinating logistically arranged product supply channels that linked points of primary production within regions of specialisation with points of end consumption and use was well developed.

The French Academy recognised the use of the word 'logistics' in a business context (in addition to its traditional military meaning) in 1960 and attached the following meaning to the word: 'All means and methods of organising a service, a business and especially the flow of materials before, during and after production' (translated version).[10]

The first textbook outside Europe to suggest the benefits of coordinated logistics management appeared in 1961.[11] Although focused primarily on physical distribution management, i.e. management of the flow of products from manufacturing to the place of consumption or use, the book also refers to the flow of goods between the origin of resources and the place of product manufacture – recognisably based on the French interpretation of business logistics.

Ruppenthal,[12] the director of the first Annual Business Logistics Forum, held in 1962 at Stanford University, published the first comprehensive overview of business logistics, which placed the concept in context. He stated:

> 'No competent military commander would dream of mounting an offensive until he was reasonably assured of logistic support. The responsible general must know that supplies will be produced in adequate number, and that they will be available when and where they were needed. This important feature of availability has long been known as logistics – the physical movement of materials and supplies from the source of supply to the place of ultimate consumption.'

In business, too, the logistics function is an essential link – in this case, between production and marketing.

> Business logistics is concerned with the inbound movement of materials and supplies, and the outward movement of finished products. Its goal is the delivery of the finished products required by the marketing department to the point where they are needed, when they are needed, in the most economical fashion.

No modern business can afford to be broken up into discrete compartments. Instead, all departments are interrelated. It is this interdependence among the departments of modern business that is the subject of business logistics. To ignore business logistics – to ignore the indivisible nature of today's business enterprise – is to court extinction.

1.4.1 Logistics analysis and operations research

Successful business logistics practice requires that decisions reached must be quantitatively sound, mainly because of the various cost trade-offs, integration and coordination involved in the logistics decision-making process. The focus of integrated and coordinated management is the lowest total process cost, and not the achievement of the lowest cost of each function in the process.[13] This statement recalls the adage that 'sub-optimisation is the name of the devil'. Logistics analysis (or systems analysis) relies on operations research. Operations research can indeed be regarded as an indispensable analytical toolkit for the logistician. The principles of systems analysis and operations research are logically consistent. Therefore, an integrated logistics process with cross-functional coordination achieved through the application of operations research methodology should lead to better results than one lacking coordinated performance.[14]

Operations research is a practice-oriented numeric discipline with a systematic and scientific approach to finding the optimal solution to problems. These problems usually have a high degree of complexity, uncertainty and conflict. The discipline is a powerful tool in the hands of managers, enabling them to make decisions that are mathematically based. Research has shown that the following eight tools are the most important instruments in this analytical toolkit:

- Forecasting
- Analysis with simulation
- Rational decision making
- Facility location
- Route planning
- Inventory control
- Scheduling (of machines, production, vehicles, crews and projects)
- Application of queuing theory

Of these eight tools, professional logisticians should first and foremost possess the following five operations research competencies:

- Making rational decisions
- Forecasting
- Scheduling
- Determining routes for vehicles
- Controlling inventory levels

The five most important operations research techniques to achieve these competencies are:
- Linear programming
- Integer programming
- Feasibility analysis
- Transportation modelling
- Deterministic and probabilistic inventory modelling[15]

Systems analysis is a dynamic, methodological goal-driven, decision-making process that was developed and used by the allied forces during World War II in large, complex operations, which could only be executed successfully through military logistics efforts. Through systems analysis, various alternative solutions to a problem and approaches to an overall plan are considered to arrive at an acceptable system with optimum performance in terms of specific criteria. Ever since World War II, the systems approach has been successfully employed in the integrated solution of business logistic problems in which goods, service and information requirements (demand); productive capacity (supply); and the operating environment vary with time.

The systems analysis process entails seven consecutive steps:

Step 1: Define business objectives and determine the levels of logistics service needed to achieve them (problem identification).

Step 2: Gain an understanding of the present business environment and system (in which the logistics system will operate) through investigation, description and simulation of the status quo (systems modelling).

Step 3: Determine all technically feasible alternative logistics investment options and operating procedures (generating alternative solutions).

Step 4: Apply optimisation and assessment techniques in order to determine the most financially viable logistics investment options and operating procedures (evaluation).

Step 5: Choose from the most viable alternative logistics investment options and operating procedures (system selection).

Step 6: Organise and introduce the selected logistics facilities, equipment and procedure(s) (implementation).

Step 7: Formulate and apply appropriate performance measures in order to judge the success of the logistics execution (monitoring and review).

If monitoring and review show that the logistics system is not serving the stated business objectives successfully and/or not consistently meeting the requirements and expectations of the clients that it serves, it means that a system problem has emerged that requires rectification. Then the cycle of analysis will start again. The arrows depicting the direction of the flow in Figure 1.5 show that the systems analysis process has no definite cut-off point: as soon as a fresh problem emerges, the monitoring and reviewing phase takes the whole process back to the first stage of the analytical cycle.

1.5 The concepts of logistics and supply chain management

1.5.1 The relationship between logistics and supply chain management

The Council of Supply Chain Management Professionals (CSCMP), the major supply chain management and logistics organisation in the USA, defines logistics management as 'that part of supply chain management that plans, implements, and controls the efficient, effective forward and reverse flow and storage of goods, services and related information between the point of origin and the point of consumption in order to meet customers' requirements'.[16]

According to the CSCMP:

'Supply chain management encompasses the planning and management of all activities involved in sourcing and procurement, conversion, and all logistics management activities. Importantly, it also includes co-ordination and collaboration with channel partners, which can be suppliers, intermediaries, third-party service providers, and customers. In essence, supply chain management integrates supply and demand management within and across companies.'[17]

Consistent with the CSCMP's definition, Palgrave describes supply chain management as follows:[18]

'The integrated managing and control of the flow of information, materials and services from the suppliers of the raw materials, through to the factories, warehouses and retailers, to the end customers. The benefits to an organisation involved in supply chain management should be lower inventory costs, higher quality and higher customer-service levels. These benefits will only be gained, however, if all those involved in the supply chain are conforming to the standards set.'

Logistics management is the performance required to move and position inventory throughout a supply chain (also called a value chain). It creates value by timing and positioning goods (i.e. raw materials, goods-in-process and finished goods). Logistics management is an integrating function that serves to link, coordinate and optimise the entire value chain as a continuous process, which is essential for effective supply chain connectivity.[19]

The broader concept of supply chain management is regarded by the CSCMP[20] as an integrating function with primary responsibility for linking major business functions and processes within and across firms into a cohesive business model. Supply chain management includes all logistics management activities as well as manufacturing operations. It drives the coordination of processes and activities in tandem with marketing, sales, product design, finance and information technology. (Aspects of applied marketing and practical sales are addressed in Chapters 2 and 4; financial aspects of product supply chains are covered in Chapter 5.)

Supply chain operations require managerial processes that span functional areas within individual firms and link trading partners and customers across organisational boundaries. Therefore, supply chain management is concerned with each firm's responsibility for and functional contribution to the chain. It does not purport to take possession of or completely control each participating firm or entity. The management focus is on what each partner or collaborator

CHAPTER 1 INTRODUCTION TO BUSINESS LOGISTICS

Figure 1.5 The coherence between systems analysis and logistics management

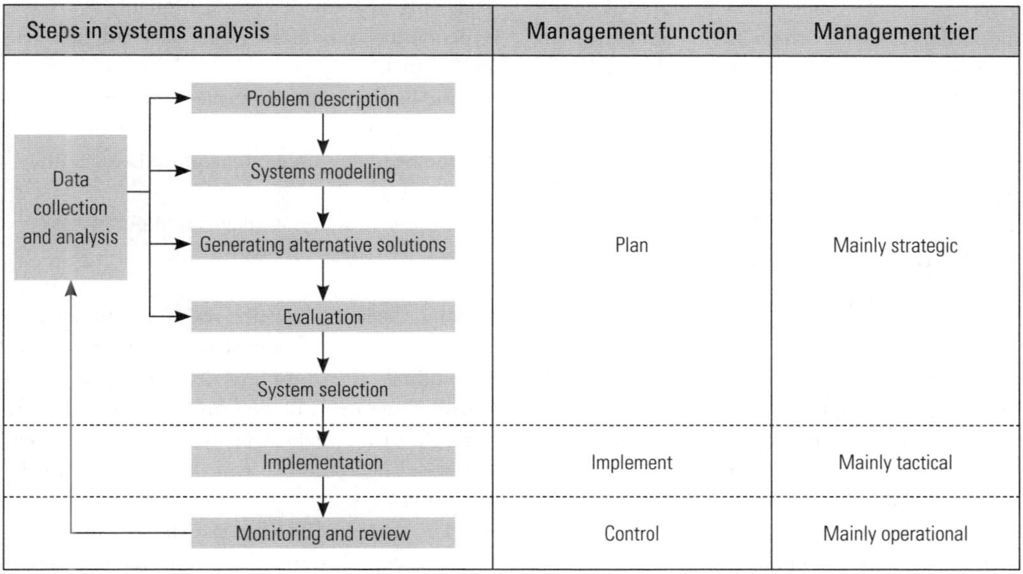

Steps in systems analysis	Management function	Management tier
Data collection and analysis → Problem description → Systems modelling → Generating alternative solutions → Evaluation → System selection	Plan	Mainly strategic
Implementation	Implement	Mainly tactical
Monitoring and review	Control	Mainly operational

brings to the party. A supply chain member may be a firm that participates in many other product supply or value chains. It is the participation, or the performance that each member is responsible for, which is managed and controlled.

> The supply chain, or value chain, are generic names of the process integration of different business activities in order to convert raw materials into finished products and to convey them to the end-user.

The supply chain may involve firms that extract raw materials or that conduct basic refinement or conversion of these raw materials. These materials are then passed on to a manufacturer which will turn them into usable parts or semi-processed goods. Parts and semi-processed goods are then converted into components, which, in turn, are assembled or processed into finished goods. These finished goods (i.e. tangible or physical products) may then pass through the hands of distributors and retailers before reaching the end-user or the consumer. Supply chains may involve several suppliers, different manufacturers and a related distribution system. Therefore, the supply chain incorporates all the costs, time, transport, storage and packaging that may be associated with the various stages of the process of conversion in order to supply a finished product.[21]

The process of converting resources into desired finished products (i.e. finished goods and services for which there is a demand) is the task of production and operations management. The ideal of production and operations management is to achieve the target production economy within an optimal balance of efficiency and effectiveness by developing manufacturing operations that increase flexibility and responsiveness while controlling unit cost and maintaining product quality. The following are some of the main activities of production and operations management:

- Plant and factory design
- Product design
- Manufacturing process design, operation and control (including lot sizing and time scheduling)
- Quality management

Production and operations management is the subject of Chapter 8.

Increasingly, nowadays, supply chains also take into account the return journey that many finished products undergo after having been used for a considerable time by the end-user. Therefore, a reverse supply chain often operates alongside the primary supply chain. This reverse system incorporates replacement parts; reusable packaging and other materials and their flow; and the disposal of waste and recycling of parts, components or whole products. The reverse system within product supply chains is addressed in Chapter 19.

1.5.2 Functions of logistics management

The CSCMP's definition of logistics management (quoted in the first paragraph of Section 1.5.1) is the generally accepted description of the concept in contemporary business logistics management literature. It is the standard definition used throughout this book. Some comments on this definition are in order.

First, as the definition indicates, logistics management is a subset of supply chain management and includes the actions required to a) prepare (plan); b) organise (implement); and c) execute (control) the activities of a firm when moving materials or finished products to customers. The planning and preparation activities include the selection of:

- facility sites (including type, number, location, size and capacity);
- durable equipment necessary for the flow of goods through the logistics network;
- distribution parties (including wholesalers, retailers and third-party service providers); and
- carriers (including choice of transport mode) necessary to offer services at the level demanded by customers to achieve the goals of the firm.

The organisational and implementation aspects of logistics include:
- the allocation and positioning of resources; and
- the fixing of production and distribution activities to respond to customer needs in an efficient manner in order to accomplish the firm's goals.

Execution includes operational aspects (such as routing of trips and scheduling of vehicles and crews) and control includes monitoring and reviewing performance (such as quality of service, expenditures, productivity and asset utilisation) to ensure that:

- the logistics process satisfies customers effectively;
- the firm's resources are deployed efficiently; and
- corrective action is taken when performance is not in line with goals.

Second, because logistics management revolves around planning, organising and executing/controlling the business logistics process, it encompasses many of the firm's activities, from the strategic to the tactical to the operational levels. Logistical decisions are typically classified in the following ways: [22, 23]

- The strategic level (i.e. preparation and planning) deals with decisions that have a long-lasting effect on the firm. Because data is often incomplete and imprecise, strategic decisions are generally based on aggregated data (obtained, for example, by grouping individual products into product families and aggregating individual customers into customer zones).
- The tactical level (i.e. organisation and implementation) includes decisions that are updated any time between once a month and once a year. Tactical decisions are often based on disaggregated data.
- The operational level (i.e. execution and control) refers to day-to-day decisions. Operational decisions are customarily based on very detailed data.

Third, an objective in logistics management is to be efficient and effective across the entire system. This objective can be achieved by minimising system-wide costs, from transport, materials handling and distribution, on the one hand, to warehousing and keeping inventory of raw materials, semi-finished goods and finished products on the other hand. This requires that a systems approach is followed whereby a product supply chain is analysed as a whole. Therefore, the emphasis is not on simply the cheapest or the fastest transport or reducing inventories, but rather on an integrated and coordinated systems approach to the logistics process. The integrated total-cost concept is the trade-off of all costs that are in conflict with each other and that can affect the outcome of a particular logistics decision. The acceptance of the systems approach, i.e. the total-cost logistics concept, has changed the relative importance of the different logistics activities and has led to cost trade-offs between transport/materials handling services and the operation of warehouse and production facilities assuming greater importance. For example, traditional wisdom dictates that materials can be handled most efficiently by using maximum-size mechanical means to reduce the number of moves needed for a given amount of material. While reducing the number of trips required is a good objective, the drawback of this approach is that it tends to support large production lots, large material handling equipment and large space requirements. Small unit loads allow for more responsive and less expensive material handling systems. Furthermore, continuous manufacturing flow processes necessitate the use of smaller unit loads.

1.5.3 The relationship between systems analysis and logistics management

The sequential steps in systems analysis and the coherence that exists between systems analysis and logistics management on the strategic, tactical and operational levels are illustrated in Figure 1.5. Logistics strategy (predominantly long-run planning) is discussed in Chapter 3; logistics organisation (i.e. tactical management) is addressed in Chapter 4; while control of logistics and supply chain operations is the topic of Chapter 20.

From the discussion above it is clear that business logistics management is a recurring and cyclical flow process within product supply chains. However, logistics can also be concerned with one-off events.

> The logistic arrangements relating to one-off events – referred to by some as event logistics – is formally known as project management. Project management entails the careful preparation, organisation, execution and control of a complicated event or operation so that it happens in an efficient and effective way.

In common parlance, logistics is perhaps most frequently thought of as the organisation and smooth execution of a complex operation. Regardless of whether the word is used in a military, recurring business flow, or one-off project context, the objective of logistics is to ensure that the desired inputs or products (i.e. goods and services) and information are made available to the client at the designated place and time, in the required condition and quantity and at an acceptable price.

1.6 Business logistics activities

The flow of goods, services and information between the point of origin and the point of consumption or application involves the following activities: demand forecasting; facility site selection and design; procurement; materials handling; packaging; warehouse management; inventory management; order processing; logistics communications; transport; reverse logistics (including return goods handling and waste disposal); and customer service.

The management of the goods flow and storage process between the point (or points) of origin of raw materials and the point where the materials are converted into finished goods is known as materials management (or inbound logistics). The management of the flow and storage of finished goods between the final point of manufacture and the point of consumption is known as physical distribution management (or outbound logistics).

> Return goods handling and waste disposal together form reverse logistics. Inbound logistics, outbound logistics and reverse logistics are collectively known as business logistics, or logistics management – the two terms are often used interchangeably.

Figure 1.6 Logistics and supply chain management comprise several activities

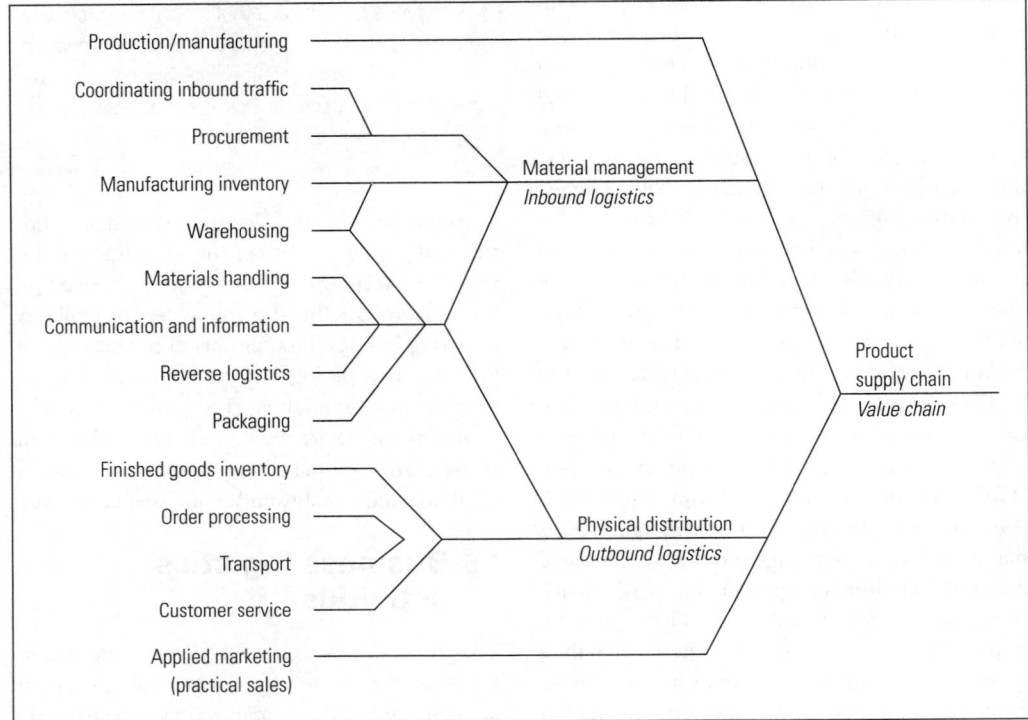

Logistics management, production management and applied marketing (i.e. practical sales) collectively constitute supply chain management. This coherence of activities is schematically illustrated in Figure 1.6. Systemic cohesion among the activities is achieved through integrated strategic, tactical and operational management, shown in Figure 1.5.

1.6.1 Demand forecasting

Demand forecasting is the process of determining the amount of product and related information that consumers will require in the future, either in the short or long term. This information is important for marketing, manufacturing and logistics management (i.e. for supply chain management as a whole).

Marketing forecasts of future demand determine promotional strategies, the allocation of sales-force efforts, pricing strategies, market research activities and manufacturing scheduling and sizing.

Manufacturing schedules determine acquisition strategies, plant inventory decisions and right-sizing production capacity in line with marketing forecasts.

Logistics management forecasts determine how much of each item manufactured by the firm needs to be transported to its various markets. Logistics management must also determine where the demand will occur so that appropriate volumes of goods can be made available in each market area. Knowledge of future demand levels enables logistics managers to plan for the activities needed to service that demand.

Forecasting supply chain requirements is the subject of Chapter 6.

1.6.2 Site selection and design of facilities

The type, layout, location, number and capacity of facilities are of strategic importance. The first consideration in selecting a site is the location

of the firm's various resources and markets. The placement of sales facilities near the firm's markets can improve customer service. Proper facility location can also allow lower total transport costs from the location of raw materials or primary producers through the logistics chain to the consumer. The needs of consumers and the location of raw materials and other resources are important when considering the inbound movement and storage of materials and the outbound product flows of a firm. The following are other important factors pertaining to site selection:
- Labour costs
- Transport costs
- Land and construction costs
- Property rates and taxes
- Availability and cost of utilities, services and infrastructure
- Security
- Legal concerns
- Local factors, such as the attitude of the community towards new industry

Facility site and design considerations form part of network integration and are addressed in Chapter 7.

1.6.3 Procurement

Procurement is the acquisition of goods, services and information to ensure that the firm's manufacturing and marketing processes operate effectively. The procurement function includes:
- Selecting resources and suppliers
- Determining the form in which the inputs are to be acquired
- Timing and coordination of the arrival of incoming goods
- Price negotiation
- Quality control of incoming goods

Procurement management is discussed in Chapter 9.

1.6.4 Materials handling

Materials handling is concerned with the (off-road) movement or flow of raw materials, semi-finished goods and finished goods at the facility's premises. Successful materials handling contributes towards smooth manufacturing operations; reduced inventory; reduced processing, storage and transhipment costs; and increased productivity within facilities. Materials handling as a function within warehouse management is dealt with in Chapters 13 and 14.

1.6.5 Packaging

Packaging performs two functions: marketing and logistics. As a marketing function, packaging acts as a form of promotion and advertising. Its size, mass, colour, appearance and printed information can attract attention and convey information about the product. From a logistics perspective, packaging serves a dual role. First, the package protects the product from damage and sometimes prevents potentially hazardous products from damaging other goods. Second, packaging can make it easier to store and move products, thereby lowering materials handling and distribution costs. Packaging is the subject of Chapter 12.

1.6.6 Warehouse management

Warehousing comprises the activities relating to managing the space needed to hold or maintain inventories. Goods must be stored for later sale and consumption unless customers need them immediately after production. Generally, the greater the time lag between production and consumption, the larger the quantity of inventory required. Specific warehouse management criteria include:
- Warehouse location, capacity and design
- Whether the storage facility should be owned or rented
- The level of mechanisation or automation
- Considerations regarding the mix of goods
- Security and maintenance
- Personnel training
- Productivity measurement
- Operational standards
- Range of services offered

Warehouse operations and management are the subject of Chapter 14.

1.6.7 Inventory management

Inventory management is a critical issue. The requirements for both manufacturing and marketing have to be met continuously. However, large volumes of inventory occupy capital-intensive warehouse space, while possession of the inventory itself requires financial sacrifice. The cost of warehouse space and the value of the inventory both have an opportunity cost. An optimal trade-off must be reached between this opportunity cost and the negative effects that result from stockouts. This illustrates again that accurate demand forecasting is important in order to satisfy customer needs without sacrificing efficiency. Inventory management is the topic of Chapter 10.

1.6.8 Order processing

Order processing is those activities associated with fulfilling consumers' orders. These include:
- Transmission of the order details to the sales section
- Verification of consumers' creditworthiness
- Transmission of the necessary packaging details to inventory-control staff for delivery to the dispatch section
- Preparation of the consignment documentation
- Communication of the order status, method of payment and delivery details to customers

The time span and accuracy of a firm's order processing are important determinants of the level of its customer service. Advanced automatic systems, such as electronic data interchange and electronic funds transfer, can reduce the time between order placement and delivery. Such systems, although initially expensive, can substantially improve both order-processing accuracy and response time. Savings in other logistics expenses, such as inventory control, transport and warehousing, or increased sales from improved customer service often justify the investment cost of the system. Value creation through effective order processing is addressed in Chapters 4, 9 and 10.

1.6.9 Logistics communications

Successful logistics requires the effective management of information and communications systems. Effective communication must take place between:
- the firm and its customers and clients;
- the firm and its suppliers;
- the major functional components of the firm (e.g. marketing, manufacturing and logistics);
- the various logistics activities, such as procurement, warehousing, order processing, inventory control and transport; and
- the various components of each logistics activity.

Accurate and timely communication is the cornerstone of successfully integrated and coordinated logistics management. The flow of information and its importance are discussed in Chapters 4 and 18.

1.6.10 Transport

The movement of goods is a key activity within, and usually the largest cost component of, logistics. Within the logistics chain, the transport system is indispensable in determining whether customers receive goods as and when required. With transport, the following factors need to be taken into account:
- Whether to operate one's own or to hire transport
- Mode, carrier and service selection
- Method of freight consolidation
- Vehicle routing and crew and trip scheduling
- Equipment selection, replacement and acquisition (i.e. whether to purchase, lease or rent)

The elements of the transport system and its stakeholders are discussed in Chapter 15. Transport cost and pricing principles are dealt with in Chapter 16. Chapter 17 concerns itself with the most pertinent decision-making and management actions that ensure that logistics requirements are met. Aspects of international transport are dealt with in Chapter 18.

1.6.11 Reverse logistics

Reverse logistics consists of returned goods handling and waste disposal.

1.6.11.1 Handling of returned goods

Handling returned goods is an integral part of the logistics process. Customers may return goods to the seller because of defects and excesses, or because they received the wrong items. Logistics systems are often not established for, or capable of handling, goods movement on return (or contra-flow) trips. Whenever customers return items for warranty repair, replacement, or recycling, costs may be high. Returned goods often cannot be transported, stored, and/or handled as easily as new goods. Returned goods handling promises to become even more important as consumers demand more flexible and lenient goods return policies, especially in instances of effective product competition. Returned goods handling is addressed in Chapter 19.

1.6.11.2 Waste disposal

Waste is a side effect of manufacturing and consumption. When waste is to be reused or recycled, its handling, storage and carriage to plants is the responsibility of logistics management. If it cannot be recycled, it must be properly disposed of. In the case of hazardous material, organisations need to conform to special disposal standards and environmental regulations. Waste disposal will assume increasing importance as recycling and environmental considerations gain greater significance. Waste disposal is discussed in Chapter 19.

1.6.12 Customer service

If a business can consistently provide its customers with the desired quality and quantity of products, where and when they are needed and at an acceptable price, it can gain market share advantage over its competitors. The firm might be able to sell its products at a lower cost as a result of logistics efficiencies, or provide a higher level of customer service as a result of logistics effectiveness, or both – thereby gaining a competitive edge.

Customer service acts as the binding and unifying force for all of the logistics activities. Customer satisfaction occurs when the firm's manufacturing, marketing and logistics efforts are successful, thus adding sufficient value (or creating enough utility) to prevent the customer from procuring the product in an alternative way. Each activity of a firm's logistics system can influence the level of customer satisfaction. Optimal customer service involves well-managed logistics in order to provide the necessary level of customer satisfaction (i.e. effectiveness) at the lowest possible total cost (i.e. efficiency) in order to contribute towards the firm's welfare.

An element of customer-service activity is providing consumers with an after-sale service. This includes providing replacement parts when products malfunction. The logistics function is responsible for ensuring that parts are available where and when the customer needs them. Product failure can be costly to the customer if it results in a production interruption. In order to ensure customer satisfaction, the firm supplying the replacement part must be able to respond promptly. Customer service is discussed in Chapter 2.

After-sale service sometimes requires faulty items to be returned to the supplier. In such cases, it forms part of reverse logistics, which is discussed in Chapter 19.

1.7 Conclusion

Increasing competition in the business world and more sophisticated consumer service requirements led to the realisation in the 1980s that product competition would be achieved through logistically arranged product supply chains, rather than through individual firms operating in isolation. This led to the introduction of logistics management as a major field of study at tertiary education institutions internationally since the 1980s.

Compared to the USA, South Africa's logistics cost represents a relatively high percentage of GDP (15,7 per cent in South Africa in 2006 as opposed to 9,9 per cent in the USA – in relative terms, 59 per cent higher).

Successful business logistics practice requires that decisions reached must be quantitatively sound, mainly because of the various cost trade-offs, integration and coordination involved in the logistics decision-making process. The aim of integrated and coordinated management is to achieve the lowest total production cost, and not the lowest cost of each function in the process.

Logistics management can be defined as that part of supply chain management that plans, implements and controls the efficient, effective forward and reverse flow and storage of goods, services and related information between the point of origin and the point of consumption in order to meet customers' requirements.

Supply chain management includes all logistics management activities as well as manufacturing operations, and it drives the processes and activities in coordination with marketing, sales, product design, finance and information technology.

Supply chain management does not purport to take possession of or completely control each participating firm or entity. The management focus is on what each partner or collaborator brings to the party. It is the participation, or the performance that each member is responsible for, which is managed and controlled.

Business logistics is a recurring, cyclical flow process within product supply chains. Alternatively, logistics can also be concerned with one-off events. The logistic arrangements of one-off events is formally known as project management. Project management entails the preparation, organisation, execution and control of a complex activity or operation so that it is executed in an efficient and effective way.

Logistics is perhaps most frequently thought of as the organisation and smooth execution of a complex operation. Irrespective of whether the term is used in a military, recurring business flow, or one-off project context, the objective of logistics is always to ensure that the desired inputs or products (i.e. goods and services) and information are made available to the customer or client at the designated place and time, in the required condition and quantity and at an acceptable price.

The flow of goods (i.e. raw materials, goods-in-process and finished goods), services and information between the point of origin and the point of consumption or application involves the following activities: demand forecasting; facility site selection and design; procurement; materials handling; packaging; warehouse management; inventory management; order processing; logistics communications; transport; reverse logistics (including return goods handling and waste disposal); and customer service.

Key terms

After-sale service	Outbound logistics
Business logistics	Packaging
Control	Physical distribution
Customer service	management
Demand forecasting	Planning
Effectiveness	Procurement
Efficiency	Return goods handling
Facility site selection	Reverse logistics
Implementation	Strategic management
Inbound logistics	Supply chain
Inventory management	Supply chain
Logistics	management
Logistics	Systems analysis
communications	Systems approach
Logistics management	Tactical management
Materials handling	Total-cost approach
Materials management	Transport
Operational	Value chain
management	Warehouse management
Operations research	Waste disposal

Questions

1. Discuss why there is a need for (a) business logistics systems and processes in the business world, and (b) logistics management to be taught as an academic discipline.
2. Briefly describe the evolution of the logistics concept and how it developed into a business process.
3. Explain the meaning of the concepts of logistics management and supply chain management and identify the difference between the two concepts.
4. What is meant by the systems, or total-cost, approach? Explain its significance.
5. Briefly describe systems analysis and show how it relates to logistics management.

6 Describe what is meant by strategic, tactical and operational logistics management, and cite examples of activities within each management tier.
7 By making use of a figure that shows the activities which form part of logistics management, indicate why (a) procurement and controlling manufacturing inventory are materials management activities, (b) order processing and customer service are physical distribution management activities, and (c) warehousing, logistics communication and materials handling occur in both materials management and physical distribution management.
8 Identify the range of activities that can form part of a business logistics process and briefly describe the function(s) of each activity.

Consult the web

Council of Supply Chain Management Professionals (CSCMP): www.cscmp.org/
European Logistics Association: www.elalog.org/
Global Institute of Logistics: www.globeinst.org/
Supply Chain Council: www.supply-chain.org/index.ww
The International Society of Logistics (SOLE): www.sole.org/
Vereniging Logistiek Management: www.vlmnet.nl/

Consult the books

Ballou, R. H. 2004. *Business logistics/Supply Chain Management*, 5th edition. Englewood Cliffs: Prentice Hall.
Bowersox, D. J., Closs. D. J. and Cooper, M. B. 2002. *Supply Chain Logistics Management*. New York: McGraw-Hill.
Council of Supply Chain Management Professionals (CSCMP). 2005. 'Supply chain management/Logistics management definitions'. Available from: www.cscmp.org/Website/AboutCSCMP/ Definitions/Definitions.asp.

Dictionnaires Le Robert. 1976. *Petit Robert: Dictionnaire Alphabétique et Analogique de la Langue Française*.
Dictionnaires Le Robert. 1996. *Petit Robert: Dictionnaire Alphabétique et Analogique de la Langue Française*.
Ghiani G., Laporte G. and Musmanno, R. 2004. *Introduction to Logistics Systems Planning and Control*. Chichester: Wiley.
Havenga, J. H., Jacobs, C. G., Pienaar, W. J. and Van Eeden, J. 2008. 'Macro-economic perspective'. In: Council for Scientific and Industrial Research (CSIR). 2008. The fourth annual state of logistics survey for South Africa. Pretoria.
Hinkelman, E. G. 2000. *Dictionary of International Trade: Handbook of the Global Trade Community*, 4th edition. Novato: World Trade Press.
Macksey, K. and Woodhouse, W. 1991. *The Penguin Encyclopedia of Modern Warfare: 1850 to the Present Day*. London: Viking.
Parkinson, R. 1977. *Encyclopedia of Modern War*. London: Routledge.
Pienaar, W. J. 2004. 'Logistics: Its origin, conceptual evolution and meaning as a contemporary management discipline'. International Logistics Congress 2004, Dokuz Eylul University, School of Maritime Business and Management, Izmir, Turkey. Dokuz Eylul Publications: pp. 3–10.
Pienaar, W. J. 2005. 'Operations research: An indispensable toolkit for the logistician'. *Orion*, 21(1): 77–91.
Plowman, E. G. 1964. Lectures on elements of business logistics. Graduate School of Business, Stanford University, Stanford (CA).
Ruppenthal, K. M. 1963. 'New dimensions in business logistics', proceedings of the First Annual Business Logistics Forum 1962. Graduate School of Business, Stanford University, Stanford (CA).
Simchi-Levi, D., Kaminsky, P. and Simchi-Levi, E. 2008. *Designing and Managing the Supply Chain: Concepts, Strategies and Case Studies*, 3rd edition. New York: McGraw-Hill.

Simchi-Levi, D., Wu, S. D. and Shen, Z. 2004. *Handbook of Quantitative Supply Chain Analysis: Modelling in the E-Business Era*. Boston: Kluwer.

Smykay, E. W., Bowersox, D. J. and Mossman, F. H. 1961. *Physical Distribution Management*. New York: Macmillan.

Supplychainforesight report. 2008. Sandton: Barloworld Logistics. Available from: www.scf.co.za.

Sutherland, J. and Canwell, D. 2004. *Palgrave Key Concepts in Operations Management*. New York: Palgrave Macmillan.

Notes

1. Pienaar, W. J. 2004: 3–10.
2. Havenga et al. 2008: 14.
3. Supplychainforesight. 2008: 1–3.
4. Dictionnaires Le Robert. 1976: 1004.
5. Dictionnaires Le Robert. 1996: 1299.
6. Parkinson. 1977: 20.
7. Macksey, K. and Woodhouse, W. 1991: 198.
8. Plowman, E. G. 1964: 1.
9. Hinkelman, E. G. 2000: 75.
10. Dictionnaires Le Robert. 1996: 1299.
11. Smykay et al. 1961.
12. Ruppenthal, K. M. 1963: xiv.
13. Bowersox et al. 2002: 463. See also Ballou, R. H. 2004: 47.
14. Simchi-Levi et al. 2004: Chapter 1.
15. Pienaar, W. J. 2005: 90.
16. CSCMP. 2005: 1.
17. CSCMP. 2005: 1.
18. Sutherland, J. and Canwell, D. 2004: 227.
19. Bowersox et al. 2002: 4.
20. CSCMP. 2005: 1.
21. Sutherland, J. and Canwell, D. 2004: 226.
22. Ghiani et al. 2004: 18.
23. Simchi-Levi et al. 2008: 12.

2 Competitive advantage created by logistics

W.J. Pienaar

Learning outcomes

After studying this chapter, you should be able to:
- identify the ultimate goal and the immediate objectives of the business logistics process;
- describe how value is created by logistics;
- understand the concepts of customer service and consumer and user satisfaction;
- describe the most pertinent logistics performance determinants in the area of customer services;
- outline what competitive advantage means and how it can be achieved; and
- describe how logistics can help to create wealth within a business.

2.1 Introduction

The ultimate goal of employing business logistics management throughout the supply chain of products (goods and services) is to increase the long-term wealth of all the member firms within the chain. In order to achieve maximum wealth in the long run, the immediate objective of business logistics practice is to be efficient and effective across the entire supply chain and to conform to the requirements of customers and clients.

An important characteristic of logistics is that it is not demanded in its own right. It is a means to ensure that the desired goods, services and information are made available at the designated place and time, in the required condition and quantity, and at an acceptable cost or price. If a business (or the supply chain of which the business might be a member) can consistently provide its customers or clients with the quality of logistics service they require, it can gain a competitive market advantage.

This chapter concerns itself with examining how logistics management principles can assist the participants of a product supply chain to obtain a competitive advantage in the market.

2.2 Logistics linkages with the value chain

The definition of logistics management used in this book is the one utilised by the Council of Supply Chain Management Professionals (CSCMP), which defines logistics management as 'that part of supply chain management that plans, implements, and controls the efficient, effective forward and reverse flow and storage of goods, services and related information between the point of origin and the point of consumption in order to meet customers' requirements'.[1]

2.2.1 From point of origin to point of consumption in a value chain

The point of origin of a supply or value chain occurs where no primary suppliers exist. All suppliers to the point of origin members are solely supporting members. The point of consumption is where no further value is added to a product and it is used without serving as an input to another supply chain.[2]

Goods may be grouped according to the stage they have reached in the series of processes within the supply chain, extending from primary production to consumption, or end-use. These

groups are raw materials, semi-finished goods and finished goods. This grouping allows one to match the physical characteristics of the goods with the appropriate storage requirements and transport technology; and to judge the goods' ability to bear logistics costs in relation to their value.
- Raw materials are the primary products of agriculture (e.g. crops and livestock); forestry (e.g. timber); fishing; and mining (e.g. ore, coal and crude oil).
- Semi-finished goods are in the process of being converted from raw materials to finished goods, but are not yet in a suitable form for consumption or final use.
- Finished goods are those goods that have been processed (e.g. manufactured and assembled) into the form required for consumption or final use.

Raw materials are generally moved from their primary production sources (the points of origin where they usually occur in an unusable form) and consolidated at a place of intermediate processing. Semi-finished goods are stored at and moved from places of intermediate processing to places of final processing and assembly. Finished goods are stored at and moved from a place of final processing via the warehouses and marketing facilities of distribution intermediaries to the consumer (the place of consumption or end-use). Waste materials are carried from places of processing and consumption to places of disposal. Returned goods – for example, empty containers, reusable packaging and defective goods – are transported from users back to suppliers.

The definition of logistics management given in Section 2.2, paragraph 1 includes the flow of goods and services in both the manufacturing and service sectors. The service sector, or the tertiary sector in economics terminology, includes wholesale and retail commercial activities; electricity supply; transport; communication; education; and financial, personal and public services.

In addition to the movement of goods and services, the definition also includes the flow of information. Normally, users want products and related information to arrive simultaneously. For example, order and shipment documentation, manuals, warranty and maintenance information and invoices are usually required by the client at the same time as the product. Similarly, the logistics service provider needs pre-transaction and in-transit communication from users to ensure that an effective service is provided.

2.2.2 Efficiency and effectiveness

The CSCMP definition of logistics management is explicit about the fact that the logistics process should be efficient and effective across the entire system. The objective is to minimise system-wide costs, from line-haul transport and short-distance distribution to inventory of raw material, semi-finished and finished goods. Therefore, the emphasis is not simply on the cheapest or the fastest transport or on reducing inventories, but rather on an integrated and coordinated systems approach to the logistics process.[3] The acceptance of the total-cost logistics concept has changed the relative importance of the different logistics activities. For example, the total-cost approach has led to logistics cost trade-offs between transport services provided and to the operating costs of facilities assuming greater importance.

> Efficiency (also called cost-effectiveness) is a measure of the way that the allocation of resources maximises outputs with the given inputs and technology, or put the other way round, a measure of the way the allocation of inputs minimises the cost to satisfy given objectives. Efficiency generally implies achieving an objective at the lowest possible cost.

> Effectiveness is a measure of how successful the supply of a product is as experienced by users and consumers, i.e. how well service conforms to their expectations or how well goods satisfy their needs. As a performance measure, effectiveness may be expressed as the degree to which the desired level of service is provided to meet stated goals and objectives.

Although the CSCMP's definition of logistics management incorporates the notions of efficiency and effectiveness, it does not address the reconciliation of these elements. Aiming for system-wide minimum costs while conforming to customer requirements is a laudable objective, but it should be dealt with in the context of a common goal. From the organisation's viewpoint, the goal is the maximisation of its long-term wealth.

Cost minimisation (efficiency) ought, therefore, to be confined only to eliminating waste and should not include pruning costs at the expense of greater revenue. Reducing logistics costs makes sense only if the foregone profits are smaller than the cost reduction. Similarly, incurring additional logistics costs is justified only if the net revenue increases as a consequence. For example, an airfreight delivery may be selected instead of a cheaper but slower mode of transport in order to prevent a loss of sales, but only if the transport cost premium that led to the sales and revenue retention is offset by lower inventory-carrying cost or other logistics cost savings.

The optimal level of expenditure to supply an output occurs where marginal expenditure (i.e. the expenditure attributed to the last unit of output) equals marginal revenue (i.e. the revenue attributable to the last unit of output).

2.2.3 Value creation as a chain of activities

Whenever a supplier converts inputs, or resources, into outputs, or products, and sells the product profitably to buyers, a value is added. The profit gained by the supplier or seller can generally be seen as the producer surplus. In turn, the price that a buyer reasonably pays for an input – the seller's output – is always less than or equal to the utility or value that the buyer hopes to gain from the input. The surplus of an input's value above the price paid by the buyer for it is known as the consumer surplus. Together, the producer and consumer surpluses form the transaction surplus. (The concept of consumer surplus is explored in more detail in Section 2.3.2.)

> The chain of transactions, or profitable activities, that span from the point of origin to the point of consumption where the finished product is supplied is referred to as the value chain, or product supply chain.

Given the objective of supplying a value-added finished product that is sought after by customers, it is clear that these activities are, or should be, integrating functions, which, in most cases, are broader than the traditional functions of a single business. In modern and diversified industrial economies, the maxim that one cannot be everything for everybody holds true: specialisation and the division of labour, with effective integration and coordination within a product's supply chain, are called for.

Competitive advantage is derived from the manner in which businesses perform their link activities in the value chain. If a business wishes to enjoy a competitive advantage in its area or span of the chain it must perform its activities in a more cost- and service-effective way than its competitors in other product chains, or than potential partners in its own chain. The activities in effectively integrated value chains should ideally be: firstly, of the minimum number feasible; secondly, effective in terms of quality or service; and, thirdly, performed at a relatively low cost. Firms ought to view each activity (link) in their value chain critically and evaluate whether they possess a competitive advantage in each of the activities that they perform. If not, they should consider outsourcing those activities in which they do not excel.

In surplus-oriented capitalist economies, especially in advanced industrial sectors, value is not only created by the focal organisation, but by all the participants connecting together. Whilst this chain of members linking together to supply a product for which there is an active demand is synonymously referred to as either a value chain or a supply chain (depending on the mindset of the speaker), there are subtle differences between the two terms. First, the supply chain concept is supply-oriented, starting at the resource point of origin and ending with the last (most downstream) supplier. In this sense, the total value created from primary resource to end supplier is the sum of all the supplier surpluses realised in the chain of transactions. The value chain concept, on the other hand, is demand-oriented. It also starts with the primary producer. However, the primary producer can be seen in this case as the demander of the natural or primary resources necessitated. The value chain ends with the final consumer, or end-user. In the value chain the total value created equates to the sum of all consumer surpluses realised in the chain of transactions. A second point of distinction – although a purely semantic one – is that a value chain is seen by some as an organisational or institutional arrangement of a product's demand chain, while a supply chain is viewed by some as a physical, functional or instrumental arrangement of the supply chain of the product. It is commonplace, therefore, to hear operations managers (involved in production and manufacturing) referring to a supply chain, and marketers (who seek to recruit and retain active demand) referring to a value chain. Both schools of thought, however, are part of the same whole: supply is often focused on cost efficiency, while demand is oriented towards service effectiveness – both create value.

As an example, the value chain of petroleum products is shown in the left-hand column of Figure 2.1. An instrumental display of the supply chain of the same products is shown on the right-hand side of the diagram.

2.3 The value-added role of logistics

2.3.1 Value-added utilities

The value of a product is reflected by the price that demanders are willing to pay for it. Willingness to pay is determined by the utility that the product

Figure 2.1 The value and supply chain of petroleum fuel products

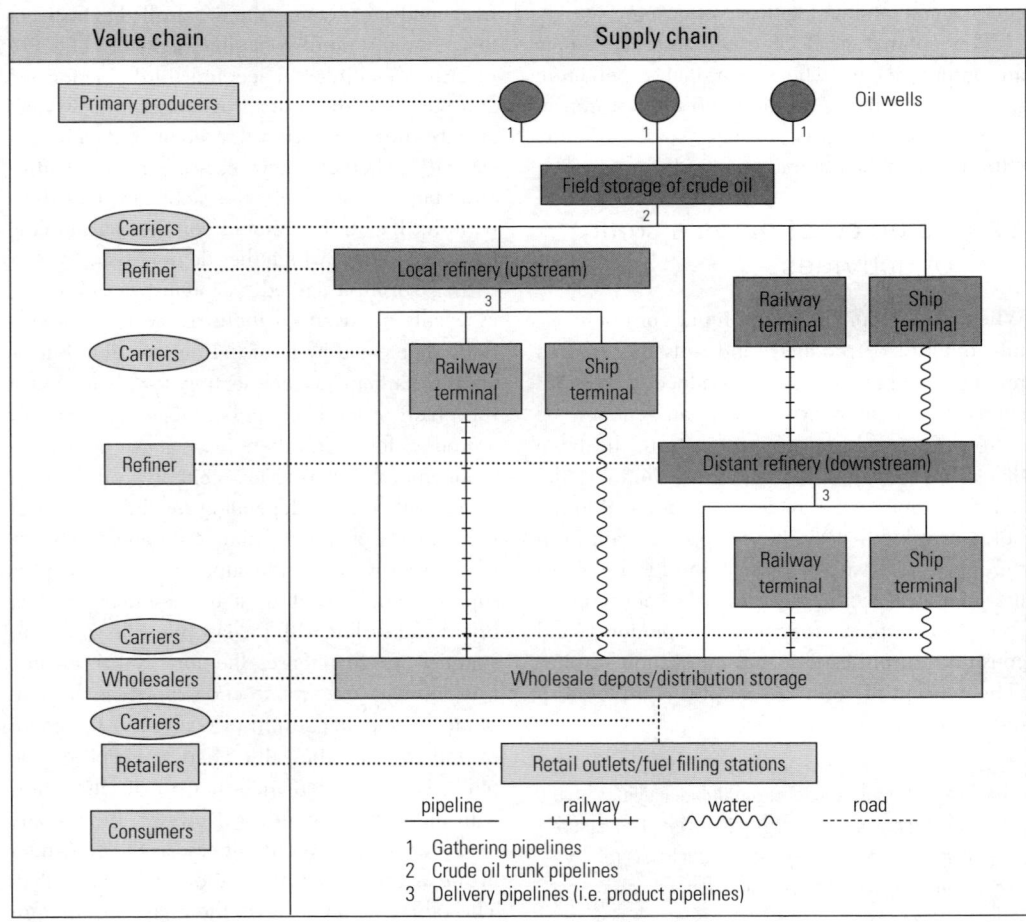

will have for the demander. Utility, in turn, is the satisfaction derived from a product, particularly its usage or consumption in whatever desired way.

Four subsets of utility can add value to a product: form, place, time and possession utility. Form utility is created by manufacturing activities; place and time utility by logistics activities; and possession utility by applied marketing activities.

2.3.1.1 Form utility

Form utility is the result of raw materials combined in the production and/or manufacturing process to make a finished product for which there is a demand. It is the level of satisfaction of a user's or consumer's needs and desires deriving from the alteration of the shape, structure, composition or other inherent characteristics of a good or combination of goods offered in the form required. The specific value attached to form utility is represented by the price (money value) that a buyer (user or consumer) is willing to pay to use a product in the desired form.

2.3.1.2 Place utility

Place utility is created by moving goods to where their value is greater, namely places where buyers are willing to pay more for them. In practice, logistics creates place utility by moving goods from places where they occur in a form that cannot be utilised, or where they are in surplus (i.e. in oversupply), to places where they are processed into a useful form or where they are relatively scarce in relation to the existing demand. For example, certain types of raw materials may be sparsely distributed and geographically separate from production facilities. In order to process them profitably, they need to be conveyed by way of efficient materials management to points of concentration or consolidation in the proximity of these facilities. Manufactured goods are furthermore in oversupply at their place of manufacture. Through physical distribution, they are delivered to places where demand for them matches their supply volume.

> In short, place utility is the value added to goods by transporting them from a place where they are not needed or not demanded to a place where they are needed or demanded.

2.3.1.3 Time utility

Time utility is the increase in the value of a good (or a service) because of it being made available (or rendered) at a more desirable time. Logistics creates time utility by storing and then delivering goods at the place of demand at a time when desired by the customer. For example, certain fresh produce (e.g. apples), which are kept in refrigerated storage will most probably sell for a higher price in their low season, when they are scarce, than in their high season. The location and capacity of the warehouses are integral to the creation of time utility. Warehouses that are located strategically and integrated with an effective transport service help ensure that delivery times match the needs of the customers. Warehouses carry the buffer of stock necessary to provide for demand fluctuations. The availability of the required stock in the desired quantity in the warehouse contributes to the time utility.

2.3.1.4 Possession utility

Possession utility is the satisfaction of needs resulting from the functional possession of, or power of disposal over, land, resources and goods. It is created through applied marketing and sales. Logistics supports and enhances possession utility, because place and time utility are prerequisites to making goods physically available to customers and therefore to the disposal of goods where and when required.

2.3.2 Consumer surplus

Consumers' willingness to pay reflects the monetary value placed by them on a product. The difference between what consumers are willing to pay and the price that they actually pay for a product is known as consumer surplus. In many cases, the purchase price of a product does not reflect the total cost of acquiring it. There might be other substantial procurement costs involved, in which case it will be more accurate to refer to the 'total cost of ownership' rather than merely the purchase price. The maximum amount of money that consumers are willing to pay is subjectively derived from the utility that a product is expected to offer them. The utility per unit is perceived to decline from consuming additional units of a product in a given period. Given this, the consumer surplus arises because consumers are willing to pay for these additional units up to the point where the value derived from the utility of the last unit (i.e. marginal utility) is equal to the unit price of the product. Business clients of the firm who are downstream in the supply chain could reveal a declining willingness to pay for additional units of a product in a given period. For example, capacity constraints within warehouses and other facilities may limit the volumes of inventory that a business entity can handle. Surplus inventory bears an opportunity cost and huge production volumes may simply not be compatible with efficient logistics practice.

2.3.3 Perceptions of value

Consumer value must be defined from the customer's perspective, based on the relative importance to the customer of the various elements of perceived price, perceived total cost of acquisition and use, and perceived benefits of owning or using the goods or service.

Zeithaml identifies four different perceptions of value among customers:[4]

- **Low price**
  For those who equate value with low price, the most significant dimension of value seems to be the small amount of money they have to pay. This perception of value has a cost-effectiveness or efficiency orientation. When goods or commodities are perceived to have a uniform or homogeneous level of output per unit, the cheapest goods are judged to be the most valuable. (See quadrant 1 in Figure 2.2.)
- **Whatever demanders want in a product in a quantitative sense**
  For the demanders (potential customers) who equate value with whatever they want in a product, the benefits seem to be the critical element in their perception of value. This might equate to a utility approach to value perceived as an absolute monetary amount. The more units that demanders get for a certain amount of money, the higher they value the purchase. (See quadrant 2 in Figure 2.2.)

- **The quality that demanders get for the price they pay**
  For demanders who view value as the quality received in exchange for the price paid, value is perceived as the trade-off between a single benefit (quality) and a single sacrifice (price) in a generalised qualitative sense. This perception of value has a service-effectiveness, or quality-of-service, orientation. (See quadrant 3 in Figure 2.2.)
- **What demanders get for what they give**
  Those who view value as what they get for what they give seem to consider all the relevant benefits as well as all the relevant sacrifices or costs and then value it as a proportional or percentage return on the investment, or the sacrifice made. This perception of value is oriented both to cost leadership (cost effectiveness) and service leadership (service effectiveness), which is the main tenet of this book. (See quadrant 4 in Figure 2.2.)

Figure 2.2 The mission of logistics and supply chain management

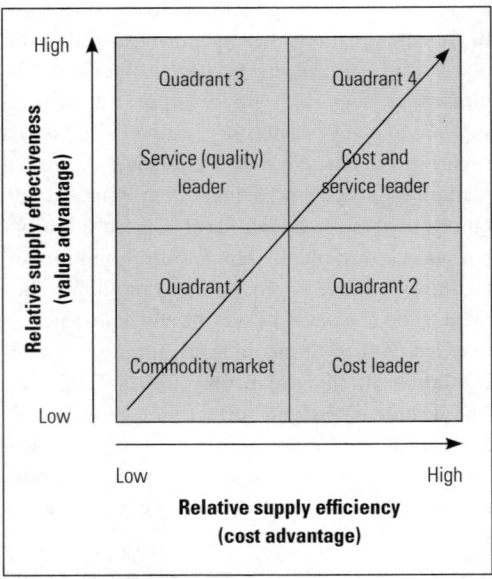

If a business can consistently provide its customers and clients with the desired quality and quantity of products where and when needed, at an acceptable

cost, it can gain market share advantage over its competitors. Competitive advantage consists of cost leadership and effective product differentiation (the direction of the arrows in Figure 2.2). It occurs when a firm implements a value-creating strategy and other firms are unable to do the same or find it too costly to imitate. The firm might be able to sell its products at a lower cost as a result of logistics efficiencies, or provide a higher level of customer and client service as a result of logistics effectiveness, or both – thereby gaining a competitive edge in the market.

The efficiency with which resources are used and organised to achieve their stated objectives will have a direct effect on the firm's competitiveness. In competitive conditions, the lower the output cost per unit – without sacrificing the quality of service in relation to the value or price of the delivered product – the greater the efficiency of the logistics process. Technically, efficiency refers to the combination of:

- the best and most modern production, marketing and logistics techniques;
- prudent management;
- a highly skilled workforce; and
- organising the business to allow its logistics function to operate at a scale or size where economy is achieved.

> Economy means that resources are used optimally so that the maximum benefit is gained from any given input.

In logistics, economies of scale may result from increasing vehicle sizes and successfully utilising their carrying and distance capacity; increasing fleet sizes and successfully utilising fleet capacity; and intensifying the use of infrastructure and facilities (e.g. warehouses, distribution centres and terminals) in cases where a business owns these. Achieving economies of scale in transport is dependent on the attainment of any or all of the following three subgroups of economies: economies of density, economies of scope and long-haul economies. These efficiency concepts are discussed in Chapter 16.

2.4 Customer service

2.4.1 Components of customer service

Customer service is the integrated series of activities between a supplier and a buyer, which enhance the sale and facilitate the effective use of the supplier's products. When rendered effectively, customer service is the overriding logistics supply chain function that can create demand and retain customer loyalty. Customer service includes a wide variety of activities, including after-sale servicing, such as maintenance, repair and replacement services; extended warranties; regular mailing of information; and free-call telephone services in the case of enquiries and complaints. The appeal of a firm's products is greatly influenced by the customer services it offers.

An objective of a well-managed product supply chain is to supply a product to customers in a way that effectively satisfies their need for the product. Technically, customer service is the entire process of customer order fulfilment. The process includes the receipt of the order; managing the payment; picking up and packing the goods; shipping and delivering the consignment; providing after-sale service for the end-user; and handling the possible return of the goods.

Customer service can be grouped according to when the transaction between a supplier and a customer takes place. These groups can be categorised into pre-transaction, transaction and post-transaction components.[5, 6]

The pre-transaction component establishes circumstances conducive to desirable customer service. It provides a written statement of the customer-service policy, such as when ordered goods will be delivered, the procedure for handling returns and back orders, the methods of shipment and informing customers of the kind of service they may expect. Contingency plans are established for times when labour action, uncontrollable external occurrences or natural disasters influence normal service provision. Another element of the pre-transaction component, in the case of suppliers of high-technology or advanced durable equipment, is to inform users or clients timeously as to when innovative or improved new models, promising to be significantly more efficient and effective than existing technology, will be available. Such proactive communication could alert users to the need to review the composition and timing of their capital investment and replacement programmes. Such action by suppliers of high-technology products could enable their clients to maintain and even increase their competitive edge in the future. In combination, all these pre-transaction aspects have the potential to enhance buyer-supplier relations.

The transaction component consists of the actions that directly result in the delivery of the product to the customer. Examples are determining inventory levels, selecting transport service and technology and establishing order-processing procedures. These actions, in turn, affect delivery times, the accuracy of order filling, the physical condition of goods when delivered and product availability.

The post-transaction component includes the spectrum of services needed to support the product during application or use after it has been sold; to protect consumers and users from defective or dysfunctional products; to provide for the return of reusable components, containers and packages (for example, returnable bottles, reusable cylinders and pallets); to handle claims, complaints and returns; and to fulfil the conditions of product warranties and product maintenance agreements after a warranty has expired. Customers' expectations of efficient and effective after-sale service are of great importance in making products competitive, and lack of customer confidence in the quality and price of after-sale services may make products unsaleable.

2.4.1.1 Elements of customer service components

The effectiveness and success of the process of supplying customer service requires continuous monitoring. In this respect, it has been proposed that each of the three time components of customer service should be broken down into at least four elements and that the supplier, or logistics service provider acting on its behalf, should continuously test each of these elements by posing one or more critical questions, which are outlined next.[7]

Pre-transaction elements
- Written customer service policy – is it communicated internally and externally? Is it understood? Is it specific and quantified where possible?
- Organisational structure – does an effective customer service management structure exist? What level of control exists over the service process?
- Accessibility – is the firm approachable and easy to do business with? Is there a single and available open-door point of contact?
- System flexibility – are the service delivery systems sufficiently adaptable to meet particular customer needs?

Transaction elements
- Product availability – what proportion of demand for each item can be met from available inventory?
- Order cycle time – how long is the time duration from receipt of an order to delivery? What is the reliability/variation?
- Order fill rate – what percentage of orders are completely filled within the stated lead time?
- Order status information – how long does it take to respond to an enquiry with the required information? Are customers informed of problems or do they have to make the contact?

Post-transaction elements
- Availability of spares – what are the in-stock levels of service parts?
- Call-out time – how long does it take for the representative or technician to arrive, and what is the first-call fix rate?
- Customer complaints and claims – how promptly are complaints and returns dealt with? Is customer satisfaction measured with response?
- Product tracing/warranty – can the location of individual products be determined once purchased? Can the warranty or service contract to customers' expected levels be maintained or extended?

2.4.1.2 Importance of service effectiveness

Customer service acts as the binding and unifying force for all of the logistics activities. Customer satisfaction occurs when the firm's manufacturing, marketing and logistics efforts are successful, thus adding sufficient value (or creating enough utility) to prevent the customer from procuring the product in an alternative way. Each activity of a firm's logistics system can affect whether a customer receives the demanded product and related information at the designated place and time, in the required condition and quantity, at an acceptable price.

Optimal customer service depends on well-managed logistics in order to provide the necessary level of customer satisfaction (through effectiveness) at the lowest possible total cost (through efficiency) in order to contribute maximally towards the firm's welfare.

The key challenge is how to outperform competitors' service effectiveness in an efficient manner. If specific goods are not available where and when required for manufacturing, it may cause a production shutdown, which entails cost wastage, possible lost sales and a potentially substantial loss of business. The more severely that a service malfunction reacts negatively upon a customer's performance, the higher the priority that needs to be placed on error-free logistics.[8]

2.4.2 Service performance control

Creating and sustaining basic logistics of customer service performance is measured through availability, operational performance and service quality.[9]

2.4.2.1 Availability

> Availability entails providing inventory to consistently meet customers' material or product requirements. It is the capability to supply inventory where and when desired by a customer.

Availability is based on three performance measures: stockout frequency, fill rate and orders shipped complete.

Stockout frequency

A stockout occurs when a business does not have the demanded product available to fulfil a customer order.

> Stockout frequency refers to the probability of a business not having inventory available to meet a customer order.

For example, a supermarket survey revealed that, at any time, the average supermarket is out of stock of approximately 8 per cent of the items planned to be on the shelves. Note, however, that a stockout only occurs when a customer demands an unavailable product. The aggregation of all stockouts across all products is an indicator of how well a firm is positioned to provide basic service commitments in terms of product availability. Although stockout frequency does not consider that the availability of a certain product may be more critical than that of another, it is a good starting point when analysing inventory availability.

Fill rate

> Fill rate measures the magnitude or impact of stockouts over time. Being out of stock does not affect service performance until a customer demands an unavailable product. For example, if a customer wants 100 units of an item, but only 96 are available, the fill rate is 96 per cent.

In order to evaluate fill rate effectively, the performance is monitored over time to include multiple customer orders. Therefore, fill rate performance can be monitored and assessed for an individual customer, product, or for any combination of customers, products, or market segments.

Fill rate can be used to differentiate the level of service to be offered on specific products. In the example cited above, if all 100 products ordered were critical to a customer, then a fill rate of 96 per cent could result in a stockout at the customer's plant or warehouse and severely disrupt operations. (Imagine, for example, an assembly line scheduled to assemble 100 cars, which receives only 96 of the required steering mechanisms.) In situations where some of the items are not critical to performance, however, a fill rate of 96 per cent may be acceptable. The customer may accept a back order or be willing to reorder the undelivered items at a later time. Fill rate strategies need to consider customer requirements for products.

Orders shipped complete

The most precise performance measure in product availability is orders shipped complete. It considers having everything available that a customer orders as the standard of acceptable performance. Being unable to provide all the items in a customer's order results in that order being recorded as zero in terms of complete shipment.

These three measures of availability collectively determine the extent to which a firm's inventory strategy handles customer demand. These measures also form the basis for evaluating the appropriate level of availability to incorporate into a firm's basic logistical service programme. High levels of inventory have traditionally been regarded as the means with which to increase availability. Nowadays, however, advanced strategies use information technology, such as electronic data interchange (EDI), to monitor customer sales turnover in real time. This enables suppliers of fast-moving consumer goods to predict replenishment volumes and times in advance of the receipt of actual customer orders. This allows some businesses to achieve very high levels of basic service performance without concomitant increases in inventory.

2.4.2.2 Operational performance

The most pertinent determinants of operational logistics service performance are suitability, accessibility/market coverage, goods security, transaction time, reliability and flexibility. The more comprehensive factor framing these determinants is consistency.

Suitability

Suitability refers to the ability to provide the equipment and facilities needed for the carriage, handling, and storage of a particular product or item. Examples of suitability are storage facilities that can provide controlled temperatures or humidity; special handling equipment; and vehicles that can carry abnormal loads.

Accessibility/market coverage

This is the ability to provide service between particular facilities throughout the geographical area of business and to gain physical access to such facilities.

Suitability and market coverage determine whether the provider can physically perform the desired logistics services.

Goods security

Goods security involves goods being delivered in the same physical condition and quantity as when tendered for storage and conveyance. Insecure logistics service results in opportunity costs of lost profits or productivity because the goods are not available for sale or use, or have to be sold at a lower price than intended.

Transaction time

This is also known as order delivery time. It is the total time that elapses from when an order is received to when the goods are delivered to the customer. This includes the time for order processing; pickup and delivery; and handling and movement between origin and destination.

Reliability

Reliability refers to the consistency of the transaction time. It is the proven record or reputation of a provider to maintain consistently punctual delivery lead times in terms of prearranged order processing, pickup and delivery times.

Flexibility

This is the proven ability, readiness and willingness to handle effectively variations in order and inventory quantities; freight consignment volumes and masses; delivery times; and delivery locations without any significant loss of overall efficiency.

Shorter transaction times, higher reliability and greater flexibility lead to lower inventory levels and lower stockout costs – the latter being a source of competitive advantage.

Generally, the most important value-adding service criterion is reliability. The impact of reliable and consistent transaction times on inventory levels, stockout costs and customer service is more important than the length of the total transaction time.

2.4.2.3 Service quality

Service reliability is a comprehensive concept concerned with punctuality and time variation in a service. Perhaps the biggest reason for customers considering reliability, or consistency, of service to be more important than transaction time is that service consistency is vital to logistical planning. For example, a customer would prefer a consignment to arrive at a specific time every time that product is ordered, rather than have it delivered early one time, late the next and on time the next. Therefore, if a firm provides a short transaction time, but is inconsistent in delivering that service, a customer is likely to choose a service provider with a longer transaction time, but greater consistency. The many benefits of a consistently punctual service include improved goodwill; marketing and sales advantages; the ability to plan more precisely; fewer product stockouts and inventory cost savings.

The key to superior service quality is accurate measurement of availability and operational performance. Only through comprehensive (or statistically representative) performance measurement is it possible to determine if overall logistical support of customer service-oriented operations is achieving its goals. Therefore, it is essential to identify and implement appropriate inventory availability and operational performance measurements.

In addition to availability and operational performance, attributes of quality may mean that consignments routinely or consistently arrive damage-free; invoices are accurate; deliveries are made to the correct locations at prearranged times; and the exact quantity of product ordered is included in the delivery. Furthermore, service quality involves the capability and willingness to provide accurate and useful information to customers regarding operations and order status. The ability and willingness of a supplier to provide such information is one of the most significant attributes of a dependable customer-service programme. Customers often indicate that advance notice of problems, such as incomplete orders, is more critical than attaining a complete order itself. Customers are usually able to adjust to an incomplete or late delivery, provided they have received sufficient advance notice of it.

2.5 Aspects of competitive advantage

> Competitiveness is the ability to compete in markets for goods or services. It is based on a combination of price and quality.

With equal quality and an established reputation, suppliers are competitive only if their prices are as low as those of their competitors. A new supplier without an established reputation may need a lower price than competitors to compete. With lower quality than competitors, a business may not be competitive even with a low price; with a reputation for superior quality, a supplier may be competitive even with a higher price than its competitors.

Competitive advantage is the leading edge over competitors and is gained by offering customers greater value, either by means of lower prices or by providing greater benefits and better servicing facilities, which may justify higher prices. This may be achieved by proactive and useful pre-transaction information; increased product performance; and superior distribution methods.

2.5.1 The role of logistics management in creating competitive advantage

Studies dealing with the role of logistics management in creating competitive advantage and wealth within supply chains have indicated the following:[10]

- The objective of logistically managing a product's supply chain is to enhance

- the competitive advantage of the entire chain, rather than improve the competitive advantage of any single member in the chain.
- The means to achieve competitive advantage is by creating greater value for downstream member clients than that offered by competitors.
- Customer value is created through cooperation and coordination to improve cost efficiency and/or service effectiveness in ways that are most valuable to key customers.
- The willingness to pay is not only based on a product's value per se, but is rather determined by the perceptions of customers and clients.
- To compete through adding customer value, a firm must clearly understand its customers' value perceptions and the product attributes demanded by them.
- Value perceptions differ among customer segments. A firm must, therefore, identify the customer segments that are important for its long-term success and adjust its capability correspondingly to deliver the value important to these segments.
- The competitiveness of several chain members can improve even if only one chain member becomes more cost-efficient and/or more service-effective.
- Delivering customer value in dimensions that are important to customers better than the competition leads to customer satisfaction and competitive advantage.
- By satisfying customers' needs and achieving competitive advantage, firms in a supply chain influence customers to make choices and respond in ways that improve the financial performance of all the members in the supply chain.

2.5.2 Customer feedback

Any serious quest to achieve and retain competitive advantage requires supply chain service performance to be stated from the point of view of the customer. In order to determine whether the desired goods, services and information are consistently made available at the designated place and time, in the required condition and quantity and at the agreed price, feedback should be obtained directly and explicitly from the customer. In doing so, the following measures are most critical:

- Percentage of consignments received at the correct place
- Percentage of consignments received on time
- Percentage of consignments received damage-free
- Percentage of consignments received complete
- Percentage of orders fulfilled accurately
- Percentage of orders billed accurately

Suppliers and customers need to ensure that their respective understandings of performance correspond. For example, they should agree on what constitutes 'on time', and who is actually to blame when a transfer of physical goods does not happen as stipulated. A supplier's perspective of order fulfilment is linked to goods delivery, while a customer's perspective is tied to receiving according to expectation. For this reason, proof-of-delivery documentation needs to be complete, accurate and verifiable. This can ensure that suppliers' claims of delivery status correspond with customers' perceptions of receiving orders. The expression 'knowing your customer' is vital, because what may mean half full to one party may mean half empty to the other. Discovering how a customer perceives value is essential, because retaining a customer is generally less costly than finding a new one.

2.6 Wealth creation through logistics

2.6.1 Drivers of wealth creation

Business logistics strategy, tactics and operations can enhance the long-term wealth of a business in four areas: revenue growth; operating cost reductions; working capital efficiency; and fixed capital efficiency.[11]

2.6.1.1 Revenue growth

Customer-service logistics can significantly influence sales volume and customer retention. Although it is not generally possible to determine the exact correlation between service level and sales volume, several studies have indicated a positive relationship between the two variables. Superior customer service (in terms of reliability and responsiveness) increases the probability that customers will remain loyal to a supplier. Experience indicates that higher levels of customer retention lead to increased sales: customers are likely to place increasing proportions of their orders with a vendor who consistently supplies superior service.

2.6.1.2 Operating-cost reductions

There is a significant potential for operating-cost savings through logistics. A large proportion of costs in many firms derive from logistics operations. Savings in transport costs, warehousing costs, lot quantity costs (i.e. the costs associated with purchasing and manufacturing in different lot sizes), information systems costs and the opportunity cost of carrying inventory all potentially represent an increased net operating profit. Logistics innovations that can reduce costs, such as time compression in the supply chain, must be recognised by top management. Businesses need to be made aware of how these savings can enhance their competitive advantage.

2.6.1.3 Working capital efficiency

Logistics can have a significant influence on working capital requirements. By their nature, long supply chains accumulate substantial volumes of inventory. The time span of transactions and the accuracy of order processing and invoicing can directly affect the ability to collect payments on time. Faster collection of payments and lower inventories make funds available for other investment opportunities. Working capital requirements can be reduced through time compression in the logistics chain and the associated improvement in cash-to-cash cycle times (i.e. the time from the payment for purchased materials until the sale of the finished product and collection of its transaction payment). The cash-to-cash cycle time can exceed six months in many manufacturing industries. Therefore, by reducing the amount of time in the logistics chain when no value is added, reductions in working capital can be achieved.

2.6.1.4 Fixed capital efficiency

Logistics is capital-intensive, and in many firms the opportunities for asset reductions are substantial. Investment in vehicles, handling equipment and facilities (such as workshops, terminals and warehouses) can be significant. Whenever the reduction of a firm's investment in fixed assets is considered, the feasibility of – and the expected value created by – pursuing an alternative strategy should be assessed.

2.6.2 Example of a wealth-creating strategy

An owner-driver scheme is one example of a wealth-creating strategy for businesses. When implemented successfully, an owner-driver scheme has the potential to add value within a firm through all of the abovementioned drivers of wealth creation.

The scheme involves outsourcing a firm's transport activities to vehicle owner-drivers who are not employees of the firm. In many cases, such individuals are ex-employees who now act as independent hauliers (third-party carriers).

The primary goal of an owner-driver scheme is to enhance a firm's long-term profitability through improved productivity. Greater productivity can be achieved through cost savings and increased returns. Cost savings are achieved by conducting the transport function more efficiently. Increases in returns may result from the fact that the firm gets the opportunity to concentrate on its core business functions and the fact that owner-drivers are rewarded for greater output and for more effectively conforming to customer-service requirements. The secondary objectives of an owner-driver scheme are the ability to reduce labour problems and empower the workforce.[12]

2.7 Conclusion

An important characteristic of logistics is that it is not demanded in its own right. It is a means to an end, a way of ensuring that goods, services and information are made available as and when they are needed.

The point of origin of a supply, or value, chain occurs where no primary suppliers exist. All suppliers to the point of origin members are solely supporting members. The point of consumption is where no further value is added to a product and it is consumed or used without serving as an input to another supply chain.

Being efficient generally implies achieving an objective at the lowest possible cost. Effectiveness is a measure of how successful the supply of a product is as experienced by users and consumers.

The optimal level of logistics expenditure is when marginal expenditure equals marginal revenue.

Four types of utility can add value to a product: form, place, time and possession utility. Form utility is created by manufacturing activities; place and time utility by logistics activities; and possession utility by marketing activities.

Customer service is the integrated series of activities between a supplier and a buyer, which enhance the sale and facilitate the effective use of the supplier's products. When rendered effectively, customer service is the overriding logistics supply chain function that can create demand and retain customer loyalty. Customer service can be grouped according to when the transaction between a supplier and a customer takes place. These groups can be categorised into pre-transaction, transaction and post-transaction components. Creating and sustaining basic logistics for customer service performance is measured by availability; operational performance; and service quality.

Consumers' willingness to pay reflects the monetary value placed by them on a product. The maximum amount of money that consumers are willing to pay is subjectively derived from the utility that a product is expected to offer them. The most pertinent logistics service performance determinants are suitability, accessibility, goods security, transaction time, reliability, and flexibility.

Competitive advantage is the leading edge over competitors gained by offering customers greater value, either by means of lower prices or by providing greater benefits and better servicing facilities, which could justify higher prices. If a business can consistently provide its customers and clients with the quality of logistics service they require, it can gain a competitive advantage in the market. Discovering how a customer perceives value is essential, because retaining a customer is generally less costly than finding a new one.

Business logistics strategy, tactics and operations can enhance the long-term wealth of a business in four areas: revenue growth; operating cost reductions; working capital efficiency; and fixed capital efficiency.

Key terms

Competitive advantage	Performance measure
Competitiveness	Place utility
Consumer surplus	Possession utility
Customer service	Post-transaction
Effectiveness	Pre-transaction
Efficiency	Product
Fill rate	Raw material
Finished goods	Reliability
Fixed capital	Semi-finished goods
Flexibility	Service
Form utility	Service quality
Goods	Stockout
Goods security	Suitability
Market coverage	Time utility
Operating cost	Utility
Operational performance	Value
	Value chain
Orders shipped complete	Wealth
	Working capital

Questions

1. Describe why successful business logistics management is a value-creating process.
2. Discuss the various types of utility that can add value to a product. Refer to the contribution of logistics in this process.
3. Describe how perceived utility is related to a consumer's willingness to pay for effective logistics services.
4. Discuss the concepts of customer surplus and customer satisfaction.
5. Why should customers and clients be made aware of the value of a logistics service provided to them?

6 Discuss the most pertinent determinants of logistics performance.
7 Describe what is meant by customer service by grouping the concept according to when a transaction between a supplier and a customer takes place.
8 Describe the process of service performance control.
9 Discuss the concepts of competitiveness and competitive advantage and supply a list of factors that can enhance competitive advantage.
10 Describe how logistics can help to increase a business's wealth.

Consult the web

American Productivity and Quality Center (APQC): www.apqc.org
Council of Supply Chain Management Professionals (CSCMP): www.cscmp.org
Delta Nu Alpha: www.deltanualpha.org
International Customer Service Association (ICSA): www.icsa.com
Operations & Fulfillment: www.opsandfulfillment.com
Supply Chain Council: www.supply-chain.org

Consult the books

Ballou, R. H. 2004. *Business Logistics/Supply Chain Management*, 5th edition. Englewood Cliffs: Prentice Hall.
Bowersox, D. J., Closs, D. J. and Cooper, M. B. 2007. *Supply Chain Logistics Management*, 2nd edition. New York: McGraw-Hill.
Christopher, M. G. 2005. *Logistics and Supply Chain Management: Creating Value-Adding Networks*, 3rd edition. London: Prentice Hall.
Christopher, M. G. and Ryals, L. 1999. 'Supply chain strategy: Its impact on shareholder value'. *The International Journal of Logistics Management*, 10(1).

Council of Supply Chain Management Professionals (CSCMP). 2005. 'Supply chain management/Logistics management definitions'. Available from: www.cscmp.org/.
Lalonde, B. J. and Zinszer, P. H. 1976. *Customer Service: Meaning and Measurement*. Chicago: National Council of Physical Distribution Management.
Nix, N. W. 2001. 'The consequences of supply chain management: Creating value, satisfaction and differential advantage'. In Mentzer, J. T. 2001. *Supply Chain Management*. London: Sage Publications.
Porter, M. E. 1984. *Competitive advantage – Creating and Sustaining Superior Performance*. New York: The Free Press.
Simchi-Levi, D., Wu, S. D. and Shen, Z. 2004. *Handbook of Quantitative Supply Chain Analysis: Modelling in the E-Business Era*. Boston: Kluwer.
Spamer, J. S. and Pienaar, W. J. 1998. 'Riglyne vir die implementering van 'n eienaar-drywerstelsel'. *South African Journal of Business Management*, 26(4).
Zeithaml, V. A. 1988. 'Consumer perceptions of price, quality and value: A means-end model and synthesis of evidence'. *Journal of Marketing*, 52.

Notes

1 CSCMP. 2005: 1.
2 Porter, M. E. 1984: 36.
3 Simchi-Levi et al. 2004: Chapter 1.
4 Zeithaml, V. A. 1998: 2–22.
5 Lalonde, B. J. and Zinszer, P. H. 1976: 281.
6 Ballou, R. H. 2004: 93.
7 Christopher, M. G. 2005: 48.
8 Bowersox et al. 2007: 52.
9 Ibid.: 49–51.
10 Nix, N. W. 2001: 62.
11 Christopher, M. G. and Ryals, L. 1999: 3–4.
12 Spamer, J. S. and Pienaar, W. J. 1998: 171.

3 Logistics and supply chain strategy planning

J. Louw

Learning outcomes

After you have studied this chapter, you should be able to:
- understand what strategy means and how it applies to an organisation;
- understand the importance and nature of strategic management;
- understand the cascading levels of strategies in an organisation;
- understand how a logistics and supply chain strategy is derived from a business strategy;
- describe the major elements and processes involved in developing a logistics and supply chain strategy;
- identify logistics and supply chain strategic focus areas;
- know what the content of a supply chain strategy document should comprise and how to summarise it in a strategy map;
- understand the importance of proper strategy implementation; and
- know how to use a scorecard and action plans to drive implementation.

3.1 Introduction

Many organisations are exposed to the effect of globalisation and increasing competitiveness in the markets in which they operate. The competitive environment has changed drastically in a number of aspects. Customers are more geographically dispersed than before and demand higher-quality products at lower costs in a shorter time. Organisations have also expanded their manufacturing operations from centralised, vertically integrated, single-site manufacturing facilities to more geographically dispersed networks of resources across the globe. Strategic partners are now incorporated into and become part of a supply network structure of suppliers and manufacturers. Businesses are faced with increasing volatility and uncertainty in the economic and competitive playing fields.[1]

Pressure for organisational change has originated from various sources. These include the presence of new suppliers; the development of new competitors; the shortening of product life cycles; technological advances; regulatory changes; new logistics options; organisations' growth goals and innovation; and tighter financial objectives related to cost and the performance of both fixed and working capital.

These developments have dramatically increased the rate of change and business complexity. Therefore, businesses need to undertake periodic reviews in order to initiate the strategic changes required. Formulating an appropriate strategic response has become a competitive necessity for most organisations to ensure long-term success. Organisations require a clear vision and a robust long-term strategic plan to focus and steer them.

A business strategy aims to build on the core competencies of an organisation, with specific goals or objectives in mind. The business strategy defines the overall direction of an organisation. Analytical and decision-making processes are followed during strategy formulation to provide answers to the questions of what to offer (products and services); when to offer (timing, business cycles etc); and where to offer (markets and segments).

Derived from the business strategy, a supply chain strategy defines how the supply chain should be configured and operated in order to be competitive. An iterative process is followed in formulating a supply chain strategy, which evaluates the cost-benefit trade-offs of all the operational components. To continue to succeed, supply chain and business strategies (i.e. sales, marketing and finance) must reflect an integrated design. Achieving full alignment between an organisation's strategic intent and its supply chain strategy, however, still remains a major challenge in terms of creating value and enabling growth.[2]

Organisations have started to examine their supply chain and logistics strategies more closely than ever before. Initially, the supply chain approach started with a cost and customer service focus. A strategic focus has now emerged. The need to think strategically about logistics and the supply chain has never been more important.

It is important to move away from a situation where the supply chain largely reacts to, but rather than aligns with and supports, the overall organisational strategy. In aligning the supply chain strategy to the organisational strategy, the supply chain focus needs to start with the customer and then work backwards through the entire supply chain.

Many organisations seeking to expand the reach of their products and services to international markets have focused their efforts on planning effective supply chains. However, the global supply chain is a complicated network and efficient processes are often elusive. Forrester Research estimates that successful cross-border transactions require participation by an average of 27 parties.[3] Companies that establish the required supply chain capabilities to deal with the business complexity at hand have proven to be more successful than their competitors.

A supply chain strategy also establishes how an organisation will work with its supply chain partners, including suppliers, distributors, customers and even its customers' customers. As the marketplace becomes more competitive, it is critical to reinforce existing relationships and work together.

The success of a strategy is only as good as an organisation's ability to fully implement and properly execute it. A great supply chain strategy – linked with operational excellence – can provide success not only for the focal business, but also its partners and customers.

3.2 What do strategy and strategic management mean?

> Strategy is a long-term plan of action designed to achieve a particular objective or goal. Strategies are used to make future challenges easier to deal with.

A good starting point to understand strategy is a typical definition used from a business perspective:

'Strategy is the direction and scope of an organisation over the long term, which achieves advantage for the organisation through its configuration of resources within a challenging environment, to meet the needs of markets and to fulfil stakeholder expectations . . . If you don't know where your business is going, any road will get you there. A strategy represents the essential course of action to reach an objective.'[4]

In other words, business strategy is concerned with the following questions:

- Where is the business trying to get to in the long term? (Direction.)
- What products or services will be offered?
- Which markets should a business compete in? (Markets; scope.)
- What kinds of activities are involved in these markets?
- How can the business outperform the competition? (Advantage.)
- What resources are required? (Skills; assets; finance; relationships; technical competence; facilities.)
- What are the external environmental factors? (Environment.)
- What are the values and expectations of all parties involved in the business? (Stakeholders.)

Managers responsible for specific functional areas in a business often only focus on their short-term objectives and do not always take note of the longer-term effect of what they are doing. This is because they are preoccupied with short-term achievements. They may neglect to balance this with a regular review of effectiveness. A fundamental part of strategic management is to match short-term and long-term objectives. It is vital to achieve a balance between doing things right (efficiency) and doing the right things (effectiveness).

Strategic management is in essence a combination of three main processes: strategy formulation, strategy implementation and strategy evaluation. Key aspects and issues covered in strategy development include vision, mission, values, objectives, goals, strategic actions, programmes and initiatives.

This chapter provides a framework and approach to follow for the development and implementation of a logistics and supply chain strategy as well as the documentation thereof. The approach of this chapter is to clarify how to develop and implement a strategy while assuring proper alignment to the overall organisational and business-unit strategy. Figure 3.1 illustrates how the different strategies fit together. These components are elucidated in this chapter. Organisations operate in a competitive environment. Within an organisation, business units are typically formed to focus on specific market segments and products. Supply chains are structured to support a business unit's strategy.

3.3 **Organisational strategy**

Strategies exist at several levels in most organisations. They range from the overall organisational, or corporate, strategy to business-unit strategies through to the individuals working in the business units.[5] These strategies align with each other to focus the organisation as a whole.

Corporate strategy is concerned with the overall purpose and scope of the organisation to meet stakeholder expectations. This is a crucial strategic level since it is heavily influenced by investors in the business and acts to guide strategic decision making throughout the business. Corporate strategy is often stated explicitly in a mission statement. It also gives direction to corporate values, culture and goals. Corporate directives are also set to be followed by business units (e.g. policies). Other functional strategies can exist from a corporate perspective, with the purpose of compliance with legislation, such as those relating to corporate governance, finance and health and safety; to safeguard a business, such as risk-management strategies and policies; and enablement strategies (e.g. human resources and information technology).

Business-unit strategy is concerned with how a business competes successfully in a particular

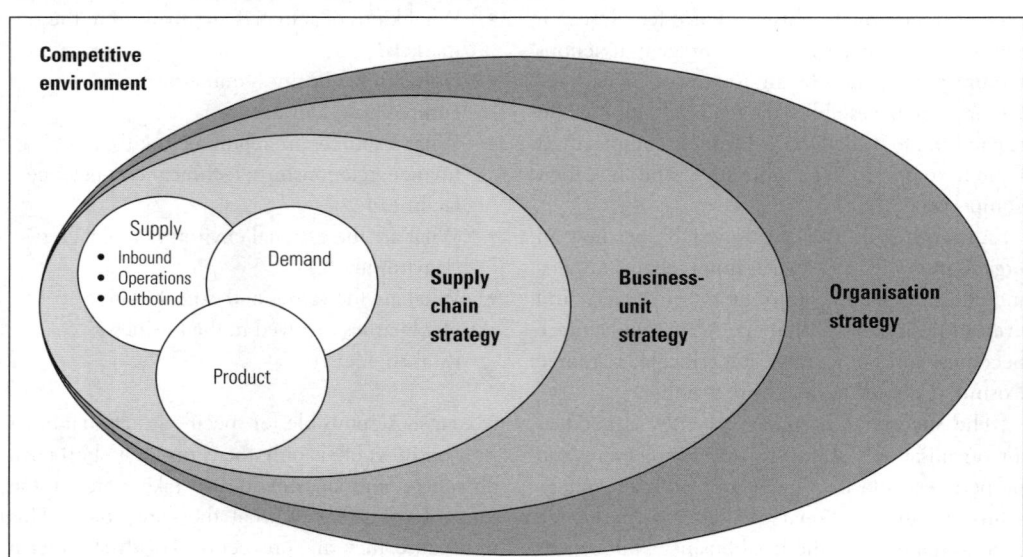

Figure 3.1 Positioning a supply chain strategy within an organisation

market. It focuses on a set of related value chains in an organisation. It relates, for example, to strategic decisions about choice of products; meeting customers' needs; gaining advantage over competitors; and exploiting or creating new opportunities. A supply chain strategy is formulated based on the products and markets selected.

Operational strategy is concerned with how each part of the business and its operations are organised to deliver the corporate and business-unit-level strategic objectives. Operational strategy is very narrow in focus and deals with day-to-day operational activities. It focuses on operational issues of resources, processes, people etc. Operations help translate strategy and vision into day-to-day reality.

Functional organisational structures (e.g. marketing, production, procurement, finance, information technology) are not always an efficient way to organise and execute strategy and focus an organisation's activities. Instead, structuring organisations according to processes or strategic business units provides better focus. These are semi-autonomous business units within a larger organisation. Each is usually responsible for its own budgeting, new product decisions, hiring decisions and price setting. A business unit is treated as an internal profit centre by the organisation. Each business unit is responsible for developing its own business strategies, which must be in tune, however, with the broader corporate strategies.

The main purpose of a business-unit strategy is to improve the focus of the company in the core areas that make it unique in its products or service offerings. A supply chain strategy should closely align with and be derived from a business unit's strategy. For the purpose of this chapter, the focus will be on business strategy as set by each business unit.

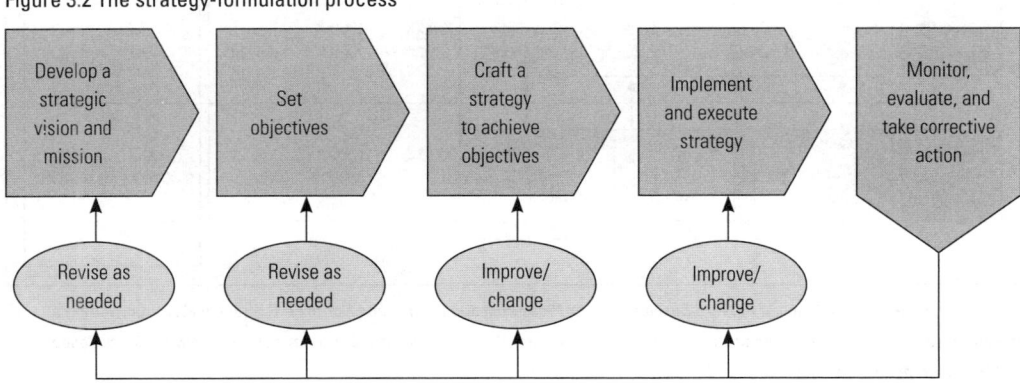

3.4 The strategy-formulation process

Strategic planning is one of the most important ways a management team can make provision for economic, demographic, competitive, technological and regulatory changes that affect the way an organisation operates. Strategic planning follows a process of collective and informed decision making that helps management and leadership teams position their enterprise for lasting competitive success, and for these teams to implement changes to their processes, systems and structures.[6]

The process of strategy formulation, implementation and evaluation is at the very heart of strategic planning. Depending on the business environment, strategies may be updated or reviewed on a yearly basis, but have a long-term focus of three to five years (and sometimes up to twenty years). Figure 3.2 indicates a typical process to follow for strategy formulation. (The terms used in the diagram are clarified in the paragraphs that follow.)

Strategy formulation starts with a proper situational analysis, self-evaluation and competitor analysis. This forms the basis for crafting a business's vision and mission. A vision is a clear picture of the business in three or more years' time, or a long-term view of the future. A vision considers future

Figure 3.2 The strategy-formulation process

Develop a strategic vision and mission	Set objectives	Craft a strategy to achieve objectives	Implement and execute strategy	Monitor, evaluate, and take corrective action
↑ Revise as needed	↑ Revise as needed	↑ Improve/ change	↑ Improve/ change	

products, markets, customers, processes, location and staffing. The mission describes the purposes of the business and indicates what the business is about. Next, objectives are set. These objectives are linked to milestone timelines; some are short term and others long term. A business's objectives are both financial and strategic. Objectives are typically defined for specific focus areas. Specific strategies, or courses of action, are derived to achieve the objectives. The available strategic options should be evaluated, however, against three key success criteria:
- Suitability (will it work?)
- Feasibility (can it be made to work?)
- Acceptability (will stakeholders work with it?)

Strategy implementation relates to the allocation and management of sufficient resources (financial, personnel, time and technological support). Strategy execution is the means to achieve the stated objectives. An action-plan approach, which constitutes a number of initiatives, can be used to make big strategic reform more manageable. Strategy implementation also involves managing the implementation process. This includes monitoring results; comparing these to benchmarks and best practices; evaluating the efficiency and effectiveness of the process; controlling for deviations; and making adjustments to the process as necessary. A sound change-management strategy should be followed during strategy implementation.

Strategy evaluation is designed to measure the effectiveness of the strategy that has been implemented. A business will evaluate whether all the objectives have been met and make any rectifications or adjustments required.

Strategy maps (developed Kaplan and Norton) are used with great success in strategic planning. A strategy map captures a business's strategy in a visual format so that managers can better execute their desired strategy (see Figure 3.3). Strategy maps make the strategy easier for stakeholders to

Figure 3.3 Strategy map, balanced scorecard and action plan

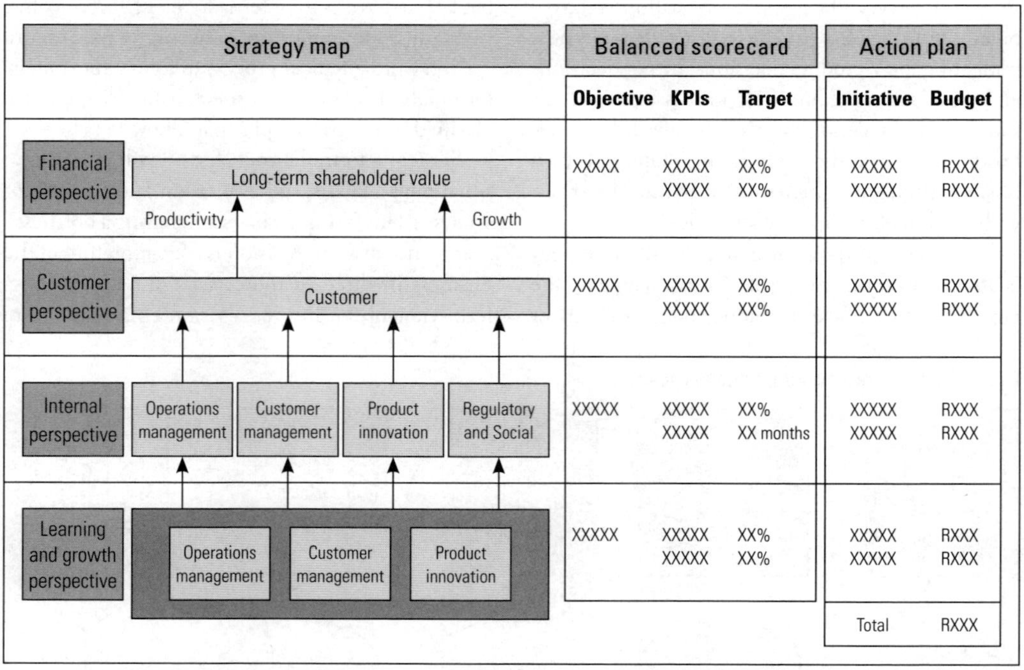

Strategy map						Balanced scorecard			Action plan	
						Objective	KPIs	Target	Initiative	Budget
Financial perspective	Long-term shareholder value					XXXXX	XXXXX XXXXX	XX% XX%	XXXXX XXXXX	RXXX RXXX
	Productivity			Growth						
Customer perspective	Customer					XXXXX	XXXXX XXXXX	XX% XX%	XXXXX XXXXX	RXXX RXXX
Internal perspective	Operations management	Customer management	Product innovation	Regulatory and Social		XXXXX	XXXXX XXXXX	XX% XX months	XXXXX XXXXX	RXXX RXXX
Learning and growth perspective	Operations management	Customer management	Product innovation			XXXXX	XXXXX XXXXX	XX% XX%	XXXXX XXXXX	RXXX RXXX
									Total	RXXX

Source: Reprinted by permission of Harvard Business School Press from Kaplan, R.S. and Norton, D.P. Strategy Maps: Converting Intangible Assets into Tangible Outcomes. Boston: Harvard Business School Press. 2004. Copyright by the Harvard Business School Publishing Corporation; all rights reserved

interpret and understand. People cannot manage what they cannot measure, and they can't measure what they can't describe. A strategy map provides a simple, one-page representation of the cause-and-effect linkages among the objectives for both the outcomes and drivers of the strategy. Specific focuses and related objectives in a strategy map are converted into a balanced scorecard of measures, targets and initiatives. The strategy map and balanced scorecard enable everyone in the organisation to have a common understanding of the strategy.[7]

A good strategy map will link together four perspectives of a business:
- The desired productivity and growth outcomes (financial)
- The customer value proposition that will be needed
- Outstanding performance in internal processes
- The capabilities required from intangible assets (learning and growth)

In summary, the contents of a business's strategy should cover the following:
- Assessment of the business's current situation (i.e. as is)
- Vision of the business in a couple of years' time (i.e. to be)
- Mission/purpose statement
- Statement of corporate values and beliefs
- Determining key objectives and goals
- Identifying key strategies for the business and major focus areas
- Defining strategic action plans (constituting a number of initiatives)

3.5 Developing a logistics and supply chain strategy

Smart businesses elevate and align their supply chain strategies to their core business strategies. They have come to realise the role that a world-class logistics and supply chain strategy can play in improving shareholder value. These smart businesses are characterised by:[8]
- a clear business strategy supported by supply chain strategies and operations;
- strategies executed well through complementary operations;
- an operating model and strategy aimed at achieving a balanced set of objectives; and
- the fact that they follow a limited number of tailored supply chain practices.

Strategic reviews are required on a periodic basis due to major changes in the business strategy (such as environment and industry developments) and the establishment of a new business or new supply chain opportunities that can be leveraged. Opportunities for improvement may be found anywhere along the supply chain, ranging from suppliers to the final customers. Long-term supply chain strategies encompass infrastructure, assets, organisation, processes and technology. As indicated in Figure 1.5, strategy predominantly focuses on long-run planning.

The following are typical steps that can be followed in order to link supply chain and business strategies:[9]
- Understanding the business context and strategy
- Defining the role the supply chain needs to play
- Identifying and prioritising improvement opportunities
- Defining supply chain objectives and goals
- Developing detailed plans to achieve these goals
- Conducting regular supply chain performance reviews
- Executing plans to achieve results
- Monitoring progress and making necessary adjustments

Most companies do not have a documented logistics and supply chain strategy – or have one that is poorly communicated to the parties involved. Managers also confess that they would not know how to write a supply chain strategy or get senior management support for it. The following sections are the elements that normally constitute the development of a logistics and supply chain strategy. These elements form the headings for documenting a logistics and supply chain strategy. The process to follow is illustrated in Figure 3.4.

Figure 3.4 Supply chain strategy development and implementation

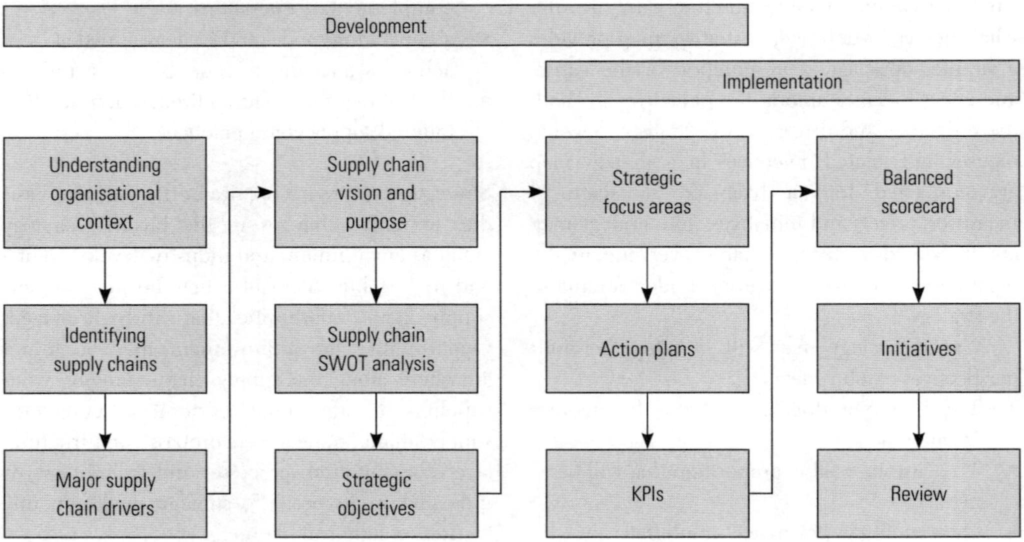

```
Development                                    Implementation

Understanding        Supply chain         Strategic            Balanced
organisational  →    vision and      →    focus areas     →    scorecard
context              purpose
    ↓                    ↓                    ↓                    ↓
Identifying          Supply chain         Action plans         Initiatives
supply chains        SWOT analysis
    ↓                    ↓                    ↓                    ↓
Major supply         Strategic            KPIs                 Review
chain drivers        objectives
```

3.5.1 Understanding organisational context

Developing a logistics and supply chain strategy starts with a thorough understanding of the business strategy. Three of the issues related to the marketing strategy provide the basis for business competition:[10]

- What products or services should the firm sell?
- What customer segments should the firm serve?
- In what geographical markets should the firm operate?

It is important to achieve a strategic fit between the competitive strategy, the product-development strategy and the marketing and sales strategy.[11] The supply chain strategy should align with these strategies and base itself on a sound understanding of customer needs and service requirements. Other issues affecting strategic fit are multiple product and customer segments; product life cycles; and competition change over time.

Understanding the competitive strategy is important not only for alignment, but to orient the supply chain operations so as to create a customer-facing entity that serves the competitive goals of the business (and not merely the isolated operational departments). For example, if the business strategy is to be a low-cost provider, then the supply chain strategy should support this. A business's competitive requirements can take any of the following forms: innovation, reduced time-to-market, responsiveness, service excellence, cost leadership, high quality, flexibility and reliability.

Related to the competitive requirements, a business's major objectives also influence the supply chain strategy. For example, these could be profitable growth, increased revenues, increased market share, low cost, lowest total delivered cost and working capital efficiency.

The international expansion of businesses has major implications for their supply chains. Supply chain strategies should be defined and implemented to deal with this increased complexity. The drivers for international business expansion are the following:[12]

- The need for new products and technology. Firms seek to complement their existing capabilities or find new technologies for developing additional products.
- The need to find new markets. Companies' domestic markets are approaching saturation or maturity and firms needs to sustain growth levels.

- The need to remain a major market player. Competitors with overseas operations are perceived by analysts to have better growth opportunities.

A business's core beliefs and values shape the way the business operates. The supply chain strategy should aim to instil similar values amongst all parties involved. This way, it will aid coordination and cooperation along the supply chain.

3.5.2 Identifying supply chains

Knowing what products a business will sell and what customer segments exist provides the basis for understanding and identifying different supply chains. The example matrix shown in Figure 3.5 is a method to identify the number and size of supply chains for a business. The columns in the matrix are focused on demand and are used to indicate customer segmentation. This also relates to marketing/distribution channels or groupings of customer demand. The lowest level entry in a column is a billable customer or entity. Adding the revenues of all the columns should equal a business's total revenue.

The rows in the matrix are focused on supply and are used to indicate major product lines/families, production locations or suppliers. The lowest entry in a row is a stock-keeping unit (SKU), related to the product hierarchy data. Adding the cost of all the rows should equal a business's total cost of goods sold (COGS). Each 'X' represents a possible supply chain. Some of these might be grouped to form a bigger supply chain if they share logistics networks, manufacturing sites or are managed together.

3.5.3 Deriving major logistics and supply chain drivers

The imperatives for business competitiveness need to be translated into supply chain drivers. These are one of the key building blocks for developing a supply chain strategy and are derived for each defined supply chain. The major supply chain drivers relate to flexibility, responsiveness, reliability and availability, lowest delivery cost and asset optimisation. They also relate to the major performance attributes that a supply chain should portray. Since these drivers are in conflict with each another, not all are applicable for a specific supply chain. For example, reliability and availability may be more important in a particular case than lowest delivery cost.

Cost as a competitive priority would correspond to cost leadership, while the others (quality, flexibility, speed etc.) would correspond to differentiation. As an example, old machinery and disparate systems may entail high operational overheads and costly process inefficiencies and

Figure 3.5 Matrix for identifying supply chains

Product	Customer or market channel			
	Retail		Commercial	
	Internet direct	Internet direct	Commercial building	Commercial major acct.
Big AirCo		X	X	Big SC
Small AirCo	X	X	Small SC	
Custom industrial			X	
Standard industrial		Commercial SC	X	X

Source: Francis, J. and Brown, M. 2006. Supply-Chain Benchmarking with SCOR. Washington DC: Supply Chain Council: 16. Reprinted by permission of the Supply Chain Council

redundancies – clearly not supportive of a low-cost provider strategy.

Supply chain drivers and the supply chain design are also dependent on the nature of the product. Products can be divided into functional and innovative categories. Functional products sell at low margins. Supply chains for functional products should be efficient since customers are buying based on price. Innovative products achieve much higher margins. Delivery and availability – not efficiency – should drive the design of such supply chains.

Another factor influencing the supply chain drivers is supply and demand uncertainties. As indicated in Figure 3.6, a supply chain strategy under supply and demand uncertainties can take any of the following forms given the alignment with the business strategy and strategic drives:[13]

- Efficient supply chains (high-cost efficiency; economy of scale; capacity utilisation; tight and effortless information integration)
- Responsive supply chains (flexible to changing needs; built to order; mass customisation; order accuracy is key)
- Risk-hedging supply chains (shared risk in supply chain; safety stock/inventory pooling with other companies; supply chain information transparency)
- Agile supply chains (combine the strength of responsive and risk-hedging supply chains; flexible and agile to customers' needs)

Demand and supply uncertainties can be used as an approach to devise the right supply chain strategy. Innovative products with unpredictable demand and an evolving supply process face a major challenge. Because of shorter and shorter product life cycles, the pressure on companies to adjust and adapt their supply chain strategy is mounting.

3.5.4 Establishing supply chain vision and purpose

From an alignment perspective, all stakeholders in a supply chain should have a shared vision and be clear on its purpose and intent.

The vision statement provides a clear picture of where the supply chain should be in the next five to ten years in terms of its appearance, performance, contribution and stature. Vision statements are written in the present tense in order to create the motivation to change from the current state to this new state. The following examples are a selection of supply chain vision statements:

- The supply chain is to realise operational excellence and ensure sustained success and support of the business.
- To have world-class supply chains creating significant value.
- A globally competitive, profitable business that delivers consumer satisfaction through efficient and effective supply chains.

The purpose statement clearly describes the role that the supply chain should fulfil within the business. A purpose statement also relates to a mission and has the primary purpose of focusing the supply chain stakeholders on their various roles in support of the supply chain intent. The

Figure 3.6 Matching supply chain strategies to supply and demand uncertainties

		Demand uncertainties	
		Low (functional products)	High (innovative products)
Supply uncertainties	Low (stable products)	**Efficient supply chains** (e.g. grocery, basic apparel, food, oil and gas)	**Responsive supply chains** (e.g. fashion apparel, computers, pop music)
	High (evolving products)	**Risk-hedging supply chains** (e.g. hydroelectric power, some food produce)	**Agile supply chains** (e.g. telecom, high-end computers, semiconductors)

Source: Lee, H.L. 2002. 'Align supply chain strategies with product uncertainties'. California Management Review, 44(3)

following are some examples of supply chain purpose statements:
- To create competitive advantage through purchasing, manufacturing and distributing products and services that provide superior value to our customers.
- We propose, deliver and leverage supply chain solutions and services to help our customers achieve their business goals, taking into account strategic and time constraints.
- We are committed to providing high-quality products with extraordinary service to our customers. Our focus is on creating value for our business partners, providing a safe and healthy work environment for our employees and complying with all regulatory requirements. Ultimately, we strive to become a leader in delivering transforming ideas that help build the businesses of an expanded network of customers.

3.5.5 SWOT analysis

> SWOT is an acronym for strengths, weaknesses, opportunities and threats. A SWOT analysis is a simple tool for understanding the current position and making best use of the opportunities available.

A SWOT analysis helps determine the true capabilities of the supply chain when compared to the best in its industry, as well as all the potential competitors. An example of a SWOT analysis is shown in Figure 3.7, with items under each heading ranked in order of importance.

Assessing the strengths and weaknesses of the supply chain involves an internal focus on its capabilities, such as efficiency. Comparative information from benchmarking of competitors in the industry or comparable industries can be used. This will highlight where the supply chain is strong and where there are weaknesses in its performance compared to actual and potential competitors.

The opportunities and threats are externally focused. Opportunities are issues that will change or assist the development of the supply chain. These may allow the supply chain to improve, in particular with respect to its competitors,

thereby establishing a competitive advantage. The competitive advantage, if sustainable, will improve the supply chain's capability to support the business's goals. Within this assessment, it is also important to consider the issues and constraints related to technological changes; environmental changes; political changes; and social changes.

Looking further ahead, the Massachusetts Institute of Technology (MIT) has identified six macro-factors that could reshape supply chains by 2020. Managers should proactively sense when any of these changes could impact on their supply chains:[14]
- Ageing of people in developed countries (impact on products and services demanded)
- Volatility of oil prices (impact on freight costs; material costs; production operating costs; packaging costs)
- Shift of economic and military power towards the East
- Tightly aligned trading blocs (three or four major blocs)
- 'Green' laws enforced globally (reverse logistics; 'green' products)
- Pervasive powerful technologies

Once the SWOT analysis is complete, some of the strategic objectives and actions may start to become apparent.

3.5.6 Strategic objectives

Formulating a logistics and supply chain strategy requires translating competitive imperatives into achievable objectives consistent with the business strategy. These objectives relate to strategic aspirations as well as gaps and improvement opportunities identified in the inbound and outbound elements of the supply chain.

The SWOT analysis, as outlined in the previous section, will bring up some of the issues that face the supply chain. The strengths must be turned into long-term, enduring capabilities to sustain the supply chain as it proceeds. Any weaknesses must be eliminated or significantly reduced. Threats must be nullified; opportunities must be pursued. Individual objectives addressing these issues must be formulated and agreed on. These

Figure 3.7 Example of a SWOT analysis

Strengths and weaknesses are internal factors:

Strengths could be (excellence):
- specialist expertise
- a new, innovative service
- location of the business
- quality processes and procedures

Weaknesses could be (inadequacy):
- lack of export expertise
- undifferentiated products or services (i.e. in relation to competitors)
- location of suppliers
- poor quality goods or services
- damaged reputation

Opportunities and threats are external factors:

Opportunities could be (favourable impact):
- a developing market, such as the Internet
- strategic alliances
- moving into new market segments that offer improved profits
- a new international market
- a market vacated by an ineffective competitor

Threats could be (unfavourable impact):
- a new competitor
- price wars with competitors
- a competitor has a new, innovative service
- competitors have superior access to channels of distribution
- taxation is introduced on product or service

objectives reflect the plans that must be put into action to enable the supply chain to be competitive in its environment, and to add specific value to all parties involved.

The plans to achieve these objectives must be articulated with appropriate measures. Measures – also known as key performance indicators (KPIs) – are used to assess progress of the agreed and implemented plans. Objectives must be specific, measurable, achievable, realistic and time-bound.

A common frustration aired by managers is that they never know whether they are staying on track strategically. The planning process becomes an isolated event, which is not linked explicitly to specific events in the business. There are inadequate early-warning systems to flag major deviations from expected outcomes and limited reporting systems to update progress against strategic objectives. Managers should be able to relate day-to-day decisions to their overarching strategic objectives for their supply chain.[15]

Overall objectives can be defined for the supply chain as a whole, as well as within the specific focus areas identified (refer to the next section). The major focus areas to improve relate to the objectives that the supply chain aspires to achieve. The current performance and targets set indicate the step changes envisioned (based on related KPIs). Objectives should be spread across a balanced scorecard's four perspectives – financial, customers, internal processes and learning. The following are examples of supply chain objectives:

- To elevate the supply chain's contribution to enhance the business's competitive position (contribute to the business's key financial indicators).
- To delight customers with order-cycle lead times that are well within best-in-class performance.
- To develop and manage efficient and cost-effective internal business processes that enable the provision of services.
- To have the appropriate capability to deal with supply chain complexity.

3.5.7 Major strategic focus areas

Major strategic focus areas are identified in order to help with focus, clarify priorities and make the logistics and supply chain strategy more manageable. Strategic objectives and their related strategic actions are normally grouped together and formed into clearly defined strategic focus areas. These strategic focus areas should not be viewed in isolation since they closely relate to each another and are interdependent as regards delivering the vision of a supply chain.

Several generic strategic focus areas are indicated in this section. The nature, challenges, possible improvement opportunities, objectives and maturity level of a supply chain will determine, however, what the strategic focus areas for a supply chain should be. Some focus areas relate closely to inbound and/or outbound logistics activities, while others relate to the supply chain as a whole (refer to Figure 1.6, see page 12). These generic strategic focus areas are:
- Network integration
- Operational efficiency and effectiveness
- Reverse logistics
- Inventory optimisation
- Risk management
- Relationship management
- Procurement management
- Organisation and people capability
- Supply chain planning
- Information management

Each of these focus areas are described below in terms of their strategic objectives, typical strategies and actions and KPIs. For each KPI, a target value should be determined and used to track progress during implementation.

3.5.7.1 Supply chain network integration

Objective: to ensure supply chain networks are optimised and provide the required capability (e.g. adequate infrastructure and capacity) to service a business's segmented markets.

Typical strategies and actions:
- Considering available sources of supply, manufacturing facilities and target markets, develop and evaluate a number of alternative supply chain networks based on sound screening criteria (e.g. service, cost, flexibility and strategy support). Carry out cost-benefit trade-offs of the alternatives available.
- Assess proactively business growth for the organisation and the logistics infrastructure requirements. Ensure the necessary supply chain capacity is in place to support growth plans.
- Derive strategic and operations requirements for transportation, warehousing, materials handling and packaging.
- Leverage supply chain network synergies across the organisation's supply chains, within an industry or across industries.

Typical KPIs: return on supply chain fixed assets; supply chain flexibility; and supply chain management costs.

3.5.7.2 Operational efficiency and effectiveness

Objective: to ensure that supply chain operations (outbound logistics, manufacturing and inbound logistics) run efficiently and effectively according to world-class standards.

Typical strategies and actions:
- Translate supply chain strategy into executable tactical and operational processes to improve supply chain effectiveness. This relates to the different operational activities of the supply chain (manufacturing, transportation, warehousing, materials handling and packaging).
- Screen the supply chain processes for improvement opportunities using appropriate best practices (e.g. standard process frameworks, such as the supply-chain operations reference model (SCOR)).
- Use appropriate benchmarks to optimise the efficiency of supply chains (inbound and outbound). The major performance attributes to screen include supply chain costs, reliability, responsiveness, flexibility and asset management.

Typical KPIs: perfect order fulfilment; delivery performance; and order fulfilment cycle time.

3.5.7.3 Reverse logistics

Objectives: to minimise the amount of waste generated in the supply chain to benefit the environment at the lowest possible costs. The returns process should address both operational and customer-retention issues.

Typical strategies and actions:
- Establish well-developed processes for the cost-effective handling, recycling, reuse and/or disposal of waste.
- Implement the ISO 14000 quality standard.
- Refine order processes to prevent wrongly delivered goods as far as possible.
- Create appropriate channels to handle the return of unsold and/or wrongly delivered goods.
- Establish cooperation between manufacturing, marketing and procurement for better demand insight on reverse logistics operations.

Typical KPIs: percentage of error-free returns shipped; return costs as a percentage of revenue; value of inventory in reverse channel; total waste-disposal cost.

3.5.7.4 Inventory optimisation

Objective: to optimise inbound and outbound inventories. This relates to raw materials, components, sub-assemblies, capital goods and final products.

Typical strategies and actions:
- Apply a consistent stock and location policy for all inventory (e.g. what and how much inventory to keep where). Factors to take into account include target availability; demand variability; production reliability; lead times; replenishment cycles; review period and safety stock.
- Work with key stakeholders (i.e. customers, marketing, operations, procurement and suppliers) with the aim of reducing variability in supply and demand to facilitate stock optimisation and consistency.
- For inbound inventories (e.g. maintenance spares), seek opportunities for standardisation and consolidation.
- Ensure stock visibility and traceability across the supply chain. This includes stock in transit, at each location and within storage facilities. Apply the correct inventory management practices and minimise stock losses. Electronic identification may be implemented where applicable (e.g. bar coding).

Typical KPIs: working capital; inventory turnover; inventory days of supply.

3.5.7.5 Risk management

Objectives: to minimise the negative effect of supply chain risks; to anticipate, avoid and neutralise risks; to capitalise on opportunities; to aim to reduce impact and probability of incidents.

Typical strategies and actions:
- Have sufficient robust practices in place to deal effectively with supply chain risks, uncertainties and complexities.
- Establish contingency actions to mitigate adverse effects of occurrences.
- Establish risk management processes that include the identification, exploration, impact and probability assessment, treatment, monitoring and reporting of risk.
- Implement plans for the internal controls required for compliance with legislation.

Typical KPIs: compliance with governance; frequency of major incidents; reportable losses.

3.5.7.6 Procurement management

Objective: to optimise a business's external expenditure related to the acquisition of goods and services. To aim for the lowest total cost of ownership (TCO).

Typical strategies and actions:
- Establish the four basic subsets of procurement – sourcing, purchasing, contracting and managing.
- Screen, select, review and optimise the number of role players in a specific supply chain (suppliers, contract manufacturers and logistics service providers). Use appropriate selection criteria.
- Engage in organisation-wide contracts/ agreements where appropriate.
- Analyse external expenditure and relate to key indices on a regular basis.
- Aim to contain the prices of goods and services at a level lower than the relevant indices.

Typical KPIs: total external expenditure; procurement cost as a percentage of external expenditure.

3.5.7.7 Relationship management

Objective: to establish and maintain mutually beneficial relationships with suppliers, internal stakeholders and customers and meet their expectations.
Typical strategies and actions:
- Establish sound external customer-relationship management practices.
- Establish sound supplier management practices.
- Have proper internal stakeholder-relationship management plans within the business.

Typical KPIs: supplier performance; customer complaints.

3.5.7.8 Organisational and people capability

Objective: to have effective organisational structures with competent and motivated people who focus on a shared vision.
Typical strategies and actions:
- Develop and refine a supply chain organisational structure with clear roles and responsibilities.
- Establish a culture that acknowledges the key role that people play.
- Cultivate constructive leadership styles.
- Develop career paths and succession plans for critical positions.
- Develop and implement a learning and development structure based on necessary competencies.

Typical KPIs: levels of motivation; skills portfolio status.

3.5.7.9 Supply chain planning

Objective: to have in place planning processes that support effective and efficient supply chain decision making, execution and monitoring.
Typical strategies and actions:
- Establish or enhance the planning process to support effective and efficient supply chain decision making (e.g. sales and operations planning process (S&OP)).
- Get commitment from the key decision makers involved in the collaborative S&OP process (e.g. marketing, sales, manufacturing, finance, logistics and external parties).
- Establish a customer-focused, demand-driven approach to plan and drive upstream supply activities.
- Ensure the use of proper feedback and reviews to improve continuously planning processes.

Typical KPIs: demand forecast accuracy; capacity utilisation; inventory turns; inventory levels; supply chain throughput.

3.5.7.10 Information management

Objectives: to have timely and accurate information available to enable supply chain business processes. To ensure information visibility. To simplify, standardise and eliminate duplication where possible.
Typical strategies and actions:
- Establish and ensure information sharing and visibility to support effective and efficient decision making and execution.
- Establish a consistent data structure throughout a supply chain.
- Automate applicable processes and interfaces to support improved effectiveness and efficiency of supply chains.

Typical KPIs: data accuracy; speed of information transfer; timely availability of information for decision making.

3.5.8 Strategy map of focus areas

A logistics and supply chain strategy map can be used for clarification and the alignment of the parties involved. A strategy map portrays a balanced view of the supply chain focus areas and related strategic actions across four perspectives of a balanced scorecard (indicating a balanced strategy). Each role player can see how their actions contribute towards achieving the various objectives of the supply chain vision.

The objective statements and strategic actions from each focus area are then converted into a balanced scorecard of measures, targets and initiatives. A strategy map and balanced scorecard enable everyone in the supply chain to have a common understanding of the strategy. An example of such a strategy map is shown in Figure 3.8.

3.6 Implementing a logistics and supply chain strategy

Poorly implemented strategies frequently result in businesses not achieving their set objectives. Less than 10 per cent of effectively formulated strategies

Figure 3.8 Example of a logistics and supply chain strategy map

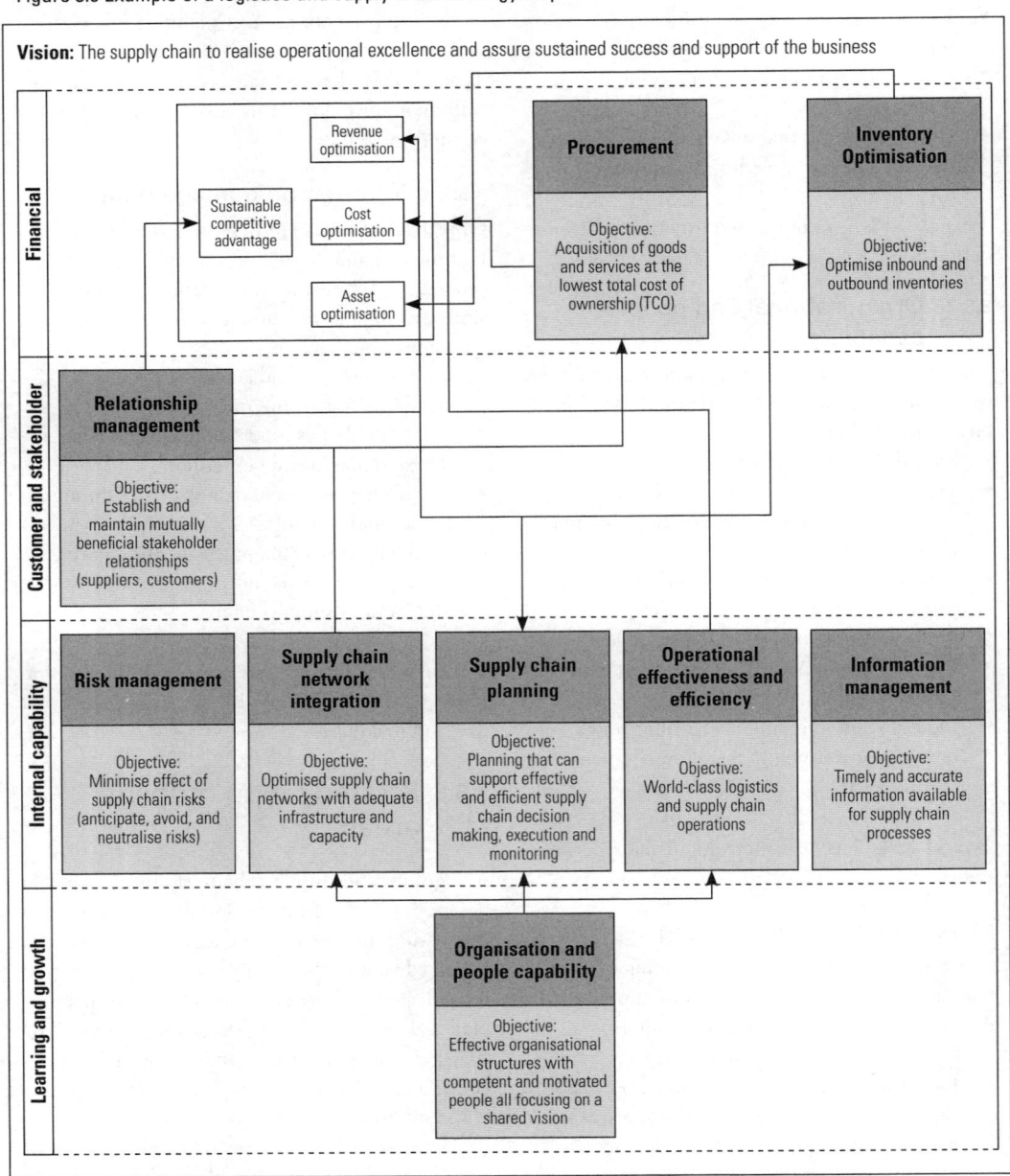

Vision: The supply chain to realise operational excellence and assure sustained success and support of the business

Financial
- Revenue optimisation
- Sustainable competitive advantage
- Cost optimisation
- Asset optimisation
- **Procurement** — Objective: Acquisition of goods and services at the lowest total cost of ownership (TCO)
- **Inventory Optimisation** — Objective: Optimise inbound and outbound inventories

Customer and stakeholder
- **Relationship management** — Objective: Establish and maintain mutually beneficial stakeholder relationships (suppliers, customers)

Internal capability
- **Risk management** — Objective: Minimise effect of supply chain risks (anticipate, avoid, and neutralise risks)
- **Supply chain network integration** — Objective: Optimised supply chain networks with adequate infrastructure and capacity
- **Supply chain planning** — Objective: Planning that can support effective and efficient supply chain decision making, execution and monitoring
- **Operational effectiveness and efficiency** — Objective: World-class logistics and supply chain operations
- **Information management** — Objective: Timely and accurate information available for supply chain processes

Learning and growth
- **Organisation and people capability** — Objective: Effective organisational structures with competent and motivated people all focusing on a shared vision

are implemented successfully.[16] Most of the time, the problem is not with strategy development. In general, strategy failures occur primarily because of failure in execution: not getting things done, being indecisive or not delivering on commitments. Supply chain strategy is no different and faces the same challenges.

Even a relatively ordinary strategy implemented with great effectiveness is worth more than a brilliant business strategy that never gets off the ground.[17]

There are many reasons why strategic plans fail (one being the overemphasis on strategic planning and underemphasis on implementation). The following are some of the major reasons:
- Failure to define objectives correctly
- Lack of focus
- Overestimation of resource competence
- Failure to coordinate
- Failure to obtain senior management commitment
- Failure to obtain employee commitment
- Underestimation of time requirements
- Failure to follow the plan
- Failure to manage change
- Poor communications

Executing a logistics and supply chain strategy means dealing with all entities involved (both internal and external). Just as it is crucial to align the supply chain strategy with the business strategy, the execution of the strategy must be in agreement with all the different groups or stakeholders. It is crucial to coordinate the implementation of strategic changes across all supply chain entities. Some parts of the supply chain may be able to implement at speeds that other supply chain entities are unable to maintain, resulting in misalignment and inefficiencies. Furthermore, some of the supply chain entities may not have adequate resources to commit and realise the shared objectives. Good communication can help to coordinate and keep the strategy implementation in sync.

3.6.1 Balanced scorecard and action plans

Implementation drives the achievement of the specific objectives of the major strategic focus areas identified. A balanced scorecard summarises the key objectives, KPIs, targets and related supply chain action plans. Scorecards are used for communication and progress tracking throughout strategy implementation.

Scorecards are designed to ensure a balance between financial and non-financial performance over long- and short-term horizons.[18] Financial performance measures, or lag indicators, are supplemented by including measures related to the underlying drivers of long-run profitability, namely business process measures; innovation and learning measures; and customer-satisfaction measures. Figure 3.3 (see page 38) indicates how such a scorecard relates to the strategy map as well as the action plans.

The KPIs and progress-in-action plans agreed must be tracked on a regular basis during implementation (refer to Chapter 20 for more information on KPIs). This allows the measurement of how successful the realisation of the objectives and goals of a supply chain strategy is in relation to the target values agreed. Linking KPIs to personal performance charters can help people understand their contribution and responsibilities. Incentive schemes can also help further motivate and mobilise individuals or groups to achieve the required performance improvement.

3.6.2 Initiatives and strategic actions

For the major strategic focus areas identified, the strategic actions must be managed and executed to reach the specific objectives. A good practice to follow is to project-manage action plans and measure progress throughout implementation. Adequate resources should be allocated to ensure capacity for implementation.

Using a 'plan-do-review' cycle maintains the progress. This cyclical process can help improve a project's quality and deliver on commitments. The success of the cycle depends on effective teamwork. Consultation with stakeholders throughout is critical to the improvement of quality. The cycle involves the following steps:
- Plan: Planning within the larger project takes place. Actions are coordinated to ensure

synchronisation (e.g. actions to be done this month before commencing).
- Do: The plans are then deployed and the actions agreed are executed through the resources committed.
- Review: Reviewing the progress and effectiveness of actions completed. Agree on any necessary changes in the plan. Continue with the cycle.

Table 3.1 illustrates how the achievement of an agreed objective can be managed through action plans. Action plans clarify the initiatives (with the related strategic actions), major deliverables (milestones and timelines), responsibilities and resources (budget) required.

3.6.3 Change management

In addition to strategy development and implementation, the embedding of strategy is also required to ensure the sustainability of changes. Embedding requires the building of a shared understanding and the acceptance of strategic choices throughout the organisation. This establishes a basis for change.

At the heart of successful change management lies the involvement and participation of those who will be affected by the change and ultimately have to take ownership for its success. By getting as many key stakeholders as possible involved through the process of strategy development and implementation, the chances of achieving enduring change improve dramatically. This process goes far beyond merely communicating, explaining and directing. Real dialogue is required with the people who can make or break the change effort. Even if the change is successfully initiated and implemented by a committed and aligned group of leaders who have a clear vision and strategy for change, the chances are slim that the daily reality of operations will change. Once people have a sense of ownership and commitment to change, however, they will not revert to the old ways of doing things. Empowering people to create the future is the most important element in transforming to an integrated supply chain.

The company and its organisational culture play a key role in developing and executing a supply chain strategy. The following are some common organisational challenges found in many organisations:[19]

- Lack of ownership – many supply chain processes do not have an owner.
- 'Tower of Babel' problem – most organisations do not speak a common supply chain language.
- Organisational focus – some managers are function- or process-oriented.
- Extending the supply chain – most supply chain initiatives involve external parties (trading partners), which makes strong collaboration a requirement.

There are several prerequisites for managing sustainable change. These include the pressure for change; a clear shared vision; the capacity for change (skills, incentives and resources) and actionable first steps. As indicated in Figure 3.9, all of these factors must be present otherwise sustainable change is not achievable and the resulting outcomes will be negative.

3.7 Conclusion

Organisations have started to appreciate the importance of developing and implementing a comprehensive logistics and supply chain strategy

Table 3.1 Achieving objectives through action plans

Focus area	Objective	Measures (KPIs)	Initiative	Key activities	Responsible party	Timeline
	Objective		Initiative			
			Initiative			

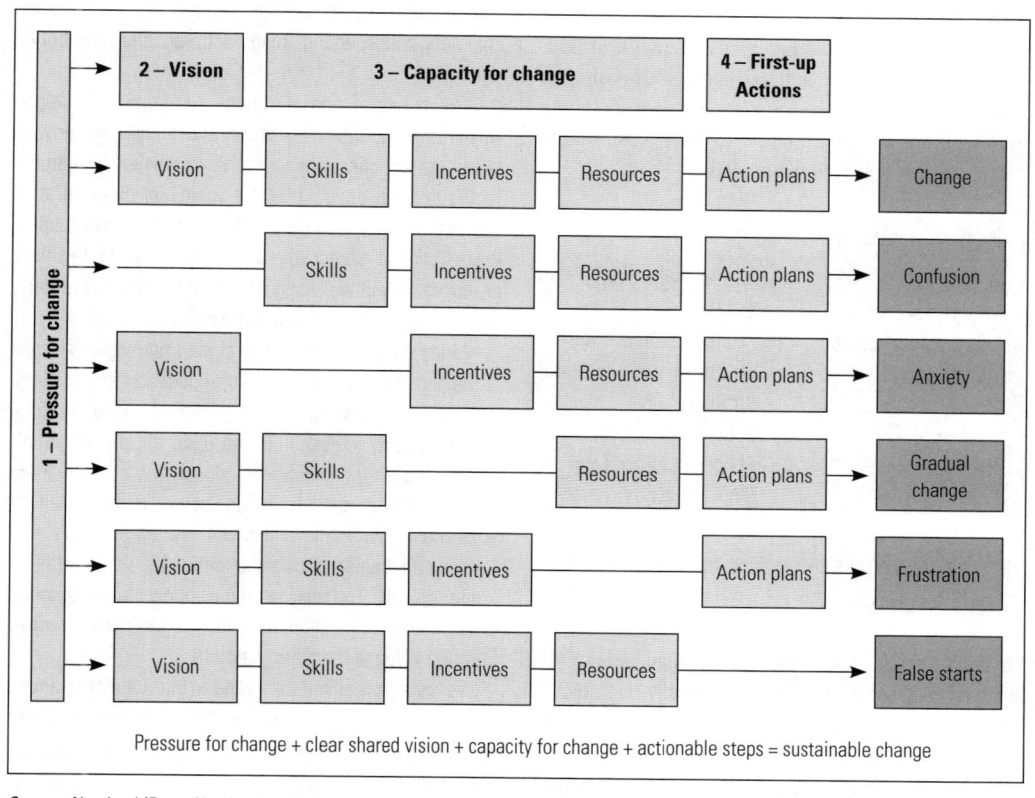

Figure 3.9 Prerequisites for sustainable change

1 – Pressure for change	2 – Vision	3 – Capacity for change			4 – First-up Actions	
→	Vision	Skills	Incentives	Resources	Action plans	**Change**
→		Skills	Incentives	Resources	Action plans	**Confusion**
→	Vision		Incentives	Resources	Action plans	**Anxiety**
→	Vision	Skills		Resources	Action plans	**Gradual change**
→	Vision	Skills	Incentives		Action plans	**Frustration**
→	Vision	Skills	Incentives	Resources		**False starts**

Pressure for change + clear shared vision + capacity for change + actionable steps = sustainable change

Source: Newland (Barry Newland, H.P Way, May 1997) as referenced by Easton, R., Brown, R. and Armitage, D. 1998. 'The dynamics of change in the supply chain: Translating supply chain strategies into action'. In Gattorna, J. (ed.). 1998. Strategic Supply Chain Alignment; Best Practice in Supply Chain Management. Aldershot, Gower: 448. Reprinted by permission of Ashgate Publishing.

that is linked to and aligned with their overall business strategy. The rate of business change and complexity and the impact of globalisation have increased dramatically. Organisations need to combat these challenges through timely strategic reform and by establishing the capabilities to leverage their core competencies. A logistics and supply chain strategy is derived from the core business drivers and defines how the supply chain should operate in order to compete successfully.

This chapter has provided a framework and approach to follow for the development and implementation of a logistics and supply chain strategy as well as the documentation thereof. A number of elements constitute the development of a logistics and supply chain strategy. The process starts off with a sound understanding of the organisation, business context and strategy. Next, the applicable supply chains are defined and key drivers clarified. All parties involved need to align along a shared understanding of the supply chain vision and purpose. A situation analysis is conducted to help identify and prioritise improvement opportunities. The development of a logistics and supply chain strategy is complete when objectives and goals are set and the major strategic focus areas agreed. Each focus area is described in terms of its strategic objective, typical strategies and actions to implement, and KPIs for tracking progress.

The success of a logistics and supply chain strategy is only as good as the organisation's ability to implement and execute it. Most of the time, the problem is not with strategy development: strategy failures occur primarily because of poor execution. Effective strategy implementation drives the achievement of the specific objectives within the major strategic focus areas identified. Balanced scorecards, action plans, well-managed initiatives, performance tracking and sound change management are the means to help sustainable strategy implementation succeed.

Key terms

Action plan
Balanced scorecard
Change management
Execution
Key performance indicator (KPI)
Purpose
Risk
Strategic focus area
Strategy
Strategy development
Strategy implementation
Strategy map
Supply chain driver
Supply chain strategy
SWOT analysis

Case study

Veragoods is a leading consumer packaged goods (CPG) business that serves retail markets locally and abroad. Veragoods has a presence in more than 40 countries and offers a product portfolio that spans the grocery store market with well-known trademark brand names. Although it has a number of manufacturing facilities for producing a wide range of products, it also makes use of contract manufacturing and supply agreements.

Many CPG organisations are struggling to align their supply chain strategy with their business strategy. A number of typical challenges face these types of businesses, including:
- growth goals and innovation streams leading to more complex product portfolios that require new capabilities;
- ever-changing customer requirements (for example, customisation, lead times and fill rates); and
- financial pressure for cost and capital performance (fixed and working).

Many challenges have emerged over time for Veragoods as product lines were purchased and sold off, product line portfolio priorities shifted, assets rationalised, new technologies introduced and customers increasingly provided with differentiated services. Veragoods has multiple supply networks rather than single chains, with each network reflecting different product families, trade channels and sourcing, manufacturing and distribution networks.

Key business considerations for Veragoods began to materialise, including brand and technology growth rates; geographic, channel and customer investment focus; and the capabilities for achieving differentiation in the market. The need to grow and innovate, coupled with financial objectives and relevant good business practices collectively suggested that strategic third-party relationships would become crucial.

Many cost-focused supply chain improvements have in the past helped to improve Veragoods' bottom line (e.g. sourcing, lean manufacturing, contract manufacturing, and third-party logistics). In the past, the organisation's supply chain was essentially thought of as little more than a required path from the factory to the retailer's warehouse. With this philosophy, Veragoods was able to focus on manufacturing and marketing, while retailers made the sale. The next strategic supply chain challenge is to achieve full alignment with the business intent of creating value and enabling growth.

Veragoods realised they need to initiate a programme that will aid them in achieving full alignment between their business strategy and their supply chain strategy approach.

Veragoods has approached you to advise them on formulating an appropriate supply chain strategy. From your understanding of what supply chain strategy entails and the business context described, explain to Veragoods how best to deal with the following issues.

1. What business imperatives are highlighted and should be used to become supply chain drivers? Discuss some of these supply chain drivers.
2. For this industry and type of business (given the level of supply and demand uncertainty), what would be an appropriate supply chain strategy?
3. Advise Veragoods on a sound process to follow for the development and implementation of a supply chain strategy.
4. What approach can be followed to help Veragoods gain strategic alignment among the parties involved within its supply chain(s)?

Case study

The global chemicals industry is highly complex and diversified, with end products often composed of a number of chemicals combined in various ways to provide the required properties and characteristics. Margin management, cost management and the ability to be price-competitive in the marketplace are some of the major challenges that bulk chemical manufacturers face. Feedstock and raw materials generally make up about 40 per cent of a bulk manufacturer's total cost. A large investment in capital equipment is required by manufacturers and drives the emphasis on asset utilisation and high occupancy. The competitive nature of the business creates ever-lower margins and as a result, bulk chemical manufacturers sometimes make a loss. Added to this are environmental and safety requirements for hazardous installations and product handling, which do not come at a small expense.

From a business perspective, this industry is characterised by boom-and-bust business cycles across the spectrum of base chemicals to higher-value chemicals. These cycles are mainly due to oversupply or shortages, which result in the rise and fall of commodity prices. Chemicals are divided into four broad categories:

- Base chemicals (ethylene and other petrochemical building blocks; ammonia; acids)
- Intermediate chemicals (waxes; solvents; polymers)
- Chemical end products (paints; explosives; fertilisers)
- Speciality end products (pharmaceuticals; agrochemicals)

Lorenchem is a global manufacturer of chemicals, comprising 12 business units that produce chemicals ranging from ethylene to polymers. Although it primarily serves commodity chemicals markets abroad, it also has a relatively big local market share for its product range. The executives leading this organisation once believed that its fragmented business approach owing to a large number of business units and country-based organisations inhibited its ability to reap the benefits of global reach and scale. Through a peer benchmarking report, Lorenchem determined that its operating cost structure was fairly high relative to that of the competition.

Lorenchem's business strategy indicated that to survive and grow its business in this industry, it will have to restructure its portfolio of businesses, lower its operational costs and create operating discipline (this all within the ever-changing demands and requirements of the customers).

Restructuring meant more sharply focusing on Lorenchem's core business and shedding a number of business units and facilities that did not strategically fit any more. This reduction would enable the organisation to concentrate on producing chemicals that are more basic, which could realise enormous near-term cost reductions. The creation of operational discipline meant the globalisation of business operations and the development of significant competence in procurement, manufacturing and distribution. Lorenchem had largely run its chemical operations on a regional basis (each having its own sales and operations group with its own set of policies and procedures). The globalisation effort would establish consistency across regions and enable Lorenchem to leverage its scale on a worldwide basis.

To create competence across the areas of procurement, manufacturing and distribution, Lorenchem thought it good to establish a project team with the purpose of formulating and implementing an appropriate supply chain strategy for each of the refocused business units.

One of the key changes anticipated was to migrate from a supply/push operating discipline to a demand/pull customer strategy. With a mandate to dramatically improve operations and become more market-focused, Lorenchem began to explore an approach to increase its effectiveness with its customers by better understanding their needs and buyer values.

1. Given the business strategy and the objectives set, what would you suggest are some of the major supply chain strategic focus areas for Lorenchem? Suggest some strategic actions in these focus areas.
2. For the proposed strategic focus areas and strategic actions, what approach would you suggest Lorenchem follows to ensure proper implementation?

Questions

1. What is the effect of globalisation and increased competitiveness on a business? Explain how this has highlighted the need for a proper logistics and supply chain strategy.
2. Briefly explain what strategy is.
3. Explain briefly the cascading levels of strategy from organisational and business-unit strategy to logistics and supply chain strategy. Use an appropriate diagram.
4. Strategic planning combines three main processes: strategy development, strategy implementation and strategy evaluation. Briefly explain what each of these processes entail.
5. Explain how a supply chain strategy is derived from a business strategy. Describe the process and the different elements that make up the development of a supply chain strategy.
6. How would you go about identifying the different supply chains for a business?
7. Explain the use of supply and demand uncertainties to derive an appropriate supply chain strategy.
8. Explain the purpose of using strategic focus areas for logistics and supply chain strategy development.
9. Why is it important to properly document and communicate a business's logistics and supply chain strategy?
10. What are some of the main reasons why strategic plans fail? How can the use of a balanced scorecard and action plans help?

Consult the web

Achieving Supply Chain Excellence through Technology: www.ascet.com
Council of Supply Chain Management Professionals (CSCMP): www.cscmp.org
Planware: www.planware.org/strategicplan.htm
Strategy formulation: www.ceo.lt
Supply-Chain Council (SCC): www.supply-chain.org
Supply Chain Management Review: www.scmr.com
UPS Supply Chain Solutions: www.ups-scs.com

Consult the books

Brewer, P. E. and Speh, T. W. 2001. 'Adapting the balanced scorecard to supply chain management'. *Supply Chain Management Review*, 5(2).

Chopra, S. and Meindl, P. 2001. *Supply Chain Management: Strategy, Planning and Operation*. Prentice Hall.

Corporate executive board. 2002. 'Developing strategy for a global supply chain'. *Initiative Snapshot*, June.

Easton, R., Brown, R. and Armitage, D. 1998. 'The dynamics of change in the supply chain: Translating supply chain strategies into action'. In Gattorna, J. (ed.). 1998. *Strategic Supply Chain Alignment; Best Practice in Supply Chain Management*. Gower.

Evans, R. and Danks, A. 1998. 'Strategic supply chain management'. In Gattorna, J. (ed.) *Strategic Supply Chain Alignment: Best Practice in Supply Chain Management*. Gower.

Francis, J. and Brown, M. 2006. *Supply-Chain Benchmarking with SCOR*. Washington DC: Supply Chain Council (Webinar).

Fuller, J. 2005. 'Strategic planning in the 21st century'. Available from: www.monitor.com/cgi-bin/iowa/ideas/index.html?article=108 (accessed 25 May 2008).

Happek, S. 2005. 'Supply chain strategy. A UPS supply chain solutions white paper'. Available from: www.ups-scs.com/ (accessed 22 February 2006).

Johnson, G., Scholes, K. and Whittington, R. 2005. *Exploring Corporate Strategy*, 7th edition. London: Prentice Hall.

Kaplan, R. S. and Norton, D. P. 2004. 'Strategy maps: Converting intangible assets into tangible outcomes'. Harvard Business School Press.

Lapide, L. 2008. 'MIT SC2020 Project: Supply chain futures'. In SAPICS 2008, 30th Annual Conference and Exhibition. Sun City, South Africa.

Lee, H. L. 2002. 'Align supply chain strategies with product uncertainties'. *California Management Review*, 44(3).

Lummus, R. R., Alber, K. and Vokurka, R. J. 2000. 'Self-assessments: A foundation for supply chain success'. *Supply Chain Management Review*, 4(3).

Mazza, J. 2003. 'Strategic planning and implementation: Organisational road maps for success'. *Los Angeles Business Journal*, October 13.

Monahan, S. and Nardone, R. 2007. 'How Unilever aligned its supply chain and business strategies'. *Supply Chain Management Review*, November 2007. Available from: www.scmr.com (accessed 25 May 2008).

Speh, T. 2008. 'Managing the state-of-the-art global supply chains'. CSCMP South Africa. Johannesburg.

Stock, G. N., Greis, N. P. and Kasarda, J. D. 1999. 'Logistics, strategy and structure: A conceptual framework'. *International Journal of Physical Distribution and Logistics*, 29(4).

Notes

1. Stock et al. 1999.
2. Monahan, S. and Nardone, R. 2007.
3. Corporate executive board. 2002.
4. Johnson et al. 2005.
5. Ibid.
6. Mazza, J. 2003.
7. Kaplan, R. S. and Norton, P. N. 2004.
8. Speh, T. 2008.
9. Lummus et al. 2000.
10. Evans, R. and Danks, A. 1998.
11. Chopra, S. and Meindl, P. 2001.
12. Corporate executive board. 2002.
13. Lee, H. L. 2002.
14. Lapide, L. 2008.
15. Fuller, J. 2005.
16. Kaplan, R. S. and Norton, P. N. 2004.
17. Mazza, J. 2003.
18. Brewer, P. E. and Speh, T. W. 2001.
19. Happek, S. 2005.

4 Tactical logistics management and supply chain integration

W.J. Pienaar

Learning outcomes

After you have studied this chapter, you should be able to:
- distinguish between the various tiers, or levels, of management;
- identify the functional supply chain activities that are implemented and organised through tactical logistics management;
- identify the main tactical management objectives in a supply chain;
- give an account of the planning systems that are used to organise the flow of goods from point of origin to point of end-use, or consumption;
- distinguish between push, pull and push-pull product supply processes and discuss the various push, pull and push-pull systems;
- explain the importance of time in the management of supply chains;
- give an account of the main causes of long production cycles and order lead times; and
- describe the steps that can be followed to enhance the efficient use of time in supply chains.

4.1 Introduction

The aim of tactical logistics management is to ensure that the most feasible operations are implemented in order to supply products to customers. This chapter deals with principles and concepts that can be utilised within tactical logistics management. Tactical logistics management within a supply chain refers to the arrangements and organisation required to ensure that the desired product and information are made available to the customer at the designated place and time, in the required condition and quantity, at an acceptable price.

Tactical logistics management follows (or is led by) logistics strategy, which is in turn led by the mission, goals and objectives that are formulated at the strategic corporate management level. The organisation of operating activities and procedures on the tactical level is, therefore, subordinate to logistics and corporate strategy (i.e. long-range planning and preparation). Tactical management is responsible for implementing logistics operations (see Figure 1.5, page 8).

The tactical management responsibilities (operations planning; organising and coordinating activities; and arranging and implementing procedures) should be performed in a coherently focused fashion to ensure that the flow of goods throughout the entire supply chain is executed in an efficient and effective manner. It is especially on the tactical management level where operational logistics processes can be tailored to give the supply chain a competitive advantage.

4.2 Tactical logistics activities

Tactical logistics activities are undertaken to implement and organise functional supply chain activities. The latter include goods processing and logistics activities, sales and other applied marketing activities.[1] Note that goods processing (i.e. making) and selling are not logistics activities, but their direct planning (i.e. implementing and organising them) are logistics activities.

Tactical activities are grouped into the following broad activities:

- Buying – involves the procurement and acquisition of raw materials, components and any other activity that is involved in obtaining resources for the supply chain.
- Making – covers processing (primary production, secondary manufacturing and assembly) and related activities, such as quality control and maintenance.
- Moving – involves the transport and handling of goods during forward and reverse flow inside, and waste removal away from, the supply chain.
- Storing – involves carrying inventory at all of the transformation levels of products, from raw material to finished state during materials management and in warehouses during physical distribution.
- Selling – includes all applied commercial activities, and more generally, those activities that concern and/or influence the outputs of the supply chain.

An objective of a supply chain is customer satisfaction. At the same time, individual components of the supply chain aim to maximise shareholder value by maximising the return on investment. This strategic objective can be translated into several short- and medium-term objectives at the tactical level. If successful, these tactical objectives enhance return on investment. The main tactical management objectives in a supply chain are to:

- minimise the time required for converting orders into cash;
- minimise the total work-in-process (WIP) in the supply chain;
- improve pipeline visibility, namely the visibility of each of the activities of the supply chain by each of the partners;
- improve visibility of demand by each of the partners;
- improve quality;
- reduce costs; and
- improve services.

4.3 Managing the goods flow[2]

In order to manage the goods flow from point of origin to point of end-use, management should know what systems can be implemented to handle this flow and the impact that the organisation of the goods flow has on logistics performance.

In Figure 4.1, a customer order starts the logistics planning system via the sales function. If the finished goods are available in the finished goods store or a distribution centre, the distribution function

Figure 4.1 Managing the goods flow

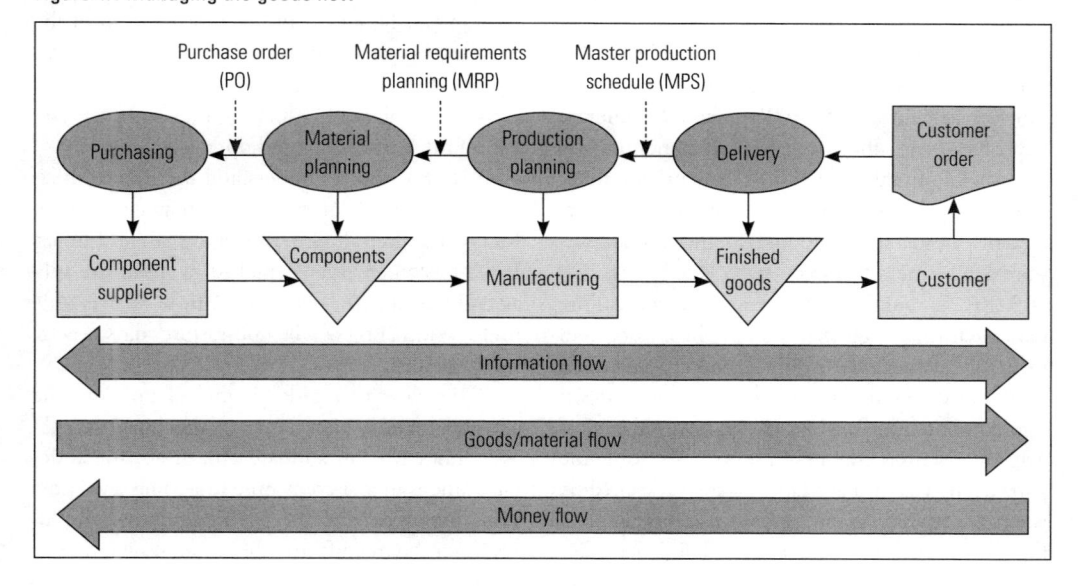

(included in 'moving' in Figure 4.5, see page 71) delivers them to the customer. The customer could be the end-user or the next party in the supply chain, for example, a wholesaler or retailer.

If the finished goods are not available, the customer demand becomes part of the master production schedule (MPS). Production planning then places a works order on the production function. The production function picks the components from the component store, manufactures or assembles the items required and forwards the finished products to the finished goods store, ready for distribution.

An MPS takes into account planned production, as well as inventory on hand.[3] The MPS has three major inputs:
- Opening inventory (i.e. stock on hand)
- Forecasts for each period in the schedule
- Customer order volumes

The outputs of the scheduling process include projected inventory, production requirements and the amount of uncommitted inventory.

The MPS is a time-phased plan that specifies how many of each product the business intends to manufacture and when. A fully integrated MPS programme combined with a material requirements planning (MRP) programme can calculate precisely how much raw material, and how many sub-assemblies or other goods are needed to make the products.

If the components are not available in the components store, the materials planning function acts through the MRP system to generate requisitions on the procurement function. By means of a purchase order (PO), the procurement function in turn orders raw materials from suppliers for delivery, so that the products for the components store can be manufactured.

MRP is mainly concerned with scheduling manufacturing activities and the associated inventory management. MRP begins by forecasting customer demand. The demand is broken down into component parts that will be required against existing inventories and then seeks to schedule the parts needed against available capacity. A schedule is produced for all component parts (including those to be purchased if necessary). The process also identifies any expected shortages due to capacity limitations. The procedure is updated at regular intervals, during which demand is forecasted and necessary adjustments made in order to fulfil this demand. MRP requires considerable data capture, (a) to accurately predict future demand and, (b) for the scheduling of all component parts required. MRP requires the following input details:[4]
- Bill of materials (BOM) (which identifies the component parts of a final output product)
- MPS (which shows the quantity of each item required and when they are needed)
- Opening inventory (which shows available inventories of all materials)
- Opening capacity (derived from the above information)
- Lead time and lot sizing rules

MRP calculates the following quantities as outputs:
- Purchase requirements
- Manufacturing activity schedules
- Expected shortages
- Surplus components inventory
- Available free capacity

A BOM aims to list all of the parts, sub-assemblies and individual items needed to manufacture a specific product. However, a BOM is more than merely a list of parts – it lists the components, sub-assemblies and other items sequentially as they should be added in the process to form the product. In other words, a BOM indicates – like a recipe – how a product is to be assembled and the precise ordering of production units and processes within the factory or workshop.[5]

It is important to understand the impact of all the above aspects on goods flow management. In Figure 4.2, the values in the circles are lead times. If the customer order is picked up from the sub-assembly store, the order lead time is five time units. (A time unit can be hours, shifts, days, weeks, months etc.)

If the customer order is picked up from the component inventory store to manufacture sub-assemblies for the sub-assembly store, the order lead time is increased by nine time units (two time units for processing the MPS requirements plus seven for the manufacture of the sub-assemblies)

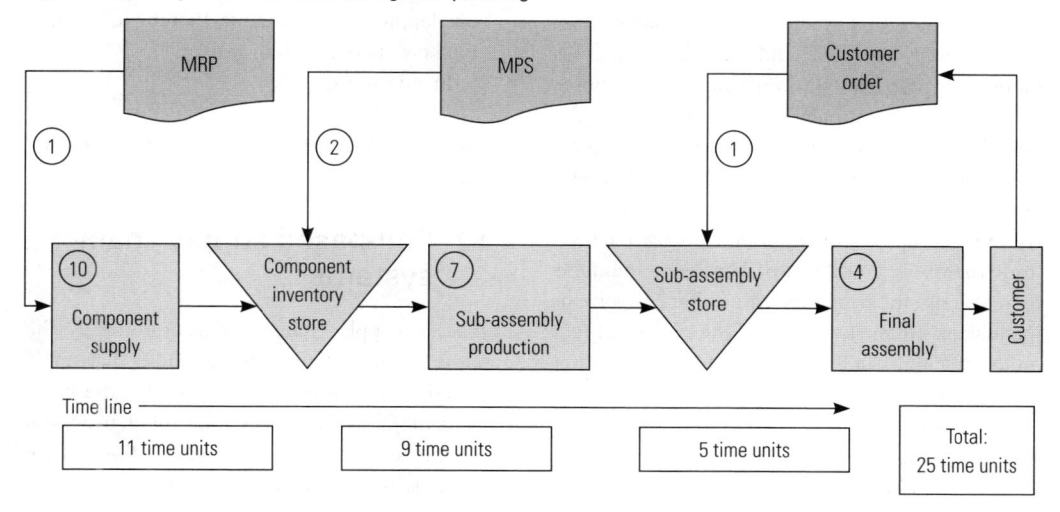

Figure 4.2 The impact of lead times on logistics planning

[Diagram: Flow from Component supply (10) → Component inventory store → Sub-assembly production (7) → Sub-assembly store → Final assembly (4) → Customer. MRP feeds into Component inventory store (1) and Sub-assembly production (2). MPS feeds from Customer order (1). Time line: 11 time units + 9 time units + 5 time units = Total: 25 time units.]

If the customer order cannot be picked up from the component inventory store, a further 11 time units are added to the order lead time (one time unit for the processing of the MRP and another ten units for the production of the components by the suppliers).

Therefore, in the above example, the total order lead time of an unexpected or unplanned customer order could amount to 25 time units (one time unit to process the order; two units to process the MPS if the sub-assemblies are not available; one time unit to process the MRP if the components are not available; ten units to manufacture the components, seven units to manufacture the sub-assemblies, and four units for final assembly). This means that, in order to guarantee customer service levels in this example, the sales need to be forecasted accurately 25 time units in advance.

Since it is unlikely for any sales forecast to be accurate 25 time units in advance, logistics systems need to be in place to accommodate the situations in the above example. The next section looks at the logistics concepts that can alter order lead times and introduce flexibility.

4.4 Product supply chain processes[6]

Product supply chain processes have traditionally been either the push or pull variety. More recently, a mixed push-pull approach has developed. These supply chain processes are at the heart of both manufacturing and inventory management. The decision to adopt one of these processes dramatically influences the manner in which manufacturing and inventory systems are handled. Each of the systems are discussed in the subsequent three sections.

4.4.1 Push-based supply chain systems

Push-based supply chain systems put the onus on the manufacturing entity to decide when – and how much of – a given product will be sent into storage. Manufacturing and distribution (mainly inventory and transportation) decisions are based on long-term forecasts of demand, and the present inventory position. In this system it is the manufacturing entity that sets the pace and determines priorities from the point of view of the supply process.

Manufacturers typically base demand forecasts on orders received from wholesalers and retailers. It will, therefore, take substantially longer for a push-based supply chain to react to changing end-user market conditions. This can lead to, first, an inability by manufacturers to meet changing consumer demand patterns, and second, the obsolescence of some supply chain inventory because demand for certain products disappears. In addition, the variability of replenishment orders received from the wholesalers and retailers is usually larger than the variability in their end-user demand. This increase or propagation in variability as one moves upstream in the supply chain is known as the bullwhip effect. This effect arises when members upstream in the supply chain are faced with a high degree of uncertainty about the time pattern and volume of replenishment orders to be received from members downstream. Upstream members therefore run the risk of carrying either excessive or inadequate buffer stock to fulfil the replenishment orders efficiently or effectively. This implies either excessive inventory-carrying cost (inefficiency) or stockout losses (ineffectiveness). More specifically, this increase in variability leads to:

- Bigger and more variable production batches
- Excessive inventories due to the need for huge safety stock
- Product obsolescence
- Unacceptable service levels due to stockouts

Because planning and managing are much more difficult in a push-based supply chain, the bullwhip effect leads to inefficient resource utilisation. For example, it may not be clear how a manufacturer should determine manufacturing capacity. If based on peak demand, the manufacturer will have expensive unutilised resources during long off-peak periods; if based on average demand, additional and expensive capacity will be required during periods of peak demand. Furthermore, it is not clear in such periods of fluctuating demand how to plan transport capacity. Therefore, in a push-based supply chain, there are often increased transport costs, high inventory levels and/or high manufacturing costs due to the need for emergency manufacturing changeovers.

Push systems usually offer suppliers economies of scale through increasing lot sizes during manufacturing and through freight consolidation during carriage. Large buffer stocks of finished products close to customers also reduce the risk of sales losses. The types of traffic consolidation tactics applied most by suppliers are:
- the transfer of goods from small to large vehicles for the part of journey that is common to all vehicles;

- traffic pooling and redistribution to prevent overlapping of movements, thereby reducing total distance travelled; and
- reduced trip frequency.

The methods of freight consolidation are discussed in Chapter 17.

4.4.2 Pull-based supply chain systems

Pull-based supply chain systems use exactly the opposite set of determinants to those that apply in push-based systems. In this case, it is the warehousing function that dictates how much of a given product is required and when. In situations where the organisation manufacturing the products does not maintain buffer stock and order information is not communicated early and effectively, pull systems can lead to some customers not being able to have their orders fulfilled when required.

In a pull-based supply chain, manufacturing and distribution are demand-driven. They are coordinated by actual customer demand rather than forecasted demand. In a pure pull system, the firm carries no product inventory and its supply reactions are order-specific. This is made possible by fast information flow mechanisms to transfer information about customer demand, for example, point-of-sale data to the various supply chain members. In comparison to push-based systems, pull-based systems offer the following advantages:

- A decrease in order/delivery lead times achieved through the ability to better anticipate incoming orders from the retailers.
- Less inventory at the retailers, since inventory levels at retail warehouses increase with order/delivery lead times.
- Reduced variability in the system and, in particular, variability faced by manufacturers due to order/delivery lead-time reduction.
- Less inventory at the manufacturer due to the reduction in order/delivery lead-time variability.

Therefore, in a pull-based supply chain, there is usually, first, a substantial decrease in system inventory levels, second, an enhanced ability to manage resources and, third, a reduction in supply costs when compared to the equivalent push-based supply chain.

Pull-based supply chain systems are often difficult to implement when lead times are so long that it becomes unrealistic to respond to demand information. In pull-based systems it is often more difficult to take advantage of economies of scale in manufacturing and transport because these supply systems are not planned far ahead in time. The advantages and disadvantages of push and pull supply systems have led firms to seek new supply chain tactics that enjoy the benefits of both. This frequently entails a combined push-pull supply chain configuration.

4.4.3 Push-pull-based supply chain systems

With push-pull supply chain approaches the upstream (i.e. initial) stages of the supply chain are often operated in a push-based manner, while in the downstream stages a pull-based approach is utilised. The interface between the push-based phase and the pull-based phase is known as the customer order decoupling point. It can be regarded as the push-pull boundary. If you visualise a supply chain timeline, described as the time that elapses between the procurement of raw material (i.e. the beginning of the timeline) and the delivery of the eventual customer order (i.e. the end of the timeline), then the order decoupling point indicates the point on the timeline when the chain's push phase switches to its pull phase. The push phase consists of the standardised (generic) stages; the pull phase consists of stages that contribute towards product differentiation.

As an example, consider a manufacturer of electronic equipment that makes to stock and, therefore, bases all manufacturing and distribution decisions on forecast. This is a pure push approach. If, however, the same electronic equipment manufacturer assembles and supplies its products to order according to differentiated customer specifications, this would be an example of a push-pull approach. This implies that component inventory is managed based on forecast, but final assembly is in response to specific (probably customised) customer orders. Therefore, in the latter case, the push phase of the supply chain is the part before assembly, while the pull phase of the supply chain starts with assembly and its execution is based on actual customer demand. In this case, the customer order decoupling point is at the beginning of assembly.

Demand for a specific component is the sum of the demand for all finished products that use the component. Because aggregate forecasts are more accurate than individual forecasts, uncertainty in component demand is smaller than uncertainty in the demand for finished goods. This leads to safety stock reduction. Therefore, manufacturers of electronic equipment (as in the example above) often use the push-pull supply concept very effectively.

Postponement, or delayed differentiation in product design, is a good example of a push-pull tactic. In postponement, the product and its manufacturing process are designed in such a way that decisions about which specific product is manufactured can be delayed as long as possible. The manufacturing process starts by manufacturing a generic, or family, product, which is differentiated to a specific finished product once demand is revealed. The phase of the supply chain before product differentiation is operated utilises a push-based approach. The generic product is built and transported based on a long-term aggregate forecast. Because demand for the generic component is the sum of the demand for all its related finished products, forecasts are more accurate, so inventory levels are reduced. Against this, customer demand for a specific finished product usually has a high level of uncertainty, so product differentiation occurs only in reaction to individual or specific demand. Consequently, the phase of the supply chain starting from the time of differentiation is pull-based.

4.4.4 Identifying the appropriate supply chain approach

This section provides guidelines on when a supplier should employ a push, pull, or a push-pull supply chain approach. Figure 4.3 shows a framework for matching the supply chain approach with different types of products. The vertical axis indicates the level of uncertainty in customer demand; the horizontal axis shows the importance of economies of scale in either manufacturing or distribution.

High demand uncertainty leads to a preference for managing a supply chain based on orders received: a pull approach. Alternatively, small demand uncertainty leads to a preference to manage the supply chain based on a long-term forecast: a push approach. The higher the importance of economies of scale in reducing unit cost, the greater the value of aggregating demand, and consequently the greater the importance of managing the supply chain based on long-term forecast and adopting a push-based approach. When economies of scale do not occur and aggregation does not reduce unit cost, a pull-based approach is more appropriate.

In Figure 4.3, the region spanned by the two dimensions 'demand uncertainty' and 'economies of scale' is partitioned into four boxes. Box 1 represents products that are characterised by high demand uncertainty and by situations in which economies of scale in manufacturing and distribution are not important, such as electronic equipment and computer products. The frame indicates that a pull-based supply chain approach is appropriate for these products.

Box 3 represents products that are characterised by low demand uncertainty and high manufacturing and distribution economies of scale. Consumables and grocery products such as beverages, toiletry, pasta, soup and easy-to-prepare meals fall into this category. Demand for these products is fairly stable, and reducing transport cost by shipping full truck and container loads helps to reduce supply chain costs. In this case, a traditional push-based retail approach is appropriate, because managing inventory based on long-term forecasts does not increase inventory-carrying costs, while delivery costs are reduced through economies of scale.

Boxes 1 and 3 represent cases in which it is relatively easy to identify an efficient supply chain approach. In boxes 2 and 4, there is a mismatch between the approaches suggested by the two attributes, demand uncertainty and the importance of economies of scale. In boxes 2 and 4, uncertainty pulls the supply chain towards one approach, while economies of scale push the supply chain in a different direction.

For example, box 4 represents products characterised by high demand certainty, which indicates a push-based supply chain, and low economies of scale, favouring a pull-based supply chain approach. Many high-volume and fast-selling books and CDs belong in this category. In this case, a more careful analysis is required, since both the traditional retail push and the more innovative push-pull approaches may be appropriate depending on the specific costs and uncertainties.

Box 2 represents product ranges for which uncertainty in demand is high, while economies of scale are important in reducing manufacturing and distribution costs. Furniture and cars with optional

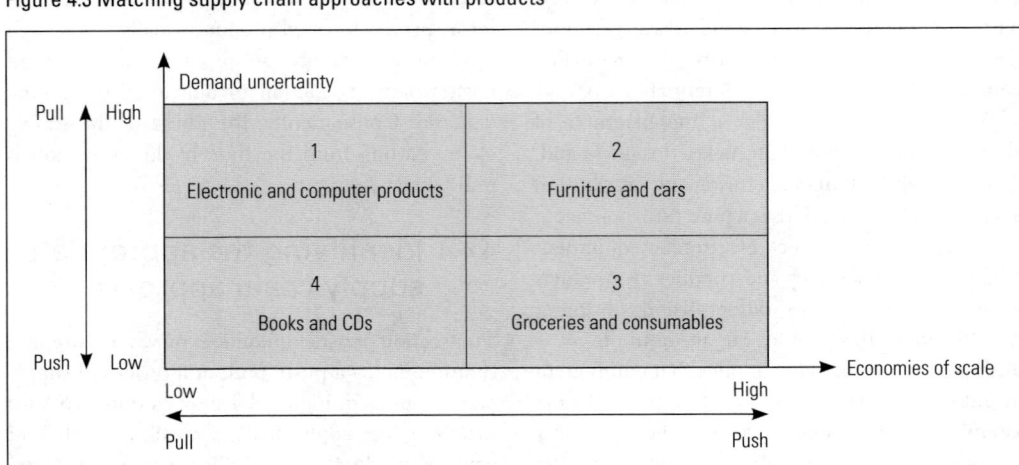

Figure 4.3 Matching supply chain approaches with products[7]

features are good examples of this category. Generally, furniture retailers offer a large number of similar products distinguished by shape, colour, material, upholstery etc. As a result, demand uncertainty is very high. However, furniture products are bulky and delivery costs consequently high.

In the case of furniture, there is a need to distinguish between the manufacturing and the distribution approaches. Manufacturing has to follow a pull-based approach since it is impossible to base manufacturing decisions based on long-term forecasts. However, the distribution approach has to take advantage of economies of scale to reduce distribution costs. This is indeed the approach followed by many retailers that do not keep inventories of furniture. When a customer places an order, it is sent to the manufacturer, who orders the material and makes to order. Once the product is ready, it is delivered together with many other products to the retail store and from there to the customer. For this purpose, the manufacturer typically has a fixed delivery schedule, which is used to aggregate all the products that are delivered to outlets in the same region, thereby lowering transport costs through economies of scale. Therefore, the supply chain approach employed by furniture manufacturers is a pull-push approach, where manufacturing takes place according to orders received (pull), but delivery according to a fixed schedule (push).

The vehicle market is another example of the conditions of box 2. Car manufacturers offer a number of similar models distinguished by engine power, shape, colour, number of doors, trimmings and other optional features. Consequently, demand uncertainty for a particular specification is very high. Delivery cost is also high.

4.4.5 Implementing a supply chain approach

Different supply chain approaches are necessary in different industries and market conditions. The approaches vary primarily as to where the customer order decoupling point is located. This is considered to be the furthest upstream point in the supply chain where a specific customer order affects inventory-level decisions directly. The concept of decoupling implies that even in cases of continuous production, if an organisation ensures that it has sufficient inventory, and that buffering has been set up between each stage of the production, all the processes on that production line can operate independently of each other.

The characteristics of the push and pull portions of supply chains are summarised in Table 4.1. In a supply chain that utilises a push-pull approach the push and pull portions interact only at the customer order decoupling point. At this point there is a need to coordinate the two supply chain approaches, which is generally done through buffer stock. Note that buffer stock fulfils a different role in each supply chain portion. At the downstream end of the push portion, buffer stock is part of the inventory generated in the tactical planning process. In the pull portion of the chain the inventory forms the feeder stock to the fulfilment process.

The location of customer order decoupling points is described in the sections that follow and illustrated in Figure 4.4. The different ways in which a supply chain can respond to customer demand are explained in the sections below[8, 9, 10] and summarised in Table 4.2 (see page 67).

Table 4.1 Characteristics of the push and pull portions of supply chains

Characteristic	Push portion	Pull portion
Objective	Minimise cost	Maximise service level through flexibility
Complexity	High	Low
Demand	High certainty	High uncertainty
Focus	Efficient resource allocation	Effective responsiveness
Lead time	Long	Short
Processes	Supply chain planning according to forecast	Order fulfilment
Product	Standard	Customised or differentiated

Figure 4.4 Customer order decoupling points

| customer order decoupling points | engineer to order | purchase and make to order | make to order | assemble to order | make to stock | pick and ship to stock |

suppliers → raw material RM → component and sub-assembly production → semi-finished goods SFG → final assembly → finished goods FG → finished goods FG → customers

raw material store — semi-finished goods store — finished goods store — distribution centre

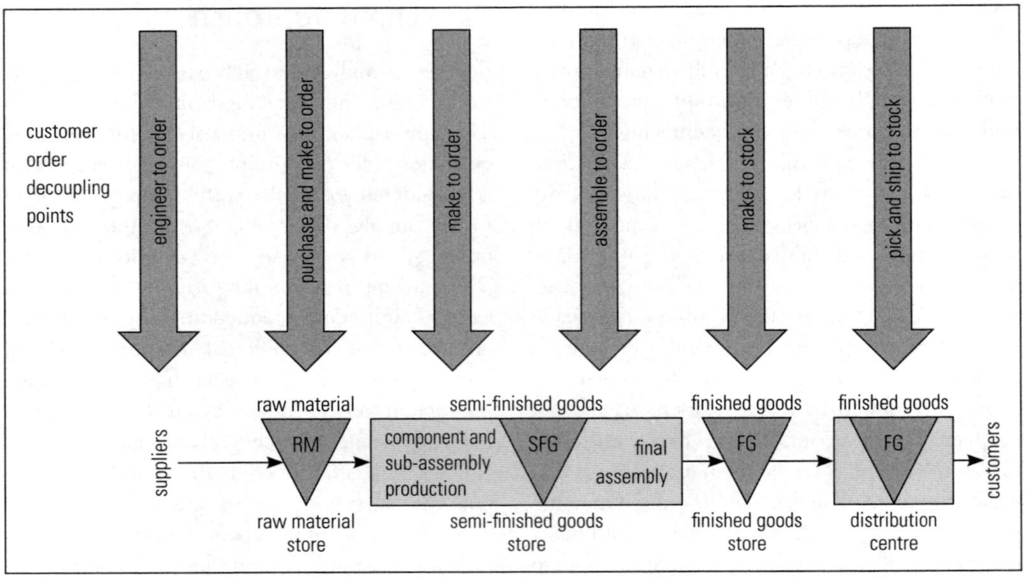

4.4.5.1 Pick and ship to stock

The use of pick and ship to stock (also called assemble and ship to stock) allows the swift delivery of products to the customer. The customer order decoupling point is located at the distribution centre. This is typical of the fast-moving consumer goods (FMCG) industry, where the finished goods inventory must be available on the shelves at all times. If the product is not available, the consumer is likely to buy a substitute product or purchase it elsewhere.

As a push supply tactic, the main challenge facing this process is demand management and more specifically the forecasting of independent demand. The major risk in this tactic lies in the inventory levels. Shortage of inventory results in poor consumer service. Surplus of inventory might result in obsolescence, either through the product shelf life expiring or demand falling away.

4.4.5.2 Make to stock

> Make to stock is a supply tactic where finished product is continually held in plant or warehouse inventory to fulfil expected incoming orders or releases based on a forecast.

The customer order decoupling point is located at the finished goods store. This is typical for consumer products that are not physically consumed, but used over time, such as domestic appliances. Relatively few products are kept for display and demonstration purposes in showrooms, but back-up inventory is kept in a central finished-goods store.

The customer order triggers the delivery of the goods from the location of the finished goods, either to the customer or to the sales outlet for replenishment. Once again, as a push supply tactic the main challenge is to manage and forecast demand and the main risk is the inventory levels.

4.4.5.3 Assemble to order

> Assemble to order is a production method in which a product is assembled after receipt of a customer's order.

The key components (bulk, semi-finished, intermediate, sub-assembly, manufactured, purchased, packing etc) used in the assembly or finishing process are planned and usually stocked in anticipation of a customer order. Receipt of an order initiates assembly of the customised product.

This tactic is useful where a large number of end products (based on the selection of options and accessories) can be assembled from common components.

The customer order extends to the final assembly line, where sub-assemblies and semi-finished goods are picked and assembled to the customer's desired configuration. All permutations of the various possible configurations must be offered, but these cannot all be kept in the finished goods store, as they would inflate finished goods inventory levels and the total logistics cost.

This customer order decoupling point is typical of markets where mass customisation is essential. An example is the laptop computer industry. Many vehicle manufacturers also utilise this process. In the manufacturing process, they allow and make provision for orders for specific options on vehicles. The inventory must be controlled at the sub-assembly level. Although assemble to order is a push-pull approach, the push element forms the minor portion. The manufacturer has to forecast the independent demand for the sub-assemblies.

This process can satisfy the customer's needs for a specifically configured item. The challenge is to keep the assembly lead times short in order to add value for the customer. Capacity constraints should not cause the final assembly to extend the delivery time. The major risks are excess stocks and subsequent obsolescence of sub-assemblies and/or components due to changes in market demand.

4.4.5.4 Make to order

> A make-to-order manufacturing approach occurs where the trigger to begin manufacturing a product is an actual customer order or release, rather than a market forecast.

For make-to-order products, generally more than 20 per cent of the value added takes place after the receipt of the order or release and all necessary design and process documentation is available at time of order receipt.

The customer order decoupling point is located at the component and sub-assembly manufacturing point. This is typical of industries that manufacture items such as custom-made furniture. The manufacturer uses special components or sub-assemblies to make the furniture. This process is more extensive than in the motor vehicle industry, where the optional sub-assemblies are standard and only the choice of the optional sub-assemblies makes the car unique to the customer.

Make to order is a push-pull approach. The push portion forms the minor part of the supply chain. The forecasting that does occur here is focused on replenishing the sub-assemblies to maintain the semi-finished goods store inventory. The assembly process of the basic item is only started once an order is received. Therefore, the independent demand for components and sub-assemblies needs to be forecasted. One of the major logistics challenges in this case is to balance the capacity of the supply chain. The people employed in this type of environment are usually multi-skilled.

4.4.5.5 Purchase and make to order

> The term purchase and make to order refers to instances when a manufacturer waits until there is a firm order for a product. All aspects of the manufacturing process, including the final assembly and packaging of the product, will only commence after the customer has confirmed the order.

The major challenge with purchase and make to order is that the business is never in a position to know precisely how many materials, components or parts will be required at any given time to fulfil customer orders. Consequently, the problem extends to the suppliers, who may be expected to deliver the necessary material to the manufacturer at extremely short notice.

Purchase and make to order is a pure 'pull' process. It is typically used in industries where the components and/or sub-assemblies are very expensive, or where the components are not used frequently. In the manufacturing process, this is the traditional so-called job-shop process. The customer order decoupling point is located at the raw material store. The business does not carry the inventory, but orders the components once the customer order has been received. Therefore, the

BOM for the components is of critical importance. An incorrect BOM will result in delays, which will impact on the production-cycle time and order lead time.

4.4.5.6 Engineer to order

> Engineer to order, often known as design to order, refers to situations where businesses undertake the engineering of products and their subsequent manufacture in line with customers' specific instructions or requirements.

Engineer to order is considerably more complex than most other forms of manufacture, as each product has to be designed to the customer's exact specification. Therefore, the business needs to be able to give the customer an accurate assessment of the delivery time, which incorporates all the lead times associated with engineering, component development, procurement, manufacture, assembly, packing and shipping.

Organisations that offer an engineer-to-order product supply need to have a fully integrated system, which incorporates close cooperation between the designers, engineers, buyers, manufacturing team and any other associated area of the business. Although each specific project may be significantly different from those which the business has already experienced, customers will expect relatively accurate indications of the stages through which their products will be developed and manufactured, as it may be a requirement of the customer to be involved in the progress and inspection of the products. Engineer to order only applies to organisations that actually design, engineer, manufacture and then fulfil the customer's specification.

The customer order decoupling point is located at the raw-material supplier level. This process is typically used to supply unique products or services and is very often undertaken as a special project. The design and construction of, for instance, a winery production cellar, bridge or seaport terminal are examples. There are no repeat orders and no economies of scale. There is also no predetermined BOM. The cost and the lead times are determined for each individual project.

4.4.6 Assessment of business response service level

The concept of service level can be used in a number of production- and inventory-based situations. When considering a pick-and-ship-to-stock and a make-to-stock system – the two push systems – the service level is the percentage of products or orders that are immediately available from the organisation's inventory.

When the term is used in connection with assemble to order, make to order, purchase and make to order and engineer to order – the four systems that have a significant pull portion – the service level is usually measured in terms of on-time delivery. The on-time delivery performance is measured as the percentage of orders that are received by the customer either by the promised or requested time. An organisation can improve its on-time delivery performance by improving the reliability (i.e. consistency) of the level of promise it gives customers by reducing its production-cycle and order lead times. These can be achieved by making use of time-compression opportunities during the production cycle and by applying service flexibility during order lead times.

4.5 Time management in supply chains

4.5.1 The importance of time[11]

Increasingly, organisations are realising that they compete on the basis of time. Reducing the time required to provide the end-customer with products is one of the major factors that impel organisations to participate in supply chain management initiatives. Adopting an integrated supply chain management approach provides the means to make significant reductions in the cycle time required to move materials between supply chain members and the end customer. Time imperatives have also been shown by several authors to be highly effective in focusing overall improvement efforts within an individual organisation. Businesses have found that in order to compete on the basis of time, other competitive capabilities in addition to reducing cycle times

Table 4.2 Supply chain responses to customer demands

Supply system	Supply concept	Inventory situation	Decoupling point	Order lead time	Examples
Pick and ship to stock	A pure push concept. Standard and generic consumer ware stored in distribution-centre inventory.	Large inventory of finished goods.	At the distribution centre.	Only the order picking and delivery time.	Order of consumer ware from a distribution centre, destined for a supermarket.
Make to stock	A pure push concept. Standard finished products are stored in inventory.	Large inventory of finished goods. Usually also has WIP and raw materials.	At the finished-goods store.	Only the delivery time from the finished goods warehouse to the customer.	Medical devices; several consumer products; white goods; standard home furniture.
Assemble to order	A push-pull concept. Semi-finished products and sub-assemblies, assembled in response to a customer order specifying from a set range of optional features.	Inventory of sub-assemblies and semi-finished products. Usually also WIP and raw materials.	At the final assembly line.	The assembly and delivery time.	Personal computers; cars; recreational vehicles; modular furniture assemblies.
Make to order	A push-pull concept. Raw materials are transformed into a customised end product.	Usually inventories of raw materials. It is possible to implement with no inventory.	At the component and sub-assembly manufacturing point.	The component and material manufacturing, assembly and delivery time.	Customised clothing; custom-made furniture; injection-moulded parts.
Purchase and make to order	A pure pull concept. Customer-specified high-value components and raw materials are transformed into a customised end product.	Potentially no inventory of high-value components. Usually some inventory of raw materials.	At the raw-materials store.	The purchase of raw materials, component manufacturing, assembly and delivery time.	Custom-made durable/ indivisible equipment – usually movable and with unique features (such as small watercraft and light aircraft).
Engineer to order	A pure pull concept. A (unique) design is developed and constructed/assembled (usually on the customer's site) for a particular customer need.	Usually no inventory. Could have limited inventory of sub-assemblies and raw materials.	At the supplier level.	The design, development and (a) construction/assembly, or (b) delivery and installation time (if built elsewhere).	Custom-built fixed construction or immovable capital equipment.

must simultaneously improve, including reliability and flexibility.

In the past, manufacturers were the drivers of the supply chain – managing the pace at which products were manufactured and distributed. Nowadays, customers require quick order fulfilment and fast delivery, complemented by reliable delivery-time performance (i.e. consistently on time). Manufacturing quality – a long-time competitive differentiator – is reaching similar standards across the board, so meeting customers' specific demands for product delivery has emerged as the next critical opportunity for competitive advantage.[12]

Cycle time is the total elapsed time required to complete a business process. Often, only a small percentage of the total elapsed time required to complete a process has anything to do with real value-adding activities. The rest of the time is typically devoted to a wide range of worthless activities and events, all of which take time. Identifying and eliminating these poor uses of time represent one of the major supply-chain-management opportunity areas. However, cycle-time reduction is not just about completing a process quickly – it is also concerned with completing the given processes consistently on time. By focusing on key processes, supply chain member organisations can make significant improvements in cycle-time performance through time efficiency and reliability, which can provide a source of competitive advantage.

4.5.2 Causes of long production cycle and order lead times

There are at least fifteen causes of long production cycle and order lead times found in product supply chains. Research has shown that whenever supply chain processes are analysed, any one or more of the following fifteen causes (analysed in the ensuing sections) will be present.[13]

4.5.2.1 Ambiguous goals and objectives

It is most important that all supply chain members are aware of and understand the strategic supply chain goals and objectives. Each supply chain member also needs to understand their role in and contribution towards the overall success of the supply chain.

4.5.2.2 Batching

Batching occurs when a volume of goods is accumulated at one step in the process or at a member in the supply chain before it is released to the next process step or downstream supply chain member. Only when batching improves overall efficiency should this tactic be implemented. An example of an efficiency tactic might be taking advantage of cheaper transport through larger consignments. In such circumstances justification of the situation should be periodically tested through trade-off analysis to establish if the economies of scale associated with the so-called batch approach are worth the time and storage required as a consequence. Very often, batching leads to inventory-carrying costs exceeding the revenue opportunities created.

4.5.2.3 Excessive controls

Excessive controls often result in too much time wasted on following the rules governing processes within and between supply chain member firms. Firms often realise that their rules and controls serve only to slow their response to customers, and that many of these control mechanisms are more of a hindrance to smooth goods flow.

For example, several signatures may be required for a purchase order, leading to a situation where these signatures are merely being rubber-stamped. Obviously, controls should not be abandoned; their purposefulness in the supply chain process should be considered periodically to ascertain if the level of control exercised is worth the associated cost.

4.5.2.4 Lack of information

It is vital for decision makers to have the correct information and in the desired format. The cycle time for supply chain decision making is often prolonged due to the time taken to collect the necessary information to make well-informed decisions. It should be recognised that the required information does not always originate within the decision maker's firm, but in one or more of the other supply chain member firms.

4.5.2.5 Lack of synchronisation in materials movement

It is necessary for goods to be moved across the supply chain in the most effective manner. For example, materials that arrive at the customer's location too early can necessitate additional storage and materials-handling activities, while delivery too late can disrupt the customer's operations and consequently damage the supplier's reputation.

4.5.2.6 Lack of proper training

Inadequate training increases the time for employees to become proficient in their jobs and can lead to improvements being delayed. Unfortunately, not all people involved in supply chain processes and activities have received adequate training to fulfil their specific duties. The tactical challenge is to provide ongoing training opportunities that focus on supply chain performance improvement in general and cycle-time reduction in particular.

4.5.2.7 Limited cooperation

Cycle time and overall supply chain performance hinge on the cooperative efforts of all the members. All supply chain members must be truly committed to the purpose of the supply chain. If not, their membership should be reconsidered.

4.5.2.8 Limited coordination

Integration and coordination of supply chain processes is a prerequisite to their success. All parties involved in a given process should recognise their respective roles and associated responsibilities. Coordinated inter-firm processes lie at the heart of any logistics-driven approach. A sound approach dictates that formal rules of engagement should exist to ensure the desired level of coordination. Unfortunately, such engagement is often lacking.

4.5.2.9 Non-value-added activities

When examining supply chain processes, it is worthwhile determining the value that is added by the overall process and individual process activities. Processes or activities within a process that add little or no value are often identifiable. Such activities should be eliminated. If an activity adds value, tactical management should ensure that it is conducted in the best way possible given current practices. For example, does the firm conduct quality inspections of purchased materials upon receipt, or does it utilise high-performing suppliers that certify that the materials they ship meet all specifications?

4.5.2.10 Outdated information technology

Supply chain members do not always make use of the best available information technology. For example, are purchase orders transmitted from the procurement entity to the supplying entity by fax, electronic data interchange (EDI), the Internet, or are they mailed? Do warehousing operations within the supply chain utilise a high level of automation or are they primarily manual operations?

4.5.2.11 Poor communication

Communications within and between businesses are critical to supply chain performance. However, it is occasionally the case that the necessary lines of communication have not been established within all supply chains. Managers within supply chain member firms often still do not know whom to contact in other functional areas within their own organisation, as well as in the allied supply chain firms. A list of key contacts in the organisations across the chain is a very simple, but valuable, resource for problem solving.

4.5.2.12 Poorly designed procedures and forms

Not all procedures and forms associated with specific processes lead to the efficient completion of the process. Indeed, some procedures significantly increase the time to complete the process by creating more work, while adding little value.

4.5.2.13 Repeating process activities

A major cause of poor supply chain cycle-time performance is having to repeat process steps due to issues relating to goods or service quality. Few situations increase product-cycle times (in terms of average cycle times and variability) more than quality issues. These problems often arise from an inability to engage in good practice the first time around.

4.5.2.14 Serial versus parallel operations

Supply chain activities are often executed in a serial manner (i.e. first complete activity 1, then complete activity 2, and so on through the process). Opportunities in the supply chain for activities to take place in a parallel (simultaneous) manner as opposed to the commonly used serial, or sequential method should be explored. For example, within a manufacturing firm, new products and the processes that are used to manufacture these products might not be developed concurrently, and the design of the product might simply be thrown over the wall, as it were, to the manufacturing section. Ideally, the manufacturing group's key supplier and customer partners in the supply chain should cooperate in any new product development and design process.

4.5.2.15 Waiting

In many supply chains significantly more time is still devoted to waiting between process steps than is actually spent in all of the processing steps combined. It is not always evident where the longest delays occur in the process, the causes of delays, or what actions can be taken to reduce or eliminate time spent waiting. Supply chain members are not always sure whether they need additional capacity in terms of facilities and equipment, or whether proper chain integration coordination is lacking.

4.5.3 Opportunities for production cycle and order lead time reduction[14, 15]

Organisations generally have significant opportunities for cycle-time improvement from a supply chain perspective. As customers increasingly focus on time-based performance, it is imperative that supply chain members have the capabilities to meet this time-based challenge. Where should the supply chain and its member organisations begin in their quest for cycle-time reduction? Opportunities for production cycle-time and order lead time reduction exist on both an intra- and inter-firm basis. An examination of the entire supply chain – from point of origin through to point of destination – is usually necessary.

Cycle-time improvement entails more than simply reducing the production cycle. It includes the time required to obtain raw materials and components, to control their quality, and to handle and, if necessary, store them until they are used. It also includes the time that finished products are stored and prepared to be shipped to retailers, the transport time and the time they are stored again before being delivered to customers – i.e. the order lead time.

To fulfil an order, it is necessary to receive the raw materials and the outsourced components on time and to ensure that the required resources, such as machines, tools, employees, transport and handling equipment, will be available on time. Minimising the time for fulfilling an order requires strong coordination between the selling, moving, manufacturing, storing and buying activities.

The buying activity consists of procuring raw material and outsourced components when required. A risky and expensive solution to reach this objective is to have ample buffer stock available. It is risky because customers' requirements can change without notice and thus make inventories obsolete. It is expensive because inventories tie up capital, and quality may suffer as a consequence of storing and handling. Thus, inventories should be avoided as far as possible in a supply chain. Selecting many reactive providers that compete with each other is the best solution for reducing the risk of running out of raw material or components.

An objective of the product supply chain system is to ensure that the manufacturing cycle of each ordered product is as short as possible, taking into account the partial schedule that exists at the time the product is launched in production. This calls for real-time scheduling that takes advantage of the idle periods of the resources. In such a scheduling approach, a product is scheduled as soon as it is launched in production and the products previously scheduled are not rearranged.

Once manufacturing is complete, the product should be packaged (end of make activity), transported to the retail location (move activity) and sold (sell activity). The storage (store activity) of finished products should be kept to a minimum, since it ties up capital and requires handling that may affect quality.

From a systems viewpoint the objective is not merely to optimise each of the previous activities, but also to coordinate them. The ability to obtain raw material or components in a very short time may result in unnecessary expense if the manufacturing system is overloaded and manufacturing cannot take place immediately. Similarly, if logistics resources are overloaded, it may be necessary to delay manufacturing of the ordered product. It is clear, therefore, that when a product is ordered, the buy, make, move and sell activities should be scheduled simultaneously, taking into account the schedule of the products that were ordered previously and the availability of external resources, such as raw material and other input suppliers. Such a system of real-time supply chain scheduling is illustrated in Figure 4.5.

Such a system enables the supply chain to meet customer demand in the shortest time and at the lowest cost by maximising the cooperation between the five activities of the supply chain. This requires determining the following:

- Whether the order can be fulfilled through existing inventory at a retail location near the customer. If not, can it be fulfilled by inventories at other locations without incurring additional transport costs?
- Whether the order can be fulfilled through manufacturing. If it can, which manufacturing plant should make it?
- Whether the partner responsible for the move activity can add value to the supply chain by consolidating different orders into one shipment, thereby reducing both cost and transport time. One should also determine whether it can handle special requests, such as deliveries direct to customers and not just between the manufacturer, wholesaler and retailer.

The remainder of this section deals with reducing the supply chain cycle time, based on the process-improvement approach presented by Harrington.[16] It consists of the following six steps:

Step 1: Establish a time management team. (TMT)

Step 2: Develop an understanding of the given supply chain process and current cycle-time and order lead time performance.

Step 3: Identify opportunities for cycle-time reduction and improvement of on-time delivery performance.

Figure 4.5 Real-time supply chain scheduling

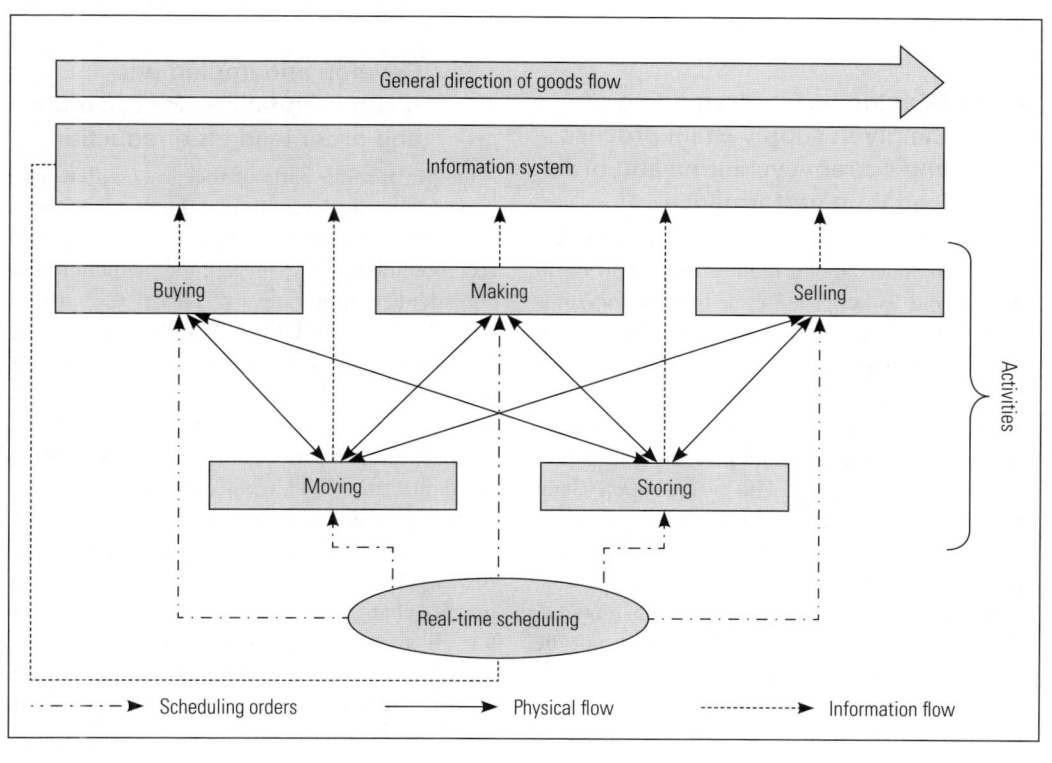

Step 4: Develop and implement recommendations for cycle-time and order lead time reduction.

Step 5: Measure process cycle-time and order lead time performance.

Step 6: Implement continuous improvement efforts for supply chain cycle-time reduction.

4.5.3.1 Establish a time management team

The first step in this process is to identify those who will conduct the cycle-time reduction effort. The composition of the TMT is important, as it will have a significant effect on the probability of success for the initiative. The TMT should include representatives of each functional area and supply chain member firm. All TMT members must possess a thorough and detailed understanding of their part of the process to ensure that the TMT collectively fully understands the entire supply chain process. In-depth knowledge of all the existing functions and activities in the chain will make it easier to identify opportunities for cycle-time reduction and make significant improvements in the entire process.

4.5.3.2 Develop an understanding of the given supply chain process and current cycle-time and order lead time performance

Once the TMT has been established, its first task is to gain an understanding of the entire supply chain process and its associated cycle-time performance characteristics. An effective way of conducting this task is to develop a process map (flow chart). Every functional area and/or member firm represented on the TMT is responsible for researching, documenting (mapping) and presenting its part of the process to the TMT. The overall supply chain process map is then consolidated from all the various composite parts of the process. Existing cycle-time performances for the overall process as well as the activities that make up the process are also required. Specific measures should include, but not be limited to, average cycle time, minimum cycle time, maximum cycle time, standard deviation of the cycle times and percentage of on-time deliveries.

4.5.3.3 Identify opportunities for cycle-time reduction and improvement of on-time delivery performance

Once the TMT has an understanding of the entire supply chain process and its existing performance, the next task is to identify opportunities for cycle-time reduction. The TMT should attempt to focus on the parts of the process that have the longest average cycle times, those with the highest levels of cycle time variability and those factors that lead to inconsistency insofar as on-time delivery performance is concerned.

In a demand pull situation a supply chain member awaiting a consignment of goods from an upstream member may request the carrier of such goods to apply flexibility tactics in order for the goods to be delivered earlier than originally arranged, or closer to on-time delivery when the consignment starts running late. By successfully capitalising on a carrier's flexibility, the business does not suffer delays or interruptions in its operations. Such flexibility tactics may include expediting, diversion, or cross-docking. Tactics used to coordinate incoming traffic are discussed in Chapter 17.

4.5.3.4 Develop and implement recommendations for cycle-time and order lead time reduction

After the specific parts of the process that offer opportunities for cycle-time reduction have been identified, the TMT must develop and implement recommendations for cycle-time reduction and consistent on-time delivery. This is the creative part of the work of the TMT. Specifically, for the opportunities identified in the previous step, the TMT must determine what can be done to improve the process cycle-time performance, given existing resource constraints. Keeping in mind that the TMT's objective is to strive for cycle-time improvements that recognise the cost, quality and technological requirements of the marketplace, it is imperative that the effects of any process changes are understood and anticipated for all parts of the supply chain examined. Simulation using computer modelling of the process and proposed changes can be helpful in this respect.

After the specific recommendations have been developed, the TMT will then present them to the management responsible for the functional areas involved. Actual implementation of the changes will normally require decision making and fund allocation on a tactical management level. However, having TMT members participate in the actual implementation efforts is advisable. These individuals should be in a favourable position to provide the context for the implementation effort due to their detailed process knowledge and motivation to live up to their recommendations.

4.5.3.5 Measure process cycle-time and order lead time performance

Once the first round of recommendations has been implemented, it is necessary to determine the effects of the changes on the actual supply process cycle-time performance. For example, did the average process cycle times decrease? Has the rate of on-time deliveries increased? How do the implemented changes affect the supply process cycle-time variability? Key performance measures should be implemented if they are not already in place. These measures need to be monitored on an ongoing basis to determine process performance.

4.5.3.6 Implement continuous improvement efforts for supply chain cycle-time reduction

Process cycle-time reduction is not a one-off event, but a continuous activity. Once one process or part of a process has been examined and improved, it is time to move on to the next process, or to improve the worst of the remaining problems first.

4.6 Conclusion

Tactical logistics activities are undertaken to implement and organise functional supply chain activities. They include goods processing, applied marketing and logistics activities, namely buying, making, moving, storing and selling.

The main objectives of tactical management in a supply chain are to:
- minimise the time required for converting orders into cash;
- minimise the total WIP in the supply chain;
- improve pipeline visibility, namely the visibility of each of the activities of the supply chain by each of the partners;
- improve visibility of demand by each of the partners;
- improve quality;
- reduce costs; and
- improve services.

Supply processes are either supply-driven (push), demand-driven (pull), or both demand- and supply-driven (push-pull).

The concept of service level can be used in a number of production and inventory-based situations. When considering a pick and ship to stock and a make to stock system, (i.e. the two push systems), the service level is the percentage of products or orders that are immediately available from the organisation's inventory.

When the term is used in connection with assemble to order; make to order; purchase and make to order; and engineer to order systems (i.e. the four systems that have a significant pull portion), service level is usually measured in terms of on-time delivery.

In the past, manufacturers were the drivers of the supply chain, and controlled the pace at which products were manufactured and distributed. Nowadays, however, customers require quick order fulfilment and fast delivery, complemented by reliable (i.e. consistently on-time) delivery time performance.

By focusing on key processes, supply chain member organisations can make significant improvements in cycle-time performance that can provide a source of competitive advantage for the supply chain.

An approach for supply chain cycle-time reduction and enhancement of on-time delivery performance consists of six steps.

Key terms

- Assemble and ship to stock
- Assemble to order
- Bill of materials (BOM)
- Decoupling point
- Design to order
- Engineer to order
- Make to order
- Make to stock
- Manufacturing
- Master production schedule (MPS)
- Material requirements planning (MRP)
- Order lead time
- Pick and ship to stock
- Procurement
- Pull system
- Purchase and make to order
- Push-pull system
- Push system
- Storing
- Time management
- Work-in-process (WIP)

Case study

Bankvas Furniture manufactures high-quality wooden home furniture. Wood that is sufficiently dry for manufacturing is bought once a year at a nearby wood auction during February. Delivery to customers takes place by road transport using a van-body truck. The furniture is manufactured at a uniform pace throughout the year. However, 60 per cent of the annual sales take place during December and January; 18 per cent during July; 6 per cent during April and the balance at 2 per cent per month during the remaining months.

Bankvas Furniture currently experiences the following problems:

- There is a great accumulation of high-value finished products. This bears high opportunity cost, risk of theft and fire, and requires big storage space.
- Some furniture remains in the display room for more than two years, which leads to it eventually being sold at substantially reduced prices.

After analysis, you recommend that Bankvas Furniture stop making standard home furniture and instead manufacture furniture to the exact design requirements of customers, after receiving a 50 per cent down payment with each order. The balance should be paid on delivery, which takes place immediately after product completion, on a time agreed with each customer at the time of receiving the order.

Bankvas Furniture accepts your proposal, but asks you to append the following to your market research report:

a) An identification and brief description of the five most likely causes that might prolong the supply chain cycle time under the proposed way of conducting business.
b) An identification and a brief description of the newly recommended product supply system. (Hint: consult Section 4.4.)
c) How the time required to convert orders into cash can be minimised by Bankvas Furniture under the proposed new supply system, using the approach presented by Harrington.

Questions

1. Indicate the various levels of management and identify the different functional activities that are organised through tactical logistics management.
2. Identify the main tactical management objectives within a supply chain and briefly indicate what each of these objectives means.
3. Describe how the flow of goods is organised in a supply chain by making use of a diagram that illustrates goods/material flow. Refer to the role of the MPS, MRP and the BOM in your description.
4. Describe the impact of lead times on logistics planning by making use of a diagram.
5. Describe the six product supply processes and identify an industry to which one can match each of these processes.
6. Why has time management become an important ingredient of gaining competitive advantage?
7. Give an overview of the 15 main causes of long production cycle and order lead times.
8. Describe the six steps proposed by Harrington that can be used to enhance the efficient use of time in supply chains.

Consult the web

APICS – The Educational Society for Resource Management: www.apics.org
Council of Supply Chain Management Professionals (CSCMP): www.cscmp.org
Council of Supply Chain Management Professionals. 2005. Supply Chain Management/ Logistics Management Definitions. Available from http://www.cscmp.org/Website/AboutCSCMP/ Definitions/Definitions.asp.
The International Society of Logistics (SOLE): www.sole.org
SAPICS – The Professional Society for Supply Chain Management: www.sapics.org.za
Supply Chain Council: www.supply-chain.org
Warehousing Education and Research Council (WERC): www.werc.org

Consult the books

Govil, M. and Proth, J. 2002. *Supply Chain Design and Management: Strategic and Tactical Perspectives*. San Diego: Academic Press.
Handfield, R. B. and Nichols, E. L. 2002. *Supply Chain Redesign: Transforming Supply Chains into Integrated Value Systems*. Upper Saddle River: Prentice Hall.
Harrington, H. J. 1991. *Business Process Improvement: The Breakthrough Strategy for Total Quality, Productivity, and Competitiveness*. New York: McGraw-Hill.
Simchi-Levi, D., Kaminsky, P. and Simchi-Levi, E. 2008. *Designing and Managing the Supply Chain: Concepts, Strategies and Case Studies*, 3rd edition. New York: McGraw-Hill.
Sutherland, J. and Canwell, D. 2004. *Palgrave Key Concepts in Operations Management*. New York: Palgrave Macmillan.
Vitasek, K. 2005. *Supply Chain and Logistics Terms and Glossary*. Washington: Council of Supply Chain Management Professionals.

Notes

1. Govil, M. and Proth, J. 2002: 65–8.
2. Use has been made of the contribution by P. Linford on pages 50 and 51 of the first edition of this book.
3. Sutherland, J. and Canwell, D. 2004: 153.
4. Ibid.: 154.
5. Ibid.: 25.
6. Use has been made of Simchi-Levi et al. 2008: 188–95.
7. Based on Simchi-Levi et al. 2008: 191.
8. Use has been made of the contribution by P. Linford on pages 52 and 53 of the first edition of this book.
9. Vitasek, K. 2005: 64.
10. Sutherland, J. and Canwell, D. 2004: 12, 93, 147 and 207.
11. Handfield, R. B. and Nichols, E. L. 2002: 53.
12. Council of Supply Chain Management Professionals. 2005: 2.
13. Handfield, R. B. and Nichols, E. L. 2002: 54–7.
14. Ibid.: 57–61.
15. Govil, M. and Proth, J. 2002: 68–72.
16. Harrington, H. J. 1991.

5 Financial aspects of logistics and supply chain management

W.J. Pienaar

Learning outcomes

After you have studied this chapter, you should be able to:
- understand the concepts of shareholder value, cost of equity, free cash flow, economic value added, and give a brief account of how these values are determined;
- identify and describe the various drivers of value;
- analyse and interpret a statement of financial position in terms of return on investment, profit margin and asset turnover;
- describe the objectives of activity-based costing, marginal costing, cost structure calculation, cost-volume-profit (CVP) analysis, breakeven analysis, and explain how these values are determined; and
- solve examples of the various abovementioned concepts numerically and interpret your answers.

5.1 Introduction

The goal of any business should be to realise the maximum net profit after tax. This way, the wealth of the owners is maximised. In the case of companies, ownership is reflected through formal shareholding. Therefore, it is generally accepted that the financial goal of the management of a company is to maximise the market value of its shares.

Accounting information, such as earnings per share, is widely published and has become the driving force of a company's performance. Management is constantly under pressure to improve on accounting information. Increasing positive cash flow has become an important success factor and a desired management goal. In order to achieve these goals, it is important to determine the drivers of the market value of shares. Logistics managers should be aware of these drivers and how they are influenced by their decisions in order to increase the market value of the shares.

In this chapter, the drivers of market value are discussed and the techniques for managing these drivers are analysed. Advanced techniques on managing costs and decisions regarding non-routine costs are also covered.

This chapter is divided into two parts. Part A provides an introduction to financial decision making. Part B deals with cost accounting and calculations for decision-making purposes.

Part A Introduction to financial management decision making

5.2 Shareholder value

Shareholder value is determined by the market value of a company's shares. Investments by shareholders in the shares of a company are referred to as the equity of the company. Shareholders require a return on their investment, which is referred to as the cost of equity. There is general agreement that the market value of shares is determined by discounting the projected free cash flows (see Section 5.4), as generated by the company to a present value, at the cost of equity. Management can increase the market value of the shares by either:
- increasing and expediting the projected free cash flow of the company; or
- reducing the risk of the company, thereby reducing the cost of equity.

Accounting measures, such as earnings per share, are only coincidentally related to share prices and not to the primary movers of share prices. Furthermore, investors have become increasingly aware of the fact that many accrual-based accounting measures do not provide a dependable picture of the future performance of a company. The benefit of using free cash flow lies in the fact that it is not affected by changes in accounting methods for financial reporting purposes, whether mandated by the International Financial Reporting Standards (IFRS) or simply dictated by management choice.

The following section concerns itself with the calculation of cost of equity; the subsequent section analyses drivers of free cash flow.

5.3 Cost of equity

5.3.1 Introduction

> Cost of equity is the return that shareholders require on their investments. On deciding to invest in a particular company, shareholders need to be compensated for the risk of investing in that company.

An investor has the option to invest risk-free (government bonds), or to invest in a company by buying shares where the return might fluctuate higher or lower than with a risk-free investment. For this risk taken, it is the shareholder's prerogative to be compensated by earning a premium above the risk-free return.

The return that a shareholder requires on an investment in shares can be summarised as follows:
$Ce = Rf + Mrp$

Where:
Ce = cost of equity (return that a shareholder requires)
Rf = risk-free rate of return
Mrp = market risk premium

5.3.2 Risk-free rate

When using the risk-free rate in the above calculation, long-term (i.e. more than ten years) government bond rates are used. The reason for using long-term government bonds is that investments in shares are considered to be long-term investments. When applying the long-term government bond rate, the after-tax rate should be used, as investors will be taxed on interest from income.

5.3.3 Market risk premium

The market risk refers to the average risk of the market as a whole in the economic system. Taking into account all the shares on a stock market, the total expected return from the market will vary. The market as a whole might either do better than the risk-free rate or it might do worse. Shareholders who invest on the stock market are exposed to a higher risk than the investors in government bonds. To compensate shareholders for this higher risk, the return that investors require from shares is higher than the return on risk-free investments. The market risk premium refers to the difference between the expected rate of return on the market as a whole that shareholders require and the risk-free rate of return over the same period.

5.3.4 The beta factor

If a shareholder wants to invest in an individual share listed on a stock market, the return that the shareholder requires from the individual share will be higher or lower than the market return, depending on whether the risk of the share is higher or lower than that of the market. The movement of this share relative to the movement of the market must be analysed in order to conclude whether the individual share is more or less risky than the market. If the movement of an individual share is more volatile than the market, the risk of the individual share is higher than the risk of the market.

This movement of one share relative to the movement of the market is represented by the beta factor. The beta factor for each listed company is available. In statistical terms, beta refers to a regression coefficient expressing the relationship of the covariance between an individual share and the market with the variance of the market. This relationship can be determined through least square regression analysis.

5.3.5 Capital asset pricing model

A model was developed to calculate the return that investors require based on the premise that investors are compensated for the risk they bear. This model is the capital asset pricing model (CAPM) and has the refinement that it recognises the risk of operating in the economic system in which the company operates (market risk) and the risk pertaining to investing in a specific company (beta factor).

The return that a shareholder requires from an individual share can be explained as follows by means of the CAPM:

$$Ce = Rf + (β \times Mrp)$$

Where:
- Ce = cost of equity (return that a shareholder requires)
- Rf = risk-free rate of return after tax
- β = beta of the individual share
- Mrp = market risk premium

5.4 Free cash flow

> Free cash flow is the cash flow from operating activities actually available for distribution to the shareholders.

Free cash flow is calculated as follows: net operating profit after tax plus any non-cash adjustments shown on the statement of cash flows less investments in working capital and in property, plant and equipment needed to sustain operations.

In order to increase a company's future free cash flow, management needs to:
- increase its profit after tax (refer to Sections 5.6.1, 5.6.2 and 5.6.3);
- decrease its investment in working capital (refer to Section 5.6.4); and
- decrease its investment in property, plant and equipment (refer to Section 5.6.5).

Taking the time value of money into account it is important to expedite the future free cash flow, as the present value of the discounted free cash flows will increase. The time value of money can be illustrated as follows. If a company is going to receive R1 000 per annum for the next three years and the required rate of return is 15 per cent, the present value is calculated as shown in Figure 5.1.

Figure 5.1 Calculating the time value of money

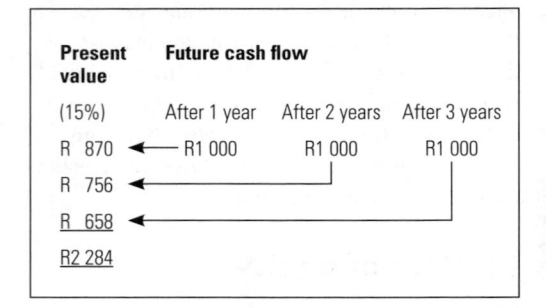

Present value	Future cash flow		
(15%)	After 1 year	After 2 years	After 3 years
R 870 ←	R1 000	R1 000	R1 000
R 756 ←			
R 658 ←			
R2 284			

From Figure 5.1, it is clear that the closer the cash flow is to the present date, the higher the present value will be.

5.5 Economic value added

Earlier in this chapter it was stated that the main financial objective of the management of a company is to maximise the market value of the shares of the company. As the profits of a company are the main driver of the free cash flow, it is the goal of management to maximise the profits of the company.

As stated earlier, when shareholders invest in a company there is a minimum return required by them, which is the cost of equity. If the required return is not achieved, the value of the shares will drop, thereby eroding shareholders' value. Earnings growth does not necessarily lead to the creation of value for shareholders. Only when management earns a rate of return higher than the rate investors expect to earn do the company's shares increase in value.

> Economic value added (EVA) is a residual income measure that subtracts the cost of capital employed (shareholders' investment in the company, i.e. equity) from the operating profits generated in the company.

A shortcoming of reporting profits according to the accounting system is that the cost of equity is not taken into account. EVA is a measuring tool that addresses this.

EVA = NOPAT − CCE

Where:
NOPAT = net operating profit after tax
CCE = cost of capital employed (return required by shareholders on their total investment in the company)
 = shareholders' investment (equity) × cost of equity

An increase in the EVA will have a positive effect on the shareholders' value. The above equation shows that a company can have a negative EVA. Negative EVA, where the cost of capital employed is greater than the net operating profit after tax, will erode shareholders' value, especially when it lasts for a long period of time.

Market value added (MVA) is calculated by calculating the net present value of all future EVAs. This can be regarded as a true measure of the value of the business to its shareholders. Another way of calculating the MVA is:

Share price × shares issued − book value of capital employed = MVA

5.6 Value drivers

Free cash flow from operations represents the difference between operating cash inflows and outflows. Free cash flow is relevant when estimating the value of the shares in a company, as it represents the cash available to compensate shareholders, thereby creating shareholder value. The following are the main value drivers of free cash flow and a strategy to maximise these value drivers must be implemented to increase the future free cash flow:

- Revenue
- Operating costs
- Tax
- Working capital
- Property, plant and equipment

These are elaborated on in the following sections.

5.6.1 Revenue

The type of product or service that the company delivers will determine the strategy to be followed to increase revenue. The volume of sales is important and the goal will be to maximise sales. (Refer to Section 2.6.1.1, page 30.)

Forces that compete against maximising revenue are the threat of new entrants and substitute products and the bargaining power of buyers. Sales volume and customer retention, therefore, are crucial, as well as the impact that logistics services might have. Customers remain loyal to a supplier if the service is reliable, responsive and meets required standards. Satisfied customers attract other potential customers and are more inclined to place bigger orders with the supplier.

5.6.2 Operating costs

All the costs pertaining to the business, such as production and distribution costs, must be taken into consideration and analysed in order to find ways to reduce them. Budgets are tools that can be used to assist management in minimising costs by controlling costs effectively. The production and distribution costs can be divided between fixed expenses and variable expenses. (See Chapter 16 for a discussion on fixed and variable costs.)

5.6.2.1 Gross margin

The gross margin refers to the following ratio: (Revenue less cost of goods sold)/revenue.

The lower the cost of goods sold in relation to the sales, the higher the gross margin. The cost of goods sold in a manufacturing environment is determined by raw materials used in production and the other expenses incurred in converting raw materials into finished products. These expenses comprise labour costs, indirect costs and other fixed costs, such as the depreciation charges of equipment used.

Direct and indirect costs of converting raw materials into finished goods must be analysed to identify where the costs of finished goods can be reduced. Factors such as better training of workers and improvement in productivity should lead to a reduction in the wage bill, as employees can do more work, which may lead to higher production figures. Better utilisation of raw materials will lead to a reduction in waste materials and savings in costs. Shorter supply chains will also have a positive effect on cost savings. Fewer members in the chain will result in less duplication of activities and faster reaction to a change in demand.

5.6.2.2 Net profit

Net profit is gross profit less expenses. If management reduces expenses without a reduction in the sales, the profits will increase. Expenses can be divided into primary activities and support activities. Primary activities comprise inbound logistics; operations; outbound logistics; marketing and sales; and services. Support activities comprise company infrastructure; human-resource management; technology development; and procurement.

Primary activities

When managing primary activities, the following should be addressed:

Inbound logistics

Operating expenses to be managed are materials handling; warehousing; freight-in; and administrative activities.

Operations

These expenses include processing; assembling; testing; and packaging.

Outbound logistics

These comprise materials handling; warehousing; freight-out; and administration.

Marketing and sales

Marketing and sales-related expenses cover the sales force; advertising; promotion; and administration.

Service

Service expenses relate to installations; training; maintenance and returns.

Support activities

When managing support activities, specific attention should be paid to the following expenses:

Firm infrastructure

Activities include general management; planning; finance; accounting; legal; and government affairs.

Human-resources management

Human-resources management includes activities involved in the recruitment, hiring, training, development and compensation of personnel involved in the primary activities.

Technology development

These are activities aimed at improving the product or any of the primary activities, for example, a computerised order-entry system.

Procurement

These expenses are related to the function of purchasing inputs used in the company's value chain.

5.6.3 Tax

The free cash flow is calculated after all taxes have been paid. Payments to shareholders by means of dividends are after-tax payments. To maximise the free cash flow it is important to minimise the taxes that should be paid. Tax regimes differ from country to country and the decision regarding the location of the operating and distribution facilities may have an important impact on taxes payable. Opportunities should be taken to minimise taxes by considering the location of assets and production and distribution activities. Governments levy taxes on many activities of a company. Examples of taxes payable by companies are tax on profits; tax on dividends declared; property taxes; taxes on fuel; and value-added tax.

5.6.4 Working capital

Companies require a certain level of working capital in order to operate efficiently. Inventory levels should be sufficient so as not to result in stockouts with resulting loss in sales. Collection policies on debtors should not be so stringent that debtors are driven elsewhere to purchase their goods. On the other hand, there is an opportunity cost where the investment in working capital is too high. The optimal working capital policy is one in which the return generated on the investment in working capital is balanced with the risk of being unable to meet commitments.

Understanding the working-capital cash-flow cycle of a company is essential when determining the investment in working capital. The activities and working-capital cycle of a manufacturing company are as follows:
- Based on its budgets and manufacturing needs, the company orders raw materials.
- The company then receives the raw materials.
- Depending on the credit terms that have been negotiated, the creditors require payment.
- As the need arises, the raw materials are then transferred to the production department.
- Labour and machines are used to convert the raw materials into finished goods.
- Finished goods are then transferred to the sales department.
- The finished goods are then sold to customers on credit.
- Cash is received from debtors at the end of the cycle.

A diagram of the working-capital cycle in a manufacturing environment, from the time the raw materials are purchased until when the cash from the sale of the goods is received, is shown in Figure 5.2.

Management should strive to shorten the working-capital cycle as much as possible in order to reduce the period for which finance is required without affecting the efficiency of operations. From Figure 5.2, it is clear that the cycle can be shortened by:
- reducing the period from raw materials purchased to production;
- reducing the time it takes to convert raw materials into finished goods;
- reducing the time taken to sell the finished goods;
- reducing the time taken to recover cash from debtors; and
- extending the time taken to pay creditors.

5.6.4.1 Cash

Cash is crucial for a company to be able to pay suppliers in order to ensure ongoing deliveries of goods and services. Buying and paying for inventories and not receiving payment from debtors will result in an extension of the period for which finance is required in the working-capital cycle. Inventories and debtors are usually financed by short-term borrowings, which is expensive.

5.6.4.2 Accounts receivable/payable

Shortening the accounts receivable period will shorten the period in which finance is required.

Figure 5.2 Working-capital cycle in a manufacturing company

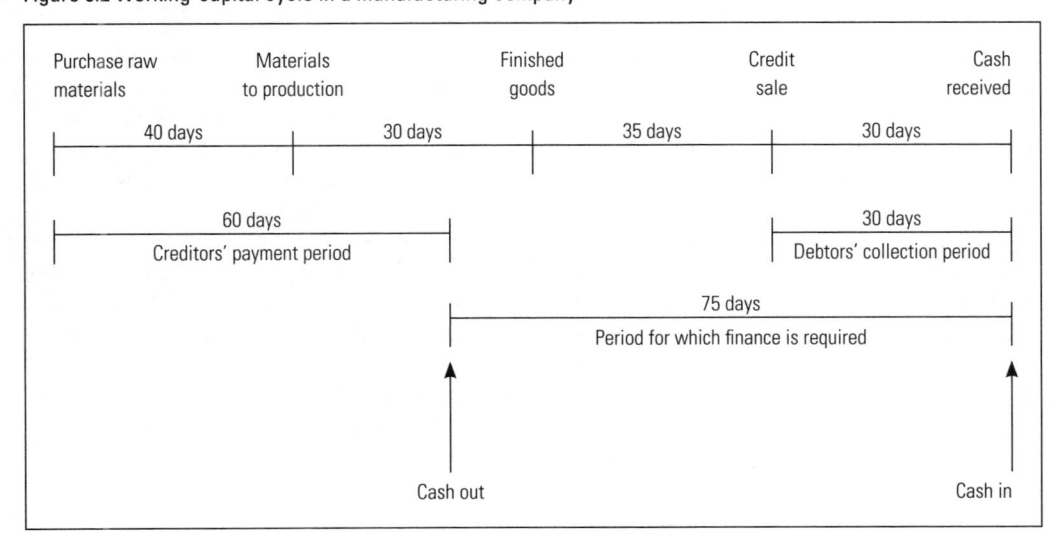

Purchase raw materials	Materials to production	Finished goods	Credit sale	Cash received
40 days	30 days	35 days	30 days	
60 days — Creditors' payment period			30 days — Debtors' collection period	
		75 days — Period for which finance is required		
		Cash out		Cash in

This way, interest is saved and the cash available enables the company to pay creditors, wages and other expenses. The opportunity to negotiate cash discount is also available. The longer the accounts receivable period, the higher the risk of bad debts and the resulting loss for the company.

Extending the accounts payable will also shorten the period in which finance is required, with the same benefits to the company as shortening the accounts receivable period.

5.6.4.3 Inventories

Inventories of a manufacturing company consist of raw materials, work in progress and finished goods. The investment in inventories can be a substantial part of the investment in the working capital of a manufacturing company. The extent to which inventory levels are monitored and managed have a major impact on profitability. (Refer to Chapter 10 for a detailed analysis of inventories management.)

5.6.5 Property, plant and equipment

The efficient deployment and utilisation of property, plant and equipment in companies where the investment in property, plant and equipment is considerable are crucial to a company's profitability.

A company can invest in its own property, plant and equipment or it can partly outsource production or physical distribution of products in order to move assets off its balance sheet. Assets on the balance sheet will be financed by equity and loans. Management has the responsibility to utilise the assets to generate income for the company. It is important for management to earn a return on assets that is greater than the costs of financing these assets. The costs of financing the assets will be determined by the costs of equity and the interest paid on the borrowings. The higher the income generated by the assets (return on assets), the higher the return on equity, as the cost of borrowing is fixed.

The advantage of partly outsourcing production and physical distribution is that management can focus on the primary activities of the company.

5.7 Return on investment

5.7.1 Introduction

The statement of financial position is a summary of the assets controlled by management and the financing of those assets. The statement of financial position can be presented as follows:
Assets = equity + liabilities

The objective of management is to increase the return on assets. The return on assets will have a direct impact on the return on equity, as explained by the following calculation:

	(R)
Income generated by the assets of the company	900 000
Less cost of goods sold	600 000
Gross profit	300 000
Less expenses incurred	150 000
Profit before interest	150 000
Interest	50 000
Profit before tax	100 000
Tax	30 000
Profit after tax (return on equity)	70 000

The ability of management to increase the return on the assets of a company is an indication of the effectiveness of management. Figure 5.3 is a summary of how to manage the return required by shareholders.

The return on equity is the product of two ratios:
- Return on assets, which is an indication of how well management is utilising the assets.
- The assets to equity ratio, which is an indication of the portion of the assets that is financed by shareholders' money.

Return on assets is important to the management of a company, as it reflects the effectiveness of management. This ratio in turn is the product of the following two ratios:
- The profit margin
- The asset turnover

Figure 5.3 Managing a company's return on equity

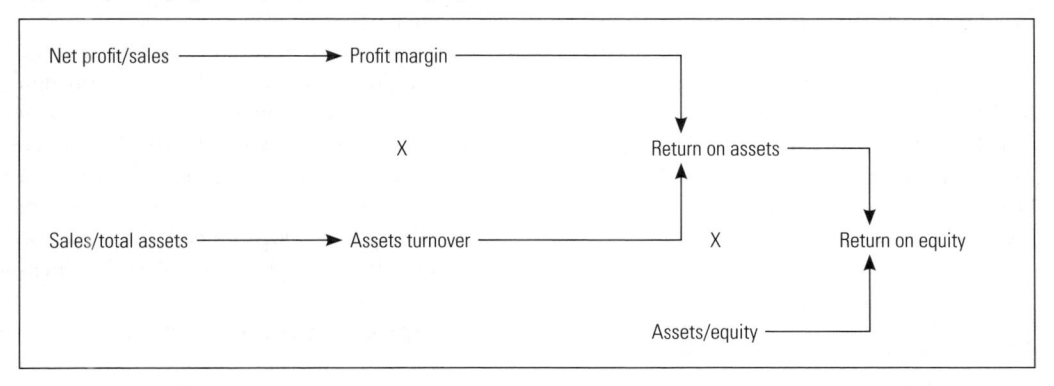

Net profit/sales → Profit margin
Sales/total assets → Assets turnover
Profit margin × Assets turnover → Return on assets
Return on assets × Assets/equity → Return on equity

5.7.2 Profit margin

The profit margin is the net profit divided by the sales. The net profit is calculated as follows:
- Sales less cost of sales = gross profit; and
- Gross profit less expenses = net profit

The strategy for increasing net profit to sales will be to reduce the cost of sales and the expenses relative to sales. The ratio of gross profit to sales, gross profit margin, is an indication of how well the management is managing its production cost.

Cost of sales in a manufacturing environment is compiled as follows:

	(R)
Inventories at the beginning of the year	240 000
Raw materials	60 000
Work in progress	70 000
Finished goods	110 000
Plus	740 000
Purchases of raw material	360 000
Labour costs	220 000
Overheads	160 000
	980 000
Less inventories at the end of the year	380 000
Raw materials	80 000
Work in progress	120 000
Finished goods	180 000
Cost of sales	600 000

From this, it is clear that in order to reduce the cost of sales the raw materials that have been used, the labour costs and overheads must be reduced. Strategies to reduce these costs are discussed further in Part B of this chapter.

The ratio used to manage the expenses is the net profit to sales ratio. The goal here is to minimise the expenses needed in order to achieve the required sales. The expenses of a manufacturing company are made up of:
- marketing and distribution costs;
- administrative expenses;
- other operating costs;
- interest payable; and
- taxation.

From this, it is clear that there should be a strategy to manage each different category of expenses.

5.7.3 Asset turnover

The asset turnover ratio is an indication of how effective the assets are utilised. The assets of a company are made up of non-current assets and current assets. Non-current assets to turnover is an indication of how many sales are generated by the non-current assets of a company. By analysing the individual non-current assets and calculating the turnover generated by each asset, management can identify assets that are not fully utilised.

Net current assets comprise inventories plus accounts receivable less accounts payable. In order to reduce the investment in net current assets, the investment in inventories and accounts receivable must be as low as possible and the investment in accounts payable as high as possible. The investment in inventories is managed by calculating the turnover of inventories. The longer it takes to sell inventory, the higher the investment. The debtor collection period is used to manage the investment in accounts receivable. The longer it takes to collect the outstanding debt, the higher the investment in debtors will be.

Part B Introduction to cost accounting and calculations for decision-making purposes

As explained earlier in the chapter, the management of cost is important in maximising net profit before tax. In order to take meaningful decisions regarding financial aspects of logistics, for example the discontinuation of a product or department, or changing the logistics chain of a product or service, it is important to understand how costs are affected by such decisions and how costs accumulate for products, services and departments.

The concepts discussed in the second part of this chapter will assist the management of a company in making the correct decisions and implementing the required action to ultimately maximise shareholder value.

5.8 Logistics costing and activity-based costing

5.8.1 Logistics costing

Logistics management integrates resources across a product's supply chain, running through the company from supplier to customer. Financial accounting and reporting, on the other hand, is based on determining product cost for external reporting purposes. Financial reporting is still based on a departmental approach, which does not allow for the measurement of the costs relating to the supply chain that flows interdepartmentally.

Recent developments in management accounting are beginning to bridge this gap. Management accounting is a function within the company that provides information for planning, control and decision making.

Basic principles of logistics costing are that the costing system should provide cost information that follows the flow of a product or service through the logistics chain and should be able to separate cost per product or customer type. A management accounting tool that can be very useful in understanding how a logistics cost system can be developed is the concept of activity-based costing.

5.8.2 Activity-based costing

> Activity-based costing, referred to as ABC, is a refined costing system that seeks to assign costs to products or services based on the manner a product or service 'causes' costs.

This approach stipulates that it is activities within a company that result in costs being incurred and that these costs must be assigned to products based on the manner in which a certain product or service causes these activities to take place. For example, if the activity is to store products in a warehouse, a product will be assigned a part of the storage costs (e.g. rental) based on its size and the period of storage, which in combination are the cause for the activity of storage. These so-called causes are known as the cost drivers of an activity.

The process of activity-based costing involves:
- identifying the main activities that take place within an organisation;
- allocating costs to these activities (cost pools);
- determining the cost drivers for these activities (causes); and
- assigning the costs to each product or service, depending on its usage of the activity.

Consider the cost of making deliveries. Initially, it may seem very difficult to assign these costs to each delivery as each delivery varies from the next. But if we apply the principles of ABC (listed above), it becomes easier, as shown:
1 Identify the delivery-related activities.
   The activities may include receiving and processing the delivery order, packaging,

travelling to and from delivery address and repairs and maintenance of delivery vehicles.
2 Allocate the costs to these cost pools. Cost of packaging materials, packaging personnel and cost of operating packaging machines are allocated to the packaging cost pool.
3 Determine the cost driver for these activities. Packaging cost may be driven by two factors: the fragility of an item delivered and the size of a package.
4 Assign the costs to each delivery based on its usage of the activity. A large package of medium fragility will get the costs calculated to be assigned to a large package plus the costs needed to package medium fragile items securely (e.g. extra bubble wrap).

In this way, the package is assigned costs for each activity as it flows through the supply chain. For example, it will also get a tariff per kilometre to assign transport costs based on the specific distance for this package. Depending on the level of accuracy needed and the cost of attaining that accuracy, the activities and cost drivers can be broken down into more depth, as shown in Figure 5.4.

Figure 5.4 Delivery costing across departmental boundaries

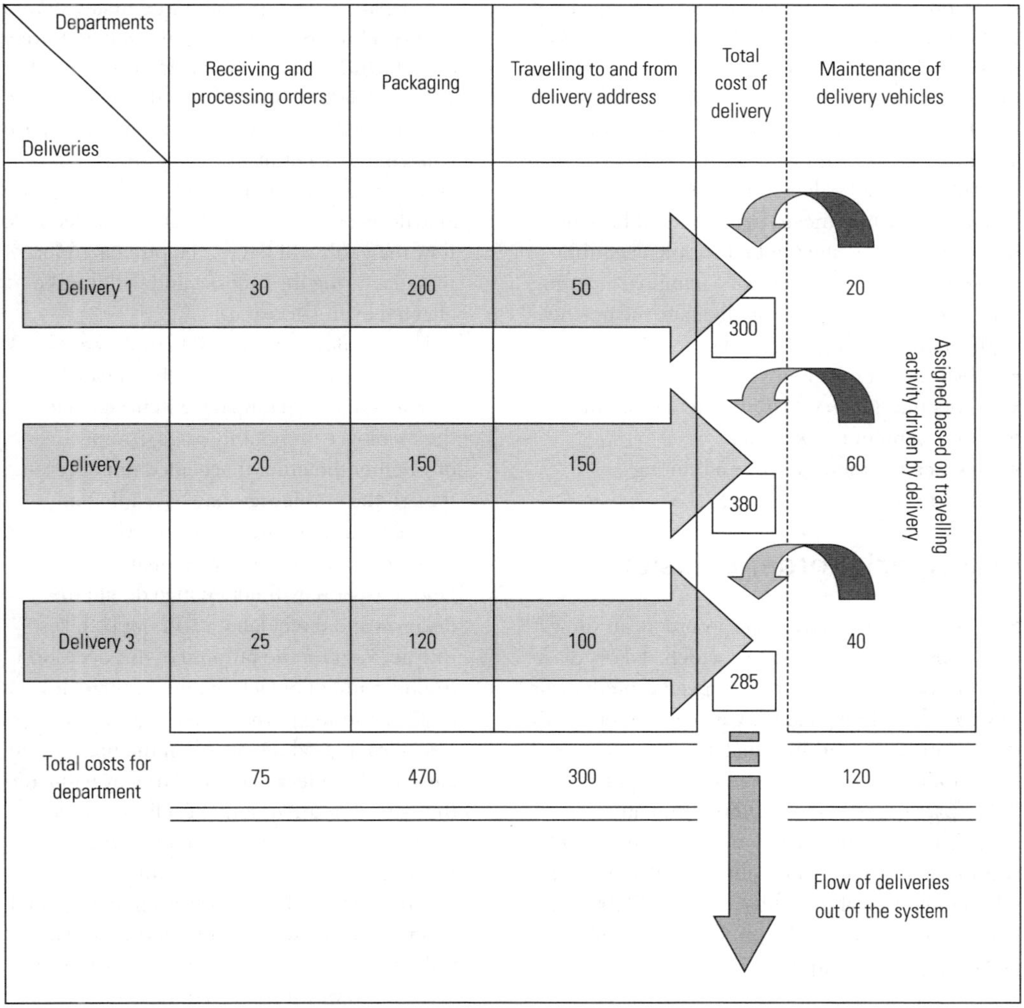

Departments \ Deliveries	Receiving and processing orders	Packaging	Travelling to and from delivery address	Total cost of delivery	Maintenance of delivery vehicles
Delivery 1	30	200	50	300	20
Delivery 2	20	150	150	380	60
Delivery 3	25	120	100	285	40
Total costs for department	75	470	300		120

Assigned based on travelling activity driven by delivery

Flow of deliveries out of the system

5.9. Marginal costing

5.9.1 Introduction to marginal costing

When management is confronted with non-routine decisions, such as changing the logistics chain of a product or closing a department, the normal cost information supplied for reporting purposes does not provide adequate information to enable management to make the correct decision.

The concept of marginal costing – also known as relevant costing – was introduced to assist management to take only the costs and benefits affected by the decision into account. Furthermore, it is important to remember that the effects of a decision normally spread much wider than its immediate functional area of impact within the company.

The key point to remember is only to take into account the costs and benefits that will change as a result of a specific decision (i.e. the relevant costs and benefits). This means that costs that have been incurred in the past are not taken into account.

Four different types of marginal costing decisions will be discussed to illustrate the practical applications of marginal costing:
- Special-order decisions
- Discontinuation of a department or product
- Replacement of equipment
- Choice of products where a limiting factor exists

5.9.2 Special-order decisions

Special-order decisions relate to orders at a lower than normal selling price, which takes place outside the main market of a specific product or service. This will typically be once-off orders to fill short-term spare capacity that the company may have available from time to time. This applies only if the spare capacity is of a short-term nature.

This is best explained by means of an example. Assume a company normally manufactures and sells product A at a selling price of R200. The manufacturing cost of the product as compiled for normal reporting purposes is as follows:

	Cost per unit (R)
Raw materials (5 kg @ R14)	70
Labour (permanent employees) (2 hours @ R20)	40
Apportionment of factory rental	35
Packaging costs per unit	10
Cost of manufacturing one unit of product A	155

If the company has capacity to manufacture 10 000 units of product A per month, but has spare capacity for three months in winter, should they accept a special once-off order at a selling price of R140 per unit (which will fill the spare capacity of 1 000 units)?

At first glance, it seems that the company should not, as the selling price is below normal cost price for manufacturing the product. However, the key concept as stated earlier is that only the costs and benefits that will be affected by the decision have to be taken into account.

Consider each component of the cost in more depth to decide whether it is relevant to the decision.
a) Raw materials will have to be purchased for manufacturing the product and will thus be affected by the decision.
b) Labour relates to permanent employees of the company. This means that it can be assumed that the company will have to pay the employees a monthly wage, irrespective of whether the order is accepted or not (even though the employees may have idle time on their hands, as there is spare capacity available). As a result, the company's total labour expense will not change due to the decision and direct labour will not be taken into account for the purpose of this decision.
c) Apportionment of factory rental is done for cost accounting purposes to assign the correct cost to each product, based on the normal capacity. It is clear that the company will pay the same amount of rental each month (as negotiated on a normal rental agreement), irrespective of the number of units manufactured. This also means that the rental will not change whether or not the special order is accepted. This amount is accordingly also irrelevant with regard to this decision.

d) The packaging cost will change, as the special-order units require packing (which can be saved if the order is not accepted). Therefore, this cost is relevant to this decision.

Let's now compare only the marginal or relevant costs to the benefit that will be gained from the special order:

	Rands per unit A
Benefit – selling price	140
Marginal cost	
Raw materials	(70)
Packaging	(10)
Marginal benefit in accepting the order (per unit of A)	60

As there is a positive marginal benefit for the company in accepting the special order, it would be wise to accept the special order.

5.9.3 Discontinuation of a department or product

When considering the discontinuation of a department or product, the same basic principle discussed above applies. The difference is that the discontinuation decision is a longer-term one and, therefore, longer-term financial implications now have to be considered. The rental, for example, was irrelevant for the decision relating to the special order, as rental would remain unchanged. However, when discontinuing a department, the rental of the premises on which the department is situated can be saved (depending on the circumstances) and hence becomes relevant to the decision.

The cost of equipment and other assets of the department under consideration are irrelevant, as this cost was incurred in the past on initial purchase. If the equipment will be sold, the possible resale value will be relevant (not the profit at disposal, as the profit takes the historical cost price into account, which, as already stated, is irrelevant).

It is also of importance to note that the company as a whole needs to be considered. In many situations, the reported cost or profit of a department is calculated by including certain head-office fees that were apportioned to that department on an arbitrary basis. If these head-office fees are not caused by the department specifically, and as a result cannot be saved by the company as a whole, then these costs must not be taken into account and are irrelevant for this decision. From a logistics point of view, the possible benefit from savings in transportation costs for the department, if situated away from other departments, should be taken into account. The same applies to any other logistical savings, such as savings regarding the communication system, or repairs and maintenance costs and so on.

When management considers the discontinuation of a product, it is necessary to take the total sales income of the product into account, less only the costs that can be saved by discontinuing the product (the marginal cost in total). This figure will mostly not resemble the profit reported on the product for normal purposes. If it is calculated that the product's sale income in total is more than the costs that can be saved by discontinuing the product, namely, the result of the calculation is positive, then the company should not discontinue the product without further investigation of whether it really is worthwhile to discontinue it. An example of when it may still be worthwhile to discontinue the product in such a case is when the capacity that will become available from the discontinuation can be used in a more profitable manner (i.e. the benefits from the alternative use exceed the positive result of the calculation mentioned for the current product).

5.9.4 Replacement of equipment

This scenario is particularly relevant when changes in equipment are considered with a view to shortening the time that a product spends in the production cycle so that the cash-to-cash cycle of a product can be optimised.

We know that the cost price of the equipment currently in use is irrelevant, but that any benefit that can be gained from the resale of the equipment will be a relevant benefit. It follows, therefore, that the cost price of the new equipment will be relevant.

A question that would be addressed by financial accounting is whether the fact that the depreciation of the currently used and new equipment will differ is relevant to the decision. Let's consider this for a moment.

Depreciation is an accounting entry to apportion the historical cost price of an asset to periods in which the asset is being used by the company. We have already dealt with the handling of the two assets' cost prices. If we were to take the difference in depreciation into account, we would be double-counting the effect of the assets' cost price. Furthermore, depreciation is only an accounting entry and has no cash-flow implications. Because of these reasons, depreciation is always irrelevant in a marginal-costing situation irrespective of the type of decision.

5.9.5 Choice of products where a limiting factor exists

When a company manufactures more than one product and it happens that there is a resource in scarce supply that prevents the company from producing as many products as it would like to satisfy demand for its products, the question arises as to how many of which product the company should manufacture to maximise its profits.

5.9.5.1 Fixed and variable costs

To answer this question, as well as other questions that will be discussed later in this chapter, the following is of great importance.
- Fixed cost does not vary in accordance with the number of units being produced. An example would be the rent of a factory building. This cost remains the same from month to month regardless of whether one unit is produced or 10 000.
- Variable costs, however, vary according to the number of units produced. Raw materials used in the production process are a good example. If one unit is produced, the company will only order enough raw materials for one unit. If 10 000 units are produced, this is multiplied by 10 000.

Consider the sales income derived from selling the units produced. In the same way, this is a variable income, as you derive extra income for each unit being produced and sold.

If you look again at Section 5.9.2 on special-order decisions, you will see that you have already applied this approach. In the example discussed in that section, you will remember that the factory rental was treated as irrelevant, as the acceptance of the special order does not result in extra rent having to be paid, as it is a fixed cost.

5.9.5.2 The concept of contribution per unit

> Contribution per unit is the sales price (which is a variable income, as explained) less the variable cost for that unit.

Contribution per unit = sales price per unit − all variable costs per unit.

Contribution per unit is the basic building block that contributes towards achieving and increasing profit. The term is appropriate, as this figure is the contribution that the sale of each unit makes towards covering fixed costs and eventually increasing profit. This is discussed in more detail in Section 5.10 on CVP analysis.

5.9.5.3 Limiting-factor decisions

In the real world, all resources are limited, but there may be one factor that limits the company's activities in such a way that it cannot function to its full potential (in other words, the factor limits the company from satisfying the demand for its products or services). The steps to identify this factor and to determine how many of which product a company should manufacture (the production mix) to maximise profits are as follows:

Step 1: Identify the main limiting factor.
Step 2: Calculate contribution per unit.
Step 3: Calculate contribution per limiting factor.
Step 4: Rank product according to preference for manufacturing based on best contribution per limiting factor.
Step 5: Calculate the production mix that will consume the available resource in the most profitable manner.

Let's look at an example to explain the concept clearly:

A company manufactures three products, Ace, Ball and Cell. The composition of each product's contribution per unit is set out below:

	Ace	Ball	Cell
Selling price per unit:	R80	R120	R62
Variable costs per unit:			
Raw materials	R32	R48	R24
(at R8 per metre)	(4 metres)	(6 metres)	(3 metres)
Labour	R20	R40	R20
(at R20 per hour)	(1 hour)	(2 hours)	(1 hour)
Contribution per unit:	R28	R32	R18
The demand for the product is:	1 000	1 500	500

The available resources are limited to 12 000 metres of raw materials and 6 000 labour hours (assuming a scarcity in labour with the skills to work on the production of these products). The steps are applied as follows:

Step 1: To see which of the two limiting factors, if any, limits the company from satisfying full demand, one has to calculate how much of each resource is needed.

	Ace	Ball	Cell
Demand for unit:	1 000	1 500	500
Usage of resource per unit:			
Raw materials:	4 metres	6 metres	3 metres
Labour	1 hour	2 hours	1 hour
Resource needed to produce enough units to satisfy demand (demand × usage):			
Raw materials:	4 000 metres	9 000 metres	1 500 metres
Labour	1 000 hours	3 000 hours	500 hours

From the calculation above, one can see that the company needs 14 500 metres of raw materials and 4 500 labour hours to produce enough units to satisfy market demand. When compared to the available resources, we see that the available raw material is less than needed, and therefore it is the main limiting factor.

Step 2: Calculate contribution per unit.

The contribution per unit is shown above (Ace: R28; Ball: R32; Cell: R18).

Step 3: Calculate the contribution per limiting factor.

One cannot just use the contribution per unit to decide on the ideal production mix, as the company has to take into account that each type of product consumes the limited resource in different quantities. For example, product Ball gives the best contribution per unit, but consumes six metres of the limited raw materials to achieve this contribution. The solution is to take the contribution per unit and divide it by the quantity of resource used to arrive at a contribution per metre of the limited resource.

	Ace	Ball	Cell
Contribution per unit	R28	R32	R18
Raw materials required per unit	4 metres	6 metres	3 metres
Contribution per metre of raw material	R7	R5,33	R6

Step 4: Ranking of products.

Next, the products can be ranked on the basis of which contributes the most towards profit per resource consumed.

	Ace	Ball	Cell
Ranking	1	3	2

Step 5: Calculate profit-maximising production mix.

The company should manufacture the product with the best contribution (ranked first) until either the resource has been completely consumed or the demand for the product has been satisfied. If there is still some of the limited resource left, the company should proceed to manufacture the product next in rank until either the resource has been consumed or the demand has been satisfied. This continues until the company cannot manufacture any further product because of the total consumption of the resource.

	Raw materials available (m)
Available	12 000
Manufacture Ace	
(1 000 units at 4 metres per unit)	(4 000)
Resource still available	8 000
Manufacture Cell	
(ranked 2nd; 500 units × 3 metres)	(1 500)
Resource still available	6 500
Manufacture Ball	(6 500)
Resource still available	0

Note that to satisfy the demand for product Ball, 9 000 metres of raw materials are needed (see Step 1). As the available resource falls short of what is needed, Ball will be manufactured until the resource is consumed. This means that 1 083 units of product Ball will be manufactured (6 500 metres available divided by 6 metres per unit Ball).

The optimal product mix will be to manufacture 1 000 units of Ace, 500 units of Cell and 1 083 units of Ball.

One can calculate the total contribution for the company by multiplying the quantity of each product to be manufactured by the product's contribution per unit and by adding up the answers for the three products.

5.9.6 Non-financial factors

Managers should remember not only to consider the calculations above, but also the non-financial factors closely related to the decision under consideration. It is important to remember to take factors such as the company's public image, environmental and legislative matters and the interrelationships between services and products into account before a final decision is reached. Costly mistakes can be prevented by ignoring, for example, what the public may think of the company when it sets off in a specific direction.

5.10 Cost-volume-profit analysis

5.10.1 Introduction to CVP and its relevance to logistics

Cost-volume-profit (CVP) analysis is the study of the effect that changes in variable and fixed costs, sales price and sales volume have on profitability. It is clear, for example, that a reduction in the volume of units sold or services rendered will result in a reduction in profit. However, the exact amount of the reduction, as well as the level to which the sales volume can decrease before a company starts suffering a loss are more difficult to assess. CVP assists in calculating these effects.

Logistics management impacts on the profit and loss of a company, as the decisions relating to logistics strategies have a material influence on a company's sales volumes and fixed costs (such as the number of warehouses to make use of and at which locations). It is imperative then that a logistics manager should have an understanding of the impact of changes in sales volumes and fixed costs on the profit or loss situation.

5.10.2 Contribution approach to CVP analysis

As discussed earlier in the chapter, contribution is the sales price of a product or service less all the variable costs of that product or service.

5.10.2.1 Breakeven point

The breakeven point is the point where total sales and total costs are even and the company shows neither a profit nor a loss. The breakeven point can be expressed in terms of either unit numbers that need to be sold or the amount of total sales (in rands) needed in order to break even.

The breakeven point in units = fixed cost/ contribution per unit.

The breakeven point in terms of sales value = number of units to break even × sales price per unit.

As more units are sold, the sales revenue, variable cost and thus the contribution earned by the units sold in total increase proportionally. The fixed costs, however, remain constant. In order to break even enough units must be sold to earn enough contribution in total to cover fixed costs. Figure 5.5 illustrates the following scenario:

Sales price of a unit: R80; variable cost of a unit: R30; total fixed cost for the period: R200. Expected sales for the period amount to six units.

Contribution per unit is calculated as: R80 − R30 = R50 per unit

In Figure 5.5, one must remember that contribution already takes variable costs into account. The only cost left that needs to be covered in order to break even is the fixed cost. When one performs the breakeven calculation, it is clear that the company in this scenario needs to sell at least four units in order to break even (R200/R50).

This analysis is very helpful for determining the feasibility of a new product or service. If one takes the budgeted cost and revenue and calculates the specific number of units needed to sell in order to break even, this number can be compared with the number of units expected to be sold. If it is expected that less of a product will be sold than the units needed to break even, then the project is not feasible, as it will probably be running at a loss unless changes can be made to the cost structure. (Refer also to the discussion on changes in variable and fixed cost in Sections 5.10.3.1 and 5.10.3.2.)

5.10.2.2 Margin of safety

The contribution of the units sold over and above the breakeven number of units will in total be the profit earned on the project (as can be seen in Figure 5.5). The contribution of the two units sold over and above the breakeven number of units (breakeven being four units) represents the profit. In this scenario the total profit will be R100 (2 units × R50 contribution per unit).

These two units also represent the number of units by which the company's sales can decrease before the company will start incurring a loss. In other words, the company has a margin of safety of two units. For comparability purposes, it is necessary to express the safety margin as a percentage of sales. This is calculated by dividing the safety margin number of units by the total number of units currently sold. This company's safety margin would be 33,3 per cent (2 units/6 units × 100 per cent).

Margin of safety = (total sales − breakeven sales)/total sales × 100 per cent

It can be calculated by either using the number of units in the calculation or the total sales value in rands.

5.10.2.3 Sales to achieve a target profit

Looking at it from another angle and assuming that one wants to achieve a profit of R100, one knows that the fixed cost amounts to R200 and that the

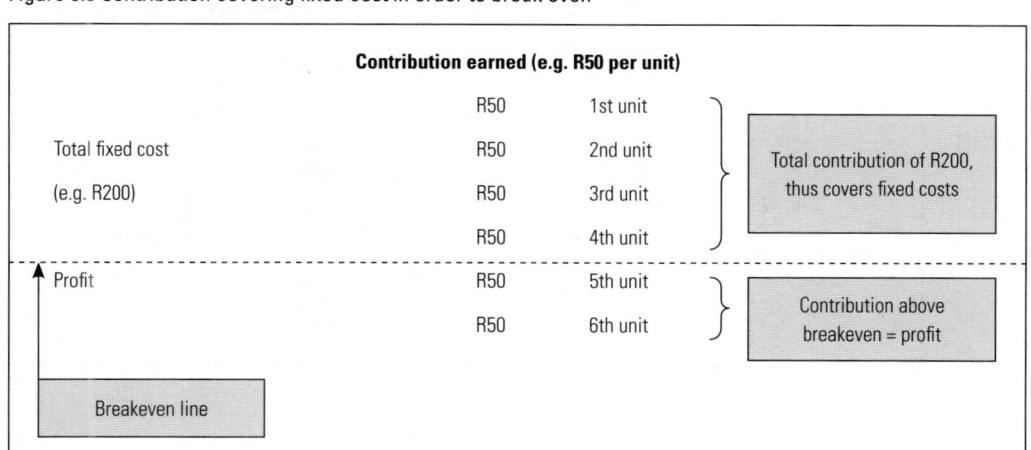

Figure 5.5 Contribution covering fixed cost in order to break even

	Contribution earned (e.g. R50 per unit)		
Total fixed cost (e.g. R200)	R50	1st unit	Total contribution of R200, thus covers fixed costs
	R50	2nd unit	
	R50	3rd unit	
	R50	4th unit	
Profit	R50	5th unit	Contribution above breakeven = profit
	R50	6th unit	
Breakeven line			

contribution per unit is R50 so one can calculate how many units have to be sold to achieve the required profit. The company will have to sell enough units so that the contribution earned will cover the fixed cost as well as the required profit. The calculation would thus be:
(R200 + R100)/R50 = 6 units
Number of units that have to be sold to achieve target profit = (fixed cost + target profit)/contribution per unit.

5.10.2.4 Breakeven graph

Breakeven graphs enable management to interpret and compare different projects' CVP analyses more successfully. Figure 5.6 is a breakeven graph that illustrates the CVP analysis of a specific project.

In Figure 5.6 the vertical axis shows total sales revenue and the total cost of a project; the horizontal axis represents the number of units sold.

Line A in the graph is the total sales line. When zero units are sold, no sales revenue is earned. The total sales revenue rapidly increases as more units are sold. Line C is the fixed cost line, which remains constant irrespective of the number of units sold. Line B is the total cost line. Total cost is R200 (only fixed cost) when no units are sold. As more units are sold, the variable cost accumulates and increases the total cost. The point where the total sales line meets the total cost line is the breakeven point. After this point the company starts earning a profit.

5.10.3 CVP analysis in decision making

Now that the functioning of CVP analysis is understood, this technique can be used to predict the effect that decisions should have on the future profit structure of a company. At this stage, the link between logistics management and CVP analysis becomes more evident. As logistics costs very often account for a substantial portion of the company's total cost, and logistics management policies will have a notable effect on the composition of fixed and variable costs, the effect of decisions on changes in fixed and variable costs on the CVP analysis of a company are considered next.

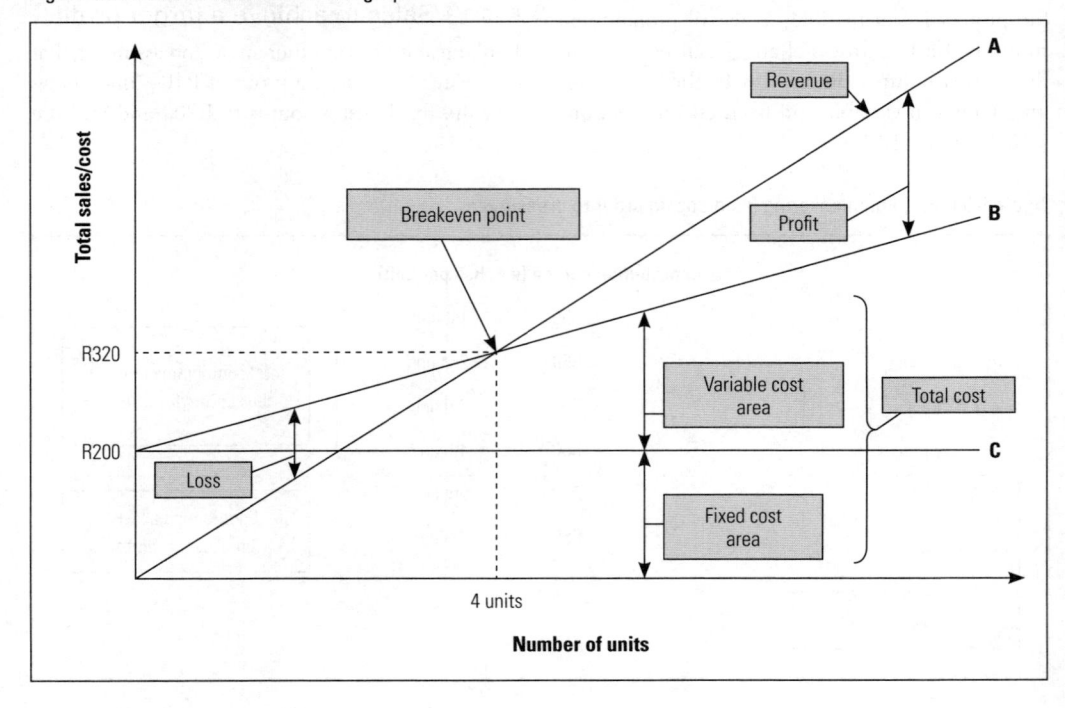

Figure 5.6 Illustration of a breakeven graph

5.10.3.1 Change in fixed cost

How many warehouses should be occupied (rented or owned)? How many permanently employed personnel are needed for logistics purposes? Should transportation be bought or hired, or should the company make use of an outside transport supplier who is paid for the volume transported and/or the distance of transportation? All are relevant questions posed by logistics managers, and all the decisions made regarding these questions will result in varying amounts of fixed and variable costs.

When we look at the example above (see Figure 5.5) where fixed cost amounts to R200, it should be clear that an increase of the fixed cost to R250, for example, will result in the company's breakeven point requiring a larger number of units to be sold (R250/R50 = 5 units in this case). This will also imply that the losses to be suffered when fewer or no units are sold will be higher, as the amount of fixed cost will still have to be paid in full. The company's margin of safety would also decrease. The opposite applies to a decrease in fixed cost.

When there is a great deal of uncertainty or seasonality surrounding the sales volume of a company's products or services, it might be a safer option to reduce fixed costs by not owning or renting as many assets and instead outsourcing these functions to a supplier who is paid per volume, distance etc. This way, the company substitutes fixed cost with variable cost.

5.10.3.2 Change in variable cost

As variable cost is deducted from the sales price per unit to arrive at the contribution per unit, an increase in variable cost will result in a decrease in the contribution per unit. In turn, the reduction in contribution per unit will decelerate the pace at which contribution can cover fixed cost and thereby result in a higher breakeven point. As the contribution per unit contributes towards profit, a reduction in contribution per unit as a result of an increase in variable cost per unit will also decelerate the pace at which profit is increased beyond the breakeven point.

High-tech industries may be more capital-intensive and as a result require more fixed cost. In this environment it is very important to keep variable costs low to enable contribution to cover fix costs more rapidly.

5.10.3.3 Change in selling price

The effect that change in selling price has on the CVP analysis, on the one hand, is very similar to the effect of a change in variable cost, as it also has the effect of increasing or decreasing contribution per unit. If the selling price is increased, the contribution will also increase, resulting in contribution covering fixed cost and contributing to profit at an accelerated pace.

On the other hand, management must remember that an increase in selling prices will almost always have a decreasing effect on the sales volume of a product. The relative size of the impact that the price increase will have on the sales volume will depend on the price elasticity of the specific product's market. The sales volume of a product that is essential to customers' needs will normally react less to an increase in sales price than would a luxury product's sales volume.

5.10.3.4 Conclusion on CVP

The logistics manager needs to keep in mind the effect that logistics policies and decisions may have on the CVP analysis of a company when developing strategies.

The following points are also worth taking into account:
- Higher fixed cost in relation to lower variable cost results in higher risk, as the breakeven point is increased, but also holds the promise of profits accelerating at a quicker pace once fixed cost has been covered.
- The effective use of fixed-cost capital, such as warehouses, transport infrastructure and other logistics capital is still the key. If one uses this fixed-cost capital less effectively, it will result in the company having to make up for it by increasing the sales volume.

5.11 Worked examples

1 *Value the shares of Trans-County Ltd on 31 December 2009 using the discounted cash-flow method.*

Trans-County Ltd transports a range of goods. It is the industry leader in this segment of the transport market. The financial director of Trans-County Ltd has provided you with the following information regarding the company:
- The free cash flow for the next five years will be R40 000 000 per annum.
- The risk-free rate of the long-term government bonds is 6 per cent after tax.
- The market risk premium is 6 per cent.
- The beta of Trans-County Ltd has been 1,2 for the past five years and it is expected to be a reliable forecast of the future beta of Trans-County Ltd.
- The terminal value of Trans-County Ltd after five years will be R400 000 000.
- There are 10 000 000 shares in issue.

Required
Calculate the value of a share in Trans-County Ltd.

Suggested solution
According to the capital asset pricing model, the cost of equity of Trans-County Ltd is:
Risk-free rate of return plus the beta of the individual share × the market risk premium = 6% + (1,2 × 6%) = 13,2%

The present value of the future free cash flows for the next five years, plus the terminal value, will be as follows:
(R000)

The present value of the free cash flow for the next five years is 140 005
(R40 000 000 × 3,500135*)

*Present value of R1 per annum for five years

The present value of the terminal value after five years is 215 192
(R400 000 000 × 0,53798)
Value of Trans-County Ltd at valuation date 355 197
Value of a share in Trans-County Ltd
(R355 197 000/10 000 000) = R35,52

2 *Return on investment.*

The summarised financial statements of RAS Ltd are as follows:

Statement of financial position at 31 December 2001

	(R000)
Assets	
Non-current assets	3 000
Current assets	2 000
	5 000
Equity and liabilities	
Equity	2 000
Non-current liabilities	2 000
Current liabilities	1 000
	5 000

Statement of comprehensive income for the year ended 31 December 2001

	(R000)
Revenue	9 000
Cost of sales	6 000
Gross profit	3 000
Expenses	2 200
Profit before interest	800
Interest	200
Profit before tax	600
Tax	200
Profit after tax	400

Required
Advise the management of RAS Ltd on a strategy to increase the return on equity by 20 per cent, taking into account that it is not possible to increase the sales or change the financial structure of the company.

Suggested solution
Currently, the return on equity is 20 per cent (R400 000/R2 000 000 × 100%). If the company wants to increase the return by 20 per cent, the return on equity must be 24 per cent. Based on an equity investment of R2 000 000 the return must be R480 000 (R2 000 000 × 24%).

As the financial structure is given, the company cannot change the assets-to-equity ratio, but should focus on the return-on-assets ratio by addressing the following:
- Reducing the cost of sales
- Reducing the expenses

Return on equity = return on assets × assets/equity
If a return of 24 per cent is required the return on assets should be:
Return on assets = 24%/(R5 000 000/R2 000 000)
= 9,6%
Return on assets = profit margin × assets turnover
Assets turnover = R9 000 000/R5 000 000
= 1,8 times

Given a return on assets of 9,6 per cent and an asset turnover of 1,8 times, the profit margin should be:
Profit margin = return on assets/assets turnover
= 9,6%/1,8 = 5,33%

The current profit margin of RAS Ltd is 4,44 per cent (R400 000/R9 000 000) and it has to be increased to 5,3 per cent.

3 Activity-based costing.

NSU Ltd provides bodybuilding pharmaceutical products to pharmacies. Management has decided to do some research on a new budgeting system to ensure that they only accept profitable orders. The system is based on the activity-based costing (ABC) system.

Each order from a customer is treated as follows. The cost of the products ordered, as well as an amount for sales and distribution cost is placed on the customer's invoice (a percentage is also added for profit purposes, but this is not applicable with regard to this analysis).

NSU Ltd currently uses a simple ratio to apportion sales and distribution costs to customer orders. The ratio is determined by dividing the sales price of the specific order by the total budgeted sales for the year. This ratio is then multiplied by the total sales and distribution cost to get the amount apportioned to the specific order. The problem with this system, according to management, is the fact that some customers place more orders (i.e. fewer products at a time), while other customers only place a few large orders. Consequently, the apportionment ratio mentioned above is deemed unreliable.

Management studied the costs in more detail and prepared the following information for the purpose of next year's budget:

Total price of products to be sold:
R6 million (for 12 000 orders for the year)

Sales and distribution cost	(R000)	Further information (see below)
Invoice processing	210	1. and 3.
Packaging	160	2.
Deliveries	140	4.
Other overheads	150	Apportioned equally to each order
Total sales and distribution cost	660	

Further information with regard to customer orders:

1. Each order is sent in one packet and leads to one delivery (you can assume that the delivery motorcycles can carry only one packet at a time) and one invoice.
2. Packaging cost is R13 per large packet and R6 per small packet.
3. On each invoice a new line is started for each type of product ordered. An estimated 32 000 invoice lines are used in a year. Management estimated that 80 per cent of the cost of processing invoices is related to the amount of invoices processed during the year and the other 20 per cent is related to the amount of invoice lines.
4. Of the delivery cost, an amount of R30 000 per annum is needed to cover the cost related to the motorcycles, which has no relation to the distance travelled during the year (apportioned equally to each order). The remainder of the delivery cost depends on the distance travelled by the motorcycles (petrol etc.). In total, the motorcycles travel 82 000 kilometres per year with deliveries.

Required

a) Calculate the sales and distribution cost that would be apportioned to two standard orders (order no. 364 and order no. 529, see below) on both the:
- currently used method, as well as on the
- ABC method.

Standard orders:

Order	Total price of products ordered	Lines on invoice	Size of packet	Distance to customer (one way)
No. 364	R1 100	2	Small	6 km
No. 529	R750	6	Large	12,5 km

(Round off your calculations to the nearest cent.)

b) Briefly discuss whether it is necessary for NSU Ltd to determine what the composition, activity bases and cost drivers of the 'other overheads' are to enable them to apportion the cost more accurately.

c) Name any two reasons why the traditional cost system provides misleading information for decision-making purposes.

Suggested solutions

a) Overhead apportionment
to two standard orders: No.364   No. 529
                          (R)   (R)

(i) Current method:
(R660 000/6 million)
× R1 100 and × R750   121   82,50

(ii) ABC method:
Invoice processing
– Invoice lines
(R210 × 20%)/32 000 = R1,31
(R1,31 × 2) and (R1,31 × 6)   2,62   7,86
– Number of invoices
(R210 × 80%)/12 000   14   14
Packaging   6   13
Deliveries:
– Fixed (R30 000/12 000)   2,5   2,5
– Distance
(R140 – R30)/82 000 = R1,34
(R1,34 × 6 × 2) and   16,08
(R1,34 × 12,5 × 2)   33,5
Other overheads   12,5   12,5
(R150 000/12 000)
                                   53,7   83,36

b) The more management refines the cost bases and drivers, the more accurate the information that management has to support their decisions. Based on more accurate information, management will be able to make decisions more efficiently, which will ultimately have the best effect on the business's profits. However, the principle of cost versus benefit will always apply. In other words, if the cost that has to be incurred to refine the cost apportionment system further exceeds the increase in return that can be generated by having access to better information, then management should not refine the system further at all costs.

c)
- The traditional system is mostly based on volume-related rates and does not consider the complicated composition of overhead costs.
- The traditional system apportions costs to departments, while the activity, which results in the costs, is given less attention.
- The traditional system does not take into account the diverse product range of the company, as overhead costs are apportioned to a single or a small number of bases.
- The traditional system uses volume-based costs only, while some costs are not driven by volumes.

4 Special-order decisions.

Stones Ltd manufactures tyres that sell for R500 per tyre. The current production is 10 000 tyres per month.

The current income of Stones Ltd is as follows:

	(R000)
Sales (R500 × 10 000)	5 000
Less:	
Marginal costs (variable costs)	4 000
Variable manufacturing costs (R300 × 10 000)	3 000
Variable selling and administration costs (R100 × 10 000)	1 000
Contribution margin	1 000
Less:	
Fixed costs	500
Manufacturing costs	300
Selling and administration costs	200
Net profit	500

According to the above calculation of the net profit, the costs per tyre sold are:

	(R)
Variable manufacturing costs	300
Variable selling and administration costs	100
Fixed manufacturing costs (R300 000/10 000)	30
Fixed selling and administration costs (R200 000/10 000)	20
	450

The total production capacity is 14 000 per month. Stones Ltd received a special order to export 3 000 tyres per month at R430 per tyre. This order will not have any impact on the current sales of Stones Ltd.

Required

Advise the management of Stones Ltd whether they should accept this order.

Suggested solution

As the total production capacity is 14 000 tyres per month, there is surplus capacity to produce 4 000 tyres per month. This special order of 3 000 tyres per month is well below the surplus of 4 000 tyres.

The variable cost per tyre manufactured is as follows:

	(R)
Variable manufacturing costs	300
Variable selling and administration costs	100
	400

The marginal income per month on the special order will be:

	(R000)
Sales (R430 × 3 000)	1 290
Less:	
Marginal costs (variable costs)	1 200
Variable manufacturing costs (R300 × 3 000)	900
Variable selling and administration costs (R100 × 3 000)	300
Contribution	90

As there is a positive contribution, the order should be accepted.

5 Discontinuation of a department or product.
A–Z Ltd currently manufactures the following spare parts:

Spare part	X	Y	Z
	(R)	(R)	(R)
Sales	900 000	500 000	700 000
Total costs	700 000	550 000	550 000
Profit/(Loss)	200 000	(50 000)	150 000

A–Z Ltd is considering discontinuation of spare part Y, as it is incurring a loss on this particular product. Management have decided to do an analysis of the costs per spare part and made the following summary:

Spare part	X	Y	Z
	(R)	(R)	(R)
Variable costs	600 000	480 000	460 000
Direct materials	180 000	150 000	140 000
Direct labour	210 000	160 000	130 000
Indirect manufacturing costs	140 000	120 000	130 000
Selling and administration costs	70 000	50 000	60 000
Fixed costs	100 000	70 000	90 000
	700 000	550 000	550 000

Required

Advise the management of A–Z Ltd on whether they should discontinue the production of spare part Y.

Suggested solution

The statement of calculating the profit in marginal costing format is as follows:

Spare part	X	Y	Z
	(R)	(R)	(R)
Sales	900 000	500 000	700 000
Less:			
Variable costs	600 000	480 000	460 000
Direct materials	180 000	150 000	140 000
Direct labour	210 000	160 000	130 000
Indirect manufacturing costs	140 000	120 000	130 000
Selling and administration costs	70 000	50 000	60 000
Contribution margin	300 000	20 000	240 000

If the management of A–Z Ltd decides to discontinue the production of spare part Y, the profits of A–Z Ltd will fall by R20 000.

6 Choice of products where a limiting factor exists.

Opt Ltd has the option to manufacture three different products. These products are all manufactured on the same production line. The capacity of the production line is 400 hours per week. The marginal costs and demand of the three products per week are as follows:

Product	X	Y	Z
	(R)	(R)	(R)
Selling price per unit	950	900	800
Less:			
Marginal costs	800	780	700
Material	300	480	500
Labour	500	300	200
Contribution per unit	150	120	100
Maximum demand of units per week	50	60	80
Production time to complete one unit (hours)	5	3	2

From the above information, Opt Ltd requires 590 ((50 × 5) + (60 × 3) + (80 × 2)) hours production time in order to satisfy the demand. As Opt Ltd is limited to 400 hours it is not possible for Opt Ltd to satisfy the demand.

Required

Determine which unit/s and how many of each unit should be manufactured.

Suggested solution

The products are all showing a contribution and there is no reason not to manufacture a product. However, as there is a constraint, the products must be ranked in order of the contribution per unit of limiting factor so that the total contribution can be maximised.

Calculation of contribution per limiting factor:

Product	X (R)	Y (R)	Z (R)
Contribution per unit	150	120	100
Production time to complete one unit (hours)	5	3	2
Contribution per production hour	30	40	50
Ranking	3rd	2nd	1st

To manufacture all the products it would need ((50 × 5) + (60 × 3) + (80 × 2)) 590 hours of production time. As the production time is limited to 400 hours, the following production plan should be followed:
80 units of product Z using 160 production hours
60 units of product Y using 180 production hours
12 units of product X using 60 production hours
Total production hours used is 400 (160 + 180 + 60).

7 Breakeven point.
Cacao Ltd manufactures chocolates which it sells for R60 per box. Current output is 10 000 boxes per month. The income per month of Cacao Ltd is as follows:

	(R)
Sales (R60 × 10 000)	600 000
Less:	
Variable costs (R30 × 10 000)	300 000
Contribution margin	300 000
Less:	
Fixed costs	200 000
Net profit	100 000

The management of Cacao Ltd is concerned that the sales of chocolates might drop in future.

Required
Calculate the breakeven value of Cacao Ltd.

Suggested solution
Breakeven in units
= fixed cost/contribution per unit
= R200 000/(R60 – R30)
≈ 6 667 units
Breakeven value
= breakeven units × sales price per unit
= 6 667 × R60
= R400 020

8 Margin of safety.
Air Ltd manufactures and sells golf balls on the local market. Market research has indicated that if they sell the golf balls at R5 per ball, they could sell 80 000 golf balls per month. Budgeted variable manufacturing costs are R3 per ball and the budgeted fixed factory overheads are R60 000 per month. Budgeted variable selling expenses are R0,50 per ball and the budgeted fixed selling expenses are R30 000 per month.

The shareholders of Air Ltd are concerned about the profitability of Air Ltd and request management to advise them on the margin of safety in rands.

Required
Calculate the margin of safety in rands.

Suggested solution
Margin of safety in rands
= budgeted sales – breakeven sales
Budgeted sales in rands
= 80 000 × R5
= R400 000
Total fixed costs
= R60 000 + R30 000
= R90 000
Breakeven units
= R90 000/(R5 – (R3 + R0,50))
= 60 000
Breakeven sales
= 60 000 × R5
= R300 000
Margin of safety in rands
= R400 000 – R300 000
= R100 000

9 Change in fixed cost.

Sens Ltd purchases and sells telephone answering machines. Sens Ltd's most recent profit calculation is as follows:

	(R000)
Sales (200 000 units)	12 000
Less:	
Variable expenses	8 000
Contribution margin	4 000
Less:	
Fixed expenses	2 000
Net income	2 000

Sens Ltd's lease on the premises expires at the end of the year. The current lease is R500 000 per annum and the landlord is planning to increase it to R800 000 per annum. In order to decide whether to sign the new lease, Sens Ltd requires the breakeven sales in units.

Required
Calculate the breakeven sales in units.

Suggested solution
Contribution per unit:

	(R)
Selling price per unit	
(R12 000 000/200 000)	60
Variable costs per unit	
(R8 000 000/200 000)	40
Contribution margin per unit	20

	(R000)
Total fixed costs:	
Current fixed costs	2 000
Increase in lease payments	300
	2 300

Breakeven units:
Fixed costs/contribution per unit
= R2 300 000/20
= 115 000 units.

10 Change in variable cost.

Chic Ltd manufactures and sells poultry feed. Three basic raw materials – bonemeal, maize meal and growth stimulants – are mixed in a predetermined ratio and packed in 50 kg bags that are sold for R2 500 per bag. The direct cost for a 50 kg bag of feed is made up as follows:

	(R)
Bone meal (10 kg at R30 per kg)	300
Maize meal (35 kg at R20 per kg)	700
Growth stimulants (5 kg at R120 per kg)	600
Bag	20
Variable production overheads	80
	1 700

The total fixed overheads of Chic Ltd are R85 000 per month.

The growth stimulants are imported and as a result of the weakening of the rand the price has increased from R120 per kg to R180 per kg. In order to determine the sales targets for the next month, Chic Ltd needs the breakeven sales in rands based on the increase in variable costs.

Required
Calculate the breakeven sales in rands based on the increase in variable costs.

Suggested solution
The total fixed costs of Chic Ltd are R85 000 per month.

Contribution per bag:

	(R)
Selling price per bag	2 500
Variable costs per bag	
(R1 700 + (5 kg × (R180 – R120)))	2 000
Contribution margin per bag	500

The breakeven units
= R85 000/R500
= 170 bags a month
The breakeven sales in rands per month
= 170 bags × R2 500
= R425 000

11 Change in selling price.

ABC Ltd imports computers from the United Kingdom and sells them on the local market. The details regarding the profit per computer sold are as follows:

	(R)
Selling price	6 000
Less:	
Variable costs	4 100
Purchase price	2 000
Import duties	1 000
Transport costs	500
Selling and administration	600
Contribution margin	1 900

The fixed costs of ABC Ltd for the year are as follows:

	(R)
Depreciation of equipment and delivery vehicles	150 000
Rent of premises	180 000
Salaries	300 000
	630 000

ABC Ltd plans to reduce the selling price in order to increase sales. The shareholders require a profit before tax of R300 000.

Required
Calculate the required sales to achieve a profit before tax of R300 000 if the selling price is reduced to R5 750 per computer.

Suggested solution
Contribution margin after the selling price is reduced
= R5 750 – R4 100
= R1 650

Number of unit sales required to earn target profit
= (fixed cost + target profit)/contribution per unit
= (R630 000 + R300 000)/R1 650
≈ 564 units per year

Required sales to earn target profit
= 564 × R5 750
= R3 243 000

Key terms

- Activity-based costing (ABC)
- Breakeven point
- Capital asset pricing model (CAPM)
- Contribution per unit
- Cost of equity
- Cost-volume-profit (CVP) analysis
- Economic value added (EVA)
- Fixed and variable cost
- Free cash flow
- Margin of safety
- Marginal costing
- Market value added (MVA)
- Shareholder value
- Value drivers

Questions

1 Value the shares of Buzzy Bee Ltd on 31 December 2007 using the discounted cash-flow method.

Buzzy Bee Ltd is a company that supplies logistics services to a range of private hospitals. You collected the following information on the company:
- The free cash flow for the next five years, discounted to a present value at Buzzy Bee Ltd's cost of equity rate will be:

Years from now	Present value of free cash flow	Future value
1	R21 477 663	R25 000 000
2	R18 451 601	R25 000 000
3	R15 851 860	R25 000 000
4	R13 618 463	R25 000 000
5	R11 699 710	R25 000 000

- The risk-free rate of the long-term government bonds is 8 per cent after tax.
- The market risk premium is 6 per cent.
- The beta of Buzzy Bee Ltd has been 1,4 for the past five years and it is also expected to be a reliable forecast of the future beta of Buzzy Bee Ltd.
- The terminal value after the five years of Buzzy Bee Ltd, discounted to a present value at the company's cost of equity rate, will be R116 997 103.
- There are 40 000 000 shares in issue.

Required

You are required to calculate the value of a share in Buzzy Bee Ltd.

2 Activity-based costing.

Hawk Ltd manufactures four types of specialised boxes, namely Squares (Product S), Triangles (Product T), Circles (Product C) and Pentagons (Product P), using the same plant and processes.

The following information relates to a production period:

Product	Volume	Material cost per unit	Direct labour per unit	Machine time per unit	Labour cost per unit
S	500	R5	$\frac{1}{2}$ hour	$\frac{1}{4}$ hour	R3
T	5 000	R5	$\frac{1}{2}$ hour	$\frac{1}{4}$ hour	R3
C	600	R16	2 hours	1 hour	R12
P	7 000	R17	$1\frac{1}{2}$ hours	$1\frac{1}{2}$ hours	R12

The production overhead costs recorded by the cost accounting system are analysed under the following headings:

Factory overheads applicable to machine-oriented activities	R37 424
Set-up costs	R4 355
Cost of ordering materials	R1 920
Handling materials	R7 580
Administration of spare parts	R8 600

These overhead costs are currently absorbed by products on a machine hour rate of R4,80 per hour, giving an overhead cost per product unit of:

Squares	R1,20
Triangles	R1,20
Circles	R4,80
Pentagons	R7,20

However, investigation into the production overhead activities for the period reveals the following:

Product	Number of set-ups	Number of material orders	Number of times material was handled	Number of spare parts
S	1	1	2	2
T	6	4	10	5
C	2	1	3	1
P	8	4	12	4
	17	10	27	12

Required

a) Calculate the production overhead cost per product unit of the four products that Hawk Ltd manufactures by using an ABC system.
b) Explain:
   (i) Why Hawk Ltd's management would favour an ABC system over the current costing system for decision-making purposes.
   (ii) How management would use the ABC system information in its decision-making process.

3 Special-order decisions.

Toxicz Ltd, is a company that produces miniature wooden chests. The costs to produce their flagship chest are set out below:

R175 for 10 cubic cm of wood
R8 varnish per chest
R10 for a rubber foot-piece to be placed at the bottom of the chest
R10 direct labour per chest
R5 royalties per chest, paid to the designer of the chest
Fixed production costs allocated to each chest:

Indirect materials	R2
Indirect labour	R3
Indirect expenses	R5
Sales, distribution and administrative overheads per chest	R10

Five chests are produced out of every 10 cubic cm of wood.

Required
Briefly discuss (supported by calculations) whether it will be worthwhile for the company to accept a once-off order by a popular hotel for 1 000 chests at R74 each (Toxicz Ltd will advertise its brand on the chests). You can assume that the company has spare capacity available.

4. Choice of products where a limiting factor exists.

Coast Ltd has the option to provide shipping services for three different types of cargo. These services will all be provided using the company's existing ships. The capacity of the company's shipping line is 1 030 000 m^3 and a maximum of 1 220 tons of freight per week. The marginal contribution made by supplying the shipping services is as follows:

Cargo type	X (R000)	Y (R000)	Z (R000)
Contribution per unit of cargo type	15	12	17,50
Maximum demand of units per type per week	120	160	110
Space needed per unit of cargo type	2 000 m^3	1 000 m^3	4 000 m^3
Weight per unit of cargo type	5 t	3 t	7 t

Required
Determine how many units of each cargo type should be shipped.

5. Change in fixed cost.

Lopez Ltd purchases and sells intercom systems. Lopez Ltd's most recent profit calculation is as follows:

	(R000)
Sales (250 000 units)	12 000
Less:	
Variable expenses	8 000
Contribution margin	4 000
Less fixed expenses	2 450
Net income	1 550

The current margin of safety is 45,56 per cent.

Lopez Ltd's factory manager will be leaving the company at the end of the year. His current salary is R550 000 per annum and the possible new manager whom the human resource department wants to appoint is looking to earn R800 000 per annum. In order to decide whether to appoint the new manager, Lopez Ltd requires the breakeven sales in units and the new margin of safety.

Required
Calculate the breakeven sales in units and the new margin of safety.

Consult the web

http://www.essays.se/essay/2994ff0eea/
http://www.lionhrtpub.com/tmr/features98/1298feature.html
http://findarticles.com/p/articles/mi_qa3705/is_199401/ai_n8727452
http://www.financialmanagement.org/

6 Forecasting supply chain requirements

W.J. Pienaar

Learning outcomes

After you have studied this chapter, you should be able to:
- distinguish between qualitative and quantitative forecasting;
- distinguish between time series forecasting and explanatory forecasting;
- identify and describe some qualitative methods of forecasting;
- establish appropriateness of time series models;
- apply relevant time series models to data;
- fit an appropriate linear regression model to data;
- interpret results;
- evaluate techniques; and
- carry out the forecasting process.

6.1 Introduction

Many factors influence all our numerous daily decisions, but if we consider decision making from a buyer's perspective, we may appreciate the value of forecasting from the seller's perspective as well. For example, we go to a car showroom, look at the vehicles and decide on a model. But the bad news is that the model we have selected is not in stock and we find our names added to a waiting list. This puts us into a bit of a quandary, as we need the vehicle, so we may change our mind and go to another dealer, or we may keep our old vehicle. This is where forecasting could have assisted the dealer: if he had projected his anticipated sales correctly, he may have had a customer for life.

The dealer who is able to correctly anticipate what a customer wants, and has the desired item in stock, will be more successful. Demand forecasting refers to the process of determining the amount of product and related information that consumers will require in the future, either in the short or long term.

The responsibility for preparing demand forecasting is usually in the marketing and sales departments. This information is important for marketing, manufacturing and logistics management (i.e. for supply chain management as a whole). Marketing forecasts of future demand determine promotional strategies, allocation of sales force effort, pricing strategies and market-research activities.

The following quote by Al Enns, director of supply chain strategies at Motts North America, illustrates the importance of forecasting:

'I believe that forecasting of demand management may have the potential to add more value to a business than any single activity within the supply chain. I say this because if you can get the forecast right, you have the potential to get everything else in the supply chain right. But if you can't get the forecast right, then everything else you do essentially will be reactive, as opposed to proactive, planning.'[1]

This quote links to forecasts and schedules. Operations-generated forecasts impact on manufacturing, scheduling, inventory requirements, resource needs and sizing. Manufacturing schedules determine acquisition strategies, plant inventory decisions and right-sizing production capacity in line with marketing forecasts.

Logistics management forecasts determine how much of each item manufactured by the firm has to be transported to the various markets the items serve. Logistics management must also determine where the demand will occur so that appropriate volumes of goods are made available in each market area. Knowledge of future demand levels enables logistics managers to plan for the activities needed to service that demand.

A leading manufacturer of roof windows and skylights noted the following:

'Demand planning is the key driver of the supply chain. Without knowledge of demand, manufacturing has very little on which to develop production and inventory plans, while logistics in turn has limited information and resources to develop distribution plans for products among different warehouses and customers. Simply stated, demand forecasting is the wheel that propels the supply chain forward and the demand planner is the driver of the forecasting process.'[2]

6.2 Features of forecasting

It is important to take note of the following features of forecasting:
- It is difficult to forecast accurately; indeed, it is impossible. Many factors cause a difference between actual demand and forecasted demand. Events such as unexpected hailstorms or competitors that enter the market or initiate special actions introduce additional uncertainty in the market. The purpose of forecasting is to generate good forecasts on average over time and to keep the forecast error as low as possible.
- Forecasts for groups of items are often more accurate than forecasting demand for single items. When items are grouped together, higher than forecasted demand for a certain item cancels out the effect of the lower than forecasted demand for another. For example, forecasting sales of all vehicles of a certain brand is more accurate than forecasting sales of a specific series within that brand.
- Forecasts for a shorter time period are usually more accurate than forecasting for a longer time horizon. Short-range forecasts entail fewer uncertainties. Vehicle sales two years ahead might be affected by unknown circumstances, such as higher or lower fuel prices, higher or lower interest rates or the world economy. In the short term, it is easier to predict vehicle sales for the next six months, for example, because economic indicators are easier to predict for the short term.
- What happened in the past can be used as an important guideline when making forecasts. This knowledge can be combined with market research for forecasting.

When making forecasts, forecasted values can be evaluated if they fulfil certain requirements. The following are the elements of a good forecast:
- Forecasts should be timely. Time is needed to respond to the forecasts. The forecast horizon should give enough time to implement changes when necessary. If the forecast indicates that capacity at the crossdock centre, for example, needs to be expanded, enough time should be allowed to implement this.
- Forecasts should be credible and reliable. It is often the case that forecasts are ignored because decision makers do not feel at ease with the results. Forecasts should deliver consistently good results: they should not be on target some of the time and way off target other times.
- There may be ineffective communication between the forecasting team and the decision makers. The assumptions and conditions under which forecasts are valid should be communicated. If these conditions change, decision makers may adapt their strategy accordingly.
- Forecasts should be in meaningful units. For financial planners, these units might be in currency, while production planners' units might be the number of products required, and schedulers might need to plan in machine hours.
- Forecasting techniques should be relevant. The data should match the forecasting technique used. If there is a definite pattern or relationship in the historical data, a

forecasting technique should be applied to incorporate that pattern.
- Forecasting should be cost-effective. The benefits of the process should outweigh the cost of the forecasting.
- Forecasts should address uncertainty. This can be achieved by providing upper and lower bounds on the forecasts. It can also be addressed by preparing forecasts for different alternative futures. A further measure for addressing uncertainty is to analyse the accuracy of previous forecasts.

6.3 Types of forecasting

When sufficient quantitative information about the past is available and it can be assumed that some aspects of the past pattern will continue in the future, one can apply quantitative forecasting techniques. Although the future is constantly changing, some aspects in history do repeat themselves. It is possible, by identifying the relationship between the variable to be forecasted and time itself (and/or between several other variables), to make an informed forecast.

There are two major types of quantitative forecasting models: time series and explanatory models.

A time series is a time-ordered sequence of observations taken at regular intervals, e.g. daily, weekly, monthly, quarterly or annually. Forecasting techniques based on time series data use the assumption that future values can be estimated from past values. No attempt is made to establish factors influencing the series. The analyst needs to identify the underlying behaviour of the series. When plotting the data, trends, seasonality, cycles or other variations can be identified. For example, a pizza home-delivery service needs to plan the number of vehicles that will be required for a particular evening. It may base its assumptions and planning on the orders received in the past, and thus allocate a particular number of vehicles in its planning.

Explanatory models, also called regression models, rely on identification of related variables that can be used to predict values of the variable of interest. A mathematical relationship is developed between demand, for example, and some other factors that cause demand behaviour. For example, daily sales of a popular cooldrink might depend on the season, the average temperature, the day of the week, the success of a recent advertising campaign, etc. This type of forecasting might also include past sales data, as in time series data. In the next section, time series data and explanatory models will be described in detail.

Qualitative forecasting techniques are appropriate when little or no quantitative information is available, but sufficient qualitative knowledge exists. It is usually a product of judgement and accumulated knowledge, and requires input from a number of specially trained people. A typical example of when this technique would be appropriate is when input from sales staff is used to forecast sales for a new region or a new product.

The following are four examples of qualitative forecasting techniques:
- **The Delphi method.** This takes advantage of the wisdom and insight of a panel of people who have considerable expertise about a particular product or demand. It also utilises anonymity among the participants. The experts – five to seven in number – do not know who the panel members are, and they never meet to discuss their views. The Delphi method follows the following steps:

    Step 1: Participating panel members are selected.

    Step 2: Questionnaires about the variables to be forecasted are distributed among the members.

    Step 3: Results are collected and summarised.

    Step 4: Summarised results are distributed amongst panel members for reviewing and further consideration.

    Step 5: Panel members revise their initial estimates, taking into account views from other panel members unknown to them.

    Step 6: The last three steps are repeated until no significant changes are observed.

Neither peer pressure nor strong personalities influence the outcome of the forecasts.
- **Jury of executive option.** The judgement of experts with years of experience may be useful in the forecasting process. A forecast is developed by combining the subjective opinions of managers and executives. These people should be selected from different functional areas. Meetings are helpful and opinions are considered. The disadvantage is that people with strong personalities may dominate the group.
- **Sales force composite.** Each sales person estimates what sales will be in his or her region and these forecasts are reviewed to ensure that they are realistic and then combined at a district or national level to reach an overall forecast.
- **Consumer market survey.** Input by using surveying techniques from customers or potential customers is analysed to establish their future purchasing plans. It may prove helpful not only for preparing forecasts, but also improving product design and planning for new products.

6.4 Long-term and short-term forecasting

Patterns do not change over a short time. This implies that they may be extrapolated to provide accurate short-term forecasts, typically measured in days or weeks. If large numbers of customers are involved, random forces have a smaller effect, and there is a higher accuracy of the short-term forecast. Short-term forecasting is crucial for day-to-day planning. Patterns may help to determine safety stock levels and production plans that may be derived from materials requirements planning (MRP) systems and resource requirements planning, for example. Shift scheduling may require forecasts of workers' availabilities and preferences.

Medium-term forecasting is usually measured in weeks or months (up to 18 months). As the time horizon increases, changes in patterns and relationships become more apparent. Economic cycles change from boom periods to recessions. Medium-term forecasts are usually needed for budget purposes, including forecasts of sales, prices and costs for the entire company and different divisions. It may also assist in forecasting economic and industry variables that will affect sales and costs. The March 1997 announcement of the permanent closure of the Renault factory in Belgium and the dismissal of nearly 4 000 additional personnel were partly caused, according to top management, by the 1996 slump in the European car market, which was not predicted.[3]

Long-term forecasting is primarily needed for capital expansion plans, selecting research and development projects, launching new projects, formulating long-term goals and strategies and adapting to environmental changes. The further the time horizon, the less accurate the forecasts. The purpose of such forecasts is to build scenarios to provide general direction to where the economy or industry is heading, to identify major opportunities and warn of dangers ahead. New technologies may develop, which will be very difficult to forecast. Long-term forecasts rely more on qualitative methods.

6.5 The forecasting process

It is important to view the forecasting process in a systematic way. The following steps provide a useful paradigm:

Step 1: Determine the use of the forecast. Specify the objectives clearly.

Step 2: Determine what to forecast. Select the items or quantities that are to be forecasted. For example, do you want to forecast the financial value of sales, or units of sales? Should the forecast be for total sales, or sales by region?

Step 3: Determine the time horizon of the forecast. Is it 1–30 days (short term), one month to 18 months (medium term) or more than 18 months (long term)? Is the forecast needed on an annual, quarterly, monthly, weekly or daily basis?

Step 4: Gather the data needed to make the forecast.

Step 5: Do the model selection. This depends on the pattern exhibited by the data, the quantity of historical data available and the length of the forecast horizon.

Step 6: Validate the forecasting models. This is done by evaluating how each model works in a retrospective sense, that is, how well the results fit the historical data that were used to develop the models.
Step 7: Make the forecasts.
Step 8: Implement the results
Step 9: Track the results. Compare the forecasts with the actual values observed during the forecast horizon.

Selecting the appropriate technique; forecasting techniques and the validation process are discussed in detail in the next sections.

6.6 Selecting appropriate forecasting techniques

In the model selection phase, the forecaster will look for patterns in the historical data and use them to predict future behaviour. The easiest way to identify patterns is to plot the data and examine the results graphically. The following example illustrates how to plot the data. Note that all illustrations are with Excel 2007.

The Belgian Trucking Company[4] needs to determine the number of cold-storage trucks to satisfy the transportation demand between Antwerp and Brussels on a daily basis. The demand for the first six weeks is shown in Table 6.1.

Figure 6.1 displays the first 20 observations, although all 30 observations were plotted.

There are four basic patterns, or combinations thereof, present in time series data, as shown in Figure 6.2 and explained below.

a Level or horizontal, also called stationary. The data fluctuates around a constant mean. The variable under investigation does not increase or decrease over time. This type of pattern is common for products in the mature stage of their life cycle, for which demand is steady and predictable.

b Trend or non-stationary time series. The data increases or decreases over time. The trend can also be non-linear.

c Seasonality. A seasonal pattern is a regular pattern that repeats itself over time. This pattern has a constant length over time. An example is an increase in sales of toys during November and December, followed by a decrease in sales in the first six months of the year. Similarly, restaurants may well experience an increase in business on Fridays and Saturdays.

d Cycles. Typical cyclical patterns are those associated with business cycles, especially products that are associated with inflation, recessions etc. Cyclical patterns vary in length and magnitude over time.

Table 6.1 Demand for the number of cold-storage trucks needed for the next six weeks

Week	Day	Time	Demand	Week	Day	Time	Demand
1	Monday	1	67	4	Monday	16	76
	Tuesday	2	54		Tuesday	17	57
	Wednesday	3	51		Wednesday	18	53
	Thursday	4	46		Thursday	19	50
	Friday	5	62		Friday	20	69
2	Monday	6	65	5	Monday	21	78
	Tuesday	7	55		Tuesday	22	60
	Wednesday	8	47		Wednesday	23	54
	Thursday	9	45		Thursday	24	53
	Friday	10	64		Friday	25	80
3	Monday	11	75	6	Monday	26	81
	Tuesday	12	58		Tuesday	27	63
	Wednesday	13	56		Wednesday	28	58
	Thursday	14	49		Thursday	29	52
	Friday	15	71		Friday	30	83

Figure 6.1 Line graph of the demand for cold-storage trucks for the next six weeks

	A	B
1	Time	Demand
2	1	67
3	2	54
4	3	51
5	4	46
6	5	62
7	6	65
8	7	55
9	8	47
10	9	45
11	10	64
12	11	75
13	12	58
14	13	56
15	14	49
16	15	71
17	16	76
18	17	57
19	18	53
20	19	50
21	20	69

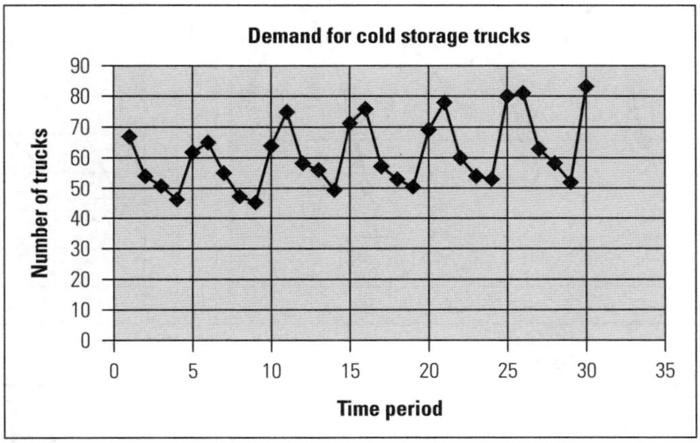

Creating a line graph with Excel

Select cells A1 to B31.
Click on Insert and select Scatter Chart.
Select Scatter with Markers only.
Right-click on one of the data points on the graph and select Format Data Series.
Click on Line Style and change the width to 1pt.
Click on Close.

Additionally, random variation occurs. This is any unexplained variation that cannot be predicted.

Any time series can be described in terms of the patterns in Figure 6.2. There are two general forms of time series models. The most widely used is a multiplicative model, which assumes that demand is the product of the four components, as follows:

Time series data = trend × seasonality × cycle × random variation

An additive model adds components together as follows:

Time series data = trend + seasonality + cycle + random variation

The first three components can be forecasted, but the random variation cannot be predicted. The more the random variation in the data, the more difficult it is to make a forecast.

Different techniques are appropriate, depending on the nature of the time series data.

Figure 6.2 Types of data patterns

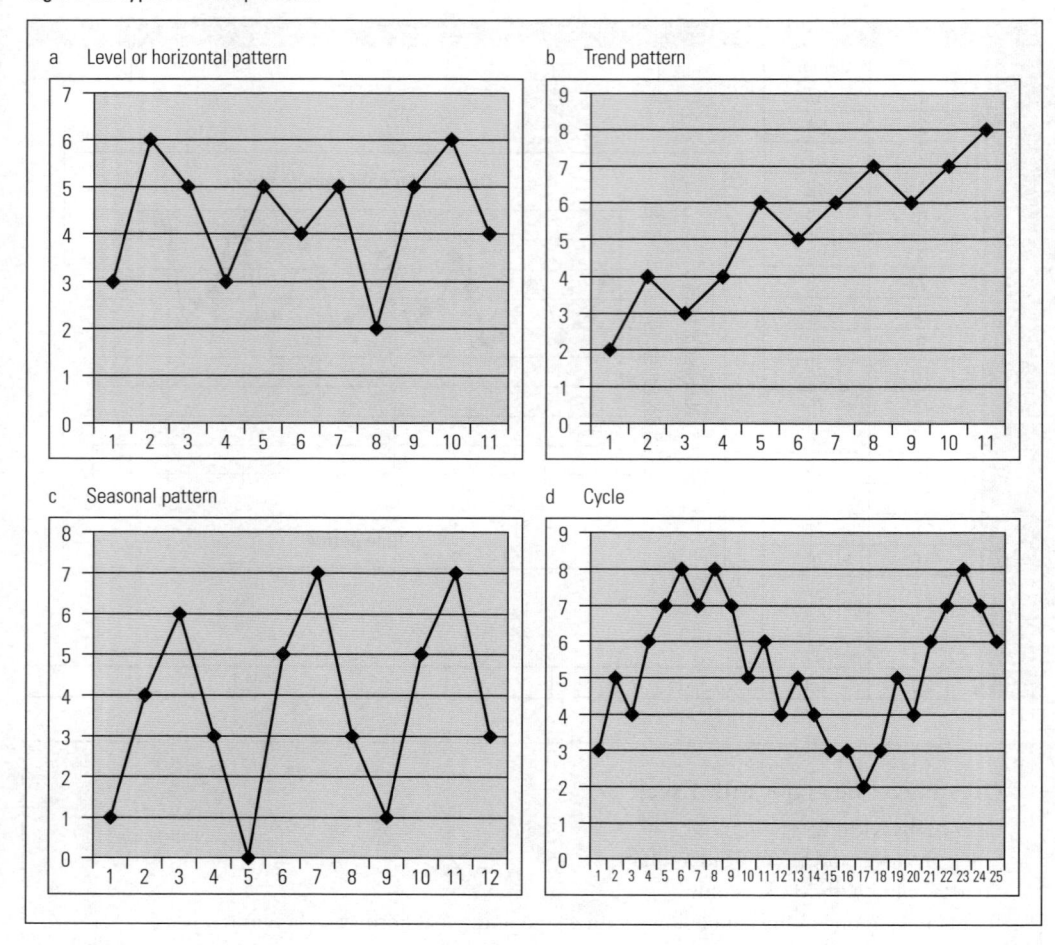

a Level or horizontal pattern

b Trend pattern

c Seasonal pattern

d Cycle

Table 6.2 is a guide for selecting a forecasting method. It takes into consideration the data pattern as described in this section, the available number of historical observations and the forecast horizon.

Table 6.2 Selecting an appropriate forecasting method

Forecasting method	Data pattern	Minimum number of observations	Forecast horizon
Naïve	Stationary	1 or 2	Very short
Moving averages	Stationary	At least the number of periods in the moving average	Very short
Exponential smoothing models: Simple	Stationary	5 to 10	Short
Holt	Linear trend	10 to 15	Short to medium
Holt-Winter's additive and multiplicative	Trend and seasonality	At least 4 or 5 per season	Short to medium
Regression-based models: (1) Time series data	Linear and non-linear trend with or without seasonality.	Minimum of 10 observations with 4 or 5 per season if seasonality is included.	Short to medium
(2) Causal (cross-sectional data)	Can handle nearly all data patterns	Minimum of 10 observations per independent variable	Short, medium and long

Source: Wilson, Keating and Galt: 57

6.7 Validating forecasting models

Many methods are available for forecasting, and it is impossible to know in advance which method will be the most effective for specific data. A common approach is to forecast using several methods and evaluate how well each explains past behaviour of the time series variable. Three of the most common quantitative measures of accuracy are as follows:

- Mean absolute deviation: $\text{MAD} = \frac{\Sigma |A_t - F_t|}{n}$
- Mean square error: $\text{MSE} = \frac{\Sigma (A_t - F_t)^2}{n}$
- Mean absolute percentage error: $\text{MAPE} = \frac{100 \Sigma |(A_t - F_t)/A_t|}{n}$

Because of different units used for different series, only MAPE can be used to compare across different series. MAD and MSE values will be dependent on the units used. These measures are used to compare different methods of forecasting on the same series.

The following strategy for evaluating any forecasting methodology is proposed:

Step 1: Divide the time series into two parts, namely an initialisation set and a test set to conduct an evaluation of the forecasting method.

Step 2: Choose an appropriate forecasting method.

Step 3: Use the initialisation set to estimate the trend and seasonal components and/or parameter values at this stage. At this stage, the measures of accuracy such as MAD, MSE and MAPE are calculated and they are used to establish fit accuracy.

Step 4: The method is then applied to the test set to see how well it does on the data that was not used in estimating the components of the model. Again, the measures of accuracy are calculated on the test set; this time, they are used to establish forecast accuracy.

Step 5: Repeat steps 2 to 4 for several forecasting techniques, and select the forecasting method which performs best with regard to forecast accuracy and which is also appropriate depending on the data pattern.

Step 6: Use the complete data set and apply the selected technique to do the forecast.

6.8 Techniques for stationary time series data

The simplest forecasting methods are for level or stationary time series data. Two methods are presented, but bear in mind that many variations are possible.

6.8.1 Naïve forecasting

The naïve method assumes that the next period's forecast is equal to the current period's actual value. For example, if a business had used 57 cold-storage trucks in the current month to deliver products to different regions, it assumes that next month it will again use 57 trucks. If in the following month the actual number is 60, then it forecasts that it will need 60 trucks for the subsequent month. The assumption is that there is little change from period to period. Mathematically, it is expressed as follows:

$$F_{t+1} = A_t$$

Where: F_{t+1} = forecast for the next period $t + 1$
A_t = actual value for the current period t
t = the current time period.

The following example shows an application using the naïve method.

The actual sales of television sets at TV Corp has been steady over the last five weeks. The company uses the naïve method to forecast sales for the next week. The data and forecasts are shown in Table 6.3 and Figure 6.3.

Table 6.3 Naïve forecast for TV sales

Row/column	A	B	C
1	Week number	Actual sales	Naïve forecast
2	t	A_t	F_t
3	1	250	
4	2	245	250
5	3	247	245
6	4	251	247
7	5	250	251
8	6		250
9	7		250
10	8		250
11	9		250

Entering the formulas in Excel:
In cell C4 enter: =B3.
Copy the formula down from cell C5 to cell C8.
In cell C9 to C11 enter: =C8.

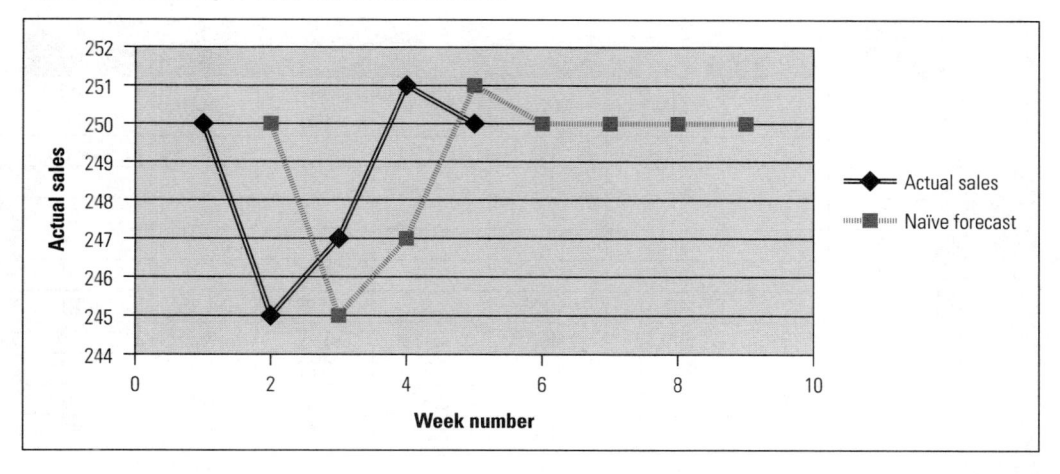

Figure 6.3 Forecasting TV sales with the naïve method

[Graph showing Actual sales and Naïve forecast across Week numbers 0-10, with Actual sales values approximately: 250, 250, 245, 247, 251, 250, 250, 250 and Naïve forecast lagging by one period]

Creating two-line graphs with Excel for Figure 6.3:
Select cells A3 to B7.
Click on Insert and select the Scatter Chart.
Select Scatter with Markers only.
Right-click on one of the data points on the graph and select Format Data Series.
Click on Line Style and change the width to 1pt.
Right-click on one of the data points on the graph and click on Select Data.
Click on Add (to add new series).
Select A4 to A11 for X-values, and C4 to C11 for Y-values.
Click OK.

For forecasting TV sales for week number 7 and further on, one can assume that the sales in the previous week are equal to the forecast. This will result in forecasting a value of 25 for each future period.

The naïve method is very simple and works well if there are few changes from one period to the next. It is often used as a method to evaluate more complicated forecasting methods. Because of the simplicity of the naïve method, it is expected that other methods should perform better than the naïve method.

6.8.2 Simple moving average

The simple moving average uses an average of n of the most recent observations in the average to create a forecast for the next period. As new data becomes available, the oldest is dropped and a new average is calculated. This model is also used when the data is stationary.

The following formula is used:

$$F_{t+1} = \frac{A_t + A_{t-1} + \ldots + A_{t-n+1}}{n},$$

where: F_{t+1} = forecast for the next period $t + 1$
A_t = actual value for the current period t
n = number of periods included in the moving average.

If we forecast the demand for the number of television sets for TV Corp for the sixth week using the average of three periods (MA-3) and an average of four periods (MA-4) respectively, the results are as shown in Table 6.4 and Figure 6.4. We will also evaluate the MA-3 and MA-4 methods.

Table 6.4 Forecasting TV sales using moving averages

Row/column	A	B	C	D	E	F	G	H
1	Week number	Actual sales	MA-3	MA-4	MAD	MAPE (%)	MAD	MAPE (%)
2	t	A_t	$F_t\,(n=3)$	$F_t\,(n=4)$	$(n=3)$	$(n=3)$	$(n=4)$	$(n=4)$
3	1	250						
4	2	245						
5	3	247						
6	4	251	247,33		3,67	1,46		
7	5	250	247,67	248,25	2,33	0,93	1,75	0,70
8	6	245	249,33	248,25	4,33	1,77	3,25	1,33
9	7	247	248,67	248,25	1,67	0,67	1,25	0,51
10	8	251	247,33	248,25	3,67	1,46	2,75	1,10
11	9	253	247,67	248,25	5,33	2,11	4,75	1,88
12	10	252	250,33	249,00	1,67	0,66	3,00	1,19
13	11	249	252,00	250,75	3,00	1,20	1,75	0,70
14	12	248	251,33	251,25	3,33	1,34	3,25	1,31
15	13	251	249,67	250,50	1,33	0,53	0,50	0,20
16	14	250	249,33	250,00	0,67	0,27	0,00	0,00
17	15	251	249,67	249,50	1,33	0,53	1,50	0,60
18	16	251	250,67	250,00	0,33	0,13	1,00	0,40
19	17	252	250,67	250,75	1,33	0,53	1,25	0,50
20	18	254	251,33	251,00	2,67	1,05	3,00	1,18
21	19	250	252,33	252,00	2,33	0,93	2,00	0,80
22	20	252	252,00	251,75	0,00	0,00	0,25	0,10
23	21		252,00	252,00				
24	22		251,33	252,00				
25	23		251,78	251,50				
26	24		251,70	251,88				
27								
28			MSE	MSE	MAD	MAPE	MAD	MAPE
29			7,27	5,38	2,29	0,92	1,95	0,78

Entering the formulas in Excel for Table 6.4:

In cell C6 enter: =AVERAGE(B3:B5).
Copy the formula down from cell C7 to C23.
In cell D7 enter: AVERAGE(B3:B6).
Copy the formula down from cell D8 to D23.
Enter in cell C24: =(B21+B22+C23)/3 (similar for C25 and C26).
Enter in cell D24: =(B20+B21+B22+D23)/4 (similar for D25 and D26).
Enter the MSE in C29: =SUMXMY2(B6:B22,C6:C22)/COUNT(C6:C22).
Enter the MSE in D29: =SUMXMY2(B7:B22,D7:D22)/COUNT(D7:D22).
In cell E6 enter: =ABS(B6–C6).
In cell F6 enter: =100*ABS((B6–C6)/B7).

Copy the formulas in E6 and F6 down from E7 and F7 to E22 and F22.
In cell G7 enter: =ABS(B7–D7).
In cell H7 enter: =100*ABS((B7–D7)/B7).
Copy the formulas in G7 and H7 down from G8 and H8 to G22 and H22.
In E29 enter: =AVERAGE(E6:E22).
In F29 enter: =AVERAGE(F6:F22).
In G29 enter: = AVERAGE(G7:G22).
In H29 enter: =AVERAGE(H7:H22).

The mean square errors (MSE) in cells C29 and D29 are calculated using the formula:

$$\text{MSE} = \frac{\Sigma(A_t - F_t)^2}{n}$$

The numerator of this formula can be calculated using the Excel function SUMXMY2(array_x, array_y), and the denominator n, which is the number of observations, can be calculated using the Excel function COUNT(array_x) or COUNT(array_y).

The MAD in cells E29 and G29 are calculated using the formula:

$$\text{MAD} = \frac{\Sigma|A_t - F_t|}{n},$$

and the MAPE in cells F29 and H29 are calculated using the formula:

$$\text{MAPE} = \frac{100\Sigma|(A_t - F_t)/A_t|}{n}$$

We want to compare MA-3 and MA-4 to decide which method gives the smaller MSE (or MAD or MAPE) value. In this case, MA-4 delivers a smaller MSE value, as well as smaller MAD and MAPE values, indicating a better degree of fit accuracy than the MA-3 method for this example.

Figure 6.4 Forecasting TV sales using moving averages

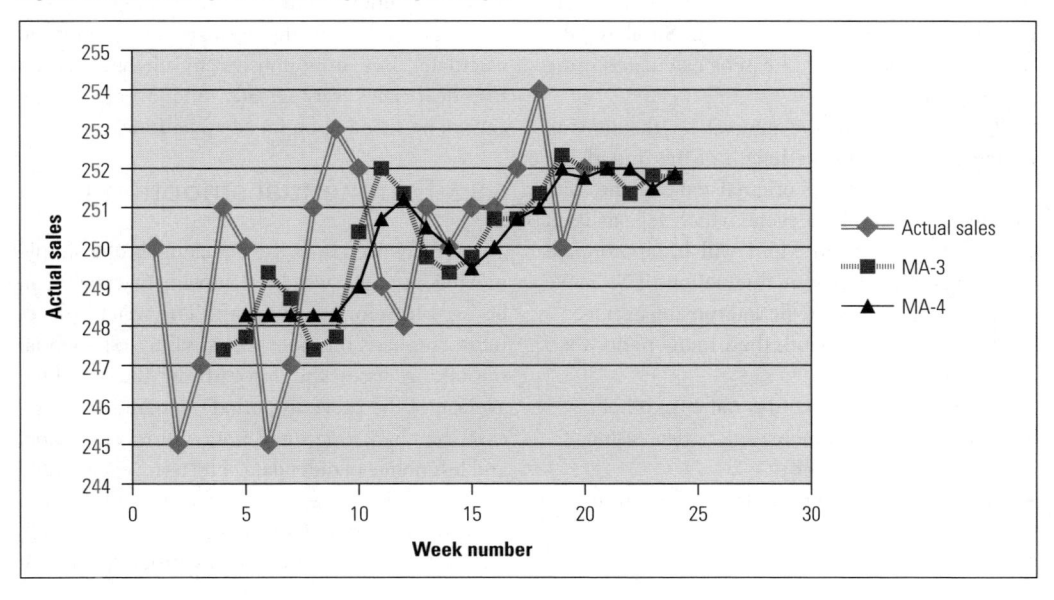

> **Creating three-line graphs with Excel for Figure 6.4:**
> Select cells A3 to B22.
> Click on Insert and select the Scatter Chart.
> Select Scatter with Markers only.
> Right-click on one of the data points on the graph and select Format Data Series.
> Click on Line Style and change the width to 1pt.
> Right-click on one of the data points on the graph and click on Select Data.
> Click on Add to add a new series.
> Select A6 to A26 for X-values, and C6 to C26 for Y-values.
> Repeat (8) and (9) but select A7 to A26 for X-values and D7 to D26 for Y-values.
> Click OK.

To forecast more than one period in the future using MA-3, for example, we must substitute the forecasted values for unobserved actual values. For example, suppose that at the end of time period 20 we want to forecast the number of TVs to be sold in time periods 21 and 22:

$$F_{21} = \frac{A_{18} + A_{19} + A_{20}}{3} = \frac{254 + 250 + 252}{3} = 252$$

$$F_{22} = \frac{A_{19} + A_{20} + A_{21}}{3} = \frac{250 + 252 + 252}{3} = 251{,}33$$

At time period 22, we do not know the actual value for A_{21}, and we substitute F_{21} for A_{21} to generate the forecast for the time period 22. Similarly, the forecast for time period 23 can be calculated using A_{20}, F_{21} and F_{22}.

The choice of n, the interval for the moving average, depends on the length of the underlying cycle or pattern in the original data. If the data exhibits, for example, a cycle, which repeats itself every four periods, an MA-4 will be appropriate to dampen the short-run fluctuation. The naïve method is actually a one-period moving average.

If we forecast demand, then many periods are best when:
- the underlying demand is static (in other words, there is no increasing or decreasing trend in demand); or
- large variations between demand occur in each period.

Reducing the number of periods in the average enables the forecast to adapt faster to a changing trend. Fewer periods are preferred when:
- there is an indication of a positive or negative trend;
- the demand is smooth (not much variation from period to period); or
- the demand in a period is dependent upon that in the previous period.

A short moving average period (n is small) gives a good response to changes in the market, but is affected by fluctuation.

In general, moving averages are simple to calculate, but unresponsive to change. When historical sales vary greatly, the average value cannot be relied upon for accurate forecasts.

6.8.3 Exponential smoothing

To partially overcome the deficiencies of a simple moving average, weighted moving averages can be used to refine the forecast. The weight places more emphasis on more recent sales. Exponential smoothing bases the forecast on the weighted average of the previous period's demand and forecast, thereby taking more notice of recent history and less notice of older data. The term 'exponential smoothing' is derived from the fact that there is a contribution from many years of data, although older data becomes increasingly insignificant as it ages. Simple exponential smoothing is applicable when there is no trend or seasonality in the data.

A new forecast is calculated by mixing a portion of the old average with a portion of the new demand. Mathematically, exponential smoothing is expressed as follows:
$$F_{t+1} = \alpha A_t + (1 - \alpha) F_t$$

where: F_{t+1} = forecast for period $t + 1$
A_t = actual demand for period t (the current period)
F_t = forecast for period t (the current period)
α = smoothing constant ($0 < \alpha < 1$)

An alternative form of the formula is:
$$F_{t+1} = F_t + \alpha(A_t - F_t)$$

This formula indicates that the forecasted value for time period $t + 1$ is equal to the forecasted value of the previous period plus an adjustment for the error made in predicting the previous period's value. It can be shown that the exponential smoothing formula is equivalent to:
$$F_{t+1} = \alpha A_t + \alpha(1 - \alpha) A_{t-1} + \alpha(1 - \alpha)^2 A_{t-2} + \ldots + \alpha(1 - \alpha)^n A_{t-n} + \ldots$$

The forecast in exponential smoothing is a weighted combination of all previous values in the time series where the most recent observation receives the heaviest weight. The value of the smoothing constant (α), therefore, determines the amount of notice, which is taken of the previous period's demand. Low values of the smoothing constant make the forecast consistent, but it does not react

Table 6.5 Forecasting TV sales using exponential smoothing

Row/column	A	B	C	D	E	F
1	Week number	Actual sales	Forecast		Alpha =	0,5
2	t	A_t	F_t			
3	1	250	250,00			
4	2	245	250,00			
5	3	247	247,50			
6	4	251	247,25			
7	5	250	249,13			
8	6	245	249,56			
9	7	247	247,28			
10	8	251	247,14			
11	9	253	249,07			
12	10	252	251,04			
13	11	249	251,52			
14	12	248	250,26			
15	13	251	249,13			
16	14	250	250,06			
17	15	251	250,03			
18	16	251	250,52			
19	17	252	250,76			
20	18	254	251,38			
21	19	250	252,69			
22	20	252	251,34			
23	21		251,67			
24	22		251,67			
25	23		251,67			
26	24		251,67			

> **Entering the formulas in Excel for Table 6.5:**
>
> Enter the value 0,5 in cell F1.
> In cell C3 enter: =B3 (initialise the forecast).
> In cell C4 enter: =$F$1*B3+(1-$F$1)*C3.
> Copy the formula in C4 down from cell C5 to C23.

quickly to changes in the data. High values make it reactive to change. Too high a value would make the forecast rely heavily on demand in the last period. If $\alpha = 1$ then the method is the same as the naïve method. If $\alpha = 0$ the forecast will be equal to the first observation in the series.

The accuracy of using various alpha values can be tested by examining the forecast error when applying various alpha values. The Solver function in Excel can also be used to identify the alpha value which will minimise MAD, MSE or MAPE. Table 6.5 illustrates exponential smoothing, and finding the optimal value of alpha when obtaining the MSE value.

The value in cell F1 represents α. The first forecasted value, F_1, is unknown, and is assumed to be equal to the first observation A_1. That is why we enter in cell C3 the same value as in cell B3. The forecasting starts in cell C4. The result is Figure 6.5.

Use the instructions in Figure 6.4 to create the graph in Figure 6.5 and future graphs.

When forecasting with exponential smoothing, the forecast for the number of TVs to be sold in time period 21 is calculated as:

$$F_{21} = \alpha A_{20} + (1 - \alpha)F_{20}$$
$$= (0{,}5 * 252) + (1 - 0{,}5) * 251{,}34$$
$$= 251{,}67$$

When we try to forecast for time period 22, the actual value A_{21} is unknown and is substituted by F_{21}, and the forecast is therefore:

$$F_{22} = \alpha A_{21} + (1 - \alpha)F_{21}$$
$$= (0{,}5 * 251{,}67) + (1 - 0{,}5) * 251{,}67$$
$$= 251{,}67$$

Similarly, all future forecasts will be equal to 251,67. Solver in Excel can be used to find the value of α that minimises the MSE. Figure 6.6 shows the solution to this problem.

Figure 6.5 Forecasting TV sales using exponential smoothing, alpha = 0,5

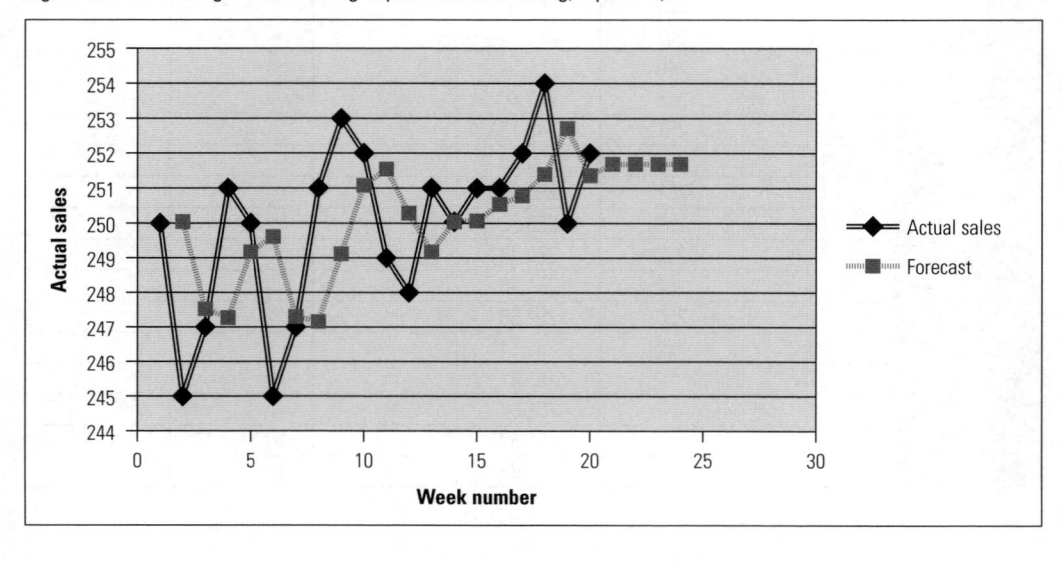

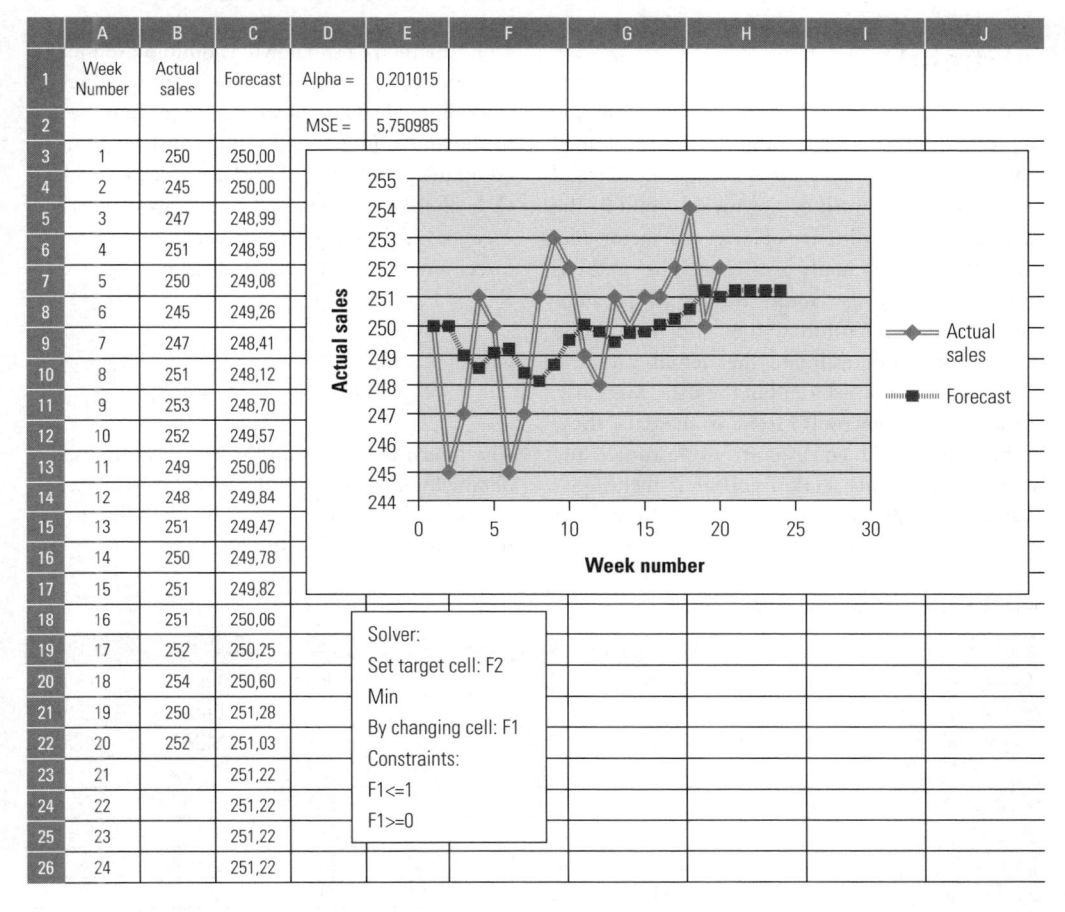

Figure 6.6 Using Solver to find the optimal value of alpha that minimises the MSE

	A	B	C	D	E	F
1	Week Number	Actual sales	Forecast	Alpha =	0,201015	
2				MSE =	5,750985	
3	1	250	250,00			
4	2	245	250,00			
5	3	247	248,99			
6	4	251	248,59			
7	5	250	249,08			
8	6	245	249,26			
9	7	247	248,41			
10	8	251	248,12			
11	9	253	248,70			
12	10	252	249,57			
13	11	249	250,06			
14	12	248	249,84			
15	13	251	249,47			
16	14	250	249,78			
17	15	251	249,82			
18	16	251	250,06			
19	17	252	250,25			
20	18	254	250,60			
21	19	250	251,28			
22	20	252	251,03			
23	21		251,22			
24	22		251,22			
25	23		251,22			
26	24		251,22			

Solver:
Set target cell: F2
Min
By changing cell: F1
Constraints:
F1<=1
F1>=0

To find the optimal value of alpha for Figure 6.6:
Enter in cell F2: =SUMXMY2(B3:B22,C3:C22)/COUNT(C3:C22).
Put the cursor on cell F2, click on Data.
Click on Solver (if Solver is not available, access the add-ins and add Solver).
The target cell is F2.
Click on Min.
The changing cell is F1.
For the constraints, click on add.
Add two constraints: F1 ≤ 1 and F1 ≥ 0.
Click on options; click on Assume Non-Negative.
Click on OK and Solve.

The optimal value of alpha is 0,20. Note that alpha is smaller than 0,5, which is an indication that the average demand level varies slowly.

6.9 Techniques for forecasting time series data with a trend

The methods discussed in section 6.8 are appropriate for stationary, or horizontally inclined time series data, when there is no significant trend over time. An upward or downward trend in the data reflects the influence of long-term factors that affect the data gradually over time. The methods discussed so far use some average of previous values to forecast future values and they would consistently underestimate the actual values if there were an upward trend in the data. Similarly, if there were a downward trend in the data, these techniques would consistently overestimate the actual values. This section considers techniques that are appropriate for non-stationary time series with an upward or downward trend over time.

6.9.1 Holt's method

Holt's method (also known as double exponential smoothing) is an extension of the simple exponential smoothing; it adds a growth factor (or trend factor) to the smoothing equation to adjust for trend. It computes an estimate of the base, or expected level (E_t), of the time series and the expected rate of increase or decrease (trend) per period (T_t). The forecasting function is represented by:

$$F_{t+n} = E_t + nT_t,$$

where: $E_t = \alpha A_t + (1-\alpha)(E_{t-1} + T_{t-1})$
$T_t = \beta(E_t - E_{t-1}) + (1-\beta)T_{t-1}.$

The forecasting function for F_{t+n} can be used to obtain forecasts for n time periods ahead, where $n = 1, 2, 3 \ldots$ and so on. The smoothing parameters α and β in the equations for E_t and

Table 6.6 Forecasting using Holt's method

Row/Column	A	B	C	D	E	F	G
1	Week number	Actual sales	Base	Trend	Forecast	Alpha =	0,50
2						Beta =	0,50
3	1	220	220,00	0,00		MSE =	9,75
4	2	223	221,50	0,75	220,00		
5	3	230	226,13	2,69	222,25		
6	4	229	228,91	2,73	228,81		
7	5	228	229,82	1,82	231,64		
8	6	234	232,82	2,41	231,64		
9	7	240	237,62	3,60	235,24		
10	8	239	240,11	3,05	241,22		
11	9	245	244,08	3,51	243,16		
12	10	246	246,79	3,11	247,59		
13	11	244	246,95	1,64	249,91		
14	12	248	248,29	1,49	248,59		
15	13	251	250,39	1,79	249,78		
16	14	250	251,09	1,25	252,18		
17	15	251	251,67	0,91	252,34		
18	16	251	251,79	0,52	252,58		
19	17	252	252,15	0,44	252,31		
20	18	254	253,30	0,79	252,59		
21	19	258	256,04	1,77	254,09		
22	20	257	257,40	1,57	257,81		
23	21				258,97		
24	22				260,54		
25	23				262,10		
26	24				263,67		

> **Entering the formulas in Excel for Table 6.6:**
> Enter in cell C3: =B3.
> Enter in cell D3: =0.
> Enter in cell C4: =$G$1*B4+(1–$G$1)*(C3+D3).
> Enter in cell D4: =$G$2*(C4–C3)+(1–$G$2)*D3.
> Enter in cell E4: =C3+D3.
> Highlight cells C4, D4 and E4 and copy from cells C5, D5 and E5 to cells C22, D22 and E22.
> Enter in cell E23: =C22+D22.
> Enter in cell E24: =C22+2*D22.
> Enter in cell E25: =C22+3*D22.
> Enter in cell E26: =C22+4*D22.

T_t can assume any values between 0 and 1 ($0 \leq \alpha \leq 1, 0 \leq \beta \leq 1$). The interpretation of the value of α is the same as for exponential smoothing. With regard to the β value, if β is close to 1, there is a definite trend in the data, which can be either upward or downward. If β is closer to 0, the trend is slight.

The data in Table 6.6 represents actual sales of DVDs for DVD View for the next 20 weeks. Holt's method is applied to forecast sales for four future weeks. Holt's formulas were applied to calculate the base, trend and forecast. Smoothing constants α and β are initially set to 0,5.

Figure 6.7 Forecasting DVD sales using Holt's method

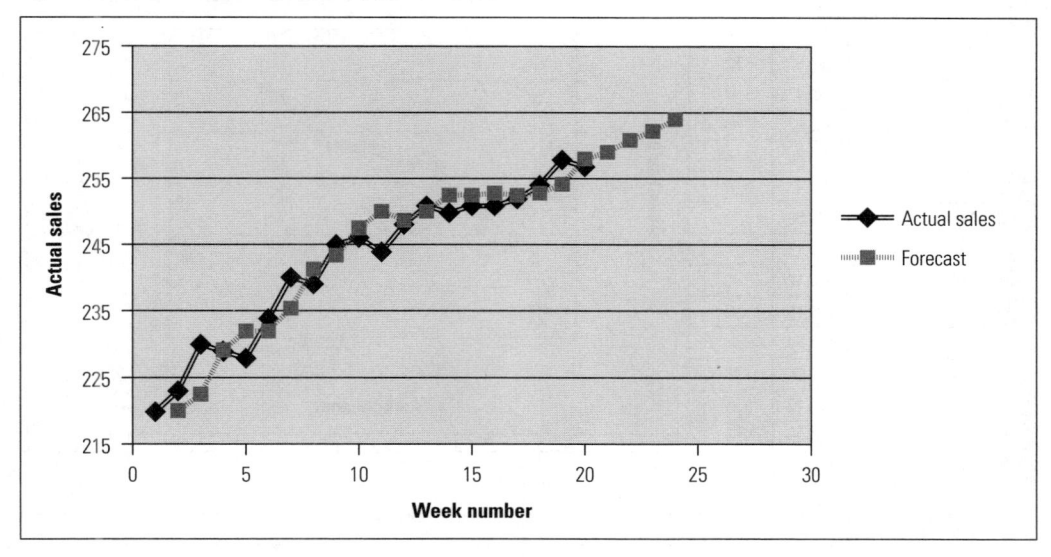

When forecasting with Holt's method, the forecast for the number of DVDs to be sold in time period 21 is calculated as:

$F_{21} = E_{20} + (1)T_{20} = 257,40 + (1) * (1,57) = 258,97$

When we try to forecast for time period 22, the forecast is:

$F_{22} = E_{20} + (2)T_{20} = 257,40 + (2) * (1,57) = 260,54$

Similarly, all future forecasts will be calculated by increasing n by 1 for each subsequent period. The forecasts will form a straight line with an upward or downward trend, depending on the sign of the last known trend value.

Solver can be used to find the values of α and β that minimise the MSE. Figure 6.8 shows the solution to this problem. The optimal values are $\alpha = 0{,}33$ and $\beta = 1{,}0$, indicating that the average demand varies slowly, but with a definite trend.

6.9.2 Time series data and linear regression

Simple linear regression might be appropriate if a scatter plot of the data suggests that a strong linear relationship exists between the time variable (independent variable) and the variable to be forecast (dependent variable). The linear trend line uses the following equation to generate the forecast:
$Y = a + bX$,

where: Y = forecast for period X
X = the number of time periods from $X = 0$
a = the value of Y at $X = 0$ (Y – intercept)
b = slope of the line.

The coefficients a and b are computed using the least squares method, which minimises the sum of the squared errors. The steps for computing the forecast using the linear trend line are as follows:

1. Compute the slope parameter b:
$$b = \frac{\Sigma XY - n\overline{X}\overline{Y}}{\Sigma X^2 - n\overline{X}^2}$$

Figure 6.8 Using Solver to find the optimal values of alpha and beta that minimise the MSE

	A	B	C	D	E	F	G	H	I	J	K
1	Week Number	Actual sales	Base	Trend	Forecast	Alpha =	0,33				
2						Beta	1,00				
3	1	220	220,00	0,00		MSE	0,61				
4	2	223	220,98	0,98							
5	3	230	224,60	3,62							
6	4	229	228,47	3,87							
7	5	228	230,92	2,45							
8	6	234	233,58	2,66							
9	7	240	237,47	3,89							
10	8	239	240,58	3,12							
11	9	245	244,13	3,54							
12	10	246	247,12	3,00							
13	11	244	248,11	0,99							
14	12	248	248,74	0,63							
15	13	251	249,90	1,16							
16	14	250	250,72	0,81							
17	15	251	251,36	0,64	251,53						
18	16	251	251,67	0,31	252,00						
19	17	252	251,99	0,32	251,98		Solver:				
20	18	254	252,86	0,87	252,31		Set target cell: G3				
21	19	258	255,13	2,27	253,74		Min				
22	20	257	257,27	2,14	257,40		By changing cell: G1:G2				
23	21				259,41		Constraints:				
24	22				261,55		G1:G2<=1				
25	23				263,69		G1:G2>=0				
26	24				265,83						

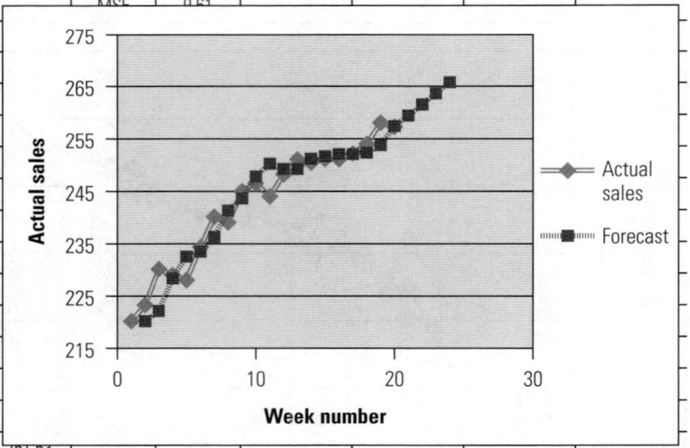

> **To find the optimal values of alpha and beta for Figure 6.8:**
> Enter in cell G3: =SUMXMY2(B4:B22,E4:E22)/COUNT(E4:E22).
> Put the cursor on cell F2; click on Data.
> Click on Solver (if Solver is not available, access the add-ins and add Solver).
> The target cell is G3.
> Click in min.
> The changing cells are G1:G2.
> For the constraints, click on add.
> Add two constraints: G1:G2 ≤ 1 and G1:G2 ≥ 0.
> Click on options; click on Assume Non-Negative.
> Click on OK and Solve.

2. Compute the intercept parameter a: $a = \bar{Y} - b\bar{X}$.
3. Generate the trend line: $Y = a + bX$.
4. Generate the forecast (Y) for the appropriate value of time period (X).

Table 6.7 Calculating the regression coefficients

Row/column	A	B	C	D
1	Week number	Actual sales		
2	X	Y	XY	X^2
3	1	240	240	1
4	2	245	490	4
5	3	247	741	9
6	4	249	996	16
7	5	248	1 240	25
8	6	245	1 470	36
9	7	247	1 729	49
10	8	251	2 008	64
11	9	250	2 250	81
12	10	252	2 520	100
13	11	249	2 739	121
14	12	248	2 976	144
15	13	251	3 263	169
16	14	250	3 500	196
17	15	251	3 765	225
18	16	251	4 016	256
19	17	252	4 284	289
20	18	254	4 572	324
21	19	251	4 769	361
22	20	253	5 060	400
23				
24	$\bar{X} = 10{,}5$	$\bar{Y} = 249{,}2$	$\Sigma XY = 52\,628$	$\Sigma X^2 = 2\,870$

Entering the formulas in Excel for Table 6.7:

Enter in cell C3: =A3*B3.
Copy this formula down from C4 to C22.
Enter in cell D3: =A3^2.
Copy this formula down from D4 to D22.
Enter in cell A24: =AVERAGE(A3:A22).
Enter in cell B24: =AVERAGE(B3:B22).
Enter in cell C24: =SUM(C3:C22).
Enter in cell D24: =SUM(D3:D22).

Using the DVD sales as an example, Table 6.7 illustrates how the formulas can be used to forecast DVD sales if a linear trend is appropriate.

Now compute the following:

$$b = 52\,628 - \frac{20(10,5)(249,2)}{2\,870 - 20(10,5)^2} = 0,45$$

$$a = 249,2 - (0,45)(10,5) = 244,53$$

Figure 6.9 Forecasting using the trend (regression) line

Row/column	A	B	C	D	E	F	G
1	Week Number	Actual sales	Forecast				
2	X	Y					
3	1	240	244,97		SUMMARY OUTPUT		
4	2						
5	3						
6	4					0,81	
7	5					0,65	
8	6					0,63	
9	7					1,99	
10	8					20,00	
11	9						
12	10	252	248,98		ANOVA		
13	11	249	249,42			Df	SS
14	12	248	249,87		Regression	1,00	131,75
15	13	251	250,31		Residual	18,00	71,45
16	14	250	250,76		Total	19,00	203,20
17	15	251	251,20				
18	16	251	251,65			Coefficients	Standard Error
19	17	252	252,09		Intercept	244,53	0,93
20	18	254	252,54		X	0,45	0,08
21	19	251	252,98				
22	20	253	253,43				
23	21		253,87				
24	22		254,32				
25	23		254,76				
26	24		255,21				

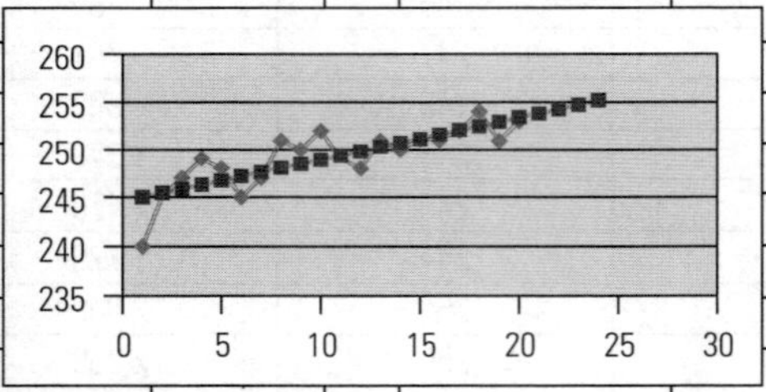

The trend line is therefore: Y = 244,53 + 0,45X.
The forecast for time period 21 is then Y = 244,53 + 0,45(21) = 253,87.

The same process can be done in Excel, as shown in Figure 6.9.
Note that the values of a and b are obtained from the intercept and X coefficients respectively.

Forecasting using the regression function in Excel for Figure 6.9:
Click on Data, then Data Analysis (use the add-ins if it is not on the options list).
Click on regression.
Input Y range: select B3:B22.
Input X range: select A3:A22.
Select output range; enter E3.
Click OK.
In cell C3, enter the following: =$F$19+$F$20*A3.
Copy this formula down from C4 to C26.

6.10 Forecasting seasonality

The techniques discussed so far allow for average demand, fluctuation in demand and trends in demand. However, no provision has been made with these techniques for cyclical or seasonal demand patterns. Many products are subject to seasonal demand patterns. These may be caused by natural seasonal factors, such as temperature and rainfall variations, or by other seasonal factors, such as holidays, festive seasons and financial year ends.

This section looks at multiplicative seasonality, in which the seasonality is expressed as a percentage of the average. The percentage by which the value for each season is above or below the mean is a seasonal index. For example, if sales in December are 1,30 of the mean sales, the sales in December are 30 per cent above the average. Similarly, if the sales in January are 0,80 of the mean, the sales in January are 80 per cent of the average.

The following steps show how to compute forecasts by incorporating seasonality if quarterly data is available.

Step 1: Calculate the forecast demand for the known observations using linear regression or Holt's method.
Step 2: Calculate the actual sales as a percentage of the trend by dividing the actual sales by the forecast sales for each time period.
Step 3: Calculate the average seasonal index for each season by adding up the values calculated in step 2 for that season and dividing by the number of years.
Step 4: Multiply the forecast by the average seasonal index for the corresponding season. This will produce a forecast adjusted for seasons.

The following example is an illustration of modelling seasonality with a linear regression model. The owner of a departmental store has collected quarterly unit sales data of a certain high-tech toy for 20 consecutive quarters. He wants to analyse this data to create a model to estimate the number of units for the following four quarters.

Figure 6.10 suggests that toy sales are affected by seasonality. In the third and fourth quarter of each year, the unit sales increase above the trend line, and in most cases the unit sales are below the trend line in the first and second quarters. It is obvious that these features can be incorporated in future forecasts, and that the trend line will not reflect these systematic or seasonal effects.

A simple way to model multiplicative seasonal effects is to develop seasonal indices that reflect the average percentage by which the sales in each season differ from the projected trend values. If these seasonal indices are known, we could multiply the trend projections by these values to increase the accuracy of the forecasts.

Figure 6.10 Plot of seasonal data with linear trend

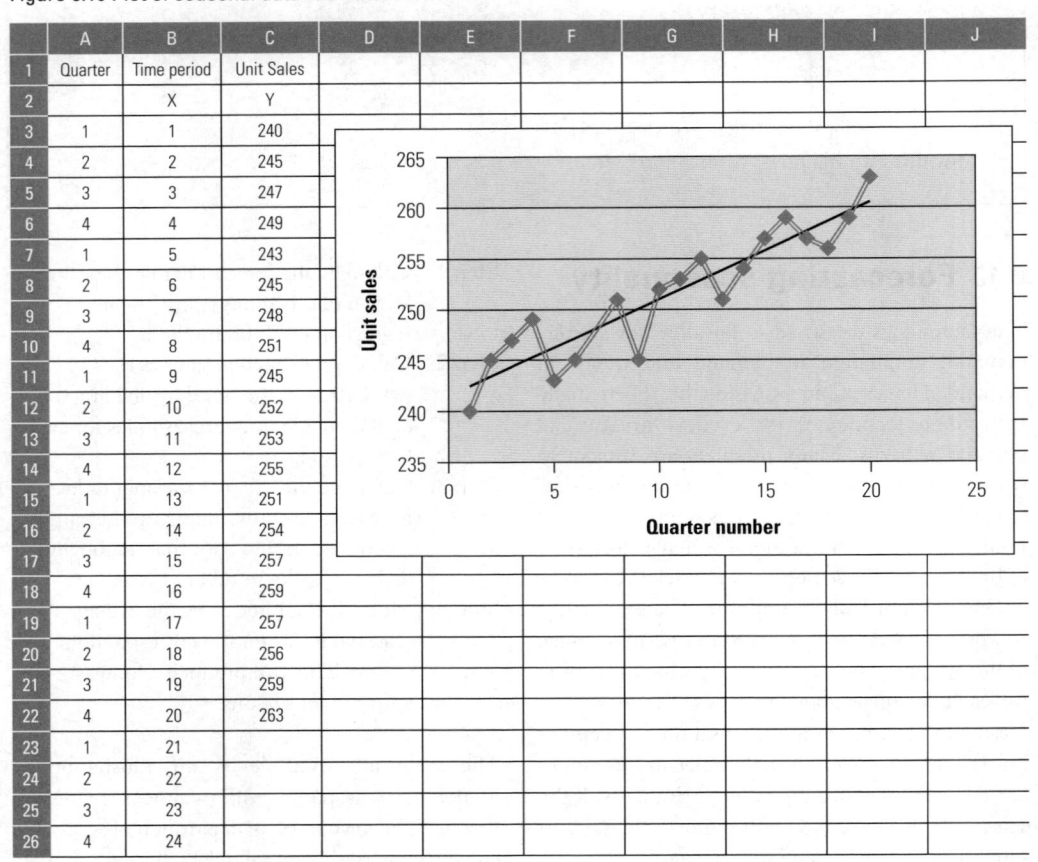

	A	B	C	D	E	F	G	H	I	J
1	Quarter	Time period	Unit Sales							
2		X	Y							
3	1	1	240							
4	2	2	245							
5	3	3	247							
6	4	4	249							
7	1	5	243							
8	2	6	245							
9	3	7	248							
10	4	8	251							
11	1	9	245							
12	2	10	252							
13	3	11	253							
14	4	12	255							
15	1	13	251							
16	2	14	254							
17	3	15	257							
18	4	16	259							
19	1	17	257							
20	2	18	256							
21	3	19	259							
22	4	20	263							
23	1	21								
24	2	22								
25	3	23								
26	4	24								

To draw the trend line in Figure 6.10:

Select cells B3 to C22.
Click on Insert and select Scatter Chart.
Select Scatter with Markers only.
Right-click on one of the data points on the graph and select Format Data Series.
Click on Line Style and change the width to 1pt.

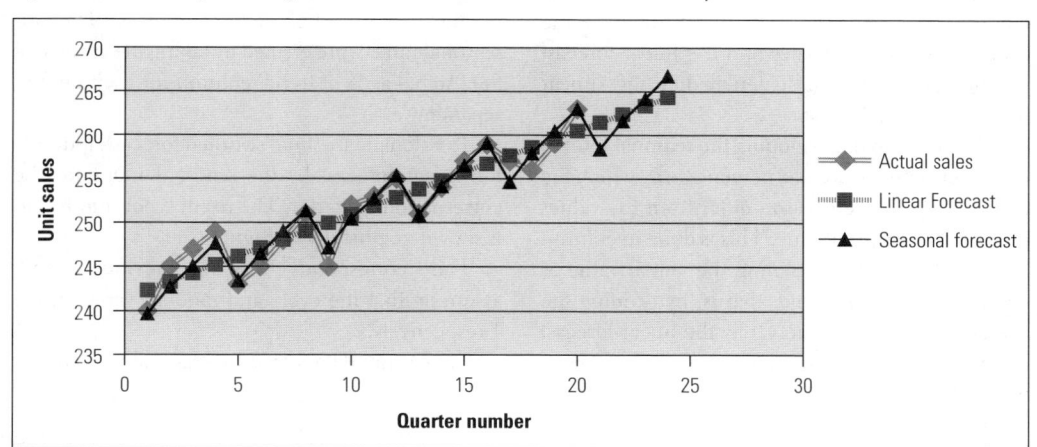

CHAPTER 6 FORECASTING SUPPLY CHAIN REQUIREMENTS | 127

Figure 6.11 Forecast plots using seasonal indices as well as linear trend of toy data

Table 6.8 Seasonal forecasting of toy data

	A	B	C	D	E	F	G	H
1	Quarter	Time period	Unit sales	Linear forecast	Actual as % of trend	Seasonal forecast		
2		X	Y					Coefficients
3	1	1	240	242,37	0,99	239,63	Intercept	241,4158
4	2	2	245	243,33	1,01	242,79	X	0,955639
5	3	3	247	244,28	1,01	245,14		
6	4	4	249	245,24	1,02	247,69		
7	1	5	243	246,19	0,99	243,41	Quarter	Seasonal index
8	2	6	245	247,15	0,99	246,61	1	0,988685
9	3	7	248	248,11	1,00	248,98	2	0,997807
10	4	8	251	249,06	1,01	251,55	3	1,003527
11	1	9	245	250,02	0,98	247,19	4	1,009983
12	2	10	252	250,97	1,00	250,42		
13	3	11	253	251,93	1,00	252,82		
14	4	12	255	252,88	1,01	255,41		
15	1	13	251	253,84	0,99	250,97		
16	2	14	254	254,79	1,00	254,24		
17	3	15	257	255,75	1,00	256,65		
18	4	16	259	256,71	1,01	259,27		
19	1	17	257	257,66	1,00	254,75		
20	2	18	256	258,62	0,99	258,05		
21	3	19	259	259,57	1,00	260,49		
22	4	20	263	260,53	1,01	263,13		
23	1	21		261,48		258,53		
24	2	22		262,44		261,86		
25	3	23		263,40		264,32		
26	4	24		264,35		266,99		

This is demonstrated in Table 6.8, in which columns B, C and D show the number of the time period, the unit sales and the linear forecast of the unit sales as calculated using linear regression analysis.

The next step in developing the seasonal indices is to determine the average percentage by which the observations in each season differ from the values projected by the trend line. This is done in column E in Table 6.8 by calculating the actual value as a percentage of the trend, that is, by dividing the actual unit sales (column C) by the linear forecast (column D) for each observation. This shows that unit sales in the first time period are 99 per cent of the linear forecast and in the fourth time period 102 per cent of the linear forecast. The four seasonal indices are created by taking the average of the 'Actual as % of trend' column for each quarter separately.

To calculate the final seasonal forecast, multiply the linear forecast by the seasonal index for the corresponding quarter. The result is column F, and is shown graphically in Figure 6.11.

This corresponds with a previous result, assuming that the cycle and random variation are 1 respectively.

Time series data = trend × seasonality × cycle × random variation.

Applying the formulas for Table 6.8:

Calculate the linear forecast: Data, Data Analysis, Regression.
Type in cell D3: =$H$3+$H$4*B3; copy down from D4 to D26.
Type in E3: =C3/D3.
Type in H8: = (E3+E7+E11+E15+E19)/5.
Copy H8 down from H9 to H11.
Type in F3: =D3*$H$8.
Multiply the rest of the values in column F by the corresponding seasonal index in column H.

Note that the seasonal forecast corresponds closely to actual values, as shown in Figure 6.11.

6.11 Example of the forecasting process

A manufacturing company of air conditioners suitable for cooling and heating large buildings recorded quarterly sales from 2003 to 2007. Sales are usually high in the summer and winter months, and lower in spring and autumn when the climate is more moderate. The data will be used to fit an appropriate model, which will then be tested on the 2008 data. After studying the plot of the data from 2003 to 2007, the analyst decided to apply the naïve forecast, Holt's method (he noticed a definite trend in the data) and a method using seasonal indices. He will use the data for 2008 as test data, and calculate forecasts using these methods for 2008. The forecast accuracy will be established by calculating the MSE, MAD and MAPE values, by comparing the forecast for 2008 with the actual data gathered for 2008. The final decision will then be made about which forecasting method to use.

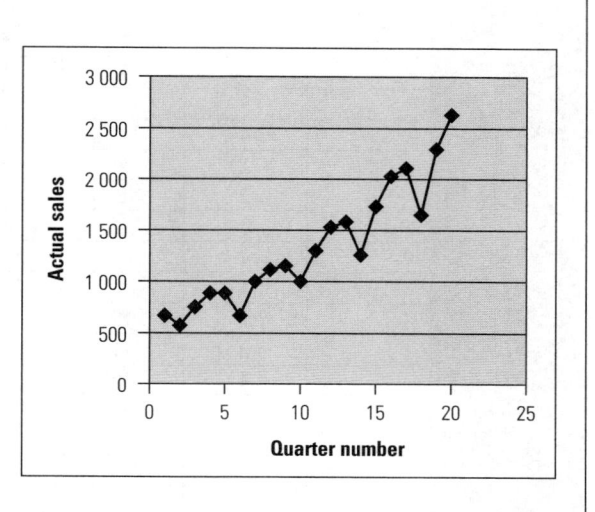

Table 6.9 Actual data and plot of quarterly sales of air conditioners (2003–2007)

Year	Qtr	Time period	Actual sales
2003	1	1	680
	2	2	585
	3	3	760
	4	4	890
2004	1	5	886
	2	6	677
	3	7	1 000
	4	8	1 120
2005	1	9	1 160
	2	10	990
	3	11	1 310
	4	12	1 540
2006	1	13	1 590
	2	14	1 260
	3	15	1 740
	4	16	2 031
2007	1	17	2 109
	2	18	1 651
	3	19	2 305
	4	20	2 640
2008	1	21	2 800
	2	22	2 200
	3	23	2 600
	4	24	2 900

Table 6.10 Forecasting quarterly sales of air conditioners using the naïve method

Row/column	A	B	C	D	E	F	G
1			Time period	Actual sales	Naïve forecast		
2	Year	Qtr					
3	2003	1	1	680			
4		2	2	585	680		
5		3	3	760	585		
6		4	4	890	760		
7	2004	1	5	886	890		
8		2	6	677	886		
9		3	7	1 000	677		
10		4	8	1 120	1 000		
11	2005	1	9	1 160	1 120		
12		2	10	990	1 160		
13		3	11	1 310	990		
14		4	12	1 540	1 310		
15	2006	1	13	1 590	1 540		
16		2	14	1 260	1 590		
17		3	15	1 740	1 260		
18		4	16	2 031	1 740		
19	2007	1	17	2 109	2 031		
20		2	18	1 651	2 109		
21		3	19	2 305	1 651		
22		4	20	2 640	2 305		
23	**2008**	1	21	2 800	2 640	160	5,71429
24		2	22	2 200	2 640	440	20
25		3	23	2 600	2 640	40	1,53846
26		4	24	2 900	2 640	260	8,96552
27							
28					72 100	225	9,05
29					MSE	MAD	MAPE

Calculating forecast accuracy of the naïve forecast in Table 6.10:

Type in cell E4: = D3.
Copy E4 down from E5 to E23.
Type in cell E24:E26: = E23.
To calculate MSE: In cell E28: = SUMXMY2(D23:D26,E23:E26)/COUNT(D23:D26).
To calculate MAD:
- In cell F23: = ABS(D23-E23).
- Copy F23 from F24 to F26.
- In cell F28 type: = AVERAGE(F23:F26).

To calculate MAPE:
- In cell G23: =100*ABS((D23-E23)/D23).
- Copy G23 from G24 to G26.
- In cell G28 type: = AVERAGE(G23:G26).

Table 6.11 Forecasting quarterly sales of air conditioners using Holt's method

	A	B	C	D	E	F	G	H	I
1			Time period	Actual sales				Alpha=	0,11909
2	Year	Qtr			Level	Trend	Forecast	Beta=	1
3	2003	1	1	680	680	0		MSE=	47 484,64
4		2	2	585	668,69	−11,31	680,00		
5		3	3	760	669,59	0,91	657,37		
6		4	4	890	696,64	27,05	670,50		
7	2004	1	5	886	743,02	46,38	723,69		
8		2	6	677	776,01	32,99	789,40		
9		3	7	1 000	831,75	55,74	809,00		
10		4	8	1 120	915,18	83,43	887,49		
11	2005	1	9	1 160	1 017,82	102,65	998,60		
12		2	10	990	1 104,93	87,11	1 120,47		
13		3	11	1 310	1 206,09	101,16	1 192,04		
14		4	12	1 540	1 334,97	128,88	1 307,25		
15	2006	1	13	1 590	1 478,87	143,90	1 463,84		
16		2	14	1 260	1 579,56	100,70	1 622,76		
17		3	15	1 740	1 687,38	107,81	1 680,26		
18		4	16	2 031	1 823,27	135,89	1 795,19		
19	2007	1	17	2 109	1 977,01	153,74	1 959,17		
20		2	18	1 651	2 073,62	96,61	2 130,75		
21		3	19	2 305	2 186,27	112,66	2 170,22		
22		4	20	2 640	2 339,55	153,27	2 298,93		
23	2008	1	21	2 800			2 492,82		
24		2	22	2 200			2 646,09	MSE=	83 969,7
25		3	23	2 600			2 799,37	MAD=	251,322
26		4	24	2 900			2 952,64	MAPE=	10,1828

Entering the formulas in Excel in Table 6.11:

In cell E3: =D3.
In cell F3: =0.
In cell E4: =$I$1*D4+(1-$I$1)*(E3+F3).
In cell F4: =$I$2*(E4-E3)+(1-$I$2)*F3.
In cell G4: =E3+F3.
Copy cell E4:G4 down from E5:G5 to E22:G22.
In cell I3: =SUMXMY2(D4:D22,G4:G22)/COUNT(G4:G22).
Use Solver to minimise MSE in cell I3, subject to I1:I2 ≥0 and I1:I2≤1.
In cell G23: = E22 + F22.
In cell G24: = E22 + 2*F22.
In cell G25: = E22 + 3*F22.
In cell G26: = E22 + 4*F22.
Forecast error:
- In cell I24: = SUMXMY2(D23:D26,G23:G26)/COUNT(D23:D26).
- In cell I25: = (ABS(D23-G23)+ABS(D24-G24)+ABS(D25-G25)+ABS(D26-G26))/4.
- In cell I26: = (100*ABS((D23-G23)/D23)+ . . . +100*ABS((D26-G26)/D26))/4.

Table 6.12 Forecasting quarterly sales of air conditioners using the seasonal method

	A	B	C	D	E	F	G	H	I	J
1			Time period	Actual sales	Linear forecast	Actual as % of trend	Seasonal indices	Seasonal forecast	Q1	1,12
2	Year	Qtr							Q2	0,82
3	2003	1	1	680	464,17	1,46	1,12	517,61	Q3	1,03
4		2	2	585	557,02	1,05	0,82	457,13	Q4	1,10
5		3	3	760	649,86	1,17	1,03	670,03		
6		4	4	890	742,71	1,20	1,10	819,79		
7	2004	1	5	886	835,55	1,06	1,12	931,74		
8		2	6	677	928,40	0,73	0,82	761,92		
9		3	7	1 000	1 021,24	0,98	1,03	1 052,94		
10		4	8	1 120	1 114,09	1,01	1,10	1 229,71		Regr.
11	2005	1	9	1 160	1 206,93	0,96	1,12	1 345,87		Coeff.
12		2	10	990	1 299,78	0,76	0,82	1 066,70	Intercept	371,3
13		3	11	1 310	1 392,62	0,94	1,03	1 435,84	Time	92,8
14		4	12	1 540	1 485,47	1,04	1,10	1 639,64		
15	2006	1	13	1 590	1 578,31	1,01	1,12	1 760,00		
16		2	14	1 260	1 671,16	0,75	0,82	1 371,48		
17		3	15	1 740	1 764,00	0,99	1,03	1 818,75		
18		4	16	2 031	1 856,85	1,09	1,10	2 049,56		
19	2007	1	17	2 109	1 949,69	1,08	1,12	2 174,13		
20		2	18	1 651	2 042,54	0,81	0,82	1 676,27		
21		3	19	2 305	2 135,38	1,08	1,03	2 201,66		
22		4	20	2 640	2 228,23	1,18	1,10	2 459,48		
23	2008	1	21	2 800	2 321,07		1,12	2 588,27		
24		2	22	2 200	2 413,92		0,82	1 981,05		
25		3	23	2 600	2 506,76		1,03	2 584,56		
26		4	24	2 900	2 599,61		1,10	2 869,41		
27										
28						MSE	MAD	MAPE		
29						23 485,67	119,18	4,79		

Entering the formulas in Excel for Table 6.12:

Calculate the linear forecast: E3=$J$12+$J$13*C3; copy from E4 to E26.
In cell F3: = D3/E3; copy from F4 to F22.
Seasonal indices: In J1: = (F3+F7+F11+F15+F19)/5; copy from J2 to J4.
Copy seasonal indices in column G.
In cell H3: = E3*G3, copy from H4 to H26.
Calculate forecast accuracy in rows 23 to 26 as before.

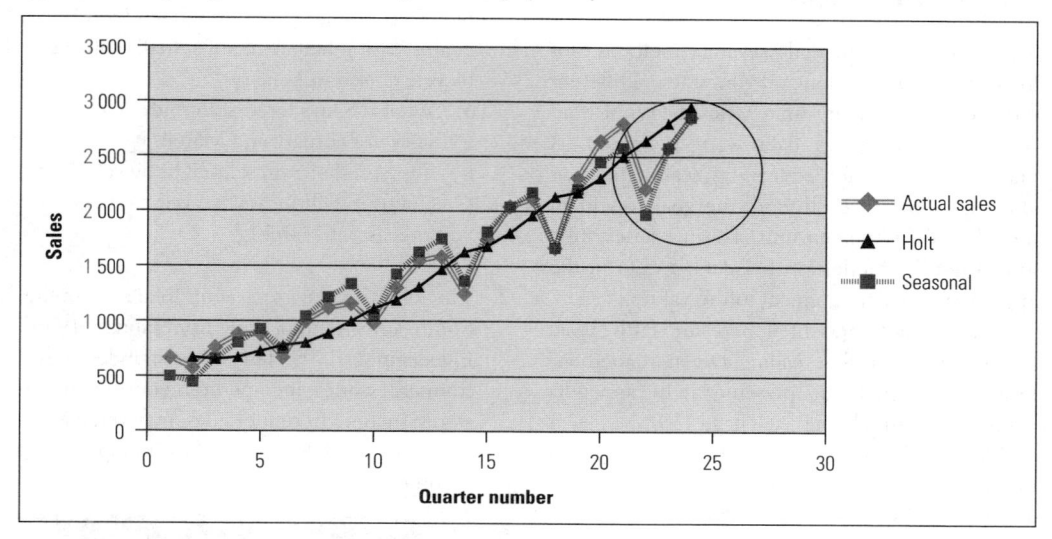

Figure 6.12 Comparing different forecasting methods graphically

The last four observations in the circle shown in Figure 6.12 indicate how well Holt's method and the seasonal method forecasted the test data. Table 6.13 is a summary of the forecasting accuracy measures. The seasonal forecasting method clearly performs better than both the naïve method and Holt's method.

Future observations will, therefore, be forecast using the seasonal method. The result is as shown in Figure 6.13.

Table 6.13 Comparing the forecasting methods

	MSE	MAD	MAPE
Naïve method	72 100,0	225,0	9,1
Holt's method	83 969,7	251,3	10,2
Seasonal forecast	23 485,7	119,2	4,8

Figure 6.13 Forecast of future sales of air conditioners using the seasonal method

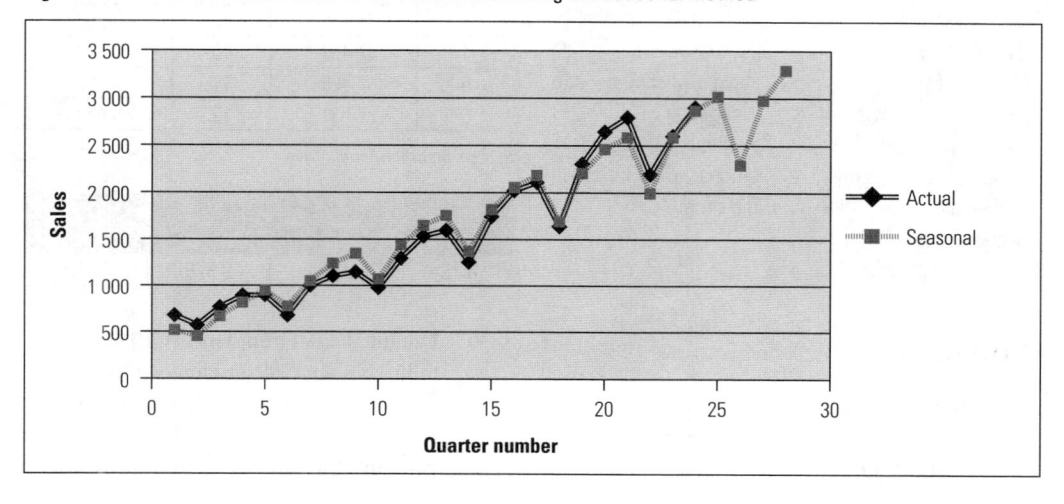

6.12 Conclusion

This chapter presented several methods for forecasting future demand or sales. Different methods for stationary time series data and non-stationary time series data were presented. A practical method for addressing seasonality was also suggested. In each case, the goal was to fit models to the past behaviour of a time series, then to first test the models on test data, and to fit the appropriate model to project future values.

The methods presented here are fairly basic techniques. For further reading, two more methods to address seasonality are presented in the appendix at the end of this chapter (see page 138).

More sophisticated approaches to time-series forecasting, such as auto-regressive moving averages (ARMA) and auto-regressive integrated moving averages (ARIMA) are superior in many respects, but difficult to implement and interpret without using specialist packages, and are beyond the scope of this book.

Key terms

- Consumer market survey
- Delphi method
- Demand forecasting
- Explanatory models
- Fit accuracy
- Forecast accuracy
- Forecasting process
- Holt's method
- Mean absolute deviation
- Jury of executive option
- Long-term, short-term, medium-term forecasting
- Mean absolute percentage error
- Mean square error
- Moving averages
- Naïve method
- Non-stationary time series
- Qualitative and quantitative forecasting
- Sales force composite
- Seasonality
- Simple exponential smoothing
- Smoothing parameters
- Stationary time series
- Time series

Problems

1. Each month, Sam's Cycle Parts uses exponential smoothing (with $\alpha = 0{,}75$) to forecast the number of bicycle chains that will be sold during the next month. In December, Sam forecast that he would sell ten bicycle chains during January. Sam actually sold 12 bicycle chains in January.
   a. What is Sam's forecast for bicycle chain sales in February and March?
   b. Suppose that Sam sells eight bicycle chains in February, what is the revised forecast for March?

2. The following data represents total sales of the South African motor trade from January 1998 to December 1999. This value includes sales from accessories; income from convenience stores; income from fuel sales; new-vehicle sales; used-vehicle sales; and workshop income.

1998			
Month	Sales (R million)	Month	Sales (R million)
1	7 449	7	8 476
2	7 954	8	7 702
3	7 941	9	7 376
4	7 714	10	7 869
5	7 660	11	7 879
6	7 692	12	7 719

1999			
Month	Sales (R million)	Month	Sales (R million)
1	7 342	7	8 376
2	7 820	8	8 535
3	7 930	9	8 590
4	7 487	10	8 700
5	7 789	11	8 665
6	7 531	12	8 424

Source: Statistics South Africa

2000			
January	February	March	April
8 184	9 454	9 378	8 752

  a. Use the dataset from January 1998 to December 1999 and forecast the South African motor trade for the next four months (January–April 2000) by computing a four-month moving average.

b Calculate the MSE value of the forecast accuracy, by comparing your forecasts with the actual values given for January 2000 to April 2000.
c Create an exponential smoothing model that minimises the MSE for the dataset (January 1998 to December 1999).
d Calculate the MSE value of the forecast accuracy using the exponential smoothing model in the previous question by comparing your forecasts with the actual values for January 2000 to April 2000.
e Plot the actual data from January 1998 to April 2000, as well as your four-month moving average and exponential smoothing forecasts on the same graph.
f Make a recommendation on which model you would suggest would be more appropriate.
g Do you think other models should be considered? If so, why or why not?

3 The following data represents actual sales of the motor trade in South Africa from January 2000 to December 2005, which is a continuation of the data series in question 2.

2000		2001		2002	
Month	Sales	Month	Sales	Month	Sales
1	8 184	1	10 633	1	12 377
2	9 454	2	11 391	2	12 852
3	9 378	3	11 655	3	12 732
4	8 752	4	10 410	4	13 113
5	9 979	5	11 421	5	13 948
6	10 255	6	11 634	6	13 310
7	10 390	7	11 716	7	14 215
8	10 846	8	11 759	8	14 833
9	10 578	9	11 062	9	14 561
10	10 592	10	12 392	10	14 736
11	11 100	11	12 324	11	15 275
12	10 411	12	12 546	12	14 122

2003		2004		2005	
Month	Sales	Month	Sales	Month	Sales
1	14 892	1	17 090	1	18 645
2	14 833	2	16 195	2	18 700
3	14 668	3	16 413	3	19 563
4	13 952	4	15 335	4	19 962
5	14 854	5	18 863	5	21 287
6	14 932	6	18 219	6	21 036
7	16 622	7	19 344	7	22 391
8	15 285	8	19 259	8	22 847
9	15 768	9	19 712	9	22 690
10	16 746	10	19 413	10	22 440
11	17 198	11	20 144	11	23 733
12	16 795	12	20 319	12	22 161

Source: Statistics South Africa

2006			
January	February	March	April
21 676	22 512	23 679	21 797

a Use Holt's method to create a model that minimises the MSE for the dataset from January 2000 to December 2005.
b Use Holt's method to forecast actual sales for January 2006 to April 2006.
c Calculate the MSE for the forecast error of Holt's method.
d Use a linear regression model to forecast actual sales for January 2006 to April 2006.
e Calculate the MSE for the forecast error of the linear regression model.
f Prepare a line graph comparing the forecasts from Holt's method and the linear regression model versus the original data.
g If you had to choose between Holt's method and the linear regression model, which would you use and why?
h Do you think other models should be considered. If so, why or why not?

4 The following data represents (in R million) retail trade for South Africa for the period January 2000 to December 2003. Two columns are presented for each time period: the constant sales (in R million) and the sales

in current value (R million). The constant sales value uses 2000 as the base year, and adjusts the current values for the effects of inflation. This will then provide us with a true reflection of whether sales (in R million) increased over time or not.

2000			2001		
Month	Constant	Current	Month	Constant	Current
1	16 454	15 862	1	16 292	16 732
2	15 758	15 223	2	15 729	16 185
3	17 150	16 721	3	17 334	17 976
4	16 788	16 604	4	17 071	17 840
5	16 907	16 788	5	17 291	18 173
6	16 509	16 509	6	17 115	18 108
7	16 455	16 636	7	17 338	18 448
8	16 229	16 456	8	17 143	18 206
9	16 389	16 684	9	16 957	18 059
10	16 980	17 354	10	17 886	19 156
11	18 136	18 553	11	18 711	20 190
12	23 853	24 426	12	24 407	26 506

2002			2003		
Month	Constant	Current	Month	Constant	Current
1	16 919	18 628	1	17 403	21 214
2	16 409	18 149	2	16 708	20 334
3	18 026	20 261	3	18 366	22 536
4	17 272	19 673	4	17 730	21 843
5	17 978	20 693	5	18 778	23 003
6	17 609	20 462	6	18 336	22 297
7	17 472	20 424	7	18 397	22 628
8	17 626	20 763	8	18 172	22 478
9	17 340	20 721	9	18 522	22 948
10	17 889	21 646	10	19 135	23 650
11	19 022	23 112	11	20 545	25 476
12	24 574	29 858	12	26 783	33 211

Source: Statistics South Africa

a Use Holt's method to create a model that minimises the MSE for the current sales from January 2000 to December 2003.

2004		
Month	Constant	Current
1	19 247	24 001
2	18 591	23 332
3	19 553	24 636
4	19 226	24 301
5	20 315	25 699
6	20 017	25 462
7	20 436	25 975
8	20 098	25 424

b Use Holt's method to forecast current sales for January 2004 to August 2004.
c Calculate the MSE for the forecast error of Holt's method.
d Use a seasonal linear regression model to forecast current sales for January 2004 to August 2004.
e Calculate the MSE for the forecast error of the linear regression model.
f Prepare a line graph comparing the forecasts from Holt's method and the seasonal linear regression model versus the original data.
g If you had to choose between Holt's method and the seasonal linear regression model, which would you use and why?

5 Consider the data in question 4.
   a Prepare a time series plot of the data for both the current sales values and constant sales values on the same graph.
   b Comment on the nature of the time series of both variables, as well as the relationship between the two time series.
   c Use Holt-Winter's additive method to create a model that minimises the MSE for the dataset from January 2000 to December 2003.
   d Use Holt-Winter's method to forecast current sales for January 2004 to August 2004.
   e Calculate the MSE for the forecast error of Holt-Winter's method.
   f Use Holt-Winter's multiplicative method to create a model that minimises the MSE for the current sales from January 2000 to December 2003.

g Use Holt-Winter's multiplicative method to forecast current sales for January 2004 to August 2004.
h Calculate the MSE for the forecast error of the Holt-Winter's multiplicative model.
i Prepare a line graph comparing the forecasts from Holt-Winter's additive and multiplicative methods against the original data.
j If you had to choose between Holt-Winter's additive and multiplicative methods, which would you use and why?

Questions

1. List and discuss four features of forecasting and seven elements of a good forecast.
2. What is the difference between quantitative and qualitative forecasting techniques?
3. Discuss the difference between time series models and explanatory models of forecasting.
4. List and discuss four qualitative forecasting techniques.
5. Explain at what stage in the supply chain short-term forecasting is appropriate.
6. What is meant by short-term forecasting (i.e. the time period)?
7. Which departments or people in the company are mostly responsible for short-term forecasting?
8. Explain at what stage in the supply chain medium-term forecasting is appropriate.
9. What is meant by medium-term forecasting (i.e. the time period)?
10. Which departments or people in the company are mostly responsible for medium-term forecasting?
11. Explain at what stage in the supply chain long-term forecasting is appropriate.
12. What is meant by long-term forecasting (i.e. the time period)?
13. Which departments or people in the company are mostly responsible for long-term forecasting?
14. Which forecasting techniques are appropriate for short-term, medium-term, and long-term forecasting?
15. List the steps in the forecasting process.
16. Which two techniques are appropriate if the time series data is stationary without any signs of seasonality?
17. Which two techniques are appropriate if the time series data is non-stationary, without any signs of seasonality?
18. Write down a strategy for evaluating any forecasting methodology.

Consult the books

Barr, D. P. 2002. 'Challenges facing a demand planner: How to identify and handle them'. *Journal of Business Forecasting* 21(2) (Summer 2002).

Dewhurst, F. 2002. *Quantitative Methods for Business and Management*, 2nd edition. London: McGraw-Hill.

Ghiani, G., Laporte, G., Musmanno, R. 2004. *Introduction to Logistics Systems Planning and Control*. New York: John Wiley & Sons.

Hill, S. 1998. 'A whole new outlook'. *Manufacturing Systems* 16(9) (September 1998).

Makridakis, S., Wheelwright, S. C. and Hyndman, R. J. 1998. *Forecasting: Methods and Applications*, 3rd edition. New York: John Wiley & Sons.

Ragsdale, C. T. 2007. *Managerial Decision Modeling*, revised edition. Thomson South-Western.

Reid, R. D. and Sanders, N. R. 2005. *Operations Management: An Integrated Approach*, 2nd edition. John Wiley & Sons.

Render B., Stair, R. M. and Hanna, M. E. 2006. *Quantitative Analysis for Management*, 9th edition. Upper Saddle River: Pearson Prentice Hall.

Wild, T. 2002. *Best Practice in Inventory Management*, 2nd edition. Rochester: Butterworth-Heinemann.

Wilson, J. H., Keating, B. and John Galt Solutions, Inc. 2007. *Business Forecasting with Accompanying Excel-Based ForecastX^{TM} Software*. Boston: McGraw-Hill.

Notes

1 Hill, S. 1998: 70–80.
2 Barr, D. P. 2002: 28–9.
3 Makridakis et al. 1998: 555.
4 Adapted from Ghiani et al. 2004: 72.

Appendix 6.1 Holt-Winter's seasonality models

Moving averages and exponential smoothing methods can deal with almost any type of data, as long as the data is non-seasonal. Where seasonality exists, these methods are not appropriate.

Holt's method was extended by Winter to capture seasonality. There are two different Holt-Winter's methods, depending on whether seasonality is modelled in an additive or multiplicative way. Figure A6.1 shows the difference between additive and multiplicative seasonality.

Note that for the additive model (a), the amplitude, or the difference in demand, between the seasons with the largest values and lowest values stays the same over time. In the multiplicative model (b), one can clearly see that as time progresses, the difference in demand between the seasons with the higher values and the seasons with the lower values increases over time.

A6.1.1 Holt-Winter's additive model

Holt-Winter's method is based on three smoothing equations, one for the level, one for the trend and one for the seasonality. It is similar to Holt's method, but an equation is added to deal with seasonality. The basic equations for Holt-Winter's additive model are as follows:

Base: $E_t = \alpha(Y_t - S_{t-p}) + (1 - \alpha)(E_{t-1} + T_{t-1})$
Trend: $T_t = \beta(E_t - E_{t-1}) + (1 - \beta)T_{t-1}$
Seasonality: $S_t = \gamma(Y_t - E_t) + (1 - \gamma)S_{t-p}$
Forecast: $\hat{Y}_{t+n} = E_t + nT_t + S_{t+n-p}.$

The forecast can be used to obtain forecasts n time periods into the future, where $n = 1, 2, ..., p$. The forecast for time period $t + n$, i.e.

$$\hat{Y}_{t+n} = E_t + nT_t + S_{t+n-p}$$

is obtained by adjusting the expected base and trend level at time period $t + n$, by the most recent estimate of seasonality associated with this time period (S_{t+n-p}). The smoothing parameters α, β and γ can assume any value between 0 and 1.

The four basic steps in the process are as follows:

Step 1: Compute the base level E_t for time period t.
Step 2: Compute the estimated trend value T_t for time period t.
Step 3: Compute the estimated seasonal factor S_t for time period t.
Step 4: Compute the final forecast $\hat{Y}_{t+n}$ for time period $t + n$.

When calculating E_t, T_t and S_t at time period t, values should exist for E_{t-1}, T_{t-1} and S_{t-p}. We start the initialising process by calculating the initial estimates for seasonality to be:

$$S_t = Y_t - \sum_{i=1}^{p} \frac{Y_i}{p}, t = 1, 2, ..., p.$$

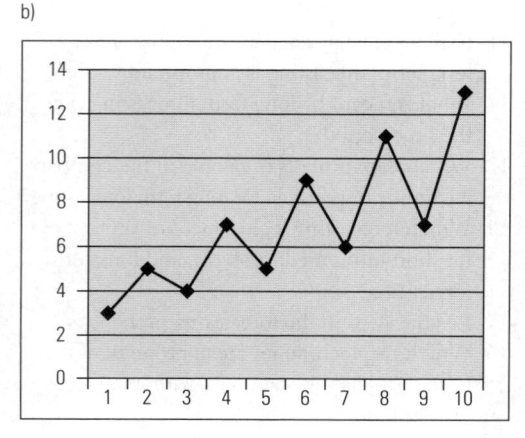

Figure A6.1 Additive and multiplicative seasonality

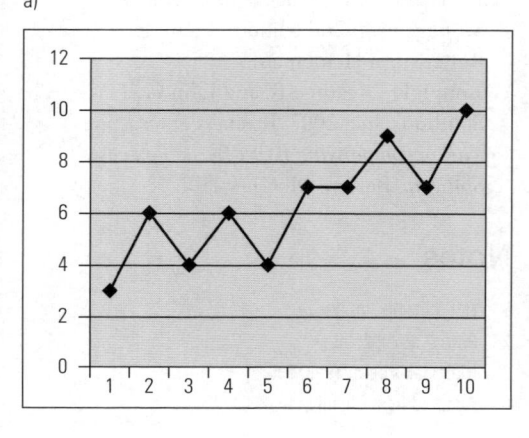

This implies that the initial seasonal estimate for each of the first p time periods is the difference between the observed value in the time period and the average value observed during the first p time periods. We initialise the first E_t value in time period p as $E_p = Y_p - S_p$, and $T_p = 0$. Other methods of initialising also exist. In practice, the process of initialising arises only once for any series, and the assumption is that enough history built up takes place for the method and that self-adjustment will take place and good values will result independently of the starting values used.

The following example illustrates the use of Holt-Winter's additive method in Excel. The data shown in Table A6.1 represents international airline passenger travel (in thousands) for a 24-month period.

Table A6.1 Forecasting airline data with Holt-Winter's additive method

	A	B	C	D	E	F	G	H	I
1	Quarters	Period	Actual	Base	Trend	Seasonal	Forecast	Alpha	0,5
2	1	1	362			−18,000	--	Beta	0,5
3	2	2	385			5,000	--	Gamma	0,5
4	3	3	432			52,000	--	MSE	1 631,073
5	4	4	341	380,0	0,0	−39,000	--		
6	1	5	382	390,0	5,0	−13,000	362,00		
7	2	6	409	399,5	7,3	7,250	400,00		
8	3	7	498	426,4	17,1	61,813	458,75		
9	4	8	387	434,7	12,7	−43,359	404,44		
10	1	9	473	466,7	22,3	−3,355	434,42		
11	2	10	513	497,4	26,5	11,423	496,31		
12	3	11	582	522,1	25,6	60,878	585,74		
13	4	12	474	532,5	18,0	−50,930	504,28		
14	1	13	544	548,9	17,2	−4,146	547,16		
15	2	14	582	568,4	18,3	12,527	577,58		
16	3	15	681	603,4	26,7	69,234	647,58		
17	4	16	557	619,0	21,1	−56,471	579,17		
18	1	17	628	636,2	19,1	−6,148	636,01		
19	2	18	707	674,9	28,9	22,322	667,82		
20	3	19	773	703,8	28,9	69,221	773,05		
21	4	20	592	690,6	7,9	−77,532	676,24		
22	1	21	627	665,8	−8,5	−22,475	692,31		
23	2	22	725	680,0	2,9	33,657	679,66		
24	3	23	854	733,8	28,3	94,696	752,10		
25	4	24	661	750,4	22,4	−83,443	684,64		
26	1	25					750,31		
27	2	26					828,88		
28	3	27					912,36		
29	4	28					756,65		

Excel instructions for Table A6.1:
In cell F2: =C2-AVERAGE($C$2:$C$5).
In cell F3:F5: copy F2 down.
In cell E5: =0.

In cell D5: =C5–E5.
In cell D6: =$I$1*(C6-F2)+(1-$I$1)*(D5+E5).
In cell E6: =$I$2*(D6-D5)+(1-$I$2)*E5.
In cell F6: =$I$3*(C6-D6)+(1-$I$3)*F2.
In cell G6: =D5+E5+F2.
Highlight D6:G6 and copy to D25:G25.
In cell G26: =D25+E25+F22.
In cell G27: =D25+2*E25+F23.
In cell G28: =D25+3*E25+F24.
In cell G29: =D25+4*E25+F25.

Use Solver to find the minimum MSE value by changing the values of α, β and γ. The result is as follows: $\alpha = 0{,}43$; $\beta = 0{,}23$ and $\gamma = 1{,}0$. The MSE value is 1 176,5.

Figure A6.2 Excel spreadsheet showing the application of Holt-Winter's additive method on airline data

	A	B	C	D	E	F	G	H	I
1	Quarters	Period	Actual	Base	Trend	Seasonal	Forecast	Alpha	0,430753
2	1	1	362			–18,000	–	Beta	0,23168
3	2	2	385			5,000	–	Gamma	1
4	3	3	432			52,000	–	MSE	1176,459
5	4	4	341	380,0	0,0	–39,000	–		
6	1	5	382	388,6	2,0	–6,615	362,00		
7	2	6	409	396,4	3,3	12,622	395,61		
8	3	7							
9	4	8							
10	1	9							
11	2	10							
12	3	11							
13	4	12							
14	1	13							
15	2	14							
16	3	15							
17	4	16							
18	1	17							
19	2	18							
20	3	19							
21	4	20							
22	1	21							
23	2	22	725	665,9	9,9	59,117	720,16		
24	3	23	854	709,1	17,6	144,903	776,68		
25	4	24	661	731,2	18,7	–70,199	650,60		
26	1	25					722,49		
27	2	26					827,64		
28	3	27					932,09		
29	4	28					735,65		

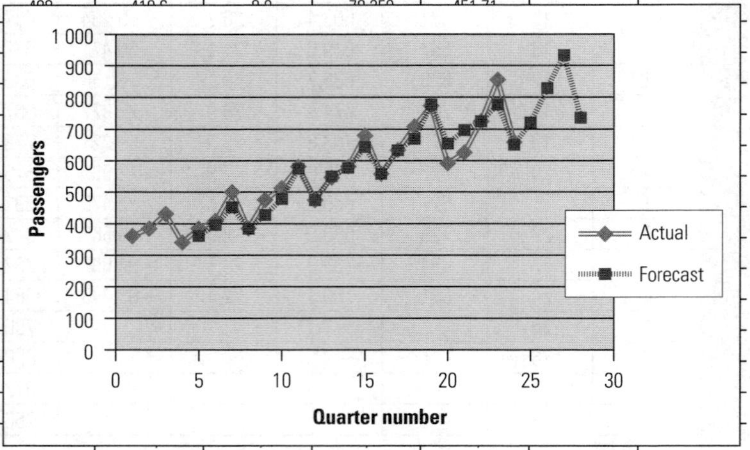

A6.1.2 Holt-Winter's multiplicative model

Holt-Winter's multiplicative method is similar to the additive method, but subtraction is replaced by division in the formulas of E_t and S_t. The forecast will also change. The basic equations for Holt-Winter's multiplicative model are as follows:

Base: $E_t = \alpha \dfrac{Y_t}{S_{t-p}} + (1-\alpha)(E_{t-1} + T_{t-1})$

Trend: $T_t = \beta(E_t - E_{t-1}) + (1-\beta)T_{t-1}$

Seasonality: $S_t = \gamma \dfrac{Y_t}{E_t} + (1-\gamma)S_{t-p}$

Forecast: $\hat{Y}_{t+n} = E_t + nT_t + S_{t+n-p}$

The forecast can be used to obtain forecasts n time periods into the future, where $n = 1, 2, \ldots, p$. The forecast for time period $t + n$, i.e.
$\hat{Y}_{t+n} = (E_t + nT_t)S_{t+n-p}$
is obtained by multiplying the expected base + trend level at time period $t + n$, by the most recent estimate of seasonality associated with this time period (S_{t+n-p}). The smoothing parameters α, β and γ can assume any value between 0 and 1.

The four basic steps in the process are as follows:

Step 1: Compute the base level E_t for time period t.

Step 2: Compute the estimated trend value T_t for time period t.

Step 3: Compute the estimated seasonal factor S_t for time period t.

Step 4: Compute the final forecast $\hat{Y}_{t+n}$ for time period $t + n$.

When calculating E_t, T_t and S_t at time period t, values should exist for E_{t-1}, T_{t-1} and S_{t-p}. We start the initialising process by calculating the initial estimates for seasonality to be:

$$S_t = \dfrac{Y_t}{\sum_{i=1}^{p} \dfrac{Y_i}{p}}, \; t = 1, 2, \ldots, p$$

This implies that the initial seasonal estimate for each of the first p time periods is the quotient of the observed value in the time period divided by the average value observed during the first p time periods. We initialise the first E_t value in time period p as:

$$E_p = \dfrac{Y_p}{S_p}, \text{ and } T_p = 0$$

The example in table A6.2 illustrates the use of Holt-Winter's multiplicative method in Excel.

Table A6.2 Forecasting airline data with Holt-Winter's multiplicative method

	A	B	C	D	E	F	G	H	I
1	Quarters	Period	Actual	Base	Trend	Seasonal	Forecast	Alpha	0,5
2	1	1	362			0,953	--	Beta	0,5
3	2	2	385			1,013	--	Gamma	0,5
4	3	3	432			1,137	--	MSE	992,7665
5	4	4	341	380,0	0,0	0,897	--		
6	1	5	382	390,5	5,2	0,965	362,00		
7	2	6	409	399,7	7,2	1,018	400,95		
8	3	7	498	422,5	15,0	1,158	462,64		
9	4	8	387	434,4	13,4	0,894	392,61		
10	1	9	473	468,9	24,0	0,987	432,36		
11	2	10	513	498,3	26,7	1,024	501,82		
12	3	11	582	513,9	21,1	1,145	607,90		
13	4	12	474	532,6	19,9	0,892	478,37		
14	1	13	544	551,8	19,6	0,986	545,34		
15	2	14	582	569,9	18,8	1,023	584,95		
16	3	15	681	591,7	20,3	1,148	674,22		
17	4	16	557	618,2	23,4	0,897	545,99		
18	1	17	628	639,1	22,2	0,985	632,95		
19	2	18	707	676,3	29,7	1,034	676,14		
20	3	19	773	689,7	21,5	1,134	810,56		
21	4	20	592	685,8	8,8	0,880	637,62		
22	1	21	627	665,7	−5,6	0,963	683,83		
23	2	22	725	680,6	4,7	1,050	682,44		
24	3	23	854	719,1	21,5	1,161	777,41		
25	4	24	661	745,9	24,2	0,883	651,65		
26	1	25					741,77		
27	2	26					833,64		
28	3	27					950,28		
29	4	28					744,11		

Excel instructions for Table A6.2:

In cell F2: =C2/AVERAGE($C$2:$C$5).
In cell F3:F5: copy F2 down.
In cell D5: =C5/E5.
In cell E5: =0.
In cell D6: =$I$1*(C6/F2)+(1-$I$1)*(D5+E5).
In cell E6: =$I$2*(D6-D5)+(1-$I$2)*E5.
In cell F6: =$I$3*(C6/D6)+(1-$I$3)*F2.
In cell G6: =(D5+E5)*F2.
Highlight D6:G6 and copy to D25:G25.
In cell G26: =(D25+E25)*F22.
In cell G27: =(D25+2*E25)*F23.
In cell G28: =(D25+3*E25)*F24.
In cell G29: =(D25+4*E25)*F25.

CHAPTER 6 FORECASTING SUPPLY CHAIN REQUIREMENTS | 143

Use Solver to find the minimum MSE value by changing the values of α, β and γ. The result is as follows: $\alpha = 0{,}97$; $\beta = 0{,}12$ and $\gamma = 0{,}0$. The MSE value is 707,9.

Figure A6.3 Excel spreadsheet showing the application of Holt-Winter's multiplicative method on airline data

	A	B	C	D	E	F	G	H	I
1	Quarters	Period	Actual	Base	Trend	Seasonal	Forecast	Alpha	0,974758
2	1	1	362			0,953	–	Beta	0,115104
3	2	2	385			1,013	–	Gamma	0
4	3	3	432			1,137	–	MSE	707,8988
5	4	4	341	380,0	0,0	0,897	–		
6	1	5	382	400,5	2,4	0,953	362,00		
7	2	6	400	402,7	2,5	1,013	408,12		
8	3	7							
9	4	8							
10	1	9							
11	2	10							
12	3	11							
13	4	12							
14	1	13							
15	2	14							
16	3	15							
17	4	16							
18	1	17							
19	2	18							
20	3	19							
21	4	20							
22	1	21	627	658,5	10,5	0,953	640,93		
23	2	22	725	714,4	15,7	1,013	677,86		
24	3	23	854	750,7	18,1	1,137	830,05		
25	4	24	661	737,4	14,5	0,897	689,86		
26	1	25					716,28		
27	2	26					776,46		
28	3	27					887,71		
29	4	28					713,72		

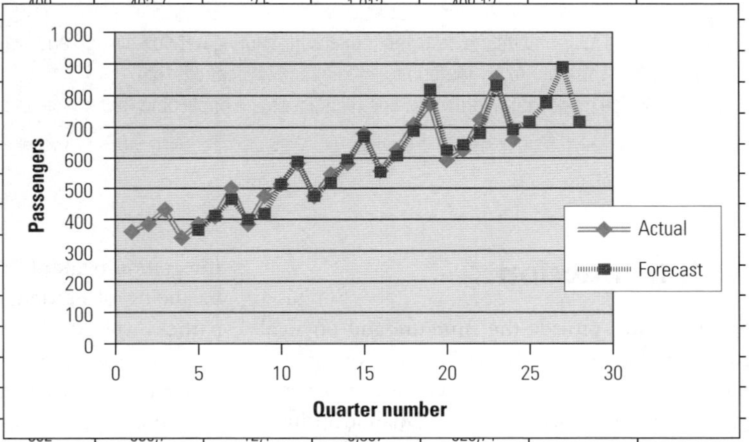

7 Network integration

J. Louw

Learning outcomes

After you have studied this chapter, you should be able to:
- understand how supply chain design facilitates network integration;
- explain why and when network redesign is required;
- know what the different stages in network design and implementation entail;
- apply the main network design and implementation steps;
- identify the major factors to be taken into account during network design and when locating facilities;
- apply the centre of gravity method for single facility locations; and
- know which modelling approaches and techniques are applicable for network design.

7.1 Introduction

Supply chains provide the structure and physical capability for manufacturing businesses to supply raw material and goods to their operations and products to their markets. Today's dynamic business environment means that many organisations have to expand, merge, contract, or otherwise redesign their supply chain networks. The various geographically dispersed inbound and outbound activities make up a business's supply chain network. The focal business is normally at the centre of this network of suppliers and customers (as illustrated in Figure 7.1). This network provides the veins, or channels, through which inventory flows. The main network activities are movement, storage and transformation, which extend from the supply sources to the consumers of final products.

Manufacturing businesses commonly outsource a number of the supply chain activities that they view as non-core capabilities (e.g. transportation and storage). The parties contracted to execute such outsourced activities become the business's external stakeholders. They form into a network that links the supply chain together. For a supply chain to function successfully, internal cross-functional integration as well as external integration across the network of organisations is required.

Integration relates to the effective interfacing and balancing of capacity between the supply chain parties involved.

It is becoming increasingly apparent that competitive advantage is derived from the combined capabilities of the network of linked organisations in the supply chain. This is a fundamental shift in the traditionally held view of a business model based upon a single firm. Markets today are more volatile than in the past and less predictable. Consequently, supply chain networks need to become more agile to respond.[1]

Decisions relating to the supply chain network have a significant effect on the organisation for a relatively long period of time (i.e. for several years). The major issues are infrastructure and overall capacity levels. The level of risk and uncertainty associated with such decisions increases as the time period extends. The reality is, however, that 80 per cent of a supply chain's cost structure is determined by up-front, long-term strategic planning decisions. Unfortunately, many supply chains networks are inherited and, therefore, not designed for or aligned with the business strategy. Such supply chains have purely evolved over time, making them less efficient and effective. Most efforts to improve supply chain efficiency fall short because they do not challenge the fundamental structure

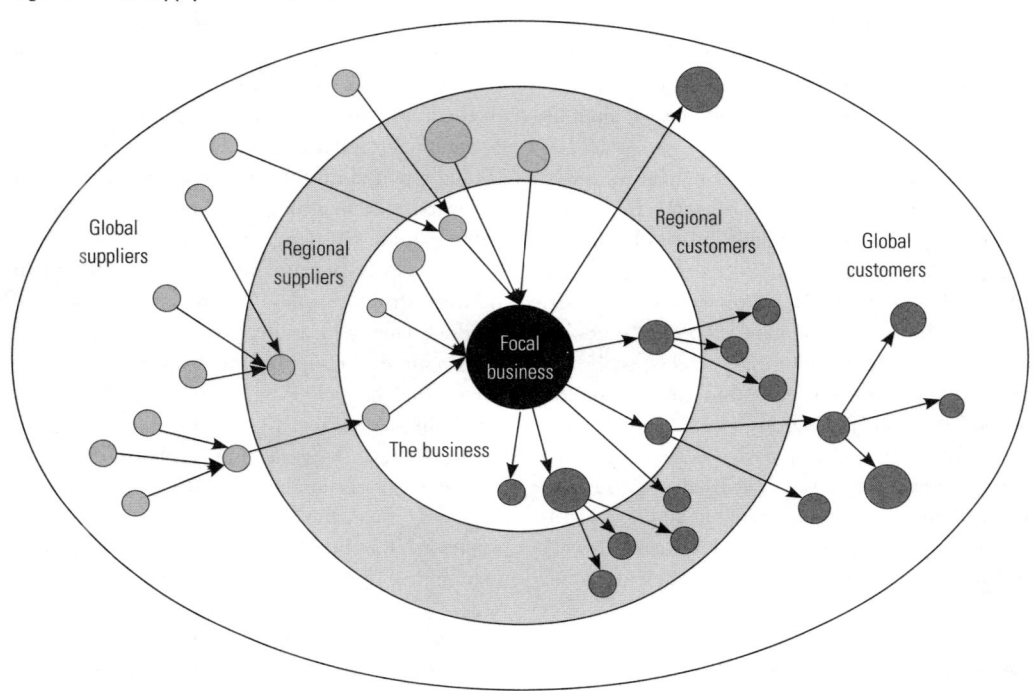

Figure 7.1 The supply chain network

of the supply chain, but instead attempt to improve performance within existing limitations.

Supply chain network design is a key focus area of supply chain strategy (see also Chapter 3) and provides the foundation for business success. It ensures that the supply chain network is optimised and provides the required capability – in terms of infrastructure and capacity – to service a particular business's market segments.

7.2 Network integration and supply chain design

Supply chain network integration requires the right design and configuration. Network design and configuration involves the structural dimensions of the network as well as the careful selection of the members in the supply chain. A supply chain network can either be designed for the material and product flows of a new business, redesigned to accommodate, for example, the expansion of a current business, or optimised to leverage opportunities. Figure 7.2 shows an approach for supply chain network design and implementation, indicating the major project stages (assessment, design, implementation and operation). These stages are described later in this chapter. Supply chains that are properly designed and have been in operation for a few years should be reassessed to ascertain if they are functioning optimally from time to time. The typical reasons for a redesign are listed in Figure 7.2. These relate to supply or business changes. A merger with or acquisition of another organisation may demand the rationalisation of the supply and distribution networks at the strategic network design level.

Network design relates to decisions regarding customer service; inventory policy; transportation modes; and the location and size of stocking points.[2] In terms of location issues, the common decisions are about the location of retail outlets; processing plant/ports; sources of supply; warehouses; breakbulk points; consolidation points; and layout of activities within a specific facility. Key considerations include the availability of supply sources, manufacturing facilities and where the target markets are located. A number of alternative supply chain networks are developed and evaluated based on sound screening criteria (e.g. service, cost, flexibility and strategy support). A detailed cost benefit trade-off analysis is then carried out on these alternatives.

Depending on the nature of the business and the environment in which it operates, the supply chain network may be relatively simple or very complex. A number of supply chain attributes that ultimately determine the supply chain complexity include the customer base; product portfolio; supplier base; manufacturing (process, scale and variety); logistics scope (inbound and outbound); and systems and applications used.

Supply chain network design is generally not a regular activity: it is usually carried out every few years, as companies do not need to add new plants or distribution centres on a routine basis. Network design and infrastructure configuration decisions have a long-term focus and usually create and establish the capacity required for future supply chain operations. These capacities then become part of the potential constraining resources used in medium-term tactical planning and short-term operational scheduling. Capacity utilisation, throughput and inventory turnover are the normal indicators used to evaluate how effective a design is with regard to satisfying future requirements.

The key determinants of a supply chain network structure relate to the markets for final product; facility locations (manufacturing, storage etc.); sources for supply; and transport links. The importance of each of these structural elements is briefly highlighted next.

To achieve a good supply chain design, a thorough understanding of the market for a business's final product is necessary. This also relates to the business's marketing strategy and competitive requirements. The different market

Figure 7.2 Stage-gate model for supply chain network design (initial design and redesign cycle)

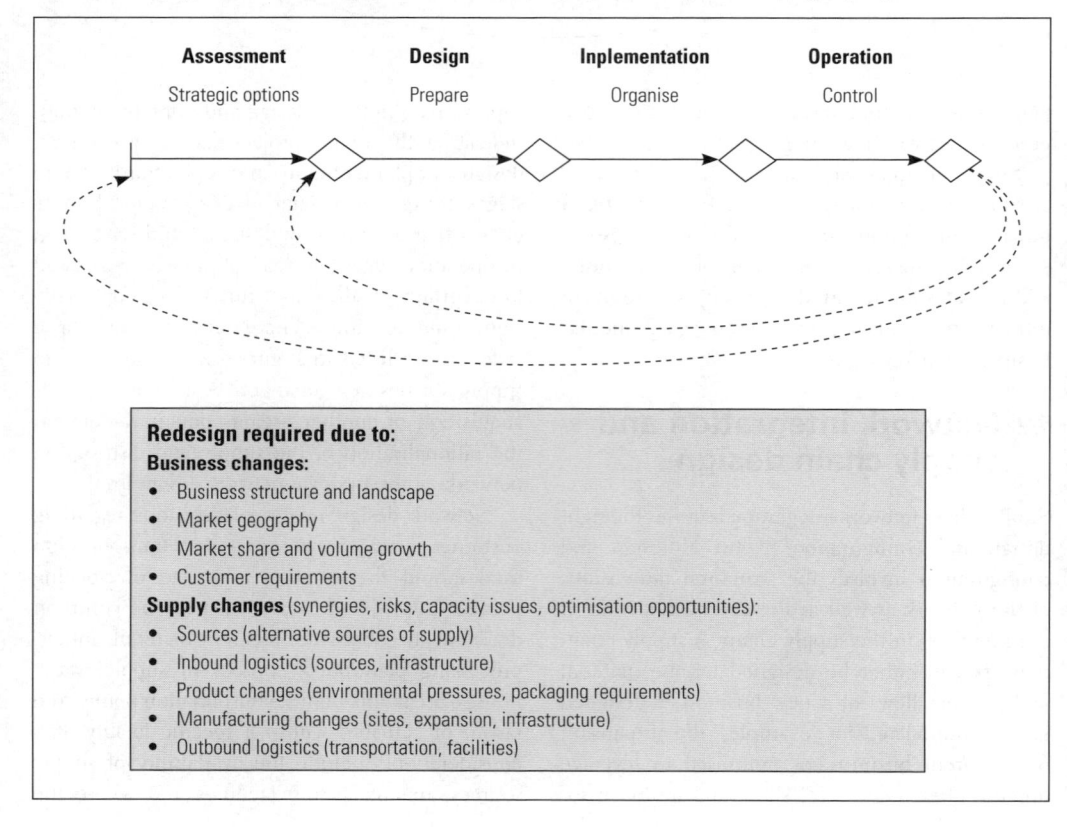

Assessment	Design	Inplementation	Operation
Strategic options	Prepare	Organise	Control

Redesign required due to:
Business changes:
- Business structure and landscape
- Market geography
- Market share and volume growth
- Customer requirements

Supply changes (synergies, risks, capacity issues, optimisation opportunities):
- Sources (alternative sources of supply)
- Inbound logistics (sources, infrastructure)
- Product changes (environmental pressures, packaging requirements)
- Manufacturing changes (sites, expansion, infrastructure)
- Outbound logistics (transportation, facilities)

segments, customers targeted, anticipated demand and service requirements form the basis for identifying future demand.

The number, size and location of facilities in a supply chain network are important strategic planning issues because major capital investments often need to be made.[3] Facility location relates to the geographic placement of production facilities, stocking points and transfer facilities. Logistics operational costs (ranging from 8 to 30 per cent of sales) are significantly affected by location decisions. Optimising the location of facilities within a supply chain network can save between 5 and 15 per cent of logistics costs.[4] Facility planning includes the following major logistics decisions:

- Whether to expand the existing facility instead of moving.
- Whether to maintain current sites and add another facility.
- Whether to close the existing facility and move to another.
- The type of facility layout (which has a major role to play in opportunities to minimise the total cost of material handling).

Closely linked to facility decisions is the selection of applicable sources of supply. The location and number of sources of material, goods and services for production as well as the nature of the manufacturing technology used can have a major influence on the supply chain network structure and, therefore, require careful consideration.

The specific manufacturing technology that businesses utilise can predetermine between 60 and 80 percent of the supply chain's costs. A good understanding of these costs and critically linking them to engineering or design trade-offs early in the design stage of a new manufacturing facility can contribute to significant cost savings. Standardisation of major equipment, spare parts and leveraging off common suppliers are some practices that can be applied.

Transport is a key activity in the supply chain, since it acts as the physical link between customers and suppliers, enabling the flow of materials and resources. Choices about transport modes (e.g. road, rail, ship, air and pipeline), the transport corridor and shipment sizes are some of the important decisions to be made in network design. With the introduction of third-party logistics providers (3PLs) (and fourth-party providers), carriers now also provide more than just physical transportation – they also provide an overall service, including value-added activities, such as inventory control and warehouse management.[5]

7.3 Supply chain configuration and functional requirements

There are numerous decisions regarding network design that affect the eventual supply chain operation. These design decision areas normally relate to network optimisation; network operation; policy formulations and optimisation; and design for robustness (or, preparedness for risk).[6] These decision areas help clarify the supply chain configuration, operation and functional requirements.

Network design and optimisation decisions ultimately determine the basic structure of the supply chain. Typical questions to be answered include:

- From the possible site locations that could be considered, which ones should be used?
- What is the fundamental network configuration in terms of structures, facilities and parties involved that will minimise the total cost of servicing the consumer demand?

The goal of network integration is the identification of the lowest total network design cost.[7] The basic concept of total cost for the overall logistical system is illustrated in Figure 7.3, which shows the relationship between a number of network facilities, inventory cost and transportation cost.

The task of structural design is to evaluate several alternative structures and select the lowest-cost network. Network optimisation models (e.g. linear or mixed integer programming) are typically used for these evaluations. An example of the contribution from such a network evaluation is shown in figure 7.4. In this example, six strategically located distribution centres were introduced and could result in the reduction of 49 small storage facilities.

Figure 7.3 Lowest total network cost

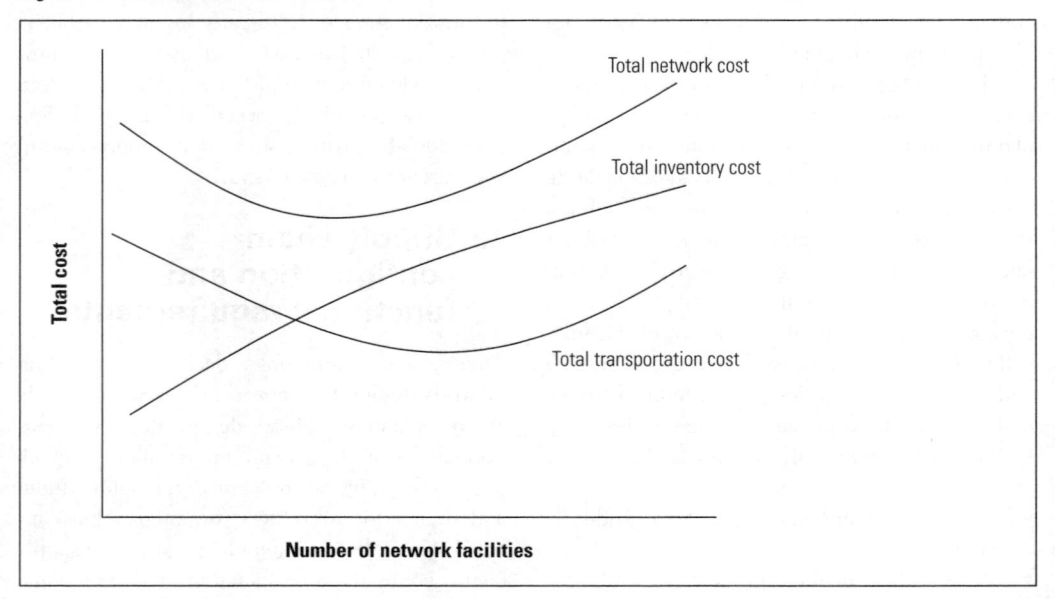

[Graph showing Total cost on y-axis vs Number of network facilities on x-axis, with curves for Total network cost, Total inventory cost, and Total transportation cost]

Network optimisation evaluates several supply chain alternatives. Each alternative is simplified and predominantly cost-focused to derive the least-cost network. Before finalising a proposed design or selecting which network design is best from various alternatives, the analysis needs to predict how each design will operate in the real world with all its variability, such as variability in demand, supply and transportation. Network simulation is used for this. Detailed models indicate how well a proposed supply chain will run (although not how it can be changed to improve it). Discrete-event simulation modelling tools are normally used to build these complicated models. Through such simulations,

Figure 7.4 An example of network optimisation

		Old	New
●	Demand clusters	80%	80%
▲	Production facilities	1	4
⬢	Distribution centres	0	6
■	Small storage facilities	65	16
♦	Small retail	101	53

the various supply chain activities are evaluated for capacity, operation philosophy and some basic functional requirements.

Once a network design is finalised and the new intended operation clarified, the best operating rules (policies) for the supply chain must be established. Policies include rules about whether or not inventory should be kept for various products, and how much and where inventory should be kept. Other examples relate to whether full truckload shipments suffice or if less than truckload shipments are needed to achieve the necessary customer service and whether the company should make or buy components for each product and main sub-assembly.

In the real world, supply chains encounter some unforeseen disruptions, unplanned events or things that might go wrong (e.g. strikes, breakdowns and storms). Risk assessment and contingency planning are sound methods to deal with such eventualities in a supply chain. With design for robustness, the aim is to evaluate what things might go wrong. This will ensure that the network does not perform poorly under other-than-expected conditions. The goal of supply chain management is not just to enable profitable business – there is an implicit goal to avoid very bad performance even under conditions that are unlikely but possible. Some deviations from the original basic assumptions might include: What if marketing was wrong about demand? What if the cost of supply doubles? What seemed like a good idea given forecasted conditions may kill the company under other conditions. Optimal answers are not necessarily the best answers. Given this paradox, a robustly designed supply chain aims to ensure the focal business's survival under nearly any circumstances.

7.4 The stages of supply chain design and implementation

The process of designing and implementing an appropriate supply chain network should be closely aligned with overall business strategies. Designing or redesigning a business's supply chain network can be complex, since many factors need to be considered to determine the optimum design. At the outset, it is important to clarify the scope, objectives and major deliverables of the supply chain network design or redesign process itself. Figure 7.5 indicates the major stages and steps that are recommended for thorough supply chain network design and implementation. These stages and steps are discussed in the following sections.

7.4.1 Assessment stage

Depending on the size of the engagement, a project or task team might be needed to conduct the supply chain design or redesign process. This team is formed early in the assessment stage. The team will familiarise themselves with the business's strategy; competence requirements and

Figure 7.5 Stages and steps in supply chain network design and implementation

Stages	Assessment	Design	Implementation	Operation
Major steps/ tasks	Business orientation	Conceptual flow design	Infrastructure establishment and construction	Stable operation
	Assessment of alternatives	Detail of functional design	Commerce/ new operations	Evaluation and refinement
	Project management			
	Change management			

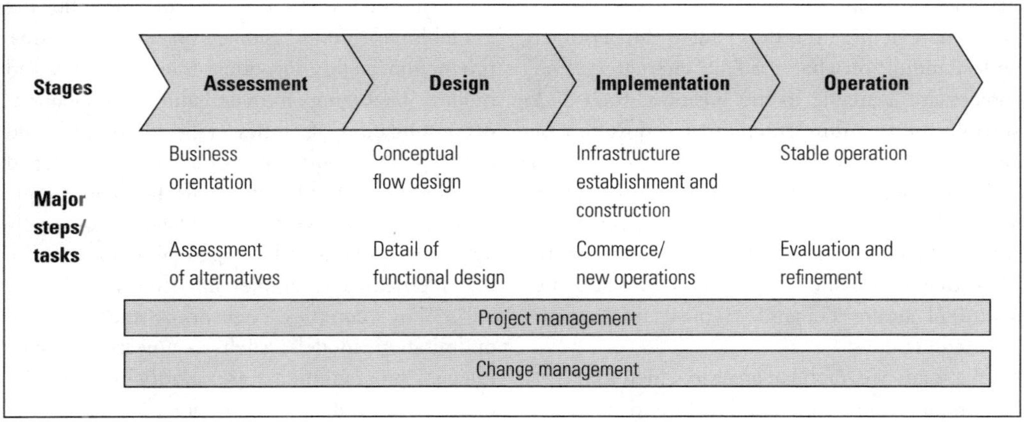

imperatives; products and markets; and elements of the supply chain strategy already drafted.

Senior management expectations of the overall design process are an essential directional input. The availability of resources – funding, people and systems – is a key element to be clarified with the management team at an early stage in the process, as it will have a major impact on the scope and extent of the design work to be tackled. A project steering committee is normally formed with representatives from all key stakeholders (including senior management, functional representation and external alliance partners). Progress feedback, recommendations and ratification of key decisions are normally made by the steering committee.

7.4.1.1 Business orientation

Since supply chain network design forms an integral part of the supply chain strategy, a thorough understanding of the business is essential. The project team will research the business strategy, value-chain structure and alternative business scenarios being considered. The existing supply chain strategies and philosophy need to be viewed and understood in order to be used in context with the production and marketing plans. Matters such as the business ownership, market scenarios, material supply issues, production process, technology considerations and facility location options must be clearly understood since they have such a big influence on the eventual supply chain network structure. For existing businesses that have been operating successfully for a number of years, alternatives might be limited or not available (for example, in the case of an existing production facility). It is thus vital to gain a proper understanding of what strategic alternatives and choices are available to the business, such as a possible joint venture, merger or acquisition or new production facility.

Product and marketing information should be obtained. Product information and characteristics define handling and storage requirements. Marketing information provides insight into the nature of future demand. Typical information required includes:

- the main geographical areas to which the product will be supplied (locally and abroad);
- estimated volumes to these areas;
- parcel sizes;
- frequency of supply;
- parcel formats required for different customers and/or geographical areas; and
- buying and selling terms and conditions.

This marketing data is critical and has a direct influence on the development of a supply chain. Information regarding materials and goods required by the manufacturing facilities must also be obtained. Usually at this stage of a new supply chain network design, marketing information is vague and unstructured. It will change frequently as the marketers gain better understanding of the future target market. Assumptions will have to be made in collaboration with marketing when information is not available. Different products' life cycle stages and the approach to new product development and introduction should also be assessed.

7.4.1.2 Supply chain network alternatives

For the various business scenarios considered, high-level, viable supply chain alternatives are developed and proposed. The primary focus is on possible supply chain networks (inbound and outbound), basic configuration and assessing key supply chain parties that could play a major role in the future. Supply chain network alternatives are primarily determined by the different market scenarios, manufacturing site options and sourcing alternatives.

The supply chain network alternatives are structured from a variety of the following available elements: storage facility locations; production facility locations; transport lanes and modes; packaging formats; and consolidation/deconsolidation facilities (e.g. harbours and transhipments). Alternatives need to be developed to indicate first-order trade-offs between supply chain cost and service levels. Diagrams of supply chain networks are developed to help visualise the alternatives (examples are shown in Figure 7.6). For complex networks, mathematical optimisation models, such as linear or mixed integer programming, are normally used to evaluate alternatives. The major points to clarify

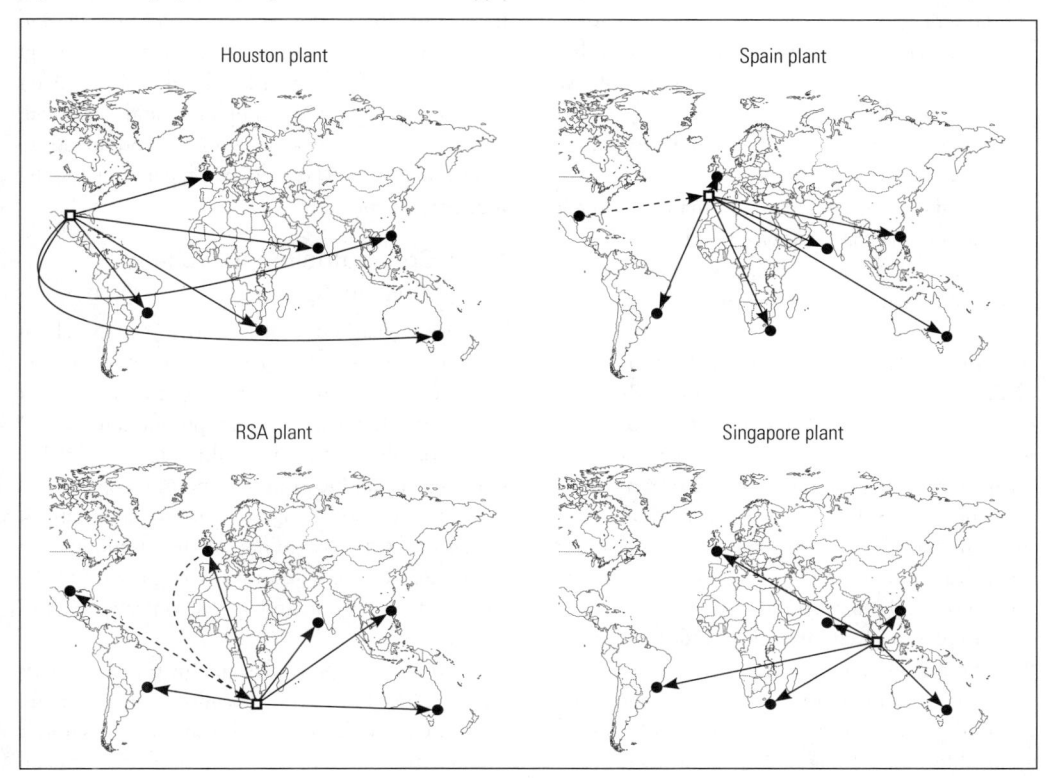

Figure 7.6 Geographical diagrams of alternative supply chains

for decision making are infrastructure availability, overall capacity levels and cost estimates. The design requirements for logistics activities at some facilities might be required before final site selection and need to be included in the development of the supply chain alternatives. Details of such requirements are explained in Section 7.4.2.

Other major issues to take into account and questions to consider at this stage include the following:

- The geographical location of current and potential new markets, production locations and sources.
- What are the associated products (outbound) and materials (inbound) of the business's direct value chain? This relates to raw materials, process materials, intermediate products and final products.
- A clear understanding of the preliminary specifications, characteristics and logistics requirements for products and materials.
- What are the major inbound and outbound supply chain activities required (transportation, storage, packaging, handling and support services)?
- The intended buying and selling terms and conditions – ex works (EXW); free on board (FOB); cost and freight (C&F); delivered duty paid (DDP).
- Are there shared interests that could provide possible structural or commercial supply chain synergies with other business units and which could affect other business units within the organisation?
- Identification of potential supply chain commercial risks (reliability, flexibility and monopoly situations relating to suppliers).
- The corporate governance issues that should be considered.

Based on the supply chain structure alternatives, the expected spend base with external suppliers is

defined and estimated. This includes raw materials; components; sub-assemblies; process materials; and logistics services. It is important to assess as early as possible which key supply chain participants will play a major role as regards:
- inbound (feedstock, process materials, hard goods, spares and services);
- manufacturing (potential toll manufacturers);
- outbound (logistics service providers); and
- internal (receiving, storage, packaging, material handling and dispatch).

A cost estimate is prepared for each of the supply chain network alternatives. The supply chain cost drivers are determined and defined. Costs need to be allocated to all the supply chain activities, normally by using the activity-based costing (ABC) principle. A distinction must be made between internal and external costs (the latter, for example, being services from external logistics service providers). Capital cost and operational cost also need to be separated for each in order to evaluate the different alternatives.

All the information used to develop the supply chain alternatives, the assumptions made and the applicable cost estimates should be documented and presented to the rest of the project team and the steering committee. Recommendations must be made on which supply chain is likely to be the optimal and most viable for the next stage of the process. Carefully selected performance indicators are used to identify the optimal supply chain (e.g. service level, total cost, throughput and working capital). If it is not clear which supply chain is the most viable, more than one alternative can be chosen and used for further development.

The outcomes of this stage are the various supply chain alternatives and their implications. A recommendation is made on the most viable supply chain or chains, indicating the specified evaluation criteria used.

7.4.2 Design stages

After the supply chain network alternatives are narrowed down to the most viable and feasible options, and the stakeholders involved have given their consent to progress to more detailed work, the next process is to design the material and product flow and the required infrastructure. Design follows a two-prompt process. First, a concept proposal is drafted with a first level of detail. After the concept study is completed and accepted, a more detailed design study is conducted to ensure a complete design in preparation for the implementation stage.

7.4.2.1 Conceptual supply chain flow design

The most feasible and effective supply chain alternatives are developed and refined in the form of a conceptual design proposal. The major sources, facility locations (e.g. production facility) and market alternatives will at this stage be restricted to the most suitable for the business. Geographical and product flow diagrams of the alternatives, which indicate the different requirements for each site, provide a sound way of presenting the supply chain's scope and spread (refer to Figures 7.1 and 7.4).

During conceptual design the prime focus is on inventory flow, buffer locations, infrastructure required as well as establishing the first-order functional and operational requirements for each of the elements or activities involved in the supply chain. The supply chain design will later provide the constraints for future supply chain planning and operations decisions. The conceptual configuration (supply chain structure and key role players) and the anticipated costs are evaluated.

Updated sourcing, production and marketing information should be obtained (as gathered and defined in the assessment stage). The potential markets (geographical spread and contracting terms anticipated), production location(s) and feedstock sources (geographical spread) are clarified. This information is used to gain better insight into the characteristics of material supply from sources through production and of product distribution to markets. A thorough understanding of the nature of the material and final product to be handled in the supply chain is essential (e.g. packaged goods vs. bulk), since this will have a major impact on what type of facility, infrastructure and equipment will be required along the supply chain. Transport variability must be clarified with the potential service providers. It will also give a good indication of the flow dynamics to be expected (e.g. volumes to flow intermittently in parcels; variability in supply and demand expected). Screening is done for suitable available transport links and facilities to establish fitness for use.

It is good practice to establish a dynamic simulation model of the supply chain at this stage. The simulation model is used to provide insight into how the supply chain will operate. A number of inputs are needed to make sure that the model is an accurate representation of how the intended supply chain will operate. These inputs typically include:

- a master transport schedule (for inbound and outbound transportation);
- shipping schedules for exported products;
- the amount of available rail and/or road trucks;
- storage sizes considered at the different applicable sites;
- expected production variability;
- required production shutdowns (maintenance);
- demand variability from possible customers; and
- the philosophies that will be applied in the execution and operation of the supply chain.

An optimised and integrated supply chain network aims to balance the capacity across all activities. The design objective is to maximise the throughput potential while using the minimum amount of supply chain resources and adhering to the service requirements. Establishing the necessary buffers (e.g. storage facilities with adequate capacity) at strategic positions along the supply chain is an important throughput enabler. A simulation model aids in testing and evaluating alternatives. It also aids in deciding what the capacity of the different resources should be and how the supply chain should operate to achieve the throughput objective. Such a model also helps with understanding some performance attributes through carefully selected indicators.

Functional logistics requirements must also be established and specified per facility as well as for all the transport links. The requirements are later used in agreements with suppliers and service providers as well as for detailed infrastructure and equipment design. These include the amount of handling equipment; storage space; packaging equipment; the amount of rail and/or road vehicles; construction materials to be used; and special handling and storage requirements (e.g. temperature control). The functional requirements and the services needed at a facility will have a direct influence on the plot size required per site for storage, handling and packaging.

Throughout the design of the supply chain network, supply risks must be identified and mitigated as far as possible. Risk assessment studies might be required, for example environmental impact assessment for facilities and transportation risk assessment on certain routes. Other risks might also relate to infrastructure availability, capacity, reliability, flexibility, variability, material/product hazardousness and so on.

As the supply chain network is designed, the performance indicators to be used are proposed (e.g. inventory turnover, total logistics cost etc.). These indicators and target values must be in line with the strategic objectives for managing the supply chain. The control limits and the logic of operation (i.e. how the supply chain will operate and operational rules) must be well defined and agreed to by all the parties involved. If these measurements and targets are well developed, understood and accepted, some of them can later be used as the basis for a service-level agreement (SLA) with suppliers and service providers.

At this stage the insourcing and outsourcing approach will be clarified and the sourcing strategy refined. This may be individual, cross-functional, cross-regional or global collaboration. The expected spend base is refined with the external suppliers that are being considered in terms of raw materials, process materials, hard goods, services and logistics expenditure. The supplier selection options and criteria are developed. For the supply chain that is being considered, the supplier base for feedstock, process materials, hard goods, spares and services is explored in terms of local and global supplier representation and locality. The supplier base to be approached for future contracts is then refined. The shared interests that could provide possible commercial synergies with other business units, or that could affect other business units are assessed and identified. Discussions can be initiated with potential key suppliers.

The refined estimate for supply chain costs must match competitive requirements. Distinction must again be made between internal and external costs, as well as between capital and operational costs per alternative. At this stage of the design of the supply chain, care should be taken that the capital costs needed for specific functional logistics requirements are included in the capital cost estimate of the project.

All the information used to develop site-specific supply chain alternatives, assumptions made and applicable cost estimates must be presented to the rest of the project team and the business. Recommendations must be made on which supply chain is likely to be the best during detailed supply chain design (see Section 7.4.2.2). The criteria to determine the optimal supply chain can include costs; the availability of site facilities; the availability and capability of the logistics service providers; and the business's preference.

7.4.2.2 Detailed functional design of the supply chain

With the conceptual supply chain flow design complete, the detailed functional, or operations, design is refined and finalised for the supply chain proposed. Interactions with potential key supply chain participants are required to confirm and refine functional design requirements before implementation starts. The supply chain and all activities included must be designed in as much detail as necessary to ensure their feasibility, functionality and interfacing. The functional/ operations design outcomes will be used later as inputs to the establishment of agreements and contracts with selected logistics service providers.

The focus is on finalising the supply chain configuration through interaction with potential external suppliers, customers and internal departments. The interactions with all key supply chain participants are important to ensure a viable supply chain design and to refine the operational- and capital-cost estimates.

The final requirements of each individual supply chain activity are determined. The infrastructure required and layout of activities for the facilities are also established. The integration of critical logistics activities for the various applicable sites are finalised (e.g. receiving, dispatch, warehousing, packaging, containerisation and terminal areas). Transport modes, vehicle and vessel types, routing, shipment frequency and load configuration are key matters to be addressed at this point.

The operating philosophy of the supply chain has to be determined based on the way in which the business will operate. The final supply chain design and operational philosophy should be tested for operability with a dynamic simulation model which addresses how the design will operate in the real world with all its variability. Assumptions are reviewed and defined to ensure the most accurate display and testing of the supply chain as it would function in real day-to-day operations. Reliability, flexibility and other related performance indicators are used for evaluation. As decisions are made and more detail is available to define the supply chain, the latest applicable information should be documented, such as detailed information about customers, logistics activities, manufacturing and suppliers. The implications of scheduling heuristics of orders, manufacturing batches and campaigns, and the impact of pre-marketing or ramp-up requirements on feedstock, process material, spares and logistical requirements must be taken into account. The inventory strategy, management policy and deployment plan are also finalised, including anticipated inventory replenishment and stock-control methods.

The sourcing strategy needs to be finalised at this stage in terms of materials, goods and services to be procured for the business. The scope for commercial and operational arrangements with suppliers is drafted and refined. A shortlist of suppliers is compiled from the available supplier base. These suppliers are contacted, interactions initiated and relationship building starts. The feasibility of design and functional requirements and assumptions can be verified with these suppliers. Where possible, identified commercial synergies are leveraged (e.g. using similar standardised spares and suppliers across various businesses in an organisation). With potential strategic relationships defined, the sourcing and negotiation processes start. These involve draft agreements, proposals, quotations and clarity on provisional terms and conditions.

The identified operational risks of the supply chain are addressed and strategies refined to reduce their impact. These strategies will address infrastructure availability, capacity, reliability, flexibility etc. The same is done for the identified commercial risks, such as supplier reliability, flexibility, monopoly and economies of scale.

A total cost evaluation of the final supply chain configuration is done, including capital and operational cost estimates. The anticipated supply chain costs are finalised.

This supply chain with all the applicable information used and assumptions made needs to be presented to the rest of the project team and steering committee. A detail report should be compiled to ensure that the environment in which the supply chain is developed and will operate in is clearly defined. All the philosophies that have been used to develop the supply chain, must be understood and agreed upon by the different role players.

7.4.3 Implementation stage

During this stage the approved supply chain design is implemented. The various supply chain activities are brought into operation in a sequenced fashion to enable the coordinated flow of materials and products.

7.4.3.1 Infrastructure establishment and construction

The implementation stage puts into operation the detailed supply chain functional design. The focus of this stage is on detail, and encompasses equipment design and manufacturing; equipment selection; infrastructure/facility construction; modification and establishing operating procedures. Functional, operational and equipment design should incorporate the country's legislative requirements regarding logistics.

The inbound and outbound logistics channels are now prepared for commencing operations. The inbound operations will deal with the required upstream supply activities – transportation, storage, handling and packaging – needed for the availability of feedstock, process chemicals, hard goods, spares and maintenance equipment for the manufacturing and maintenance functions. Outbound operations will deal with the required downstream supply activities – transportation, storage, handling and packaging – of intermediate and final products for customers.

Communication plays a vital role during the implementation stage. It is crucial to have alignment amongst all participants regarding the new supply chain's operating philosophy. Any infrastructure changes at this stage will be costly and hamper implementation timelines. Logistics, production, marketing and sales personnel should visit key customers; this helps establish relationships. The same applies to maintenance and production personnel, who should visit key suppliers. Establishing regular contact with selected logistics service providers also helps build relationships. Clarifying the roles and responsibilities of each participant in the supply chain prepares the path for smooth operations.

All marketing and sales plans are finalised and supply agreements established with major customers. This includes projected demand during product launch and market ramp-up requirements. An integral part of this stage is to finalise the specifications for feedstock, production and marketing materials. Any unnecessary changes in these specifications may entail expensive, time-consuming alterations to some of the supply chain activities and should be avoided at all costs.

All inbound and outbound activities must be operational in time for start-up so that product can be shipped on time. It should also be ensured that facilities are ready in time to handle reverse logistics (return and waste streams). Feedstock and start-up spares must be available in time before operations commence – production and maintenance departments are the key stakeholders.

A number of operating procedures must be established. Actions in this regard include the following:
- Ensuring that each entity in the outbound supply chain has developed the required operating procedures to aid in control.
- Establishing reverse logistics procedures.

- Developing and agreeing on quality and quantity assurance and control procedures.
- Translating operating procedures into work instructions.
- Operating procedures should be incorporated in operational agreements with outbound supply chain contracting parties.
- Dispatch, proof of delivery (POD) and stock control procedures should be in place.
- Customs and excise documentation should be in order.

Potential deviation analyses are conducted for all inbound and outbound logistics activities with all stakeholders present to establish contingency plans for foreseen eventualities. These analyses could include transport risk assessment (TRA) and preventative and contingency measures before the business operation commences.

Commercial, operations and service-level agreements are drafted and expectations clarified amongst all contracting parties. During all negotiations with external parties integration, cooperation and strategic fit requirements must be ensured. A number of agreements are normally required for:
- external feedstock or components;
- process materials;
- third-party utilities (water, power etc.);
- spares and maintenance equipment (mission-critical);
- office goods (non-critical);
- maintenance and operations support services;
- handling of waste and recovery streams;
- emission permits; and
- inbound and outbound logistics services (facilities, transport, support services).

The total supply chain operational cost estimates are concluded. The cost structures and currency split must be understood by all involved. All the applicable information that relates to the operational procedures that have been created during the implementation stage (including supply chain configuration) needs to be documented.

7.4.3.2 Commence new operation

At this stage the entire supply chain (inbound and outbound) must be fully functional and ready for operations. This milestone will normally be in sync with the timeline of the new or revised business launch. The focus is on ensuring operational readiness and commencement of the related activities along the supply chain (inbound and outbound). Synchronising the readiness and start-up of these activities helps the business reach its product-launch objectives.

All contracts with feedstock suppliers, logistics service providers and customers should be in place. These contracts will typically include commercial agreements, operational agreements and SLAs.

During the commencement of a new operation, the sales and operations planning process (S&OP) fulfils a key role in integrating and balancing supply and demand across the supply chain network. Operations might initially be quite variable and proper inventory planning and buffering will be required to ensure that customer service expectations are met. Production ramp-ups, initial shutdown requirements and customer take-off agreements need to be taken into account.

A sound communication plan ensures that all stakeholders are fully apprised of progress and start-up dates. A good practice is to conduct a roadshow (both internally and externally) to inform and educate all interested and affected parties on the supply chain activities. Where hazardous goods are involved, the required emergency response information is provided to the appropriate local municipality and fire stations.

All the necessary logistics procedures and documents are finalised. These procedures relate to inbound and outbound logistics; on-site logistics; reverse logistics; waste strategies; surveying and testing; intermediate processes; and international logistics. From a quality management and control perspective, the documents will assist in creating a unified approach in the general storage and handling of new products.

A useful tool during start-up is a pre-operation audit. This should be set up in such a fashion that all elements concerning the supply chain are covered. The pre-operation audit will run parallel to all other activities during the implementation stage. It can be used as a checklist to ensure that all the necessary elements of the supply chain activities have been dealt with, to specify the people

responsible for each activity and to monitor the progress made until completion. The pre-operation audit is a screening procedure to ensure that:
- all inbound and outbound logistics activities are in place and ready for operation;
- all relevant processes and procedures are in place;
- transport companies start scheduling the provision of required transport capacity to meet anticipated product schedules;
- safety and emergency response measures required along the routes are arranged and implemented; and
- equipment interfacing and compatibility tests are performed in order to ensure compatible linking operations (e.g. offloading and loading equipment etc.).

The physical inspections activities during the start-up stage are carried out on all the newly developed infrastructure. These activities will ensure that the infrastructure is capable of handling the new product and that the supply chain operations will run smoothly after the final start-up.

With all the infrastructure, facilities and equipment ready and in place across the supply chain, the focal business starts receiving materials, goods and spare parts. Inventory becomes available from manufacturing ready for customer orders. The intended inventory policy and replenishment controls for inbound material and outbound product are initiated. The required operational performance measurements are initiated and compared with the agreements that are in place.

7.4.4 Operation stage

As soon as stable operations have been achieved, a post-implementation evaluation of the supply chain is made to compare the actual configuration and performance with what was originally intended. The focus is on assessing how close the actual supply chain configuration is to the design intent. An operations assessment and benchmarking can be utilised for the evaluation.

The assessment should investigate all aspects of the supply chain and compare it to the original supply chain design. Any major deviations should be noted and documented. The reasons for a deviation from the original design could either indicate a sound justification for the course of action and highlight potential problems or it could indicate a move away from the original supply chain design and require serious management intervention to rectify.

Benchmarking with carefully selected performance indicators, such as service and cost, and best practices can highlight areas in the supply chain that are meeting or exceeding expectations, or where attention is needed.

A customer-satisfaction survey can indicate how well the supply chain is serving customers' needs. An organisation's external and internal customers (e.g. production and maintenance) should be covered in these surveys. Any shortcomings should be highlighted and addressed as soon as possible.

A supplier evaluation related to industry structure, conduct and performance might also be required. This can provide an indication of how well inbound and outbound participants are fulfilling their roles and whether they are aligned with the supply chain's objectives.

Once the post-implementation evaluation has been completed, all major problems and improvement areas should be addressed. A philosophy of continuous improvement in supply chain configuration and network integration should be adopted to sustain the business's competitive requirements.

7.5 Factors to take into account in supply chain design

Several factors should be taken into account during the process of designing a supply chain network. Ignoring these could lead to missed opportunities, a suboptimal design or placing the supply chain at risk. The following are some of these major factors applicable to large-scale organisations; they are described in more detail in the sections that follow:[8]
- Understanding a specific business's context
- Interdependencies with other related supply chains
- Master agreements within an organisation

- Country-specific logistics infrastructure
- Factors that affect location decisions

7.5.1 Understanding the business context

The primary activities of a business provide the context for the supply chain network design. The market demand, sales history, material and product information, production facilities used and sources of supply normally indicate the scope of a business's activity. In addition to this information, the current supply chain(s) may have a significant influence on alternatives. The current supply chain philosophy and preferences may, for instance, already promote outsourcing. The same applies to the existing supply chain configuration, coverage and agreements in place.

7.5.2 Interdependencies with other related supply chains

Within larger organisations numerous supply chains exist to supply product to specific market segments. Portions of these supply chains will most probably overlap in some facilities or movement-related activities, such as a distribution centre. While designing a new supply chain network, cognisance should be taken of where potential overlaps may occur. These overlaps could either provide an opportunity to leverage synergies or create potential risks, one such being capacity constraint.

By scanning geographical and process flow diagrams, common elements can become apparent. The following are physical characteristics in supply chains that can help identify common elements:
- Compatible products
- Similar packaging
- Same geographical areas (including origins, intermediate storage and destinations)
- Similar delivery routes and standards
- Similar storage and handling methods/conditions

Interdependencies also exist between supply chains that require tight integration. The dependence on upstream supply and risk/difficulty of transportation – an example is the supply of large volumes of propylene gas – may limit a number of facility location or logistics network options. Due to infrastructure capacity limitations, the addition of a supply chain to an existing logistics network might require additional capital investment to create the required capacity (e.g. rail infrastructure and shunting capacity at a specific facility). The investment decision cannot be taken in isolation and needs cooperation between all parties involved. Economies of scale can also be leveraged if the movement of compatible products are consolidated along applicable corridors of movement (e.g. overland and sea transport).

7.5.3 Master agreements within an organisation

In large-scale organisations, supplier management is a key enabler to ensure that external spend is optimised. The total cost of ownership related to the procurement of raw materials, goods and services is proactively managed. Consolidated/master agreements are established with the purpose of leveraging economies of scale and creating strategic alliances with key suppliers.

During supply chain network design it is important to take into account these master agreements for certain raw materials, spares, goods and services. When evaluating potential outsourcing parties to participate in a supply chain, the current available master list of all approved vendors should first be consulted and subsequently utilised. Should no current agreement exist for specific materials or services, a supplier selection process is initiated to follow strategic sourcing practices. Establishing agreements without taking into consideration the organisation's approach to supplier management could put a business at risk and reduce its ability to manage its spend base proactively.

7.5.4 Country-specific logistics infrastructure

Multinational and global businesses utilise supply chains that reach across the globe. These businesses normally make use of applicable trade lanes, or corridors, that can provide business benefit in the face of demand and supply imbalances.

A country's logistics infrastructure is what is available for the movement of materials and products (roads, railways and waterways) as well as key facilities for storing, handling and flow-through (e.g. terminals and trade zones). Certain countries have a well-developed logistics infrastructure with adequate capacity, while others may struggle to sustain and grow their infrastructure availability and capacity. A country's macroeconomics and political dispensations may have a big influence on its approach to sustaining and growing its logistics infrastructure. National legislation may also be applicable in some countries, which could inhibit logistics activities or require very specific practices. A country's specific logistics infrastructure, trends, planned interventions and legislation, therefore, need proper consideration if one is to avoid making the wrong decisions about the supply chain network.

7.5.5 Factors that affect location decisions

Once a company commits to a location, many costs are fixed and become difficult to change. Up to 25 per cent of a product's cost is influenced by the location of the manufacturing facility.[9] The factors that affect location decisions are not the same for countries, regions, communities and sites – within these zones different factors come into play. Table 7.1 indicates the applicability of some location factors. The proximity to markets, suppliers or competitors are location factors that can differ significantly between industries or the position within the value chain. For example, heavy manufacturing facilities prefer proximity to raw materials, while retail facilities require proximity to their customers.

7.6 Modelling approaches

Modelling is the process of creating a representation of the real world by using statistical and/or mathematical techniques for the purpose of analysis and experimentation. A number of modelling applications and techniques can be used to support supply chain network design decisions. These applications can model, optimise and simulate the trade-offs in manufacturing, inventory, logistics, and buyer-seller relationships during supply chain design. With supply chain network design the goal

Table 7.1 Important factors that influence location decisions

Location factor	Country	Region	Site
Regional trade agreements	X		
Competitiveness of nation	X		
Federal taxes and incentives	X		
Currency stability	X		
Environmental issues	X	X	X
Access and proximity to market	X	X	X
Labour issues	X	X	X
Proximity to supplies	X	X	X
Transportation issues	X	X	X
Utility availability and cost	X	X	X
State taxes and incentives		X	X
Local taxes and incentives			X
Land availability and cost			X

is to determine the optimal number and location of manufacturing facilities, distribution operations and sourcing relationships while finalising transportation modes and inventory strategies (under the condition that all customer demand requirements are met). These applications are typically used on a quarterly, biannual or annual basis to evaluate the overall structure of the supply network.[10]

Some of the modelling techniques frequently used for support in logistics and supply chain network design and location planning are:[11]
- approximate methods;
- mathematical optimisation;
- simulation; and
- heuristics.

7.6.1 Approximate methods

The weighted-factor rating method is a popular approximate method employed to compare the attractiveness of several alternatives against a number of quantitative and qualitative dimensions. This method can be used for comparing the attractiveness of alternative facility sites or alternative supply chains.[12] The main steps to follow include:
- identifying the factors;
- assigning weights to each factor (0,00–1,00; all weights add up to 1);
- subjectively rating each alternative against each factor (0–100, 100 being the best);
- multiplying the factor rating by the weight, then adding the weighted scores; and
- selecting the alternative with the highest total weighted score.

Table 7.2 is an example of a weighted-factor rating model applied to a facility location problem. In this example, three alternative sites are available. The factors serve as the criteria used for evaluation. The importance of each factor is reflected in the weights (0 = no importance; 1 = highest importance). The rating of the sites relates to their favourability in relation to the criteria (0 = worst rating; 100 = best rating). In this example, Site 2 has the highest score and therefore should be considered.

7.6.2 Mathematical optimisation models

Optimisation models for complex strategic logistics planning centre around logistics network models.[13] Facilities, transportation and inventory are the core focus for logistics network models. This section expands on the key issues that can be resolved with the aid of optimisation models:
- Facilities and their functional operations
  - Which existing facilities should be left open or expanded?
  - Which existing facilities should be shut down?
  - Which new facilities should be opened with how much throughput capacity?
  - Which facility or facilities will serve each customer or market?
  - Which suppliers will replenish each facility?

Table 7.2 Weighted-factor rating model – site selection

Factors (or criteria)	Weight	Rating of alternatives					
		Site 1		Site 2		Site 3	
		Rating	Score	Rating	Score	Rating	Score
Labour pool and climate	0,25	80	20,00	65	16,25	90	22,50
Proximity to suppliers	0,15	100	15,00	91	13,65	75	11,25
Wage rates	0,10	60	6,00	95	9,50	72	7,20
Community environment	0,15	75	11,25	80	12,00	80	12,00
Proximity to customers	0,10	65	6,50	90	9,00	95	9,50
Distribution cost	0,20	85	17,00	92	18,40	65	13,00
Air service	0,05	50	2,50	65	3,25	90	4,50
Total			78,25		82,05		79,95

- Transportation alternatives (mode, routing, cost)
  - Inbound transportation
  - Inter-facility transportation
  - Outbound transportation
- Materials/inventory management
  - Relates to activities that cut across the entire supply chain

Linear programming (LP) models and methods for optimising them play a central role in all types of supply chain applications. The models and methods were originally devised to optimise the allocation of scarce resources to economic activities in a complex system. Logistics network models (including transportation models) are also well suited for the application of linear programming.[14]

Mixed integer programming (MIP) models are generalisations of LP models, in which some variables, called integer variables, are often strained to take on only non-negative integer values. MIP is used to model a variety of strategic supply chain options. These include fixed costs, economies of scale and production changeovers. It also provides for multiple-choice and other non-numeric constraints. A typical application of MIP is for multiple distribution centre location models and supply chain network optimisation models.[15]

Most of the logistics network models are structured around an objective function, constraints and variables.[16] The following is an example of how to determine the optimal customer service policy given the objective of minimising the total logistics costs (TLC). The TLC includes inventory-carrying costs, response time costs (warehousing and transportation) and lost sales costs.[17] The constraints are the availability of inventory and the response time requirements that make up the core of the customer service policy. Mathematically, it is expressed as follows:

Minimise:
Total logistics costs = inventory-carrying costs
  + response time costs
  + lost sales cost

Constraints:
1. Inventory availability > customer-service inventory target
2. Response time < customer-service response time target

7.6.3 Simulation models

Simulation models have been applied to supply chain problems for a long time. They are intuitive and easy to understand (compared with optimisation models). Simulation models, which are defined as descriptive models, permit managers or analysts to study the dynamic behaviour of supply chain systems.[18] There are two broad categories of simulation models:
- Deterministic simulation (describes system behaviour with no random effects)
- Stochastic simulation (describes system behaviour with random effects)

The basic concept of simulation constitutes the abstraction of a complex system in preferably a computerised model and the use of the model to evaluate various alternatives.[19] Since simulation modelling is time-consuming and costly, the most important factors that justify their use are complex interactions between system components, the variability of such components and the variability in certain parameters over time. Simulation is ideally suited to analysing systems with multiple sources of variation and interdependencies and balancing resource capacity in the supply chain.[20] Simulation tools normally provide animation capabilities that allow the process designer to see how customers and/or work objects flow through the system.

7.6.4 Heuristics

Heuristic methods are narrow search methods that attempt to find a good solution to problems quickly.[21] Heuristics can use rules of thumb about a given decision problem in an attempt to determine a feasible solution. However, they are not guaranteed to find an optimal solution or even a feasible solution to the problem. Heuristics are ad hoc search methods customised to a specific problem based on rules established by humans about the problem.

A simple, well-known heuristic method used in facility location problems is known as the centre of gravity method.[22] This technique involves mapping a number of locations on an x-, y-coordinate grid and then finding a central location closest to all. These could, for example, be the locations of suppliers or customers. The volume supplied or demanded per location (weight) pulls the centre of gravity location in the direction of the higher concentration of volume. To calculate the coordinates of the centre of gravity, the following is used:

x-coordinate =
$$\frac{\text{sum of (each location's x-coordinate} \times \text{weight)}}{\text{total weight}}$$

y-coordinate =
$$\frac{\text{sum of (each location's y-coordinate} \times \text{weight)}}{\text{total weight}}$$

As an example, a single distribution centre must be located to serve several store locations in a geographical region. Table 7.3 indicates the coordinates and demand of the various stores.

To calculate the x- and y-coordinates of the centre of gravity:

x-coordinate of the centre of gravity:
$$= \frac{(30)(2\,000) + (90)(1\,000) + (130)(1\,000) + (60)(4\,000)}{2\,000 + 1\,000 + 1\,000 + 4\,000}$$
$$= 520\,000/8\,000$$
$$= 65$$

y-coordinate of the centre of gravity:
$$= \frac{(120)(2\,000) + (110)(1\,000) + (130)(1\,000) + (40)(4\,000)}{2\,000 + 1\,000 + 1\,000 + 4\,000}$$
$$= 640\,000/8\,000$$
$$= 80$$

For this example, a distribution centre must be located as close as possible to the x-, y-coordinates (65, 80), as indicated in Figure 7.7.

Table 7.3 Coordinates and demand of stores for location example

Store location	x-coordinate	y-coordinate	Demand
A	30	120	2 000
B	90	110	1 000
C	130	130	1 000
D	60	40	4 000

Figure 7.7 Centre of gravity – example for locating a single distribution centre

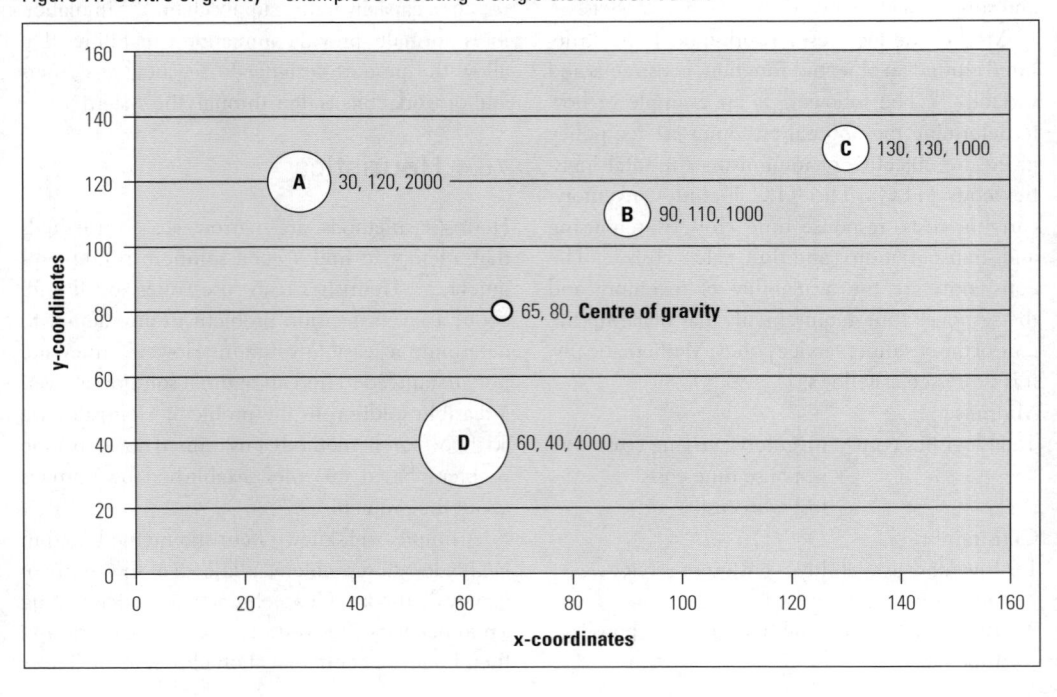

7.7 Conclusion

Supply chains provide the structure and physical capability for manufacturing businesses to supply raw materials and goods to their operations and finished products to their markets. Designing an optimal supply chain network is one of the cornerstones of competitive, world-class organisations. Together with the right physical network, strategically selected suppliers form a network of organisations that represent the supply chain configuration. Network integration focuses on the physical structure and arrangement of supply chain activities, as well as the right interfacing and balancing of capacity amongst all participants involved.

Many supply chains networks are not intentionally designed, optimised or aligned with the business strategy. They have purely evolved over time, making them less efficient and effective than they could be. Most efforts to improve supply chain efficiency fall short because they do not challenge the fundamental structure of the supply chain, but instead attempt to improve performance within existing limitations. Proper network design aims to address these management oversights and can help businesses to have integrated supply chain networks that enhance their competitiveness.

Supply chain network design and implementation typically goes through a number of stages to ensure sound decision making. These stages are assessment, design, implementation and operation. Supply chain network decisions are made infrequently and have a significant effect on the organisation for a relatively long period of time – decisions that are not easily changed once implemented. The operational costs of logistics (ranging from 8 to 30 per cent of sales) are significantly affected by locational decisions. Optimising the location of facilities within a supply chain network can save between 5 and 15 per cent of logistics costs.

In the process of designing a supply chain network, many factors should be taken into account. Ignoring these can lead to missed opportunities, a sub-optimal design or putting the supply chain at risk. These factors normally relate to the business's context; interdependencies with other related supply chains; the logistics infrastructure and legislation specific to particular countries; master agreements within an organisation; and facility location criteria.

Various types of modelling can play a major support role during supply chain network design to help in decision making.

Key terms

Assessment	Integration
Audit	Location
Capacity	Market
Complexity	Modelling
Conceptual design proposal	Network
	Network design
Configuration	Redesign
Constraint	Risk
Contingency planning	Robustness
Criteria	Source
Design	Structure
Facility	Survey
Implementation	Throughput
Infrastructure	

Case study

Pretoria Portland Cement (PPC) has been in operation since 1892 and is one of the largest manufacturers of cement in South Africa, with a market share of around 40 per cent. PPC is the leading supplier of cement in southern Africa, with manufacturing facilities and depots in South Africa, Botswana and Zimbabwe. Together, these facilities are capable of producing more than 6 million tons of cementious products each year.

PPC has a fairly complex supply chain network. In 2003, the supply of raw materials to six factories came from nine separate quarries. Inbound raw materials, components and sub-assemblies to the factories were provided by 35 separate suppliers. Customer and packaging requirements comprise 48 product packaging combinations for the three mainstream cement products. Eight depots and warehouses were utilised to provide 1 415 sales nodes with product and were increasing annually. The transportation modes used were road, rail and conveyors. The supply network consisted of 150 inter-facility links and 12 800 customer links.

PPC's geographically dispersed customer base contributes to relatively high outbound logistics costs.

Approximately 500 deliveries were made to customers each day within South Africa and across the border in Zimbabwe, Botswana, Namibia, Mozambique and Swaziland.

In 2003, PPC started to experience a huge growth in demand for cement of more than 13 per cent per annum (with demand rapidly rising every month). The six factories responsible for the production of cement were starting to reach their economically viable lifespan. In addition to this, some equipment needed replacing and the quarries were running out of capacity.

Economic growth in South Africa, with additional implications on cement demand from projects such as Coega, Gautrain and the 2010 FIFA World Cup forced PPC to reconsider its future capacity-expansion programme.

PPC needed to consider some key strategic decisions. Should they establish new manufacturing facilities to expand their existing capacity? Can they economically refurbish and expand their existing manufacturing facilities? Should they consider reopening some of their previous mothballed facilities? What other supply options are available?

Other questions facing PPC that also needed answers include:

- What product quantities (by facility and by process) should be produced and stored in each period to support customer demands at minimum supply chain cost?
- From where should raw materials, components and sub-assemblies be sourced?
- What products should be produced in each manufacturing location?
- What is the cost versus service trade-off of alternative distribution strategies?

Barloworld Logistics was appointed as the consultant to advise the business on the course of action to be taken.

1. What process would you suggest Barloworld Logistics should follow to redesign the PPC supply network?
2. How would the various strategic decisions regarding the manufacturing expansion be incorporated into this redesign process?
3. Propose and briefly explain what modelling technique(s) you suggest Barloworld Logistics should use to help answer the questions and decisions faced by PPC.

Case study

Rising from a humble start, Inamed has established itself as a progressive manufacturer and supplier of medical devices internationally. The company is credited with a clear business strategy of growth through acquisition and new product innovations. These acquisitions have contributed to making Inamed's supply chain networks extensive and complex, with additional sources of supply, many added manufacturing facilities and a spread of global markets served.

Anticipating its continued growth and business success, Inamed needs to ensure that its supply chain networks provide the capability for the expanding organisation. Inamed faces several challenging supply chain questions:

- What is their optimal distribution network?
- Are there potential network synergies between the different supply chains to be leveraged?
- Where are the potential supply chain risks that could have adverse effects on the business?
- Should they outsource some supply chain activities?
- How would they go about identifying the requirements for selecting outsourced parties?
- What are the correct network modelling techniques that could be used for decision support in network optimisation?

As a result of these questions, Inamed initiated a global supply chain opportunity assessment to identify potential network enhancements in terms of service, cost and competitiveness.

As well as identifying the current supply chain network improvement opportunities, Inamed is also looking for a methodology and practical tools to evaluate future acquisitions for its supply chain and the impact they will have on the supply chain.

1. What approach and process would you propose that Inamed should follow for the supply chain network opportunity assessment?
2. What obvious factors should the study take into account and use as criteria for evaluating alternative improvement proposals?
3. Make a proposal for the major components of a guideline/methodology to evaluate the supply chain impact of future acquisitions by Inamed.

Questions

1. What are typical supply chain network decisions and why do they have a significant effect on the organisation for a relatively long period of time?
2. Describe the supply chain design and implementation stages and the associated major steps.
3. Why is it important to establish a project or task team to conduct a supply chain design or redesign study?
4. What are the major factors that should be taken into account in the process of designing a supply chain network?
5. List and explain a number of typical reasons why a supply chain redesign is required and when it should be done.
6. What are the supply chain attributes that ultimately determine the supply chain's complexity?
7. What are the major supply chain design decision areas and how do they assist in clarifying configuration, intended operation and functional requirements?
8. What are the key determinants of a supply chain network structure?
9. During the process of designing a supply chain network, several factors should be taken into account. What are these factors and why are they important?
10. Describe the factors that affect location decisions and how they differ in terms of country, region/community and site-specific considerations.
11. What are some of the more frequently used modelling techniques that are suited for decision support in logistics and supply chain network design and location planning problems?

Consult the web

AMR Research: www.amrresearch.com
Barloworld Optimus Supply Chain Specialists: www.barloworldoptimus.com
i2 Technologies: www.i2.com
LogicTools – ILOG: www.logic-tools.com
SAP Supply Chain Management (SAP SCM) application: www.sap.com/solutions/business-suite/scm/
Supply Chain Brain: www.supplychainbrain.com
Supply Chain Digest: www.scdigest.com
Supply Chain Management Review: www.scmr.com

Consult the books

Ballou, R. H. 1995. 'Logistics network design: Modeling and information considerations'. *International Journal of Logistics Management*, 2(6).

Bowersox, D. J., Closs, D. J. and Cooper, M. B. 2007. *Supply Chain Logistics Management*. 2nd edition. Boston: McGraw-Hill.

Chizzo, S. A. 2005. 'Supply chain strategies for a commercial launch'. *The Journal of New England Technology*. Available from: www.masshightech.com (accessed 22 September 2005).

Christopher, M. and Towill, D. 2001. 'An integrated model for the design of agile supply chains'. *International Journal of Physical Distribution and Logistics*, 31(4).

De Villiers, G. 2004. 'Logistics channel strategy and network design'. 2004 Supply Chain Business Forum. Hosted by Logistics News. Johannesburg Sandton Convention Centre. 13–14 September.

Frazelle, E. H. 2002. *Supply Chain Strategy: The Logistics of Supply Chain Management*. New York: McGraw-Hill.

Hicks, D. A. 1999. 'Introduction to SC operational strategy'. *IIE Solutions*. Available from: http://solutions.iienet.org/ (accessed 15 March 2002).

Kasilingam, R. G. 1998. *Logistics and Transportation: Design and Planning*. Dordrecht: Kluwer Academic Publishers.

Langley, C. J. (Jr.), Coyle, J. J., Gibson, B. J., Novack R. A. and Bardi E. J. 2009. *The Management of Business Logistics: A Supply Chain Perspective*, 9th edition. Mason: South-Western/Thomson Learning.

Lapide, L. 1998. *Supply Chain Planning Optimization: Just the Facts*. Boston: AMR Research. The Report on Supply Chain Management, May 1998.

Louw, J. J. 2002. 'Practical supply chain design and optimisation methodologies'. In *Logistics Workshop*. Hosted by CSIR & Georgia Tech. Pretoria: CSIR. 5–7 August.

Meyer, I. A. 1995. 'Simulation applications in logistics'. SAPICS '95, 17th International Conference. Port Elizabeth: Feather Market Centre.

Naim, M. M. & Potter, A. T. 2008. 'The five principles of integrated tailored logistics'. SAPICS '08, 30th International Conference and Exhibition. Sun City 29 June–2 July.

Quinn, F. J. 2000. 'The master of design: An interview with David Simchi-Levi'. *Supply Chain Management Review*, 4(5).

Rogers, D .S. 1997. 'Simulation takes pain out of trial and error'. *Transportation and Distribution*, 38(4).

Russell, R. S. and Taylor, B. W. 2006. *Operations Management*, 5th edition. New Jersey: Wiley & Sons.

Shapiro, J. F. 2001. *Modeling the Supply Chain*. Duxbury.

Simchi-Levi, D., Kaminsky, P. and Simchi-Levi, E. 2008. *Designing and Managing the Supply Chain: Concepts, Strategies, and Case Studies*. 3rd edition. New York: McGraw-Hill.

Suleski, J., Cecere, L. and Souza, J. 2005. *Optimizing Inventories: A Network Design, Inventory Configuration, and Inventory Policy Vendor Landscape*. Boston: AMR Research. The Report on Supply Chain Management, January 2005.

Tompkins, J. A., White, J. A., Bozer, Y. A. and Tanchoco, J. M. A. 1996. *Facilities Planning*. New York: Wiley.

Wisner, J. D., Leong, G. K. and Tan, K. 2005. *Principles of Supply Chain Management: A Balanced Approach*. Mason: Thomson Business and Professional Publishing.

Notes

1. Christopher, M. and Towill, D. 2001.
2. Ballou, R. H. 1995.
3. Ibid.
4. Kasilingam, R. G. 1998.
5. Naim, M. M. and Potter, A. T. 2008.
6. Hicks, D. A. 1999.
7. Bowersox et al. 2002.
8. Louw, J. J. 2002.
9. Tompkins et al. 1996.
10. Suleski et al. 2005.
11. Ballou et al. 2000.
12. Tompkins et al. 1996; Russell, R. S. and Taylor, B. W. 2006.
13. Shapiro, J. F. 2001.
14. Ibid.
15. Ibid.
16. Kasilingam, R. G. 1998.
17. Frazelle, E. H. 2002.
18. Shapiro, J. F. 2001.
19. Meyer, I. A. 1995.
20. Rogers, D. S. 1997.
21. Shapiro, J. F. 2001.
22. Langley et al. 2009.

8 Production and operations management

J. van Eeden

Learning outcomes

After you have studied this chapter, you should be able to:
- explain what is meant by the term operations management;
- understand some of the basic concepts of operations management;
- understand the relationship between operations and strategy;
- explain the roles of operations within strategy;
- understand the concept of planning operations capacity;
- understand the importance of product design and transformation process design;
- understand the concept of quality management;
- explain the cost-of-quality concept;
- understand the importance of inventory management within operations management;
- understand the most recent operations management approaches and philosophies; and
- understand the importance of operations management in the services environment.

8.1 Introduction

8.1.1 Definition of operations management

All organisations must produce value for their customers. Value can be described by the price customers are willing to pay for the benefits they perceive a product holds. The difference between the price a customer is willing to pay for a product and the cost to produce it is the profit, and for a company to make a profit, the product cost needs to be as low as possible and the perceived product value as high as possible.

> Operations management is the decisions made about the operations function and the management of the transformation process to ensure that value is provided to the customer at a cost that will ensure a profit to the company's shareholders.[1]

Three keywords emerge from this definition: decision, function and process.

- Decision: All managers make decisions, but decision making in operations management puts emphasis on the areas of process, quality, capacity and inventory. The rest of this chapter expands in more detail on each of these decision areas.
- Function: Operations is a key function in any company and is responsible for creating the product or service that the company sells to its customers.
- Process: Operations managers plan and control the operations function, which is in essence the transformation process and all its interfaces to internal and external role players.

Schroeder[2] explains the decision-making activity in operations as consisting of a framework with four responsibility areas. These four areas are groupings of decisions of a similar nature or consequence and can be described as follows:
- Process: Decisions in this area are concerned with the process by which and the facility through which the product is produced and the workforce policies that are associated with

the process. It includes decisions about the equipment and technology employed, the facility's physical design and layout, process design, individual job design and workforce policy and structuring. These decisions are long term and not easily altered overnight. Many other functions, like finance and human resources, are involved in these decisions to ensure that the strategic planning of the organisation as a whole is incorporated into the operational decisions. Large infrastructural decisions regarding assets and human capital are made about the process that will be utilised, therefore an integrative approach is essential.
- Quality: Operations are responsible for the quality of products and services. Quality decisions are aimed at designing the quality into the products and manufacturing processes. Operations management also has to ensure that an acceptable level of quality is determined, standards set, employees trained to comply and quality monitored throughout the process to ensure quality products to the customer. Although operations management fulfils the key role in quality decisions, other functions have to collaborate to ensure that the desired quality is defined and met. For example, marketing should determine the expectations of the customer and obtain feedback on the achieved service level.
- Capacity decisions relate to determining the correct amount of facilities and people to ensure that enough products can be produced and delivered at the right time and place.

Capacity decisions have short-, medium- and long-term consequences, as facility decisions are primarily long term, whereas day-to-day production scheduling and work shift planning are short-term capacity decisions. In the short term, capacity can be supplemented by subcontracting, extra shifts or hiring extra equipment.
- Inventory decisions relate to the flow of raw materials and finished goods within the organisation and the total supply chain. They concern the volume, position and timing of inventory ordered from suppliers and manufactured for customers. The primary focus is to have enough of each stock-keeping unit (SKU) available to ensure that the customer can be serviced and that production is never stopped due to a shortage of raw materials.

8.1.2 Operations management as a transformation process

The transformation process (also known as the conversion process) is depicted in Figure 8.1. Operations utilise inputs and transform them as efficiently as possible into outputs via this transformation process. Outputs are products or services. Inputs can take on a variety of forms and are grouped into two categories – transformed and transforming resources,[3,4] as follows:
- Transformed resources: raw materials; information; customers (services).
- Transforming resources: labour; facilities; consumables; capital; energy.

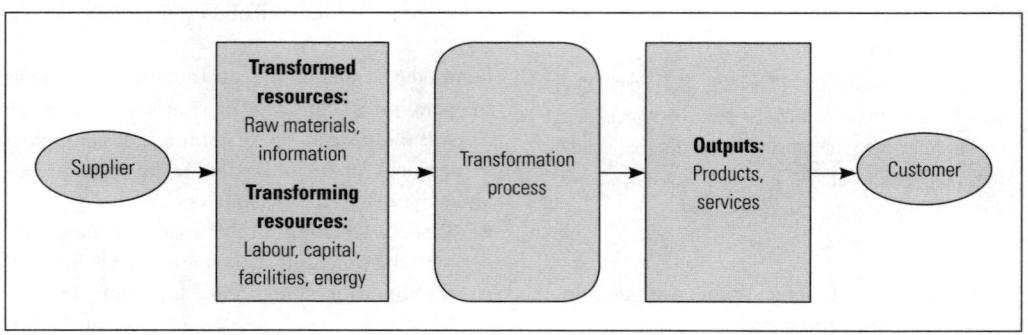

Figure 8.1 Operations as a transformation process

For the logistician it is important to understand the principles of decision making within the operations environment in order to understand the importance of the timely arrival of raw materials from suppliers and the shipping of final products to customers.

8.1.3 The supply-chain operations reference (SCOR) model

The Supply Chain Council – a professional organisation for supply chain management professionals – advocates that companies should have a wider view on their total supply chain in order to understand the flow of raw materials, sub-assembly products and final products between the various players in the supply chain. The SCOR model, shown in Figure 8.2, illustrates this concept by referring to each company in the supply chain by means of five core management processes[5] – plan, source, make, deliver, return.

- Planning is the process of balancing the demand and supply. It includes the strategic and tactical planning for the other four management processes and communicating decisions to supply chain partners. It also includes financial planning, asset management, business rules, compliance and regulatory issues.
- Sourcing is the process of acquiring raw materials and ensuring that deliveries are made on time. It also includes the process of evaluating, selecting and managing suppliers' performance according to preset standards.
- Making is the process of manufacturing the actual product into stock or for shipping directly to the customer. This includes production scheduling, physical production, testing and quality control and packaging and releasing for shipment.
- Delivery refers to the process of managing customer orders through warehousing control, transportation, installation and billing.
- Return refers to the process through which items (in excess, for maintenance or which are defective) are returned to suppliers or from customers.

Data management, business rules and regulatory issues are an important subset of business processes across all the five groups mentioned above and must be controlled separately, but also collectively in an integrated fashion.

The 'make' management process group essentially encompasses the operations management function within each player in the supply chain. The 'source', 'deliver' and 'return' process groups cover the logistics management function in the supply chain and relate to the interacting functions between the supply chain partners. Although the 'make' process group is an isolated function within each supply chain partner individually, it has an intricate role in the rest of the supply chain's effectiveness and therefore in every aspect of the product delivered to the final consumer.

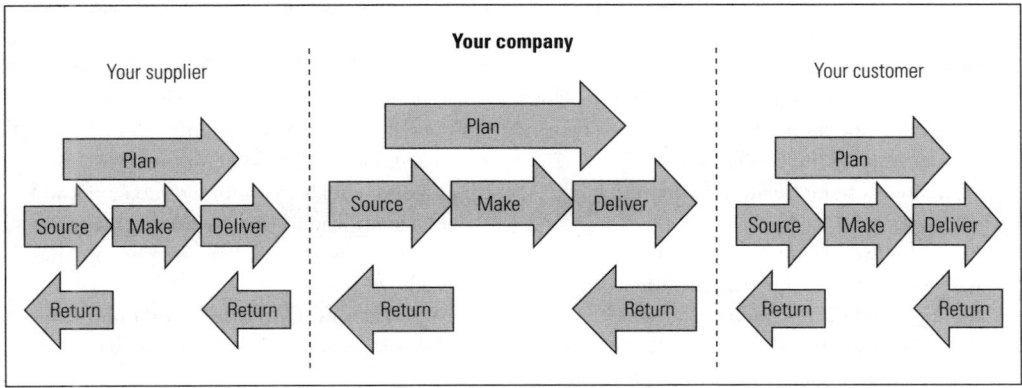

Figure 8.2 The SCOR model indicates the position of operations in the supply chain

It is important to remember the interactive role that all supply chain partners have to play in the combined product design and manufacturing in order for it to be the most effective and efficient supply chain to meet the final consumer's requirements.

8.2 Strategic and planning concepts

8.2.1 Strategy and operations

Strategy exists at three levels in an organisation: corporate, business and functional levels. Strategies at these different levels address the questions of what business the company is in, and how and in what way the company plans to compete in this business. Strategy at all three levels consists of the decisions that a company makes in order to survive and prosper in its current environment over the long term.[6] Various functions in an organisation need to make individual decisions consistent with the overall strategy of the company in order to create a synergy that will make the whole better than the components together.[7]

The major strategic decision areas can be divided into two overarching groups: structural and infrastructural decisions.[8] Structural decisions include:
- Facilities: These decisions relate to the location, size, geographic service area and product focus of each facility.
- Capacity: These decisions are concerned with the specific utilisation of facilities in terms of shifts, working hours and staff levels. Capacity determines the number of products that can be produced and hence the geographic area that can be supplied from each facility.
- Process technology: This determines the extent of automation; the skills required by employees; and the configuration of equipment used in relation to the number of people employed.
- Supply network: This concerns itself with the extent to which operations are outsourced or managed in-house. It includes various decisions about the evaluation, selection and management of the relationship with suppliers.

Infrastructural decisions include:
- Planning and control: The systems and philosophies used for planning and controlling production.
- Quality: Policies and practices followed to ensure quality management.
- Work organisation: The organisational structure and decisions about the assignment of responsibility and accountability.
- Human resources: Decisions about the recruitment, selection, training and development of employees at all levels within the operations process.
- New product development: The decisions that govern the design, development and selection of new products and services
- Performance measurement: Decisions about financial and non-financial performance linked to recognition of individual and collective performance.

Many of these strategic decision areas are very industry-specific as to their implementation, whereas others are fairly generic and applicable to all industries. Four of these generic decision areas are discussed briefly in subsequent sections: the concepts of capacity planning, product design, transformation-process design and planning and control.

8.2.2 Strategy and performance objectives

The way in which a company deploys its operational resources determines how successful the strategy will be to achieve its performance objectives. Pycraft[9] lists five key operations performance objectives:
- Quality: Doing things right, or the ability to produce at the desired quality level consistently and without errors.
- Speed: Doing things fast, or the ability to respond quickly to customers' demands and offer short lead times between the customer placing an order and delivering the ordered products.
- Dependability: Doing things on time, or the ability to consistently deliver products when promised.

- Flexibility: Changing what you do, or the ability to change the operations to meet the specific needs of the customer with respect to volume, production lead time, product mix and innovative new product introductions.
- Cost: The ability to produce at low cost.

Excelling in any one or more of these performance objectives is critical in order for a business to obtain a competitive advantage. The decision as to which of these objectives to excel in is governed by what the customer sees as advantages in the specific industry. Excelling at all of these objectives, however, is costly and does not provide competitive advantages in all industries. It is, therefore, of utmost importance to get the balance of these strategic objectives correct by using trade-offs between them to find an optimum mix for the sector. It might mean focusing on one key aspect and being the best in the one area that the customer considers to be the non-negotiable element of the product offering.[10]

8.2.3 Capacity planning

8.2.3.1 What is capacity planning?

Capacity planning is an integral part of supply chain management and with the increasing focus that companies are placing on the supply chain, there is a corresponding increased focus on capacity planning to identify opportunities to reduce cost and increase revenue while better satisfying the demand of the customer. Capacity planning, however, means different things to different people depending on the industry in which they operate.

> Capacity planning can be broadly defined as '... the process of determining the production capacity needed by an organisation to meet changing demands for its products. In the context of capacity planning, capacity is the maximum amount of work that an organisation is capable of completing in a given period of time'.[11]

The two main drivers of capacity planning, encapsulated in the above definition, are changing demand and limited production capabilities. First, an organisation ideally needs to supply according to its customers' demand. If it produces too little, there will be unsatisfied customers who will look elsewhere to satisfy their needs, or the organisation may produce more than its customers are willing to buy, resulting in waste and unnecessary cost. Another characteristic of demand is that it fluctuates over time – over the short, medium and long term and a business needs to be aware of these fluctuations. Second, a company has a finite production capacity. If it invests in too much capacity it will incur unnecessary expenses in capital outlay, which would amongst others negatively affect its cash flow and maintenance requirements. On the other hand, if the demand exceeds the production capacity, the company will have to acquire additional capacity by either developing such capacity in-house or outsourcing production to other companies. Again, the company should be very aware of and properly understand any fluctuations in demand.

Other factors that affect the production capacity of an organisation include:
- the number of staff that it employs and the level of education and skills they have;
- the quality and availability of raw materials and other production inputs;
- the quality, type and availability of its equipment;
- the quality of the maintenance on its equipment;
- the layout and efficiency of its equipment;
- the techniques and procedures that it follows; and
- regulatory requirements.

Capacity could, therefore, be calculated by multiplying the available production units by the available time, utilisation and efficiency in the system. Capacity planning should not be seen as purely an output maximisation exercise, but rather an optimisation effort. During capacity planning the organisation endeavours to match its production as closely as possible to customer demand. Since demand is a moving target, the organisation needs to take this into consideration in its strategic planning processes.

8.2.3.2 Capacity-planning strategy

Barnes[12] further classifies the timing of capacity planning into one of three primary strategies, namely lead, lag or match strategies. These are also shown in Figure 8.3:

- Lead strategy means adding capacity in anticipation of an increase in demand. This enables an aggressive strategy where the competition can be challenged by flooding the market with products. The disadvantage is that it results in excess inventory, which is costly and could be wasteful.
- Lag strategy refers to adding capacity only after the organisation is running at full capacity or over capacity due to overtime or around-the-clock shifts. Lag strategy allows the company to increase the utilisation of assets and reduce the fixed cost per unit. It reduces the risk of waste, but may result in the loss of possible customers in the case of a sudden demand increase above available capacity levels.
- Match strategy is adding capacity in small amounts in response to changing demand in the market. This more moderate strategy allows a company to grow with demand and as funding is available. Match strategy enables the company to keep up with the market and therefore not run the risk of losing customer loyalty as a consequence of not being able to supply products when required.

As mentioned above, these strategies should be formulated in the context of the different strategic time frames, since each of these time frames require different perspectives.

Figure 8.3 Capacity-planning strategies

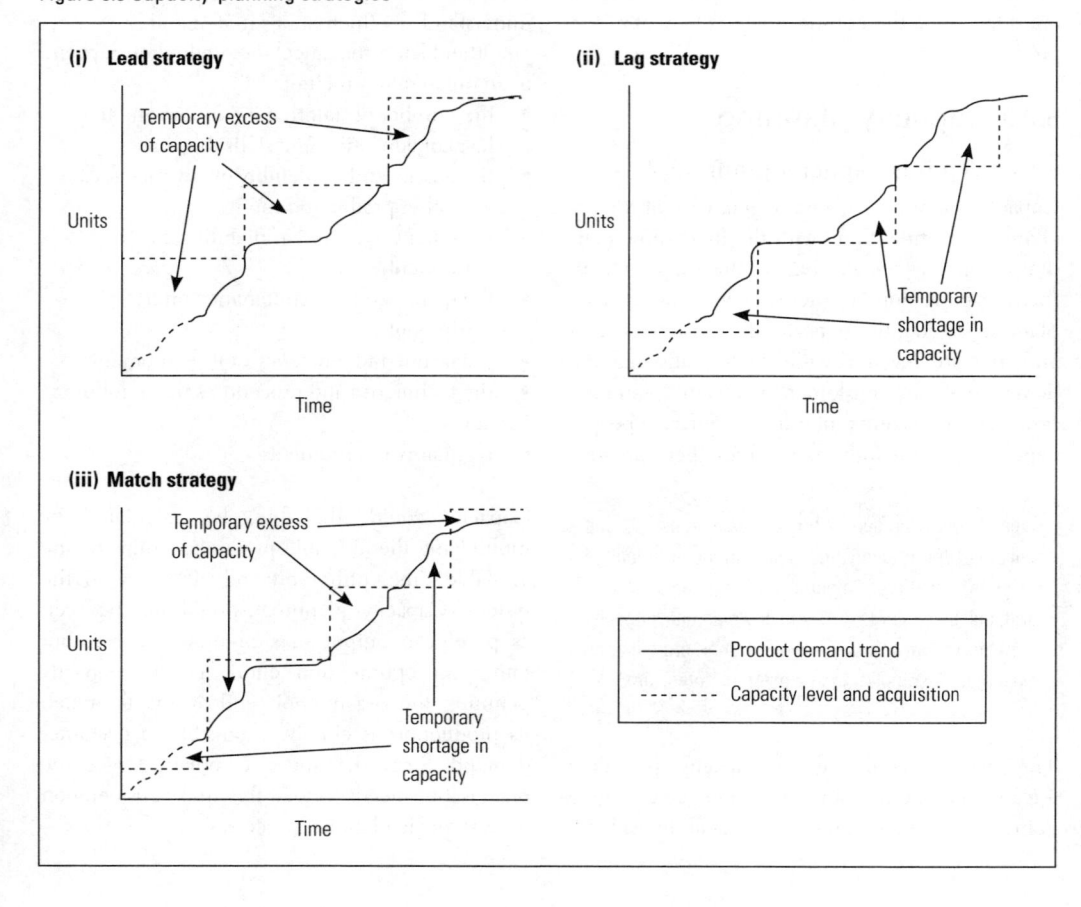

8.2.3.3 Time perspective of capacity planning

It is important to ensure that a company not only prepares capacity growth to meet growing demand, but reviews its requirements with an integrated approach to the long-, medium- and short-term needs for capacity. The determinant of what is short, medium and long term differs by industry, but in general can be described as follows:

- Long-term capacity planning involves strategic issues relating to the firm's production facilities and is interrelated to location decisions. Furthermore, long-term capacity planning also relates to the technology that an organisation elects to use.

  When planning for the long term, the organisation needs to project demand over the long term to determine at what stage its current capacity (facilities, equipment, techniques and practices) would no longer be able to supply to meet that demand.

  Given the extended lag time associated with location and facility planning, the time frame for long-term capacity planning would typically be between two and five years, but in some industries could be up to, or even more than, 30 years. Long-term capacity planning normally involves expensive capital investments to increase capacity.

- Medium-term capacity planning mainly relates to seasonal fluctuation in demand, providing customers and suppliers with information on correct quantities and locations in order to meet forecasted demand. It also relates to employee levels, budgets and subcontracting needs. Medium-term capacity is generally planned in a time frame of between three and 18 months.

- Short-term capacity planning relates to scheduling, staffing, balancing resource capacities and achieving results. The focus of short-term capacity planning is to react to unforeseen shifts in demand in a cost-efficient manner. The time frame for short-term capacity planning is up to six months, but usually in the region of a few weeks.

8.2.3.4 The capacity-planning process

The capacity planning process can be divided essentially into three stages. The first stage involves the estimation of future demand. This estimation has to be performed for each of the three time perspectives mentioned above. The second stage entails determining the organisation's current capacity, which leads to the third stage – planning to meet the gap between future requirements and current capacity. This planning has to address everything from location, plant, equipment, people and supply to financial aspects, and has to address all three time perspectives mentioned above.

8.2.4 Product design

When the word design is mentioned, many tend to think that it only applies to the design of tangible products. Both products and services, however, need to be created to the required specifications. The fact that a customer has unique needs makes it necessary for the producer in the manufacturing sector or the service provider to create products and services that contribute uniquely to the final customer's requirements. Different types of design processes give rise to different products. The responsibility of the operations manager is to create design processes that will have a positive influence on the final product. The product design process itself is not stagnant; it too should be seen as an activity going through transformation, starting off as a concept that is then transformed into logical specifications of something that can be created.

All design activities have performance objectives that are fundamental to all designs. These objectives are: a design should be of high quality; it should be produced quickly, on a dependable basis, flexibly and at low cost. The design activity involves identifying and evaluating options from its inception through the different stages until the final concept. The designer should take stock of these options, and then assess the value of each. This will involve assessing each option against a number of design criteria – the three broad design categories being the feasibility of the design, the acceptability of the design and the vulnerability of each design option.

It is important to note that the processes through which the company endeavours to create the service all have an impact on the operation's ability to meet customers' needs. This is discussed in the next section on transformation-process design and the design process should keep those principles in mind when designing a product or service. Each product should not only be fully functional, but the transformation process (or production process) should be as efficient as possible and located at the correct position in the organisation.

8.2.4.1 Concurrent engineering

> Concurrent engineering is a term used to describe the process of collective product design by all affected functions in an organisation.

Concurrent engineering allows all the functions – marketing, the customer, research and development, product design, process engineering, operations, procurement, logistics and finance – to voice their requirements and limitations collectively during the design process with the goal of designing the product with the customer specifications in mind first, but also to meet the various functions' requirements as far as production, distribution, cost etc. are concerned.

Historically, the design process was often done sequentially, with each party providing their inputs one after the other. This often led to a situation where the requirements set by one function did not meet the requirements or limitations of another function, and the process had to start all over again. Concurrent engineering has the advantage that all parties are involved from the outset and limited or no repetition is required to design an optimal product whose specifications suit all the functions. This has a positive impact on the duration and cost of the product design cycle, which is continuously shortened by customers' requirements for new products.[13] The outcome of concurrent engineering is usually that a product is designed to be suitable for:

- Manufacturability. The product is designed with the understanding that it should be easy to manufacture in the current operational facility with minor layout changes, little additional financing cost and minimal disruption to the current production set-up. This allows the operations to have an influence on whether the product should be a standardised low-cost product that can be manufactured with high efficiency, or a customised higher-cost product that is more complex to manufacture. (Read more about this in Section 8.2.5 on transformation-process design.)
- Procurement. The components and sub-components are designed using standard specifications to ensure that procurement is easily done through existing supply channels and by using existing components as inputs to reduce time-to-market, added cost and complexity.
- Storage and transport. The product is designed with its packaging in order to use minimal space in storage and to be easily transported at minimum cost. This includes elements like stacking properties, dimensions, strength, durable shelf life etc.
- Environmental friendliness. More and more emphasis is placed on products that are environmentally friendly and can be easily recycled or disassembled and destroyed with no or minimal impact to the environment. This involves decisions regarding which materials and production processes are used.

8.2.4.2 Quality function deployment

Quality function deployment (QFD) is a planning tool used to fulfil customer expectations through a disciplined approach to product design, engineering and production. It provides in-depth evaluation of a product, with the focus remaining on integrating the customer's specifications and quality requirements throughout the product design process. It is employed to translate customer expectations, in terms of specific requirements, into directions and actions, in terms of engineering characteristics, which can be deployed through product planning, part development, process planning, production planning and service design.[14]

QFD enables the design phase to concentrate on the customer's requirements, thereby spending less time on redesign and modifications. The saved time has been estimated at one-third to a half of the time taken for redesign and modifications using traditional means. This saving means reduced development cost and additional income because products enter the market sooner. An organisation that correctly implements QFD can improve engineering knowledge, productivity and quality and simultaneously reduce costs, product development time and engineering changes.

8.2.5 Transformation-process design

In the same way that the customer is more involved in the product design process, the customer is also increasingly involved in the actual production of the product, and thus in the transformation process itself. This requires new thinking from the operations department to ensure that the various processes involved interrelate optimally. Process design needs to be driven by the competitive position that a company wishes to have in the market. There are four main areas that should be considered in designing this value-adding system:[15]

- Flexibility: Historically, transformation processes were designed to be repetitive, efficient, and isolated from the customer to produce standardised products. With the customer being more involved, the transformation process needs to be more flexible in nature, which reduces the repetitive nature and efficiency. The value that is added through more responsive processing and providing a customised product should be offset against a higher price for the product, or by using the following three criteria to maintain efficiency.
- Technology has been the driver and simultaneously the enabler of the increased demands set by customers on the transformation process. Technology is a critical component of any transformation process and can be exploited to significant competitive benefit by maintaining efficiency in the transformation process while increasing flexibility, customer involvement and facilitating supply chain configuration.
- Customer involvement: Standardised production processes do not involve the customer, while customised products have to involve the customer to ensure that each product is supplied according to the specific requirements. The extent of customer involvement has an influence not only on production efficiency – and therefore product cost – but also on customer satisfaction with the final product.
- Supply chain configuration: The extent of the company's involvement in the supply chain and the location of the various supply chain partners' facilities with regard to the customer play a significant role in the types of transformation processes that can be achieved. In a complex environment with highly customised products, smaller facilities closer to the customers can be more efficient than one large facility far from the customers. On the other hand, the distance from the suppliers can be detrimental with many small facilities and cause an increase in lead time of components from these supply chain partners, which is a constraint on efficiency. Thus the individual competitive criteria for the company's industry need to be determined to ensure that the correct supply chain configuration is used to support the other three competitive areas above.

The four competitive criteria outlined above inform the decision as to which of the following four types of transformation processes should be deployed.

- Job shops utilise highly skilled labour and general-purpose equipment (at a low fixed cost) to produce small numbers of customised products, often prototypes. This process type is known for exceptional flexibility and complete customisation, but comes at a higher price and a slower speed of manufacturing, and sometimes at a lower level of quality consistency. Custom prototypes of an engineering nature are examples of this process, such as luxury yachts and customised machinery.
- Batch processes produce a limited number of similar items simultaneously or sequentially

according to customised requirements. Flexibility and customisation are lower than in a job shop environment, but unit costs are lower, product consistency higher and delivery speed faster. More specialised equipment is often used at a higher fixed cost than found in the job shop environment. Examples include winemaking and batches of paint or fabric.
- Repetitive processes produce a high volume of standardised products of consistent quality, at a very low unit cost. Low-skilled workers are used with dedicated and specialised equipment that has a high fixed cost. Flexibility and opportunities for customer involvement is limited to non-existent, and the use of technology is very high. Examples of repetitive processing include bottled beverages, canned processed food and motor vehicles.
- Continuous-flow processes are similar to repetitive processes, but the product is manufactured in a continuous flow in non-discrete units. This is used for products like chemicals, flour, or cement, which are eventually packaged in discrete (countable) units, but which are manufactured in a non-discrete continuous process. The same principles that apply to repetitive processes apply here as well.

From these discussions it can be concluded that every company needs to devise a coherent strategy for product design and process design that support its overall strategic operations and performance objectives, are supported by its production capacity planning and use an applicable process to plan and control its production facility. This strategy should include the decisions about the customer order decoupling point discussed in Chapter 4. The company needs to determine which of the make to stock, assemble to order, make to order and engineer to order approaches it will follow to implement their transformation process to fulfil their strategic objectives.

8.2.6 Planning and control

Now that we have introduced the transformation process model, the product design process and the transformation design process, we need to describe the day-to-day running of the transformation process. The purpose of planning and control is to make decisions to ensure that operations run effectively and make the correct products in the appropriate quantities, at the appropriate time and at the appropriate level of quality.[16]

Consider the operations that go into a service like a music festival. Ticket holders arrive at the weekend and enjoy the performances, the food stalls and the atmosphere, oblivious to the months of planning work that went into putting together the festival. Decisions need to be made on the dates; the number of performers and specific performers; forecasting the number of festival visitors and sound engineers required; the type of atmosphere that needs to be created; infrastructure planning, marketing; and the operational aspects of selling tickets; arranging the details, like merchandise sales and security. During the event itself, adjustments need to be made for specific circumstances and unforeseen issues that might arise. All of these are the planning and control tasks.

Planning is usually concerned with activities that occur before the transformation process, with the purpose of taking all aspects into account and predicting the timing of material and resource requirements and finished goods.

However, everything does not always go according to plan and control is applied during the transformation process to alter the planning to cater for unforeseen circumstances. The planning and control processes become so intertwined in a manufacturing environment that it is often difficult to distinguish between the two.[17] The transformation process is set up to use inputs and transform them into outputs. Transformation process inputs are planned according to the output requirements. During the process all aspects are measured to determine whether the intended outcome is achieved. If not, control processes are triggered to change the plans accordingly to move closer to the desired outcomes.

There are many reasons why an initial plan is not achieved. Customer demand might be different from the forecast with respect to volume, mix of goods and timing required. The resources that are involved in the transformation process will then

have to change from the original plan to meet the latest requirements. These resources are:
- people (customer or employees);
- materials (being processed or consumed);
- information; and
- equipment.

Some of these resources are easy to change, others more difficult. For example, employees work according to a shift roster and can be changed over the medium term, but not necessarily on a day-to-day basis. On the other hand, the scheduling of manufacturing equipment can be altered within certain limitations, as can the material requirements, depending on the ability of the suppliers to change their processes relative to the lead time involved.

Timescales play a significant role in planning and control activities, with longer timescale activities usually being planning activities and short timescale activities being control activities. The different planning and control activities are:[18]
- Strategic operations planning: This is long-term planning that needs to tie in with the company's corporate strategic plan. It involves large-scale capital and investment decisions.
- Aggregate planning: These are medium-term plans (usually 12 or 24 months ahead), which consider the demand for the total product mix and how the company should meet this demand on a month-by-month and facility-by-facility basis. Aggregate planning needs to assess whether sufficient capacity is available and address shortcomings.
- Master production schedule (MPS): This planning determines on a week-by-week and product-by-product basis how forecasts or customer orders will be filled. The forecast looks at the next 12–24 weeks and at individual products. The scheduler aims to match supply with demand by scheduling current resources as efficiently as possible.
- Activity scheduling: The schedule determined by the MPS is now planned into detailed activities at each work centre to determine the sequence and routing of work orders and the loading of each work centre on a day-to-day basis. This leads to work order schedules, human resource schedules, equipment schedules and material schedules.
- Expediting: Short-term changes to plans inevitably have to be made. Sudden changes or demand from priority customers, the illness of a specialist operator or an equipment breakdown might require the MPS and activity schedule to be altered to ensure that a deadline is met. These interventions to day-to-day activities are known as expediting. Although it is advisable to limit these interventions to a minimum to ensure that efficiencies are maintained, it is unrealistic to believe that such interventions can be completely eliminated.

The different levels of planning and control activities have to be integrated and interlinked to ensure that the various time-horizon activities support one another. Constraints for people, equipment and materials in terms of cost, capacity, timing and quality need to be kept in mind during these planning processes. The normal timescales of the various types of planning and control activities are shown in Table 8.1.

Table 8.1 The timescales of planning and control activities

Planning and control activities	Typical timescales
Strategic operations planning	two to five years (and more)
Aggregate planning	one to two years
Master production schedule	three to six months
Activity scheduling	one to four weeks
Expediting	Real time

Source: Barnes, D. 2008. Operations Management – An International Perspective. London: Thomson Learning: 238. Reprinted by permission of Cencage Learning Services Ltd.

8.3 Quality management

8.3.1 Quality concepts and principles

The conscience of quality emerged in the 1950s, with Japan as the key instigator of the awareness of and desire for exceptional product quality. In Japan's attempt to re-establish its industry in the post-war era, it found that it could significantly increase its sales of products by implementing several quality-focused initiatives that were based on the teachings of quality gurus from the West, like Deming and Juran.[19] This caught most of the industries of the West by surprise and Japanese product quality quickly became a benchmark that everybody else was trying to keep up with. 'Made in Japan' became a guarantee of quality and is nowadays seen as an emblem for striving for zero defects.

The definition of good enough quality is measured by a product being fit for a customer to use. Companies have used many processes to establish this fit-to-use level of quality. Four stages can be identified in the progression of the concept of quality, outlined next.

- Quality inspection is usually done at the end of the transformation process to confirm whether a product to be sold is of an acceptable standard, needs rework or needs to be scrapped. In this form, often a 100 per cent inspection rate is required to ensure that good-quality products leave the factory floor, which is a costly exercise. With a lower percentage of inspection or by only sampling some of the products, there is a significant chance that products below acceptable quality will leave the factory without being noticed. A quality department is usually responsible for quality inspection and the operations function often see quality as not being their problem.
- Quality control is the next level of concern. Inspection is carried out in a more scientific way and quality defects are analysed to find the cause of the bad quality and to take corrective action. Quality control also attempts to control the process to some extent by implementing statistical process-control methods. Despite this, quality control still has a reactive nature and only results in an acceptable level of defects, not a zero-defect environment.
- Quality assurance is the next level over quality control where a quality management system (QMS) is often implemented to ensure that quality is not a by-product, but pro-actively planned and designed into the transformation process. Quality of inputs is assured by buying only from approved suppliers that also practise quality-assurance principles. In this environment the product design focus is extensively on designing quality into both the product and the transformation process and eliminating any possibilities of defects during the design process. The cost-of-quality concept is used to determine where improvements should be made to reduce the cost of bad quality rather than the approach of spending enough money to achieve only an acceptable defect level.
- Total quality management (TQM) is an approach that targets the attitudes of every person in the organisation to focus on quality and quality improvement. With TQM, the focus is on cultivating beliefs and values for everyone in the company to respect quality as the all-important factor for the organisation. TQM sees quality as a source of competitive advantage and acceptable quality is determined by the customer's point of view. TQM also takes a continuous improvement view, with an understanding that the pursuit of quality is not a one-off goal, but a never-ending journey to always become better. (Read more on this concept in Section 8.5.4.)

Quality has become such an important aspect that two prestige quality awards have been implemented by the US presidency and the Japanese presidency: respectively the Malcolm Baldrige National Quality Award and the Deming Prize. Companies are in fierce competition to achieve these quality awards and to win the national prize in order to ensure that their product quality is recognised by their customers and competition. Various quality certifications under the protection of the International Standards Organisation (ISO) also exist, which companies strive to achieve – in some cases they are compelled by their customers in order to obtain sales. Some of these are the ISO 9000 series of quality standards and the ISO 14000 series of environmental impact standards.

8.3.2 Balancing the cost of quality

Bad quality costs money to correct; good quality costs money to maintain. It is important to balance the cost of prevention with the cost of errors. Pycraft et al. identify four cost elements that influence the total cost of quality:[20]

- Internal failure cost. These are expenses associated with raw materials, sub-assemblies and products that failed or were found to be defective before they left the company's premises. These costs include the cost of scrapped materials and sub-assemblies, reworked parts and lost production time.
- External failure cost. These are expenditures associated with products that are found to be defective after they were transferred to the customer. These costs include the loss of customer goodwill; customer management; guarantees and warranty costs; and litigation due to faulty products.
- Appraisal cost. This is expenditure to verify whether defects were produced in the transformation process. It includes setting up statistical process-control systems; the time consumed to inspect the process and products; investigating quality problems; and conducting customer interactions to determine the level of quality acceptance achieved.
- Prevention cost. These are expenditures to prevent defects from occurring in the first place. Prevention cost includes cost for designing the product to reduce the opportunity for quality problems; identifying the process issues that could cause defects and correcting them; and providing training to employees that will reduce the occurrence of defects.

These four costs have to be balanced to achieve the best level of quality for the least cost. Figure 8.4 illustrates the principle of achieving the optimum level of quality for the least cost by balancing the cost of quality provision and the cost of errors. Although this is a novel idea, it must be remembered that acceptable quality is a customer perception and therefore the level of quality that means the lowest cost of quality will not necessarily be acceptable to the customer and might result in lost sales.

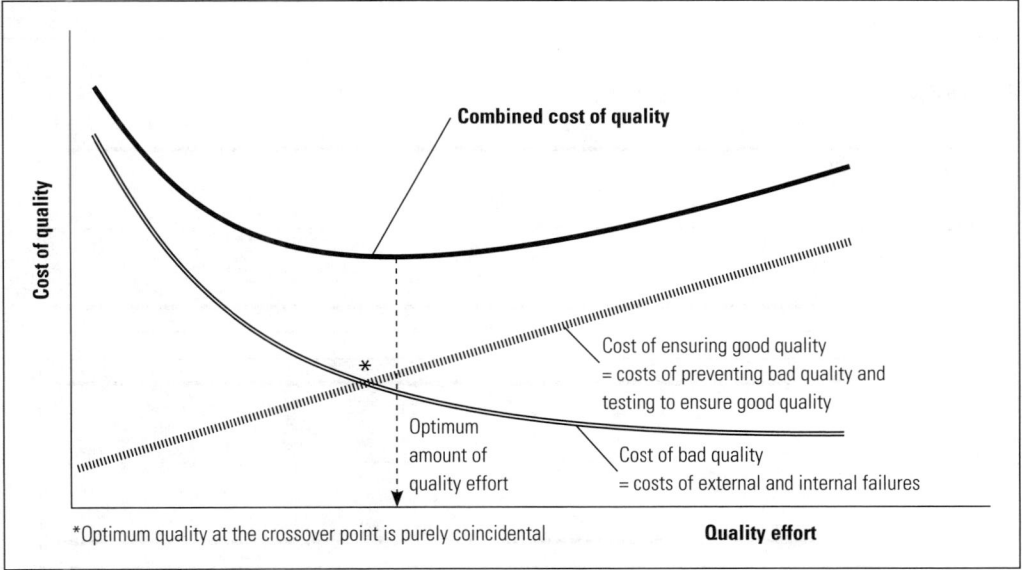

Figure 8.4 The traditional cost-of-quality model

*Optimum quality at the crossover point is purely coincidental

Combined cost of quality

Cost of ensuring good quality
= costs of preventing bad quality and testing to ensure good quality

Cost of bad quality
= costs of external and internal failures

Cost of quality (y-axis)
Quality effort (x-axis)

Optimum amount of quality effort

TQM, however, rejects the optimum quality-level concept and strives to eliminate all known and unknown causes for failure. With customers' perception of defects becoming more and more negative, what used to be known as acceptable levels of defects are now found to be unacceptable. This move towards zero defects has changed the cost-of-quality graph to the one shown in Figure 8.5. From this graph, one can see that the cost of errors has changed with the high cost assigned to customers who are less tolerant of poor quality. Thus the drive towards ever-improving quality and zero defects will continue.

8.3.3 Statistical process control

Statistical process control (SPC) is used by many companies to monitor and control the quality

Figure 8.5 The traditional cost-of-quality model with additions for TQM

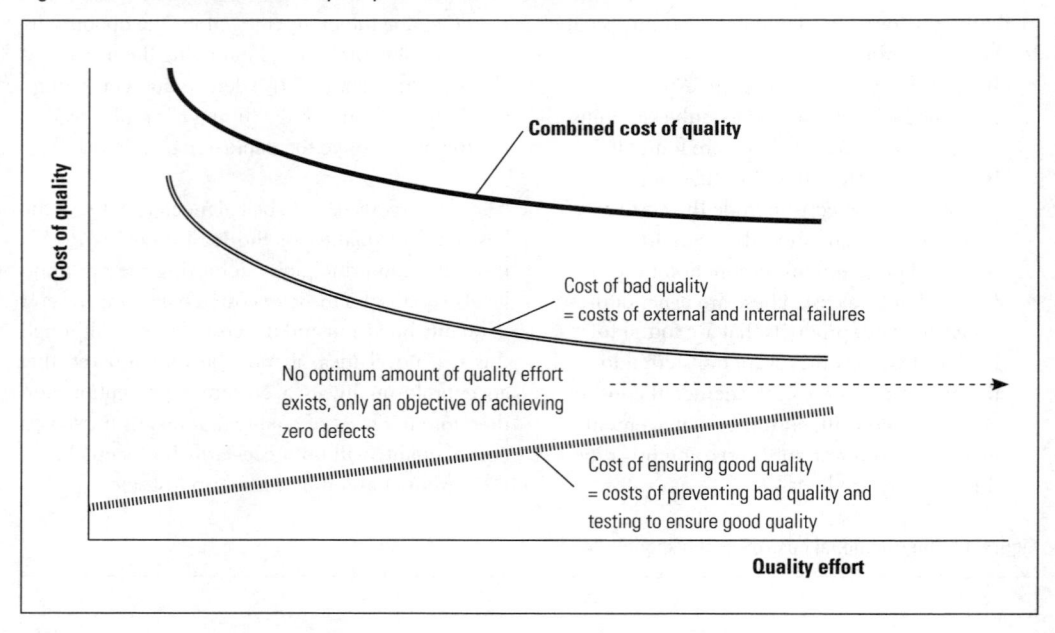

Figure 8.6 X and R charts for cement-bag filling

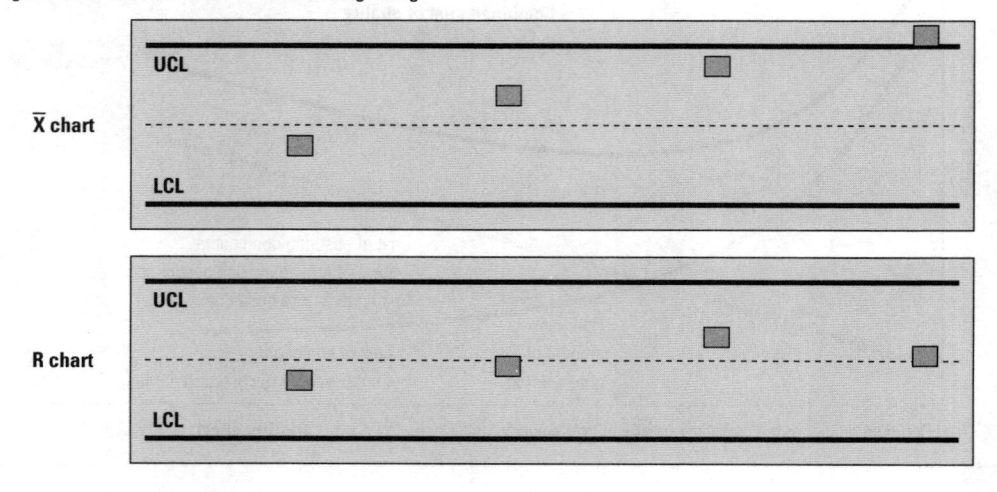

attributes and variability of a product during its production. SPC aims to monitor the current specifications of produced items in order to determine whether trends exist that indicate a shift in the process that signals that future products might not meet specifications.[21] There are four main issues to address in creating a control chart: sample sizes; the number of samples; the frequency of samples; and the control limits. The principle is briefly explained next by means of an example in cement production.

Example: cement bag weight control

Cement is sold in 50 kg bags. During the filling process the filling machine needs to fill each bag as closely as possible to 50 kg. A bag that is too light will cause a customer to be unhappy; a bag that is too heavy means a loss of product given away for free and could lead to vehicle overloading and possible litigation from the freight company. In SPC, the $\overline{X}$ chart (see Figure 8.6) will be used to determine how close to the mean of 50 kg each cement bag weighs. The R chart will be used to determine the variability of the cement bags' weight around 50 kg. In order to set up the process, a number of samples need to be taken of a predetermined size to calculate what the control limits should be. Once defined, the $\overline{X}$ and R charts will have a mean, an upper control limit (UCL) and a lower control limit (LCL), which signal the range that all samples need to stay within to indicate that the process is still in control. The mathematics behind calculating the control limits is beyond the scope of this text. Figure 8.6 illustrates the concept of an $\overline{X}$ and R chart for the cement bag example.

The aim of SPC is to monitor whether the transformation process is still in control and capable of producing the products within the specified tolerance limits. The result of the SPC charts indicates whether the process is accurate and precise. To maintain good-quality products the transformation process needs to remain both accurate and precise. Figure 8.7 illustrates the principles of accuracy and precision.

Figure 8.7 Accuracy and precision – the cornerstones of quality control

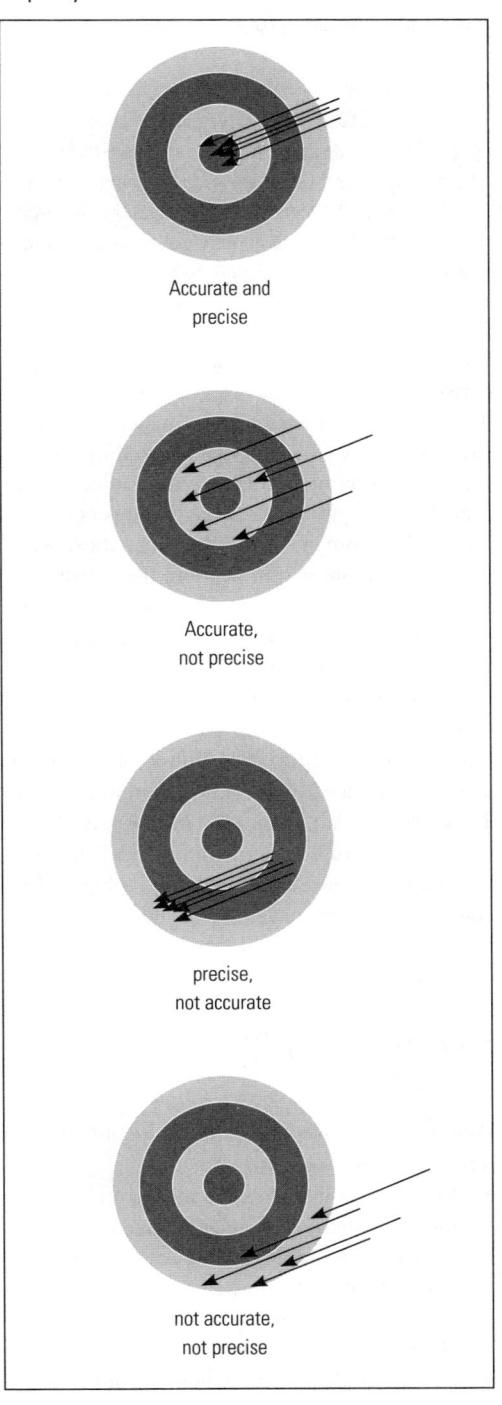

Accurate and precise

Accurate, not precise

precise, not accurate

not accurate, not precise

8.4 Inventory management

8.4.1 What is inventory?

> Inventory refers to material resources that are stored for usage at a later stage either through transformation from a raw to a finished state, or through use in the current state. Inventory can be seen at different categories, such as raw materials inventory, work-in-process inventory and finished goods inventory.

Inventory results from management strategies derived from external expectations of market demand (customers) and material supply (suppliers), as well as internal constraints, such as capacity constraints and financial resources. It can exert either a positive or negative impact on the business's bottom line. Inventory is beneficial when it enhances customer satisfaction, but detrimental if it creates complexities in planning and inhibits the smooth flow of processes. Since inventory is a servant to higher strategies, it must be in support of higher organisational objectives.

Inventory, therefore, plays an important role in the planning and control of operations facilities, and needs to be discussed in this context. These are explained briefly in this chapter to highlight the important planning and scheduling interactions between operations philosophies and inventory management. The concepts of inventory management are discussed in detail in Chapter 10.

8.4.2 Inventory types and positions

Four types of inventory can be identified with regard to operations management:[22]
- Buffer/safety inventory is a minimum level of inventory that is kept as a contingency against demand and supply variations. For example, buffer stock is useful when shipments are delayed at a port due to port congestion or clearance inefficiencies.
- Cycle inventory occurs when one or more stages in the operation cannot produce all items simultaneously. Hence, the operation process is run in batches for each item, which must be large enough to meet demand when the item is not under production.
- Anticipation inventory is kept as a cushion against demand fluctuations that are significant but relatively predictable.
- Pipeline inventory is the inventory that has been prepared by the supplier for shipment to the customer. The stock is said to be in transit (in the pipeline) from the time it is allocated to the customer to the time it arrives at the customer's destination.

Inventory also needs to be classified according to the position it has in the different stages of operations.[23]
- Raw materials are commodity materials and components used at the input side of the production facility to produce the products that the company sells. These items are usually kept on site or shipped in to arrive when required by the operations process.
- Work-in-process (WIP) comprises the materials, components and sub-components that are still in the process of being transformed into finished goods. These materials are kept in and between different workstations in the facility.
- Finished goods are the finished products that are available and ready to be sold immediately to customers when orders are placed. Finished goods are usually at the end of the operations process and either stored or immediately shipped away to a different location.

Some operations, such as retail stores, only have finished goods ready to be sold, whereas a complex manufacturing environment, like an automotive plant, has inventory in all three positions.

The strategic focus of the organisation will determine which of these various inventory types and positions are utilised more and which less. In an environment where customisation and flexibility of the finished goods are critical, no finished goods inventory are kept, but higher levels of raw materials are kept. Within a low-cost environment where production efficiency is critical to reduce cost, finished goods inventory is held to enable a level production strategy, while low WIP and raw-material inventories are kept.

8.4.3 The purpose of inventory

Inventory management is performed by all companies in all sectors. In the case of a manufacturing industry, inventory management can be the differentiating factor between success and failure. The reason for this is because inventory management is so key to the business that the true value of a detailed inventory management strategy is often taken for granted. According to Wild, inventory management controls the activity which organises the availability of items to the customers.[24] Inventory management coordinates the purchasing, manufacturing and distribution functions to meet the marketing needs.

The purpose of inventory management can be summarised to optimise three targets:
- Customer service. Customer demand seldom matches the level of production supply completely. It is often important to keep inventory to offset the variance in supply and demand by using inventory to decouple the production and customer orders from each other. This allows the company to meet customer demand and maintain a preferred level of customer service at various locations by buffering against uncertainties in demand and supply.
- Operating costs. Raw materials and sub-assemblies need to be available when production facilities require them. If material is not available at the correct quantity and place, it has a detrimental effect on production efficiency and can incur huge costs in lost production time, with machines and labour being idle.
- Inventory costs. The cost of ordering, handling and storing inventory has to be minimised, as storage itself does not add value. The previous two targets prefer to have as much stock available as possible in order to always supply production and customers on demand. Inventory provides value solely by the fact it is available when required by customers or production facilities, but the cost of carrying excess inventory needs to be offset with the cost of a stockout.

These three targets of inventory management need to be in balance according to preset values of customer service levels, production facility requirements, and to minimise inventory cost.

This balancing act refers to the streamlining of resources, which leads to the global optimisation of the entire logistical supply chain so that supply and demand are in phase to create greater customer value. From the operations strategy perspective, inventory management policies should be implemented to enhance the business's profitability. This means keeping inventory levels within productive limits and totally avoiding surplus and excess stock. Effective inventory management is critical to business success and directly affects a company's financial performance. Businesses are at all times faced with mixed push/pull factors and inventory has to be well managed to cater for customer needs, while simultaneously preventing overstocking. Inventory management policies should be aimed at lowering holding costs through higher inventory rotation without triggering substantial stockouts and back orders caused by demand peaks and/or lead-time delays.

Leading companies are now aiming for more customer-aligned inventory strategies, rather than the traditional crisis-response signals. In the past, the business environment was more supply-driven, but there has been a rapid progression to demand-driven operations, and this has greatly impacted on the way that inventory is managed. It is now critical to link inventory requirements to customer requirements for high quality, quick response and low cost. Hence the quest for continuous improvement and competitiveness leads businesses to pay close attention to scrutinising their inventory.

In managing inventory, careful attention should be given to the symptoms and problems that exist. The symptoms are normally the initial indicators that something is wrong. For instance, inventory can be described as too much or too little. However, symptoms will not point to the root cause of the problem. Inventory managers must be careful to investigate and eliminate the underlying causes of inventory problems. Long-term solutions should be implemented that will arrive at greater customer value.

8.5 Operations management: current approaches and philosophies

There is a number of contemporary operations management approaches and philosophies adopted by companies to structure their operations so as to improve efficiency and effectiveness. Some of these approaches bring numerous small improvements, while others promote large once-off changes with a significant once-off impact. A number of these are discussed briefly next, with the emphasis on the effect they have on planning and controlling the internal operations processes and the external supply chain. Each of them is well suited to a particular transformation process type and functions well in this particular environment, but not in others. It is important, therefore, that the operations manager understands the principles of each of these approaches in order to make the correct decision regarding which approach to implement in his or her own environment.

8.5.1 Just-in-time

Just-in-time (JIT) is an inventory strategy implemented to improve the return on investment of a business by reducing in-process inventory and its associated carrying costs. JIT was first used by Toyota in its Toyota Production System (TPS), which later came to be known as JIT. In a nutshell, JIT means producing only what is needed, in the amounts that are needed, when they are needed, using the minimum amount of materials, equipment, labour and space. The ideal environment for JIT includes:
- a stable customer demand;
- a high volume of products;
- a limited number of standardised products;
- a repetitive value-adding system;
- employee involvement in the improvement of the production process; and
- long-term supplier relationships that exist or can be cultivated.

Key elements of JIT are that it is intended to stabilise and level the mass-production system with uniform plant loading to create a uniform load on all work centres through constant daily production. JIT environments favour a situation with excess capacity, rather than excess inventory. JIT as far as possible reduces or eliminates set-up times; reduces lot sizes (manufacturing and purchase); reduces lead times; and promotes preventive maintenance. JIT can only be achieved by a combination of strategic capacity considerations, strategic supply chain management and detailed ways to make work flow using pull systems, such as *Kanban* (Japanese for card system). With the *Kanban* system, work is authorised by means of a signalling system that instructs the start of work only once a new product is required by a downstream activity. This way, products are pulled through the system only as they are required, which significantly reduces WIP inventory.

One of the major steps in implementing JIT is to identify waste in the production process. This requires managers and workers to look at their workplace in a different way. Toyota has documented seven types of waste that need to be eliminated:[25]
- Over-production: Producing more than required or producing early into WIP, which is only required much later in the process.
- Product waiting: This is idle time, or time when no value is added to the product and it is waiting to be processed further towards becoming a finished item.
- Transportation: This refers to handling products more than once or delays in moving materials from one process to the next incurred by unavailability of transport equipment.
- Processing: Some processing of the product adds no value to the final product or to the customer's perception of value.
- Storage: Unnecessary raw materials, WIP and finished goods are kept in stock for no apparent reason.
- Motion: Movement of equipment or people, which adds no value to the products.
- Defects that need to be reworked or scrapped.

The philosophy of JIT is to expose these wastes and eventually reduce or eliminate them, rather than use high levels of inventory to hide the wastes in order to maintain customer service levels. Carrying inventory is costly and could be eliminated effectively in the environments where JIT can be implemented. The major advantage of implementing JIT is the reduction of cost through the reduction of inventory and the increased responsiveness by means of shorter production lead times created by the reduced inventory and smaller lot sizes.

8.5.2 Lean systems

Lean systems are often linked to, or confused with, JIT principles. While similar, it is a distinctly different concept. JIT can be seen as part of lean systems, but is not the same thing as lean systems. Where JIT is primarily internally focused on inventory and production, lean systems is a broader concept, focusing on more than only the internal operations, but applied to all aspects of the business. The focus of lean systems is external – it is on the customer and the customer's expectations and perception of value. It focuses on eliminating waste by eliminating all activities that do not add value to the customer, and can be applied to both services and manufacturing. In this text the focus is on manufacturing.

Lean systems have the same approaches as JIT to:
- scheduling and control;
- waste elimination,
- reducing lot sizes; and
- reducing set-up times.

The lean system is also elaborated on both sides of the supply chain through several supply chain partners sharing the concepts and implementing lean thinking, not only locally but throughout the supply chain. The focus of lean systems rests on three pillars:
- Eliminating waste. This includes the seven wastes of JIT (explained in Section 8.5.1), but broader than only internal waste.
- Involving everyone. This means extending respect to all people, their person and ideas.
- Continuous improvement – this is not a destination, but a journey that continues.

In the process of implementing lean systems an operation is designed that is fast moving, dependable and produces higher-quality services at a lower cost. Key improvements that have been reported by implementing lean-systems thinking in manufacturing are: increased innovation in products and process improvements; safety improvements; reduction of scrap; increased inventory turnover; increased labour efficiency; and a reduction in shift and machine changeover times. Some of the lessons learnt are as follows:
- Improvements have to be sustained by daily follow-up to ensure that they are engraved into the culture of the organisation.
- The value and importance of good, open communication should never be underestimated in problem solving and the implementation of innovative ideas.
- A team-based approach to problem solving is non-negotiable and produces significantly better results than individual attempts.
- Results and success should be celebrated by the team, as this cultivates the process and the importance of excelling even more.

8.5.3 Theory of constraints

The theory of constraints (TOC), developed by Dr Eliyahu Goldratt, is a management methodology that states that organisations or systems must have constraints, otherwise the system will generate infinite amounts of the end product.

> A constraint can be defined as anything (an activity or resource) that restricts a system, organisation or process from achieving its best possible performance in its entirety.

Goldratt states that 'an hour lost in a bottleneck is an hour lost to the entire process'.[26] This hour is not only lost to the process, but is lost forever and will never be reclaimed – it is lost profit. TOC also advocates that by identifying constraints, managers will be able to implement continuous improvement through constant evaluation and thereby allow organisations to achieve their ultimate goal: to make money, now and in the future.

TOC prescribes different approaches for different environments. In the production environment, the drum-buffer-rope concept is applied; in the project environment, on the other hand, the critical-chain concept is applied. Both these applications can be implemented using a technique known as the Five Focusing Steps.[27] This technique describes a structured approach for identifying and elevating the bottleneck's capacity within a system or an organisation. The steps are:

Step 1: Identify the system's constraints.
Step 2: Decide how to exploit the system's constraints.
Step 3: Subordinate everything else to the above decisions.
Step 4: Elevate the system constraint's capacity.
Step 5: If in the previous steps a constraint has been broken, go back to step 1, but do not allow inertia to cause a system constraint; in other words, don't stop.

TOC has many implications for the scheduling of operations. Figure 8.8 illustrates the principle of drum-buffer-rope scheduling.

The bottleneck (D) is the critical resource and should be scheduled to achieve maximum output for the total operation. All scheduling of other non-bottleneck resources (A, B, C) should then be subordinated to the bottleneck's schedule to ensure that it does not starve the bottleneck of raw materials needed as input. Subordinated processes should not create too much inventory that clogs the buffer area in front of the bottleneck process. In TOC scheduling, the bottleneck is called the drum because it sets the pace of the whole facility, while subordination is called the rope, which is used to communicate the release of new material to the other subordinated resources. Other resources do not need to produce at maximum capacity, but just fast enough to provide sufficient inventory for the bottleneck buffer to remain constant and, therefore, not starve the bottleneck at any time of the raw materials and sub-components it requires.[28]

Another element of TOC is that it has a unique outlook on quality. Any item processed by the

Figure 8.8 Theory of constraints: drum-buffer-rope concept

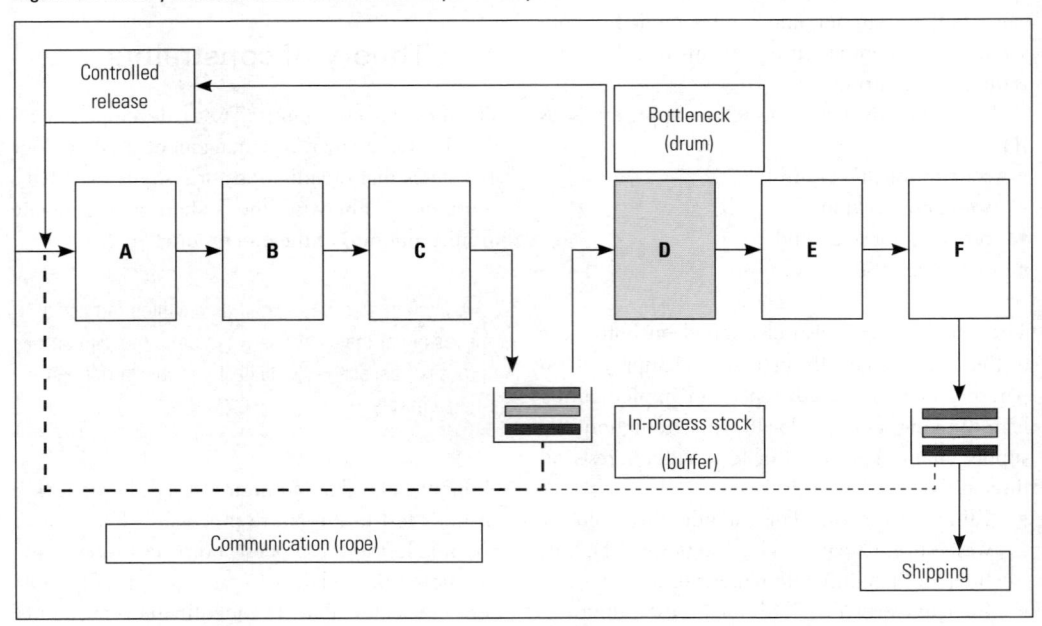

bottleneck and later scrapped due to quality issues is an item lost forever. Therefore, the aim is to thoroughly inspect all items for defects before the bottleneck and to be especially quality-conscious with all processes (E, F) after the bottleneck in order to reduce any losses of process time at the bottleneck.

Goldratt claims that many of the traditional measurements used in operations are misleading and should be seen as secondary to the ultimate goal of making money. He argues that the concept of making money can be broken down into three measurements – throughput, inventory and operating expenses – which are more accurate than the traditional measurements used in operations:[29]

- Throughput is the sale of products that are manufactured in the plant and actually sold, minus the cost of raw materials used to manufacture them. Any item that is manufactured and not sold is not seen as throughput, but instead creates inventory that is most likely to become obsolete. The focus thus shifts away from local efficiencies of single machines and work centres to producing only products that can be sold now.
- Inventory is the cost of any raw material that is in inventory before or within the transformation process. Goldratt does not add the value from direct-cost elements, like labour and machine time, to work-in-process inventory, but adds these transformation costs to operating expenses. According to Goldratt, the direct cost allocation to WIP inventory can often cause misleading value perceptions about items that cannot necessarily be sold to customers.
- Operating expenses are the total cost of turning raw materials into throughput (i.e. sales). They include indirect overhead expenses and expenses that are otherwise seen as direct labour and machine expenses normally allocated to WIP inventory's unit cost.

By focusing all its management attention on increasing throughput while simultaneously reducing the inventory and operating expenses, an organisation gets closer to its ultimate goal of making money.

8.5.4 Total quality management

Quality as a differentiating factor is more important today than ever before because price is no longer sufficient on its own as a differentiating factor. The quality of products and services relies on capable processes and the mindset of people. Many a total quality management (TQM) implementation has failed because of a lack of either top management buy-in or worker involvement. TQM is not merely a philosophy, but an overall quality improvement system. It encompasses all facets of the organisation and is based on the principles of total customer satisfaction, employee involvement, continuous improvement and long-term relationships with suppliers and customers.[30]

Toyota believes that no process can ever be declared perfect and that, therefore, there is always room for improvement. *Kaizen* is a Japanese word meaning to continually aim for improvement. TQM, as developed at Toyota, is a concept that should embrace all functions across the company. The belief is that every worker in every department contributes to quality, no matter how indirectly. It is the responsibility of managers and other workers to learn as much as they can about their work environment, thus employees at all levels are educated and empowered to identify and eliminate waste. In Toyota, *Kaizen* leads to reduction in costs by getting everybody involved, and making small improvements all the time. Toyota was very successful with its implementation of TQM, because TQM became the very fibre of the organisation and part of the everyday culture of the organisation as a whole, and not only operations.

Quality has become such a hot topic that TQM has over the past few years been under the spotlight, both from management gurus as well as the business media. The reason for this is its suspected lack of impact on financial performance. 'Is TQM dead?' 'Is Total Quality Management yesterday's news or does it still shine?' These are just some of the questions raised in publications such as the *Wall Street Journal*, *USA Today* and the *Washington Post*. The results from many studies, however, have shown that the success of TQM implementation is not a function of the understanding of the TQM concept, but rather the focus and determination shown by management in the implementation process. There is clear evidence that companies that have successfully implemented TQM as a management philosophy, and dedicated the necessary resources to maintaining it, have reaped the benefits in terms of financial success and long-term sustainability.

TQM as a management philosophy is alive and well, and although many companies have successfully adopted the TQM principles, its continuous reinforcement and the involvement and participation of employees and managers at all levels of the organisation are needed for the full benefit of TQM to materialise.

8.6 Operations management in the service sector

In South Africa (and the rest of the world), the service sector's contribution to GDP has grown significantly over the last 40 years to overtake the other sectors, as can be seen in Table 8.2. It is important, therefore, for operations managers to understand the functioning of operations in the service sector so as to be able to implement the principles in their environment.

The services sector is characterised by a wide array of economic activities that can be executed across a heterogeneous spectrum of providers, ranging from individuals to large corporations. The characteristics of services include:

- Intangibility: A service cannot be physically experienced prior to its purchase.
- Inconsistency: Service quality is dependent on the ability and skill sets of the people who deliver the service. These issues affect the way the service is promoted, priced and experienced.
- Inseparability: The user of the service cannot separate the product from the deliverer.
- Inventory: A service cannot be stored and the problems related to its 'inventory' is subjective in that it relates to idle production, namely when the service provider is available, but there is no demand.

With reference to the issue of inseparability, key characteristics of a services environment are that the delivery is dependent on people and that either the client or the provider or both must travel to where the transaction occurs. Furthermore, with the impact of knowledge and information the boundaries between industries are shifting and becoming blurred. The offerings companies are bringing to the market range from product-dominated to service-dominated packages, with an increasing number of companies being concentrated within the middle range of what is known as the service continuum.[31] This area is where services become the value-add for goods-based offerings and where goods become the value-add for service-based offerings.

As the services sector becomes increasingly important in world economies, the manner in which it uses capital, labour and knowledge creates greater diversity, which adds to services' unique characteristics. The Organisation for Economic Co-operation and Development (OECD) has therefore recently refined the general classification of services with the notion of 'knowledge-intensive services'. These are defined as services that use more research and development, technology and

Table 8.2 Composition of the South African economy by sector

Sector	1970	1980	1990	2000	2006
Primary sector (agriculture; mining)	19,6%	14,2%	12,3%	10,8%	9,0%
Secondary sector (manufacturing; construction)	27,1%	30,6%	28,9%	24,2%	23,6%
Tertiary sector (services; wholesale and retail trade; transport; storage; communication)	53,2%	55,2%	58,8%	64,9%	67,4%

Source: Derived from South African Statistics 2008:14.3–14.4

highly skilled workers compared to other types of service industries. They further separate market services, such as the communication sectors, financial sectors and business activity sectors from non-market services, which are predominantly provided by the public sector. A range of services are excluded from this definition of knowledge-intensive, which include tourism, hospitality and retail, as their growth potential is limited due to the non-tradeable nature of the service on the global market.

Most of the operations principles are also applicable to the service environment. The challenge to the operations manager in the service sector is to establish ways to implement these principles and apply them correctly in his or her own operations. The day-to-day operation of a service is a constant challenge because the environment is in a continuous state of change.

8.7 Conclusion

This chapter has dealt with various issues of operations management. It discussed the concept of the transformation process as the core of the operations of any company, and the relationship of this transformation process to the company's surrounding supply chain. It discussed the importance of strategic decisions regarding the design of products, transformation processes and capacity and work-floor planning and control. The importance of quality and inventory management where highlighted as critical to efficient and effective operations management. Some of the latest philosophies behind, and approaches to, the planning and control of operations were highlighted. The emergence of the service industry was also discussed in terms of its own particular challenges to the field of operations management.

Key terms

Capacity planning
Concurrent engineering
Continuous improvement
Control
Customer involvement
Environmentally friendly
Flexibility
Inventory
Inventory management
Job shops
Just-in-time (JIT)
Lead time
Manufacturability
Operations management
Quality assurance
Quality function deployment (QFD)
Stock-keeping unit (SKU)
Supply-chain operations reference (SCOR) model
Total quality management (TQM)
Transformation process
Work-in-process (WIP)

Case study

Dell Computers was founded by Michael Dell in 1984. At the age of 19, Dell's interest in computers caused him to drop out of medical school and start up his own company. Dell's concept was simple: selling computer systems directly to customers. This direct business model eliminates retailers and can distribute computers much more quickly than slow-moving indirect distribution channels.

Dell's assemble-to-order model

Dell achieved a great innovation in supply chain management by adopting a direct sales model; that is, a demand-driven supply chain in which the traditional make-to-stock approach is replaced by the assemble-to-order model. At this stage, no other computer manufacturer had used this model, and it was seen as against the norm. However, Dell was proven to be a visionary in the industry and his foresight has paid off. Through the direct ordering system, Dell has created the opportunity to increase significantly the flexibility of what it offers customers. The company keeps inventory of numerous sub-assemblies that can be assembled into almost any configuration depending on the customer's specific request. With this configuration of its transformation process Dell has increased customer involvement and utilises Internet technology to increase connectivity with the customer throughout the process. The amount of freedom for the customer to choose a product has provided a competitive advantage above rivals like IBM and HP.

Dell has expanded its JIT practices from the company to the entire supply chain as suppliers have been integrated into Dell's operations through means of well-designed IT systems. A well-managed supply chain reaps the best fruit from the assemble-to-order tree. Dell has over time created efficiencies through its materials-management process. It was able to meet the demand of customer orders by building the customised system in a timely manner. Dell has enhanced its procurement process, resulting in almost 90 per cent of the company's procurement being done online and leaving only two hours of inventory on the factory floor.

The Internet and web services

Dell's assemble-to-order model utilises the Internet efficiently. The Internet provides Dell not only with a channel for direct sales, but also a great opportunity to manage and control its supply chain.

1. Explain the competitive advantage gained from the assemble-to-order operations strategy that Dell uses.
2. Discuss the spread between the inventories that you would find on Dell's factory floor with respect to the positions of inventory, raw materials/components, WIP and finished goods.
3. There are four main areas that need to be included in the transformation process design: flexibility, technology, customer involvement and supply chain configuration. Explain how Dell has used all four in a collective fashion to differentiate itself from its competition.
4. What do you think the competition has done to counter Dell's strategy?

Case study

Company XHST began implementing the concepts of JIT in 2004. The company facility has 5 400 m^2 underroof, comprising 17 manufacturing cells. It employs 280 people whose average age is 32. Company XHST produces 1,8 million parts per annum and had annual sales of $83 million in 2007. Most of the products are exported to automotive manufacturers in Europe and North America, while some of the products are utilised by automotive manufacturers throughout South Africa. The company's facility is located in Port Elizabeth close to the local automotive manufacturers.

Company XHST produces catalytic converters, which reduce the emission of harmful gases. This is in keeping with one of the key focuses of Company XHST, namely to create a healthier and greener environment for all. The completed products are boxed and shipped abroad or locally to find their ways into the engine systems of cars worldwide. Company XHST's vision is to be the number-one supplier of catalytic converters in the world. Its mission is to deliver a cleaner environment for humanity. Core values that it strives to achieve are trust, honesty, respect, teamwork, embracing diversity and the pursuit of excellence.

The JIT model starts with a pull created by the customer placing an order. The completed catalytic converters that have already been boxed and transported by truck are freighted in containers and loaded onto a ship to be transported to the customers. An empty container on a two-bin system with a *Kanban* order card provides the trigger for replenishment of the finished catalytic converter. The ready-boxed finished products have been sent to a truck to be distributed to the customer, and new stock needs to be produced to meet the next customer request. Raw materials are replenished from the suppliers as needed and purchase orders are triggered by *Kanban* systems. Some of the suppliers are located far from their facility in Port Elizabeth and communication needs to be excellent to ensure that JIT principles are used to replenish raw materials and components with minimum stockout issues and low inventory levels.

1. How well does Company XHST's transformation process fit with the criteria for JIT implementation set out in this chapter?
2. How do you think the distance between Company XHST and its suppliers influences the feasibility and effectiveness of JIT?
3. To what extent would it benefit Company XHST to source alternative suppliers that are located closer to their facility, or motivate its suppliers to move closer to its facility?
4. How will forecasting and information systems facilitate Company XHST in managing the distance factor from its suppliers?
5. What do you think were the challenges in implementing JIT at the company?
6. Do the values of the company fit the requirements for JIT?

Questions

1. What is the transformation process?
2. Using the terms quality, timeliness, low cost, and flexibility, describe the competitive priorities of:
   - McDonalds
   - BMW
   - A one-hour photo shop
   - Your university
   - A medical specialist
3. Compare make-to-stock, make-to-order, assemble-to-order and engineering-to-order policies. How do the differences between these relate to businesses' competitive priorities?
4. Is there a difference between meeting the specifications of a hamburger in a fast-food restaurant and achieving customer satisfaction?
5. What is the difference between precision and accuracy? How would you apply this concept to a target-shooting competition? Who would win the competition?
6. How is the concept of design for manufacturability inherent in the modern concurrent engineering approach to product design?
7. Explain what is meant by buffers.
8. How can an understanding of the bottleneck scheduling concept influence the cost of production?

Consult the web

A guide to implementing the theory of constraints (TOC): www.dbrmfg.co.nz
Association for Operations Management (APICS): www.apics.org/
Council of Supply Chain Management Professionals (CSCMP): www.cscmp.org/
Supply Chain Operations Reference model: www.supply-chain.org/cs/root/scor_tools_resources/scor_model/scor_model
TOC Southern Africa: www.tocsa.co.za
Wikipedia: http://en.wikipedia.org/wiki/Capacity_planning

Consult the books

Barnes, D. 2008. *Operations Management – An International Perspective*. London: Thomson Learning.
Chase, R. B. and Aquilano, N. J. 1995. *Production and Operations Management – Manufacturing and Service*, 7th edition. IRWIN.
Goldratt, E. M and Cox, J. 1986. *The Goal*. North River Press.
Hanna, M. D. and Newman, W. R. 2007. *Integrated Operations Management – A Supply Chain Perspective*, 2nd edition. Thomson.
Kerin, R. A., Hartley, S. W., Berkowitz, E. N. and Rudelius, W. 2006. *Marketing*, 8th edition. New York: McGraw-Hill/Irwin.
Pycraft, M. Singh, H. and Phihlela, K. 1997. *Operations Management* (South African edition). Pearson Education, South Africa.
Roux, A. 2005. *Everyone's Guide to the South African Economy*, 8th edition. Cape Town: Zebra Press.
Schroeder, R. G. 2008. *Operations Management: Contemporary Concepts and Cases*, 4th edition. McGraw-Hill.
Wild, T. 2002. *Best Practice in Inventory Management*, 2nd edition. Oxford: Butterworth.

Notes

1. Schroeder, R. G. 2008: 4.
2. Ibid.: 8–9.
3. Hanna, M. D. and Newman, W. R. 2007: 5.
4. Barnes, D. 2008: 5–6.
5. Hanna, M. D. and Newman, W. R. 2007: 86–9.
6. Barnes, D. 2008: 22–5.
7. Hanna, M. D. and Newman, W. R. 2007: 37.
8. Barnes, D. 2008: 35–6.
9. Pycraft, M., Singh, H. and Phihlela, K. 1997: 48–9.
10. Barnes, D. 2008: 24–5.
11. Wikipedia. 2008: http://en.wikipedia.org/wiki/Capacity_planning
12. Barnes, D. 2008: 144–6.
13. Hanna, M. D. and Newman, W. R. 2007: 258.
14. Schroeder, R. G. 2008: 43.
15. Hanna, M. D. and Newman, W. R. 2007: 293–4.

16 Pycraft, M., Singh, H. and Phihlela, K. 1997: 343.
17 Barnes, D. 2008: 236–7.
18 Ibid.: 238–9.
19 Ibid.: 273.
20 Pycraft, M., Singh, H. and Phihlela, K. 1997: 741–3.
21 Chase, R. B. and Aquilano, N. J. 1995: 215.
22 Pycraft, M. Singh, H. and Phihlela, K. 1997: 746.
23 Ibid.: 423–4.
24 Wild, T. 2002: 4.
25 Barnes, D. 2008: 257–8.
26 Goldratt, E. M. and Cox, J. 1986.
27 Hanna, M. D. and Newman, W. R. 2007: 698.
28 Ibid.: 702–5.
29 Schroeder, R. G. 2008: 300–1.
30 Chase, R. B. and Aquilano, N. J. 1995: 163.
31 Kerin et al. 2006: 319.

9 Procurement management

W.J. Pienaar

Learning outcomes

After you have studied this chapter, you should be able to:
- explain the difference between purchasing in the narrow sense (to gain ownership of items) and procurement as a holistic process to support the operations of a business;
- define and describe the objectives of procurement management;
- discuss the strategic, tactical and operational roles of procurement in an inter-organisational and intra-organisational sense;
- describe the five principal steps of the procurement process;
- discuss the nature and classification of goods and services that businesses procure;
- give an account of the dimensions of the quality of physical products and service delivery;
- discuss the procurement-related activities that can enhance supply chain success;
- outline the methods used to curb procurement expenditure; and
- give an account of electronic procurement tools and supply a classification of electronic business-to-business marketplaces.

9.1 Introduction

All businesses need inputs of goods, services and information from external suppliers to support their operations. It is impossible for a manufactured product to reach the market without the constituent parts for its processing first having been acquired through numerous transactions. It is axiomatic, therefore, that procurement is an inevitable function within the supply chain of all finished products.

This chapter looks at the objectives of procurement management; the strategic role of procurement in the business context; the various tiers of procurement management; the nature and classification of the various products that are purchased; selecting and managing suppliers; procurement-related activities that enhance supply chain success; procurement cost management; and electronic procurement.

The procurement management process consists of five principal steps:
Step 1: Identifying a procurement need
Step 2: Supplier survey
Step 3: Investigation and assessment of suppliers
Step 4: Choice of supplier(s)
Step 5: Establishing relationships with suppliers.

Steps 2, 3 and 4 collectively form the supplier selection phase.

9.2 The objectives of procurement management

Procurement management is the function responsible for the interface with suppliers. Procurement management has to ensure that the business acquires the right quantities of goods and services at the right time, at the right place, at the right price, to the right quality specification and from the right source(s). These objectives, however, encompass more than meets the eye. For example, the right price may not necessarily be synonymous with the lowest total input cost. Buying from low-price vendors can prove financially damaging. This is evident when the goods are frequently defective; or delivered unacceptably behind schedule; or when the supplier demands immediate payment upon delivery; or – in the case of capital assets – when the vendor is ineffective in fulfilling its post-transactional obligations. Low price is only one facet of the lowest total cost of ownership (TCO) of procured items. Just like the right price, the other 'rights' in the statement above need amplification.

A more encompassing viewpoint of the objectives of procurement management will take into account the following nine objectives:[1]

1. To improve the business's competitive position. Being of strategic importance, procurement management should focus on contributing to the business's strategy, goals and objectives. Procurement managers must identify and exploit opportunities that can enhance revenue, asset management and cost reduction. Procurement should aim to achieve the lowest total cost of supply; gain access to innovative technologies, high-quality goods and services and product design; and negotiate flexible delivery arrangements, quick response times and technical support.
2. To provide an uninterrupted flow of goods and services required to support the business's operations. Stockouts of items and interruption to services can be very costly in terms of lost production, lower revenues and profits and diminished customer goodwill.
3. To minimise inventory investment and loss of revenue. A tactic for ensuring an uninterrupted flow of operations is to hold large inventories. However, carrying excessive inventory requires the use of capital that cannot be invested elsewhere – an opportunity cost that may be even higher than the financially detrimental effect of a stockout.
4. To maintain and improve quality. A certain level of quality is required for each physical product or service input, otherwise the finished product's performance will not meet expectations or will have costly repercussions.
5. To find or develop best-in-class suppliers. Procurement success depends on the ability to link purchasing decisions to business strategy by finding suppliers and working with them to develop continuous improvements. Only if the final vendor selection results in suppliers which are continuously both responsive and responsible will the business obtain the goods and services it needs.
6. To standardise, where appropriate, the inputs and the associated procurement processes. Standardisation often leads to lower risk, lower prices through volume purchase agreements and lower inventory and tracking costs, while maintaining service levels.
7. To procure items and services at the lowest total cost of ownership. Purchased goods and services usually represent the largest share of a business's total costs. Purchase price is often the most convenient method to compare competing vendor proposals. However, the role of procurement management is to acquire the required goods and services at the lowest *total* cost of ownership. This necessitates consideration of other factors (e.g. quality levels; after-sales service; warranty costs; inventory; spare parts requirements; and the salvage value of the item at the end of its service period). In the long term, these exert a greater cost impact on the business than solely the original purchase price.
8. To achieve cooperative, productive internal relationships. Procurement management will not accomplish its goals and objectives without effective cooperation with the appropriate individuals elsewhere in the business.
9. To accomplish organisational procurement objectives at the lowest possible operating cost and as efficiently as possible. Achieving business objectives successfully requires financial sacrifice over the short and long term.

> By way of brief summary of these nine points, we can define procurement management as that part of supply chain management that plans, implements and controls the efficient, effective acquisition of all raw materials, semi-finished goods, finished goods, services and information in order to support the core operations and ancillary activities of the organisation.

9.3 The strategic role of procurement within a business

Procurement management needs to ensure the efficient and effective sourcing of the inputs needed to conduct the business. In order to fulfil this strategic requirement, procurement management should identify and exploit opportunities to ensure an uninterrupted flow of inputs to support the business's operations. These inputs may be:
- the raw materials, intermediate goods, services and information that are needed as feedstock for the products the business produces;
- the finished goods, services and information required as marketing inputs if the business purchases items for resale; and
- the capital goods, moving assets, consumables, services and information needed to equip and support the business's management, administration, ancillary and other secondary activities.

The contemporary strategic procurement management focus is on, first, fostering lasting relationships with existing and newly recruited suppliers to help ensure ongoing access to external markets, with a view to contributing to long-term revenue enhancement and, second, on total expenditure over the long term, which implies the maintenance of an integrated, interactive relationship with the other management functions of the business in order to enhance efficiency and effectiveness in their ongoing business activities.

9.3.1 Access to external markets

A business can gain contact with the external market by establishing a network of informants and by appointing suppliers – both locally and from abroad. External informants supply the business with information regarding emerging fashion trends; innovations; product developments; new kinds of materials; new technology; and potential suppliers.

The business should select and develop the external suppliers in such a way that they will contribute to its success. The suppliers can be incorporated into the activities of the firm, which may lead to substantial cost and time savings in the development of new products. An example is the automotive industry, where the computer network of each subsystem of manufacturers is linked to those of their major external suppliers. When the principal design office of a vehicle manufacturer designs a new vehicle, the designers of the different components are connected to the computer system of the principal design office. They can design vehicle subsystems (for example, the auto-electrical system, the brake system etc) simultaneously with the principal vehicle design process. This can lead to savings in design and development time without the designers of the components having to be present in the principal design office.

9.3.2 Intra-firm management relations

The procurement function has an integrated and interactive relationship with all the functional entities within the business. One should consider what the procurement entity can contribute to the ongoing activities of other entities and what these entities can, in turn, contribute to the mission of the procurement entity. The procurement function is a support function: it supports and supplements the activities of the other functions within the business. The procurement process is initiated by a user entity determining and specifying a procurement need. This is the first step in the broadly defined five-step procurement process (see Section 9.1). Consequently, the procurement section receives its requisitions for inputs to be acquired from the other business entities.

Firstly, all the entities within a business need to be equipped with capital goods (such as electronic equipment, computerware, furniture, copying equipment, telecommunication equipment, vehicles, handling equipment etc.), which are purchased, rented or leased through the procurement entity. Secondly, internal entities require movable assets of a non-capital nature (tools, small office equipment, accessories etc.)

and operational consumables (such as stationery) to perform their activities, also requisitioned via the procurement entity. Thirdly, the business may decide to outsource certain non-core activities to professional service providers through collaboration with the procurement entity. These services may include financing, warehousing and inventory management, transport, vocational training, expert advice and consultation. Fourthly, the entire business requires information. The success of any supply chain is based on the comprehensiveness, quality, accuracy and timeous availability of information, such as information on inventory levels, lead times and suppliers. The procurement entity fulfils the role of acquiring the appropriate information system to enable other entities in the business to perform successfully.

The ongoing activities of the procurement entity are dependent on support and inputs from the other entities in the business. For example, procurement is informed by marketing of forecasted the sales volumes of the various product ranges for which inputs need to be obtained.

In cooperation with the manufacturing entity details are obtained of the specific form and volumes of input material required for production runs, and of the required time pattern of arrival of inputs to match production schedules.

The finance entity plays a role in negotiating the financial settlement and payment agreements of inputs from vendors. To minimise the cash-to-cash cycle time within a business, the finance entity negotiates the most lenient credit arrangements with the business vendors, while endeavouring to fix debit arrangements with customers as firmly as healthy business relationships permit. Furthermore, the finance entity is involved in determining the size of the procurement budget (to pay for production inputs, merchandise for resale and the procurement of inputs for its ancillary needs), and whether inputs ought to be purchased, hired or leased.

The human-resources entity is often responsible – or co-responsible – for arranging the staffing needs of the procurement entity. These may include recruitment, appointing, placing and developing employees, and administering the procurement entity's day-to-day staff matters in harmony with the business's mission.

9.4 Tiers of procurement management

9.4.1 Strategic procurement management

Strategic management, or long-term planning, involves the visualisation, even amidst uncertainties, of what a business wishes to achieve in future. The formulation of long-term goals and objectives forms the basis of strategic management. Specific, practical objectives regarding time frames and quantitative terms are then derived from the business's overall long-term goals and objectives on the tactical (medium-term) and operational (short-term) levels.

Strategic procurement planning should take place at top management level, as it involves long-term planning in line with the owners' vision and mission. Long-term planning carries a high risk, therefore it is the responsibility of procurement management to plan proactively. The strategic procurement objectives should enable the business to:

- ensure the availability (at competitive prices) of the inputs needed to produce or sell the kind of end products that the owners of the business have identified for their business;
- be suitably located to gain easy, efficient access to its physical resources without jeopardising the effectiveness with which it interfaces with its customers; (a manufacturer of products that lose a large proportion of their mass during production would be wise to locate its business close to its suppliers and resources);
- decide on the size and shape of the organisational structure of the procurement entity, and the level of authority or seniority that will be assigned to procurement management;
- institute procedures through which precisely specified needs are reported, for example, formal requisitions from user entities and bills of materials generated through the material requirement system, which support the manufacturing process (see Chapter 4, Section 4.3); and

- select new suppliers and develop and maintain long-standing and mutually beneficial relationships with them.

9.4.2 Tactical procurement management

Tactical procurement management is typically executed at middle-management level. It involves planning for the medium term, which includes implementation of the procurement organisation that strategic management has decided upon, and coordination of the procurement operations. Tactical procurement objectives include:
- conducting ongoing logistical analysis, including trade-off analysis, to ensure that the most economical levels of inventory are maintained; the objective is to ensure a sufficient and timeous flow of procured items to support operations, while avoiding excessive inventory volumes that tie up capital that could be invested productively in alternative opportunities;
- conducting informant networking about new products, materials development and technological innovations;
- studying the various inventory-control systems available in the market and implementing the most appropriate one for the business;
- studying the most appropriate materials-flow systems and implementing the best one;
- receiving and processing intra-organisational requisitions and bills of materials to ensure the continuation of operations (see Chapter 4, Section 4.3);
- advising top management (in conjunction with the finance entity) on entering into contracts with chosen suppliers; and
- developing current and new suppliers.

9.4.3 Operational procurement management

Operational procurement management comprises short-term planning and the execution, monitoring and control of procurement operations. Operational procurement management is conducted by lower management. Monitoring and control refer to the efforts of management to achieve the formulated objectives and standards for procurement activities. Certain performance boundaries within which the business can operate are determined. Whenever the performance of procurement actions deviates significantly from the acceptable performance range, management should find reasons for these deviations and rectify the problem. For example, usually only a certain proportion of orders in a procurement department should be backorders. The moment the number of backorders exceeds the stated maximum, management must determine the cause and solve the problem.

The operational objectives are based on the tactical planning performed and guidelines provided by middle management. These objectives are usually firmly stated and in quantitative terms. The objectives of operational procurement are to:
- conduct inventory analyses and stock-taking;
- reduce inventories through scheduling;
- maintain and improve relationships with suppliers;
- assist suppliers by supplying technical and administrative support;
- communicate operations schedules with suppliers and order on time;
- pay supplier invoices on time (but not too early);
- adhere to suppliers' contract clauses; and
- coordinate incoming traffic with a view to receiving procured inputs on time and returning goods that do not meet requirements.

9.5 The nature and classification of purchased products

9.5.1 Product variety

No business can escape entirely from the need (identified in Sections 9.1, 9.2 and 9.3) to procure inputs. Even if a business endeavours to self-produce all the inputs that it presently purchases, leases or hires because of direct need, it will be unavoidably trapped in a lower tier of procurement – procuring the indirect inputs to enable it to produce its directly needed inputs itself. Consequently, one can identify the need to acquire an input as the first step in the five-step procurement process.

A variety of inputs, or products, can be procured by a business. Products are divided into goods and services. Goods, in turn, can be grouped according to the stage they have reached in the series of processes within the supply chain of a product, extending from primary production to consumption, or end-use. These groups are raw materials, semi-finished goods and finished goods:

- Raw materials are the primary output of agriculture (e.g. crop harvests and products stemming from livestock); forestry (e.g. timber); fishing; mining (e.g. ore, minerals, coal and crude oil); and water sources (e.g. for use in irrigation, cooling processes, water-suspended products and the production of beverages).
- Semi-finished goods are in the process of being converted from raw materials to finished goods, but are not yet in a form for consumption or use.
- Finished goods have been processed (e.g. manufactured and assembled) into the final form required for consumption or use.

In a product's supply chain, raw materials are generally procured by other primary producers and intermediate manufacturers. Semi-finished goods (goods-in-process) are generally procured by manufacturers that transform the goods-in-process into finished (manufactured) goods. Semi-finished and finished goods are the productive output of the secondary (industrial) sector of the economy.

Finished goods can be divided into final goods and intermediate goods. Final goods are used by consumers (rather than by businesses as inputs for production processes), such as clothing, foodstuffs and beverages. Final goods are also known as consumer goods and are generally procured by marketing intermediaries (distributors, wholesalers, retailers etc.) in the outbound or physical distribution portion of a product's supply chain for downstream resale to consumers.

Intermediate goods are used in the production of other goods and services, rather than for final consumption. Examples of the latter are finished vehicle spare parts (e.g. car batteries) and capital goods (such as durable handling equipment, commercial vehicles and workshop machinery). Intermediate goods are also known as producer goods because the purchaser is a supply chain member in the inbound (materials management) portion of a product's supply chain. Goods can often be used for dual purposes, for example, raw materials, like water and coal, used in the making of steel and the generation of electricity, are producer goods, while coal used to fuel a furnace in a private home, and water consumed domestically are consumer goods. Similarly, finished goods (e.g. cars purchased by a business for commercial use and cars bought by private individuals) can be both intermediate and final goods. Where the classification of goods into raw materials, semi-finished goods and finished goods is a technical one, the distinction between producer goods and consumer goods refers to the use of the goods. This chapter is primarily concerned with goods procurement for business purposes, often referred to as business-to-business (B2B) goods.

Services are non-physical, or, intangible, products. They are highly perishable and are consumed immediately upon production, therefore services cannot be transported to a place of consumption elsewhere or stored for later consumption. The client is part of the service process. Therefore, the response time (order lead time) of a service is very short: if a service is not consumed immediately upon delivery it cannot be recovered or used later. To illustrate, a cargo aircraft that has flown an empty flight can never recover this under-utilisation.

Services are the productive outputs of the tertiary sector of the economy. Examples are financial services (such as loan funding, hire-purchase funding and lease funding) provided by lenders and financiers; transport services provided by professional goods carriers; logistics services provided by third-party logistics service providers; vocational training provided by training providers; and professional or expert advice provided by specialist consultants.

9.5.2 Quality of physical products

Much of the service emphasis in supply chain management is to consistently deliver physical products undamaged, on time and with all the attributes necessary to conform to customer service requirements. However, in the context of physical product form, customers often have different viewpoints of a particular item's quality features. The quality of a physical product is often judged in terms of the following seven competitive dimensions:[2] performance, reliability, durability, conformance, features, aesthetics and serviceability. These are each discussed in the following sections.

9.5.2.1 Performance

From a procurement viewpoint an obvious aspect of quality is how well a product actually performs in comparison to how it was designed to perform. For example, computers may be judged in terms of their processing speed. The performance level of a physical product is usually objectively measurable – it can be compared between different items and models. However, an item may possess multiple performance features, which complicates performance comparison. Computers are not judged only by their speed, but by other capabilities, such as their hard-disk capacity and range of applications.

9.5.2.2 Reliability

This refers to the likelihood that an item will continually maintain its ability to perform at a given output level. As with performance, reliability is a quality feature that is objectively measurable, such as the number of a certain item's malfunctions encountered during a specified period.

9.5.2.3 Durability

Although related to reliability, durability is a different quality feature. It refers to the longevity of an item and is usually expressed as the actual or expected length of service life in terms of the time or volume of output. For example, the expected technical service life of a vehicle can be judged to be 12 years or 240 000 km. Through more robust design features this period may be extended, thereby most likely increasing customers' judgement of its quality. However, service life may also be extended through preventive maintenance and effective repairs.

9.5.2.4 Conformance

Conformance refers to whether a supplier's product meets the exact design specifications. Conformance is often measured by judging a manufacturer's relative quantity of scrap, remanufacturing and defects within its attempted output. For example, if 98 per cent of the supplier's products meet the design specifications, it performs at a 2 per cent defect rate.

9.5.2.5 Features

Customers often judge the quality of a product solely on the basis of the number of extra features (accessories) it possesses in addition to its primary function. For example, a vehicle model with additional features, such as speed control, a factory-installed security system, safety airbags and concealed crash roll bars, might be judged to be of higher quality than the basic model. However, the more accessories a product possesses, the higher the likelihood that other quality attributes may be lacking, such as reliability and durability.

9.5.2.6 Aesthetics

The visual appearance of, and types of materials used in, a product often influence customers in their judgement of quality. In the procurement of production inputs by businesses that target market segments in which popular fashion trends are of lesser concern (often in product supply chains with a strong pull orientation where the end-users have a low price sensitivity), one needs to take account of the fact that the users of such products are strongly influenced by aesthetics, and prefer products that are made of choice-grade or sought-after materials. In vehicles, for example, the use of leather rather than cloth for seats, and wood rather than plastic for panelling are aesthetic features that typically imply quality.

9.5.2.7 Serviceability

Serviceability means the ease with which a product malfunction can be repaired or rectified. It is an important quality aspect for many customers of capital products especially. For example, equipment that contains diagnostic ability, which warns users that a malfunction is imminent, affords users the opportunity for proactiveness. Ideally, easy serviceability should allow the user to solve a malfunction with minimal cost and operational disruption.

Like beauty, quality is in the eye of the beholder; it is the customers who are the final judges of product quality, as they perceive a product's performance and determine how efficiently and effectively it fulfils the purpose it was acquired for. The total quality of a physical product is an aggregate of these seven quality dimensions outlined above; and total quality is determined by how effectively this mix matches the quality composition desired by the procuring business, or how this composition is perceived by the end-customer. The circumstances that prevail where a product is used and the value judgements of its end-customers result in the composition of its required quality dimensions. These are the factors that lend direction to the procuring entity when formulating its input specifications to the supplier.

9.5.3 Service quality

The various dimensions of customer service are discussed in Chapter 2, Section 2.4 (see page 25). That section describes how in the supply of physical products there are two accompanying, essential service domains (customer service and logistics service), the quality of which, together with the inherent characteristics and quality composition of the physical product, helps to determine the value of the purchased physical product delivered to the customer. The first service domain in the supply of physical products is their required transaction service. This is defined according to when the transaction between a supplier and a customer takes place, namely the pre-transaction, transaction and post-transaction components of customer service (described in Chapter 2, Section 2.4.1). The second service domain is the logistics service provided in a product's supply chain. The determinants of the quality of logistics service are:
- suitability;
- accessibility and market area coverage;
- goods security;
- transaction or order lead time;
- reliability; and
- flexibility.

The quality aspects of logistics service delivery within procurement management are presented in Chapter 2, Sections 2.4.1.2 to 2.4.2.3; the quality aspects of transport service (as a subset of logistical service) are presented in Chapter 17, Section 17.2.2.3.

9.6 Selecting and developing suppliers

Suppliers are present throughout the whole supply chain – from the producers of primary goods and manufacturers of semi-finished and finished goods, to marketing intermediaries, like distributors, wholesalers and retailers, to service providers. It is necessary for the focal business in every supply chain to collaborate with and coordinate the performance of the suppliers in their chain effectively. This can be done by selecting and appointing the most suitable suppliers and then forming long-standing collaborative relationships with them.

9.6.1 Steps in the supplier selection process

The following three steps can be followed in the selection of suppliers:
Step 1: Supplier survey
Step 2: Supplier investigation and assessment
Step 3: Supplier choice

These three steps constitute the second, third and fourth steps in the broad five-step procurement process explained in Section 9.1.

9.6.1.1 Supplier survey

In the survey phase potential suppliers are identified. A search is conducted to find suppliers that are likely to be able to supply the inputs that the business needs for its operations. This likelihood is based on the apparent similarity of vendor outputs in relation to the type of inputs required by the surveying purchaser. This survey needs to be conducted thoroughly, as the alternatives for not finding a suitable supplier are to self-produce the required inputs, or not to embark on the business venture at all. In many cases, suitable suppliers will be found abroad – especially where capital goods with advanced custom-made features are concerned. Such items are often manufactured in large, developed economies where an effective market for them exists.

The following sources can be used in the search for potential suppliers:
- Trade journals. These often contain indexed sections of different industry sectors.
- Trade registers and directories (e.g. the publications of Braby's Directories).
- The Internet (especially supplier websites that are registered with search engines).
- Telephone directories (e.g. the *Yellow Pages*).
- Suppliers' sales personnel and field representatives.
- Suppliers' catalogues, price lists, mail promotions and advertisements.
- Trade shows and exhibitions.

The purchasers of fast-moving consumer goods, standard domestic appliances and standard furniture (i.e. products of pure push-oriented supply chains) often make use of, firstly, computer-aided, vendor-managed procurement with input from suppliers' sales personnel, and are made aware of new products and promotions through the field representatives of suppliers, and, secondly, from supplier catalogues and standard price lists.

The purchasers of customised consumerware (mostly model clothing, stylised and modular furniture, electronic equipment and computers and recreational vehicles – i.e. the products of combined push-pull-oriented supply chains), typically make use of trade journals, registers and directories, the Internet and trade exhibitions in their search for suppliers.

Apart from merely identifying possible suppliers whose range of outputs may cater for the prospective procuring business's needs, the survey stage can go one step further and identify all parties that are interested in being considered for supplier assessment. In the case of standard items in a push-oriented supply chain, the only required information at this stage may be whether the vendor is capable of supplying and willing to supply certain volumes of standard products at certain destinations at certain times, and a preliminary indication of its price and payment conditions. In the case of non-standard (differentiated) items, more initial information might be required, as desired production lots might become smaller and more careful goods treatment may be required. The likely approach is to establish whether suppliers of non-standard items are willing to be listed for investigation and assessment upon exact product specifications that will be furnished at a later time.

A business can also make use of an open pre-qualification tender system, which allows suppliers to tender in response to advertisements and open invitations in the media and on the Internet. The solicitation of vendor response through an open tender or on invitation is usually used in a pull-oriented supply chain where the objective is to procure specialised and custom-made products. This form of vendor identification is like a form of reverse marketing. After obtaining all the relevant information, a list must be drafted with the names, addresses and the relevant information to enable an investigation and assessment of possible suppliers.

9.6.1.2 Supplier investigation and assessment

Once a list has been compiled of the vendors who, first, supply a similar form of inputs to those that are mission-specific to the procuring business, and, second, have indicated during the survey phase a willingness to supply such inputs to the business, the investigation and assessment phase follows. This phase is initiated by an exchange of information. First, exact product specification or tender documents are furnished to identify potential suppliers and preferred bidders. Second, sufficient assessable information should be made available to the investigating purchaser. The purchasing business should consider the following factors when assessing potential suppliers:
- Specific production capability
- Corporate standing
- Specific logistical supply capability

Specific production capability

This refers to whether a supplier has:
- the appropriate facilities and equipment;
- the technical expertise;
- access to the factors of production, coupled with effective resource procurement arrangements;
- healthy labour relations;
- capacity for technological research and product development;
- the ability to supply maintenance and technical after-sales service; and
- adequate operational controls to supply the procuring business with:
  - the specific form of physical goods;
  - to the exact quality specification;
  - at the desired time; and
  - in required quantity sustainably over the specified period.

A failure to identify at least one supplier that passes the assessor's technical standards test terminates the selection process.

Corporate standing

Having found technically capable suppliers of the specific item(s), the assessment proceeds. Given the impact that a supplier can have on a procuring business's performance and the sustainability of its operations, the next selection criteria to assess are firstly the likelihood that it will remain in business to fulfil the promises it makes, and secondly whether it is the kind of organisation that the purchaser would like to be seen doing business with. In this regard, the following supplier factors are important:
- Reputation
- Quality of management
- Financial stability and viability
- Corporate image

With respect to the supplier's reputation, present and past customers should be able to provide first-hand information. It may be difficult to investigate the quality of the business's management. However, companies that are listed by JSE Limited[3] are easier to investigate, as they must provide financial reporting publicly. Extensive business details and performance measurements of each JSE-listed company (and many non-listed companies) appear in the data register of McGregor BFA.[4] The McGregor reports are diversified, of a high standard and supply detailed information on the financial results and business performance of companies. In some cases, visits to a potential supplier's business operations should give the investigators an insight into the quality of management and operational housekeeping. Discussions with the personnel of the supplier can be an effective source of information.

A supplier whose financial position is precarious will most probably not be able to guarantee continued supply of its products. The purchaser also runs the risk of the supplier becoming insolvent at an inconvenient time. Any serious potential vendor should be willing to disclose its most recent audited financial statements, annual report and a qualified statement on its deemed goodwill to a prospective long-term customer.

The potential supplier's labour relations are of great importance, as poor labour relations can lead to operational stoppages, erratic supply and inconsistent product quality. Sources of information for investigation are the supplier's labour strike records and its labour turnover records.

In addition to a supplier's annual report, website and press releases, the archives of the printed business media and news-clipping agents could be information sources on a supplier's adherence to sound ethical and good corporate governance principles (like those proposed in the King codes of corporate conduct); its approach with respect to disadvantaged groups; and its support of charities.

The strategic importance of the item(s) to be procured; the anticipated duration and monetary size of the procurement agreement; the complexity of the supply process; and the amount of organisational interaction that will be involved will determine the closeness, degree of mutual trust and the nature of the supply chain alliance to be established. In the case of an intimate long-term business alliance it is advisable that the prospective supplier voluntarily provides an exhaustive disclosure of all the relevant information – in auditable and verifiable format – to assist the procuring business to reach a trustworthy and well-informed decision.

In addition to evaluating positive attributes of potential suppliers, one needs to take into account any possible aspects that would disqualify a supplier. For example, in the case of an input forming a relatively large part of a patented product, which requires a supplier to share confidential intellectual property of the purchaser, it would most likely preclude that supplier from also being a vendor to the purchaser's direct business competitors. Therefore, with the possible procurement of strategically sensitive and specialised items, the investigation and assessment phase might be concluded with an analysis of the strengths, weaknesses, opportunities and threats – or SWOT analysis – of the potential suppliers.

Logistical supply capability

Once the production capability and corporate standing of potential vendors have been established, the logistical supply capability of the candidates needs to be determined.

Over and above the capability of storing, handling, transporting and containing the required quantity of items safely and securely, logistical supply capability refers to the ability to deliver items timeously. This concerns, firstly, delivery (replenishment) lead time; secondly, delivery reliability; and, thirdly, delivery flexibility. As delivery lead time increases, or delivery frequency decreases, the volume of buffer (safety) stock that needs to be held by the purchaser grows. This increase is proportional to the square root of delivery lead time (see Chapter 10 for more information). Delivery lead time has a direct bearing on the delivery frequency and the lot sizes a purchasing business will require. With increasing lot sizes, the cycle stock at the purchasing business also increases; consequently the inventory-holding cost also increases. (See Chapter 10 for further information on inventory management.) Assessing suppliers' delivery lead time and frequency performance enables the purchasing business to evaluate and compare the impact of all suppliers' performance on the cost of carrying buffer and cycle stock.

Reliability of supply is determined by the record of the supplier to consistently deliver the purchaser's inputs punctually. Consistent punctuality translates into consistent lead times. In its investigation, a prospective purchasing business should take into account a vendor's reliability (e.g. by interviewing customers of the supplier).

Delivery flexibility is the proven ability, readiness and willingness to effectively handle variations in delivery volumes, specific delivery times and delivery locations, without any significant loss of overall efficiency. The internal flexibility of a supplier is the ability to apply corrective procedural steps to preserve its service reliability and to keep its promises to a purchasing customer, while external service flexibility is the ability to efficiently and effectively accommodate ad hoc and unforeseen service requests from a purchasing client (see Section 9.6.1.3 and Chapter 17, Section 17.4.3).

9.6.1.3 Supplier choice

During the choice phase, interviews and arms-length talks are held with the potential suppliers that have been included in the prioritised shortlist of candidates in order to choose the most suitable one. The supplier that conforms best to the requirements stated in the investigation and assessment phase at an acceptable total cost of product ownership is chosen (see Sections 9.2 and 9.3). The purchasing business can decide to purchase similar items from more than one supplier to ensure that the required input is always available at an acceptable price and in the required volumes. This is known as dual (or horizontally split) sourcing.

In addition to dual sourcing, supplier choice and appointment can also provide a vertically split supply configuration. This can take place in the following ways:
- A supplier is appointed that conducts both the production and logistical aspects of the sourced item(s).
- The item is purchased from a producer, but all (or most) of the logistical arrangements are procured from a third-party logistics service provider.
- The item is purchased from a producer, and all (or most) of the logistical arrangements are taken care of by the purchasing business.

Whatever vertical supply arrangement is chosen, the procuring business should keep its options open to have deliveries expedited should they

not take place on time. The coordination of incoming traffic with a view to rectifying the time performance of the party responsible for deliveries could entail any of the following:
- Tracking and tracing
- Expediting and cross-docking of in-transit shipments
- Shipment diversion and reconsignment
- Making use of in-transit privileges
- Demurrage and detention

These measures are discussed in Chapter 17, Section 17.4.3. It is sometimes a plausible option to assign the duties of incoming traffic coordination to a fourth-party logistics service provider, who may conduct this coordination effectively from within the procuring business's facilities.

9.6.2 Establishing relationships with suppliers

The establishment of relationships with suppliers is the fifth step in the broad procurement process. (see Section 9.1) Procurement management should foster lasting relationships with the business's suppliers to motivate them to provide the goods as and when required. It is desirable for a business to be in a sound long-term alliance with its suppliers, as this will potentially enhance mutually beneficial interaction and cooperation. Formal partnerships with vendors can ensure the continuous flow of goods from the raw material suppliers through to the end-users. Inter-business partnerships help silo-type functional barriers to disappear, thereby reducing the reaction time of a business's supply to any change in demand. Shared information enables cooperative parties in the supply chain to reach common goals more easily, such as responding quickly to a change in demand to ensure lean and flexible supply (see Section 9.6.1.3). All the operational and transactional activities that are described in Section 9.4.3 can also be grouped as a constituent subset within the supplier relationship step of the procurement process.

A significant trend in the business world today is the tendency to outsource. Outsourcing enables businesses to focus on their core competencies and to outsource secondary, or ancillary, activities to expert businesses that possess the necessary know-how to avoid what are known as foreign-territory pitfalls. It may also be the case that a supplier through its larger size manages to gain better economies of scale and other efficiencies than the procuring entity itself can achieve. For example, transport operations often lie outside the area of expertise or competitive advantage of a manufacturer, namely industrial legislation, labour conventions and trade-union practices. Similarly, professional freight carriers may achieve better vehicle utilisation and freight consolidation opportunities through lower transport unit costs than an ancillary operator.

9.7 Procurement-related activities that enhance supply chain success

There are a number of procurement-related activities that can contribute to supply chain efficiency and effectiveness. The most important are:
- just-in-time (JIT) scheduling;
- value analysis; and
- coordinating incoming traffic.

9.7.1 Just-in-time scheduling

JIT scheduling is common in business operations. In JIT manufacturing the systems are coordinated to provide the business with raw materials, goods-in-process and finished intermediate goods inputs just before they are needed for manufacturing. The effects of this are that minimum inventory is carried and waste is reduced. In the case of wholesalers and retailers, the JIT system reduces the monetary amount invested in inventory. An effective JIT system, therefore, improves the efficiency of the supply chain. For more information on JIT see Chapter 8.

9.7.2 Value analysis

Value analysis is the examination by a task team, think tank or committee of the design, functioning and cost of goods and services. The purpose of value analysis is to reduce costs by improving efficiency. This can be done by changing the design of the product, by replacing a component with an alternative new innovation, by eliminating the need for a component or procedure currently in use, or by changing the source of supply. The quality and reliability of the finished product should, however, be better than they were before the change.

Members of the following areas normally serve on committees that conduct value analyses: procurement, marketing, product design, operations management, finance and costing and sometimes also the supplier, in the case of a closely allied or integrated supply chain partner. The committee members must cooperate closely to formulate the best design for a product. Only certain products should be chosen for value analysis. These must be products:

- on which a substantial amount if money is spent annually;
- of an intricate design;
- of which large quantities are purchased;
- with a high percentage of waste and remanufacturing costs; and
- which form parts of other components (intermediate goods).

Posing critical questions about the goods or service forms the basis of value analysis. The so-called 'ten tests for value' consist of the following ten questions:

1. Does the use of the item hold any advantage for the business?
2. Is the TCO of a procured item less than the value it has for the business?
3. Must the item have all the existing features?
4. Is there a better item than the existing one which can be used for the same purpose?
5. Can the business use a better item than the existing one?
6. Can a cheaper, standardised item be used?
7. Is the best manufacturing process being used?
8. Is the cost of procured materials, labour, overheads and all other inputs, plus a reasonable profit close to the potential value of the item, or can it be sold at a higher price?
9. Is there another reliable supplier who can supply a similar item at a lower price?
10. Is there another buyer who buys the same item at a lower price?

9.7.3 Coordinating incoming traffic

The aim of coordinating incoming traffic is to have physical inputs delivered as closely as possible to the originally arranged delivery times, and to arrange for a change of a shipment's place of delivery to a new destination should an unforeseen stockout occur at the new place of delivery (see Section 9.6.1.3 and Chapter 17, Section 17.4.3).

9.8 Procurement cost management

The cost of input procurement forms a relatively large part of the total expenditure of any business. Saving money through effective cost control has a leverage effect: the net profit of the business increases. Proven tactics to reduce procurement costs are expenditure-reduction programmes; speculative buying; forward buying; price-change management; volume contracts; and stockless purchasing.

9.8.1 Expenditure-reduction programmes

Expenditure-reduction programmes should continually form part of business policy in order to instil a culture of efficiency. If top management does not initiate expenditure-reduction schemes themselves they should be seen to support these programmes. The results of the programmes must be monitored and controlled continuously to ensure that their goals are met. For example, the size of expenditure reduction should always exceed any consequential drop in income. The most important expenditure-reduction schemes are value analysis; supplier development; volume buying; reduction of waste; and standardisation.

9.8.2 Speculative buying

Speculative buying, or lucrative hedging, takes place when goods that are not meant for internal consumption are purchased with the aim of reselling them at a lucrative profit at a later date. For example, a sales representative of a liquor distributor makes the following offer on a certain kind of brandy to liquor stores: the liquor stores get one free case for every five bought. The cost price of the liquor will increase the following month. This special offer ends one week before the price increase.

The management of a liquor store may decide to buy, for instance, 100 cases of the liquor. When the price increases, a substantial profit can be made. The business will only do this speculative buying if the money to be made through the price increase and the special discount is substantially more than the additional warehousing, inventory-carrying and transport costs.

9.8.3 Forward buying

Forward buying is when a business enterprise anticipates future shortages of its raw materials, which may lead to production interruption and price increases. A furniture manufacturer, for instance, may be aware of a possible industrial action at the sawmill that provides it with timber. It may then take precautions by purchasing the timber needed for a specific period in advance. Businesses that use a JIT system are more inclined to buy forward, as a shortage of raw materials can disrupt their operations.

9.8.4 Price-change management

Procurement managers should continually challenge supplier price increases to ensure lowest prices. Long-term and medium-term contracts must be negotiated thoroughly. Suppliers need to be informed of the negative effect that exorbitant price increases will have on the finances of their customers. Sales may also be affected negatively by price increases. Price increases can be mitigated through shorter delivery lead times, by using more efficient, state-of-the-art technology and by using inventory management models, such as JIT and material requirements planning (MRP).

9.8.5 Volume contracts

Volume contracts can limit the effect of price increases over a period. The different sections of a business can combine their purchases in order to reduce the purchase prices and administrative costs. Through boosted purchasing power a buyer can negotiate with the supplier for cumulative volume discounts on successive purchases through the year. Businesses using JIT systems can also benefit from these discounts – despite the fact that they buy smaller volumes at a time, they purchase frequently.

In the case of non-cumulative discounts the price is based on the monetary value of each order. Suppliers can quote annually, or they can fix the future prices through contracts. Bigger orders lead to lower prices if they bring about savings in the transport, administrative, and order costs, which, combined, offset the increased inventory cost. This arrangement can be viewed as a proactive, but mutually agreed upon, form of hedging.

9.8.6 Stockless purchasing

With stockless purchasing the business does not carry inventories of purchased materials. This reduces material-related costs, such as transport, inventory, and administrative costs, as well as the purchase price per item. This purchasing method is especially suited to frequently bought, low-priced materials of which the administrative and carrying costs are relatively high in comparison to the unit prices. Based on contractual agreement between the suppliers and their customers, a predetermined volume of items is purchased over a specified period. These items are then delivered as required by the purchaser for its operations, so that inventory holding by the purchaser is eliminated.

Integrated supply is an important part of stockless purchasing. A business may decide to order all its stationery, for instance, from one supplier because better prices can often be negotiated with a single supplier rather than dealing with multiple suppliers. In the case of a single supplier, the purchasing and delivery costs are reduced with time.

9.9 Electronic procurement

The materials management function of business logistics can and does benefit from the efficient procurement of goods and services through e-business, especially the Internet.

The Internet supports the purchasing process through electronic catalogues, electronic auctions, electronic marketplaces, and on-line requests for quotes (RFQs). Businesses can also use the Internet to develop collaboration relationships.[5]

The main market tools for e-procurement are electronic catalogues, electronic exchanges and electronic auctions, as explained in the following sections.

9.9.1 Electronic catalogues

Electronic catalogues function in much the same way as traditional paper catalogues. Items normally have fixed prices, but discounts and negotiations are also possible. Although various catalogues reside on different websites, search engines can be used to facilitate selection among different items and different suppliers. The customer makes use of so-called one-stop shopping by browsing and searching in the catalogue for different items from different suppliers through product descriptions, images and technical specifications. Various products can be chosen and placed into a virtual shopping basket. At the end of the selection process, the customer confirms the order and makes the payment. The suppliers can update catalogue information in real time to ensure that the latest products and prices are accurately reflected.

9.9.2 Electronic exchanges

Electronic exchanges function in much the same way as traditional stock exchanges, with buyers and sellers bidding and asking for the same products and services in real time. Prices are not fixed, but determined by general conditions of demand and supply. These exchanges are mostly used for commodities, sufficiently standardised items and large transaction volumes.

9.9.3 Electronic auctions

E-auctions fall into two main categories: direct auctions (one seller and many offering buyers, who drive the price up) and reverse auctions (one buyer and many bidding sellers, who drive the price down). It is also possible to distinguish between open and sealed auctions. The former is conducted in real time, where bidders follow the auction and raise their bids. The latter is generally conducted through a process of sealed bids, with the best bid winning the auction. This sealed process could, however, occur more than once.

The benefits of e-procurement derive from the fact that the entire procurement process becomes more effective, as Table 9.1 shows.[6] E-procurement reduces manual interfaces (and consequently time and paperwork), and automates the process of finding suppliers.

Table 9.1 The benefits of e-procurement

Benefit source	Purchased unit cost reduction	Process improvement	Intangibles
Software-related benefits	• increased use of price agreements	• reduction in transaction costs, procurement and accounts • lead-time reduction	• availability of procurement data • simplification of user interface • harmonisation of systems
Process change benefits	• strategic sourcing leverage • compliance enforcement • better demand management	• logistics/inventory cost reduction • simplification of the control system	• automated controls and audit trails • end-user efficiency • increased customer satisfaction

E-procurement of materials for the manufacturing process is still in its development phase. However, various large corporations have formed joint ventures to create industry-specific B2B marketplaces on the Internet where they can source both maintenance, repairs and operating (MRO) supplies and raw materials by tying all their suppliers into one marketplace.

Currently, most of the opportunities for cost saving with the Internet exist in the area of MRO items. Desktop purchasing (DP) – a term for purchasing software applications – is used for the procurement of goods with low strategic importance and a high potential for automation. Given the fact that these items can make up as much as 40 per cent of the total operating expenses, even a small saving in procurement costs can have a significant impact on earnings.[7]

9.9.3.1 E-procurement: the example of P&O Nedlloyd

Perhaps the most enthusiastic e-procurement client in the shipping industry has been P&O Nedlloyd. This company bought two years' worth of paint supplies through an Internet auction in 2000.[8] At the time, the paint contract was, in terms of value, the largest single shipping purchase ever made via the Internet. P&O Nedlloyd estimated that it has saved 15 per cent by buying this way.

The paint auction was structured so that many factors were resolved off-line first. Coverage rates, payment terms and delivery ports were negotiated during an off-line process that lasted six weeks. Only then did the on-line auction take place. The winning bidder was awarded 60 per cent of P&O Nedlloyd's paint business, while two other suppliers shared the rest.

The number of B2B marketplaces is increasing rapidly, while the marketplaces themselves are growing. These marketplaces provide an opportunity for huge value creation through the reduction in transaction costs, improved supply chain visibility, and the more efficient allocation of supply and demand. Three kinds of B2B marketplaces are formed based on industries, products or functions.[9] These are vertical, horizontal, and functional marketplaces.

9.9.4 Vertical marketplaces

A vertical B2B marketplace is industry-focused and revolves around a specific industry sector (see Figure 9.1). Such a marketplace comprises a wide range of industry-specific upstream and downstream segments.

For example, in the automotive industry, Chrysler, Ford, General Motors, Nissan, Renault, Commerce One and Oracle have developed Covisint, an e-business exchange that provides the industry with an Internet-based procurement tool.[10] The aim of this B2B marketplace is to reduce costs for all the respective businesses. The vision for

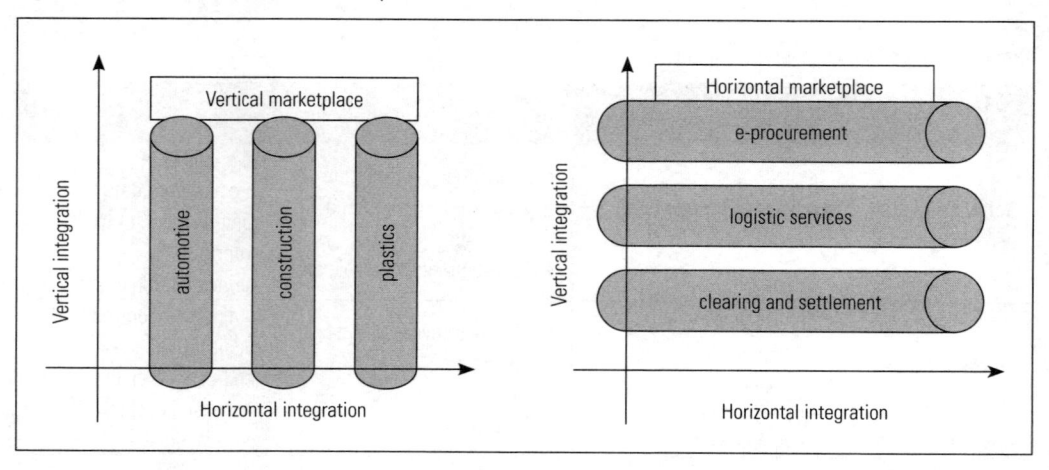

Figure 9.1 Vertical and horizontal marketplaces

Covisint is to build an on-line environment that enables individual businesses and the automotive industry in general to achieve, among other things, vehicle development cycles ranging between 12 and 18 months; compressed order-to-delivery cycles; greater asset efficiency and utilisation; more integrated supply chain planning; and reduced business process variability.

9.9.5 Horizontal marketplaces

A horizontal B2B marketplace is based on products and is formed around a supply market segment that cuts across several industries. A need in any service or product segment across industries is addressed through horizontal B2B solutions. These marketplaces are usually set up to buy and sell products that are used on the plant floor or in the company offices, but which do not become part of the finished product. An example of such a marketplace is Econia, where anything from office furniture and printing paper, to hardware, software and peripheral devices can be bought at on-line auctions.[11]

9.9.6 Functional marketplaces

Marketplaces that focus on functions emerge when value can be gained from concentrating functional skills. The functional skills may, for instance, be maintenance businesses or ones that supply truck tractors for moving trailers. Such marketplaces create value in the form of less paperwork and easier ways for suppliers to find businesses that procure or offer such services. TradeOut is an example of such a marketplace – it concentrates on the sale of excess inventory that could otherwise end up as dead stock.

9.9.7 Types of transactions

B2B marketplaces foster various types of transactions. The most basic are spot purchases, or sales of goods. These can be done through a variety of transactional means, such as auctions; reverse auctions; fixed-price transactions (one buyer and one seller); and bid/ask auctions (in which multiple buyers and sellers bid). These transactions are often conducive to short-term relationships, but marketplaces can also provide value for long-term relationships, where tight integration is beneficial.

9.10 Conclusion

Procurement management is the part of supply chain management that plans, implements and controls the efficient, effective acquisition of all raw materials, semi-finished goods, finished goods, services and information in order to support the core operations and ancillary activities of the organisation.

The broad procurement process consists of the following five steps:
Step 1: Identifying a procurement need
Step 2: Supplier survey
Step 3: Investigation and assessment of suppliers
Step 4: Choice of supplier(s)
Step 5: Establishing relationships with suppliers

A variety of products can be procured by a business. Products are divided into goods and services. Goods can be classified according to the stage they have reached in the series of processes within the supply chain of a product, extending from primary production to consumption, or end-use. These groups are raw materials, semi-finished goods and finished goods. The division of goods into producer (intermediate) goods and consumer (final) goods refers to the use of the goods.

Much of the emphasis in supply chain management is to consistently deliver the required quality of physical products on time, and with all the attributes necessary to conform to customer-service requirements, at an acceptable (usually low) price. The quality of a physical product can be judged in terms of the following seven competitive dimensions: performance, reliability, durability, conformance, features, aesthetics, and serviceability.

A low price is only one facet of the lowest TCO of procured items. With a holistic approach, procurement management's responsibility is to acquire goods and services at the lowest total cost of ownership. This means considering other factors, which in the long term can exert greater cost impact on the business than the original purchase price.

A business needs to coordinate the performance of suppliers in the chain effectively. This can be done by selecting and appointing the most suitable suppliers and then forming long-standing collaborative relationships with them. These steps can be followed in the selection of suppliers:

Step 1: Supplier survey
Step 2: Investigation and assessment
Step 3: Choosing the most suitable supplier(s)

It is desirable for a business to be in a sound long-term alliance with its suppliers, as this will potentially enhance mutually beneficial interaction and cooperation in the future business between them.

The most important procurement-related activities that can contribute to supply chain efficiency and effectiveness are:
- JIT scheduling;
- value analyses; and
- coordinating incoming traffic.

The cost of input procurement forms a relatively large part of the total expenditure of any business. Proven tactics to reduce procurement costs are expenditure-reduction programmes; speculative buying; forward buying; price-change management; volume contracts; and stockless purchasing.

The materials management function of business logistics has benefited from the efficient procurement of goods and services through e-business. The main market tools for e-procurement are electronic catalogues, electronic exchanges and electronic auctions. The number of electronic B2B marketplaces has grown rapidly. There are three kinds of such marketplaces, based on industries, products or functions; these are known as vertical, horizontal, and functional marketplaces.

Key terms

Aesthetics
Assessment
Capital goods
Conformance
Coordination
Corporate standing
Durability
Electronic procurement
Features
Final goods
Finished goods
Forward buying
Functional marketplace
Goods
Goods-in-process
Horizontal marketplace
Intermediate goods
Investigation
Just-in-time (JIT)
Logistical supply capability
Manufacturing
Operational procurement management
Performance
Planning
Procurement
Production
Purchasing
Raw material
Reliability
Selection
Semi-finished goods
Services
Serviceability
Specific production capability
Speculative buying
Stockless purchasing
Stockout
Strategic procurement management
Surveying
Tactical procurement management
Top management
Total cost of ownership (TCO)
Value analysis
Vertical marketplace

Case study[12]

Sasol is an integrated oil and gas company with substantial chemical interests. Founded in 1950 by the South African government, Sasol has grown into a multinational, publicly listed corporation. Sasol's turnover for the financial year ending June 2008 was R129 billion and its market capitalisation was R311 billion. The business is structured around a group of companies (joint ventures or wholly owned). Each of the group of companies consists of a number of divisions and business units that focus on the value chains of specific petrochemical product clusters.

In pursuit of its vision of world-class supply chains, Sasol's procurement and supply management team launched a project called Netgain in the late 1990s in order to implement best-practice procurement and supply methodologies to extract maximum shareholder value from its external spend on procured goods and services. Sasol recognised that the extraction of maximum shareholder value requires a focus on TCO, and not only purchase price. Sasol breaks down TCO into four buckets: direct spend; internal spend; related spend; and opportunity spend. Opportunities for TCO reduction are always pursued, with due regard given to the impact of purchasing decisions on sustainable development matters, such as safety, stakeholder relations and environmental performance.

One of the many commodities that Sasol purchases is low-voltage (LV) motors. Electrical motors have a large impact on plant reliability and life-cycle costs. Sasol's direct spend on LV electrical motors amounts to approximately R11 million per annum, including all operational and capital direct spend. Approximately 80 per cent of Sasol's total electricity consumption consists of electricity consumed by electrical motors.

As early as 1990, Sasol identified the sourcing of LV motors for existing plants and capital projects as an opportunity to optimise its procurement and supply practices. At that stage, sourcing LV motors was uncoordinated across the business, with an individual cost-centre mentality. Independent divisions did their own procurement and no business-wide purchases were considered.

Sasol was faced with a number of challenges to optimise the procurement of LV motors. Some of the key questions it faced were:
- How should Sasol approach the procurement of this commodity across the group of companies?
- Could the business leverage off the volumes purchased?
- Would it benefit from standardisation?
- How many different suppliers should it use?
- What type of relationship should it establish with suppliers and how should it manage the suppliers' performance?

1. Following the TCO-reduction practice introduced, how should it be applied to benefit the total procurement and supply cost of LV motors?
2. What approach should Sasol follow to decide on the suppliers to use in future?

Case study

Cisco Systems[13] is a global technology company offering products ranging from network interface cards and remote-access devices to routers and voice-over-internet-protocol communications. Cisco uses the Internet to do business and has opened portals for its customers (Cisco Connection Online – CCO), suppliers (Manufacturing Connection Online – MCO) and employees (Cisco Employee Connection – CEC). This expansion of access to intellectual capital has increased operational efficiency and reduced costs.

The CCO portal contains a number of customer-facing applications. Customers can use CCO to order products, diagnose network problems and find answers to technical questions. They can configure, price, route and submit orders electronically to Cisco on an automated order-flow system. Most of these orders go directly to Cisco's third-party suppliers, who then ship directly to customers. The site is also linked directly to FedEx and UPS package trackers, which enables customers to determine the status of their shipments in real time. This system has shortened Cisco's order cycle by 70 per cent and saved the company $440 million in 1999 by streamlining the process from order entry to shipment. It has also contributed to an increase in customer satisfaction.

1. Draw a flow diagram in which you outline the product and information flows that take place through CCO. Identify at least one level of upstream and downstream participants in this supply chain. (If you have access to a computer, you can draw the flow diagram in Microsoft PowerPoint.)
2. How do these flows differ from product and information flows in a more traditional supply chain?

Questions

1. Discuss how procurement provides access to the external markets of the business.
2. Discuss the relationship of procurement with the other entities within a business.
3. Discuss the objectives of procurement management.
4. What is the difference between the purchase price of a product and the total cost of ownership (TCO) of a product?

5   Define procurement management in the context of supply chain management.
6   Discuss the different management tiers and tasks of procurement management.
7   Describe the nature of the different categories of goods that can be purchased.
8   Discuss the characteristics of services that differentiate them from other products.
9   In your own words define finished goods and final goods.
10 Discuss the processes of surveying, evaluating and choosing suitable suppliers.
11 Describe the objectives of each tier of procurement management, and group these into the five broad steps within the procurement process.
12 Discuss the activities that ensure an efficient logistics channel.
13 Explain the best ways of reducing procurement costs.
14 How does e-procurement improve the procurement of goods and services?
15 Identify an example of either a vertical or a horizontal B2B marketplace. Identify the services that this marketplace offers, the benefits that can be gained from using it, and the ways in which the use of this marketplace may impact on a supply chain.

Consult the web

Cisco Systems: http://www.cisco.com
Covisint: http://www.covisint.com
Econia: http://www.econia.com
Electronics Supply Chain Association: http://www.electronicssupplychain.org
JSE Limited: http://www.jse.co.za
www.manugistics.com
www.mapnp.orgillibrary/ops_mgnt.htm
McGregor BFA: http://www.McGregorBFA.com
TradeWorld: http://www.tradeworld.net

Consult the books

Baitler, J. 2003. 'The power of effective procurement and strategic suppliers'. *Strategic Finance*, 85(2): 36.

Bowersox, D. J., Closs, D. J. and Cooper, M. B. 2007. *Supply Chain Logistics Management*, 2nd edition. New York: McGraw-Hill.

Chopra, S. and Meindl, P. 2007. *Supply Chain Management: Strategy, Planning and Operations*, 3rd edition. Upper Saddle River: Pearson Prentice Hall.

Fairplay. 2001. 'Box portals set to open'. *Fairplay*, 1 March 2001.

Garvin, D. A. 1987. 'Competing on the eight dimensions of quality'. *Harvard Business Review*, November/December 1987.

Hadamitzky, M. C. 2000. 'E-Business – Strategische Herausforderungen und Entwicklungstendenzen'. *Konstanz*, 24 November 2000.

JSE Limited. 2009. 'Corporate identity'. http://www.jse.co.za (accessed on 2 March 2009).

Leenders, M. R., Johnson, P. F., Flynn, A. E. and Fearon, H. E. 2006. *Purchasing and Supply Management*, 13th edition. New York: McGraw-Hill/Irwin.

McGregor BFA. 2009. 'OURDATA'. http//www.mcgregorBFA.com (accessed on 2 March 2009).

Peck, B. 2000. 'Buy-side pays the bills'. In *The E-Commerce Handbook 2000: Your Guide to the Internet Revolution and the Future of Business*. Cape Town: Trialogue.

Notes

1   Leenders et al. 2006: 29–32.
2   Bowersox et al. 2007: 79–81; Garvin, D. A. 1987: 101–9.
3   JSE Limited. 2009.
4   McGregor BFA. 2009.
5   Peck, B. 2000.
6   Hadamitzky, M.C. 2000.
7   Peck, B. 2000.
8   *Fairplay*. 2001.
9   Covisint. 2005.
10 Ibid.
11 Econia.
12 Case study compiled by Louw, J. J., Department of Logistics, University of Stellenbosch. Printed here by permission of Sasol Limited.
13 Cisco Systems. 2005.

10 Inventory management

J.N. Cronjé

Learning outcomes

After you have studied this chapter, you should be able to:
- provide reasons why it is necessary to hold inventory;
- differentiate between the various types of inventory;
- explain some basic inventory concepts;
- identify inventory-ordering costs and inventory-carrying costs;
- determine a suitable carrying-cost percentage;
- set optimum inventory levels;
- describe contemporary inventory replenishment systems; and
- perform effective inventory control.

10.1 Introduction

The importance of proper inventory management is evident when one considers that inventories have led to the demise of many a business. The downfall of some companies results from the fact that they are simply unaware of, or do not consider, the cost of inventory.

Inventory is generally considered as a safety factor, the lubrication between different parts in the supply chain that enhances the smooth functioning of the total chain. In recent times, however, inventory has come to be considered more and more as a liability. Yet the basic function of inventory, namely saving in other areas and providing 'insurance', cannot be denied. The challenge is to balance the need for inventory against the cost of carrying inventory.

The inventory problem can be compared to the groceries that are kept in the average household. The grocery cupboard and fridge may contain certain items that are used frequently (such as bread and milk) and other items that are seldom used (like certain spices). Some items are kept just in case they are needed, for example ensuring stocks of sufficient meat, milk, cold drinks and ice cream are available in case unexpected visitors show up. There may also be more of an item than actually required because a price increase is expected or the possibility exists that the item might not be available for some time. The reason why groceries are stored this way is obvious – it would cost a great deal in transport if groceries were bought on a daily basis as and when required. On the other hand, keeping a year's supply of groceries would also be unfeasible because many of the items would become obsolete or exceed the recommended shelf life and occupy space in the kitchen that could be used for other purposes. The ideal would be to keep what is needed for a relatively short period of time – not too much, but sufficient to prevent driving to the shops on a daily basis or more.

The same arguments are valid for inventories in the supply chain. The key to effective inventory management is to plan optimum inventory levels (not too much and not too little), and to control these levels. The starting point for such a strategy is accurate forecasting (estimating the demand in the supply chain). Due to the importance of forecasting in logistics, this topic is fully addressed in Chapter 6 and serves as an input to effective inventory planning. The main objective of this chapter is to address the basic principles of inventory management that will assist management in supporting decisions on optimum inventory levels.

The chapter starts with some basic considerations about inventory management. Particular attention is given to the reasons why most businesses keep stock, various types of inventory found in the supply chain, concepts that are essential to understanding inventory management and the cost of inventory.

This is followed by a detailed discussion on inventory planning, which focuses on optimum inventory levels with due consideration to demand and supply uncertainty.

The chapter concludes with useful techniques for inventory control.

Note that throughout the chapter, the terms 'inventory' and 'stock' are used as synonyms.

Multi-echelon inventory management, involving the use of stochastic models falls outside the scope of this book and is therefore not addressed in this chapter.

10.2 The purpose of inventory

There are various reasons why businesses on different levels in the supply chain hold inventory. The functions of inventories can be classified into the following broad categories:
- Decoupling
- Balancing supply and demand
- Buffering against uncertainties in supply and demand
- Geographical specialisation
- Preventing the cost of a stockout

10.2.1 Decoupling

Decoupling provides maximum operating efficiency in a logistics environment by keeping inventories at different stages or different locations in the supply chain. Holding inventory at different stages may lead to economies of scale.

First, inventory of semi-finished products (called work-in-process, or WIP) is held between different phases of the production process to prevent bottlenecks or stoppages in the production process. This prevents slowing down the speed of the total production process due to constraints elsewhere in the process.

Second, decoupling allows for economies of production. Products are often manufactured in economical lot sizes that are larger than the immediate market demand. The excess is then kept in inventory. Manufacturing in small quantities results in short production runs and high changeover costs. Plant capacity is better utilised and manufacturing costs per unit are lower when long production runs are scheduled with fewer line set-up changes.

Third, transport economies are achieved in the case of large-volume shipments. The transport cost per unit decreases as the volume of the shipment increases. However, to benefit from these savings, larger inventories of either raw material, WIP or finished goods are required than the immediate need or demand for them. The lower transport costs per unit result from greater utilisation of transport equipment. (Transport economic principles and pricing are discussed in more detail in Chapter 16.)

Last, inventory is held to reduce the cost of purchasing. Ordering goods frequently in small quantities involves high delivery costs, handling costs and administration costs. Furthermore, ordering small quantities may result in missed opportunities for bulk discounts. It is clear that there is a trade-off between the cost of holding inventory and the cost (and missed opportunities) of ordering in small quantities.

10.2.2 Balancing supply and demand

Inventory is necessary to reconcile supply with the demand for a product. Balancing is concerned with the elapsed time between consumption and manufacturing and links the economies of manufacturing with variations in consumption.

The balancing function of inventory is most prominent in seasonal supply and/or demand. This seasonality can take two forms:
- Seasonal production, but year-round consumption
- Seasonal consumption, where supply must meet peak demand

In the first instance, the demand for a product may be relatively stable throughout the year, but raw materials may be available only during certain times of the year. This is the case with most agricultural products. Typical examples are canned fruit and frozen vegetables. Fresh fruit and vegetables can only be harvested during their season, while consumption takes place throughout the year. This kind of seasonality requires the manufacturing of finished products in excess of current demand.

Many products have some seasonal variation in demand. A typical example is the demand for beverages during the festive season. The cost of providing sufficient manufacturing capacity to handle the peak demand would be substantial. The alternative is to maintain relatively stable production throughout the year and holding inventory.

10.2.3 Buffering uncertainties

The buffering function of inventory involves protecting the business or supply chain against three types of uncertainty:
- Uncertainty of future demand. This type of uncertainty results from the fact that demand usually fluctuates from period to period, causing a probability that demand may be more than the forecast. The more that demand varies from period to period, the more the uncertainty and the more difficult it becomes to forecast demand accurately.
- Lead-time uncertainty. Lead time refers to the elapsed time from order placement to order receipt. This type of uncertainty results from variability in the lead time that may be due to unforeseen delays in order processing or transportation.
- Uncertainty in supply. This refers to uncertainty about whether a specific product will be available at the time it is needed from the supplier. For example, raw materials in excess of those required for manufacturing can result from speculative purchases made because of the possibility of a strike or the unavailability of natural resources.

Related to the buffering function of inventory is the speculative reason for holding excessive inventory.

If a price increase is expected, management may opt to hold large amounts of inventory.

10.2.4 Geographical specialisation

A major function of inventory in the supply chain is to provide for geographical specialisation of members of the supply chain. The economic location of factories is often based mostly on the availability and cost of the factors of production, such as land, power, materials, water and human resources. The factors of production are not necessarily close to the markets where the final product is consumed.

Geographical specialisation requires inventory in the form of materials, semi-finished goods or components and finished goods across the supply chain. Each location (or member in the supply chain) requires a basic inventory. Furthermore, in-transit inventories are necessary to link manufacturing and distribution.

Although difficult to quantify, the savings gained through geographical specialisation are expected to be more than the increased inventory and transport costs that result from specialisation.

10.2.5 Preventing the cost of a stockout

The most important function of inventories is to ensure the availability of products – either raw materials, semi-finished goods or final products. If these are not available the result is the cost of a stockout. There are three possible costs attached to a stockout. In order of severity, these are:
- The cost of a backorder
- The cost of a lost sale
- The cost of a lost customer

The cost of a backorder involves the additional costs of processing and expediting an order that cannot be met from inventory on hand.

The cost of a lost sale incurs when the customer goes elsewhere for the purchase. These costs can be measured in terms of the contribution or profit that is lost on the particular sale.

Unavailability may result in a customer permanently seeking another supplier. Once again, the cost can be measured in terms of the total contribution or profit that is lost on all orders that the customer would have placed in future.

In conclusion, one could say that the most important functions of inventory are to save costs in other areas and to ensure superior customer service through product availability.

The challenge is to plan for optimum inventories, as discussed in Section 10.6.

10.3 Types of inventories

An understanding of the purpose of inventory, as discussed in Section 10.2, reveals that there are various types of inventories. These can be classified in terms of either the position of the inventory in the supply chain or in terms of the purpose that it serves in the supply chain.

10.3.1 Classification of inventory based on its position in the supply chain

Inventory can be classified in terms of where it is held in the supply chain. The more it moves downstream from the factory towards the final consumer, the higher the value of the inventory. This increase in value results from the form utility that is attached to it. For example, the value of iron ore is much lower than the value of metal sheets manufactured from the iron ore. Similarly, the value of metal sheets used to manufacture body parts for cars is lower than the value of the body parts. As discussed in Section 10.5.2, the value of inventory is a main determinant in estimating the cost of holding inventory.

10.3.1.1 Raw material

This is inventory of the materials required to manufacture either components or the final product; it is usually low in value and high in volume. Iron ore, water, crude oil and sugar cane are examples of raw materials.

10.3.1.2 Work-in-process

Inventory of WIP is usually held to support manufacturing. It may consist of semi-finished goods between different stages of the manufacturing process or components that are used during the manufacturing process. WIP goods can be manufactured either in the factory as part of the total manufacturing process or obtained from a supplier that specialises in a particular component. The value is usually higher than that of raw material.

WIP is often held between manufacturing stages within a factory to avoid a shutdown or to ensure a balanced (equalised) flow. All manufacturing stages within the total manufacturing process do not happen at the same rate – some operations take longer than others. WIP inventory allows for maximum economies of production without work stoppages. Businesses are increasingly focusing on minimising or eliminating the need for WIP inventory through just-in-time (JIT) manufacturing initiatives.

10.3.1.3 Packaging material

Inventory of packaging material plays a similar role to WIP. In many operations it forms part of the manufacturing process. However, different types of packaging materials can be used in different stages of the total logistics process. Cold-drink cans, for example, are a packaging material used in the manufacturing process. By contrast, shrink-wrapping is used in various stages of the logistics process.

10.3.1.4 Finished goods inventory

The final product may be held in inventory at various locations throughout the supply chain, including a finished goods warehouse at the factory, a central distribution warehouse, field warehouse, wholesaler or retailer. The value of finished goods is naturally much higher than that of raw materials, WIP or packaging material.

10.3.2 Classification of inventory based on its purpose

It is evident from Section 10.2 that inventory can be classified in terms of the purpose the products serve.

10.3.2.1 Cycle stock

From a manufacturing perspective, cycle stock is often defined as the amount of stock that is produced in an average production run. From a distribution perspective, cycle stock can be described as the inventory that is required to meet normal or average demand for the product. Cycle stock is sometimes termed base stock.

The amount (or level) of cycle stock depends mainly on the average demand and lead time under conditions of certainty – that is when demand and lead time can be predicted accurately. For example, if the demand is constant at 50 units per day and the lead time is always ten days, the maximum cycle stock would be 500 units (on the day it is delivered). Since certainty is assumed, no inventory other than the cycle stock would be required. As time goes on, the cycle stock on hand will reduce daily by 50 units until it is depleted on the tenth day.

More formally, cycle stock can be defined as '... inventory that results from the replenishment process and is required in order to meet demand under conditions of certainty ...'[1]

10.3.2.2 Transit inventory

Transit inventory is inventory that is en route (either moving or awaiting movement) from one location to another. Transit inventory should be considered as part of cycle stock even though it is not available for sale until it arrives at the destination. Depending on the terms of sale, transit inventory is owned by either the supplier or the receiver and, therefore, constitutes a cost to one of these parties in the supply chain. If ownership is transferred at shipment destination, inventory in transit is owned by the supplier. Conversely, when ownership is transferred at origin, inventory in transit is owned by the receiver. Either way, transit inventory is part of somebody's inventory and is therefore a cost to that party.

10.3.2.3 Safety (buffer) stock

Safety stock is held over and above the cycle stock to make provision for the uncertainties mentioned in Section 10.2.3. The level of safety stock would depend mostly on the severity of these uncertainties as reflected in the extent to which they vary. For example, if there is much variation from the average sales, more safety stock would be required. Similarly, the less consistent the replenishment lead time, the greater the requirements for safety stock.

Uncertainty, however, is not the only determinant of the level of safety stock. The duration of the lead time, the service level objectives of the business in terms of availability and the order quantity also influence the level of safety stock. The longer the lead time, the wider the absolute variation in demand and, therefore, the higher the safety stock requirements for a given service level.[2] Furthermore, longer lead times complicate forecasting, resulting in increased safety stock. Although the duration of the lead time does affect the level of safety stock to a certain extent, it is rather the *variability* in, or inconsistency of, lead time that plays a significant role. The lead-time duration has a greater effect on the level of cycle stock than on the level of safety stock.

The service policy of the business is a major determinant of safety stock. The higher the service level objective in terms of availability, the more the safety stock requirements. The cost of availability increases at a faster rate once a certain level of availability is exceeded. (This concept is explained in more detail in Section 10.6.)

Order quantities also affect safety stock requirements. The smaller the order quantity, the more safety stock is required. Availability is highest when a delivery has just been made and lowest before a new replenishment is expected. The risk of running out of stock is greatest when the stock is at its lowest. Frequent deliveries of smaller order quantities increase the number of times when stock is at a lower level.[3] (These relationships are explained more in section 10.6.)

In conclusion, safety stock is determined mainly by the following factors:
- Demand uncertainty
- Lead-time uncertainty
- Duration of the lead time
- Service level policy of the business
- Order quantity

10.3.2.4 Speculative stock

Speculative stock is inventory held for reasons other than satisfying normal day-to-day demand (and the safety stock to provide for uncertainties in this demand). Businesses may purchase merchandise in volumes larger than necessary for the following reasons:
- To qualify for quantity discounts
- When a price increase in goods is expected
- When a shortage of the goods is expected
- To protect against a strike
- To provide for the promotion (marketing campaign) of a certain item
- To provide for seasonal sales

10.3.2.5 Dead stock

Dead stock is items for which there has been no demand for a specified period of time. Such stock is normally obsolete and should be disposed of, since it occupies space that could be put to better use.

10.4 Important inventory concepts

A thorough understanding of certain inventory-related concepts is essential in effective inventory management. This section describes the major concepts that are crucial for understanding the planning of optimal inventory levels.

10.4.1 Availability

Reference has been made above to availability and its importance in the level of safety stock. This attribute of customer service is also explained in Chapter 2. In this section, the importance of availability and its measurements are briefly explained in the context of inventory management.

Availability is a key factor in inventory management, as it refers to the capacity of the business to have inventory when desired by a customer. The rationale for holding inventory is to have items available. The way in which availability is measured plays a key role in planning optimal inventory levels.

Availability can be defined in its broadest sense as:[4]

$$\text{Availability} = \frac{\text{demand satisfied}}{\text{total demand}}$$

For single items, this definition can be expressed as:

$$\text{Availability} = \frac{\text{total number of items supplied}}{\text{total number of items ordered}}$$

For a complete shipment, availability can be defined as:

$$\text{Availability} = \frac{\text{total number of complete orders supplied}}{\text{total number of orders}}$$

Within this broad framework, there are mainly three ways in which availability is commonly measured in practice – stockout frequency, fill rate and orders shipped complete.

10.4.1.1 Stockout frequency

A stockout occurs when demand exceeds availability. Stockout frequency refers to the probability that a stockout will occur and measures how many times the demand for a specific product exceeds availability. The total of all stockouts for all products supplied by the business gives an indication of how well a business succeeds in basic customer service commitments.

10.4.1.2 Fill rate

While the stockout frequency refers to the probability of a stockout, the fill rate measures the magnitude or impact of stockouts over time. The mere fact that a product is out of stock does not mean that demand is not going to be met. For example, if a customer orders 100 units and only 90 are available, the fill rate is 90 per cent.

A distinction can be made between a case fill rate and a line fill rate. A case fill rate defines the percentage of cases (units) ordered that can be supplied. For example, a 95 per cent case fill rate indicates that 95 cases out of 100 are filled from available stock. The remaining five cases are back-ordered or deleted.

The line fill rate refers to the percentage of individual items (product lines) that could be supplied in totality. Suppose, for example, that a customer orders 80 units of product A and 20 units of product B. This order consists of 100 items and two product lines. If there are only 75 units of product A on hand, but 20 or more of product B, the case fill rate would be 95 per cent [(75 + 20) ÷ (80 + 20)] and the line fill rate would be 50 per cent.

10.4.1.3 Orders shipped complete

Orders shipped complete (or order fill) is the strictest measure of availability. It is a measure of the number of times that a business can supply all the items ordered by a customer from the available stock. Order fill is expressed as the percentage of customer orders that can be filled completely. In the example in 10.4.1.2, the order fill would be zero, because the order could not be filled completely.

10.4.2 Average inventory

Average inventory consists of the materials, WIP, components and finished products that are typically held in inventory. Average inventories include cycle stock, safety stock and transit inventory components.

Determining the average inventory is crucial in the calculation of inventory-carrying costs. Average inventory for a specific item is calculated as half order quantity plus safety stock. Where applicable, transit inventory must also be added. This relationship is explained by means of the following practical example and Figure 10.1.

First, assume a situation where there is no uncertainty with a constant demand of 50 units per day and a lead time of ten days. Assume further that ownership of the inventory is taken upon delivery and that the replenish order quantity is 500 units. Since the stock on hand exceeds 250 units half of the time (five days) and is less than 250 half of the time, the average inventory is 250 units. Therefore, under conditions of certainty, the average stock is one half of the order quantity.

Now, assume that safety stock of 50 units is necessary to protect against uncertainty. This safety stock should always be there, regardless of the order quantity or lead time. In this case, the average inventory would be 300 (half the order quantity plus the safety stock).

The average inventory can be reduced by changing the order quantity. Instead of receiving a delivery of 500 units every ten days, the replenishment strategy can be changed to receive

Figure 10.1 Average inventory

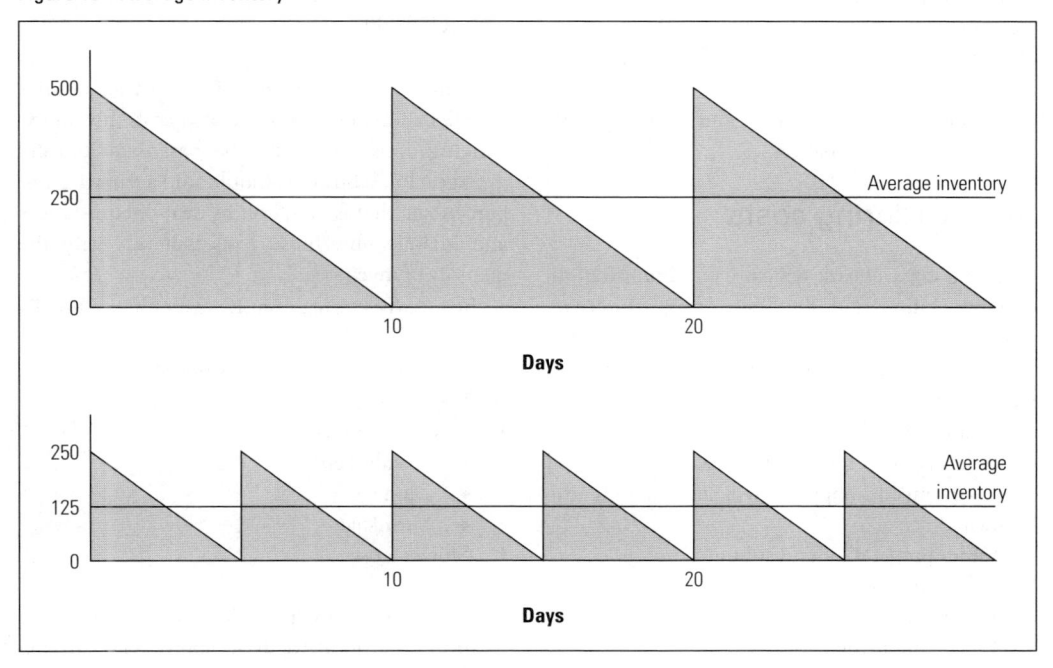

a quantity of 250 every five days. However, as mentioned in 10.3.2.3, a decrease in the order quantity will result in an increase in the safety stock. Assume, therefore, that safety stock will increase to 60 units. The average inventory will therefore be 185 units (125 + 60).

The average value of inventory for a specific product in monetary terms can be calculated as follows:

Average inventory value = unit cost × average inventory.

10.4.3 Inventory turnover

Inventory turnover (or stock turnover) is a measure of how well stock is managed. It gives an indication of how many times during a year the average stock is used up and can be expressed as follows:

Inventory turnover = total annual sales ÷ average inventory.

10.5 Inventory costs

Total inventory costs consist of purchasing costs, ordering costs and carrying costs (also termed holding or maintenance costs). Some inventory-related decisions, in particular decisions on order size, are based on the relationship between these elements of inventory costs. While purchasing costs simply depend on the purchase price of merchandise, ordering costs and carrying costs require further explanation.

10.5.1 Ordering costs

Ordering costs consist typically of administration, communication and handling costs, which are associated with order placement, processing and receiving. The extent of ordering costs depends on whether inventory is replenished from an outside supplier or from the manufacturer's own plant.

Ordering costs for merchandise that is ordered from an outside supplier typically include the following:
- Order preparation and submittal
- Receiving the product
- Placing it in storage
- Processing invoice for payment

When inventory is replenished from the factory warehouse, ordering costs would include:
- transmitting and processing inventory transfer;
- handling the product if in stock, or cost of setting up production and handling if not in stock;
- receiving at distribution warehouse; and
- processing associated documentation.

10.5.2 Carrying costs

Inventory-carrying costs are the costs associated with holding products in stock. Together with transport costs, these are regarded as one of the major components of logistics costs.

Inventory-carrying costs are calculated by multiplying the carrying cost percentage by the monetary value of average inventory. Standard practice is to base inventory value on the purchasing price or standard manufacturing costs rather than on the selling price. For example, assuming a carrying cost of 25 per cent, the annual inventory cost for a business with R1 million in average inventory is calculated as follows:

Inventory-carrying costs
= value of average inventory × carrying cost %
= R1 000 000 × 25%
= R250 000

Determining the carrying cost percentage requires the allocation of inventory-related costs. Inventory-carrying costs should not be based on industry averages. Each business should find a carrying cost percentage that is based on its own circumstances and include only those costs that vary with the quantity of inventory.

Inventory-carrying costs can be broadly categorised as follows:
- Capital costs on inventory investment
- Insurance
- Inventory risk costs:
  - Obsolescence
  - Damage
  - Shrinkage
- Storage costs

These elements and possible ways of quantifying them in order to arrive at an appropriate carrying cost percentage are discussed next and summarised in Table 10.1 (see page 222).

10.5.2.1 Capital cost

Money used to purchase goods that are kept in inventory could have been used for other types of investment. Capital is therefore tied up in stock, regardless of whether this money is borrowed from financial institutions or obtained from internal sources. The appropriate percentage to use for capital invested in inventory can range from the prime interest rate to a higher rate, determined by the return on investment of alternative investment opportunities. This rate is often termed the hurdle rate. The question to be asked is what rate of return will be foregone on the capital invested in inventory.

10.5.2.2 Insurance

Inventory needs to be insured against theft and fire. Insurance cost is not proportional to the level of inventory since it is incurred to cover a certain value of product for a specified time. Insurance cost is therefore based on the estimated risk or exposure over time. Risk and exposure depend on the nature of both the product and the place where it is held in inventory (i.e. the warehouse). For example, high-value products, products that can be stolen easily and dangerous goods that are combustible result in higher insurance cost. Preventative measures aimed at reducing risk within the warehouse, such as security cameras and sprinkler systems, also influence the insurance cost.

Insurance cost can be estimated by using the actual amount spent during the past year expressed as a percentage of that year's inventory value.

10.5.2.3 Inventory risk costs

Inventory risk costs typically consist of obsolescence, damage and shrinkage.

Obsolescence refers to the deterioration of products and is not covered by insurance. The cost of obsolescence is the difference between the original cost of the product and its salvage value. Calculations are based on past experience in terms of the number of products that must be marked down, given away or destroyed.

The allocation of obsolescence cost should be limited to the direct loss related to inventory storage and the cost expressed as a percentage of average inventory.

The cost of damage should be included only for the portion of the damage that is incurred within the warehouse while inventory is stored. Damage incurred during transit should be regarded as a throughput cost (and not inventory cost), since it does not occur as a direct result of holding inventory. Damage cost, as part of inventory risk cost, is the net amount after insurance claims have been paid (the excess) and expressed as a percentage.

Shrinkage is a serious problem for South African companies. Shrinkage refers to those losses that are not easily identifiable and traced to a specific instance of theft. It cannot, therefore, be claimed from insurance.

10.5.2.4 Storage costs

Storage costs refer to the use of warehouse space for storing products in inventory. These costs are not related to the value of the product, but rather to the size of individual products, which determines the storage space required.

In the case of privately owned warehouses, the total annual depreciated expense of the warehouse must be calculated in terms of a standard measure, such as cost per day per cubic or square metre. The cost of total annual occupancy for a given product can then be calculated by multiplying the daily occupied space by the standard cost factor for the year. This figure can then be divided by the total number of units processed through the warehouse to determine the average storage cost per unit.

In the case of public warehouses, charges typically include a storage component that is assessed on inventory at the end of each month. This charge is based on the space occupied in the warehouse.[5] Care should be taken not to include the handling cost charge of public warehouses as inventory storage costs because the handling cost (or throughput cost) is associated with warehousing costs rather than inventory-carrying costs.[6]

Table 10.1 Determining the inventory-carrying cost percentage

Cost element	Determinants and quantification	Example
Capital investment	• Prime interest rate (cost to replace money invested in inventory). • Return on investment (funds invested in inventory lose earning power and limit other more lucrative investment).	17%
Insurance	• Direct levy based on estimated risk or exposure. • Insurance cost percentage on average inventory value of past year. • Product value. • Risk and exposure of product and storage facility. • Preventative measures.	2%
Obsolescence; damage; shrinkage	• Deterioration of product while stored (cost of each unit that must be disposed of at a loss because it can no longer be sold at regular price). • Damage: net amount after claims. • Problematic to quantify. • Percentage of average inventory. • Direct loss related to inventory storage.	2%
Storage space	• Depends on types of warehouses used (own, public or contract). • Allocated to specific products (not directly related to inventory value). • Private warehousing: find standard cost per day per square or cubic metre. Multiply daily standard cost with space occupied per year for the specific product. • Public warehousing: storage charges (not handling). Normally based on maximum required storage space.	5%
Total		26%

10.5.3 Impact of carrying-cost percentage on financial records

Unlike other logistics cost elements, such as transport and warehousing, inventory-carrying costs are not apparent in the financial statements of a business. Although inventory appears as an asset in the balance statement, there is no entry of inventory-carrying cost in the income statement. This could be misleading with regard to the financial soundness of the business. Although inventory-carrying costs are not a direct entry, they have a significant impact on the business's financial activities.

10.5.4 Impact of carrying-cost percentage on logistics decisions and strategies

It is evident from the discussion in Section 10.5.2 that there is some discretion in determining the carrying-cost percentage. Some businesses may use a low percentage based on the argument that the appropriate capital cost is their internal cost of funds, which is lower than external costs. On the other hand, a business may opt for a higher percentage based on the argument that capital invested in inventory should be based on the same rate as capital invested for other uses, resulting in a high percentage.

The importance of using an appropriate percentage becomes crucial when making strategic logistics decisions, such as the number and size of warehouses in the supply chain. An unrealistically low carrying-cost percentage reduces the impact of inventory-carrying cost on total logistics costs and makes transport cost relatively more important. As a result, total logistics cost decisions would attempt to minimise transport costs by using more warehouses, resulting in more safety stock. Thus, a lower carrying-cost percentage results in strategies that replace expensive transport with relatively cheaper inventory. Conversely, a relatively high percentage would result in strategies focused on centralising inventory in fewer warehouses and allow for longer (and more expensive) transport movements.

The carrying-cost percentage must accurately reflect the capital cost component, since the relative magnitude of inventory-carrying cost resulting from the percentage used will significantly influence the optimal logistics strategy.

10.6 Inventory planning

Inventory planning involves the setting of optimum inventory levels in the supply chain, with due consideration for the lowest total logistics costs and uncertainty in demand and supply.

A very important issue in the planning of inventory throughout the supply chain is the distinction between dependent and independent demand. The reason why this distinction is important is to reduce the reliance on accurate forecasting in the supply chain. Inaccurate forecasts may result in either excess inventory or stockouts. Therefore, the less one relies on an accurate forecast, the more effective and efficient the supply chain operations.

Independent demand, as the name implies, exists when the demand for an item is not related to, or dependent on, the demand for another item. Examples of independent demand are finished goods, such as toothpaste, coffee, cans of cold drink and maintenance spares. Independent demand needs to be forecasted.

Dependent demand refers to items whose demand is related to the demand for other items. Typical examples are sub-assemblies, raw materials and packaging materials. Since the demand for these items depends on the demand for the final product, it can be calculated and there is no need to forecast dependent demand. Dependent demand can be planned for based on the forecast for independent demand. A master production schedule is a typical example of such planning.

The starting point for proper inventory planning is reliable and accurate forecasts of independent demand. Forecasting techniques are discussed in detail in Chapter 6. Naturally, circumstances dictate which methods and techniques should be used. These circumstances relate mostly to variability in demand, changes in the average level of demand, indicating possible cycles or trends and the seasonality of demand.

10.6.1 Cycle stock

The planning of cycle stock to ensure optimum inventory levels involves answering two crucial questions:
- How much should we order?
- When should we order?

There are various inventory planning systems that can be implemented to answer these two questions. The most popular systems are the review level system and the target stock level system. In the review level system, the order quantity is fixed, while the order frequency varies. The target level system involves a fixed order frequency and varying order quantities. These two systems are discussed in more detail in the next sections.

10.6.1.1 The review level (reorder point) system

How much to order

The question of how much to order can be answered by calculating the economic order quantity (EOQ) for a specific item. The EOQ is simply a trade-off or balance between inventory-ordering costs and inventory-carrying costs. If only one order is placed per year, the annual ordering cost would be very low, but the inventory-carrying cost would be very high. By contrast, ordering each day would mean high ordering costs, but low carrying costs. The key is to find a balance (trade-off) between these two costs by finding the optimum order quantity, namely the EOQ.

$$EOQ = \sqrt{2AS/CV}$$

Where EOQ = economic order quantity
A = cost of an order
S = annual sales or demand in units
C = annual inventory-carrying cost percentage
V = value or cost of one unit

This relationship is shown graphically in Figure 10.2 (see page 224).

Figure 10.2 The economic order quantity

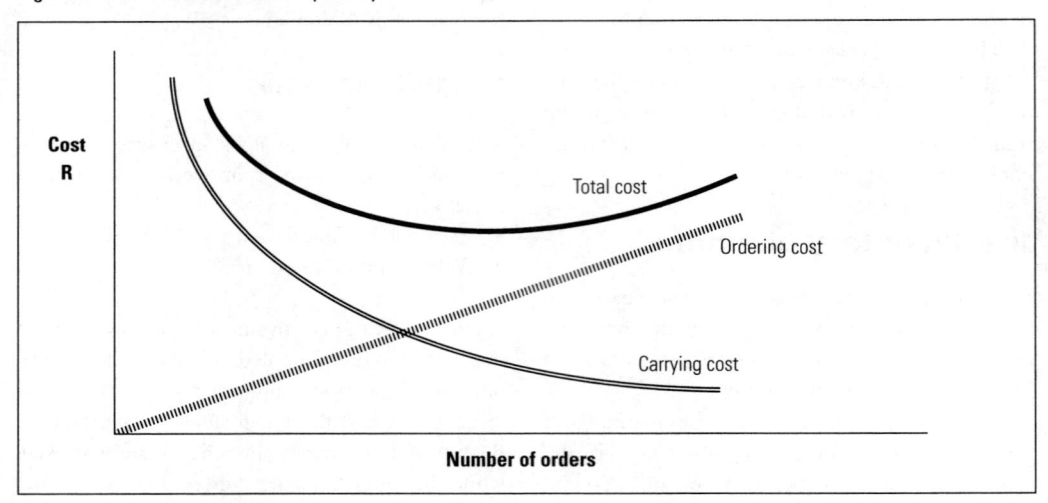

Worked example

Given annual demand of 2 000 items, cost of replenishing an order of R400, a carrying cost percentage of 25 per cent and the purchase price per item of R100, the EOQ is calculated as follows:

$EOQ = \sqrt{2AS/CV}$

$EOQ = \sqrt{2 \times 400 \times 2\,000 / 0{,}25 \times 100}$

$EOQ = 252$ items

If 50 units fit on a pallet, the order quantity would be established at 250 units.

In this case, total annual cost can be calculated as follows:

Total ordering costs per annum:
Number of orders = 2 000/250
 = 8 orders
Ordering cost = 8 × 400
 = R3200

Inventory-carrying cost:
Average inventory = ½ order quantity
 = 0,5 × 250
 = 125
Carrying cost per unit = 0,25 × 100
 = R25
Annual carrying cost = R25 × 125
 = R3125

Total annual cost = R3 200 + R3 125
 = R6 325

Although the EOQ model is widely used in industry, it has its limitations. These limitations result from the assumptions of the model, outlined as follows:

- All demand is satisfied (no stockouts are permitted)
- Continuous, constant and known rate of demand
- Constant and known lead time
- Constant purchase price that is independent of quantity ordered or time ordered
- Constant transport cost independent of quantity ordered or time ordered
- Infinite planning horizon
- No interaction between multiple items of inventory – only one stock-keeping unit (SKU)
- No inventory in transit
- No limit on capital availability

Some of the limitations posed by the assumptions can be overcome by allowing for uncertainty (planning for safety stock) or by adjusting the order quantity to allow for volume transport rates or discount on purchasing large quantities. Furthermore, the EOQ solution is relatively insensitive to small changes in the data used for the calculation. This results in the EOQ curve being relatively flat around the solution point. The relatively flat curve means that there is not much difference between the total cost for ordering quantities around the minimum cost point. For example, the total cost for an ordering quantity of 200 in the above example amounts to R6 500 (a difference of only 2,7 per cent); for an order quantity of 300 it amounts to R6 417 (a difference of only 1,4 per cent).

EOQ adjustment for volume transport rates

As a general rule, the larger the order, the lower the transport cost per unit because the transport cost is spread over more units. One could, therefore, expect that lower transport rates can be negotiated for larger order quantities.

In the above example, assume that a transport operator quotes R10 per unit for transporting the product and offers a discount of 25 per cent for shipments larger than 400 units. The total annual transport cost for order quantities of 250 would therefore be R20 000 (2 000 × 10). For order quantities of 400, it would amount to R15 000 (2 000 × 7,50). The difference in the total costs is shown in table 10.2. It is clear that the most economic order quantity, considering transport costs, would be 400 units.

EOQ adjustment for quantity discounts

When buying large quantities, discounts can also be taken into account by adjusting the EOQ. This logic is similar to that of the adjustment for volume transport rates. Negotiating discounts on larger purchase quantities results in the carrying cost being lower due to the lower inventory value and lower product cost. The total cost could therefore be adjusted by adding a column 'Annual product cost' to the above table and adjusting the inventory-carrying cost.

Using the same example as above, assuming no volume transport rates, but 10 per cent discount on purchases larger than 400 units, produces the results indicated in Table 10.3.

Clearly, the business would order in quantities of 400 rather than in quantities of 250.

Other adjustments to the EOQ

There may be other situations for which the basic EOQ solution can be adjusted. These include:
- Production lot size. These refer to the most economical quantities from a manufacturing perspective.
- Multiple-item purchase: more than one product is bought at the same time and transport and quantity discounts may come into play.
- When capital is limited: budget restrictions prevent purchasing all product lines at the EOQ. Multiple product orders must frequently be made within budget limitations.
- Specialised (dedicated) transport can influence order quantities. Since the vehicle cannot be used for other products, purchases should be made that fully utilise the available space on the vehicle.
- Unitisation: case or pallet sizes need to be considered.

Given these adjustments that can be made to the basic EOQ solution, it is clear that the limitations of the model, as imposed by its assumptions, can be overcome to a large extent.

Table 10.2 EOQ modification for volume transport rates

Order quantity	Number of orders	Ordering costs (R)	Carrying costs (R)	Transport costs (R)	Total costs (R)
250	8	3 200	3 125	20 000	26 325
400	5	2 000	5 000	15 000	22 000

Table 10.3 EOQ modification for purchase quantity discounts

Order quantity	Number of orders	Ordering costs (R)	Carrying costs (R)	Transport costs (R)	Product costs (R)	Total costs (R)
250	8	3 200	3 125	20 000	200 000	226 325
400	5	2 000	4 500	20 000	180 000	206 500

When to order

Once the order quantity is established the question of when to order can be addressed. The reorder point (ROP) defines the time when a replenishment order should be initiated. The ROP is expressed in terms of units. In other words, when a certain number of units are in stock, a new order has to be placed. The ROP therefore depends on the average demand until a new order arrives and the lead time (the time from placing the order until it is received) and can be expressed mathematically as follows:

$$ROP = D \times T$$

Where ROP = reorder point in units
 D = average daily (or weekly) demand in units
 T = average lead time in days (or weeks)

Worked example

Assume daily demand of 50 units and a lead time of ten days. The ROP in this case would be 500 units (50×10). This means that once the level of inventory on hand reaches 500 units, a new order has to be placed. The size of the order would depend on the EOQ, or the adjusted EOQ as discussed above.

Note that this calculation will only be valid under conditions of certainty (demand being fixed at 50 units per day and lead time exactly ten days every time). When safety stock is necessary to make provision for uncertainty, the formula will change slightly:

$$ROP = D \times T + SS$$

Where SS = safety stock and the other symbols have the same meaning as in the previous formula for ROP.

10.6.1.2 Target stock level system

Often circumstances make the use of the review level system inappropriate. Sometimes, suppliers encourage orders at fixed intervals. In other instances, the grouping of orders for different items from the same supplier may result in transport cost savings. Furthermore, some situations do not lend themselves to continuous monitoring of inventory levels. Many retailers, including pharmacies and small grocery stores, find themselves in one of these categories. Instead of using the review level system, they would use the target stock level (TSL) system for ordering.

The TSL (fixed order interval) system is used, therefore, when orders are placed at fixed time intervals, such as weekly, bi-weekly or monthly.

The TSL is a level to which inventory is topped up when the cycle time for ordering comes up (for example, every Thursday). The procedure follows these steps:

Step 1: Specify a day each week or month on which an order is going to be placed.
Step 2: Review the stock on a chosen day.
Step 3: The order quantity is calculated, using the formula:

$$Q = TSL - \text{stock on hand} - \text{supply orders outstanding within the current lead time}$$

The calculation of the TSL is very similar to that of the review level system. The main difference is that the replenishment quantity now needs to cover the period until the review cycle comes round again. The following formula is used:

$$TSL = D \times (T + P) + SS$$

Where TSL = target stock level
 D = daily (or weekly) demand
 T = average lead time in days (or weeks)
 P = review period in days (or weeks)

The demand in the review cycle is included because inventory may not be checked continuously or deliveries may only be made once a month. If the extra time is not included in the process, the risk of running out of stock is increased.

Worked example

Assume deliveries take place once a week. The average demand is 20 units per week and the supply lead time is five weeks. There is no uncertainty in demand and lead time.

$$\begin{align} TSL &= D \times (T + P) + SS \\ &= 20 \times (5 + 1) + 0 \\ &= 120 \text{ units} \end{align}$$

This means that once the review period comes round, the business must order a quantity to top inventory up to 120. Assuming that there are 30 items on hand and no outstanding order, the order quantity would be 90 items ($120 - 30$).

10.6.2 Safety stock

Certainty seldom prevails, if ever, in business. Planning optimum inventory levels must, therefore, include planning for safety stock. The question is how much safety stock should be provided for. As discussed earlier, this depends mainly on the variability of demand; the variability and duration of the supply lead time; the service level policy of the business; and the order quantity.

The more the demand varies from period to period, the more safety stock required. Similarly, the greater the lead time variation, the higher the safety stock level required. There are several ways of measuring variability, but the most popular measurements are the standard deviation and the mean absolute deviation. This section covers the use of the standard deviation, as it is regarded as being more accurate.

The calculation of the standard deviation is based on historical data and probability theory. The probability of occurrences assumes a pattern around a central tendency, which is the average value of all occurrences. While a number of frequency distributions are possible, most sales patterns assume a normal distribution. For this reason, safety stock calculation in this text is based on the normal distribution theory. A normal distribution is characterised by a symmetric bell-shaped curve, as indicated in Figure 10.3. The main characteristic of a normal distribution is that the mean (average) value, the median (middle) observation and the mode (most frequently observed) value are the same.

It can be statistically proven that in a normal distribution:
- 68,27 per cent of all events would fall within one standard deviation either side of the mean;
- 95,45 per cent of all events would fall within two standard deviations either side of the mean; and
- 99,73 per cent of all events would fall within three standard deviations either side of the mean.

The use of the normal distribution to find safety stock levels is explained in sections 10.6.2.1 (for protection against demand variability) and 10.6.2.2 (for variability in lead times).

It is also obvious that the higher the service level policy of the business in terms of availability (thus minimising stockout events), the greater the safety stock requirements.

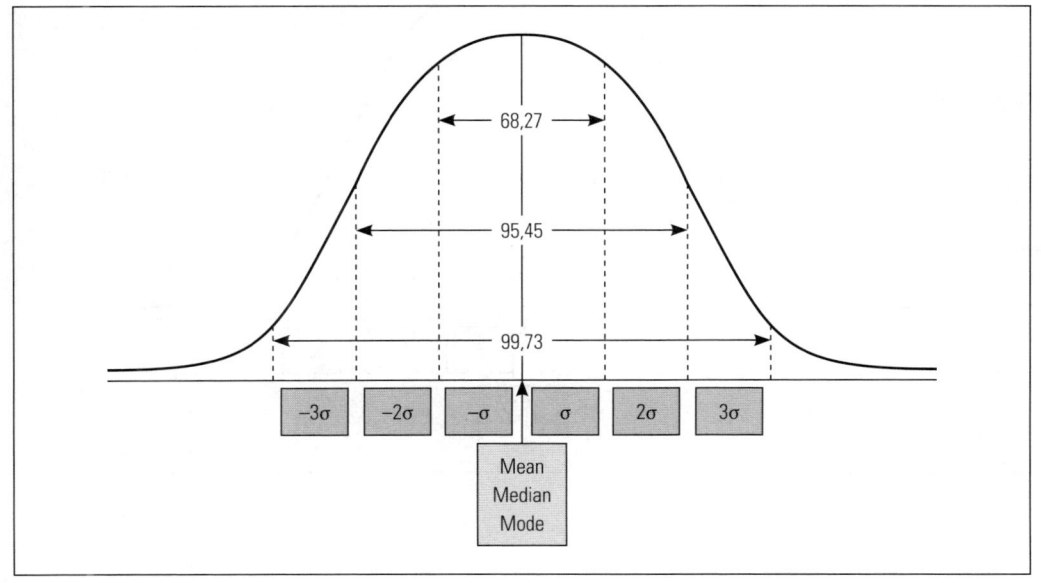

Figure 10.3 Normal distribution

10.6.2.1 Demand uncertainty

When applying probability theory and the normal distribution to demand history, it can be estimated that in approximately 68 per cent of occasions demand would be within plus or minus one standard deviation from the mean; that in approximately 95 per cent of occasions demand would be within two standard deviations either side of the mean; and in 99 per cent of occasions, demand will be within three standard deviations either side of the mean.

However, the only situations of concern are when demand is more than the average. When demand is lower than the average, no stockouts occur. Demand will be lower than average approximately 50 per cent of the time. Therefore, the probability of a stockout will occur only during 50 per cent of the time when demand is above the average. In other words, attention must be focused on the area of the curve to the right of the mean. This is illustrated in Figure 10.4, which shows that one standard deviation will protect against a stockout in 84 per cent of the occurrences (50 + (68,27/2)). Two standard deviations will protect against 98 per cent and three standard deviations will protect against 99,9 per cent. One can say that to offer a service level of 99,9 per cent three standard deviations of safety stock should be kept.

The formula for calculating the standard deviation is as follows:

$$\sigma = \sqrt{\Sigma(x_i - \mu)^2/n}$$

Where σ = standard deviation
 n = the number of observations (e.g. days in the case of daily sales)
 x_i = the value of observation i
 μ = the average of all observations

When a large number of observations are considered, the formula can be expressed as follows:

$$\sigma = \sqrt{\frac{\Sigma F_i D_i^2}{n}}$$

Where σ = standard deviation
 F_i = frequency of event i
 D_i = deviation of event i from mean
 n = total observations

The calculation is illustrated in Table 10.4, using an example of the sales for 25 days.

Figure 10.4 Stockout protection for variability in demand

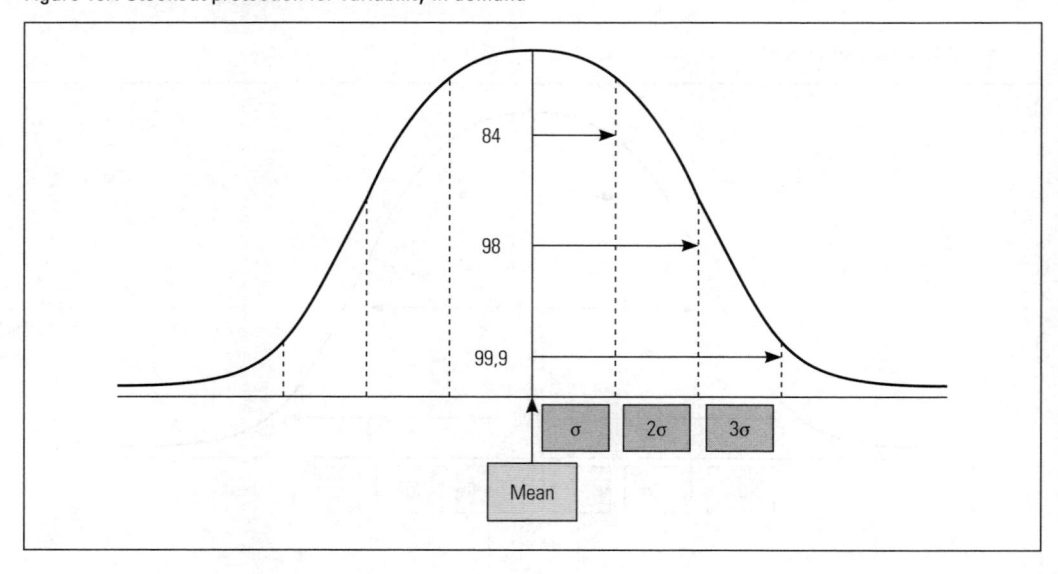

Table 10.4 Calculation of standard deviation of daily demand

Day	Demand	Deviation from mean	Deviation squared
1	4	−2	4
2	3	−3	9
3	4	−2	4
4	6	0	0
5	7	1	1
6	8	2	4
7	6	0	0
8	5	−1	1
9	6	0	0
10	10	4	16
11	8	2	4
12	7	1	1
13	5	−1	1
14	6	0	0
15	4	−2	4
16	2	−4	16
17	5	−1	1
18	6	0	0
19	7	1	1
20	6	0	0
21	6	0	0
22	5	−1	1
23	7	1	1
24	8	2	4
25	9	3	9
Total	150		82
Average	6		3,28
Standard deviation			1,81

The standard deviation is the square root of the average of the squared deviation. It can be rounded off to 1,8.

10.6.2.2 Lead time uncertainty

The provision for safety stock due to inconsistent lead times is calculated in the same way as for variations in sales. The actual lead time will be measured over a number of deliveries and the standard deviation of the observations calculated. Table 10.5 (see page 230) serves as an example in which 40 observations of the actual lead time were recorded. Due to the large number of observations, the alternative formula for the standard deviation is used.

Table 10.5 Calculation of standard deviation of lead time

Lead time Days	Frequency F_i	Deviation D_i	Deviation squared $(D_i)^2$	Product $F_i D_i^2$
10	4	−2	4	16
11	8	−1	1	8
12	16	0	0	0
13	8	1	1	8
14	4	2	4	16
Total	40			48
Average	12			1,2
Standard deviation				1,1

The standard deviation of the lead time can be rounded off to 1,1 days.

10.6.2.3 Combined effect of lead time and demand uncertainty

A business is typically confronted with both demand and lead time uncertainty. Planning sufficient safety stock to accommodate both uncertainties requires combining the two variables so that the joint impact of both uncertainties can be determined. The combined standard deviation can be calculated using the following formula:

$$\sigma_c = \sqrt{TS_s^2 + D^2 S_t^2}$$

Where σ_c = combined standard deviation
T = average lead time
S_s = standard deviation of daily sales
D = average daily sales
S_t = standard deviation of lead time

Building on the previous example, the combined standard deviation would be:

$$\begin{aligned}\sigma_c &= \sqrt{TS_s^2 + D^2 S_t^2} \\ &= \sqrt{12(1,81)^2 + 6^2(1,10)^2} \\ &= \sqrt{(39,31) + (43,56)} \\ &= \sqrt{82,87} \\ &= 9,10\end{aligned}$$

Based on this calculation, safety stock of nine units will ensure availability in 84 per cent of occurrences. To protect against 98 per cent of all possibilities, 18 units of safety stock are required; to protect against 99,9 per cent, 27 units are required.

The establishment of a safety stock commitment is in reality a customer service and inventory availability policy. The calculations show the safety stock requirements to protect the business against stockouts at various levels of probability. Additional calculations are required to determine the specific fill rate when a stockout occurs.

10.6.2.4 Calculating fill rate

While the probability theory determines the probability of a stockout, the fill rate gives an indication of the magnitude of a stockout. The fill rate represents the percentage of units of a total customer order that can be supplied from the inventory on hand.

The order quantity plays a significant role in the calculation of the fill rate, which confirms that the order quantity indeed plays a role in the level of safety stock. Figure 10.5 illustrates that the smaller the order quantity (and by implication, the more the number of deliveries) the higher the risk of running out of stock. For both examples shown in Figure 10.5, the lead time, average daily demand and safety stock (based on the probability theory) remain the same. However, the sketch with the smaller order quantity shows two instances where inventory may be depleted during a 20-day period – that is at the end of each cycle. If the order quantity is doubled, there is only one instance during the 20-day period where a stockout can occur.

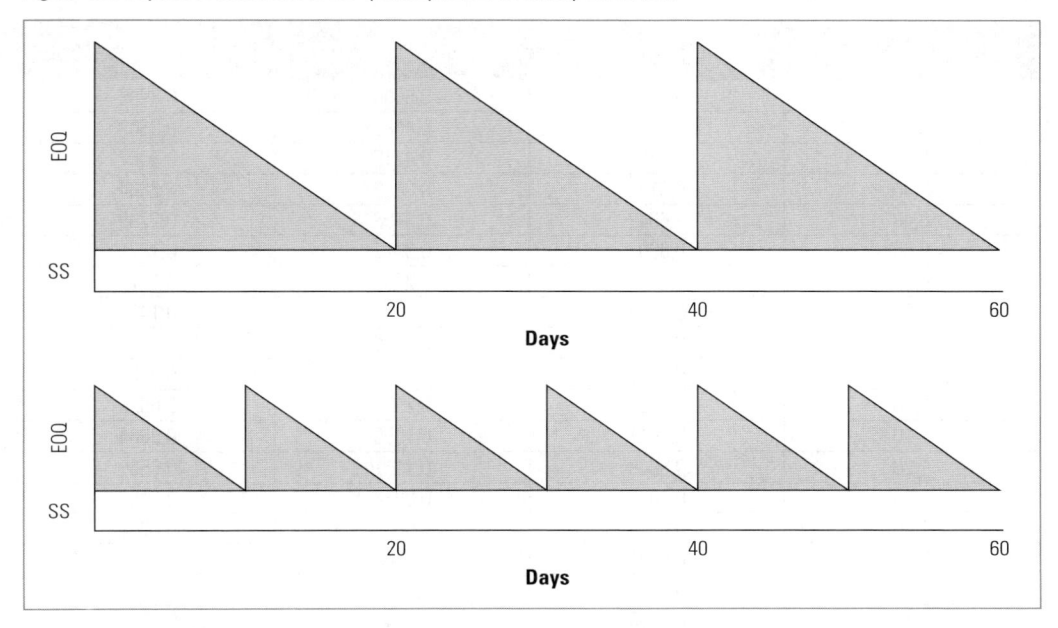

Figure 10.5 Impact of economic order quantity (EOQ) on safety stock (SS)

While both situations feature the same demand, the one with the smaller order quantity has a greater potential for inventory shortages. One can conclude that increasing the order quantity for a given safety stock level reduces the relative magnitude of potential stockouts. Conversely, a reduction in the order quantity increases the relative magnitude of potential stockouts.

The relationship between order quantity and safety stock can be expressed as follows:

$$FL = 1 - \frac{f(k)\sigma_c}{Q}$$

Where FL = fill rate (the stockout magnitude or product availability level)
f(k) = a function of the normal loss curve (see Table 10.6)
σ_c = combined standard deviation considering both demand and lead time variability
Q = order quantity

K (the safety factor) represents the number of standard deviations to protect against the probability of a stockout, as discussed in 10.6.3.1. For example, 1 K protects against 84 per cent; 2 Ks protects against 98 per cent; and 3 Ks against 99,9 per cent.

K can be calculated as follows:

$$K = \frac{SS}{\sigma_c}$$

The corresponding f(k) values for $K = \frac{SS}{\sigma_c}$ are given in Table 10.6. The f(k) values are statistically calculated values based on the desired number of standard deviations and termed service function magnitude factors.

Worked example

Using the above example, assume it is decided to keep 18 units of safety stock and the order quantity is 36. (The combined standard deviation was calculated as nine units). The fill rate can be calculated as follows:
The first step is to calculate K:

$$K = \frac{SS}{\sigma_c}$$
$$= 18/9$$
$$= 2$$

The corresponding value for f(k) when K = 2 can be found in Table 10.6 as f(k) = 0,0086. Now apply the formula for FL:

$$FL = 1 - \frac{f(k)\sigma_c}{Q}$$

Table 10.6 Loss integral for standardised normal distribution (safety stock factors)

Safety factor K or σ	Stock protection	Stockout probability	Service function (magnitude factor) f(k)
0,00	0,5000	0,5000	0,3989
0,10	0,5394	0,4606	0,3509
0,20	0,5785	0,4215	0,3067
0,30	0,6168	0,3832	0,2664
0,40	0,6542	0,3458	0,2299
0,50	0,6901	0,3099	0,1971
0,60	0,7244	0,2756	0,1679
0,70	0,7569	0,2431	0,1421
0,80	0,7872	0,2128	0,1194
0,90	0,8152	0,1848	0,0998
1,00	0,8409	0,1591	0,0820
1,10	0,8641	0,1359	0,0684
1,20	0,8849	0,1151	0,0561
1,30	0,9033	0,0967	0,0457
1,40	0,9194	0,0806	0,0369
1,50	0,9334	0,0666	0,0297
1,60	0,9454	0,0546	0,0236
1,70	0,9556	0,0444	0,0186
1,80	0,9642	0,0358	0,0145
1,90	0,9714	0,0286	0,0113
2,00	0,9773	0,0227	0,0086
2,10	0,9822	0,0178	0,0065
2,20	0,9861	0,0139	0,0049
2,30	0,9893	0,0107	0,0036
2,40	0,9918	0,0082	0,0027
2,50	0,9938	0,0062	0,0019
2,60	0,9953	0,0047	0,0014
2,70	0,9965	0,0035	0,0010
2,80	0,9974	0,0026	0,0007
2,90	0,9981	0,0019	0,0005
3,00	0,9984	0,0014	0,0004
3,10	0,9990	0,0010	0,0003
3,20	0,9993	0,0007	0,0002
3,30	0,9995	0,0005	0,0001
3,40	0,9997	0,0003	0,0001
3,50	0,9998	0,0002	0,0001
3,60	0,9998	0,0002	
3,70	0,9999	0,0001	
3,80	0,9999	0,0001	
3,90	0,9999	0,0001	
4,00	0,9999	0,0001	

Source: Stock and Lambert. 2001: 250, adapted from Brown, R. G. 1977. Materials Management Systems. New York: John Wiley & Sons: 429

FL = 1 − (0,0086 × 9)/36
   = 1 − 0,00215
   = 0,99785 or 99,785%

The fill rate would therefore be 99,8 per cent. This means that for every 100 units of the product demanded, 99,8 will be on hand when 18 units are kept as safety stock and the order quantity is 36.

From previous discussions it is clear that such a high level of service could be costly to the business. Suppose the business would be happy with a fill rate of 95 per cent and establishes safety stock to achieve the target of a 95 per cent fill rate. The same formula can be used to calculate the safety stock:

$$FL = 1 - \frac{f(k)\sigma_c}{Q}$$

In this case, FL is given as 0,95 (95 per cent), σ_c is known as nine units and the order quantity remains at 36. The service function, f(k), however, needs to be calculated:

Rearranging the formula for FL:
f(k) = (1 − FL) × (Q/σ_c)
    = (1 − 0,95) × (36/9)
    = 0,05 × 4
    = 0,2

The corresponding K-value for f(k) = 0,2 is approximately 0,5 (from Table 10.6).

If K = $\frac{SS}{\sigma_c}$, then
SS = K × σ_c
   = 0,5 × 9
   = 4,5 rounded to 5

Should the order quantity be halved to 18 units, f(k) would be:
f(k) = (1 − FL) × (Q/σ_c)
    = (1 − 0,95) × (18/9)
    = 0,05 × 2
    = 0,1

The SS would be 0,9 × 9 = 8,1 rounded to 8.

The above discussion shows that when order quantities are taken into consideration, the safety stock requirements change considerably.

10.6.2.5 Conclusion on safety stock

Due to increased competition and the need for greater efficiency, businesses worldwide are searching for ways to reduce inventories without compromising service levels. While very little savings are possible in cycle stock, safety stock reductions may offer substantial savings.

In a recent study,[7] the calculation of safety stock is viewed on the basis of probability theory and the calculation of the fill rate as being two separate measures of service level. The authors see the combined standard deviation approach (based on probability) as a 'prespecified risk of no stockout per replenishment cycle' and regard it as an unfair and flawed service measure because it does not take the order quantity and number of delivery cycles into consideration. By contrast, they define the fill rate as a 'prespecified fraction of demand to be satisfied from stock on hand'.

Their research focuses on the comparison of the two measures for different order quantities (using different modes of transport) and comes to the conclusion that the probability measure favours transportation modes with a small carrying capacity in the calculation of safety stock. They prove that substantially less safety stock is required when the order quantity is increased. Under certain circumstances, using the probability measure can cause a decision maker looking to minimise cost to select the wrong transport mode to replenish inventory.

It is, therefore, of paramount importance to consider the fill rate approach in any analysis of safety stock levels.

10.6.3 Logistics requirements planning

10.6.3.1 Definition and scope of logistics requirements planning

Logistics requirements planning (LRP) is a scheduling technique which ensures that the right goods are available at the right place, at the right time and in the right quantities. It is a logical integration of distribution requirements planning (DRP) and material requirements planning (MRP) across the supply chain.

Central to an understanding of LRP is the difference between independent and dependent demand – as discussed earlier – because DRP is driven by independent demand (demand for the final product), while MRP operates mainly in a dependent demand situation.

LRP aims to reduce total inventory in the supply chain by reducing the reliance of the demand for all items on forecasting. In the discussion on dependent and independent demand, it was mentioned that independent demand must be forecast, but dependent demand can be calculated based on the demand for the final product.

Figure 10.6 illustrates the scope of LRP where the integration of DRP and MRP is apparent. While DRP involves forecasting and planning availability of the final product, MRP involves planning the availability of all resources and materials required for production. MRP is driven by a production schedule, which, in turn, is based on the demand for the final product.

The top half of Figure 10.6 illustrates the DRP system that allocates finished inventory from the factory to distribution warehouses and customers. The bottom half of Figure 10.6 illustrates an MRP system that time-phases raw material arrivals to support the production schedule. The MRP and DRP systems interface at the factory. Close coordination of the two systems results in minimal need for safety stock.

10.6.3.2 The logistics requirements planning process

The important LRP planning tool is the schedule, which integrates and coordinates requirements across the supply chain for a specified planning period. There should be a schedule for each SKU at each node (plant warehouse or distribution warehouse) in the supply chain. To implement the process, a certain procedure is followed using predetermined variables.

The variables (information) required to implement the LRP process are mostly the inventory-related concepts that have been addressed in the previous sections of this chapter. The first important variable is the monthly, weekly or daily demand for the final product (independent demand). This is obtained through applying appropriate forecasting techniques. The second variable is safety stock levels for each SKU

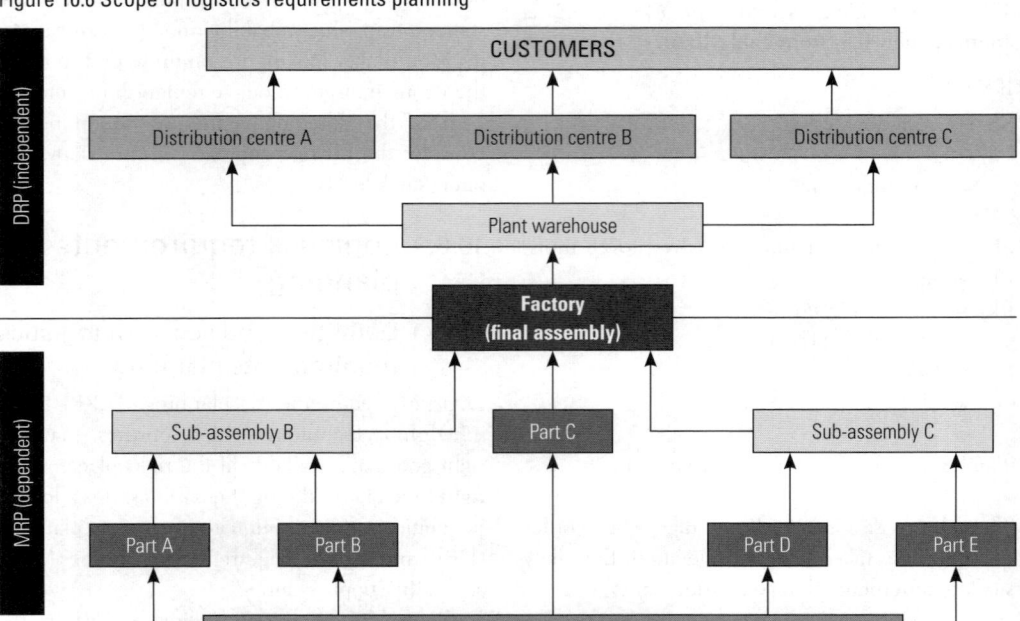

Figure 10.6 Scope of logistics requirements planning

to accommodate uncertainty in demand and lead time. A third factor is the lead time. The next variable is the ROP, which is determined by the lead time and the demand during the lead time. Finally, the order quantity is an equally important variable. As discussed in Section 10.6, the EOQ depends mainly on inventory-carrying costs, ordering costs, and volume discounts.

The procedure involves using the above variables according to the following steps:

Step 1: Start with distribution (independent demand).
Step 2: Do demand forecasting covering periods as short as possible. (Most LRP applications forecast weekly demand.)
Step 3: Calculate how long (e.g. number of days or weeks) the current stock will last.
Step 4: Deduct the safety stock requirement. (There should always be provision for uncertainty. The projected inventory on hand, therefore, should never fall below the required safety stock level.)
Step 5: Add stock that may be in transit.
Step 6: Calculate the date when safety stock will be reached – this is the date on which a new batch should arrive.
Step 7: Calculate the date of shipment, allowing for lead time between placing and receiving the order for finished products.
Step 8: Plan production via the master production schedule.
Step 9: Calculate the delivery date of raw materials.
Step 10: Calculate the date of shipment, allowing for lead time between placing and receiving the order for materials.

A practical example of the implementation of LRP is explained in the next section.

10.6.3.3 Practical application of LRP

Consider a distribution network for a certain product (a single SKU) with a central warehouse in Johannesburg (close to the factory) and regional distribution warehouses in Windhoek, East London, Cape Town, Bloemfontein and Durban.

The estimated demand in Windhoek for the next eight weeks is indicated in Table 10.7 (a). The current (week 0) inventory level is 500 units, of which 250 constitute safety stock. The lead time is assumed to be two weeks, while the most economic order quantity has been calculated as

Table 10.7 Practical application of LRP: Windhoek warehouse

a)

Lead time = 2 weeks Order quantity = 300				In stock = 500 SS = 250			
Week	0	1	2	3	4	5	6
Estimated demand		100	120	90	110	120	100
In transit	0	0	0	0	0	0	0
Estimated stock	500	400	280	190	80	−40	−140

b)

Lead time = 2 weeks Order quantity = 300				In stock = 500 SS = 250			
Week	0	1	2	3	4	5	6
Estimated demand		100	120	90	110	120	100
In transit	0	0	0	0	0	0	0
Planned receipt				300			300
Estimated stock	500	400	280	490	380	260	460
Planned order		300			300		

being 300 units. The estimated stock is calculated by deducting the following week's estimated demand from the existing stock. The estimated stock on hand in week 1 is therefore 400 units (500 – 100). Similarly, the estimated stock in week 2 (280) is calculated by deducting the estimated demand (120) from the estimated stock in week one (400). In week 3, the estimated stock (190) will fall below the safety stock level and in week 5, the warehouse will be out of stock. This warehouse, therefore, requires an order for delivery in week 3. With a lead time of two weeks, the order should be placed in week 1, as indicated by the planned receipt and planned order in table 10.7 (b). This consignment will ensure adequate stock up to week 6, when safety stock will have to be used and another 300 units would have to be received.

Similar situations in respect of the other distribution warehouses are shown in Tables 10.8 to 10.11. The lead times, order quantities and safety stock levels differ for each warehouse. Note that East London expects to receive an order, which is in transit in week 2. The stock in transit is added to the estimated stock.

The planned orders reflected in the schedule for each warehouse indicate when and how much should be ordered from the central warehouse to meet demand in each area.

Table 10.12 summarises the combined dispatch requirements for the various distribution warehouses. These can now be entered in the master production schedule and production can be

Table 10.8 East London warehouse

Lead time = 2 weeks Order quantity = 150				In stock = 160 SS = 75			
Week	0	1	2	3	4	5	6
Estimated demand		40	50	45	50	40	45
In transit	0	0	150	0	0	0	0
Planned receipt							150
Estimated stock	160	120	220	175	125	85	190
Planned order					150		

Table 10.9 Cape Town warehouse

Lead time = 2 weeks Order quantity = 150				In stock = 140 SS = 50			
Week	0	1	2	3	4	5	6
Estimated demand		20	25	15	20	30	25
In transit	0	0	0	0	0	0	0
Planned receipt						150	
Estimated stock	140	120	95	80	60	180	155
Planned order				150			

Table 10.10 Bloemfontein warehouse

Lead time = 1 week Order quantity = 150				In stock = 120 SS = 50			
Week	0	1	2	3	4	5	6
Estimated demand		25	15	20	25	20	20
In transit	0	0	0	0	0	0	0
Planned receipt					150		
Estimated stock	120	95	80	60	185	165	145
Planned order				150			

Table 10.11 Durban warehouse

Lead time = 1 day Order quantity = 300				In stock = 400 SS = 150			
Week	0	1	2	3	4	5	6
Estimated demand		105	115	95	90	100	110
In transit	0	0	0	0	0	0	0
Planned receipt				300			300
Estimated stock	400	295	180	385	295	195	385
Planned order				300			300

planned so that 300 units are ready for dispatch in week 1; and 600 cases in week 3 and so on.

Based on the number of units that have to be produced, MRP can be carried out in a similar way to the planning of distribution requirements. The inventory levels and lead times in respect of the various ingredients, WIP, sub-assemblies and packaging material must be considered. Even the number of staff involved, as well as transportation requirements can be determined beforehand and the necessary arrangements for dispatch can be made.

In conclusion, LRP ensures that the right product is available at the right place at the right time in the right quantities. When implemented effectively, LRP can save a business thousands, if not millions, of rands.

10.6.4 Just-in-time

10.6.4.1 General approach and features of just-in-time

Just-in-time (JIT) is one of several approaches to inventory management that have special relevance to supply chain management (others being MRP and DRP).

JIT suggests that inventories should be available when a business needs them – not earlier and not later. The main principle underlying a JIT system is, therefore, that a business has inventory when needed and none when it is not needed.

Conventional inventory management involves predicting demand, calculating requirements and then procuring that quantity. In JIT operations, stock is acquired only as a result of demand.

Characteristically, JIT is a pull system. In a pull system, the first action in the supply chain is demand for an item. The demand for one item then triggers the demand for another. In contrast, a push system involves providing stock for the next stage of supply.

The JIT concept is based on the *Kanban* system, which was developed by the Toyota Motor Company in Japan. *Kanban* refers to signboards attached to carts delivering small amounts of required components and other materials to locations within Japanese plants. Each signboard precisely details the necessary replenishment quantities and the exact time when the supply activity must take place. Production cards (*kan* cards) establish and authorise the number of items to be produced, while requisition cards (*ban* cards)

Table 10.12 Combined dispatch from plant warehouse

Week	0	1	2	3	4	5	6
Windhoek		300			300		
East London					150		
Cape Town				150			
Bloemfontein				150			
Durban				300			300
Total	0	300	0	600	450	0	300

authorise the withdrawal of required materials from the feeding or supply operation.[8]

The main features of a JIT system are:
- zero or minimum inventory;
- short lead times;
- small, frequent replenishment quantities; and
- high-quality or zero defects.

10.6.4.2 Difference between conventional and JIT systems

Table 10.13 shows the major differences between conventional and JIT inventory management.[9]

10.6.4.3 Application possibilities

The application of JIT systems is not possible in all situations and is more appropriate to certain stages of the supply chain than others. It can be suitable in many manufacturing companies. However, for the retail sector it is important to have stock and as a result JIT supply would not be appropriate.

In high-volume manufacturing, items can be transferred fairly easily from one production stage to the other, and lead times and cycle times can be controlled to a large extent. In distribution operations where demand is variable and uncertain, the application of JIT is more difficult, but not completely impossible.

The typical features of the ideal company for JIT concepts to be applied can be summarised as follows:
- Narrow product range
- Manufacturer
- High volume
- Stable market
- Influential business

- Good-quality management
- Local suppliers of goods and services
- Dependent and reliable suppliers of goods and services
- Fast-cycle processes
- Personal commitment by management and operators

According to Wild:[10]

'An obvious application of JIT is for manufacturers producing large quantities of similar products. They can set up a flow line and have in-line stocks of a single item or a small batch between each process stage. The trigger for manufacture is simply "use one so make one", starting from the last process and feeding back gradually to the first.'

10.6.4.4 Requirements for JIT

The requirements for a JIT system can be summarised as follows:
- Short timescale/short lead time: processes are suitable for JIT if the timescale is in hours rather than days.
- Long-term agreement with suppliers in respect of throughput levels, quality management and commitment.
- Suppliers should be treated as an intrinsic part of the organisation.
- Local suppliers. (Many suppliers locate to the vicinity of a major customer.)
- More frequent deliveries from suppliers.
- Close cooperation and liaison with suppliers of distribution services as well as of goods. (Longer-term, higher-volume commitments with suppliers can result in reduced prices.)

Table 10.13 Contrasts between conventional and JIT systems

Conventional system	JIT system
• Push system	• Pull system
• Satisfied with status quo	• Continuous improvement
• Fixed lead time	• Reducing lead time a continuous challenge
• Product range is a sales issue	• Product range reduction an inventory issue
• Stock in case of customer demand	• Purchase to meet demand rate
• Convenient purchase batch size	• Buy singly or small quantities

Source: First published in Wild, T. 2002. Best Practice in Inventory Management, 2nd ed. Rochester: Butterworth-Heinemann: 60 (copyright Elsevier)

10.6.4.5 Benefits of JIT

A JIT system may bring about several benefits, the most important being a saving in logistics costs due to a reduction in inventory requirements. The most significant savings are in the following areas:

- Reduction in warehousing costs because less space is required.
- Reduction in average inventory values due to a smaller investment in inventory.
- Operational cost savings, particularly in manufacturing, due to fast changeovers. (For example, a change in production set-up from one brand to another provides an opportunity for less inventory. Furthermore, there is less stock that needs to be counted and controlled.)
- There could be a reduction in delivery costs even though delivery quantities are smaller. Smaller delivery quantities means smaller loads, allowing for different transport methods (for example, parcel post instead of a truck load). In addition, frequent fixed route deliveries enable a carrier to have a base load upon which to build other business; frequent deliveries on fixed routes do not require planning and management effort once set up; discounts can be negotiated on contracts based on regularity of service; standard-pack quantities and containers are smaller and less expensive, while recycling is also faster.

Additional costs usually occur because methods have not been changed to suit JIT, for example information systems and agreements with suppliers.

10.6.5 Collaborative inventory initiatives

There are several concepts or methods for collaborative inventory replenishment. Most are based on sound relationships and joint planning among supply chain participants, with the purpose of rapidly replenishing inventory. The initiatives support time-based logistics with the intention of reducing reliance on forecasting in the supply chain and instead moving towards positioning inventory on a JIT basis. Effective collaborative inventory initiatives require a great deal of cooperation and information sharing among the supply chain participants. The most popular collaborative initiatives are briefly discussed next.

10.6.5.1 Collaborative planning, forecasting and replenishment

Collaborative planning, forecasting and replenishment (CPFR) is probably the most widely used collaborative effort between supply chain participants. CPFR is a process that was initiated by the fast-moving consumer goods (FMCG) industry to coordinate the individual forecasts of different participants in the supply chain.

Instead of retailers, distributors, manufacturers, transport providers (and any other participants in a specific supply chain) each producing their own forecast, they share, discuss, coordinate and rationalise individual plans to create a joint plan. A common sales forecast is created and shared between retailer and supplier based on shared knowledge of each participant's plan. Using a consensus forecast, production, replenishment and shipment plans are developed. Internet-based technologies are frequently used to facilitate such collaborative planning.

10.6.5.2 Quick response

Quick response (QR) involves the sharing of retail sales information among supply chain participants. Continuous sharing of information as regards availability and delivery reduces uncertainty in demand and supply across the total supply chain. It reduces the need for safety stock and increases the flexibility of the supply chain.

The primary purpose of QR is 'to enable a company to react faster to market changes and run operations in a more cost-effective manner to ... better satisfy the end-consumers' needs'.[11] QR is based on the following principles:

- Activities concerning inventory flow must be driven by and synchronised with the demand and behaviour of end-consumers.
- QR may be considered as the application of JIT in a distribution (as opposed to a manufacturing) environment.
- The focus should be on reducing lead times.

- Access to and sharing of information in the supply chain is crucial for the QR concept. It relies on trust and openness among the participants.

10.6.5.3 Vendor-managed inventory

Vendor-managed inventory (VMI) is very similar to QR, but eliminates the need for the downstream customer to place a replenishment order. With VMI, the supplier (vendor) manages the customer's stock and plans replenishment orders based on inventory balances and demand information. The supplier commits to maintaining appropriate inventory levels on the customer's premises.

10.6.5.4 Profile replenishment

Profile replenishment (PR) is an extension of QR and VMI, whereby the supplier anticipates future demand based on overall knowledge of the market for a specific product category. A category profile provides details about the combination of sizes, colours and associated products that usually sell in a particular retail store. Under this collaborative arrangement, the supplier can simplify retailer involvement by eliminating the need for the retailer to keep records of sales and determine appropriate inventory levels.

10.7 Inventory control

10.7.1 The purpose of inventory control

The purpose of inventory control is to optimise three objectives:
- Superior customer service
- Relatively low inventory costs
- Lowest possible total operating costs

The challenge is to find a good balance between these three objectives. A good balance results in greater efficiency of the supply chain and increased profits for an individual business.[12]

Customer service in this context relates mainly to availability from current inventory. The second objective (low inventory costs) requires a minimum possible amount of cash tied up in inventory and space. The value and volumetric size of individual items are major considerations in this regard. Minimising total operating costs involves a trade-off among the costs of the major logistics activities. The major operating costs are warehouse operations, inventory, purchasing and transport.

Effective inventory control requires a method whereby management spends more time and effort on inventory that is crucial for balancing the above objectives and less time and effort on less significant items. Such a method involves an ABC classification of inventory.

10.7.2 ABC analysis (Pareto analysis)

10.7.2.1 The Pareto Principle

In a study of the distribution of wealth in Milan during the 18th century, economist Villefredo Pareto found that 20 per cent of the people controlled 80 per cent of the wealth. This logic of the minority having the greatest importance and the majority having little importance has been broadened over the years to include many situations and is termed the Pareto Principle.[13]

Evidence of this principle can be found in our everyday social and economic lives. Examples of the Pareto Principle in business are legion:
- 20 per cent of customers or products account for 80 per cent of sales.
- 80 per cent of stock value is caused by 20 per cent of the stock lines.
- 80 per cent of purchased items come from 20 per cent of the suppliers.
- 80 per cent of warehouse space is occupied by 20 per cent of the stock lines.
- 20 per cent of stock lines give 80 per cent of the turnover.

10.7.2.2 ABC analysis using the Pareto Principle

Pareto analysis forms the basis of inventory control and is an important management tool that can be used to minimise effort and obtain the best results. To gain the best control, effort has to be directed at the most important areas. The Pareto Principle, as illustrated graphically in Figure 10.7, is often called the 80/20 rule. However, the value can be determined at any convenient point. For example,

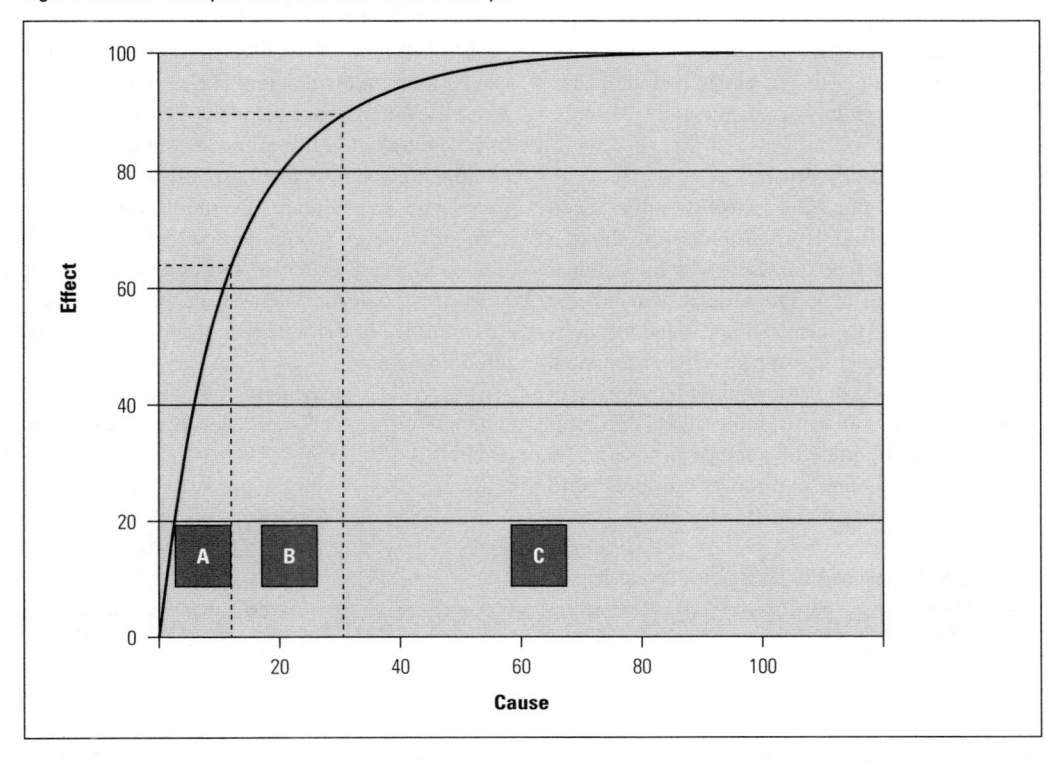

Figure 10.7 ABC analysis based on the Pareto Principle

the graph shows that 50 per cent of the product lines account for 97 per cent of the sales (and that the other 50 per cent account for only 3 per cent of the sales).

The shape of the curve arises from the range of volumes and values combined in a statistical distribution. The shape of the curve does not always give exactly an 80/20 relationship and can vary from business to business. However, this does not affect the principles of applying Pareto analysis to inventory management.

The Pareto Principle can be applied to minimise effort in control and obtain the best results towards achieving the objectives of inventory control. Effort and control should focus on high-cost or high-impact areas, for example high-value items or fast-moving product lines. The 20 per cent of the stock lines that cause 80 per cent of the cost should be subject to tight control to reduce costs. Similarly, tight control on the 20 per cent of the lines that contribute to 80 per cent of the turnover could contribute to excellent customer service.

The ABC classification of inventory can be based on a variety of measures. The most common are annual sales; profit contribution; inventory value; usage rate (demand); and the nature of the item.[14] Since product value is probably the most important determinant of inventory-carrying cost, a combination of annual sales and product value would probably be the most appropriate measure. Annual turnover expressed in monetary terms represents such a combination. Product lines are ranked in relation to the annual turnover using the following formula:

Annual turnover = annual demand × unit cost.

Based on the annual turnover, product lines are classified as follows:

A class = 10 per cent of lines contributing to 65 per cent of turnover

B class = 20 per cent of lines contributing to 25 per cent of turnover

C class = 70 per cent of lines contributing to 10 per cent of turnover

It is important to ensure that ABC analysis is based on turnover, but less important that the exact percentages are adhered to. In some instances, a further classification (D) is useful to include a large number of items with very low turnover.

Example of classification

An example of the ABC classification is given in Tables 10.14 and 10.15. Table 10.14 shows a number of different product lines with their annual demand and unit cost. The annual demand and unit cost are used to calculate the annual turnover. The annual turnover percentage is then calculated and used to rank the items in order of size of annual turnover value. In Table 10.15 the items are arranged in order of annual turnover. The cumulative percentage of turnover is calculated to classify all items as either A, B or C class.

10.7.2.3 Policy and control based on ABC classification

As shown in Table 10.16, different systems of control can be used for the different classes of inventory.[15] Since the A items have the highest value, they have to be controlled tightly using accurate systems in conjunction with market expertise and product knowledge to maintain inventory at the lowest appropriate level. Computerised techniques, with little additional expertise and interference, are most appropriate for B items. Category C items can be controlled by a simple system and with minimal administration.

The ABC classification may also be used to differentiate between service levels, as indicated in Table 10.17.

Table 10.14 Example of ABC classification: ranking

Item	Demand	Cost	Turnover	Turnover %	Rank
101	55	18	990	2,2	5
102	265	28	7 420	16,2	2
103	5	38	190	0,4	10
104	125	13	1 625	3,5	4
105	25	35	875	1,9	6
106	990	30	29 700	64,9	1
107	15	20	300	0,7	8
108	1 250	3	3 750	8,2	3
109	30	10	300	0,7	9
110	10	63	630	1,4	7
			45 780	100	

Table 10.15 Example of ABC classification: identifying A, B and C classes

Item	Demand	Cost	Turnover	Turnover %	Cumul. %	Rank	Class
106	990	30	29 700	64,9	64,9	1	A
102	265	28	7 420	16,2	81,1	2	B
108	1 250	3	3 750	8,2	89,3	3	B
104	125	13	1 625	3,5	92,8	4	C
101	55	18	990	2,2	95,0	5	C
105	25	35	875	1,9	96,9	6	C
110	10	63	630	1,4	98,3	7	C
107	15	20	300	0,7	98,9	8	C
109	30	10	300	0,7	99,6	9	C
103	5	38	190	0,4	100,0	10	C
			45 780	100			

Table 10.16 Policy and control based on ABC inventory classification

Class	Characteristics	Policy	Methods
A	• Few items • Most of turnover	• Tight control • Personal supervision • Communication • Balanced safety stock	• Frequent monitoring (daily) • Accurate records • Sophisticated forecasting • Service level policy (high)
B	• Important items • Significant turnover	• Lean stock policy • Typical stock control • Fast appraisal methods • Manage by exception	• Less frequent monitoring (weekly) • Calculated safety stocks • Limited order value • Computerised • Exception reporting
C	• Many items • Low turnover value • Few movements of low-value items	• Minimum supervision • Supply to order where possible (keep stock centrally) • Large order quantities • Zero or high safety stock policy	• Simple system • Avoid stock shortages or excess • Infrequent ordering • Automatic system

Table 10.17 Different customer service levels for inventory categories

Class	Turnover value (%)	Customer service level (%)	Weighted customer service level (%)
A	66,8	98	65,5
B	23,2	90	20,9
C	10	85	8,5
Overall service level			94,9

10.7.3 Stock cover

Inventory control aims to drive stock towards appropriate levels. These levels are determined by supply and demand factors. Balance is important in ensuring the maximum service is offered with the minimum inventory-carrying cost.

The inventory performance of each item can be monitored using a measurement of stock balance. An appropriate measure to use is the stock cover, which can be defined as the time in which inventory will be depleted at an average demand. It can be calculated as follows:
Stock cover = current stock × 52/annual demand.

The result of this calculation is the number of weeks that the current inventory will last. This is illustrated in Table 10.18 (see page 244), which is a duplication of Table 10.15, but where the current stock balance is added. Using the above formula the stock cover is calculated for each item.

Stock cover shows whether the stock is 'in the right ballpark' and gives an insight into the priority for action. It is not a perfect guide, but it does indicate when review is required. For example, the analysis in table 10.18 shows that action should be taken for item 102. Current stock will last for only half a week. Stock cover should, however, not be used for calculating reorder levels because there are more accurate and appropriate methods for determining the ROP.

Stock turnover is the reciprocal of stock cover and can be used to measure the effectiveness of inventory management. It can be calculated as follows:
Stock turnover = value of annual demand/value of stock.

The result of the calculation gives the number of times that inventory is used up in a year.

Table 10.18 Stock cover

Item	Demand	Cost	Turnover	Turnover %	Cumul. %	Rank	Class	Current stock	Stock cover
106	990	30	29 700	64,9	64,9	1	A	1 025	1,0
102	265	28	7 420	16,2	81,1	2	B	125	0,5
108	1 250	3	3 750	8,2	89,3	3	B	2 500	2,0
104	125	13	1 625	3,5	92,8	4	C	185	1,5
101	55	18	990	2,2	95,0	5	C	165	3,0
105	25	35	875	1,9	96,9	6	C	125	5,0
110	10	63	630	1,4	98,3	7	C	20	2,0
107	15	20	300	0,7	98,9	8	C	60	4,0
109	30	10	300	0,7	99,6	9	C	205	6,8
103	5	38	190	0,4	100,0	10	C	13	2,6
			45 780	100					

Worked example
Value of stock in the warehouse: R150 000
Issues for last 12 months: R900 000
Stock turn: 900 000/150 000 = 6
Thus stock value would be used up completely six times per year.

10.7.4 Setting stock targets based on ABC

Stock cover should not be used for determining reorder levels, but for control purposes to reduce stock levels.

Stock cover ratios can be used to calculate the broad ranges of weeks' cover for each inventory category. An allowable stock cover range can be set for ABC inventory categories in a ratio which is theoretically 1:3:7. Acceptable ranges could be as follows:[16]

- A class: between one and four weeks
- B class: between two and eight weeks
- C class: between three and twenty weeks

10.8 Conclusion

Together with transport costs, inventory costs constitute probably the most significant portion of total logistics costs. Many supply chain decisions are based on the cost of holding inventory. The effective management of inventory throughout the supply chain is therefore of paramount importance. A balance should be found between the levels of inventory required for day-to-day business and the cost involved in holding this inventory.

There are various reasons why it is necessary for businesses in a supply chain to hold inventory. These reasons can be summarised as follows:

- To allow for operating efficiency through economies of scale.
- To balance supply and demand, particularly when seasonality of products occurs.
- To buffer against uncertainties in demand and supply.
- To allow for geographic specialisation.
- To prevent the cost of a stockout.

Inventory can be classified in terms of either the position of the inventory in the supply chain (e.g. raw material, WIP, packaging material, finished goods) or in terms of the purpose that they serve in the supply chain (e.g. cycle inventory, transit inventory, safety stock, speculative stock and dead stock).

A thorough understanding of certain inventory concepts is essential in effective inventory management. The most important concepts are:

- Availability, which can be measured in various ways.
- Average inventory, which can be defined in general as half the order quantity plus safety stock.
- Inventory turnover, showing how many times the inventory is used up in a specific period and gives an indication of the effectiveness of inventory control.

Total inventory costs consist of purchasing costs, ordering costs and carrying costs. Purchasing cost is merely the price of the product. Most supply chain decisions involving inventory are based on ordering costs and carrying costs. Ordering costs consist typically of administration, communication and handling costs that are associated with the placement, processing and receipt of an order. Inventory-carrying costs consist mainly of capital costs, insurance, storage-space costs and obsolescence. An annual carrying-cost percentage can be estimated based on the quantification of inventory-carrying costs. This carrying-cost percentage is used to calculate total inventory-carrying costs. Too high or too low a carrying-cost percentage may result in wrong supply chain decisions.

Inventory planning involves the setting of optimum inventory levels in the supply chain, with due consideration to lowest total logistics costs and uncertainty in demand and supply. The starting point for proper inventory planning is reliable and accurate forecasting of independent demand (the demand for the final product).

Planning cycle stock comprises two major questions: how much to order and when to order. There are various inventory planning systems that can be implemented to answer these two questions. The most popular systems are the review level system and the target stock level system. In the review level system, the order quantity is fixed while the order frequency varies. The target level system involves a fixed order frequency and varying order quantities.

The simple EOQ involves a trade-off between inventory-ordering costs and inventory-carrying costs. Adjustments can be made to the EOQ to provide for volume transport rates and purchase quantity discounts. The ROP (when to order) depends on the lead time (the period between placing an order and receiving it), the forecast demand during the lead time and safety stock requirements. The ROP is expressed in numbers of units.

The TSL system is used when orders are placed at fixed time intervals, such as weekly, bi-weekly or monthly.

While very little savings are possible in cycle stock, safety stock reductions may offer substantial savings. To achieve these savings safety stock levels need to be carefully planned. Safety stock levels depend mainly on the variability of demand, the variability of the supply lead time, the duration of the lead time, the order quantity and the service level policy of the business. The calculation of safety stock involves the application of statistical methods. The standard deviation (which is a measure of variability) is used to estimate the probability of a stockout. A combined standard deviation to accommodate both demand and lead-time variability can be calculated. Based on probability theory and the combined standard deviation, safety stock requirements can be calculated to protect against the probability of a stockout. The magnitude of a stockout can be estimated by calculating the fill rate, based on the combined standard deviation and the order quantity.

LRP is a scheduling technique that aims to reduce total inventory in the supply chain by reducing the reliance on forecasting for all items. It involves the integration of DRP and MRP. Whereas DRP involves forecasting and planning availability of the final product, MRP involves planning the availability of all resources and materials required for production. MRP is driven by a production schedule, which, in turn, is based on the demand for the final product.

JIT purchasing is regarded as one of several approaches to inventory management that have special relevance to supply chain management (other approaches being MRP and DRP). JIT involves having inventory when needed and none when not needed. Although the ideal would be to operate with zero inventory, this is hardly possible in any situation. JIT is more applicable to manufacturing than to distribution operations.

There are several concepts involving collaborative inventory replenishment. Most of these concepts are based on sound relationships and joint planning among supply chain participants. The initiatives support time-based logistics with the aim of reducing reliance on forecasting in the supply chain and moving towards positioning inventory on a JIT basis. The most popular collaborative initiatives are CPFR, QR, VMI and PR.

Inventory control involves finding the suitable balance between superior customer service (ensuring availability), reduced inventory costs and lowest possible logistics operating costs that will result in greater efficiency of the supply chain and increased profits for the business. Based on the Pareto Principle, an ABC system is used to categorise all product lines or SKUs. The Pareto Principle is applied to minimise effort in control and obtain the objectives of inventory control. Management effort and control should focus on high-cost or high-impact areas, for example high-value items or fast-moving product lines. The 20 per cent of the stock lines that cause 80 per cent of the cost should be subject to tight control to reduce costs. Similarly, tight control on the 20 per cent of the lines that contribute to 80 per cent of the turnover could contribute to excellent customer service.

The A class includes typically the 10 per cent of the items that contribute 65 per cent to the turnover. B class items usually constitute some 20 per cent of the product lines that contribute 25 per cent to turnover and C class items consist of the remaining 70 per cent of the items that contribute 10 per cent to turnover.

Stock balance is important in ensuring maximum service is offered with a minimum inventory-carrying cost. Stock cover, which is defined as the time in which inventory will be depleted at an average demand rate, is a valuable tool to find such balance. Stock cover ratios can be used to calculate the broad ranges of weeks' cover for each inventory category. An allowable stock cover range can be set for ABC inventory categories in a ratio which is theoretically 1:3:7.

Key terms

ABC analysis (Pareto Analysis)
Availability
Average inventory
Collaborative inventory replenishment
Collaborative planning, forecasting and replenishment (CPFR)
Cycle stock
Decoupling
Dependent and independent demand
Distribution requirements planning (DRP)
Economic order quantity (EOQ)
Fill rate
Inventory-carrying costs
Inventory-ordering costs
Inventory turnover
Just-in-time (JIT)
Logistics requirement planning (LRP)
Material requirements planning (MRP)
Orders shipped complete
Profile replenishment (PR)
Quick response (QR)
Reorder point (ROP)
Review level system
Safety stock
Speculative stock
Standard deviation
Stock cover
Stock-keeping unit (SKU)
Stockout frequency
Target stock level system (TSL)
Transit inventory
Uncertainty
Vendor-managed inventory (VMI)
Work-in-process (WIP)

Case study

JNC produces a number of dairy products – amongst others, condensed milk. The two major ingredients for condensed milk are fresh milk and sugar. The plant is in Van der Bijl Park, situated in Gauteng. While milk is freely available in the area, sugar is sourced from a factory in Durban. After processing, the condensed milk is canned and packed into boxes of 24 units each for distribution. After thorough market research, the following points were determined:

- The demand for the product justifies distribution facilities in Johannesburg, Cape Town, Durban and Bloemfontein.
- Fluctuations in demand and lead time necessitate safety stock of approximately half the average weekly consumption at each distribution facility as indicated as 'SS req.' in Table 10.19.
- Sugar can be ordered and transported in units of 1 000 kg. The average lead time from date of order

to delivery for sugar is two weeks, but in view of possible delays it was established that 6 000 kg of sugar is desirable as safety stock.
- It takes approximately one week to process and pack the final product.

JNC uses a planning period of six weeks, during which the demand for the number of boxes of condensed milk has been established as shown in Table 10.19.

Assumptions
- Most economical transport arrangements: minimum of 100 boxes and always in units of 100 boxes.
- 10 kg sugar are required for one box (24 cans) of final product.
- We are now in week 0.
- JNC wants to keep minimum stock due to high interest rates and therefore did not establish a specific order quantity.
- Apart from the final product in stock at the distribution centres as shown in the table, the following additional stock is available:
    - Van der Bijl plant: 40 000 kg sugar and 1 000 boxes of final product
    - In transit to Cape Town: 600 boxes of final product for receipt in week 2

Based on this scenario, you are required to:
1 Prepare a schedule that will ensure that the demand at the different centres for the duration of the planning period is met at the lowest cost.
2 Indicate how much sugar should be ordered during the planning period to produce enough cases of the final product.

Case study

Logic Building Supplies (LBS, Inc), a Gauteng-based company, specialises in the supply of ten exclusive items required in the building industry to estate developers and construction companies across the country. The weekly demand, unit price and current stock of the items are given in Table 10.20.

Due to the high cost of certain items, the fast turnover of others and the fear of unavailability to the industry, LBS management spends much time and effort on inventory decisions, while also experiencing substantial inventory-carrying costs. Even with all the time and effort, they do not seem to get it right.
1 What suggestions can you put forward to LBS to assist in its inventory control?
2 What immediate action should be taken?

Table 10.19 JNC's planning period

Depot	In stock	SS req.	Lead time	Week					
				1	2	3	4	5	6
Jhb	1 200	500	1 day	1 000	900	1 100	1 050	950	900
C Town	1 000	200	3 wks	500	300	500	400	350	450
Dbn	1 200	350	2 wks	700	650	650	700	650	700
Bfn	300	120	1 wk	200	220	250	250	200	220

Table 10.20 Logic Building Supplies' stock, price and demand

Item	Weekly demand	Unit price (R)	Current stock
1	200	3 000	600
2	200	8 000	1 000
3	2 000	4 000	5 000
4	4 000	500	6 000
5	1 000	65 000	5 000
6	100	9 000	5 000
7	300	1 000	1 200
8	100	170 000	500
9	1 000	3 500	2 000
10	2 200	500	500

Questions

1. Holding inventory in the supply chain involves numerous risks. Explain why companies in the various stages of a supply chain find it necessary to hold inventory despite the risks attached to it.
2. Differentiate between the various types of inventory found in the supply chain.
3. Briefly explain the following concepts:
   a) Average inventory
   b) Reorder point
   c) Inventory turnover
   d) Inventory-ordering costs
   e) Inventory-carrying costs
   f) The economic order quantity
4. Explain fully how you would calculate inventory-carrying costs. Clearly indicate how each component of inventory-carrying costs can be quantified to arrive at an appropriate carrying-cost percentage.
5. Mandla Liquors, a local retailer of alcoholic drinks, sells, among others, XXX Beer.
   a) What would be the most economic order quantity for XXX Beer, given the following information (show all your calculations and base your answer on the total of annual ordering costs, annual carrying costs and annual transport costs):

Annual demand volume:	2 400 cases
Case value at cost:	R50
Inventory-carrying cost percentage:	20% annually
Ordering cost, including handling:	R190 per order
Transport cost for quantities below 480 cases:	R10 per case
Transport costs for quantities of 480 or more cases:	R7,50 per case

   b) Calculate the safety stock requirements for XXX Beer, given the following information:

Standard deviation of weekly sales:	10 cases
Standard deviation of the lead time:	0,25 weeks
Average weekly sales:	200 cases
Average lead time:	1 week
Service level requirement:	98%

6. An analysis of the daily sales and lead time of a certain kind of wine produced the following results:

Standard deviation of daily sales:	20 cases
Standard deviation of lead time:	1,634 days
Average lead time:	10 days
Average daily sales:	100 cases
Most economic order quantity:	700 cases

   Corresponding f(k) values for certain safety factors (K) based on a normal distribution are as follows:

K	f(k)	K	f(k)
0,3	0,2667	1,0	0,0833
0,4	0,2304	1,1	0,0686
0,5	0,1977	1,2	0,0561
0,6	0,1686	1,3	0,0455

   a) Calculate the combined standard deviation.
   b) How many cases of safety stock should be kept to protect against stockout occurrences for 98 per cent of all order cycles?
   c) What is the fill rate with a safety stock of 190 cases?
   d) How many cases of safety stock should be kept to maintain a fill rate of 95 per cent?
   e) What would be the resulting average inventory to maintain a fill rate of 95 per cent?
   f) How would a change in order quantity influence the safety stock if a fill rate of 95 per cent is to be maintained?
   g) Explain the difference between the probability of a stockout and the magnitude of a stockout.
7. Differentiate between dependent and independent demand and explain how this difference affects logistics requirements planning (LRP).
8. Fully discuss the just-in-time (JIT) philosophy for inventory management. Pay particular attention to:
   - the features of JIT;

- the difference between conventional systems and JIT;
- JIT application possibilities;
- the requirements for JIT; and
- the benefits of JIT.

9 In modern supply chains, collaborative inventory replenishment becomes increasingly important to reduce total costs. Fully discuss collaborative inventory replenishment with particular emphasis on the most popular collaborative initiatives.

10 Fully explain how you will use ABC stock classification (based on the Pareto Principle) and stock cover to effectively control inventory.

Consult the web

The Association for Operations Management of Southern Africa: http://www.sapics.org.za

Just Enough Demand Management: http://www.justenoughuniversity.com

RFID Institute SA: http://www.rfidtec.co.za

Six Sigma Systems: http://www.sixsigmasystems.com

http://www.supplychaininfo.co.za

Consult the books

Bowersox, D. J. and Closs, D. J. 1996. *Logistical Management. The Integrated Supply Chain Process*. New York: McGraw-Hill.

Bowersox, D .J., Closs, D. J. and Cooper, M. B. 2007. *Supply Chain Logistics Management*. New York: McGraw-Hill.

Chopra, S., Reinhardt, G. and Dada, M. 2004. 'The effect of lead time uncertainty on safety stocks'. *Decision Sciences*, 35(1): 1–24.

Coyle, J. J., Bardi, E. J. and Langley Jr, C. J. 2003. *The Management of Business Logistics: A Supply Chain Perspective*, 7th edition. Mason: South-Western, Thomson Learning.

Dullaert, W., Vernimmen, B., Aghezzaf, E. and Raa, B. 2007. 'Revisiting service-level measurement for an inventory system with different transport modes'. *Transport Reviews*, 27(3): 273–83.

Grant, D. B., Lambert, D. M., Stock, J. R. and Elram, L. M. 2006. *Fundamentals of Logistics Management: European Edition*. McGraw-Hill.

Jonsson, P. 2008. *Logistics and Supply Chain Management*. McGraw-Hill.

Stock, J. R. and Lambert, D. M. 2001. *Strategic Logistics Management*, 4th edition. New York: McGraw-Hill.

Wild, T. 2002. *Best Practice in Inventory Management*, 2nd edition. Rochester: Butterworth-Heinemann.

Notes

1   Stock, J. R. and Lambert, D. M. 2001: 232.
2   Chopra et al. 2004; Wild, T. 2002: 121.
3   Bowersox et al. 2007: 149; Wild, T. 2002: 123.
4   Wild, T .2002: 20.
5   Bowersox, D. J. and Closs, D. J. 1996: 256.
6   Stock, J. R. and Lambert, D. M. 2001: 200.
7   Dullaert et al. 2007.
8   Coyle et al. 2003: 247.
9   Wild, T. 2002: 60.
10 Ibid.: 76.
11 Jonsson, P. 2008: 377.
12 Wild, T. 2002: 7–8.
13 Stock, J. R. and Lambert, D. M. 2001: 256.
14 Bowersox et al. 2007: 162.
15 Wild, T. 2002: 38.
16 Ibid.: 47.

11 The design of storage and handling facilities

J. Vogt

Learning outcomes

After you have studied this chapter, you should be able to:
- explain why it may become necessary to amend the design of an existing logistics facility;
- define the purpose of the facility and explain why understanding the initial requirements of the facility is important;
- realise the importance of planning for growth;
- realise the importance of operations and warehouse management systems in facility design;
- understand the factors affecting the size of a facility;
- explain how to use vertical space (height) to achieve cost-effective storage;
- define a product process category (PPC) and give an example of one;
- identify and define the PPCs in a facility;
- plan and design the storage and handling areas of the building for each PPC;
- define and allocate the times of operation for different PPC areas;
- assemble the PPCs into a composite building that is efficient and cost-effective;
- calculate the total floor area required for a storage facility, including aisles and racks;
- define the loading and unloading requirements in terms of floor space and doors for transport;
- understand the requirements for security and the limitations thereof;
- understand the primary requirements for fire protection and the legal requirements for building protection; and
- specify the overall building shape and orientation to suit logistics, as opposed to architectural, requirements.

11.1 Introduction

Logistics networks normally consist of a number of different physical logistics facilities, such as manufacturing warehouses, distribution centres and terminals. The design of these facilities influences the long-term ability to meet customer requirements and provide value. A poorly designed facility can lock management into a non-competitive situation and be very expensive to correct.

The design of the building structure falls within the sphere of expertise of the architect and building professionals. The orientation of the building and the space allocation within it are the domain of the logistics professional. Poor orientation and space allocation will cause the operation to be inefficient and costly throughout the life of the facility. Therefore, spending time and effort up front on designing the building to suit the logistics requirements of the organisation holds future benefits. The principles of good design are applicable to all facilities, whether the design is for a new facility or an existing one.

This chapter examines the methodologies for designing changes in an existing facility in order to make it more efficient and effective. The design of a new facility is a specialised function and beyond the scope of this text. However, the principles of design for an efficient facility must be understood, since no facility exists without changes occurring in the product mix handled, the customers serviced and the value-added services offered. These issues impact on the layout and design of the most efficient facility. As the products handled change, the demands on the facility also change, so the facility should be altered to make it as efficient as possible.

It is important to understand the principles involved in the design of an efficient facility so that as the demands on the facility develop and change they can be translated into changes to the facility in order to maintain its efficiency. It is recommended that the entire facility be reviewed as to the correct layout and slotting used for the products at least twice a year. Since this cannot be done by outside consultants this regularly without significant cost, the logistics personnel at the facility should bear this responsibility.

11.2 Initial requirements

The requirements for the facility to satisfy customers need to be known and recorded. These should be documented so that the reasoning is available for future reference. As changes occur, the facility's layout and operation can then be reviewed with an understanding of the basis of the original design and layout. This facilitates modification to the facility without the concern that the changes might overlook an inherently important reason to maintain a specific process or layout.

Two aspects determine the initial requirements for the design of a facility:

- The first is the purpose of the facility. This includes whether the facility is to be a storage facility, a distribution facility, a cross-dock facility or combinations of any or all of these (these are more fully explained in Chapter 14), and whether the service promised is next-day or same-day delivery.
- The second is the growth forecast for the facility over its lifetime. In other words, a forecast of its future storage and handling requirements is required. The facility can then be sized and orientated to allow for these future needs. It is not sufficient merely to allocate space or additional land for expansion – a plan needs to be developed to allow this to happen in a measured fashion.

There are restrictions on the design of any facility. The size of the land may restrict the orientation, and slopes may restrict truck access. The design should accommodate these restrictions. However, it is of primary importance to remain as close to the ideal design as possible, and then to amend the design accordingly to deal with restrictions. The restrictions should not be introduced before the basic needs are identified and translated into design aspects. The design should focus on enabling the facility to service the needs of the customers, and not on the restrictions.

11.2.1 Purpose of the facility

The needs of the customers must be translated into the functions required from the facility, which is in the supply chain in order to promote the flow of the correct products to the customer to match or exceed the customers' service standard. Therefore, the facility has to match the various products and processes required by product ranges offered to the customer. Each product and process group is called a PPC.

> A product process category (PPC) is a product or group of products that are stored in a similar manner and/or require the same handling processes.

A new PPC may be created if the handling processes or the storage requirements differ sufficiently from other products. For example, there may be different PPCs for different temperature zones (based on product differences), and for different storage and cross-dock processes within the facility (based on handling differences). PPCs are defined in more detail in Chapter 14.

Every restriction in a supply chain introduces a source of potential inefficiency. The same is true when new PPCs are created. They need to be in different areas of the building, introducing additional travel and handling. For example, there is little to be gained from storing different produce in separate temperature zones that differ by only 2°C, as some facilities do. This merely increases the number of restrictions, resulting in poor use of space; an increased number of walls; resulting in increased capital cost; and an increased number of doors in the facility, resulting in increased travel problems, all of which reduce the efficiency of the operation. Each PPC requires different processes and areas to operate in. It will be extremely difficult and costly to expand later if the requirements for expansion are not considered initially when designing a warehouse with multiple PPCs.

11.2.2 Growth forecast for the facility

The use of a facility generally entails a commitment for a number of years. A new facility is unlikely to have an expected life of less than ten years – and perhaps longer. A facility that is too small, or does not have the flexibility to grow, is a nightmare for any operation. The operation becomes more and more inefficient, and the existing facility commitments preclude the creation of a new facility. It is therefore essential to estimate the future growth of the facility and to design into the facility the ability to expand.

The future needs (for the next five years or more) for each of the PPCs must be estimated. Each PPC has different growth rates and imposes different requirements on the facility. Part of a responsible design process is forecasting what is required over the lifetime of the facility. This forecast cannot be entirely accurate, as the market may alter in ways that were not foreseen. However, the design will be considerably better if the forecast is used. The need to do this forecast at PPC level is evident when there are significant differences in the growth from one PPC to another. Plans must be in place to allow each of these areas to be expanded. These might involve, for example, moving one PPC into an existing PPC, with the displaced PPC moving into a new expansion. Whatever the expansion plans involve, the important issue is the continued efficient operation of the facility in line with the growth forecast.

11.3 Sizing the warehouse

A warehouse is more than just a structure. It is part of the supply chain and needs to integrate the inbound and the outbound transport for the chain. To achieve this it must incorporate the transport area and access to roads and other essential services. A good rule of thumb is that the building itself should only occupy 40 to 50 per cent of the land, with the remainder set aside for transport manoeuvring, parking and access.

11.3.1 Cost factors affecting the size of a warehouse

The cost of a warehouse is significant in the total logistics chain. The warehouse needs to be designed to be cost-effective in the supply chain. Once the land is acquired, the principal cost lies in the base of the building, the floor and the roof. The cost of the walls is a small percentage of the total cost. It is estimated that the floor and the roof account for 80 per cent of the building cost. It is therefore significantly cheaper to expand storage space vertically than to create additional floor area. Storage in racks is a very cost-effective means of increasing the volume of goods in a given floor space.

11.3.2 Other factors affecting the size of a warehouse

Some of the most important factors affecting the size of a warehouse are:[1]
- Customer service levels
- Size of market(s) served
- Number of products marketed
- Size of the products
- Materials-handling system used
- Inventory turnover
- Aisle requirements
- Office area requirements
- Production lead times
- Types of racks and shelves used
- Level and pattern of demand

Changing market conditions and business strategies may result in a change in these factors, which, in turn, will impose new requirements on the optimal size of a warehouse. For example, increasing customer service levels and market demand are usually associated with an increase of inventory, which requires more warehousing space. Similarly, if the market demand becomes more volatile it creates uncertainty with planners and may necessitate increased safety stock and, therefore, more warehousing space. In general, greater warehousing space is required when products are large; inventory turnover rates are low; manual materials-handling systems are used;

production lead times are long; and the warehouse requires many office-based tasks.[2]

11.4 Operations and warehouse management systems

As part of the design process, it is necessary to choose and define the principles of operation and the capabilities of the operations and warehouse management systems (WMS). The principles of operation that influence facility design are discussed in the following sections.

11.4.1 Method of receiving goods

The partial receipt of a load of goods reduces the size of the receiving bay dramatically. For partial receipts to be effective there must be the capability of moving the goods quickly from the receiving bay while unloading continues and the receipt is recorded into the WMS at the same time.

11.4.2 The use and control of equipment in the warehouse

The appropriate equipment must be chosen to transfer the goods from the storage area and move them to the dispatch assembly area. The size of the warehouse and the operational processes must be taken into account when choosing such equipment.

11.4.3 Picking capability

If an order is big enough to necessitate full pallets, these are taken from where they are stored. The remaining products needed to fulfil the order are taken from the pick face. The full pallets taken from storage as part of an order are moved directly to the order assembly area and not to the pick face. As the product in the pick face is removed, it must be replenished by moving a full pallet from storage to the pick face. Ideally, the full pallet should be taken from a reserve and moved to the pick face just as the last item in the pick face is removed. Systems cannot operate to this tight time tolerance, and the reserve pallet must be moved to the pick slot just before the final items are removed from the pick face. If the reserve pallet is moved too early, the items in the pick face must be removed and placed on the new full pallet from the reserve and the total placed into the pick slot. If the pallet is late in being moved to the pick slot, then the selector either has to wait, or will be forced to return to the slot. Both of these processes are very inefficient.

One must have a clear understanding of what needs to be achieved with the proposed operation and WMS. Every step in the operation requires equipment or storage/rest areas that have to be considered in the design.

11.5 The design process

11.5.1 Assumptions

Once the number of PPCs, their requirements and the growth forecast have been determined, then the design can be realised in detail.

In all cases, it is assumed that the transport is operated as one fleet for all products from a facility. This is the most cost-effective and efficient manner of utilising transport. It is not efficient or effective to maintain fleets for each PPC in a facility. Different transport is only required when a product differs so radically from the other products that it requires special attention. The most common example of this is frozen products, which need to be stored at -20°C and which cannot be transported together with any other grocery items without special enclosures.

The detailed design must include the space and capabilities required for handling each PPC. The design should be centred on five operational processes: storage, receiving, order picking and dispatch. The principles of these are discussed in the following sections.

11.5.2 Stages in the design process

Various methods are suggested for approaching a design. Some texts recommend that the design start with the storage area, then look at operational flows and then at the receive and dispatch areas.

Others recommend this process in reverse. The best approach, however, is to consider all of these in an iterative process (i.e. the process is repeated until it is sufficiently refined). The demands for each area impact on other areas. One should seek the appropriate balance between the number of PPCs, the storage areas, operating areas and the flow into and from the warehouse. Each aspect should therefore be considered and one should determine the best combination to suit the current and future needs of the customers.

The iterative process is simple. After each PPC is identified, the design should define the following aspects:
- Storage requirements
- Handling and moving areas
- Assembly areas for transport loading and unloading
- Receiving requirements

The next stage of the process is to combine the requirements for each PPC into a common facility that is efficient and cost-effective. This is done in three stages by deciding:
- which areas are unique to each PPC;
- which areas can be shared with other PPC operations, and the impact of the increased traffic on the size of the common areas; and
- the periods when the various PPC operations will take place.

If one PPC operates in a completely different period from another operation, all the areas (except the storage) can potentially be used as common areas. This immediately presents an opportunity for saving space. Where PPCs share a space such as a moving area, the storage areas need to be located near one another. Storage for each PPC requires specific space that cannot be shared with any other PPC. Moving areas, loading and unloading areas, and assembly areas can potentially be shared. Each of these possibilities should be assessed on the basis of the requirements for individual PPCs.

The above discussion reflects the stages of the design process. A practical example towards the end of the chapter illustrates how to apply this information.

First, however, it is important to understand how to use calculations to assign the appropriate areas to each operation. To make this information more accessible, one PPC will be discussed in detail – starting with storage (see Section 11.5.3).

This process is essential for the correct operation of a facility. It is highly unlikely that facilities will not have new products, new transport and new operations introduced on a regular basis. The ability to adapt to these changes is founded in a correct understanding of the principles of layout and the ability to undertake simple calculations to determine the areas and layout alternatives. Without this, adaptation of the facility will be sub-optimal and inefficient. Instinct or intuition alone will not produce an efficient operation – it must be founded on calculated outcomes.

11.5.3 Storage

The basic storage modes are:
- block stacking;
- racking (various forms with different pallet handling);
- drive-in racking; and
- mobile racking.

For the example, we chose a PPC that is stored in racks, but the calculations that follow can be adapted for other modes of storage.

As discussed in Chapter 13, the use of racking increases the storage density of the warehouse. (Storage density refers to the amount of goods per square metre of floor space). In addition to the space taken up by the racks, the design must include space to allow access to the racks. The equipment chosen to move the pallets to and from the rack slots determines the aisle width. The equipment must be able to travel up and down the aisle and turn to place the pallets in the racks. Most warehouses use reach trucks for placing pallets and these require an aisle width of approximately 2,8 m. Narrow aisle stackers require approximately 1,5 m, but cost significantly more than reach trucks. This is a design trade-off: one has to determine whether the cost-effectiveness of the increased number of racks per square metre offsets the price of the narrow aisle stacker.

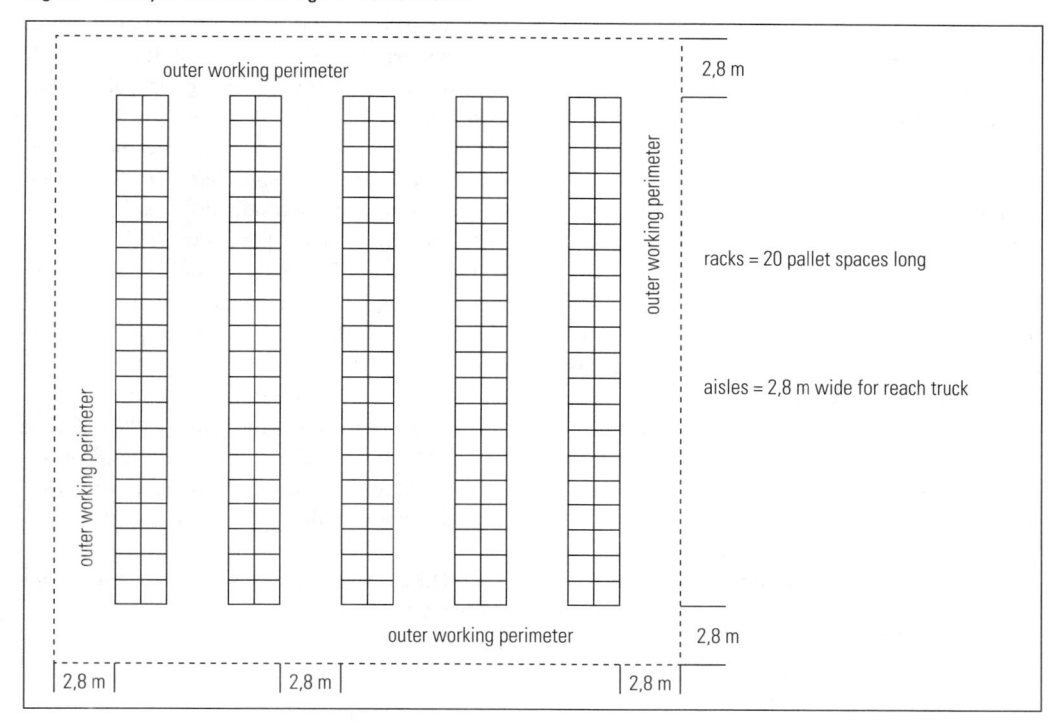

Figure 11.1 Layout of rack storage in a warehouse

Once the choice of equipment is made, the aisle width is then determined. The equipment must also be able to move from one aisle to another. The space required for this is shown in Figure 11.1, with the outer working perimeter shown by a dotted line.

11.5.3.1 Example

A business requires storage for 1 000 pallets. Racks are the most economical storage method. The warehouse is therefore designed to have ten rows of racks. Each row of racks is five spaces high and twenty spaces long. The racks are placed with two rows adjacent (back-to-back) to each other. The pallets are placed in the rack spaces by a reach truck, which requires a 2,8 m wide aisle. To provide appropriate storage space, the area that is required is determined as follows:

Each rack (a single space for a pallet of goods) occupies:
1,2 m from front to back (depth)
1,4 m from side to side (length)
1,8 m from top to bottom (height)

Four aisles are needed between the racks. Two aisles are needed to service the outer racks, and aisles are needed at both ends to move the reach stacker from one aisle to another (see the outer working perimeter in Figure 11.1).

Floor area of the racks

Floor area per rack space = length of racks × depth of racks
= 1,4 m × 1,2 m

Floor area for one row of racks = number of racks in the length × floor area per rack space
= 20 × 1,4 m × 1,2 m
= 33,6 m² per rack

Floor area for ten rows of racks = 336 m²

Total floor area

Length of the storage area = rack length + outer aisles
= (length of a rack × number of racks per row) + (aisle width × 2)
= (1,4 m × 20) + (2 × 2,8 m)
= 33,6 m

Width of the storage area = width of racks + width of aisles
= (width of racks × number of racks) + (aisle width × number of aisles)
= (1,2 m × 10) + (2,8 m × 6)
= 28,8 m

Total area = length × width
= 33,6 m × 28,8 m
= 967,68 m^2

It is important to note that, although the racks cover only 336 m^2 of floor space, the total floor area needs to be approximately 968 m^2 to operate equipment in this area – nearly 2,9 times bigger than the rack area itself. The floor area needs to be calculated correctly in the design, otherwise the operations will be inefficient.

Any storage area, irrespective of the storage method, must be evaluated in the same manner.

11.5.3.2 Design principle: storage

The density of the storage is directly dependent on the width of the aisles and the height of the racks. The higher the racks or the smaller the aisle, the greater the density.

11.5.4 Receiving

The size of the largest truck commonly received is used as the basis for the design of the receiving area. If larger trucks are occasionally received, the operation needs to be adapted to handle it.

Two important steps dominate the process of receiving a truck. The first step is to identify the quantity and quality of the goods. The second step is to record the receipt into the warehouse.

The size of the area required for the receipt is equal to the size of the largest load that must be placed on the floor to determine the quantity and quality of the goods. If the WMS and the processes can handle a partial receipt (namely, a part of the load which is received and sent to storage while the remainder is still being unloaded), then the size of the area needs to be only a portion of that required for the total load. In such a case, there must be a working aisle for identifying and moving the items.

An aisle must be created to allow equipment to move the pallets and to allow for the identification of individual pallets. The size of the aisle will depend on the configuration of the pallets, but good practice deems that the pallets be placed into two rows. These rows start one movement-aisle width from the door. There should be one movement aisle on each side of the pallet rows, as well as on the far side of the rows. This is shown in the Figure 11.2, where it is assumed that the next receiving bay has a similar configuration and allows access to the second row of pallets. This allows any pallet to be removed from the received pallets. If it is not necessary to remove specific pallets from within the rows and pallets can be removed as they arrive (i.e. from the end of the row furthest from the door), then movement aisles along the length of the rows are not required.

Figure 11.2 Layout of the receiving bay for a truck size of 22 pallets

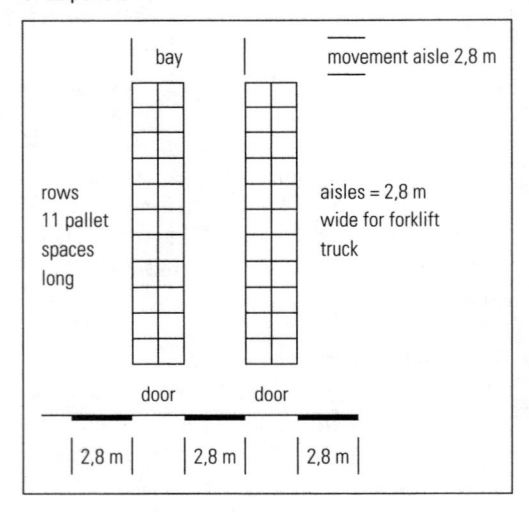

11.5.4.1 Example 1

Assume the largest truck commonly received is 15 m long and can hold 22 pallets of goods. This is used to size the receiving bays, as the WMS and the operation of the warehouse do not allow for the receipt of partial shipments. The receiving bay, therefore, needs to be bigger than the area of the pallets. Two rows of 11 pallets each are made. A forklift truck is used to move the pallets and requires a width of 2,8 m in which to operate.

Pallet area = number of pallets × area of a pallet
= 22 × (1,2 m × 1,4 m)
= 36,96 m²

Aisle area = length of row of pallets × operating width
= 11 × 1,4 m × 2,8 m
= 43,12 m²

Bay area for rows and adjacent movement aisle
= 80,08 m²

11.5.4.2 Example 2

The WMS may also allow for the immediate receipt of each pallet from a truck the same size as above. This can be done if the pallets are inspected manually and the goods do not require detailed inspection or withdrawal from the rows in the bay.

As it is highly likely that no pallet truck will be available at times to move the pallets, some will be placed on the floor. A suitable design will include an area big enough for approximately 50 per cent of the pallets, with a walk aisle of 1 m between pallet-unloading areas for successive doors. As there are 22 pallets, each row should be at least five pallets long.

Area of pallets = 2 rows of 5 pallets
= 5 × 2 × (1,4 × 1,2)
= 16,8 m²

Aisle = 5 pallets long × width of aisle for walking between stacks
= 5 × 1,2 × 1
= 6 m²

Total area = 22,8 m²

11.5.4.3 Design principle: receiving

It is important to design for the current limitations, while identifying the potential for improvement from these limitations.

Example 2 (Section 11.5.4.2) allows for a more effective use of the floor area, which results in a far more cost-effective warehouse. These decisions are important. If the warehouse is laid out for less effective WMS and operations (as in Example 1), the introduction of more effective WMS and operations will improve the floor utilisation. However, if the design assumes very effective systems and operations, but these are not in place, then the warehouse will have inadequate space and will be highly inefficient because of congestion.

11.5.5 Pick area

If items are picked manually from storage, the picking is done in the aisles between the storage areas. As space is already allocated for the reach stacker or similar equipment to move in the aisle, no additional space is required for item picks (i.e. those which are not full pallets). Where a pick requires one or more full pallets plus additional items, the pick occurs from the pick face (at ground level) and the reach truck takes the full pallet or pallets from storage or reserve stock (generally in the upper racks).

If the reach truck takes the pallet to the dispatch bay, no additional space is required. However, reach trucks are specifically designed to move pallets vertically. The primary function of the equipment in the aisle is to feed the pick face and remove the required full pallets from the upper rack reserves. If this is not done, the selection or picking process is interrupted and the entire process becomes inefficient. If the reach truck remains in the aisle and the picked pallets are moved to the dispatch bays with faster equipment, such as pallet trucks, a handover area is required near the aisles. The reach truck places the pallets in the handover zone and the high-speed pallet truck picks them up and takes them to the dispatch bay.

11.5.6 Dispatch area

Transport usually constitutes a significant portion of the land-based part of the logistics chain. The goods must be transferred to the transport as fast as possible to reduce the cost of transport waiting time. The goods must, therefore, be assembled as they are picked to create a truck load. The full load, which consists of goods from different parts of the warehouse, needs to be assembled in one area.

The various items are picked in different sections of the warehouse and then made into full pallets. An order rarely comprises full pallets only, as the probability is that each section of the warehouse will send a partially full pallet. Partial pallets can be consolidated once the pallets are in the assembly bay (or dispatch area). This is done by moving items from one partially filled pallet to another until no more than one partially filled pallet remains for the total load. It is therefore recommended that the assembly area is approximately 10 per cent bigger than the area covered by the largest truck load. As the truck size determines the limits, the size of the assembly area is determined by the transport needs and not directly by the number of PPCs. The need to limit the number of sections in the facility is emphasised again here, as consolidating the incomplete pallets is a direct result of these limitations, and involves additional work.

Trucks often have more than one destination. Consolidating two or more destinations into routes is an efficient use of transport. To allow the assembled pallets for one destination to be moved from one dispatch assembly area to another door for loading necessitates an aisle of approximately 2,8 m between the door and the start of the assembly area. An aisle is also required between the pallets to allow for the manual consolidation of partial pallets.

Pallets are often wrapped with plastic to make a stable load. Wrapping the consolidated pallets in the dispatch assembly aisles is an inefficient use of space, as it necessitates an increase in the width of the aisles to 1,5 m to allow for a pallet jack to be operated. It is better to wrap the full pallets before they are placed in the assembly area. The consolidated pallets are either wrapped before being placed in the dispatch assembly lane, or just prior to loading into the vehicle. The latter would be done in the space between the assembly areas and the loading door. No real delay occurs if the consolidated pallets are moved to one side in the movement aisle between the door and the beginning of the assembly area rows and wrapped while the full, wrapped pallets are checked and loaded onto the truck.

The size of the total assembly area is then determined as follows:
- The length of the lane of pallets in each bay is determined by the largest truck capacity, or
- Two lanes of pallets, where each of the pallet lanes are half the length of the pallets from the largest transport size. The lanes will be segregated by 800 mm to allow inspection and wrapping, and
- The number of routes of delivery at a time determines the number of bays.

11.5.7 Movement zones

The movement of a pallet from the pick area to, say, the dispatch area must be done via a clear floor area. These movement aisles should be 20 to 25 per cent wider than what is needed for the largest piece of equipment. If the aisles carry one-way traffic, they need to accommodate only the largest machine. If they carry two-way traffic, they must be wide enough for two machines to pass each other at speed. There must not be the continual need to slow down when two machines approach each other in a movement aisle.

With careful planning, the movement aisles can serve various PPC areas. While the traffic density will make the common aisle slightly wider than an aisle for a single PPC, considerable space is saved using common aisles. The common aisle also facilitates better management of the warehouse.

11.5.8 Flows

Separate PPCs may result in separate storage areas, movement areas and processes. In a warehouse where there will be continual, fast movement of goods by machines, the places where intersections of traffic flow occur need to be planned carefully. Movement at intersections is restricted, as equipment must slow down and, in some cases, give way to other equipment. The number of such intersections has to be minimised through careful design. It is poor design if they occur near racks and in doorways that have curtains over them to protect temperature zones. The visibility at intersections must be good so that the impact on equipment movement is reduced. This means that, at the most, one vehicle speeds up or one slows down slightly. One must also demarcate wide turning areas so that the equipment can negotiate the intersection and the changes in direction without delays.

It is important to chart the flow of goods to prevent cross-flows that will reduce the efficiency of operations. The simplest way to do this is to draw the flows on a plan of the proposed building and identify where the flows intersect. The movement aisles can be depicted with lines of three different thicknesses, proportional to the density of the traffic – scaled as light, medium, or heavy. Each line indicates movement in one direction only. Movement in the opposite direction must be indicated with a second line. This way, both the density and direction of the traffic are represented. Different colours can be used for different PPCs where necessary. Once these lines are drawn on the plan, it will be much easier to identify the appropriate aisle widths and layout changes to minimise common intersections.

The most frequently occurring challenge pertaining to warehouse layout and design is when the operating staff need to accommodate a new product group in an existing facility. This may well require consideration of all these aspects, and it is unlikely that the change will warrant the use of specialised personnel or consultants. Even if the change is of sufficient magnitude to contract consultants, the operating staff need to understand the design principles and processes discussed above, and use them to query and modify the design proposed by the external personnel.

11.5.8.1 Example

Two different PPCs exist in a warehouse. Both are stored in pallet racks. One is stored at ambient temperature; the second in a temperature-controlled environment. Figures 11.3 and 11.4 represent two different designs.

In Figure 11.3, the temperature-controlled partition is built around the racks, without changing the flows in the warehouse. The flow is from receiving to dispatch and the only restriction the temperature-controlled section has added is the two doors into and out of the area.

In Figure 11.4, the temperature-controlled section is built against the walls of the warehouse to reduce the building cost. The indicated flows reflect the problems. An additional movement aisle is required within the temperature-controlled portion to allow movement in both directions. The doors are placed in the best possible location, facing the existing movement aisles. Even so, on average, the goods need to be moved further than in the alternative design (Figure 11.3). The design in Figure 11.4 also leaves room for fewer doors and fewer receiving and dispatch assembly areas, even though there is the same number of racks in the temperature-controlled area.

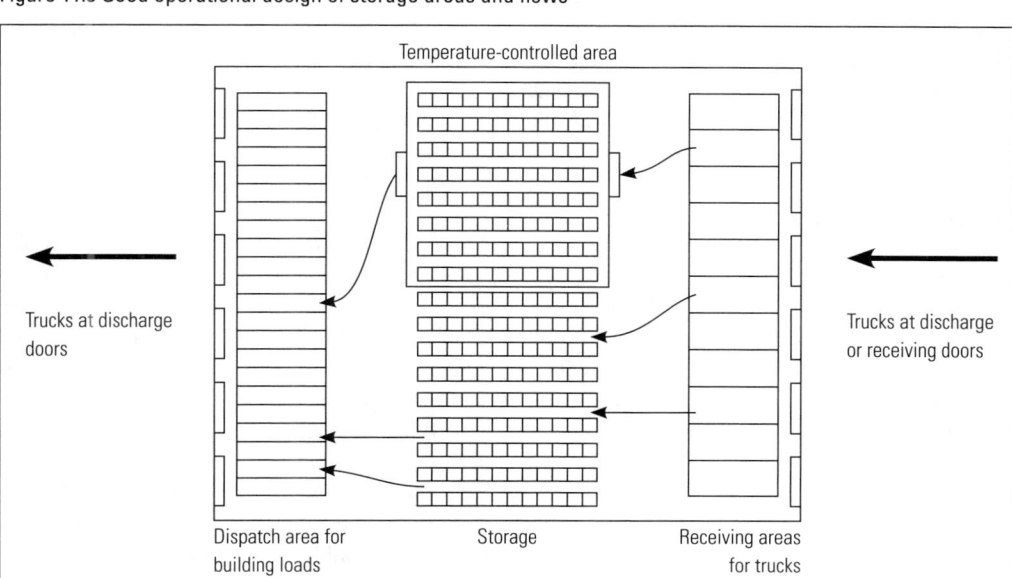

Figure 11.3 Good operational design of storage areas and flows

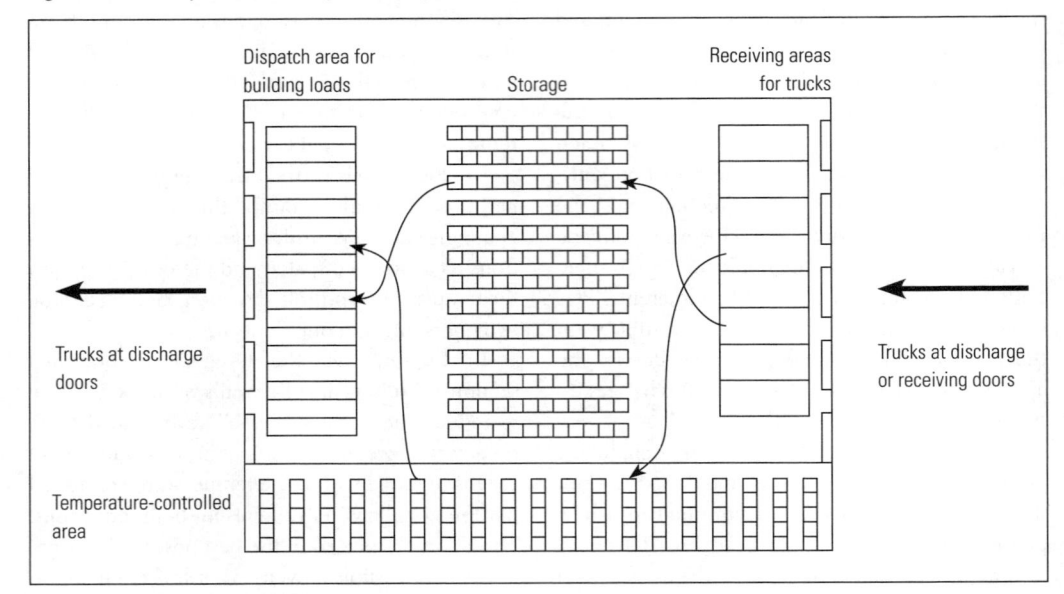

Figure 11.4 Poor operational design of storage areas and flows

11.5.8.2 Design principle: flows

It is very important to consider all the flows in the facility. A cheaper building design should not be accepted without checking whether it will introduce operational inefficiencies. The savings in the capital invested in the building must be balanced against the costs of inefficient operations.

As additional PPCs are introduced, the potential for poor flows is increased. The flows of each new PPC must be charted and the best areas allocated for storage, dispatch assembly, receiving areas and, most importantly, movement aisles. This way, the operation as a whole can be planned.

11.5.9 Loading doors

Warehouses are designed to interface with transport in some form – trucks, rail, containers, or even individual pick-ups. These interfaces must be operated in a disciplined and efficient way. This discipline and efficiency ensure there is a steady flow of work in the facility. Peaks and troughs of work reduce efficiency, create queues of trucks and delay the handling of goods received or sent.

The loading doors may need to have the following features:

- The door must be easily accessible for transport.
- The door must have a dock leveller on it to match the level of the floor of the warehouse with the level of the floor of the truck (or other transport medium).
- The door often requires a foam seal around it for temperature-controlled products. The trailer backs up against the seal and the temperature is preserved both in the truck and in the warehouse while goods are transferred.
- When products that can be adversely affected by water are moved from transport into a facility, a canopy must be erected over the facility entrance to protect the products at the interface.

More doors mean greater flexibility for handling trucks and transport. However, doors are relatively expensive when the price of the door, canopy, dock levellers, and the space needed for movement are added up. The number of doors must at least equal the number of loads received or dispatched at the peak time. However, this design does not take into account the inefficiencies of having to move loads from the assembly area to a distant door. A more realistic minimum is the greater of either one door for every two assembly bays, or the minimum number of routes to be serviced at the peak loading time.

11.5.10 External areas

When a truck arrives at a warehouse, two checks need to be carried out: to make sure that the truck is indeed destined for the facility and that it carries the desired goods. Well-managed warehouses give scheduled time slots for specific trucks to be unloaded. Where this is the practice, the time slot is checked when the truck arrives. If the truck is early, a parking area may be required. If the truck is late and cannot be received by the facility, the truck leaves without discharging or it waits until all other scheduled trucks have discharged. Trucks that need to discharge must be able to reverse up to the door without restrictions and delays.

The total area of good-quality roadway needed for this is calculated by determining:
- the length of the truck and trailer from the door;
- the turning circle; and
- the boundary area.

The approximate turning circles of some standard trucks and trailers are given in Table 11.1.

For layout purposes, the width of the roadway should be approximately 2,5 m for one-direction traffic.

In addition to the roadway for moving and loading/unloading trucks, a parking area is required for waiting vehicles. If managed well, the parking area should take up only a small space. Leaving trucks waiting on a continual basis is not cost-effective. However, as tractors are far more expensive than trailers, additional trailers are often used. The parking space needs to be sized to contain the total number of trailers and tractor-trailers expected to be on the premises of the facility at any time.

Trucks used for dispatch are treated in a similar manner. They first pass a checkpoint before being loaded. The above specifications for doors and external areas also apply for dispatch trucks. If loading and unloading take place at different times, only one area is required.

11.5.11 Combining areas

The previous sections have defined the requirements for individual PPCs. These determine the ideal sizing and shape of the areas designated to each PPC without restrictions and preconceived notions. We have also discussed the process of defining the methods of operation in accordance with the WMS capability across all of the PPCs.

Now a method is needed to combine these PPCs into a composite warehouse. There are mathematical models for doing this, but they are only justified in very large, complex facilities. As these are not often built in the market for lower-to-medium-volume movement, we recommend the following simple procedure.

The storage space for PPCs cannot be shared, as each demands storage of a specific size. Therefore, the storage areas should be the starting point for a rough building layout. If the information can be placed on a computer-aided design (CAD) figure, then so much the better. If not, the solution is to make a large-scale drawing of the site (the largest sensible size would be A0) and use paper cut-outs on the same scale for the following areas of each PPC:
- Dispatch
- Receiving
- Storage
- Movement
- Transport

Table 11.1 Approximate turning-circle diameters and lengths of various truck and tractor-trailer combinations

Type	Turning diameter (m)	Length (m)
3-axle truck, 2-axle trailer	21	18
2-axle truck, 3-axle trailer	17	18
Truck and trailer	24–30	15
Articulated pantechnicon van	24–30	15
Rigid body – long (not articulated)	24	8
Rigid body – short (not articulated)	15	6,5

Mark each PPC with a separate colour. Mark each of the cut-outs according to its function.

Place the cut-outs for the receiving and dispatch transport areas (not the parking) on the site drawing. The transport areas should be located preferably near the entrance road on the boundaries of the site. Depending on the shape of the land and the number and types of PPCs, the receiving and dispatch transport areas can be either on two sides of the site boundary or both on one side of the site boundary. The flows of individual PPCs tend to show which of these choices is preferable, but the most attractive option is determined by the processes for receiving and dispatch. If these processes occur at the same time, the potential for congestion must be considered. This should be balanced against the increased efficiency (if the doors are all on one side) of the equipment in the facility, which can take pallets from the receiving dock and do a put-away into a reserve, and then return with a pallet for the pick face that is short or a full pallet for delivery to a dispatch bay. If these receiving and dispatch flows do not overlap, then the processes have less congestion potential, and the doors on one side are an advantage for reducing the travel distance.

One can argue that the receiving and dispatch areas need to be on the same side for security reasons. While this is a valid argument, it is more important to concentrate on good flows, as the movement of the goods is generally the largest single cost factor. The size and orientation of these areas needs to be determined first, and then it is possible to identify the area that remains for the warehouse.

Arrange the storage areas so that those with the most similarities are adjacent to each other. For example, dry groceries and haberdashery have different racks. There is a bigger difference between a grocery area and, for example, a cross-dock area, where not only the storage, but also the operation, is different. Arrange the storage areas in a linear fashion between the transport areas. Between the storage and assembly areas add the movement areas. Overlap the movement areas of one storage area with those of the next area. Determine the density of the combined traffic in these movement areas by indicating the traffic from each PPC on the drawing. Add the appropriate receiving and dispatch assembly areas between the storage area and the transport area.

11.5.11.1 Design principles: combining areas

When allocating space for temperature-controlled zones, place them against the outer walls of the building. The walls have to be erected anyway, and the cost of insulating them is significantly less than the cost of erecting new walls in the warehouse.

If there are, say, three PPCs and the traffic density is categorised as low, medium, and high respectively, assign a number (1, 2, and 3) to the traffic density of each PPC. Then write the numbers in the appropriate common movement areas. Add up the totals to determine the potential traffic density. Now you can make changes to create the desired traffic patterns, such as low (1 to 4), medium (5, 6, or 7), and high (8 or 9). If there is two-way traffic, the split should reflect each direction – for example, 3 to 8 for low density, 9 to 13 for medium density, and 14 to 18 for high density.

The size of the areas allocated for storage, assembly, and so on, is calculated in terms of square metres. Their shape, however, needs to be altered until all the PPCs fit. This iterative process should take place when all areas are designed. Play around with different shapes to find the best combination. It is laborious doing it with paper cut-outs, but the process gives you a visual understanding of the warehouse, its operation and layout. It ensures that the best choices are made at the design stage. The time taken to design the desired warehouse is insignificant compared with the misery a poorly designed facility will continue to impose on its operators.

At the end of the processes discussed in these pages, you will have derived the best warehouse that operational experience and capability will allow. The unoccupied areas allow for growth and determine the direction the growth can take.

11.6 Fire

A storage facility needs to be prepared for fires. This requires that there is at least a sprinkler system in the roof of the building. Sprinkler systems are fitted with quartz iodide bulbs, which break above a certain temperature.

Insurance companies often insist on sprinklers in the racks. These prevent fires from spreading to the point where they activate the roof sprinklers. The sprinkler pipes and iodide bulbs in the racks can be easily damaged in the course of storing and picking operations, resulting in water release that may damage goods. Make sure that this type of damage is covered by the insurance.

Both the local fire brigade and the insurance assessors need to approve the system. Note that not everything that these parties ask for is compulsory: discuss the system with them and make rational, economical choices.

11.7 Security

Security measures need to be taken to prevent break-ins and theft of primarily individual items (pilferage) from within the warehouse. Both these forms of theft impact on the design of the warehouse.

Preventing theft from within the warehouse involves a thorough check of goods loaded into trucks. Additional staff and space may be needed for this purpose. Remote or hidden areas where theft can take place should also be identified. If such areas exist, the design should allow for cameras to be installed. In addition, the design must include an appropriate security system (to protect the warehouse against break-ins) and secure the perimeters of the property (to prevent theft of or from trucks).

One can distinguish between passive electronic security, such as an alarm that gets triggered when a door or window is opened, and physical-presence security, which refers to human labour. The best mix depends on the risks for and the access to each facility. It is unlikely that the security measures will need to consist entirely of either passive or physical security. All facilities should have some form of fencing, either around the building or around the complex. Perimeter beams detect movement and can be used to protect the perimeter with or without physical security.

The next sections provide a short summary of the various security options for the warehouse itself.

11.7.1 Guards

A physical security presence provided by guards is required in cases when personnel need to be searched when they enter or exit a building. The verification of the handover of physical goods is also best done with a physical check by an independent person.

The disadvantage of security guards is that they work in the same environment as the operations staff, and eventually cannot be deemed independent unless they are rotated regularly and randomly.

11.7.2 Alarms

A local, audible alarm to indicate a forced entry may cause burglars to flee. The use of an alarm linked to an armed-response unit may significantly reduce the time available for removing the goods. These alarms are triggered either when a door or window is opened or when the passive infrared (PIR) beams record movement inside the warehouse.

A refinement of infrared beams used to measure movement is the use of infrared to measure temperature. In addition to detecting movement in the warehouse, this advanced beam system also rings an alarm when there is a fire.

11.7.3 Video cameras

Video recording cameras provide visual records of remote or obscure corners of the facility. The recordings can either be watched continually by security staff or checked only if a problem is detected. As searching these tapes is time-consuming, they are not very useful for determining whether a problem exists or not. It is more effective to use them to find the cause of a problem once the problem has been identified.

A useful development is to save the images to a computer. Software is available for identifying a specific item or place in the warehouse. It also allows one to search for periods when movement occurred in the area, making it easy and quick to track a problem.

11.8 Lighting

Generally, the lighting inside the building is left to the architect. This is a mistake. There are guidelines for lighting intensity in the building codes that the architect will utilise, but these do not take the operations into account. Poor lighting cannot be corrected easily or cost-effectively once the facility is established. Operations may take place at night or at times when the external ambient light levels are low. The operations may involve, for example, storing a pallet up to 15 m from the floor or reading the bar code of the product on this pallet. Similarly, pallets may need to be moved frequently at high speed, inspected and checked. While bar coding reduces the need to read information during the operation, it does not eliminate it.

Lighting is a science. Two primary factors must be considered. The first is the amount of light and the second is the colour rendition of the light. The amount of light can be increased by using yellow lights, as the human eye sees the greatest intensity of light in this range. However, this gives problems with differentiating between colours, and in some cases, even depth perception. The intensity and colour rendition of the lighting are both important in the design of an operating facility.

Consult with a lighting specialist when deciding on the intensity and colour requirements. Identify the areas where very good lighting is needed. The storage area may need to be free of shadows that might inhibit the safe and effective storage of a pallet. Lighting specialists will design the lighting to provide sufficient intensity in all the working areas and economic colour rendition to eliminate glare – making the operation both safer and more efficient. A chart of the lighting intensity should be reviewed as part of the design.

The replacement of tubes or lamps must also be considered, as this can be very disruptive to operations. For example, the lifetime of an incandescent light is 2 000 hours, or 83 days, on average. If the warehouse has one thousand lights that burn on average for 12 hours per day, six bulbs need to be replaced every day. Alternative types of tube or lamp can reduce the maintenance load by up to 90 per cent. New lighting tubes and lamps are far more energy-efficient and provide long life with good intensity and colour rendition. The various options are shown in Table 11.2.

11.9 Conclusion

The optimal design of physical logistics facilities is a critical task in the logistics system. Markets change and so do businesses and the requirements placed on facilities such as warehouses. From time to time, it becomes necessary, therefore, to reassess and redesign an existing warehouse. This chapter discussed the methodology for designing changes in an existing warehouse in order to make it more practical and logical for operations. The chapter explored how to make decisions about segregating and combining different processes. By applying these design-review principles, the logistics manager will acquire a far more effective and efficient facility than before.

Key terms

Colour rendition
Forecast
Lighting intensity
Loading door
Picking
Product process category (PPC)
Turning circle
Warehouse management system (WMS)

Table 11.2 A comparison of lighting lifetimes and intensities

Type	Lumens	Lamp life (hours)
Incandescent	12–29	Up to 2 000
Fluorescent	40–83	Up to 12 000
Mercury vapour	50	Up to 16 000
Metal halide	100	10 000 to 20 000
High-pressure sodium	120	Up to 24 000

Case study

A certain warehouse has been in operation for more than seven years with the same products flowing successfully through the facility, which is operating at capacity. The market has been stable until recently, when a major shift in the throughput occurred. The cause of the shift has been determined as the entry of a competitor into the market. The throughput has decreased by more 20 per cent. The management have looked for additional products, and have found two new potential customers. One of these customers would increase the existing products handled by 10 per cent. The other would increase the throughput by 20 per cent, but these are very different products from the existing ones in both handling and processes.

1. Which of these options would you choose and why?
2. Would you need more information to make a final decision and, if so, what information would be required?
3. When making the decisions posed in Question 1 above, would you need knowledge of the layout and design of facilities to make informed decisions, or could you always rely on a consultant?
4. What part of the organisation was at fault or did not perform correctly if the warehouse lost 20 per cent of its business?

Case study
(by P. Kilbourn)

A company distributing fast-moving consumer goods has had to cope with 10 to 15 per cent growth per year in sales and an increase in the number of stores served in the last two years. Management have decided that the existing warehouse needs be expanded to accommodate the growth in output.

In the redesign of the warehouse the logistics manager needs to make a decision on the optimum size of the storage area. He or she needs to accommodate at least 600 extra pallet spaces and has an additional 770 m² to work with. The preferred storage method is racks and the materials-handling equipment available are reach trucks that need aisles 2,8 m wide. The warehouse is designed to have ten rows of racks. Each row of racks is four pallet spaces high and 15 spaces long. The racks are placed with two rows adjacent to each other. Four aisles are needed between the racks and two aisles are needed to service the outer racks. Two aisles are needed at both ends to allow movement to the reach stacker. Each rack provides space for a single pallet and occupies:

- 1,2 m from front to back (depth)
- 1,4 m from side to side (length)
- 1,8 m from top to bottom (height)

1. Given the above information, what is the floor area required for the ten rows of racks only?
2. What is the total floor area required to provide the extra storage space?
3. What would the total required floor area be if a much cheaper forklift truck requiring aisles 3,7 m wide were to be used and the number of racks and aisles stayed the same?

Questions

1. Comment on the following statement: The design of a warehouse involves a large amount of calculations and repeated work. There seems to be little value in the logistics manager getting involved, as professionals – such as architects – design the building.
2. Placing aisles around storage racks is complicated. Block stacking is much simpler and easier to design. Could the design be simplified by using block stacking initially and then adding racking once the warehouse is operational? Motivate your answer.
3. It is determined that a facility's loading doors need dock levellers, additional movement aisles, plus canopies. As these doors are expensive, either the very minimum number of doors must be supplied or the extra items must be omitted to leave only basic doors. Is this a sensible argument? Motivate your answer.
4. The plan for the growth of a facility should simply consist of building a new extension when additional space is required. Determining growth is so difficult that the problem is best left to the future, when the issues are better known. Comment on this statement.

Consult the web

www.fbk.eur.nl/OZ/LOGISTICA/
www.inventoryops.com
www.mmh.com/article/CA215467.html

Consult the books

Bowersox, D. J., Closs, D. J. and Cooper, M. B. 2002. *Supply Chain Logistics Management*. New York: McGraw-Hill.

Chopra, S. and Meindel, P. 2004. *Supply Chain Management: Strategy, Planning and Operation*. New Jersey: Prentice Hall-Pearson Education International.

Frazell, E. 2002. *Supply Chain Strategy: The Logistics of Supply Chain Management*. McGraw-Hill.

Gattorna, J. L. 2003. *Gower Handbook of Supply Chain Management*, 5th edition. Gower Publishing.

Stock, J. R. and Lambert, D. M. 2001. *Strategic Logistics Management*, 4th edition. McGraw-Hill.

Notes

1 Stock, J. R. and Lambert, D. M. 2001.
2 Ibid.

12 Packaging and containerisation

U. Kussing and P. Kilbourn

Learning outcomes

After you have studied this chapter, you should be able to:
- understand the logistics functions of packaging and the benefits thereof;
- explain the cost and service trade-offs involved with the use of packaging in logistics;
- identify and discuss the factors involved in the development of packaging solutions;
- describe the similarities and differences between containers and ULDs; and
- identify ways in which technology can be integrated with packaging, and the benefits that can be derived from such integration.

12.1 Introduction

Packaging has been with us in one form or another since humans first started to store food and water for later consumption or for trade purposes. Ancient packaging was made of natural materials, for example, baskets of reeds or pottery vases. Modern packaging materials are often technologically advanced to meet the changing needs of manufacturers, distributors and consumers. Packaging plays an indispensable role in modern society. Any product that is consumed or used at a place removed from its point of origin has been transferred in one or more forms of packaging at some stage.

Packaging also plays an important role in the supply chain. Although it seldom adds any value to the product that is contained in it, packaging increases efficiency in the supply chain and contributes to the effectiveness of a warehouse and of transportation if it is designed properly.

Containerisation plays such a role in that it seldom adds value to products, but contributes towards greater efficiency and effectiveness in the supply chain, mainly during intermodal and international transportation.

In any supply chain, numerous decisions have to be made that involve packaging and containerisation. This chapter provides the student with an overview of the characteristics of – and issues around – packaging and containerisation, and examines the identification technologies associated with them.

12.2 Definition and functions of packaging

> Packaging is the art and technology of enclosing and protecting goods for distribution, storage, sale and use. Packaging is also the material used to wrap a product and to convey information to the customer. The main logistics functions of packaging are to apportion, contain, protect/preserve, unitise, transport and inform/sell.

The current manufacturing environment is characterised by long production runs in order to gain economies of scale. Most products are manufactured in bulk, but need to be sold in small quantities to consumers. Packaging fulfils a function of apportionment in that it allows the original bulk volume to be divided into smaller, more manageable, quantities. For example, consumers can buy packets containing six or twelve bread rolls instead of the quantity of a whole baking tray.

The physical form and the nature of the product influence the design of packaging for effective containment. Packaging for a liquid, for example, has to be non-porous and non-absorbent. If the liquid is corrosive and odorous, one should be able to tightly seal the container and the container will have to be made from a material that is insusceptible to corrosion.

Protection is the prevention of physical damage, while preservation inhibits chemical and biological changes. Packaging has to protect its content against vibration, mechanical shocks, abrasion, deformation, temperature, humidity and tampering. The probability of these conditions occurring during storage and transit will influence the physical characteristics of the packaging. Through its preservation function, packaging also plays a role in the extension of food shelf life beyond the natural life of the product. It also helps to maintain sterility in food and medical products.

If products have to be handled and transported individually, the risk of damage increases greatly. Unitisation refers to the bundling of products into larger handling units. An example of such a handling unit is a pallet, which contains multiple cartons with multiple units of product in each carton. Unitisation reduces the number of times that a product needs to be physically handled, thereby saving time and reducing handling costs and damages.

Most products are not able to withstand the stresses of transportation and distribution without additional packaging designed to isolate or cushion them from external forces. In order for products to be transported efficiently, they need to be packaged in a way that enables optimal utilisation of the mode of transport. Cube-shaped cartons of uniform size make it easier to fill a truck to its capacity, while also reducing damages by preventing the products from moving around and knocking against each other during transportation.

Packaging has an important role to play in communication. The packaging has to make the product attractive to potential buyers. It also needs to conform to laws and regulations by displaying certain messages. DVD covers, for example, have to display the viewing age restrictions as determined by the relevant film and publications board. Distribution packaging communicates acceptable ways of handling. Food packaging most often provides information on ingredients and nutritional values.

Packaging consists of different levels, each playing a part in one or more of the functions of packaging:
- Primary packaging – the first layer of packaging, which contains the product and preserves or protects the product for sale. Example: a foil bag containing potato chips.
- Secondary packaging – the second layer of packaging that contains the product in its primary packaging. Example: a carton containing 50 bags of potato chips.
- Unit load – numerous distribution packages that are unitised into a single entity for the purpose of more efficient handling, storage and shipping (also sometimes referred to as tertiary packaging). Example: a pallet loaded with 20 cartons of potato chips.
- Distribution packaging – a form of packaging whose purpose is to protect the product during distribution and to aid efficient handling.

Figure 12.1 Primary and secondary packaging contained in a unit load

Example: a box designed to contain an exterior door panel for a truck. (Note that the door panel could be shipped without a box, but the likelihood of in-transit damage would be greater. The box is also easier to handle than the panel on its own.)

12.2.1 Benefits of packaging

Most modern businesses rely on comprehensive packaging systems to deliver their products and manufactured items to consumers in a timely manner. The sophistication of the packaging materials varies from simple, plastic carrier bags to complex, multi-layer packages. Each type of packaging fits a specific purpose and often requires a large technological investment.

Packaging can offer manufacturers and consumers a variety of specific benefits. Not all of the benefits listed below are realised in all types of packaging, but most often a few of them will apply.

- Protection – packaging protects against robust handling during distribution so that products reach the consumer in the condition required.
- Preservation – food and pharmaceuticals can be preserved from deterioration through proper packaging.
- Facilitation of distribution – goods can be easily moved from one place to another and efficiently stored, not only by companies but also by consumers.
- Information and instruction – the quantity of content, sell-by dates, use-by dates, ingredients, allergens, warning notices and directions for use can appear on packaging, making it easier for the consumer to make a purchasing decision.
- Consumer convenience – packaging caters for the changing needs of consumers by incorporating time-saving features for easy and efficient handling, for example, by incorporating the means of dispensing into the packaging.
- Containing of costs – products can be pre-packaged on a production line at a lower cost than if each product were wrapped separately in a store.
- Hygiene and safety – medical equipment and products, such as syringes, needles and blood-transfusion kits, can be sterilised and packaged in a controlled environment, thereby creating safer products and providing the patient with peace of mind.
- Waste minimisation – resealable packs allow consumers to use then reseal products that would otherwise spoil, enabling them to buy larger quantities at a time instead of lots of smaller quantities over time.
- Silent salesperson – the packaging displays and describes the product it contains, thereby enabling consumers to choose the product best suited to their requirements and tastes.
- Risk elimination – poisonous substances and medicines can be packaged in childproof bottles, thereby reducing the risk of accidental poisoning or overdosing.
- Innovation – packaging can be redesigned to meet new demands, such as space research. (The modern-day can is said to have developed from the military needs of Napoleon.)

12.3 The role of packaging in logistics

Packaging impacts on various activities in a logistics system. The main impact is in the areas of warehousing, materials handling and transport. Within each of these areas, packaging has to meet certain requirements in order to contribute to the efficiency and effectiveness of the supply chain.

12.3.1 Warehousing and materials handling

The warehousing manager should be concerned about the packaging of goods for a number of reasons. Packaging has an impact on the stacking height of products in a warehouse and thereby on the utilisation of space and costs. Many public warehouses determine rates according to the space used by the client.

Packaging also affects the protection of products during their storage and handling. Damaged products cause a lot of additional costs in a supply chain and have a negative impact on customer service. Package size affects the type of storage and materials-handling equipment used by companies. Information contained in packaging facilitates the recording of information into warehouse management systems, and putting away and retrieving items.

In many logistics systems, products can be found that are packaged in a way that does not allow full utilisation of warehouse space and materials-handling equipment. Packaging may be too wide, too high or not durable enough. This is a costly error, which may take a considerable amount of time to resolve. It is important, therefore, that packaging decisions are coordinated with warehousing and materials handling.

12.3.2 Transport

Each mode of transport offers its own particular hazards and constraints to shippers from several perspectives – including packaging. An increasing trend towards multi-modal transportation complicates matters further and requires adaptable cargo. It is important for shippers to consider the full transportation and handling cycle when a decision is made on the optimal packaging of products.

12.3.2.1 Air transport

As an alternative to other modes of transport, air transport offers greater speed along with ease and flexibility for handling and distribution. Time- and handling-sensitive goods, such as high-value goods and emergency items, are best suited to air transit. The shipper needs to know that cargo transported by air can be subjected to environmental forces during flight. These include fore and aft pressures during take-off and landing, and turbulence. The impact of atmospheric changes on products during flights should also be considered. A shipper should also know that airlines have their own packaging requirements. The packaging of air shipments is regulated by the International Air Transport Association (IATA).

The packaging of goods for air transport is also affected by the relatively limited carrying capacity in cargo bays and doorway restrictions, which may encourage improper stowage and rough handling. Packaging affects the weight and density of products and consequently has an impact on the rates charged by carriers. Airlines assess freight charges based on either the actual weight or the dimensional weight of a shipment, whichever is greatest. A special type of container, called a unit load device (ULD), is used to load freight on aircrafts. (ULDs are discussed in section 12.7 of this chapter.)

12.3.2.2 Road and rail transport

Road transportation normally requires balanced, stackable distribution packaging in order to maximise the use of trailer space. When transporting goods by truck, the proper use of bedding and strapping can reduce the likelihood of packaged goods being damaged during transit. Transportation by truck exposes goods to shocks and vibrations caused by the conditions of the road and driver behaviour. Transportation by road is also greatly affected by weather conditions.

Rail transportation requires secure and stable packaging. Movement via rail systems is caused by acceleration and deceleration and severe impacts can occur during shunting operations. Significant shock and vibration can be caused by the conditions of the rail bed.

12.3.2.3 Ocean transport

There are many risks confronting shippers when making use of sea transport. Cargo can be exposed to high humidity, condensation, rain and sea water – individually or in combination. These conditions can easily change otherwise stable cargo into a ruin of wet, stained, mildewed and rusty products. Compounding the problem is the fact that a ship in rolling seas can encounter almost any pattern of movements, such as rolling, pitching and centrifugal forces. Other common hazards in sea transport include salt spray driving across the deck of a vessel; rain-swept storage areas; condensation dripping from the interior of a ship's hold or intermodal container; and 'sweat' forming on cargo itself. If cargo is subjected to moisture damage it must be appropriately protected by various means, including preservatives, corrosion inhibitors, waterproof wrapping, and resistant external packaging and interior lining.[1] A large percentage of goods shipped by sea are containerised. (Containerisation is dealt with in section 12.6 of this chapter.)

12.3.3 Packaging and logistics trade-offs

Packaging has an impact on both cost and customer-service levels in a logistics system. Issues such as packaging design; types of materials used in packaging; packaging information; and standardisation of packaging affect the efficiency and effectiveness of various logistics activities. With the design of packaging it is important that cost and service trade-offs are considered between packaging and various logistics activities. Table 12.1 shows examples of packaging and logistics costs and service trade-offs.

12.4 Marketing

Product, place, price and promotion are the major elements of marketing. Packaging has a role to play in each of these elements. A product is more than just its physical content: it also has an image that can be enhanced through well-designed and attractive packaging. A product can only be sold if it is available in the right place and right condition. Packaging enables the containment and preservation of products so that they can be sold in perfect condition at places far from where they originated. The cost of packaging also influences the cost of the final product. Not only does packaging contribute directly to the manufacturing cost of the product, but it can also influence the logistics costs of getting the product to the shelf through increased warehouse and transport efficiencies. Furthermore, packaging plays a critical role in the promotion of its content. Of all the levels of

Table 12.1 Packaging cost and service trade-offs with other logistics activities

Logistics activity	Packaging characteristics	Trade-off
Transportation	Increased package information	• Reduces shipment delays • Reduces tracking of lost shipments
	Increased package protection	• Reduces damage and theft in transit • Increases package weight and transport costs
	Increased standardisation	• Reduces handling costs • Reduces vehicle waiting time for loading and unloading • Increases modal choices for shipper • Reduces need for specialised transportation equipment
Inventory management	Increased product protection	• Reduces theft; damage and insurance • Increases product availability • Increases product value and carrying costs
Warehousing	Increased package information	• Reduces order-filling time and labour cost
	Increased product protection	• Increases cube utilisation (stacking), but reduces cube utilisation by increasing the size of the product
	Increased standardisation	• Reduces material-handling equipment costs
Communications	Increased package information	• Reduces other communications about the product (e.g. telephone calls to track down lost shipments)

Source: Adapted from Cook, L. R. 1991. In Grant, D. B., Lambert, D. M., Stock, J. R. and Ellram, L. 2006. Fundamentals of Logistics Management: European Edition: *280. McGraw-Hill*

packaging, primary packaging is probably the most important. Primary packaging has to be attractive, needs to capture the consumer's interest and must provide information that will persuade the consumer to buy it.

Point-of-purchase (POP) packaging plays an important marketing role with consumer products. POP includes any displays, signs and related materials in a retail location. POP packaging contains units of a product in their primary packaging and is used to draw attention to products and provide information about them in the hope that this will increase sales or strengthen a specific brand name. For example, Simba chips might place a corrugated-board display at the end of a supermarket aisle. This is to display the products, indicate the price and possibly advertise a new flavour. In this case, the location and design of the stand is important to the company's marketing and sales effort.

The role of packaging, therefore, is much more than to protect a product; it is also an attention-grabbing device that can create impressions and ideas about a product. This image can differentiate products and make them seem better than competing products.

12.5 Development of packaging solutions

When a packaging solution is developed, it focuses on two broad categories of packaging: industrial packaging and consumer packaging. Consumer packaging is often developed by the marketing department, with the focus on attracting customers through innovative and attractive packaging. The aim of industrial packaging design is to create, amongst others, cartons, cases, barrels, bins and bags, in which multiple units of products can be transported and warehoused safely and effectively.

12.5.1 Factors influencing packaging design

Packaging design should follow a systems approach. Very often, packaging is designed with only the end-customer in mind. Marketing is the main objective, while storage and transportation are often ignored. With a systems approach, however, the product design, manufacturing, warehousing, distribution, retailing and the end-consumer are all taken into account during packaging design and redesign. Of these factors, consumer requirements probably exhibit the most variability and most often drive the need for redesigned packaging. To give an example, the growth in single-person households has led to an increasing demand for smaller, more convenient portions of pre-packaged food. Packaging has evolved over time to meet this demand.

A product's physical form and nature will determine what kind of packaging is required to contain it. A product's susceptibility to damage can be investigated and its various fragility factors quantified. For example, if a product is potentially temperature-sensitive, one would need to determine the critical temperatures that will lead to deterioration in its quality. If a product is susceptible to compression, the safe working load has to be determined.

The size and shape of packaging should aim to optimise the area utilisation during storage and the volumetric (cubic) utilisation during transport. Warehouse space usually has a cost associated per square metre. If more units of a product can be put into one square metre, the storage cost per unit will be lower. When designing packaging for a product with low density (i.e. a low ratio between weight and volume), the volumetric capacity of a vehicle has to be taken into account, as maximum utilisation of space makes it possible to transport more units per trip. The dimensions of packaging should be considered in terms of possible packing orientations in a shipping container, pallet patterns and space utilisation.

12.5.2 Packaging materials

Wood, paper and cardboard, glass, metal and plastic are the five basic types of materials used to manufacture packaging. Each of these materials has principal properties that influence whether they will be used to package a specific product. Packaging often includes more that one type of material in order to take advantage of the strengths of different materials.

Glass is a high-quality packaging material with good gas and liquid barrier properties. It provides the best level of clarity. Glass can be recycled and reused more easily than other materials. It is more fragile than plastics, but provides better packaging for liquids and gases that corrode or contaminate.

Paper is a very versatile packaging material with a high potential for recycling and reuse. Paper and cardboard products used for packaging include corrugated board, carton board, liner board, bags and sacks. Paper and board provide good strength and protection at low cost, while enabling good print quality. More than half of the paper and board manufactured in South Africa is consumed by the packaging industry.

Plastics are very versatile, lightweight, resin-based, artificial products that can be transformed into numerous shapes and sizes. Each of the 60 or more categories of plastic resins has an identification number that aids in the sorting process during recycling. The most common plastic resin types used in packaging are:
- polyethylene terephthalate (PET);
- high-density polyethylene (HDPE);
- polyvinyl chloride (PVC);
- low-density polyethylene (LDPE);
- polypropylene (PP); and
- polystyrene (PS).

Metal is commonly used in primary packaging, but seldom in secondary packaging. It is a good gas and liquid barrier of great strength and versatility. Metal packaging is relatively expensive, but can most often be completely recycled or reused.

Wood is a strong, rigid material that can be used to manufacture custom-made packaging. For example, wood can be used to crate paintings and other valuables that can be easily damaged. It is also easier to make pallets from wood than plastic. There are strict regulations, however, regarding the import of wood packaging materials into various countries, making it a less attractive packaging material in those cases.

The use of packaging materials has had to become more efficient over the last three decades, as rising costs of raw materials and increasing environmental concerns have compelled the packaging industry to become more responsible and innovative. Glass containers and cans are on average 30 per cent lighter than 30 years ago, while plastic bags are 45 per cent lighter than 20 years ago. This trend is referred to as 'thinwalling' or 'lightweighting' and has made a major contribution towards waste minimisation in the packaging industry.

12.5.3 Palletisation

A pallet is a flat, rectangular structure on which a number of smaller units of product can be stacked, so they can be transported and stored in a stable manner by mechanical means (e.g. forklifts or pallet jacks). Pallets (also called skids in some countries) are conventionally made of wood or plywood, but can also be manufactured from metal, plastic or corrugated cardboard. The type of material used is influenced by the product to be transported; returnability of pallets; mode of transport; handling systems and cost considerations. In general, the design of a pallet must balance its requirements in terms of strength, stiffness, durability, functionality and cost.

Two broad categories of pallets can be identified – block pallets and stringer-type pallets. Each design type can also be found in a range of variations:
- Reversible pallets – both sides can be used as load-carrying platforms, as they have similar top and bottom decks.
- Wing pallets – these are designed to be handled by slings.
- Two-way-entry pallets – stringer pallets can mostly only be entered from two ends by forklifts and pallet jacks.
- Four-way-entry pallets – handling equipment can enter the pallet from all four directions.

Pallets can be either one-way or returnable. Returnable pallets, which can be retrieved and reused, are more cost-effective. The lifespan of a pallet is influenced by the type and quality of material used in its manufacture. Pallet pools can be used for the management of returnable pallets. Within a pallet pool, the pallets normally have standardised sizes. For example, the standard pallet in most European pallet pools is an 800 mm × 1 200 mm block-style pallet with an undirectional base. Internationally, a standard pallet is 1 000 mm by 1 200 mm.

The pallet pattern, namely the arrangement of units on a pallet, is critical to compact loading and an efficient storage and distribution system. Patterns should be designed to accommodate maximum loading of the pallet while maintaining structural strength. Pattern design is influenced by the product itself; any primary and secondary packages in which the product may be contained; the distribution method and size of conveyance; and warehousing space considerations. For example, 10 kg bags of oranges can be stacked on a pallet in layers that are at right angles to one another. If netting is placed over the bags to secure them to the pallet, the stacking height can be increased.

The base of a pallet can also be incorporated into a form of bulk packaging. Pallet boxes are a good example, where a pallet is incorporated into a bulk bin. This is often used in the fruit industry, where fruit is picked, placed in the pallet bin and then transported to a packing facility. The bulk-carrying characteristics of the bin are thus enhanced with the pallet base for easier transport and handling within the packing facility.

12.5.4 Bulk-packaging systems

Bulk-packaging systems can be successfully used for the containment of large volumes of, for example, chemicals, liquids, grains, powders, rice and other food items. This type of packaging is also referred to as industrial packaging. Its only requirement is that it must survive the storage and transportation process, with marking on the packaging limited to the essential requirements of identification (i.e. product name, grade and batch number). The main priority of bulk packaging is to package goods at the lowest cost per delivered unit quantity.

The packaging method used depends on the physical form of the product. Gases are contained in cylinders or accommodated in specialised facilities within ships. Liquids are contained in drums, lined containers, tanks and tankers or directly loaded onto ships. Solids are packaged in bags, sacks, boxes and containers or loaded directly onto rail wagons and ships. The most commonly used materials in bulk-packaging systems are bags, corrugated cardboard, metal, rigid plastic and wood. These materials have their advantages and disadvantages, and are selected according to various product and supply chain requirements.

Corrugated containers are low in weight, have good stacking strength, can be reused and are easy to dispose of, but can be vulnerable to moisture. Corrugated board can be single-, double- or triple-walled. If containers have been packed to less than 100 per cent volumetric capacity, they can be cut down to save space. This is especially important if transport cost is based on or influenced by volumetric weight.

Bags are mostly used for bulk packaging of dry products and can be manufactured from various films and laminations. The strength of bags can be increased through the use of rubberised plastic films. Special extrusion coatings or protective liners can be used to meet particular product requirements. Bags are generally durable, easily collapsible, light and can be reused.

Metal drums were among the first types of modern bulk containers. Although metal containers have a high tare weight and are expensive to manufacture, they are versatile, highly reusable, very durable, resistant to environmental influences and can be easily recycled. Metal stillages and returnable containers are commonly used for delivering automotive parts and assemblies directly from suppliers to production lines.

Containers made from rigid plastics can be designed to be collapsible, lightweight and highly resistant to numerous shipping environments. Although these containers are generally more expensive to manufacture than others, the total logistics system cost can be lower because of reuse and recycling. Plastic containers are frequently used in closed-loop systems for handling and movement within or between plants of a single company.

Wooden bulk containers are good in terms of reuse, disposability, tare weight, durability and resistance to the shipping environment, although not the best if compared to the materials listed above. They can be easily adapted for different product requirements and taken apart when empty. Box liners can be used to meet special product needs that are not covered by wood alone.

The following factors should be taken into account when planning a bulk-packaging system:
- Product-related requirements. These include atmospheric (temperature and moisture) and physical protection; loading and unloading; compatibility with packaging materials; retention gases and emission of vapours; production volumes; storage methods and shipping quantities.
- Product weight and volume. These influence the type of material that will be used as packaging. Metal and rigid plastic can carry most weight, while wood is sufficient for low-density products. Bulk containers may weigh between 1 ton and 3,5 tons.
- Container cost. The physical cost of the container itself and the freight and storage costs need to be taken into account. Containers should be designed for optimum cube utilisation in storage and during transportation. Stacking strength for better warehouse space utilisation is important in the case of heavy products. Container base dimensions should be related to both storage and the transport vehicles' size and incorporate a solid base for handling. Base dimensions often correspond to pallet dimensions or the dimensions of warehouse bin locations.
- Container type. Markets served, distribution needs and customer requirements are important factors. Reusable containers reduce total costs, while disposability at the end of the container's life is also important. The automotive industry frequently uses returnable metal or plastic bulk containers for parts and assemblies that feed their production lines. Containers can be designed to facilitate product-specific filling and emptying requirements, and must be able to accept the necessary materials-handling devices.

12.5.5 Cost trade-offs

Efficient and cost-effective packaging is essential in today's competitive business environment. The overall cost of packaging needs to be considered. The first cost element is the cost of getting the packaging to the point in the supply chain where a product can be placed in the packaging, including the cost to manufacture or buy the packaging. Once it has arrived at that point, there is also the cost of filling the packaging and the cost of handling the filled package. The package will then most likely incur storage and distribution costs. Finally, the packaging will have an influence on the sales of the product itself.

The total cost of packaging has to be traded off against an increase in sales and savings in costs elsewhere in the supply chain. For example, the strength of primary packaging has to be traded off against distribution packaging. A weak primary package may be inexpensive to manufacture, but will need stronger, more expensive distribution packaging if stacking is required for more efficient space utilisation during storage and transport. Efficient packaging may sometimes be expensive to manufacture, but will lead to savings in storage cost per unit and transportation cost per unit due to better space utilisation. Sturdy protective packaging is more expensive to manufacture, but protects its content better, which leads to lower losses from in-transit damage. Fewer incidences of damage may even lead to a reduction in insurance cost. In this case, the value of the product and its susceptibility to damage will influence the amount invested in protective packaging.

12.5.6 Legislative considerations

Legislation regarding the use of packaging and packaging materials varies from country to country. In some cases, the legislation holds the producer of the packaging responsible for compliance, irrespective of whether the producer resides in that country or not. Legislation pertaining to packaging includes:
- environmental regulation that focuses on recycling;
- hazardous waste and hazardous product laws;
- special labelling laws;
- food-contact laws;
- customs regulations; and
- local and international standards.

In general, legislation requires the manufacturer and/or retailer of a product to state on the packaging what it contains. Most labels of food products have to carry a full declaration of the ingredients, or at least a declaration of certain types of additives (e.g. colourants and preservatives). Packaging also has to provide purchasers with a name and address to which they can write if they require further information on the product or if they wish to complain about or exchange the product. No claims can be made on packaging about the value or benefit of the product contained in it if these claims cannot be justified or proven. Specific prescriptions regarding labelling apply to the sale of poisonous substances. Legislation can even dictate the graphics and physical design of packaging, for example, by prescribing the language and size of the lettering on a label. Labelling is especially important in the case of dangerous goods, which have to be labelled according to UN regulations and carry the appropriate UN certificate number during transportation.

12.5.7 Environmental concerns

Businesses are facing relatively new challenges in the packaging arena. Not only must packaging be attractive, protect products, provide information and protection – it must also be more environmentally friendly. This is true for consumer product companies and non-consumer-facing companies alike. Although packaging cannot be completely environmentally friendly, the aim should be to reduce the negative environmental effect of packaging. A life-cycle assessment (LCA) can be used to evaluate the potential environmental effects of packaging options. When considering changes in packaging, LCA can show whether these changes are likely to cause more or fewer environmental burdens than what is currently in use. (See Chapter 19 for more information on LCAs.)

Households and businesses should try to reuse and recycle as much packaging material as possible. Consideration should also be given to reusability or recyclability when designing and purchasing anything contained in packaging. Glass bottles, for example, are easier to reuse or recycle than plastic bottles. Corrugated boxes made only from paper are easier to recycle than those with a plastic lining. Legislation is often used to compel companies to recycle packaging that moves through their supply chain.

The European Parliament passed a directive on packaging and packaging waste in December 1994, which covers all packaging placed in the market of the European Community and all packaging waste. Original targets set in the directive require that member countries recover 50 per cent or more of their used packaging; that at least 25 per cent be recycled; and that no more than 15 per cent be disposed of without being recycled. The directive has the aim of harmonising the national goals of packaging recycling. It is up to each country to set up its own system of taxes, deposits and/or industry collection fees. Individual companies are not covered by the directive, but have to comply with the legal requirements that are laid down at their respective national levels.

Germany probably has the most stringent and expensive packaging legislation in the world in terms of environmental focus. It places an absolute direct take-back obligation on the whole packaging chain, from manufacturers and wholesalers to distributors. Each party in the packaging chain has to take back used packaging and must ensure that it is reused or that the material is recycled. This applies to 100 per cent of all packaging handled, although manufacturers and distributors can pass on this obligation to third parties.

Plastic bag legislation came into effect on 9 May 2003 in South Africa, with the aim of reducing the amount of litter from plastic shopping bags and to encourage their reuse and recycling. The legislation covers all plastics bags given to shoppers at the point of sale and prohibits the use of plastic bags that are too thin. Since 2003, numerous other countries have adopted similar legislation or are in the process of drafting such regulations.

12.6 Containerisation

Containerisation refers to the system by which containerised freight is transported intermodally.

Containers have become a common feature in most supply chains in the last 50 years. These box-like structures (see Figure 12.2) enable shippers to consolidate a number of items into a single freight unit, which can then be loaded and sealed intact onto container ships, railcars, planes and trucks.

Containerisation has led to vast improvements in handling efficiency, as multiple items can now be handled as a single unit, thereby reducing per-unit handling costs and increasing the flow of goods through freight terminals. The risk of damage to items is also reduced, as they are only physically handled twice during a multi-modal transport process – once during loading of the container and once during destuffing of the container.

12.6.1 ISO containers

As early as the 1830s, wooden and iron boxes were used as early forms of containers that could be transported by rail and ship. Over time, completely different and incompatible sizes of containers developed in various countries. Containers were generally small and not always stackable. The current standardisation of size, fitting and reinforcement evolved out of a series of compromises between international shipping lines, railways and trucking companies.

Between 1968 and 1970, four ISO recommendations were introduced in order to standardise containerisation by defining terminology, dimensions and ratings; defining identification markings; making recommendations about corner fittings; and setting minimum internal dimensions for general-purpose freight containers.

According to the ISO standard, there are five standard container lengths: 20 ft, 40 ft, 45 ft, 48 ft and 53 ft. The two most commonly used in international freight movement are the 20 ft and 40 ft containers. Container capacity of transport equipment or container terminals is often expressed in terms of twenty-foot equivalent units (TEU). One TEU of capacity is equivalent to one standard 20 ft container. Two TEUs are equivalent to one FEU or forty-foot equivalent unit.

Standard 20 ft and 40 ft containers are 2,438 m (8 ft) wide and 2,591 m (8 ft 6 in) high, with payload capacity of approximately 21,6 t and 26,5 t (weight) or 33 m^3 and 67 m^3 (volumetric) respectively. A 40 ft high cube container has the same base dimensions as a standard 40 ft container, but an extended height of up to 2,896 m (9 ft 6 in). High cube containers have a smaller payload capacity in terms of weight and are mostly used for volumetric cargo.

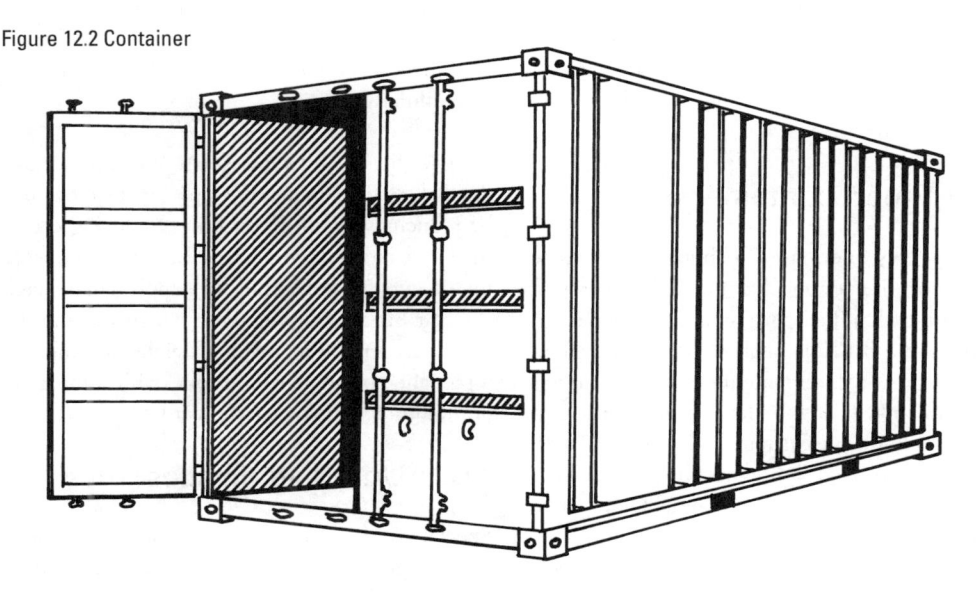

Figure 12.2 Container

Although the outside dimensions of containers are standardised, there is still some variation in the internal dimensions. When planning a container load, the true internal dimensions of the container that will be used have to be determined. Also take note that the door height and width differs from the container's height and width, and have to be taken into consideration when determining whether a large product can be shipped.

Various types of containers are available to meet general or specific logistics needs:
- Dry cargo – general-purpose ISO containers for boxes, cases, pallets, bags, drums etc.
- Reefer – temperature-controlled for perishable goods
- Ventilated – for products requiring ventilation (e.g. fresh produce)
- Insulated – to avoid environmental contamination or impact
- Open top – for bulk commodities and heavy machinery
- Flat rack – for heavy, bulky or out-of-gauge cargo
- Platform – for barrels, drums, cable drums, machinery and processed timber
- Collapsible – for lower cost of returning containers to owners

The type of container chosen by a shipper will depend on the characteristics of the cargo that needs to be shipped, as well as the freight cost and availability of container types on the origin-destination lanes on which it is to be shipped.

12.6.2 Smart containers

A smart container uses technology to sense certain occurrences and has the ability to report these to pre-identified parties via radio frequency identification (RFID), satellite or cellular communication. The development of smart containers is closely linked to the development and cost of new technology. Currently, the use of smart containers is limited, but as technology becomes more sophisticated and more affordable, it can be expected to increase.

The exact characteristics of smart containers are determined by the needs of the entity using them, but they should at least be able to detect:
- any unauthorised breach through any part of a container;
- the internal environment of the container; and
- the presence of potentially hazardous or illegal cargo.

A further frequent characteristic is the ability to detect the container's location. In the case of geo-fencing, the container detects whether there is a variance between where the container is and where it should be at a given point in time.

Breaches into containers can be detected using magnetic switches, light, vibration and temperature. Satellite positioning is used to pinpoint the location of containers. Technology that is able to detect chemical and biological agents, explosives, drugs and other undesirable material is still in a developmental stage and not readily available at a reasonable price. The ideal future smart container will use multiple technologies to track, communicate and detect occurrences at various levels.

Further challenges posed by the adoption of smart containers are:
- non-uniform global RFID frequencies and standards;
- infrastructure required for satellite communications; and
- different cellular protocols worldwide and cellular security.

Despite these obstacles, smart containers have the potential to increase supply chain efficiency by reducing overall transit times, reducing excess inventory and reducing losses through theft, while increasing the availability of supply chain data. There is no reason why these benefits cannot be achieved currently for national freight movement or for freight movement within zones with compatible or uniform technological standards.

12.6.3 Unit load devices

Special types of pallets or containers are used to load freight into aircraft. These are referred to as unit load devices (ULDs). As with standard

Figure 12.3 ULD container

12.7 Integrating technology with packaging and containerisation

12.7.1 Bar codes

A bar code is a series of high-contrast rectangular bars, blocks and spaces arranged according to the encoding rules of a particular specification in order to represent data. Its purpose is to represent information in a form that can be read automatically by a machine. Scanners are used to read bar codes and are programmed to decipher the structure of the bars, blocks and spaces. The encoded data can then be transmitted in an electronic format and stored in a file or transmitted to a computer for processing.

The layout of the rectangular bars, blocks and spaces in a bar code influence the amount of information that can be encoded. One-dimensional (1D) bar codes are the most basic and consist of only black bars with white spaces in between. These are the most common and can be found on virtually every product bought at a retail outlet. When this bar code is scanned, the product is identified and further information on it can then be drawn from a database. The bar code acts as a form of licence plate to encode a reference number to access information in a database.

Two-dimensional (2D) bar codes can encode more information than 1D bar codes or the same amount of data in less space. Enough information can be encoded in 2D bar codes to drive applications without database access. Two main categories of 2D symbologies can be identified: stacked and matrix. Stacked symbologies consist of two or more rows of linear bars and spaces. They basically look like a series of small 1D bar codes that have been stacked on top of each other. Matrix bar codes consist of dark and light geometric elements arranged in a grid. The relative position of each element to the centre of the grid is a key element during encoding. These bar codes can contain a lot of information in a relatively small area, making them suitable for use on small items. Matrix bar codes can only be read by area imagers and not by laser scanners.

pallets and containers, the ULDs allow for the simultaneous handling and movement of a large quantity or freight, thereby saving ground crew time and enabling quicker turnaround times. They also allow air cargo carriers to better utilise their volumetric carrying capacity. Each ULD has its own packing list, or manifest, and can be tracked as a single unit. Third-party logistics service providers consolidate the freight of multiple clients into one ULD, creating one master airway bill (MAWB) from each client's individual house airway bills (HAWBs).

ULDs can be found in two forms: containers and pallets. ULD containers are traditionally made from aluminium and may have refrigeration units built into them, for example, for the transport of temperature-sensitive pharmaceuticals. The shape of the container is determined by the type of aircraft in which it will be transported and the position into which the ULD will be loaded into the aircraft. An IATA ULD code is used to identify types of ULD containers. IATA develops and updates standards and guidelines around ULD containers on a continuous basis.

ULD pallets do not look like normal wood pallets, but are in fact large metal sheets with rims onto which cargo can be loaded and secured with net lugs. The cargo on the ULD pallet can be loose, boxed or palletised. The largest advantage of using such a pallet is that it reduces handling of cargo and enables airlines to offload their aircraft at a greater speed. With a premium service such as airfreight, this speed is of great importance.

Figure 12.4 Two-dimensional bar codes: stacked (above) and matrix (below)

The main advantage of 2D bar codes over 1D bar codes is that data can travel with the product and that access to the manufacturer's information systems is not required. Manufacturers of consumer goods and pharmaceuticals, for example, can use 2D bar codes to supplement identification labels with lot codes and expiry dates. Wholesalers, retailers and other organisations can get the product identification and expiry data they need directly through scanning.

A number of different bar code systems and standards are available. The Universal Product Code (UPC) and European Article Number (EAN) are the most commonly used within supply chains. The UPC is widely used in the USA and Canada, while EAN is a superset of the original UPC system and is used worldwide. EAN-13 bar codes consist of four parts containing a total of 13 numerals. Together, these numerals identify the country in which a manufacturer is registered, a manufacturer code and a product code. Further digits can be added to indicate serial numbers or the selling price, for example, of a book.

The main benefits of bar codes are speed and accuracy of data transfer, and a reduced need for printed information. Information on a product does not have to be printed any more, while the paper-trail accompanying a product's movement can now be replaced by an electronic information trail. A scanner can read a bar code in a fraction of a second – quicker than reading or manually capturing. Area imagers can even read bar codes in any orientation, upside down and sideways, thus saving further time during scanning.

12.7.2 Radio frequency identification

RFID is a type of carrier technology that falls within the field of automatic identification. It first gained prominence when retailer, Wal-Mart, and the US Department of Defence told their top suppliers that they would need to equip all cases and pallets supplied to them with RFID tags by 2005; all other suppliers had an extra year to comply. These two organisations, which both have large and extended supply chains, wanted to use RFID to increase supply chain efficiency by increasing control over their supply chain through better availability of data.

An RFID tag can be applied to or incorporated into any product or animal. It contains at least two parts: an integrated circuit or microchip and an antenna. The microchip is used for storing and processing information, while the antenna receives and transmits radio signals. Passive tags have no internal power supply, but have to be activated by external radio waves. Active tags have their own power supply and can transmit at higher power levels than passive tags. Semi-passive tags have their own limited power, which is only used to power the microchip.

Chipless RFID is the latest development in RFID, in which the RFID tag contains no power source and no microchip or other integrated circuit technology. Instead the tag consists of fibres or materials that reflect a portion of the scanner's or reader's signal back. The unique return signal is then used as an identifier. The advantage of this technology is that it is more cost-effective than traditional RFID tags, can function over a wider temperature range and is less sensitive to radio frequency interference.

In June 2003, Wal-Mart announced its plans to implement RFID technology in its supply chain by January 2005. Wal-Mart's plans envisaged compliance from its top 100 suppliers, which would enable the retailer to track pallets and cases from suppliers coming into its distribution centres. This type of RFID system is referred to as an open-loop system: RFID-tagged goods travel between facilities of multiple supply chain partners, with data shared between organisations and supply chains. In contrast to this, closed-loop RFID systems are implemented within the confines of one company. Although RFID-tagged goods may travel from one location to another, they remain solely in the primary company's supply chain.

Traditionally, RFID applications have focused on tracking goods at an item or box level, such as tracking a packet of pharmaceuticals from manufacturing to shelf and to POS. Non-traditional applications of RFID technology have started to look at, amongst others, the use of RFID in the following areas:
- Automotive ignition systems
- Managing highly complex manufacturing supply chains
- Asset and yard management
- Tracking the movement of livestock as part of disease control
- As a method to eliminate shipping errors

For Kimberly-Clark, a corporation that produces mostly paper-based consumer products, such as Kleenex and Huggies, RFID proved to be ideal for tracking the locations of trailers filled with finished goods and raw materials at one of its manufacturing facilities. This facility had five separate lots for trailer storage in 2008. Without RFID technology, it could take up to three hours for workers to locate a specific trailer at this site.[2] A system of passive RFID tags and GPS technology made it possible for the workers to locate a trailer within minutes, leading to increased labour productivity. This is an example of a closed-loop RFID system.

12.7.3 Multi-technology integration

Multiple technologies can be integrated to provide information about assets and products as they move through the supply chain. RFID has probably gained most from this conversion of technologies. In the past, an RFID tag was just an information carrier that had to interact directly with the rest of the RFID infrastructure in order to convey this information.

Within an integrated environment multiple sensors could, for example, be placed inside containers filled with frozen produce to monitor the temperature inside each container. RFID can be used to identify each container. If any variation in temperature occurs outside predetermined standards, cellular and GPS technology can be used to notify a control room. The control room then has information on the extent of the problem and the exact container that needs to be pulled in for inspection. The integrity of the frozen produce can, therefore, be managed and action taken as soon as a problem has been identified, localised and communicated to the control room.

12.8 Packaging: a supply chain perspective

There is an increased tendency to manage packaging as an interdependent component of a larger integrated system involving various actors throughout a supply chain.[3] Package design influences the efficiency and effectiveness of the entire supply chain in terms of functions, features, information and cost aspects.[4] Normally, a packaged product is handled many times in a supply chain and by a variety of means, human or mechanical. The packaging design process must, therefore, be part of a wider process where the demands of all partners in a supply chain should be considered rather than only internal costs and profits.

Currently, many material-flow systems are still hampered due to a lack of conformity between different parties in the supply chain. For example, different packaging needs exist amongst supply chain members and these needs are not all addressed in the design of the packaging unit upstream in the supply chain. As a result, a need for repacking is invariably created downstream in the supply chain and additional cost and delays are incurred. Packaging optimisation in a supply chain depends on countless variables that are unique to each company and facility in the system. Whilst a supplier may prefer the use of slip sheets instead of pallets in order to have more productive utilisation of space in transport modes, the opposite preference may exist with a customer who wishes to increase the speed of the materials-handling processes. Many of the problems in a supply chain can be resolved, however, through better communication and collaboration. One of the main reasons for the lack of conformity between different parties in the supply chain is insufficient information flow between different parties.[5]

Increased environmental restrictions and the need for more environmentally friendly packages throughout the supply chain will be one of the greatest packaging challenges of the future. Most current industry trends are focused on delivering excellent supply chain performance with reduced impact on the environment and energy sources. This has major implications on how companies in a supply chain design and use the packaging of products. Such an approach also requires a high level of supply chain cooperation for best results. An increasing number of major companies have recently announced initiatives to reduce packaging waste in their supply chains. Hewlett-Packard announced a goal to reduce energy used in its supply chain by 20 per cent, whilst Wal-Mart made it known that it wants to cut packaging waste at its stores by 25 per cent in three years.[6] In a survey conducted by consulting firm, AT Kearny, 50 per cent of the companies said they would deselect suppliers if they do not meet some form of sustainable metrics ranging from eco-efficiency in packaging, to carbon footprint, to full life-cycle costing.[7]

12.9 Conclusion

Packaging is an important activity in logistics management. It affects most of the other logistics activities and has a significant impact on total logistics costs and customer service levels in the supply chain. Packaging also has a major impact on the environment and energy sources and it is becoming increasingly important that companies design their packaging according to international requirements in this regard. It is essential, therefore, that packaging decisions are made systemically and that an integrated logistics and supply chain approach is followed.

Key terms

Bar code
Bulk packaging
Containerisation
Distribution packaging
Forty-foot equivalent unit (FEU)
ISO container
Life-cycle assessment (LCA)
Packaging
Pallet
Point-of-purchase (POP) packaging
Primary packaging
Radio frequency identification (RFID)
Secondary packaging
Smart container
Tertiary packaging
Twenty-foot equivalent unit (TEU)
Unit load
Unit load device (ULD)
Unitisation

Case study

UTi Sun Couriers was founded in 1981 and specialises in the movement of parcels, envelopes and freight to and from any address in South Africa and the BNLS countries. Its distribution network consists of 36 branches, including six hubs and four BNLS branches, and reaches 400 towns on a daily basis and a further 1 044 towns on a bi-weekly or ad hoc basis. During an average month, UTi Sun Couriers collects and delivers 1,2 million parcels through this network.

In 2008, UTi Sun Couriers launched its UTi Pak^2 and Pak^5 prepaid boxes. The Pak^2 box measures 10 × 30 × 40 cm and is designed for shipments of up to 2 kg in weight. The Pak^5 is 20 × 30 × 40 cm in size and can safely carry up to 5 kg. The boxes are custom-designed to be tamperproof and sturdy.

The Paks are sold to customers at a flat rate (i.e. the cost of the box includes both the packaging and the transport of the shipment). A special bar-coded prepaid dispatch note was also designed to assist in clearly identifying prepaid shipments. This dispatch note is pasted onto each Pak before it is sold to the client.

The Paks are targeted at freight originating in regional towns, with the intention of increasing freight coming out of those towns to which freight flow has traditionally been relatively one-directional. They can be sent to any main or regional centre serviced by UTi Sun Couriers within South Africa. Clients can use the bar-coded dispatch note number to track their parcels on Sun

Courier's website (www.sun.co.za) or they can call the national contact centre.

1. What possible benefits can UTi Sun Couriers and its clients gain from using the prepaid boxes? Refer specifically to the logistics benefits that UTi Sun Couriers will experience.
2. What role do the bar-coded dispatch notes play in the logistics process? Where in the supply chain will they contribute the most to increased efficiency?

Case study

Imagine that you have been appointed as supply chain manager for Tutti-Frutti Drinks, a Durban-based South African manufacturer of fruit juices and carbonated beverages. Tutti-Frutti currently sells its products in KwaZulu-Natal, Gauteng and the Free State, but wants to expand its market into the rest of South Africa and the African continent. Market research has indicated that its products are well suited for the Zambian, Tanzanian, Ghanaian and Egyptian export markets. Market research further indicated that Tutti-Frutti Drinks should initially export a selection of fruit juices in quantities of 1 litre and 340 ml, and carbonated beverages in quantities of 1 litre and 500 ml.

Currently, Tutti-Frutti sells its fruit juices in 1-litre plastic sachets in the local market, and the carbonated beverages in 340 ml clear glass bottles. The glass bottles are packed in wooden crates with limited stackability for distribution to spaza stores, supermarkets and restaurants. The plastic sachets are placed in stackable plastic crates for distribution.

Tutti-Frutti realises that it will have to change its packaging for export purposes. You have been asked to provide input as to the logistics requirements that the new packaging will have to meet.

1. What cost trade-offs have to be considered by Tutti-Frutti when redesigning its packaging?
2. Make a recommendation as to the packaging shape and packaging materials that should be used as primary packaging for both the fruit juices and the carbonated beverages. (Make sure that you motivate your recommendation by referring to the logistics benefits of the chosen shapes and materials.)
3. Would you recommend that Tutti-Frutti also designs secondary packaging? If yes, what type and shape of secondary packaging would you recommend? Why?

Questions

1. By looking at the definition and function of packaging, do you think that containerisation and palletisation are just forms of packaging? Motivate your answer.
2. Imagine that you are an exporter of frozen fish from Walvis Bay, Namibia, to Europe. What factors would you take into account when designing packaging for the fish?
3. Refill packages for fabric softener are sometimes packaged in plastic pouches. What benefits do these pouches hold for the manufacturer, retailer and consumer?
4. In addition to the RFID applications mentioned in this chapter, what other innovative applications of RFID technology can you think of or find on the Internet?

Consult the web

Ckdpack Inc. (Automotive Global Returnable Packaging): www.ckdpack.com
Industry Council for Packaging and the Environment: www.incpen.org
Institute of Packaging Professionals: www.iopp.org
Integrated Solutions Magazine: www.integratedsolutionsmag.com
Intermec Technologies: www.intermec.com
Reusable Pallet and Container Coalition: www.rpcc.us
RFID Journal: www.rfidjournal.com

Consult the books

Amendola, V. 2008. 'Closed-loop RFID deployments offer control'. *Integrated Solutions Magazine*. April 2008.
Brody, A. L. and Marsh, K. S. (eds.) 1997. *The Wiley Encyclopedia of Packaging Technology*, 2nd edition. New York: John Wiley & Sons.

Byett, J., Bruyns, O., Glover, T., Oakley, B., Smithard, E. and Tinkler, R. 1997. *Packaging Technology*. Pinegowrie: The Institute of Packaging (South Africa).

Chan, F. T. S., Chan, H. K. and Choy, K. L. 2006. 'A systematic approach to manufacturing packaging logistics'. *International Journal of Advanced Manufacturing Technology*, 29(9–10).

Cook, L.R. 1991. In Grant, D.B., Lambert, D.M., Stock, J.R. and Ellram, L. 2006. *Fundamentals of Logistics Management: European Edition*. McGraw-Hill.

Giermanski, J. 2008. 'Logistics and supply chain technology: Tapping the potential of smart containers'. *Logistics Management*. 1 March 2008.

Glass, T. 2008. 'Improve supply chain efficiency'. *Material Handling Management*, 63(5).

Hatteland, C. J. 2004. In Chan, F. T. S., Chan, H. K. and Choy, K. L. 2006. 'A systematic approach to manufacturing packaging logistics'. *International Journal of Advanced Manufacturing Technology*, 29(9–10).

Intermec. 2007. *The 2D Revolution: How evolving business needs and improved technology are driving explosive growth in two-dimensional bar coding*. Everett, W. A.. Intermec Technologies Corporation.

O'Connor, M. C. 2008. 'Kimberley-Clark sees positive results with PINC trailer tracking system'. *RFID Journal*. 1 May 2008.

Olsson, A., Petterson, M. and Jönson, G. 2004. 'Packaging demands in the food industry'. *Food Service Technology*, 4.

Soroka, W. 1999. *Fundamentals of Packaging Technology*, 2nd edition. Herndon: Institute of Packaging Professionals.

Stewart, B. 2007. *Packaging Design*. London: Laurence King.

Sullivan, M. and Happek, S. 2005. *Demystifying RFID in the Supply Chain*. Atlanta: UPS Supply Chain Solutions.

Tarnef, B. M. 1993. 'Safeguarding shipments when going global'. *Risk Management*, 40(9) September 1993.

Notes

1. Tarnef, B. M. 1993: 20–6.
2. O'Connor, M. C. 2008.
3. Hatteland, C. J. 2004. In Chan et al. 2006: 1088–1101.
4. Olsson et al. 2004: 97–105.
5. Chan et al. 2006: 1088–1101.
6. Glass, T. 2008: 24.
7. Ibid.: 24.

13 Equipment used in facilities

J. Vogt

Learning outcomes
After you have studied this chapter, you should be able to:
- identify the most important types of equipment that are encountered in logistics;
- understand the advantages and disadvantages of each type of equipment;
- evaluate and make the correct choice of equipment for a specific need; and
- identify the principles of the operation of the equipment in the logistics chain.

13.1 Introduction

This chapter introduces the various types of equipment that a logistics professional may encounter in the facilities within a logistics chain. Only the broad categories of equipment are presented, but there are many variations of equipment available from different manufacturers. These variations need to be investigated once the requirements for the equipment have been determined. Once these requirements have been established, each offering in the marketplace should be investigated and the most appropriate equipment chosen. This can be done initially by exploring the information provided by the various manufacturers. A number of Internet sites have been included at the end of this chapter for further reference (Consult the web, page 301). The purchase of equipment from a catalogue, which is not tested in the environment under conditions of service is not recommended. A far better way is to require the supplier to visit the site, and demonstrate the equipment doing the work required.

You will need to be familiar with the following definitions:

> Picking, or order picking, or selection is the process of assembling items from a storage location or locations in response to an order.

> The pick face is the location from where orders that require less than full pallets are taken or picked. Pick faces are designed to make goods readily available to the picker and are located, therefore, where access is simple and easy (such as floor level).

13.2 Selection of equipment

The selection criteria for equipment are discussed in the various sections in this chapter. When choosing equipment, one should always have a clear understanding of the needs of the facility. The needs should be expressed in terms of simple criteria with measurable values. The equipment may, for instance, need to be able to lift 2 tons or travel at 30 km/h. Each criterion must be assigned a priority, i.e. one must decide whether the need is:
- a prerequisite;
- required, but not a prerequisite; or
- liked, but not required.

While different or even additional criteria can be used, it is important to prioritise them when doing all assessments. The market can be tested against these needs and priorities. Suppliers can be rated according to their compliance with the criteria. Only those that satisfy the prerequisite criteria should be considered. When there are suppliers that satisfy both the prerequisite and required criteria, the impact of the liked criteria is used to make the final decision. This method is by far the best to ensure the most appropriate equipment is obtained from the best supplier. Gut feeling or choices made solely on suppliers' recommendations or because the equipment has a high profile are rarely as successful. A logistics professional should analyse purchases with the aid of measurable criteria to avoid decisions based on opinions and biases. The equipment is a significant investment, and the wrong choice means that the operation will suffer for the life of the equipment.

13.3 Risks involved in purchasing equipment

A business does not purchase equipment every day. Identifying needs and obtaining the appropriate equipment is a project. The risks of such projects reach a peak on two occasions. The first is when the decision is made to purchase equipment. This decision commits the facility to a specific technology and supplier and to spending a large amount of money. If the equipment is not suitable for the facility, a large amount of time, effort and expense will have been wasted.

The second peak is when the equipment is delivered. It must be tested and the testing recorded in detail to ensure the equipment performs to the purchasing criteria and the satisfaction of the operator. Failure to do so may result in the facility paying money to modify or replace the equipment, or working with inappropriate equipment that makes the operation inefficient.

13.4 Storage methods for small items

Smaller products in many industries cannot be stored on or picked from a pallet. The products that fit into this category include such diverse items as boxes of toothpaste; torch batteries; electronic components; and mechanical parts that are small or fragile. For these items, different forms of storage, such as shelves and bins, are needed.

13.4.1 Shelving

Smaller products can be arranged on shelving (Figure 13.1), which provides ample small storage space and makes access to the products easy. The size of the space created by shelves can be adjusted simply and quickly to suit the products. With careful planning, the box in which the product is transported can be placed onto the shelf and used as the storage container. This simplifies the storage of the product and makes it unnecessary to unpack boxes.

Because the products stored on shelves are generally lighter, the shelves can be multi-tiered (high-rise shelving, as it is sometimes called, can be up to 15 m high) or have long spans to create more storage space.

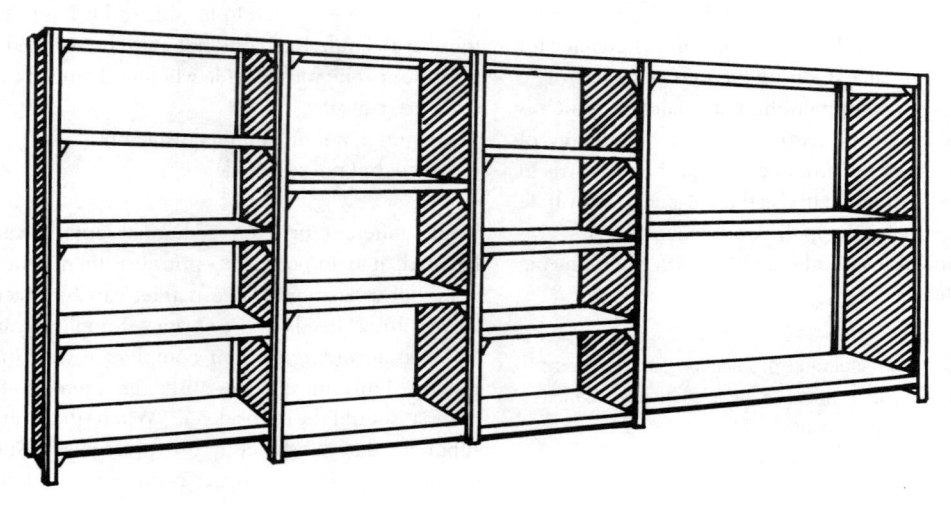

Figure 13.1 Shelving

13.4.2 Bins

Smaller items can be stored in small containers called bins (Figure 13.2). These are designed so products can be stored safely and accessed easily for counting and picking. Bins are often colour-coded to make it easier to identify products. Bins vary in shape and size, and are made from a variety of materials, mainly plastic. Plastic bins are generally lightweight, easy to stack and transport, robust and durable. The more common bins range in size, from units with a face that is 30 to 40 mm wide and high to units that are 500 mm wide and 400 mm high and have a capacity of around 50 000 cm^3.

The bins may be inserted into shelves or hung from a vertical back panel. These panels are made with special supports that allow the bins to hang anywhere on the panel. The panel can thus be fitted with the size and number of bins suitable for storage and picking.

Figure 13.2 Bins

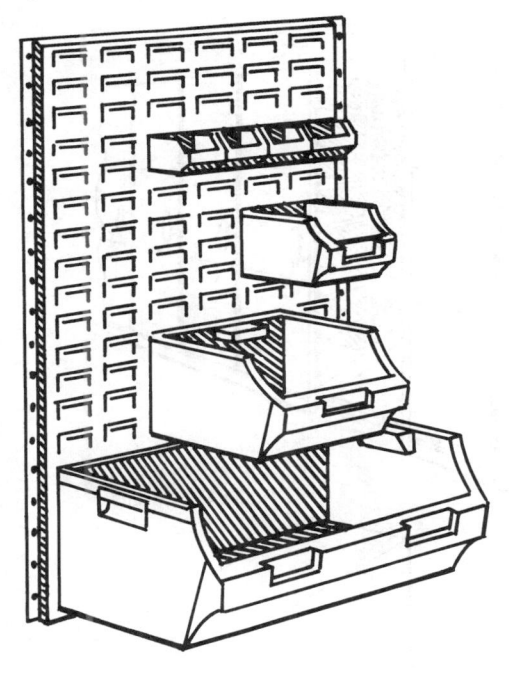

13.4.3 Live storage or case flow racks

Some products have a faster turnover, which cannot easily be handled utilising a shelf, or require a larger stockholding or strict stock rotation. If these products are in boxes or containers, they can be stored effectively in live storage systems (Figure 13.3). These consist of trays of inclined wheels or rollers. Boxes placed in the live storage move down the rollers towards the front of the racks until they rest on boxes already in the racks. As the boxes can only be removed in the sequence in which they are inserted into the live racking, stock rotation is ensured. The density of storage is also higher than that of basic shelving.

This storage method is particularly suitable for perishable items in containers, pharmaceutical products and high-movement products distributed in cases or boxes.

Figure 13.3 Live storage system

13.4.4 Mobile shelving

Shelving requires aisles for accessing goods. These aisles occupy space, which reduces the density of storage. One way to increase the density of storage is to use shelves that can be moved, manually or powered, on rails (Figure 13.4). The shelves are moved apart to create the aisle from which the product can be picked. This way, a number of shelves can be fitted into a much smaller area. If the shelves are powered and operated by remote control, the aisle can be created while the picker moves from one pick to the next.

This storage method is suitable for products that do not need to be accessed frequently. As the frequency of access increases, the delay in opening an aisle to reach the products renders this method less efficient. This method is commonly used in pharmacies, as the large amount of items carried cannot be stored in normal shelves without occupying an inordinate amount of space.

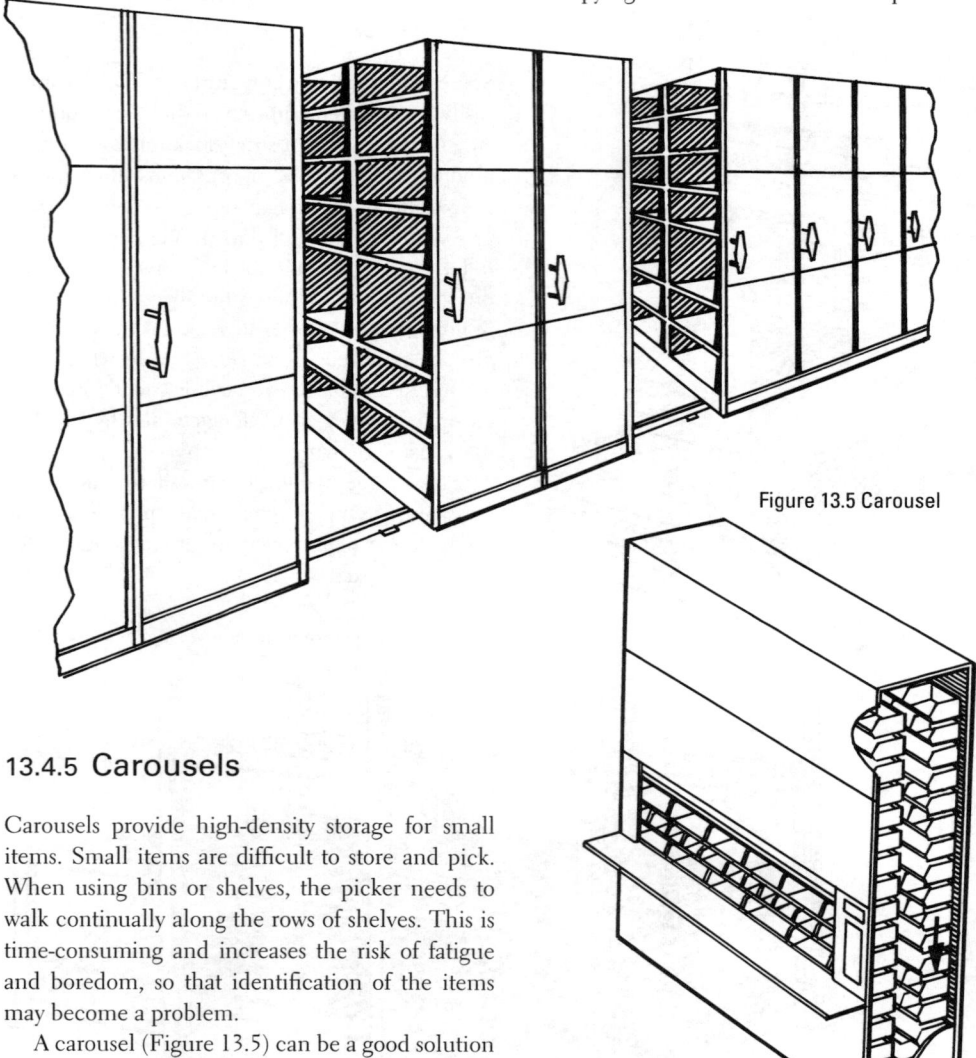

Figure 13.4 mobile shelving

Figure 13.5 Carousel

13.4.5 Carousels

Carousels provide high-density storage for small items. Small items are difficult to store and pick. When using bins or shelves, the picker needs to walk continually along the rows of shelves. This is time-consuming and increases the risk of fatigue and boredom, so that identification of the items may become a problem.

A carousel (Figure 13.5) can be a good solution to these problems, since it brings the product to the picker. It is a series of trays connected to a moving mechanism. The trays may be divided into sections to produce a row of storage locations within each tray. These multiple compartments are housed in a cabinet. As a particular item is required, the trays are rotated until the appropriate tray is available through an access slot. The rotation may be done automatically or manually. As the cabinet can be locked, it also provides excellent security for expensive items.

13.4.6 Storage cabinets

Small- to medium-sized goods can be stored effectively in cabinets fitted with drawers (Figure 13.6). The drawers are arranged as in a filing cabinet and may have compartments of various sizes. The system increases storage density and allows for secure storage, as the drawers can be locked. The size of these units may be extended vertically to give more drawers. Access is limited to one drawer at a time in an operating area.

Figure 13.6 Storage cabinet

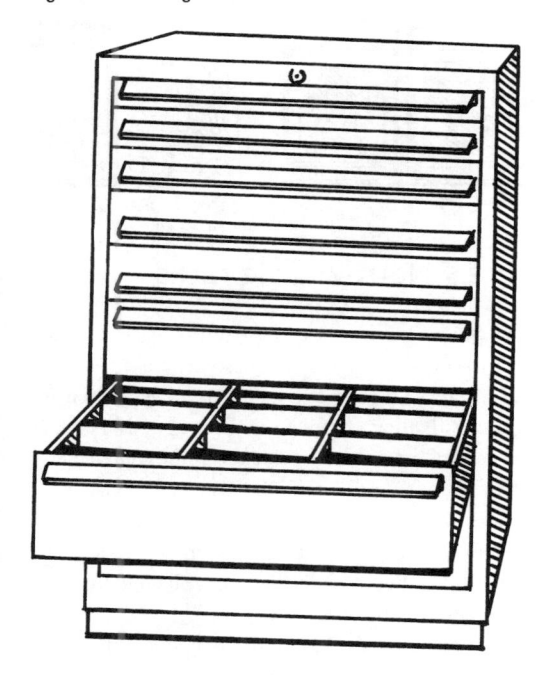

13.5 Pallets and their storage

13.5.1 Pallets

Pallets provide a simple and efficient means of consolidating goods into a unit on a single base that can be moved and stored effectively. Often, products cannot be handled individually by mechanical equipment, but as a consolidated unit they can be handled quickly and with common equipment.

The design and materials of pallets vary. The most basic pallet is made of wood, measuring 1,2 m long × 1 m wide, with a height of 0,2 m, as shown in Figure 13.7. The ease and low cost of the construction make this a popular type of pallet. Wood pallets get damaged with continual

Figure 13.7 Stacking goods on a pallet

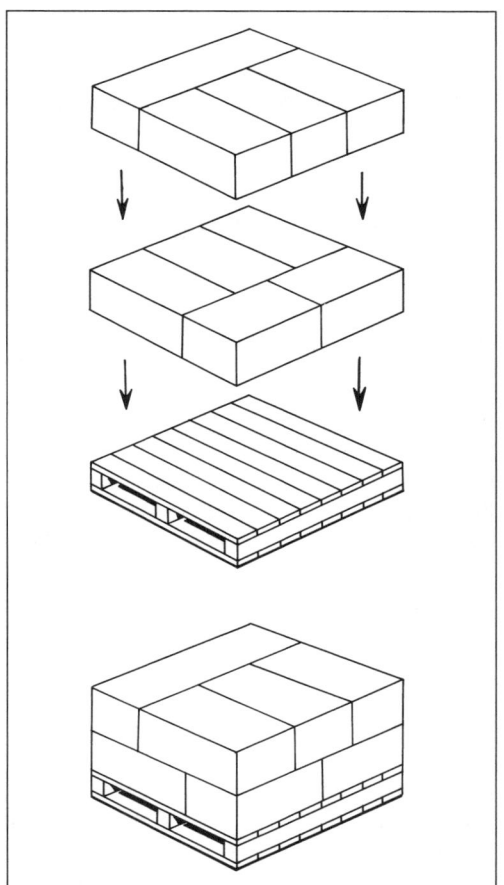

use and are not as robust or durable as those made from plastic or metal. Metal is the most durable, but is heavy to manoeuvre and transport. Plastic is probably the best compromise, as it is reasonably lightweight. Goods are stacked on the pallets up to a height of approximately 1,6 m. For each product, a standard configuration of boxes is chosen so that one can see at a glance whether all pallets carry the same quantity of the product. The boxes chosen are generally suitable to fill the base of the pallet and are then stacked one on top of another (see Figure 13.7). When a single product type is loaded on a pallet, the number of boxes on the base of the pallet is known as the Ti (or tier) of the pallet, and the number of layers is the Hi (or height).

13.5.2 Block stacking

Boxes can be stacked one on top of another. The weight of the boxes and their contents, as well as the strength of the boxes, determine the height to which the boxes can be stacked. Pallets can also be stacked in this way, but only when the boxes are strong enough to support the weight. The weight generally limits this stack to two pallets high.

13.5.3 General pallet storage racks

Racks provide access to goods from the front and allow one to stack higher than with block stacking. Whereas the goods support the stack in the block-stacking method, in this case the structure of the racks supports the goods. Static racks are a reasonably dense way of storing goods. However, the aisles that allow access to the goods take up a significant amount of floor area. In the sections that follow static storage racks (13.5.7–13.5.9), we discuss various configurations of racks which increase the density of storage at the expense of the unlimited access that static storage racks provide.

13.5.4 Static storage racks

Static storage racks (Figure 13.8) can be erected and altered with relative ease and speed. Two rows of racks are usually assembled back-to-back. This allows access only to the front of each row, but reduces the aisle space, thereby increasing the storage density. The height of racks may vary, but practical considerations limit it to approximately 11 m (approximately six to eight pallets).

This type of rack is particularly useful when the storage density of palletised goods needs to be improved. The bottom shelves of racks are ideal for pick faces. The reach stackers needed for storage or removal are relatively inexpensive, so capital costs are low.

Figure 13.8 Static storage racks with reach stacker

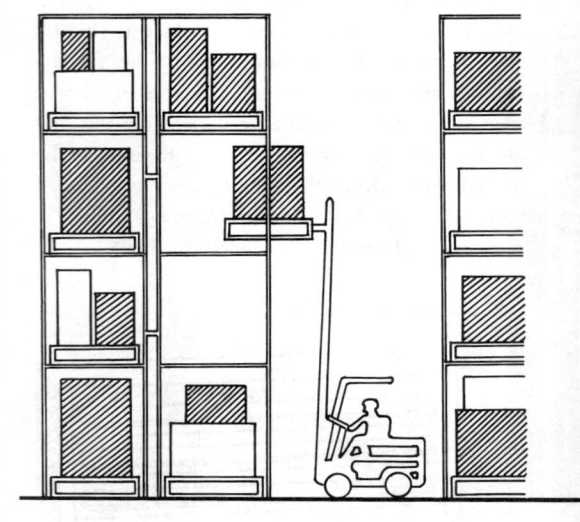

13.5.5 Narrow-aisle racks

As the name implies, these racks have a much narrower aisle than general static racks. Narrow-aisle racks (Figure 13.9) increase storage density, while still allowing access to all the goods. Narrow-aisle reach trucks and stacker cranes service this type of racking. Because the aisle is too narrow for the equipment to turn, the truck or crane moves laterally along the aisle. To prevent the aisle being blocked, pallets are placed in, or collected from, an area outside the aisle.

A narrow-aisle reach truck can reach up to 12 m high, and some versions, which elevate the operator, reach up to significantly higher levels. This is sometimes called the man-up version of the equipment. This specialised piece of equipment is much more expensive than a standard reach truck and runs on rails. It also requires more rigid and sturdier racks. A stacker crane reaches even higher than elevated-operator, narrow-aisle equipment.

Figure 13.9 Narrow-aisle racks with reach truck

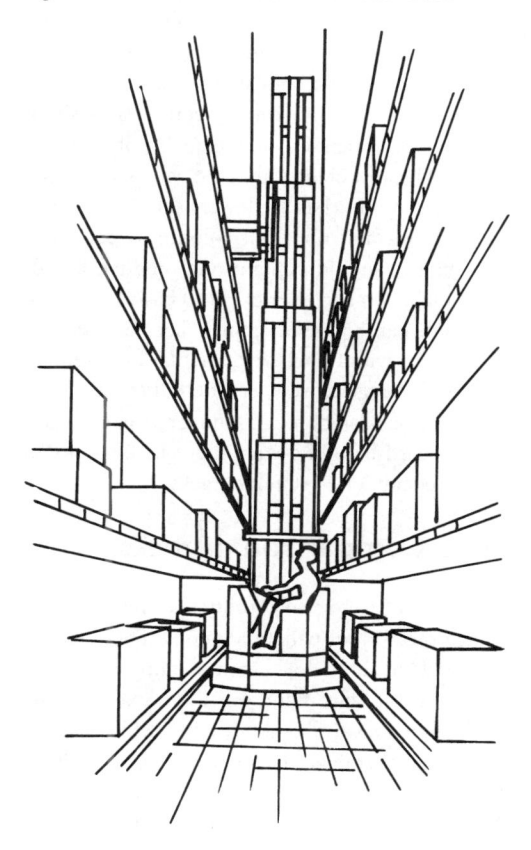

13.5.6 Drive-in and drive-through racks

To increase the density of storage, racks can be placed three or more deep. These racks have side supports for pallets that are inserted into the racks with a forklift or similar equipment. Drive-in and drive-through racks (Figure 13.10) do not cost more than general racks, but access to the goods is limited.

Drive-in racks give access to equipment from only one side. As there is only one aisle, storage density can be increased significantly, depending on the depth of the racks. Goods can only be extracted from the same side of the racks into which they were placed. The goods are rotated on a last in, first out (LIFO) basis.

Each column of racks should store only one product, as all the goods must be removed from the one column before moving on to the next column. Goods in any position in one column of these racks preclude the access to the next column of goods. If there are different products on the different levels

Figure 13.10 Drive-in racks

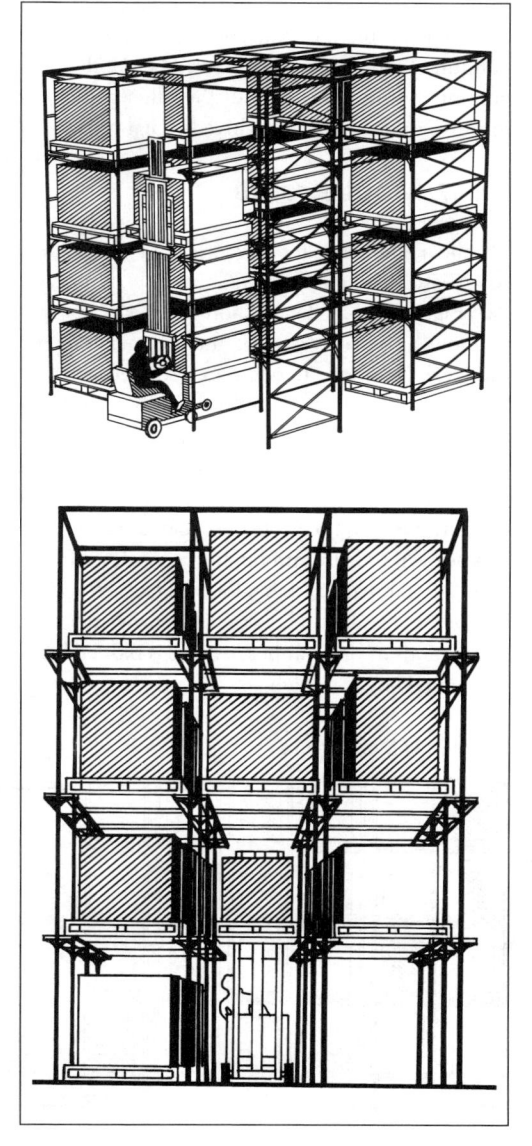

of the racks, slower-moving stock will prevent the equipment from accessing the faster-moving products until the slower-moving stock is removed. The potential for repeated handling of goods is high with these racks.

Drive-through racks provide access from two sides so that equipment can drive through the racks. Whereas the rotation of stock is a problem when using drive-in racks, with drive-through racks the goods can be rotated on a first in, first out (FIFO) basis. However, the storage density is somewhat reduced due to the need for the second aisle. The problem remains of the product in each column of the rack being removed before the next column can be accessed. All the other principles for drive-in racks apply for drive-through racks.

13.5.7 Mobile racks

Mobile racks consist of two rows of racks on a solid base that moves on rails in one dimension (see Figure 13.11). There should be space for one or more aisles between the mobile racks so that the racks can move to open an aisle between any two racks. This can be automatically controlled with a remote control on equipment travelling towards the racking. The aisle provides access that is restricted only when two pieces of equipment concurrently require access to separate racks. This can be overcome by introducing two aisles. Mobile racks are not really suitable for pick faces. Rotation of stock is feasible. The storage density increases significantly as the number of aisles is reduced, but the capital costs are high.

13.5.8 Live storage racks (pallet flow racks)

In this system, the static racks are fitted with rollers in the slots where the pallets are inserted (see Figure 13.12). The rollers are inclined from the back of the rack to the front so that the weight of the pallet carries it from one side to the other. Access is needed on both sides, necessitating two aisles. The rack depth can be comfortably six or more pallets, depending on the quality of the roller system. The advantage is that the pallets are always presented to one (i.e. the lower) side of the rack. Each level – and not each column as per drive-in racking – should contain one product. Goods are available on a very strict FIFO basis so that the lower side can be used as a pick face. Live storage racks are very useful where particular lines require increased storage density, or where there is a need for strict stock rotation. The moderate capital cost and standard handling equipment make them an attractive addition to standard racks.

13.5.9 Comparison of racks

A number of factors may influence the choice of storage method for palletised goods. These factors are listed in Table 13.1, with a rating of 1 to 4, where 1 is the lowest and 4 is the highest. In any installation, however, other variables will influence the choice of storage. If, for instance, a facility is short of space and cannot be expanded, high-density storage methods are required and other factors are not significant.

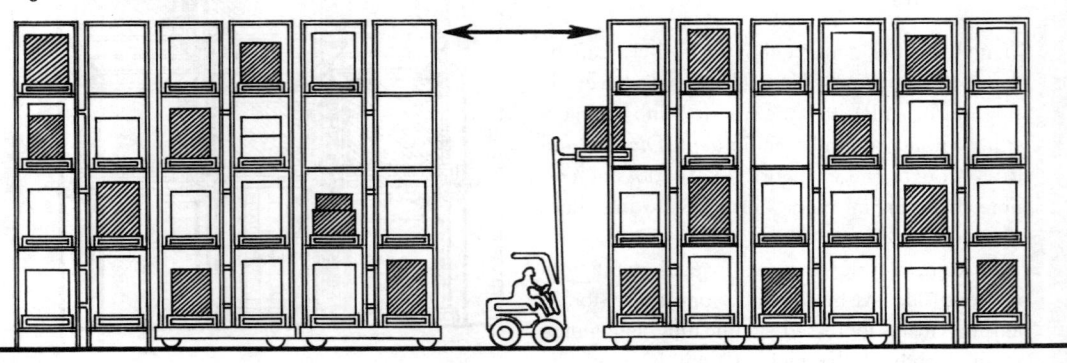

Figure 13.11 Mobile racks

Figure 13.12 Live storage racks

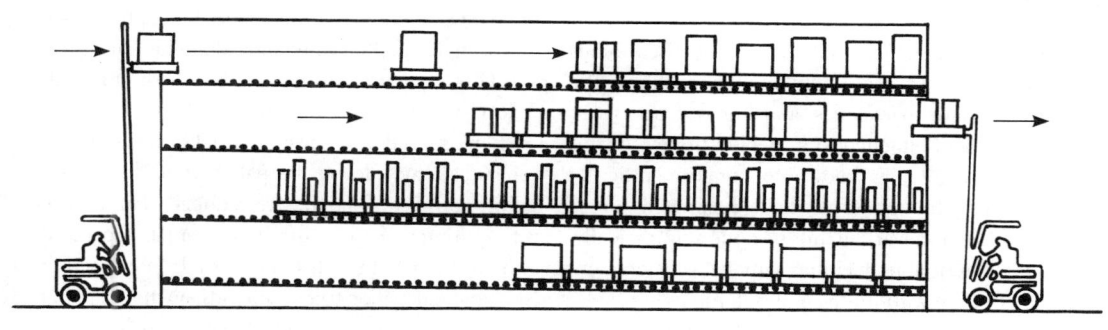

Table 13.1 Comparison of the attributes of various storage methods by rank

Storage method	Capital cost	Storage density	Rotation of goods FIFO	Access to all goods	Handling equipment cost	Used for pick face	Speed of throughput
Block stacking	1	3	1	1	1	2	3
Racks	2	2	2	4	2	4	3
Narrow-aisle racks	3	3	2	3	4	1	3
Drive-in racks	3	3	3	2	2	/	2
Mobile racks	4	4	2	3	2	/	2
Live racks	3	4	4	1	2	2	2

Note: The ranking (of 1 to 4 – 1 is the lowest, 4 the highest) is relative to the other methods of storage compared in the table.

13.6 Hanging rail systems

Certain goods are best moved on a rail or suspension system. The prime example of this is clothing, but some food products can also be moved in this way. The following description is based on clothing, but the principles are applicable to any product that should be moved and stored in a hanging configuration.

13.6.1 Hanging rails

This is a rail on which trolleys move (see Figure 13.13). It contains equipment to push trolleys up an incline or control them down an incline. The rail may also have switches to divert trolleys to other rails. The rail is supported from one side and underneath, so that the trolleys only operate on one side of the rail. When designing the merging of rails, one should take care, therefore, that the trolleys all have the same orientation.

Figure 13.13 Trolley on a rail

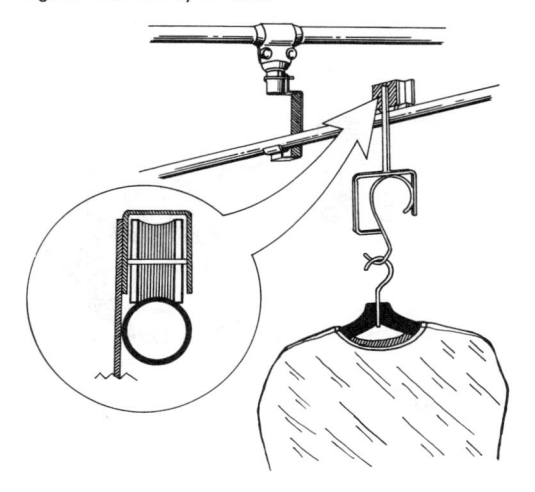

13.6.2 Trolleys

Trolleys can be used for one or several garments (see Figure 13.13). In automated facilities, the trolleys have bar codes and the garments are scanned and attached to a specific trolley. In this way, the trolley is known to contain particular garments. The trolleys also have designated storage areas. The retrieval can thus be done automatically. Large throughput facilities can be very efficient and effective with this type of system.

Manual facilities often use the trolleys for a number of similar garments that have to be moved quickly and efficiently from a truck into storage and vice versa. The advantages are rapid movement without lifting and ease of identification. The system also allows the use of the vertical space in a facility, as the garments can be stored on multiple levels.

13.7 Moving loads

13.7.1 Manual and powered pallet trucks

The most common piece of equipment for moving pallets quickly is the pallet truck (Figure 13.14), sometimes also called a walker-rider or a pallet taxi. Two forks, which fit into the pallet base, are attached to it. The forks can be raised to lift the load up to approximately 20 to 40 mm above the floor. The optimal load is 1 600 kg to 2 000 kg. The forks fitted may be one pallet in length or two, allowing two pallets to be moved at one time.

The operator supplies the hydraulic lift effort for the manual truck. A DC battery system is used for powered trucks. Because the operator may ride on the pallet truck, his or her effort and risk of fatigue are reduced. The choice of equipment is primarily based on the speed at which the pallet needs to be moved. The speed of the manual pallet truck depends on the walking speed of the operator. The powered pallet truck can attain speeds of up to 10 km/h (or 3 m/s).

13.7.2 Forklift (or counter-balance) truck

The forklift, or counterbalance, truck (so called because the load is raised on one side of the truck and counterbalanced by a fixed weight in the truck) is used for lifting pallets and moving them at a high speed. This piece of equipment (see Figure 13.15) can attain speeds of up to 15 km/h. It can lift pallets to a height of 3,5 m; with special masts, this height can be extended to approximately 8 m. These trucks can lift loads that are significantly heavier than 2 tons. They often have long forks to move two pallets at a time. This saves time and ensures that the services of both the equipment and the operator are utilised more efficiently – especially if the pallets need to be moved far distances.

Figure 13.14 Manual and powered pallet trucks

Figure 13.15 Forklift (or counter-balance) trucks

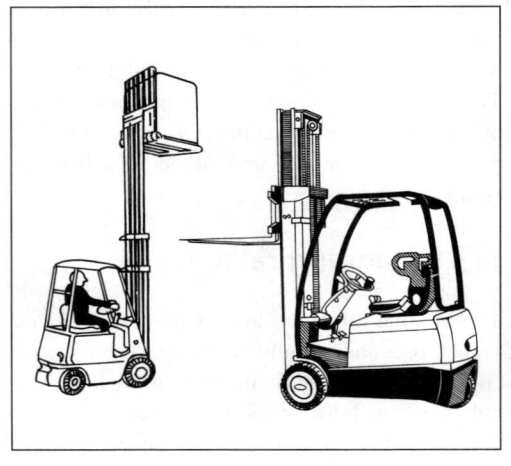

13.7.3 Reach trucks

Reach trucks (Figure 13.16) are designed to perform the specialised tasks of lifting and lowering pallets with greater ease and speed than counter-balanced trucks. The vision through the lifting mast is improved to increase the ease with which pallets are handled while elevated. Nowadays, there is very little variation in the more advanced units in which the principal functions – lifting power and speed – are combined.

These multi-purpose units are more expensive than a forklift, but the versatility is often worth the additional cost. The horizontal speeds very nearly equal those of fork-lifts. The reach truck can operate in narrower aisles, and therefore the density of storage is increased and the travel distance reduced.

Figure 13.16 Reach truck

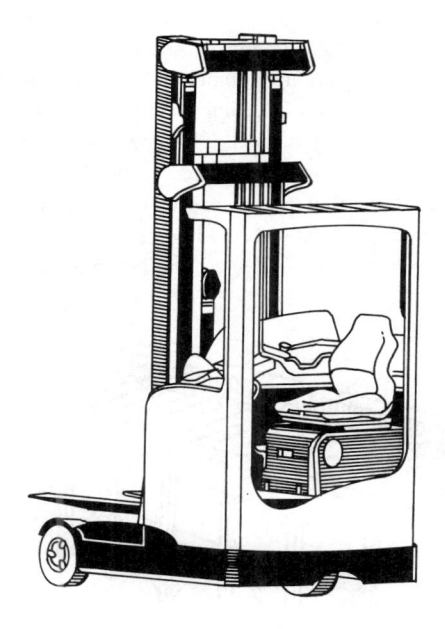

13.7.4 Turret trucks, narrow aisle trucks and cranes

When racks are very high, it may be dangerous to lift pallets to the top racks with a counterbalance or reach truck. The operator on the floor cannot see up to the top rack, as narrow-aisle racking may be as high as 12 m. The solution is the turret, or narrow-aisle, truck, which allows the cab for the operator to lift with the load (see Figure 13.17). This way, the operator has good visibility of the complete operation. The equipment can service either side of the aisle by swivelling the load. The result is that a much narrower aisle (just larger than the pallet) can be used than when general-purpose forklifts or reach trucks are utilised. The narrow-aisle equipment requires very smooth and level floors to maintain stability. The turret truck is ideally suited for long, high racks with narrow aisles. Movement can be sped up by using rails or guide wires that automatically centre the truck in the aisle.

Turret trucks running on rails or overhead cranes can service racks higher than 12 m. These racks often support the roof of the building and are built to be an integral part of the facility. This is more common in Europe, where high volumes and high land costs make such high racks more economically viable.

Figure 13.17 Turret truck

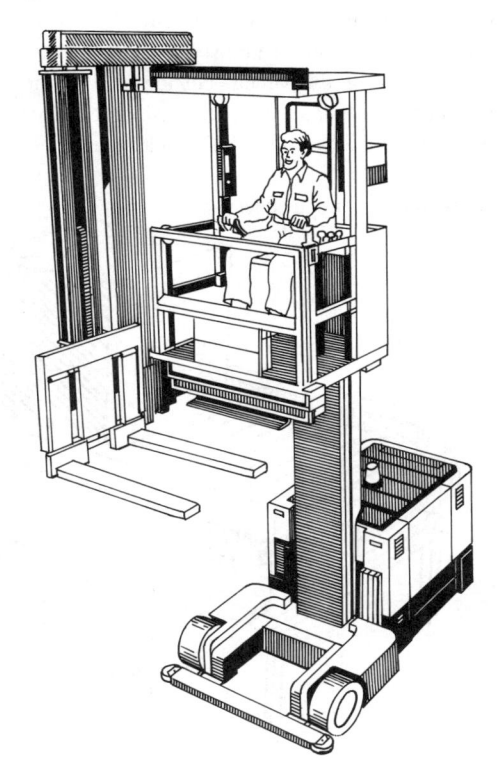

13.8 Moving and sorting

Mechanical transport systems move goods without operator intervention. This way, products can be sorted and the mass and dimensions determined without touching the goods.

When choosing equipment, one should carefully determine the level of sophistication needed. Some large facilities in which high volumes of goods are moved and stored are fully automated and computer-controlled. This is rare in the global economy; and in economies in transition, volumes are generally too low to justify such investment. In these countries, unfavourable exchange rates increase the capital cost and the cost of replacement parts for sophisticated technology.

The combined effects of very high land costs, high throughputs and the availability of skilled labour explain why many European companies opt for this type of operation. American operations generally do not adopt such sophisticated technology. The Federal Express (FedEx) main hub in Memphis, for example, handles approximately 2 million parcels between 22:00 and 01:30 every night. While mechanical handling equipment is present, approximately 8 000 employees scan and (in a limited area) sort the parcels. The lower cost of land and quality of labour allow this facility to operate efficiently and effectively with such a system.

13.8.1 Conveyors: belt and roller bed

The continuous movement of boxes or pallets down a specific route lends itself to the use of mechanical transport methods such as belt conveyors and roller-bed conveyors (Figure 13.18).

Belt conveyers are used where the goods need to move in straight lines, upwards, or downwards and when speed varies.

Roller beds are a series of rollers that turn in one direction and consequently move the goods. With these conveyors, goods can be diverted by installing bends or equipment between the rollers. The disadvantages are that goods may slip on the rollers and that goods may move at different speeds.

13.8.2 Accelerator belts

Goods that must be sorted, measured or massed need to be spaced in order to allow automated sortation and/or accurate measurements. To obtain a specific minimum distance between goods on a conveyer without slowing their throughput, an accelerator belt is used. The goods are first fed onto the feeding belt. The accelerator belt, which moves faster than the feeding belt, catches the first box and accelerates it to a higher speed than that of the feeding belt. The second box moves at the

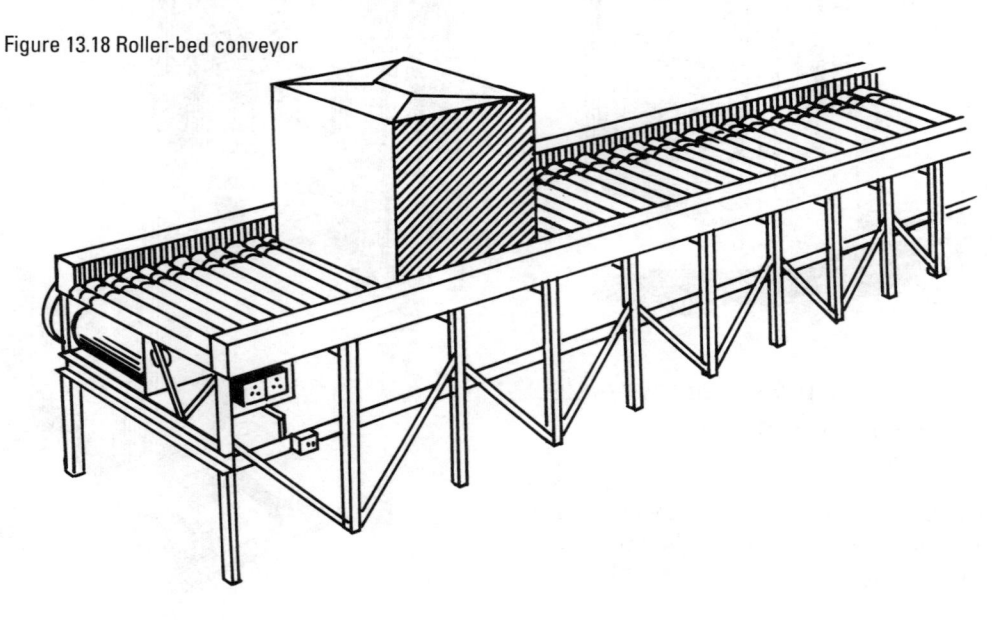

Figure 13.18 Roller-bed conveyor

slower speed of the feeding belt until the accelerator belt catches it. The first box is, therefore, a specific distance – proportional to the difference in speed between the two belts – ahead of the second box. The throughput remains stable because the faster speed of the accelerator belt compensates for the space introduced between the boxes.

13.8.3 Merge systems

A merge system is applied where two or more conveyors feed into one conveyor (Figure 13.19). The two conveyors cannot feed onto the merge conveyor simultaneously, as the boxes would fall off the conveyor or jam it. To merge successfully, one of the conveyors must be able to delay the feeding in order to take turns with the other conveyor.

Figure 13.19 Merge system conveyors

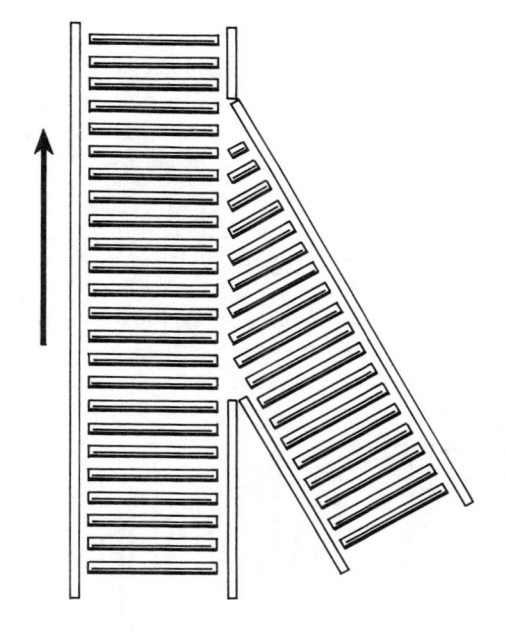

13.8.4 In-line bar code scanners and radio frequency identification devices

In-line bar code scanners are able to read bar codes while products pass through the scanner, irrespective of the orientation of either the item or the bar code. This facilitates the automatic identification of goods. For the bar code scanners to be able to see the bar code requires that the item be placed in a particular orientation so the bar code and scanner are in line of sight of one another. This complicates the use of this technology in high-speed sortation systems.

Radio frequency identification (RFID) tags (see Chapters 12 and 14 for more detailed descriptions of this technology) and readers do not have to be in line of sight of one another and for this reason a number of applications have started to use this technology for sortation as well as stock management. This technology still has issues, but these are slowly being overcome. In specific applications, the use of these is of great advantage to the operations.

13.8.5 In-line weighing and measuring

Scales that can accurately measure the weight of an item passing over them can be fitted to the belt or roller bed. Provided that the belt is travelling at a known and constant speed, the length of the item can be determined by measuring for how long the item blocks a beam. Beams reflected from the item can also determine its height, width, and depth.

13.8.6 Diverters and sorters

Items can be sorted by diverting them from one path onto another (see Figure 13.20, page 298). Light items that travel at slow speed can be sorted with an arm that swings across the line and diverts the item to the new path. In some installations, the arm does not move the item, but it moves blocks on the side of the conveyor into a 45° angle across the conveyor. The item is then pushed sideways by these blocks. This is a gentler move than striking an arm, which moves into the line of travel. This type of sorter cannot do high-speed diversions.

An alternative is to use a diversion system called a pop-up sorter. A pop-up sorter has wheels that are installed between the rollers. The wheels are driven in the direction to which the item must be diverted. When the item is above the pop-up sorter, the wheels rise and drive the item in the required direction.

Figure 13.20 Block and pop-up diverters

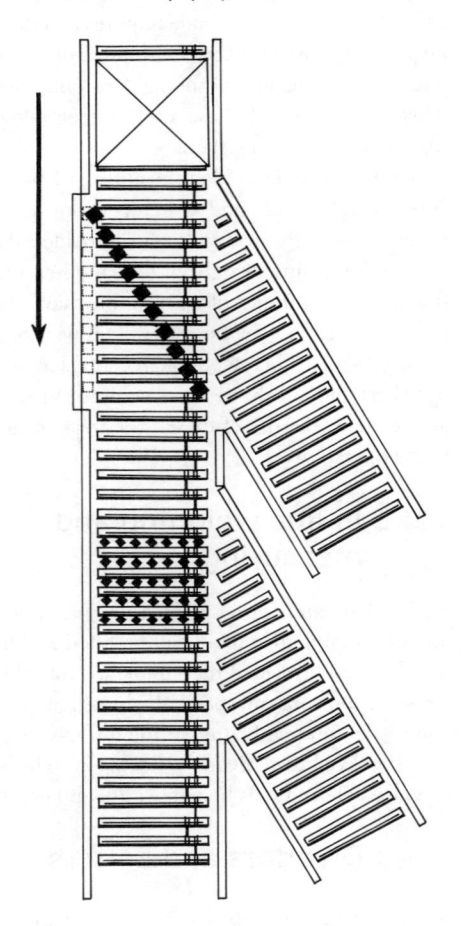

Another alternative is a tilt-tray diverter. A lighter type of parcel is carried in a tray. The tray tilts to discharge the parcel onto another conveyor. This is particularly used in situations where the parcels are all relatively light, such as within the courier industry.

13.8.7 Angled roller belt

A newer product is starting to appear as a great way to convey, sort goods and orientate goods in a material-handling system. This is the angled roller belt (ARB). It comprises a belt with roller balls extending both above and below the belt. The balls are spaced close enough so that the goods are carried on the balls above the belt. The balls below the belt can be rotated in any direction. This allows a single piece of this equipment to move items down one side faster than the other, or move the items to one side or to alternate sides and so on. Thus this equipment is a combined conveyor, sorter and arranger of goods. The ability to use the rollers in any configuration allows true two-dimensional latitude for moving items. The equipment is proven to be of great value in the design of a system.

13.9 Containers

The ability to consolidate a load into a container (Figure 13.21) that can be shipped anywhere in the world is probably the greatest advance

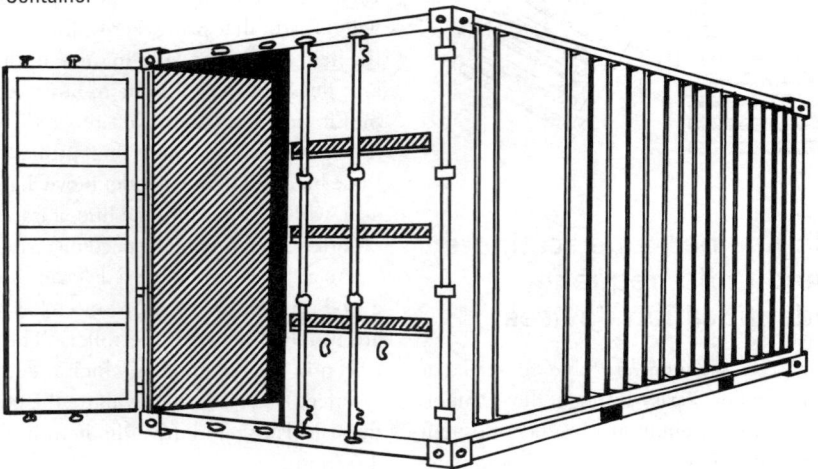

Figure 13.21 Container

the shipping industry has seen in the last fifty years. Cargo – from furniture, to motor vehicles, to rolls of paper – is now transported around the world in a standard, economical way. Containers come in two lengths: 20 feet (approximately 6 m) and 40 feet (approximately 12 m). All containers can be lifted either from the four corners or from the base. This makes it possible to use special container-handling equipment to cope with heavy loads – a 6 m container can carry a load of approximately 22,5 tons. Table 13.2 provides the standard sizes, volumes and payload weights for common containers.

Table 13.2 Approximate container sizes and weights

Container (20 feet)	Measurement
Length	5,9 m
Width	2,3 m
Height	2,4 m
Cubic capacity	6,13 m^3
Tare weight	3,1 tons
Payload weight	27,4 tons

13.9.1 Spreaders and twistlocks

Containers themselves offer a tremendous advantage over the handling of individual goods. To realise the advantage of the container, a simple means to connect handling equipment to the container is required. An attachment called a spreader is used to connect containers with other handling equipment. This attachment spreads the load from the mast of the equipment, such as a reach stacker, to the couplings at the four corners of the container. A twistlock (Figure 13.22) couples the spreader with the container. This device on the spreader extends a rectangular pad through a matching rectangular hole in the container structure. The rectangular pad is then twisted 90° so that part of it now connects with the structure of the container and provides a point for lifting. Prior to bearing weight, it is locked into this position. It is easy and quick to engage or disengage, and can be done automatically. Without the spreader and the twistlock, the advantages of containers would be largely negated.

Figure 13.22 Twistlock

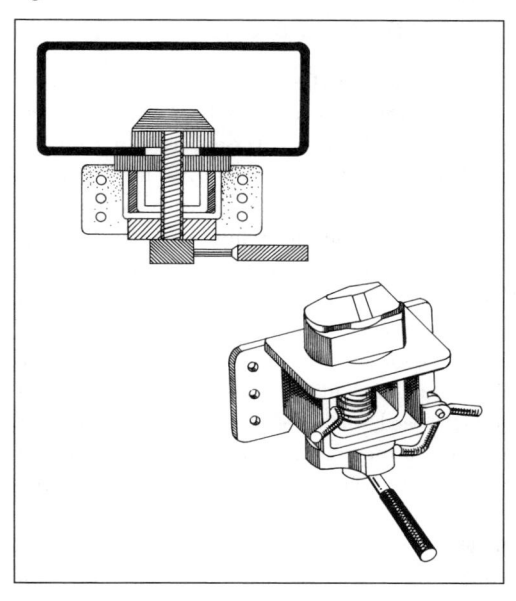

13.9.2 Reach stackers

A standard reach stacker (Figure 13.23) can handle single 20-foot containers. Larger ones can handle a 40-foot container or two 20-foot containers. Reach stackers can stack containers up to six high. They can also place a container in a rear stack by lifting it over another container. The reach stacker lifts the container via a spreader attached to the top of the container.

Figure 13.23 Reach stacker

13.9.3 Straddle carriers and straddle cranes

A straddle carrier (Figure 13.24) is a special type of mobile crane which has been developed for containers. The larger version is also called a straddle crane. This device carries the container within the structure of the crane, thus straddling the container. The carrier lifts the container using the spreader and twistlocks and then moves the container to other locations. The straddle carrier has wheels on each of the four corners of its frame. It is a versatile mover and stacker of containers. The straddling allows it to move containers at higher speeds than the reach stacker, which has to balance the container against a counterweight while moving. The limitation of the straddle carrier is that containers need to be stacked in such a way that the frame of the carrier can move over the container stack, so that an aisle is needed between every stack.

Figure 13.24 Straddle carrier

13.9.4 Quayside container cranes

Large container cranes situated on rails on the quayside generally handle the movement of containers onto and off ships. The cranes can traverse along the rails to service different parts of the ship. They lift the containers from the quayside and stack them on the ship, and vice versa. (See Figure 13.25.)

Figure 13.25 Quayside container crane

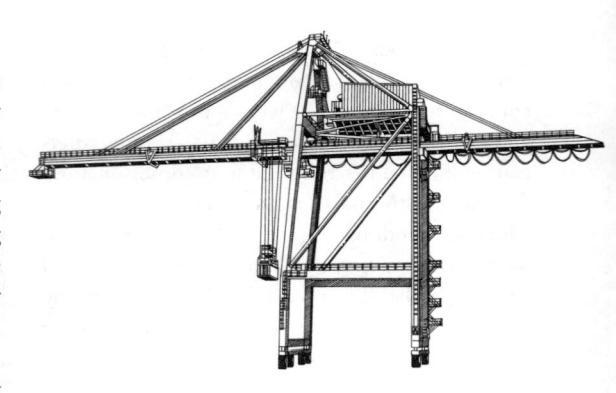

13.10 Conclusion

It is important to choose the most appropriate equipment. Equipment is expensive and should be used intensively in order for the investment to be financially justified. The cost of inappropriate equipment includes not only the capital sum, but also the consequent reduced efficiency and effectiveness of the operation. In most cases, there is one piece of equipment which is the most appropriate, and the procedure to identify such equipment has been the focus of this chapter.

Key terms

Accelerator belt	Pallet
Aisle	Pallet truck
Bar code scanner	Pick face
Bin	Radio frequency
Block stacking	identification (RFID)
Carousel	Reach stacker
Container	Reach truck
Conveyor	Roller-bed conveyor
Diverter	Shelving
Drive-in racking	Sorter
Drive-through racking	Spreader
First in, first out (FIFO)	Static racking
Forklift truck	Straddle carrier
Hanging rail	Straddle crane
Last in, last out (LIFO)	Trolley
Live storage rack	Turret truck
Merge system	Twistlock
Narrow-aisle rack	

Questions

1. The choice of equipment is made after the choice of racks. Motivate why you agree or disagree with this statement.
2. What are the advantages and disadvantages of a sorting system that automatically sorts the products into lanes compared to a manual sorting system? If the volume of products to be sorted increases by 100 per cent and the number of customers who need to be serviced also increases by 100 per cent, what are the implications for the manual and automatic systems?
3. Modern facilities utilise a vast array of equipment. Assume a specific facility has chosen racks (not narrow aisle) and that this is the most appropriate storage method. What will the primary problems be when the equipment ages and if the volume handled doubles?
4. On which primary criteria should a firm that is planning a new warehouse for the following range of products choose the storage? Which storage method should be chosen, and how does it satisfy the primary criteria?
   - Groceries, such as breakfast cereal and other dry products
   - Toiletries, such as shampoos
   - Household items, such as brooms and dustpans
   - Spices
5. A container is delivered to a facility on a trailer. The container needs to be removed from the trailer, placed inside a warehouse for unloading, and the goods stored in racks six levels high. The container is filled with palletised goods. Which equipment would you use for the operations and why?
6. Conceptually, a sea container, an air container and a pallet perform the same functions. Comment on this statement.

Consult the web

Cranes and heavy lifting on the quayside:
   www.noellcranesystems.com
General news on cargo handling in ports:
   www.worldcargonews.com
Lifting and moving equipment:
   www.boss-gb.co.uk
   www.crown.com
   www.hyster.co.uk
   www.linde.com
Reach stackers and straddle carriers:
   www.boss-gb.co.uk
   www.catracom.com
   www.fantuzzi.com
   www.hyster.co.uk
Twistlocks:
   www.william-cook.co.uk
Warehouse sorting and moving:
   www.cartercontrols.com
   www.egemin.co.uk
   www.sld.ch

Consult the books

Lambert, D. M., Stock, J. R. and Ellram, L. M. 1998. *Fundamentals of Logistics Management. International Edition.* McGraw-Hill.

Morreale, R. and Prichard, D. 1995. *Logistics Rules of Thumb, Facts and Definitions III.* Southern California Round Table/Council of Logistics Management.

14 The operation of a warehouse

J. Vogt

> **Learning outcomes**
>
> After you have studied this chapter, you should be able to:
> - identify the 13 processes that are prerequisites for the smooth operation of a facility and review and describe these processes;
> - list the methods of stock counting;
> - describe the principles of efficient operation;
> - set the principles for efficient transport operation;
> - describe a cross-dock operation and how it differs from a storage facility;
> - describe the advantages and disadvantages of bar-coding and scanning in a facility; and
> - identify the focus that world-class operations require.

14.1 Introduction

The operation of a warehouse is a complex series of processes. It makes little difference whether the facility handles steel coils on a berth in a port or whether it is a large distribution facility for groceries – the processes are essentially the same. The function of a warehouse is conceptually very simple: to receive goods into the facility, to store these goods and, when required, to dispatch the goods. This seemingly simple function hides a complex set of operations, all of which must be performed well for the facility to operate efficiently and effectively. There are usually also stringent time limits and little room for errors.

To manage a facility successfully, the personnel must be able to work under time pressure. Every stage of each operation needs to be recorded so that the progress can be monitored. The right person for this job is not someone who seeks a quiet life!

14.2 Warehouse processes

This section looks at the processes that support the activities of receiving, storing and dispatching. In Figure 14.1, the processes are shown as flows. There are 13 different flow processes in a warehouse. Each of these must be provided for and performed precisely. Each flow needs to happen at the right time and must be recorded correctly. Failure to do so will result in faulty stock records, so that finding the stock will become problematic and time-consuming, leading to an exponential drop in efficiency.

All the processes have a direct or indirect influence on the stock, either on the physical quantity in the facility or the records of where the stock is located. These 13 processes are discussed in some detail in this chapter so that the processes themselves and their interrelationships are clear. If one of these processes is faulty, the stock quantity (either the physical or recorded stock), will be influenced, and there will be problems in shipping the stock. Hence the centre of all the operations is stock management, for in essence that is the underlying requirement in order for the facility to be able to operate. While the facility receives, stores and dispatches the product, all these functions can only be done efficiently and effectively if the location of the stock is known precisely.

Other processes may be needed for specific operations. These include bond storage for imported goods that have not been released by the customs department, or the combination of several existing

CHAPTER 14 OPERATION OF A WAREHOUSE | 303

Figure 14.1 Processes in a warehouse facility

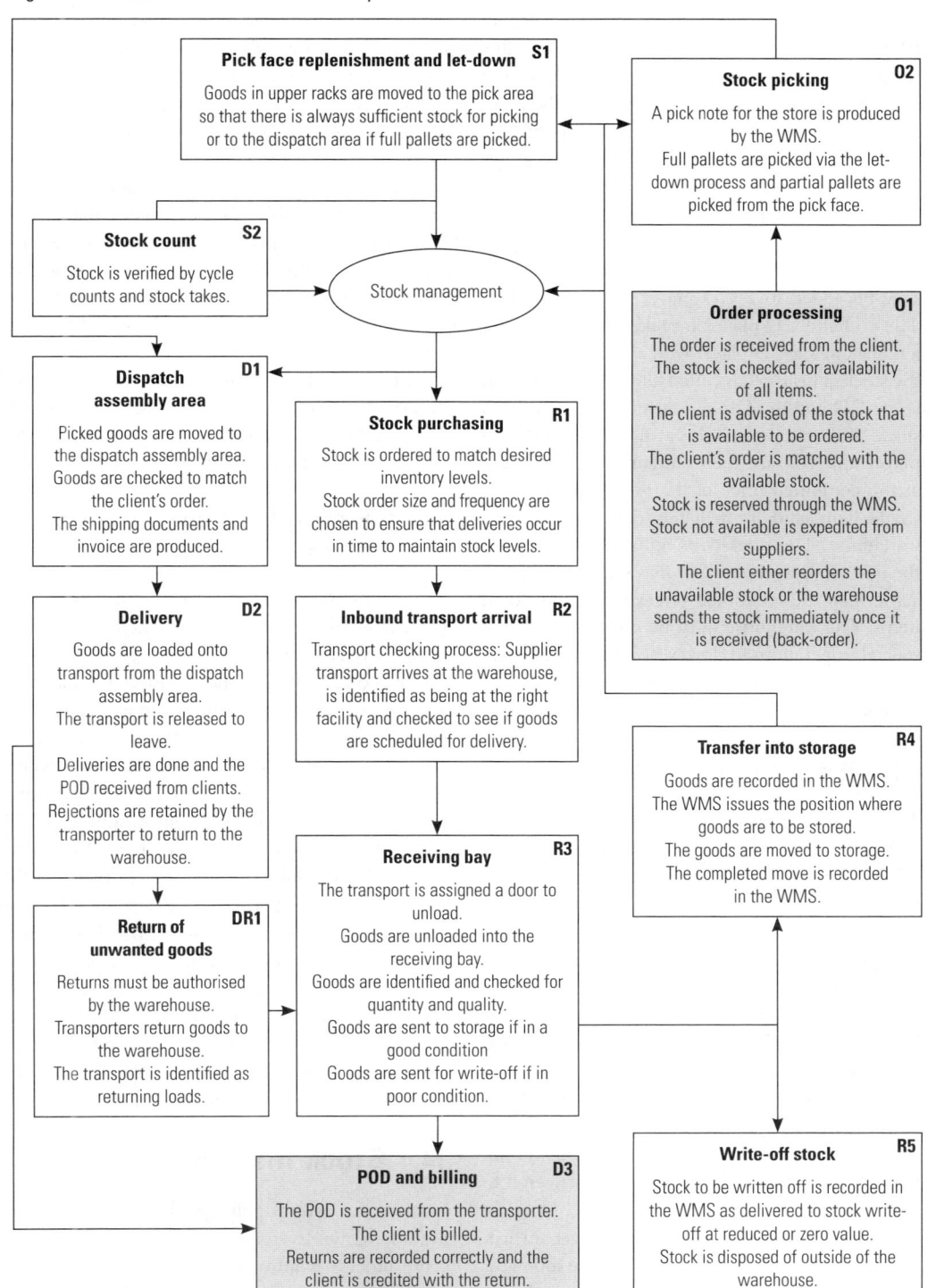

Pick face replenishment and let-down S1
Goods in upper racks are moved to the pick area so that there is always sufficient stock for picking or to the dispatch area if full pallets are picked.

Stock picking O2
A pick note for the store is produced by the WMS.
Full pallets are picked via the let-down process and partial pallets are picked from the pick face.

Stock count S2
Stock is verified by cycle counts and stock takes.

Stock management

Order processing O1
The order is received from the client.
The stock is checked for availability of all items.
The client is advised of the stock that is available to be ordered.
The client's order is matched with the available stock.
Stock is reserved through the WMS.
Stock not available is expedited from suppliers.
The client either reorders the unavailable stock or the warehouse sends the stock immediately once it is received (back-order).

Dispatch assembly area D1
Picked goods are moved to the dispatch assembly area.
Goods are checked to match the client's order.
The shipping documents and invoice are produced.

Stock purchasing R1
Stock is ordered to match desired inventory levels.
Stock order size and frequency are chosen to ensure that deliveries occur in time to maintain stock levels.

Delivery D2
Goods are loaded onto transport from the dispatch assembly area.
The transport is released to leave.
Deliveries are done and the POD received from clients.
Rejections are retained by the transporter to return to the warehouse.

Inbound transport arrival R2
Transport checking process: Supplier transport arrives at the warehouse, is identified as being at the right facility and checked to see if goods are scheduled for delivery.

Transfer into storage R4
Goods are recorded in the WMS.
The WMS issues the position where goods are to be stored.
The goods are moved to storage.
The completed move is recorded in the WMS.

Receiving bay R3
The transport is assigned a door to unload.
Goods are unloaded into the receiving bay.
Goods are identified and checked for quantity and quality.
Goods are sent to storage if in a good condition
Goods are sent for write-off if in poor condition.

Return of unwanted goods DR1
Returns must be authorised by the warehouse.
Transporters return goods to the warehouse.
The transport is identified as returning loads.

POD and billing D3
The POD is received from the transporter.
The client is billed.
Returns are recorded correctly and the client is credited with the return.

Write-off stock R5
Stock to be written off is recorded in the WMS as delivered to stock write-off at reduced or zero value.
Stock is disposed of outside of the warehouse.

items or components into a new item. Bond storage is much like a special product process category (PPC). The requirement is to retain stock in this special area, which needs to be fenced, so the goods that have not yet had duty paid on them are retained for inspection by the customs department. Records need to be maintained for all the goods received into and removed from the bond store, and duty must be paid on the goods removed.

The combination of products is more complex than one initially conceives. For example, a CD may be added to a CD player for a promotion. The CD and CD player are taken from stock and a new item – a CD player with a CD – is added to the stock. This is often called kitting. The problem is the CD and the CD player must be taken from stock, and effectively 'sold' at no profit. The CD player and CD are then concurrently purchased at the combined price of the two items, but as a single item, and immediately delivered into the warehouse. The stock costs remain the same, but the new CD player with CD may sell for a different value than the combined prices of the individual items. The warehouse must be prepared for these special operations. However, those processes shown in Figure 14.1 are the essential ones that all warehouses must follow all the time.

14.3 Errors in operation

The essential purpose of any warehouse is to be able to manage the stock in storage, the stock received and the stock dispatched in such a way that the warehouse can supply the right stock at the right time and place. If the wrong item is delivered, it implies that there is an operational error.

The same applies for late delivery, delivery of damaged items or failure to deliver. This discussion confirms the definition of logistics and its focus on supporting the marketing effort. The cost-effective delivery of goods is only possible if the correct goods are received into the warehouse, the stock is managed while in the warehouse and the correct stock is picked in time to be delivered to the customers.

Any error needs to be detected and corrected first, and then the correct procedure must be followed. As information records need to be matched, this is a labour-intensive process. Errors effectively quadruple the workload because, first, an incorrect process occurs; next, the second step is to identify the error; the third step is to rectify the error; and the last is to follow the correct process. Errors also place time constraints on operations. Personnel make more mistakes under time pressure. More mistakes mean additional time pressure and even more mistakes. This is a vicious circle that is very difficult to break. Any increase in the error rate will result in a reduction in customer satisfaction, as the expected service level will deteriorate. Customers may then start to make complaints, absorbing further time and effort.

Errors need to be monitored and minimised, as they result in stock losses or sales losses. These affect both the financial performance of the warehouse and the service delivery to the customers.

14.3.1 Example of a warehouse error

The consumer industry seeks to maximise its December sales so salespeople do their best to offer prospective customers the service they require. In a certain store, it often happens during the year that a prospective customer is interested in a particular range of goods, consisting of three models. The store then orders all three models, and the customer chooses one. The other two are immediately returned to the warehouse as an unwanted stock order. If this practice is increased in December by, say, 20 per cent, and the sales in that month increase 25 per cent over the year average, then the rate of returns to the warehouse will be 50 per cent higher than in other months. (This is calculated from 120 per cent and 125 per cent, or $120 \times 125 = 150$ per cent of the original 'error' rate). A 50 per cent increase in the returns to a warehouse can easily throw an efficient warehouse into chaos and turn it into a highly inefficient warehouse.

14.4 Stock management

Stock is the central point of all the processes in the warehouse. Every process affects the stock and every process is affected by the stock. For these reasons, having the wrong stock in the facility, or having stock that cannot be found immediately, is a big problem. If the stock is not available to be sent to customers, the processes cannot be completed and the result is dissatisfied customers. Stock losses are also immediate financial losses to the company. These losses can quickly erode profitability, as the lost goods are far more costly to replace than the profit derived from performing the logistics function. For the delivery of an item costing R1 000, the charge may be R20. If the facility's profit on this is 20 per cent of this fee, the profit is R4. If the item is lost during the delivery process and has to be replaced by the facility, the cost is R1 000 to replace the item plus the cost to deliver the item of R20. In comparison to these two costs, the profit of R4 is insignificant.

Stock is managed by three control processes:
- Each pick and delivery of stock must be completed accurately and recorded accurately as completed.
- Each receipt of stock must be completed accurately and recorded accurately as completed.
- Stock must be audited continually (i.e. counted, and the physical goods matched to the information recorded in the system) via cycle counts. (These are described later in this chapter.)

It is important to note that each process must include two separate actions: the physical operation and the recording of the physical operation with the warehouse management system (WMS). To do either of these incorrectly means that the information on the system and the physical goods no longer match. The result is further errors and associated problems.

14.5 Types of warehouses and facilities

There are many different types of facilities. These range from a terminal in a harbour that receives a product from a production facility inland and loads it into a ship for export, to a large distribution centre (DC) where finished goods are accumulated and sent to the store or customer. Some supply chains have a manufacturer's warehouse, a third-party or a common-user warehouse and a regional DC delivering to a retail store. All these operations have a receive and dispatch function and they all track stock and final deliveries. The only exception is a cross-dock facility, in which the storage function is absent, and the processes of storing and picking are combined into a sorting operation. (See Section 14.6 for an explanation of a cross-dock facility.)

Different facilities reflect their operational focus in the supply chain. Based on this there will be differences in a manufacturer's warehouse and a DC. A manufacturer's warehouse generally has to cater for the receipt of large batches of product as they come from production. This requires a storage method that keeps the batch together and allows the efficient receipt of the product into the facility. Production is generally done in a batch of a specific product, with a period between the production of the particular product while other products are made. The storage required is for sufficient product for the period between the end of one batch and the start of the next. If the warehouse is integrated with the manufacturing process, the delivery to the warehouse may be done with automated material handling, and the receipt may be automated.

A DC operation is very different from a manufacturing warehouse. Its aim is to be able to select stock and deliver it to customers in a short timescale. A DC only requires sufficient stock to cater for its existing orders, and can replenish the stock regularly and in smaller quantities. Its process is oriented, therefore, to fast selection and continuous receipt of multiple products. It is clear, therefore, that the source of product, the delivery and the focus or function that the facility serves in the supply chain will determine the layout, the equipment and the operation.

14.6 Cross-dock operations

A cross-dock is a very different operation from a normal warehouse, be it a manufacturer's warehouse or a DC. In both of these cases one of the primary functions is the storage of goods. A cross-dock is a particular type of facility in the supply chain where goods are received from suppliers, sorted without storage of the goods, and then efficiently moved on to downstream customers.

> A cross-dock is a facility in a supply chain that receives goods from suppliers and then sorts these goods into alternative groupings based on the downstream delivery point. There is no reserve storage of the goods, and staging occurs only for the short periods required to assemble a consolidated, economical load for its immediate onward carriage via the same mode used for its receipt, or a different mode.

Rather than a warehouse, a cross-dock is more like a continuous process of removing goods from one inbound transport and sorting them directly into an outbound transport. A cross-dock is only valuable for goods that are suitable for this process. The factors that determine whether utilisation of a cross-dock is appropriate are as follows:
- Products have a continuous flow to all the stores (downstream customers).
- The suppliers are highly reliable.
- There are no unpredictable fluctuations in the sales and hence the amount of product moving through the cross-dock.
- The products have uniform handling methods.

These determinants relate to products that tend to be the staple items in a store – in the case of a grocery store – or the non-fashion items in an apparel store. For example, socks are required at a constant rate every week and every year, with consistent changes for Christmas and so on. Similarly, detergents and items such as paper towels and so on are used continuously.

To enable the supply chain to operate with a cross-dock, the supply chain needs to meet certain criteria. The cross-dock operates within the supply chain, and because of the nature of a cross-dock with regard to speed of movement of the products, it must have the following characteristics:
- The supply chain must be integrated, including the systems.
- The vendors need to be reliable, accurate and offer high service levels.
- There must be frequent loads delivered.
- Multiple products that have to be married together add significantly to the staging requirements and reduce the effectiveness of the cross-dock.

The value of a cross-dock in a supply chain is, with the correct products, that it brings a reduction in inventory in the supply chain and the ability to move products through the supply chain in the most efficient manner possible. The only potential drawback is that the operation is onerous, since there is no storage to buffer the inbound and outbound processes. The goods must be in transit to the downstream customers for an extra period from the placing of an order as the order is placed on the suppliers further upstream in the supply chain. This is more than offset by the lower inventory and greater efficiency. Indeed, for really efficient supply chains, the use of point of sale (POS) information offsets this extra period, and the products are moved continuously into the store, very much as the store utilises them.

14.6.1 Types of cross-docks

There are a number of different types of cross-docks. There are three primary considerations in defining the different types:
- Where in the supply chain the identification of the specific items for a customer is performed.
- Where the sorting of goods is done for the items to be sent to one customer.
- Whether the supplier provides one product or multiple products to the sort.

From these factors there are nine potential alternatives. Only three are practical and have unique characteristics:
- Cross-dock-managed load (CML)
- Joint-managed load (JML)
- Supplier-managed load (SML)

In any traditional DC-based supply chain, the supplier selects the ordered goods, confirms that these are selected, loads transport and delivers these to some form of distribution capability, either a DC or a cross-dock. Further work is done in the distribution capability to receive, identify and – if a DC – store these items, and then to select these items and effect the distribution. In cross-dock operations some of these stages are eliminated, making the cross-dock more efficient than the

DC. These are briefly described in the following explanations of the three types of cross-docks:

14.6.1.1 Cross-dock-managed load

A CML has the identification and the sort of the items done within the DC. Thus a supplier will provide goods which the DC must check against the delivery note, identifying each item, and then sort these items to the appropriate downstream customers. Both identification and sort are done in the cross-dock.

14.6.1.2 Joint-managed load

A JML is where the supplier labels the individual items and delivers them to the cross-dock where the individual items are then sorted to build a load. This removes the identification from the cross-dock staff, which is important where the items are similar and the cross-dock staff are under pressure and not skilled in the identification of the different items, which can result in errors. This method reduces the potential for these errors significantly.

14.6.1.3 Supplier-managed load

An SML is where the supplier identifies and labels the items and sorts them into downstream customer groups. The items for a downstream customer are then consolidated into a unit load – on a pallet, for example. The only work then done in the cross-dock is the sort of the pallets from inbound to outbound transport. This is the most efficient supply chain, as the identification and sort is done once only and right at the beginning of the supply chain so the entire supply chain benefits.

14.6.2 Cross-dock processes

The operation of a cross-dock is very different from that of a normal warehouse. The facility operates without the inbound and outbound processes being two distinct, separate and non-interacting processes. In a warehouse, these two processes are separated, or buffered, by the storage, so that there is no direct interaction between the inbound and outbound processes. This is also called decoupling of the two processes. In the cross-dock, however, the processes are one continuous process. This introduces a very different focus and requires a different type of facility.

The operation of a time-sensitive process, which has no decoupling by storage, means that any delay in the process is a major problem. The introduction of a delay results in accumulation of goods in the facility while the problem is resolved. There is no space for the accumulation of goods, so the result is an immediate deterioration of efficiency as the accumulated goods inhibit movement and increase drive time in the movement of other goods. This means that the quality of the staff needs to be very high. They must understand the processes and the means to effect rectification when any problem or error occurs. The staff need to be highly trained and flexible. A cross-dock cannot operate with unskilled staff or rigid task definitions.

The cross-dock operates as a continuous process, not dissimilar to a manufacturing process that fluctuates day by day with regard to loads. What is required for the efficient operation is a continuous load throughout the day, so that the operation works at an approximately constant rate each hour. Peaks and valleys caused by poor scheduling of inbound transport severely reduce the potential efficiency. It must be remembered that most supply chains have moderately different flows each day, and the types of product may alter fairly dramatically each day. These require the ability of each operator to solve problems immediately; to be able to see where there are constraints to the smooth flow of the goods; and the ability to move staff to eliminate these constraints.

It is obvious from the above that one of the success factors is the ability to ensure that the facility receives a continuous quantity of goods each hour. This allows the process to move towards a more continuous and balanced process. While the different products received will require different amounts of work in the cross-dock, the overall workload should be planned and held to as constant a level as possible. A lack of goods is a cardinal sin, as this means the staff and facility are idle. Time without goods for the operation is lost time. It comes at a cost to the facility – the cost of labour and equipment (and may include not just the time lost, but the potential overtime to complete the work later than is necessary).

The systems that need to be in place for this type of facility are more complex than those for normal warehouse operations. The inbound loads need to be scheduled to give a constant workload in the facility. The workload is dependent on the goods being received, with each type requiring different amounts of work. Consequently, to schedule the transport to give a constant workload requires knowledge of the goods in the transport inbound as well as the arrival time. The amount of product allowed into the facility will be as close to or match the throughput capacity of the facility. This latter point is important. The introduction of excess product into the facility above what the staff can handle feasibly and consistently will result in errors, problems and the accumulation of goods in the facility. This will rapidly reduce efficiency, and quickly clog the entire facility.

A cross-dock is also shaped very differently, as it has no storage. It therefore needs a width that is sufficient for the sortation and any other specific work in the facility and to accumulate a load in front of a dispatch door. This latter should only occur if the transport has more than one delivery point. In this case, the goods for the first delivery must be staged on the dock until the transport is loaded with the goods for the second delivery. The length of the building is essentially chosen to fit the required number of doors for both receiving and dispatch. While the facility's shape can vary from a rectangle to other shapes as the number of doors increases, it is highly unlikely that in South Africa a cross-dock would require so many doors that a different shape is necessitated.

14.7 Efficiency in a warehouse

Three principles underlie the efficient operation of any facility. These reflect the criteria against which all operations must be measured for efficiency. The facility controls the operation from its boundaries as goods are moved into the warehouse, handled and stored, and moved from the warehouse to the customers. The operation encompasses not only the operation within the building, but also the interaction with the transport. For the purpose of this chapter, transport refers to either the rail or road vehicles used to move goods overland or onto ships.

14.7.1 Efficiency principle 1

Goods at rest within the boundaries of a facility outside a designated storage area reflect an inefficient operation.

There are only two desired areas of storage in a facility: the long-term storage areas (including the pick faces) and the dispatch assembly area, where goods are accumulated to build a load. Any other areas where goods are at rest, for example, the receiving area, are reflections of inefficiency.

14.7.2 Efficiency principle 2

The location of goods within the boundaries of the facility must be known to ensure an efficient operation. The processes of the warehouse require that the whereabouts of goods must be known at all times. If not, the goods may not be available for efficient delivery, or problems may arise with the receipt of additional goods.

14.7.3 Efficiency principle 3

People will perform their operations efficiently only if they are trained to do each job in the best way, and are given sufficient time to do the job without errors. Time and effort are required to rectify errors. Proper, formal training is the best way of preventing errors.

Training should focus on the specific manner in which each job should be performed and the sequence in which it should be performed. This requires that every job be defined as a set of written procedures that specify the actions in the appropriate sequence. This way, the personnel are trained to do the job right the first time and every time. Personnel become efficient if they understand and practise a job. This should not stifle innovation or improvement. Everyone should be encouraged to effect changes, but these changes cannot be made by individuals as and when they decide to try something new. A proposed change may improve the local operation, but have a detrimental effect on the overall performance. Changes should be carefully tested and measured. Improvements must be recorded in the procedures and communicated to all employees.

Leaving training to chance or to the individual operators will result in fluctuating performances between different operators, and varying standards of operations for different teams. After some time of allowing this ad hoc training, inefficiencies in the way the work is done will be transferred to new employees and the operation will fall far short of its most efficient level.

14.8 Processes and operations

14.8.1 Overview

There is no single perfect model for operating all warehouses. The design, goods and time pressures vary from facility to facility. The principles that underlie all good operations are presented in this section. (The references in brackets refer to the processes described in Figure 14.1, page 303.) Any facility that fails to comply with these principles operates ineffectively or inefficiently.

The following processes are inherent in all facilities:
- Stock purchasing (R1)
- Inbound transport arrival and identification of loads (R2)
- Receiving bay (R3)
- Transfer of stock into storage (R4)
- Pick face replenishment and let-down of stock (S1)
- Order processing (O1)
- Stock picking or picking goods from storage (O2)
- Dispatch assembly area or assembly of the goods to create a transport load (D1)
- Delivery of goods and obtaining proof of delivery (POD) (D2)
- POD and billing (D3)
- Return of unwanted goods (DR1)
- Stock write-off (R5)
- Stock count (S2)

The principles in the operations that form part of these processes are described in the next sections in some detail. Stock purchasing is covered in more detail in Chapter 9. Financial aspects are covered in Chapter 5.

14.8.2 Stock purchasing (R1)

For a facility to perform its function it must possess the correct stock, otherwise the purpose of the facility, namely to provide a cost-effective and efficient means to supply customers, is no longer tenable.

The purchasing of stock is geared to the replenishment of the inventory in the facility. This is covered in Chapter 10. The aim is to alter either the quantity or the frequency of the buying process so that a continual flow of product is moved into the facility to match the uncertainty in the inbound supply channel, while matching the orders received from the customers.

Placing orders results in inbound transport arriving at the facility in a continual process. If this is coordinated and carefully managed, the transport can be as efficient as possible. However, wildly changing purchase levels on a day-to-day basis cause problems in the planning, space and staffing required for unloading. As the whole aim of optimising the supply chain is to achieve the lowest costs, the purchasing function must ensure there is as close as possible to a continuous flow of transport into the facility to maintain the required inventory levels.

The purchasing function is described in more detail in Chapter 9.

14.8.3 Transport arrival and identification of loads (R2)

Transport must be scheduled. This may sound difficult and restrictive, but it is essential for the successful operation of any facility. The arrival of transport must be planned so that the facility can provide the staff to handle the unloading, the equipment to move the goods and the capacity to handle any discrepancies between the stock ordered and delivered. Without this planning, the workload in the facility will fluctuate excessively. Time delays will result in irate transporters. The pressure on the operations staff increases in peak times and this reduces efficiencies and the accuracy of the receipt.

The recommended process for handling transport is as follows:
- The supplier books the transport load to be delivered to the facility.
- The load details are confirmed with the facility.
- Transport arrives at the facility within the scheduled arrival period and the check is merely a confirmation of the load.
- The order number is checked.
- With good planning, the door where the truck should be discharged can now be allocated.
- The truck waits for the door to become available; it is then discharged quickly and efficiently.

There are practical considerations in this process. Preparation and planning on the part of the facility are essential. On arrival, the transporter should present the documentation for the order to the transport management section. This section must have arranged the allocation of doors with the facility operations. This ensures that all loads are allocated to doors where the load can be received by the appropriate number of personnel and equipment. The transport management section often gives the transporter authorisation identification, such as a numbered coloured disk, for a particular door. This indicates that the order has been confirmed against the WMS; the transporter is in the queue for a particular door; and the operations staff can receive the load without rechecking the time and validity of the order.

Failure to follow these procedures may result in the delay of transport and problems in receiving goods and matching them to orders. The efficiency of the facility suffers dramatically as the workload fluctuates and personnel and equipment need to be moved from one area to another in unplanned patterns. The following example illustrates this.

14.8.3.1 Example: poorly managed transport

A certain facility receives transport on a first come, first served basis. Trucks arrive early in the morning and begin to queue in front of the receiving area. The facility receives the documentation from each of the transporters as they join the queue, and begins to process the documentation. One by one, the loads are received. More trucks arrive than can be handled by the facility. The transport area becomes congested and trucks trying to leave have to manoeuvre their way out of the area. This delays the next truck trying to get to the receiving door. Some of the trucks still in the queue by mid-afternoon can see that they are unlikely to be discharged, as the queue is too long. However, their documentation is with the facility and has been entered into the facility's system, so they cannot leave. The warehouse closes the receiving function early to record the return of the documentation for loads it is unable to receive on that day. This documentation is then handed back to the transporters who can return the next day to try to deliver the goods.

Such delays may add more than 50 per cent of the usual transport cost to the costs of the suppliers. Taking back full loads and then recommitting the loads the next day to the same warehouse causes a considerable increase in processes for the supplier. However, the most distressing part of this example is that the warehouse does not have the right goods at the right time, as the receipt of goods is random and based on who arrives first.

Sounds fanciful? This example actually describes the operations of many retail stores.

14.8.4 Receiving bay (R3)

Once the receipt of transport has been arranged, the orders can be unloaded. The facility must transfer the goods into storage. In so doing, the facility incurs the financial responsibility for the purchased goods. The process, therefore, involves not just accepting goods, but also checking the quantity and the quality. The packaging must be in good condition and suitable for storage and sale. The unloading must be efficient and cost-effective for all parties, yet allow for checking the quality and quantity of the goods. The best method for achieving this is to:
- allocate the receiving bay for the goods;
- choose a door that minimises the distance the product has to travel to its storage location; and

- load the goods from the truck and place them on the floor, starting as far from the truck as possible in the first of the demarcated rows.

This process is illustrated in Figure 14.2.

Figure 14.2 Fill sequence of the receiving area

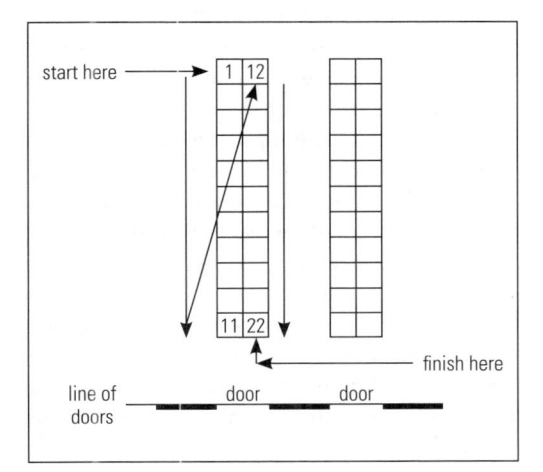

```
start here ──▶ | 1 |12|
               |↑  |  |
               |   |  |
               |   |  |
               |   |  |
               |11 |22|
                ↑
                ◀─────── finish here
line of        door      door
doors
```

This sequence is recommended for various reasons. The goods from the truck need to be moved the minimum distance in order to utilise the available demarcated areas – in the case illustrated, 22 spaces. While this is being done, the warehouse staff can begin to identify the received goods and start the storage process. The warehouse staff will take the goods from slot 1 first and progress down the fill sequence as the goods are unloaded from the transport. The transporter can begin to fill up the second row while the warehouse is processing the first row. As long as the warehouse completes the move from the first row before the transport has filled row 2 (or spaces 12 to 22), there will be no delay to the unloading of the goods, as the transporter can begin filling row 1 (spaces 1 to 11) again. This reduces the space required, minimises delays in the unloading and makes the operation as efficient as possible. It does mean that the operation has to be coordinated correctly so that there are enough personnel and equipment available to perform the WMS data entry and the storage.

Placing goods into more than two rows limits access and restricts the ability to move the goods efficiently. Goods cannot be identified if three or more rows are used. Two rows give the greatest amount of useful space at the greatest level of utilisation.

The rate of receiving stock into the warehouse is dependent on the ability to store stock. Closing a receiving bay because stock has clogged the storage process is as inefficient as having excess capacity and not enough stock to store. By matching the truck schedules with the capability to receive and store, the operation proceeds smoothly and at a reasonably consistent rate.

14.8.5 Transfer of stock into storage (R4)

The goods must be moved into the designated storage space. Once there, the move must be confirmed with the WMS. This is very important: until the confirmation is received, the WMS assumes the goods are in transit between the receiving bay and the stock location and therefore not available for picking.

Clear marking of all storage locations, whether permanent or temporary, will eliminate a large portion of the errors. However, errors do occur. The error of a product in the wrong slot is a major problem because product required for an order is now unavailable, and has to be located by visual means, as the physical stock and the WMS are out of synchronisation. The most common error is the storage of goods into the location adjacent (above, below or beside) the correct location. A simple and highly effective method helps to eliminate this error. A code number is allocated for each slot, which is used to confirm that the process has been completed correctly. The code number is unrelated to the normal rack locations designation, and is translated by the computer into a check that the correct slot was accessed. It can be used for put-away as well as removal from the slot.

Racks are often identified by designating three alphanumeric characters to each space. Thus A05E may refer to a location in the row of racks marked 'A', the '05th' column of spaces in the row (two characters are used in this group as the number of columns may exceed ten), and the space marked 'E', which is the fifth space vertically in this column. These numbers reflect a three-dimensional view of the facility: the A is the x direction, the 05 is the y direction and the E is the z direction. This location number is used on the storage instructions issued at the receiving bay. At the storage location, the operator places the goods into the designated slot. To ensure this process is correct, the operator needs to read another, different code to confirm that the goods have been stored in the correct space. The WMS knows that the location code and this confirmation code refer to the same space. The use of these separate codes reduces errors significantly. The second code can be simply a two-digit code designated to each space, in sequence or not as the case may be. In storage racks, the first space may be AA, the next AB, and so on. In the example above, the confirmation code for A05E would be BC if the racks were six spaces high (see Table 14.1).

14.8.6 Replenishment and let-down of stock to pick face (S1)

One of the processes in the facility is the let-down of pallets. Full pallets are generally stored in the upper levels so that the easily accessible levels are left for pick faces. The process of removing the full pallets from these upper storage levels – either to the pick face or to the dispatch area – is known as let-down.

14.8.6.1 Pick-face replenishment

> The pick face is the place where the selection, or pick, of a product for dispatch occurs. It is usually near the floor or walkway level, where the goods can be accessed easily.

As stock is picked from a pick face, it needs to be replenished. The correct way to do this depends partly on the design and partly on the operating process.

With racks, the biggest challenge is to fit a full pallet into the pick face while there is still stock in the pick face. In a general rack configuration, the rack height is only just higher than the pallet height to maximise the utilisation of the rack volume. This rack configuration should not be used for the pick face, as the remaining stock in the pick face will prevent the full pallet from being added. This problem cannot be solved by simply leaving the full pallet in the aisle. Instead, rack heights in the pick face should be higher than those in the standard storage racks. This allows operators to place the existing stock on top of a full pallet in the pick face. If, for example, the WMS automatically lets down a pallet once 90 per cent of the stock has been removed from the pick face, then the pick face height should be 10 per cent more than the standard height.

Pick-face replenishment must be done as the highest priority activity in the pick cycle. If the pick face is not replenished in time, the result may be a stock shortage at the pick face, delaying the pick process.

14.8.6.2 Let-down for full pallet stock pick

When an order is received for more goods than are held on one pallet, the less sophisticated operation will pick what stock is available in the pick face. A full pallet will then be let down. The new pallet will be moved to the pick face. The stock will be confirmed to be available to the WMS. If still more goods are needed to fulfil this order, a

Table 14.1 Rack location and location identification by row, column and vertical space

	Column 01	Column 02	Column 03	Column 04	Column 05
F	AF	AL	AR	AX	BD
E	AE	AK	AQ	AW	BC
D	AD	AJ	AP	AV	BB
C	AC	AI	AO	AU	BA
B	AB	AH	AN	AT	AZ
Ground: level A	AA	AG	AM	AS	AY

further let-down will be required and further delays will occur.

The ability to take full pallets of stock as part of an order will prevent these problems. The best WMS logic is always to allocate full pallets first. Only the remaining part of the order is then picked from the pick face. In the above example, only one pallet will be moved to the pick face, while another full pallet will be moved directly to the dispatch area. This is far more efficient and less time-consuming. The replenishment of the pick face is time-critical, as a lack of stock in the pick face halts the picking process.

14.8.6.3 Example

A storage facility receives an order for 100 units. Of these, 40 units are stored on each pallet. There are 25 units in the pick face when the order is issued for picking.

If the stock is only moved via the pick face, the transactions will occur as shown in Table 14.2.

There are fewer delays when full pallets are moved directly to the assembly area. The impact on the picking is also less, as Table 14.3 shows.

14.8.7 Order processing (O1)

A customer submits an order. This order must be processed to check that the products carried fall within the supplier's range, there is product available and it is feasible to ship the products. The latter may be an issue if a product cannot be sold outside of a border or particular location. Once these issues are resolved, the order is sent to the facility from which the products will be shipped and the products are selected or picked ready for dispatch.

Order processing and the stock in the facility work in two primary, different processes. In the type of operation where a customer is promised the delivery, such as an Internet-based selling organisation, the customer places the order. As the order is placed, the stock is reserved for the customer. This reserved product is essentially removed from the available stock, so that the stock is removed from the stock available to subsequent customers. In this case if there is no further stock available so the customers cannot order the product, the stock is allocated in the sequence of receipt of the orders.

Table 14.2 Products taken from the pick face only

Action	Pick face stock	Let-down pallets added to pick face	Items picked from pick face	Let-down pallets to the dispatch assembly area
Start	25		25	
Delay for one pallet let-down		40	40	
Delay for one pallet let-down		40	35	
Finish	5		100	
			Total pick = 100	

Table 14.3 Products taken from both the pick face and storage

Action	Pick face stock	Let-down pallets added to pick face	Items picked from pick face	Let-down pallets to the dispatch assembly area
Start	25			
Pallet let-down				40
Pallet let-down				40
Pick face			20	
Finish	5			
			Total pick = 100	

In the type of operation where there are multiple customers all belonging to a single organisation, the customers may be treated equally as a block if there is insufficient stock available, and the available product is allocated to the customers pro-rata to the original orders.

14.8.8 Stock picking or picking goods from storage (O2)

Most facilities will at some point get orders for less than a full pallet of goods, or whatever the delivery unit is. The storage unit must then be broken up into smaller parts so that these smaller quantities of goods can be picked for each customer.

The instruction to pick a certain quantity of a particular product comes from the WMS in the form of a pick note. The pick note contains information regarding the order and the location of the pick face where the product is stored (in a racked system, this is a location such as A05A). It can also contain other information, such as the full description of the product, to assist the picker. The pick note can be in the form of a printed form or on a wireless terminal carried by the picker. A newer method is a wireless voice-activated picking method. The picker has a headphone and a microphone headset. The picker receives audible commands from the system via the headset as to the actions to perform in order to proceed to the correct location and the number of products to pick. Once done correctly, the picker speaks a confirmation into the unit, which advises the WMS that the task is completed and sends the next set of instructions to the headphones to commence and complete the next task. Known as voice picking, this is a highly efficient method.

It is difficult to detect errors in picks. Double-checks of the picked goods are not effective, as one generally does the check to look for occasional errors. Boredom will mean the check is of little value, unless there are major errors. Random checks are more useful, as boredom is not an intruding factor. The consequences of incorrect picks are physical stock and information records that do not match, and customers who receive wrong goods or even no goods. If errors occur frequently, the stock in the pick face may differ so much from what is recorded in the WMS that the WMS does not provide the replenishment via let-down and the pick is delayed. One then has to resort to manual methods of letting down stock, which is inefficient. The stock in the pick face must be reconciled with what has been picked to discover the extent of the errors. This is a mammoth task, especially when there are significant numbers of pick errors.

Many WMSs compound the problems associated with the pick face. The WMS issues a pick note and allocates stock in the pick face to the pick note. This is done in order to calculate the amount of stock left and to determine when the pick face should be replenished. The removal of goods from the pick face is generally only confirmed when the system records them in another position. This confirmation often only takes place once the goods are ready to transport, which may be hours later. The stock in the pick face can therefore not be reconciled while there is a pick note in the facility and while the goods are not confirmed to be in the dispatch assembly area. A scanning system, however, can record the removal of the stock immediately. This alleviates the problem somewhat, but the goods are still in transit until they are recorded in a new location, so that stock reconciliation is still not simple or even practical.

A practical method to speed up the replenishment process in the case of an unsophisticated WMS system is to allocate a disk for each product pick face. The disk identifies the product in the pick face. The picker takes the disk from the pick face as soon as the bay is, say, 50 per cent empty. The picker places the disk on a hanger or board adjacent to the storage area. The disk may be colour-coded to reflect the rate at which the item is ordered. One colour represents very fast (e.g. red); another fast (e.g. blue); and another moderately fast (e.g. yellow). The personnel moving stock from the storage to the pallet area see these disks and know from the colour which stock has to be moved first for the replenishment of the pick face. The disk is returned to the pick face with the replenishment stock. This method originates from the Japanese *Kanban* system (see also Chapter 8).

As the negative consequences of wrong picks are substantial, the pickers must be the most competent personnel to ensure efficiency and accuracy.

14.8.9 Dispatch assembly area or assembly of goods to create a transport load (D1)

In the assembly area, goods from all the sections or PPCs in the facility are accumulated into suitable loads for transport. This must be done very systematically, as the goods need to be loaded onto the transport in the shortest possible time and in the most efficient way to minimise the transport costs. The goods should be recorded as they are received in this area so that the outstanding goods are easy to identify.

The best way to accumulate loads is to allocate a lane for each customer. The lanes must be segregated from one another so that items on partially filled pallets can be manually consolidated onto pallets in the same lane. This increases the density of the goods loaded into the vehicles, making the delivery more effective. Loading the product into the vehicles must be recorded to ensure that the correct product is loaded. The driver of the transport must be held accountable for the product and the loading process, as the driver is responsible for the product once the vehicle leaves the loading dock.

14.8.10 Delivery of goods and obtaining proof of delivery (D2)

There must be a positive means of confirming the transfer of the goods to the customer. The ownership and risk pass to the customer on handover of the goods, and there cannot be confusion over when this happens and how. Some firms require that a company stamp be added to the signature of a senior employee authorised to receive the goods. Some businesses allow receiving bay clerks with little or no supervision to sign for valuable goods, with no formal authorisation or procedures. The latter process reflects poor management of assets and leads to problems. A POD document, signed in accordance with an agreed procedure, is a prerequisite for transferring goods to the customer. It records the completion of the facility's task. Without it, the business will not get paid and may be held liable for loss of the goods.

14.8.11 Proof of delivery and billing (D3)

The POD authorises a facility to bill for the service it renders. Inevitably, customers will query some of the deliveries. It is difficult for a facility that delivers significant quantities of goods to keep accurate records and find the record for a specific query. A computer record of the delivery date and time is insufficient in most cases, as customers will need the POD and the signature and/or company stamp as proof that delivery was effected.

There are a number of practical solutions to this. A very comprehensive and practical method is to have the POD imaged onto a computer system. The POD images are sorted according to the reference number on the POD. When a customer queries a delivery, the POD image can be found very quickly and faxed to the customer for confirmation of the delivery.

An even better solution is to bar-code the goods. The customer should have the ability to read the bar code information into their system. The system will print a receipt and send the facility a copy of the information received from the scanned bar codes.

14.8.12 Return of unwanted goods (DR1)

Goods might be returned to a facility because stock was delivered in error, over-ordered or damaged.

- Stock delivered in error means the stock was not delivered to the correct customer. The process includes returning the stock to the facility and crediting the customer to whom the goods should have gone with not having received the goods.
- Stock damaged in transit should be returned to the facility and the customer credited with not having received the damaged goods.
- Stock that the facility agrees to accept back from the customer should be recorded as returned stock.

Goods that are returned to the facility must be credited to the appropriate customer at the price charged by the facility. The returned goods, whether damaged or not, should be received into the facility as an increase in the stock. This is important, as the value of the goods must be retained when returned to the facility and when crediting the customer for these goods (the double-entry concept of accounting). If the returned goods are immediately suitable for stock, then the goods must be put into storage.

Damaged goods need to be stored in a separate area and dealt with as described in the next section.

14.8.13 Write-off of stock (R5)

Damages may be incurred during operation, transport and loading or unloading. Damaged stock has to be removed from the stockholding in the facility. In the WMS, the goods should be sent to a specific zone designated for goods that are sold at a reduced price (where the goods can still be sold) or have zero value (where the goods are scrapped). Once any value received is recorded, the stock should be removed from the facility and the stock value loss recorded.

14.8.14 Stock counting (S2)

All errors are ultimately reflected as stock problems because the WMS records and the physical stock do not match. Counting stock is imperative to eliminate such stock errors. There are two prime methods for counting stock: a full stock count and a cycle count.

A full stock count is carried out by two independent teams, which verify each other's results. This is often done to confirm the stock for the financial auditors. If the teams agree on the numbers, these are inserted into the WMS as the correct stock quantities. If there is a discrepancy between the results of the two teams, a third team is introduced to recount the stock. This process is repeated until two of the teams agree. The agreed figure is inserted into the WMS. The process relies on the controlled counting of the stock and the figures obtained from counting the physical goods override the WMS figures. Even though the physical and WMS stock figures need to be reconciled later, the initial figures recorded in the WMS reflect the physical counts.

Cycle counts reconcile small sections of the facility on a continuous basis. The pick faces are counted every morning when all picks are completed and recorded in the WMS. (Remember that if a pick note is issued, one cannot know whether the stock has been removed from the pick face or not until it is confirmed to be in the dispatch assembly bay.) The stock count and the WMS are reconciled immediately. The storage areas are also checked continuously. Cycle counts do not interfere with the operations of the facility and they ensure that discrepancies between the WMS and the physical stock are minimised or eliminated. When effective cycle counting is performed, facilities often do away with a large and time-consuming full stock count, as it adds no value to their operations.

The stock is often categorised for the purposes of cycle counting. One system is to distinguish between high-, medium-, and low-value stock. High-value stock is counted more frequently than medium-value stock; medium-value stock is counted more often than low-value stock. Another system is to distinguish between fast-, medium-, and slow-moving stock. In this case, fast-moving stock is counted more frequently than medium- and slow-moving stock. These categorisation systems are generally based on financial considerations and are an attempt to minimise the risk of storing stock. The above systems do not really address the problems related to the operation of the facility. The facility operators need to know where all stock is, irrespective of how the stock is categorised because an error in any category could delay an order. Each category should be counted regularly. A method to make the cycle count more effective is to count each day all the pick faces where the stock level is below a particular amount. This means the stock is continually rectified, and the stock in the pick face is corrected near the point where it becomes critical, namely at the point where the WMS has to decide to introduce a let-down task to replenish the pick face.

Considering the above, stock takes for financial audits – whether carried out once a year or more frequently – are of value only to the auditors. The operation has to do cycle counts every day to eliminate a build-up of errors in the stock.

14.9 Delivery-transport operations (D2)

As transport usually accounts for a substantial portion of the supply chain cost, when capital charges are correctly included, the transport must be used efficiently. Transport efficiency is achieved by packing full loads and utilising the transport for as long as possible each day.

The operation of the transport system must allow for trucks to be loaded to the maximum volume or mass, without compromising the standards of service required by the customers. The loads must be built up from goods picked from the various sections of the facility. Separate transport fleets for various sections of the facility constitute gross inefficiency. The transport should be regarded as one fleet serving all customers. Loads must be accumulated in a dispatch assembly area in the facility. The loads should be built to fill the truck. Where the load does not fill the truck, the orders of two or more customers must be loaded into the same truck. This truck then travels a route that services the customers in sequence.

Trucks can complete a limited number of deliveries in a trip, as they have to travel between the stops, discharge the goods and then complete the documentation before moving to the next stop. The number of stops that are feasible depends on the distances, the time taken to unload and the times when customers will accept goods. Many customers accept goods not only during office hours, but also very early in the morning and later in the evening. The utilisation of a truck that normally operates from 8:00 to 16:30, or for 8,5 hours, can be significantly improved if it is allowed to discharge goods between 07:00 and 08:00 while peak traffic occurs in cities. The same applies for the evening.

Planning transport is a complex exercise. Accumulating goods into loads in one area may be difficult, particularly as various customers may have different size orders on different days. This also means that the routes are constantly changing. It is very difficult to plan the truck utilisation manually. It is better to have an information system that can analyse the data to find the best combinations of loads and truck routes. Such systems range from simple to very sophisticated and can improve transport efficiency and effectiveness significantly.

Whether the transport is optimised by a system or not, extended hours and flexible delivery times significantly improve productivity. These are negotiated between the customers, suppliers and facilities within the logistics chain. Again, the reduction of restrictions – in this case, customer receiving times – improves the potential for increased efficiency.

14.9.1 Example: improving delivery efficiency

Parts and accessories for the motor industry are regularly moved to service centres to replace items used in repairs.

A certain service centre maintains a stock facility, but items only arrive one day after they are ordered. At first, the parts were delivered before 14:00 the next day using a courier service. This was expensive, and it was often midday by the time the parts were placed into the stock facility. This affected the centre's ability to repair vehicles and often left the customers unhappy. A new system was devised. The parts and accessories were placed into a cage on wheels (called a rolltainer) and sealed. Each centre created a locked storage area large enough to store the rolltainer. The transporter could access the storage area after hours. The transporter then delivered a rolltainer at night, at a time that suited its transport capability. There were no delays for traffic congestion, or for the handover of the goods. The customer had the opportunity to check the rolltainer into the store in the first hour of the morning when vehicles were still being accepted into the centre. Parts became available to the technicians by 08:00 and at a lower cost.

14.10 Bar-coding, scanning and radio frequency identification technology

The description and principles of the operation of a facility are the same whether the stock records are kept on bin cards (sheets of paper held in each pick face) or the most advanced WMS. The practical operation of a WMS requires a significant amount of data capturing. Every movement of goods from one location to the next, every receipt and every dispatch must be recorded. The operator performs the action, notes the action and the information is captured into the WMS. This action is usually the factor that holds up the operation. For example, a pallet of goods is let down from storage and placed in the pick face. The move must first be recorded in the WMS as complete before the system will allow further picks to be issued from that pick face. The faster the recording process, the more efficient the operation.

14.10.1 Bar-coding and scanning

Scanning and bar codes reduce the delays associated with data capturing, increase the accuracy of data capturing and provide more detailed information of where goods are in the process than manual data capturing. The scanning allows the operator to record the action into the terminal (the equivalent to noting the action in the manual process). The terminal automatically updates the WMS. The scanning system speeds up data collection and reduces the need for written records. The communication between the scanner and the WMS can also be via:

- a hand scanner connected directly to a computer terminal;
- a portable scanner that stores data and transfers a batch of data to a terminal when placed in a docking station; or
- a portable scanner communicating with a wireless system to the WMS.

Wireless scanning eliminates the time taken for the scanner to update a terminal, which then progressively updates the WMS. Wireless communication also allows instructions and information to be downloaded from the WMS and displayed on scanners or terminals in vehicles.

Bar codes can be introduced to identify products. The bar codes reflect a number that is specific to a product and a pack size. This is known as the universal product code (UPC). For example, a pack of six red lipsticks has a specific number. Different numbers are given for other colours in the same pack size. A single scan will identify the product and the pack size.

Once the product is recorded as received, the movement to storage can be much more efficient if wireless communication is available. The driver of the movement vehicle scans a received pallet, and the WMS sends a message to the driver's terminal with instructions about the storage location of the pallet. Once the pallet is put into the correct rack, the rack code is scanned, and the WMS checks the scanned slot number to ensure it is the correct slot before recording the movement as complete. This requires significant time if done with a paper record system and manual data capturing. The advantages of bar coding and scanning are similar for the majority of processes in the system.

Because scanning yields such a speedy response, it allows for the receipt of cases, boxes, or pallets rather than the entire load. This reduces the area required for receiving. Similarly, the pick and dispatch process can be made much more efficient. The product and quantity to be picked can be displayed on a terminal. The completion of the pick of each product can be confirmed to the WMS. The WMS can instruct a vehicle to move picked goods to the appropriate assembly area bay and confirm the arrival of goods at the bay, all without operators having to record the information, capture it into the WMS, or wait until instructions for picking are printed.

Bar code scanning in conjunction with wireless communication introduces additional checks in the system. The processes – and the management of the processes – benefit from these. However, it also speeds up the processes that can complicate operations if there is a lack of capacity and training to control this. Unlike with a manual system, operators now perform the physical tasks and the data capturing simultaneously. This places pressure on the operators, who must be carefully selected and trained. Supervisors must also be able to rectify errors quickly and effectively, as these will cause the process to grind to a halt fairly quickly in this type of operation. For example, a pallet (called pallet X) is stored in the wrong space in the rack. The storage vehicle arrives to store a pallet in the slot which pallet X is wrongly occupying. The let-down truck arrives to take pallet X to a pick face, but the pallet slot is empty. Two drivers and two vehicles are now idle, while picking and storage slow down. A supervisor must be able to rectify the problem under great pressure.

More sophisticated labels can be used to assist in cross-dock operations. The use of bar coding and scanning is of value to any operation, and even more so when the same bar code information can be retained throughout the supply chain. This extends the benefits to all the supply chain processes. This integration of the chain as regards information is a major area for improvement in the local market – very few manufacturers, distributors or retailers have managed to achieve it.

14.10.2 Radio frequency identification

Radio frequency identification (RFID) devices are relative newcomers to the world of logistics. While they have been available for some time, they have yet to gain wide acceptance. The device comes in two parts. The first is a transmitter, or tag, that transmits an embedded code to a receiver. The second is the receiver, which performs two functions of asking for the code, and then deciphering the code to sensible data. The transmitter can be either passive or active. In an active transmitter, the device has a power source and can transmit longer distances. With the passive type, the receiver provides the power via radio waves and the distance of transmission is much less.

The great advantage of RFID is that the receiver and transmitter do not have to be in the line of sight of one another. This allows for rapid checking of the tags in an area. The great potential of this technology is that if the tags could be applied to every item in a warehouse, then all the items could be read in a few minutes with 100 per cent accuracy. While the potential for near 100 per cent accuracy of inventory exists, technology and cost remain issues. The consequence of this would be the automatic checkout in a store of all the items without them being removed from the trolley. This has yet to be realised, and at this point, the technology remains only associated with pallet identification.

The use of RFID remains one of the potentially great improvements for supply chains, but technical issues need to be resolved. For global use, the types and standards have been defined by the EPC (Electronic Product Code) Global Group. While the device standards are agreed globally, the frequencies for the devices are not. There are different frequencies available in different parts of the world, making the use of the devices globally more complicated and expensive. The transmission to and from passive units suffers from some other technical problems. The use of cans and metal containers is common in many industries. With these, the passive transmitters, when blocked from direct radio waves emanating from the receiver, do not always respond. This makes the technology unreliable for item-level identification, but applicable for pallet-level identification. The code and the details in the code are now under scrutiny for invasion of privacy, which is further slowing development.

There is no doubt that the use of RFID technology is here to stay. At this point, the tags remain at the pallet level and, in some select areas, at case level. Sortation and stock management is simpler than the bar code methods that have been traditionally used. If RFID comes to fruition, bar codes will be rapidly replaced, but until that time, bar coding remains the only universal method of identifying items along the supply chain.

14.11 The challenge of managing continuous change

Operations that continually improve are those that offer added value to their customers, suppliers and shareholders. The research into organisations that are setting worldwide standards and the reasons why they have achieved this status isolate a number of issues that directly reflect on how facilities should be operated. Irrespective of whether a facility is the most modern or not, or whether it has the best WMS or a less sophisticated one, research records that 'world-class competency is a managed result'.[1]

To be world-class, the research shows, there are four areas of competency:
- Strategy
- Measurement
- Integration
- Agility

The strategy has no bearing on the day-to-day operation of a facility, but the remaining three areas do. Operations can only aspire to world-class standards if they adopt the issues surrounding measurement, integration and agility. These directly influence the operation and its ability to grow.

The secret to a world-class operation is that the fundamental principles of the operation – sometimes called the 'drivers' of the operation – are sought and measured. Measurement allows for improvements to be prioritised, justified and implemented.

Integration comprises a number of factors:
- Supply chain unification
- Information technology
- Information sharing (key information is given to all parties)
- Connectivity (the capability to exchange data in a timely, responsive and compatible format)
- Standardisation (common operations designed to be the most efficient and effective)
- Simplification
- Discipline (doing the right action, at the right time, in the right way each time)

Agility is the ability to be flexible in areas that add value to all parties.

One of the cornerstones of world-class logistics is that continuous improvement is necessary. More efficient and effective processes need to be pursued at all times. In all cases, the improvements must benefit the entire chain and not just individual segments. In other words, local optimisation is eschewed for supply chain optimisation.

14.11.1 Example of continuous improvement

A large range of grocery items are manufactured and packed into small bottles. The manufacturer wraps six bottles of each product with plastic. Twelve of these packs are placed in a box. The box is the minimum unit for delivery. The distribution centre has to purchase the boxes from the supplier. After receipt, it has to open the boxes and store the goods as packs of six. The receipt, opening of the box and storage of the packs of six into stock require physical movement and data capturing for each step to be correctly recorded in the WMS. The box is disposed of, so it adds unnecessary cost to the process. Using returnable containers instead of boxes is an alternative that will save costs and simplify the processes in both manufacturing and at the DC.

14.12 Lean and six sigma operations

The concepts of six sigma and lean have direct applications in the operation of a supply chain and particularly in the operation of a warehouse. Six sigma is primarily the use of statistical methods to find causes of inefficiency and to help eliminate them. The method used is called the DMAIC process, which is a different way to approach a problem as a project. DMAIC stands for the steps to be taken in the project to eliminate inefficiency:
- Define
- Measure
- Analyse
- Implement
- Control

The process is powerful and useful for controlling operations and achieving improvement. The good part is that it forces a structured approach based on measurement, and a clear definition of the aim of the operation and the project.

Lean is a different concept, but a perfect complement to the six sigma process. Lean is about identifying waste in the use of time, movement, space, people, packaging and so on. The concept is to identify the waste in a process; this is one of the reasons why the detailed knowledge process is so valuable to warehouses. The warehouse utilises the lean process for physical flows and information to enable receipt, stock and dispatch. The ability to 'lean' these by reducing waste

benefits operational efficiency. Lean also espouses the issue of clean and neat facilities. There is a visual-effects programme called 5S, which works on this. 5S addresses:
- Sorting (identifying unnecessary items and removing them)
- Straightening (organising workplace for safety and efficiency)
- Scrubbing (tidiness with accountability)
- Standardising (documented expectations and procedures)
- Sustaining (maintaining good work habits and a problem-solving mindset)

Section 14.7 looked at the efficiency of operations in a warehouse. Lean and six sigma are structured methods for approaching the process of improving efficiency. The use of lean to drive out waste and six sigma to help control the process that has been improved offer great advantages to an operation.

14.13 Safety

The statutory requirements for safety in facilities in South Africa are laid out in the Occupational Health and Safety Act.[2] The Act prescribes the actions that must be taken to provide a safe working environment. It also prescribes that accidents must be reported to inspectors who have the power to investigate the accident and fine the organisation, or even recommend prosecution.

The cost of an accident is significant when the lost time is added up for the personnel involved in the accident, as well as for the personnel who are involved in investigating the cause of the accident. It is cheaper to ensure a safe working environment.

No facility can be operated efficiently or effectively and be dirty, cluttered with goods or badly maintained. A clean and orderly facility, with all areas clearly demarcated, has the potential to be efficient and effective. Housekeeping renders far more value than the effort taken to achieve it. It offers a good impression to prospective customers and sets a professional standard for the people who work there.

14.14 Conclusion

Three themes recur when discussing the operations of facilities:
- The facility must be organised.
- All the operations need to be coordinated.
- All the processes must be performed correctly first time, every time and at the proper time.

To achieve this, staff need to be well trained and operations continually improved. This requires that information (which requires measurement) and feedback be given to operators. The location and movement of stock must be managed and stock must be reconciled to the WMS continually. While technology in the form of WMS and scanning systems offer improvements, the 13 fundamental processes (outlined in Figure 14.1) need to be managed at all times and errors in all processes carefully controlled.

Key terms

Bar code	Product process
Competency	category (PPC)
Cross-dock	Radio frequency
Cycle count	identification (RFID)
Distribution centre (DC)	Stock count
Full pallet	Stock write-off
Let-down	Universal product code (UPC)
Location code	Warehouse
Manufacturing warehouse	management system (WMS)
Pick face	

Case study

The stock records in a certain facility have been giving problems. The stock as physical items and the computer-based WMS are not reconciled. The selection precision is suffering and the percentage of problems is continuously rising. These issues are also showing up in the amount of work the cycle-count staff have to perform and correct. This is now causing major problems. The task of finding the cause has been left to Joseph, the inventory foreman. He is trying to figure out the cause and is starting to

wonder just where to start. As a logistics expert, you are asked to help Joseph.
1 Advise Joseph of the processes that can cause the problems.
2 How would you contain the problem until you have found the cause?
3 If you knew that the staff had not altered, how would you isolate the cause of the problem?
4 The financial staff are claiming that the only way to fix the problem is to count the stock in the entire warehouse. What is your advice? Justify your advice.

Questions

1 There are a number of principles that underpin efficient operation in facilities.
   a) Describe the principles in your own words and explain why a facility benefits from adhering to them.
   b) During a short visit, how would you determine whether a facility has recognised these principles and is applying them?
2 The training in a certain company consists of an experienced operator showing new employees how the processes have been performed for the last ten years. Is this the best way to train new operators? If not, which is the best way? Give a specific example of how you would train someone in a process of your choice.
3 Stock counting in a facility should be done only once a year, as intermediate stock counts are a waste of time and effort. Do you agree with this statement? What operational and financial value can intermediate stock counts add to the business?
4 A cross-dock operation is simpler to introduce and to run than a warehouse. Comment on this statement, discussing the importance of ensuring that the workload of the operation is maintained at a constant level throughout the period of operation.
5 All facilities must move with the times and introduce bar coding and scanning in order to be effective. Comment on this assertion and motivate your arguments.
6 Economies in transition should not look at world-class standards, as these standards are not applicable to operations in such countries. Is this statement valid? Motivate your answer.
7 Give one example each of a successful and an unsuccessful operation that you have encountered as a consumer. Try to think of reasons for the success or lack of success. Could you trace it to superior or inferior facility operation, or to the purchasing aspect of the stockholding?

Consult the web

http://conted.clayton.edu/warehouse.shtml
http://www.inventoryops.com/articles.htm
http://www.mmh.com/article/CA215467.html

Consult the books

Bowersox, D. J., Closs, D. J. and Cooper, M. B. 2002. *Supply Chain Logistics Management*. New York: McGraw-Hill.

Chopra, S. and Meindel, P. 2004. *Supply Chain Management: Strategy, Planning and Operation*. New Jersey: Prentice Hall Pearson Education International.

Frazelle, E. 2002. *Supply Chain Strategy: The Logistics of Supply Chain Management*. McGraw-Hill.

Gattorna, J. L. 2003 *Gower Handbook of Supply Chain Management*, 5th edition. Aldershot: Gower Publishing.

Goldsby, T. J. 2005. *Lean Six Sigma Logistics*. J. Ross.

Notes

1 The global logistics research team at Michigan State University, 1995: 31.
2 Occupational Health and Safety Act of 1993.

15 The transport system

W.J. Pienaar

Learning outcomes

After you have studied this chapter, you should be able to:
- explain the role of transport in the business logistics process;
- discuss the service characteristics of the basic modes of transport;
- identify the various components of the transport system and discuss the role(s) of each component;
- discuss the characteristics of goods, and explain the way in which each characteristic influences the transport cost of different groups of goods;
- identify the four types of service providers and discuss the functions of each;
- discuss the ways in which freight forwarders and freight transport brokers can add value in the logistics channel; and
- discuss the various reasons why governments involve themselves in transport.

15.1 Introduction

The carriage of goods from one place to another, known as freight transport, is a key activity, and usually the largest cost component, within the business logistics process. Freight transport adds value to this process by creating place and time utility.

> Place utility is the value added to goods by transporting them from a place where they occur in a useless form or where they are plentiful (i.e. in oversupply) to a place where they are processed into a useful form, or where they are relatively scarce in relation to needs (i.e. effective demand exists).

Place utility can be seen as the value of the availability of goods at a place where they satisfy customers' needs.

> Time utility is the value added by making goods available at the time they are required for processing, consumption or use.

Goods may be grouped according to the stage they have reached in the series of processes within the supply chain, extending from primary production to consumption or final use. The groups are raw materials, semi-finished goods and finished goods. This grouping allows one to match the physical characteristics of the goods with the appropriate transport technology and to judge the ability of the goods to bear transport costs in relation to their value.

- Raw materials represent the primary products of agriculture (e.g. crops and livestock); forestry (e.g. timber); fishing; and mining (e.g. ore, coal and crude oil).
- Semi-finished goods are in the process of being converted from raw materials to finished goods, but are not yet in a suitable form for consumption or final use.
- Finished goods are those goods that have been processed (e.g. manufactured and assembled) into the form required for consumption or final use.

Raw materials are generally moved from their primary production source (i.e. the point of origin, where they usually occur in an unusable form) to a place of intermediate processing. Semi-finished goods are moved from a place of intermediate processing to a place of final processing. Finished goods are moved from a place of final processing via the warehouses and marketing facilities of distribution intermediaries to consumers (i.e. the place of consumption or final use). Waste materials are carried from places of processing and consumption to places of disposal. Returned goods, such as empty containers, reusable packaging and defective goods, are transported from users back to suppliers.

In this chapter, the physical components and constituent members of the transport system are identified and discussed. The main physical components of the transport system are the various modes of transport, terminals and the goods carried (freight). The main stakeholders of the freight transport system are service providers, transport users and the authorities.

15.2 Operational characteristics of the various modes of freight transport

15.2.1 Classification

There are three basic forms of transport: air, land, and water transport.

The two forms of surface transport, i.e. land and water transport, can be further divided into sub-forms or modes of transport, distinguishable by the physical right of way (or the fixed route the mode must travel) and the technology on which they rely.
- Land modes are represented by road, rail and pipeline transport.
- Water carriage can be grouped into sea transport and inland water transport. The latter includes navigable rivers, lakes and artificial waterways, or canals. Given that inland water transport is only common in some countries in North America, Europe and Asia, this mode of transport is not discussed in detail in this text.

The following five modes of freight transport are discussed in the next sections: air, road, rail, pipeline and sea.

15.2.2 Air transport

15.2.2.1 Operational overview

In most countries, air carriers convey less than 1 per cent of freight traffic. Although increasing numbers of users are using airfreight, it is mostly viewed as an emergency service because of the higher costs. In instances where an item must be urgently delivered to a distant location, or in the case of highly perishable goods, airfreight offers the shortest time-in-transit of any transport mode. However, such time-sensitive shipments are generally relatively few in number or frequency.

Aircraft have cruising speeds of up to 1 000 km/h and they travel internationally. With respect to intercontinental shipments, the major competitor for airfreight is water carriage. Domestic airfreight carriers compete directly with road freight carriers over long regional distances, and to a lesser degree with rail freight carriers.

Air carriers generally handle valuable items. The high price of airfreight would represent too great a proportion of the total cost for less valuable products to be viable. Customer service considerations may influence the choice of transport mode in the case of lower-value items, but only if service considerations are more important than cost considerations.

Although air transport provides short transit times, delivery delays and congestion at terminals may substantially reduce some of this advantage over short distances. The total origin-to-destination transit time is more important to the shipper than the transit time from terminal to terminal. In a domestic market, road transport often matches or outperforms the total transit time of airfreight.

The frequency and reliability of airfreight service is generally very good, but services are usually limited to movements between big cities over relatively long distances.

15.2.2.2 Typical strengths of air transport
- Aircraft attain high speeds over long distances. If utilised productively, this leads to increased revenue to the user. This feature of air transport has expanded the geographical range of markets for high-value perishable goods, such as cut flowers.

- The mode does not encounter physical en route obstacles as other modes do. Aircraft can follow a straight flight path, while the routes of other modes are circuitous. For example, the flight distance between Cape Town and Johannesburg is 1 271 km, and the shortest route by road between the two cities is 1 393 km.
- Airfreight is not exposed to unfavourable in-vehicle conditions for long periods.
- Standardised packing units and air cargo containers are used, which reduces packaging costs. Relatively little protective packaging is required, with the understanding that products are handled with care at terminals.
- Air transport has a good security record, which can be ascribed to stringent self-regulation; government safety and technical control; and the employment of well-trained and specialised staff.

15.2.2.3 Typical limitations of air transport

- Feeder and distribution services are needed.
- Carrying capacity (weight and volume) is limited.
- Congestion at airports can increase total transport time.
- Frequent flights are not always available, although the high speed may compensate for this.
- Air transport is directly influenced by inclement weather conditions, such as thunderstorms, gusting wind, fog and snow at airports and turbulence and headwinds during flights.
- Low accessibility – airports are often situated far from industrial and commercial areas.
- The unit cost per consignment is high.

15.2.2.4 Freight characteristics

Air transport is the favoured mode of transport for the conveyance over long distances of perishable items of high value; exotic products; fashion wear; collectors' items; pets; items for which a short lead time is vital; and courier/mail consignments. Theoretically, these are all items for which the air cargo tariff is less than the value added by receiving the goods sooner than by the next-fastest mode of transport.

Conveying items by air is the most desirable form of transport under the conditions listed next. When the commodity is:
- perishable;
- subject to quick obsolescence;
- required at short notice;
- valuable relative to weight; or
- expensive to handle or store.

When the demand is:
- unpredictable;
- infrequent;
- in excess of local supply; or
- seasonal.

When the distribution problems include:
- the risk of pilferage, breakage or deterioration;
- high insurance or interest costs for long in-transit periods;
- the need for heavy or expensive packaging for surface transportation;
- the need for special handling or care; or
- the need for warehousing or stock in excess of what would be required if airfreight were used.

15.2.3 Road transport

15.2.3.1 Operational overview

Road transport has replaced rail carriage as the dominant form of long-distance freight transport. Road freight carriers can transport goods of various sizes and masses over long distances. On long hauls (also called through-traffic), road freight carriers are able to transport certain primary products of an organic nature, such as timber, fish and agricultural products (e.g. livestock, fresh and frozen meat, fruit, vegetables and dairy products); some semi-finished goods; and most finished goods.

Road freight transport is more flexible and versatile than other modes because of the availability of extensive road networks. It can offer point-to-point service, therefore, between almost any origin and destination. It is this flexibility and versatility that has enabled road freight transport to become dominant in most countries.

Road freight carriage offers the client reliable service with little damage or loss in transit. It generally provides much faster service than rail transport and compares favourably with air carriers on short hauls. Many road freight carriers, particularly those involved in just-in-time (JIT) services, operate according to a scheduled timetable. This results in reliable transit times. Road freight carriers are able to compete, therefore, with air transport for small shipments – i.e. partial loads, or less-than-truckload (LTL) consignments – and with rail transport for larger shipments.

15.2.3.2 Typical strengths of road transport

- Door-to-door service. Road transport is not limited to a fixed route or fixed terminals. Consignments can be conveyed directly from a shipper (or consignor) to a receiver (or consignee) without the need for special terminals.
- Accessibility. Road carriers can deliver in every country, or economically active region, in the world. Therefore, deliveries are usually prompt.
- Freight protection. As a result of the ability to supply a door-to-door service, little handling and few transhipments take place between origins and destinations. Separate feeding/collection and line-hauling are often not necessary, and neither are delivery or distribution activities.
- Speed. This mode maintains short door-to-door transit times, especially over short distances. When delays occur as a result of traffic congestion or other incidents, it is often possible to follow alternative routes.
- Capacity. The carrying capacity, although relatively small compared with other modes of transport, is adaptable and can be readily increased.
- High frequency. A high frequency of service can be maintained as a result of the small carrying capacity and high speed of road vehicles.

15.2.3.3 Typical limitations of road transport

- Limited carrying capacity. The dimensions and gross mass of road vehicles are limited through legislation.
- High environmental impact. Road vehicles create considerable noise and air pollution.
- Vulnerability to external factors. Inclement weather conditions and traffic congestion can impact on the reliability and punctuality of road transport operations, especially in countries with severe climatic conditions, such as heavy fog and snowfalls.
- High energy consumption. Road vehicles consume more fuel than other forms of surface transport to convey the same unit of freight.
- Shared right of way. On public roads, the right of way is shared with other traffic, which increases safety and security risks and the occurrence of unexpected delays. An accident involving a truck with hazardous goods on board may result in a road closure lasting several hours. In addition to high accident risk, road vehicles are vulnerable to theft and hijacking.

15.2.3.4 Freight characteristics

Road transport is the most accessible and comprehensive mode of transport. It is very suitable for conveying high-value finished products over relatively short distances. It is, therefore, also suitable for collection and distribution in intermodal operations (i.e. operations where more than one mode of transport is used). Road vehicles are well suited for transporting small consignments due to their relatively limited carrying capacity.

15.2.4 Rail transport

15.2.4.1 Operational overview

In some countries, especially in Eastern Europe and Asia, rail is the dominant form of transport. In most countries, rail freight services are available between almost every metropolitan area, although rail networks are not as extensive as road networks. Because rail transport is limited to fixed routes, it lacks the flexibility and accessibility of road freight carriers. Rail transport provides a terminal-to-terminal service rather than a point-to-point service for clients, unless they have a rail siding at their facilities. If a facility is not connected to a rail link, another transport mode has to be used to gain access to the rail service.

Another disadvantage is the long transit time. Load consolidation in marshalling yards adds to the slow transport speed. Furthermore, rail transport cannot offer such frequent service as road transport. However, since the deregulation of land freight transport, rail transport has improved significantly in these areas. Transport deregulation increases competitive pressure to lower rail rates, resulting in the increasing use of contract rates by rail carriers.

In an effort to increase freight traffic volumes rail carriers are entering new markets and are participating increasingly in intermodal transport. Freight trains do travel on timetable schedules, but departures are less frequent than those of road freight transport. If a client has strict arrival and departure requirements, road transport has the competitive advantage over rail. Some of these disadvantages of rail transport may be overcome through the use of intermodal transport, which offers the advantages of rail transport combined with the strengths of other forms of transport.

15.2.4.2 Typical strengths of rail transport

- Almost any type of commodity can be conveyed by rail in special train compositions.
- Large volumes of bulk loads can be carried in single trains over long distances, which can reduce air pollution and ease the traffic burden on roads.
- Rail transport generally costs less (relative to weight) than air and road freight transport, especially over long hauls.
- The mode is not as vulnerable to traffic congestion as road transport. Theoretically, trains can be scheduled more reliably than road and sea transport.
- Rail transport is less affected by inclement weather conditions than other modes.
- Rail wagons cannot be stolen or hijacked as easily as road vehicles.
- High average trip speeds can be achieved by trains over long hauls when shunting and special composition of train sets is not necessary (e.g. unit trains).
- Private sidings can connect the facilities of clients to the rail network to allow for loading and unloading.

- Rail transport is cost- and energy-efficient over long distances and when the carrying capacity is well utilised.
- The accident safety record of rail transport is good, especially with the transport of hazardous goods.

15.2.4.3 Typical limitations of rail transport

- Owing to the limitations of a fixed track and specific terminals, rail services often need to be supplemented with additional feeder and distribution services.
- Rail transport has a high damage record. Because strong packaging is required to safeguard the goods, the packaging costs are high.
- Users often still perceive rail services to be of lower quality because of damage to freight and inconsistent service, despite the efforts of rail transport carriers to become more competitive since the economic deregulation of land freight transport.
- Rail transport requires enormous capital investment.
- Rail transport is vulnerable to pilferage when rail wagons remain stationary in marshalling yards for long periods.
- Directional traffic volume imbalances cause a high degree of empty running, so that return freight revenue often does not cover the costs of the return journey.

15.2.4.4 Freight characteristics

Rail transport can carry large and high-density commodities and bulk consignments over long distances at low cost. Rail transport is well suited, therefore, to carrying raw materials and semi-finished goods, such as mining and agricultural products. The introduction of containers has promoted the conveyance of high-value finished products.

In the bulk, long-distance transport market throughput and price are more important to the client than transit time. For example, as long as stockpiles of iron ore or coal at a port are sufficient, the arrival times of individual trains are not important. However, in many transport segments, such as containers and parcels, rail transport is losing ground because road freight carriers offer regular, shorter, and more consistent transit times.

15.2.5 Pipeline transport

15.2.5.1 Operational overview

Pipeline transport has unique characteristics:
- The infrastructure is also the carrying unit.
- It does not necessarily require a return journey or return pumping process. This eliminates joint costs.
- Product intake, haulage and discharge are combined in one process.

Pipelines are suitable for long hauls of fluids, like crude oil, petroleum products, liquid chemicals, water, and gas. The greatest utilisation can often be accomplished by using the same pipeline for different products at different times. Excessive mixing of these products is limited by the use of physical separators.

Pipeline transport offers superior reliability at a relatively low cost. Pipelines are able to deliver commodities punctually for the following reasons:
- Pipelines are not labour-intensive; they are largely automated and only a few employees are needed to control pumps and valves, or undertake maintenance.
- Worker strikes and absence have relatively little effect on their operations.
- Commodity flows through pipelines are electronically monitored and controlled.
- Weather conditions do not disrupt service.
- Losses from pipeline leaks or damage are very rare.

15.2.5.2 Typical strengths of pipeline transport

- Pipelines are environmentally sound. They do not generate fumes or noise, and can be disguised to prevent visual intrusion. Pollution or spillage only occur if they are damaged. The monitoring of pipelines is advanced and effective, which enables early detection of any defects that might cause pollution.
- Pipelines are able to move voluminous slugs of fluids and gas very reliably over long distances at a low unit cost and at low risk. Pipeline transport is highly reliable because it is both secure and punctual.
- Once the investment is made, the variable costs are low. There is also no joint cost (because a return journey – or reverse pumping – is not necessary), resulting in the highest level of economies of scale of all modes of transport.
- Although the transit speed is low – between 10 km/h and 15 km/h – the product is immediately discharged into storage tanks upon arrival. This, coupled with the fact that the pumping process can take place continuously, without the need for a return journey, reduces the total transit time. For example, at a pump speed of 15 km/h through a pipe with a 40 cm diameter, the effective delivery rate can exceed 1,8 million litres per hour, which cannot be matched by any other mode of transport.
- Because pipelines can be constructed and operated through difficult terrain, production points and areas that may not be accessible by other modes of transport can be reached by pipe, making the gathering of crude oil from such origins a viable proposition.

15.2.5.3 Typical limitations of pipeline transport

- Pipelines are able to transport only a limited range of products commercially, mainly fluids and gases.
- Pipelines are geographically inflexible as they are designed to serve fixed locations. Access to pipelines is limited due to their fixed right of way. Clients whose facilities are not connected to a pipeline must use another accessible mode of transport.
- There is a finite capacity that cannot be altered to accommodate sudden surges in demand.
- Pipelines require a high investment cost. This cost is fixed (i.e. unavoidable) and it rises rapidly per unit when throughput falls. Pipeline transport is not appropriate, therefore, for businesses that need small product volumes on an irregular basis.

15.2.5.4 Freight characteristics

In South Africa, petroleum products account for the majority of commercial pipeline traffic, followed by crude oil and gas. The USA employs pipelines to convey slurry coal, while slurry copper ore is conveyed from certain copper mines to refineries in Brazil. (Slurry is a substance suspended in a liquid, often water, so that it can be transported more easily.) Commercial water pipelines serve irrigation purposes in agricultural activities and cooling purposes in power-generation plants in the USA. Considering the world's dependence on energy products, pipelines will probably become more important in the future.

15.2.6 Sea transport

15.2.6.1 Operational overview

Ocean carriage is the most cost-effective way of transporting high-bulk commodities over long distances and is, therefore, the most widely used international shipment method. It is used for both inbound and outbound shipments, although there is usually an unbalanced flow of freight. The development of large bulk carriers has enabled sea transport to assume a vital role in the transportation of bulk materials, such as ores and minerals; grains; timber products; and especially coal, crude oil, and petroleum products between energy-producing and energy-importing countries. Because there is such a big demand for energy resources in industrialised countries, sea transport will continue to play a significant role in the transportation of these products.

In many countries, water transport is limited to international deep-sea transport and coastal shipping between local ports. Inland water carriers are dependent on the availability of navigable lakes, rivers, and canals. In North America, Europe, and Asia, for example, a significant portion of the total intercity freight tonnage is transported on inland waterways by river barges and small vessels.

Shipping has become highly specialised since the 1960s – each type of specialist ship being designed to be more productive than the ship it replaces.[1] Specialisation has resulted in ships becoming complementary to other modes of transport in the logistics chain. They are, therefore, often designed for a specific trade route and commodity type, with little prospect of employment on other trade routes.

- Bulk carriers carry cargoes with low value-to-weight ratios, such as ore, grain, coal and scrap metal.
- Tankers (mostly crude-oil vessels) carry the largest amount of cargo by tonnage.
- Roll-on/roll-off (Ro-Ro) ships carry cargo that is driven directly onto the ship, and allow for standard road vehicle trailers to load and unload cargo.
- Oil-bulk-ore (OBO) vessels are multi-purpose bulk carriers able to carry both liquid and dry bulk products.
- Container ships have greatly expanded the use of sea transport for many commodities. Most international shipments involve the use of internationally standardised containers suitable for intermodal carriage.

15.2.6.2 Typical strengths of sea transport

- A low-cost service can be supplied. Large volumes of high-density freight can be conveyed over long distances.
- Standard intermodal containers can be utilised to facilitate freight handling and transhipment.
- Traffic congestion is virtually non-existent on the open sea.
- Sea transport offers a very safe and secure service.

15.2.6.3 Typical limitations of sea transport

- A service can only be rendered to and from seaports that have the facilities to receive the ship and conduct the required transhipment. A door-to-door service is not possible.
- Because transhipment is unavoidable at both ends of a voyage, more freight handling takes place than with other surface transport modes.
- Ships are vulnerable to inclement weather conditions. This can delay delivery and in some cases prevent it altogether.
- Sea transport offers a slow and low-frequency service.

15.2.6.4 Freight characteristics

Almost any kind of freight can be conveyed by ship at a relatively low cost. Short delivery times are not of critical importance as far as the vast majority of commodities that are transported by ship are concerned. Clients make a trade-off between the long transport times and relatively low tariffs offered by sea transport.

15.3 Terminals

15.3.1 Overview

> A terminal is a special area situated at the end of a route or where different routes meet, branch out, or cross. Terminals include structures and equipment where in-transit goods are transferred between different carriers, modes of transport, or vehicles of the same mode.

It was explained in Section 15.2.1 that the technologies that provide movement or mobility within the transport system are classified as modes of transport. Terminals are a specific class of node.

> A node is a fixed point or place in the logistics chain where goods come to rest.

Other examples of nodes are the points of origin of raw materials; places of processing; warehouses; marketing facilities; and points of consumption or use. However, out of all the nodes in the supply chain, only terminals serve primarily a transport function. Examples of freight terminals are airports, seaports, tank farms, rail terminals and road terminals.

The following meanings should be attached to the various terminal facilities referred to in this book:

- Airport: a facility where the transfer of freight (air cargo) takes place between different aircraft or between aircraft and vehicles of another mode of transport.
- Seaport: a facility where the transfer of freight (sea cargo) takes place between different ships or between ships and vehicles of another mode of transport.
- Tank farm: a facility where pipelines link, or transfer takes place between a pipeline and another mode of transport or a storage facility (i.e. a tank).
- Rail terminal: a facility where the transfer of freight between rail wagons or between rail wagons and vehicles of another mode takes place.
- Road terminal: a road transport terminal.

In addition to accommodating the temporary storage or direct transhipment of freight, terminals also provide the maintenance, repair, parking and garaging of vehicles.

Terminals perform various value-adding activities to facilitate the transport of freight:

- Terminals provide a freight consolidation function by receiving small consignments and combining them into larger loads. Consolidation can maximise the utilisation of vehicle payload capacity.
- Terminals provide a bulk breaking (i.e. dispersion) service. This is the opposite of consolidation and involves separating larger units of freight into smaller units, usually for delivery to a final destination. Consolidation and dispersion are often performed simultaneously at terminals.
- Terminals perform a buffering, warehouse and transfer service. This involves the storage and protection of those consignments that are awaiting transhipment onto vehicles which are dispatched to destinations different from those of the vehicles on which the consignments arrived at the facility.
- Terminals often provide vehicle services. These may include refuelling, garaging and maintenance of vehicles and equipment, and sometimes also repairs. Examples of repair facilities at terminals are dry docks at some seaports and workshops at airports and road terminals.

15.4 Goods carried in the transport system

15.4.1 The characteristics of goods

Goods can be grouped into raw materials, semi-finished goods and finished goods. From the characteristics of goods, five factors can be isolated that determine the type of storage, handling, stowage and carriage they require.[2, 3] These five factors influence the transport cost. They are:
- in-transit care – necessitated by the intrinsic properties of goods;
- density of goods – represented by their mass-to-volume ratio;
- size and divisibility – determined by the physical dimensions of a consignment;
- stowage ability and ease of handling – determined by the form of goods; and
- potential liability of goods, determined by their value-to-mass ratio, fragility, susceptibility to theft and pilferage and potentially hazardous characteristics.

15.4.2 In-transit care

In-transit care refers to special arrangements required to secure goods while stowed on board a vehicle. Special vehicle features and other in-transit precautions to keep goods secure are significant determinants of transport costs.

The intrinsic properties, which determine the special care and treatment that goods require while in transit, are as follows:
- Form. The distinct differences between solids, liquids and gases have a significant influence on the required methods of packaging, handling and carriage.
- Animation. Live animals require confinement, handling and carriage different from those suitable for inanimate materials to protect them from hunger, thirst, injury and undue stress.
- Destructibility. During transportation, goods may be exposed to fire, the elements, vibration, jerking, jolting, chafing and violent impact. Goods that can withstand these hazards without damage can be regarded as indestructible. Examples of such goods are stone, ore, minerals, sand and soil.
- Fragility. Not all destructible goods are fragile. Fragility implies that goods are delicate and can easily be damaged, broken, destroyed or become dysfunctional. Glassware, electronic items, mechanical instruments, and lightwood products are examples of fragile goods.
- Wetness. Some goods are moist, or their physical characteristics result in the exteriors of their packaging being wet. Such goods are often classified as wet goods. The significance of the classification is that proximity of wet goods to dry goods is usually undesirable.
- Potential danger. Some goods have inherent characteristics that can potentially threaten health and safety. This necessitates precautions when storing, handling, stowing and moving them. The packaging sometimes creates a potential hazard, for example when gases are compressed into liquid form. The various broad commodity classes, their potential hazards, and examples of specific dangerous products are summarised in Table 15.1.
- Perishability. Goods may perish because of natural physical deterioration and obsolescence.
    - Natural physical deterioration includes the over-ripening and decay of fruits, vegetables, and flowers; the maturation and decay of wine, cheese and certain yoghurts. This may be accelerated in the transport process. Natural chemical actions within the goods may be accelerated by exposure to external bacteria, shaking, humidity and heat. Edible goods may be rendered unfit for consumption through contamination or vermin. Grains, for example, may be rendered inedible through premature germination.
    - Obsolescence includes news printed in the press, which becomes out of date after a lapse of time. There is a similar time limit for the transportation of goods for special occasions; fashion items designed for a particular season; and medication required urgently to meet an emergency (e.g. vaccines).

Table 15.1 Broad classes of dangerous goods

Commodity group	Type of hazard	Example
Combustibles	Fire, heat and smoke damage; suffocation	Crude oil; cotton; wood products
Contaminators	Pollution or tainting of other goods due to direct contact and vapours	Petrochemical products
Corrosives	Vapour and chemical actions causing damage to persons and other goods through direct contact	Sulphuric acid
Explosives	Devastating explosions and fire	Blasting material; compressed gases
Inflammables	Ignition by spontaneous combustion or external heat	Petroleum products
Malodorous materials	Disagreeable odours	Manure
Oxidisers	Rapid oxidisation and combustion	Nitrates; chlorates
Poisons	Noxious to life and health of living beings	Arsenic
Radioactive materials	Emission of harmful rays causing injury and damage	Radium
Water reactors	Harmful reaction with water	Calcium carbide

15.4.3 Density of goods

The density of goods refers to their mass-to-volume ratio, expressed in kilograms per cubic metre. Density is an important factor when classifying goods because both the payload space and the payload mass limit the carrying capacity of vehicles. Low-density goods, namely those with a small mass-to-volume ratio, are usually per kilogram more expensive to transport than high-density goods. Low-density goods absorb the space capacity without attaining maximum load mass, while high-density goods attain the maximum permissible load mass before the space is filled. By transporting goods with a density equal to the mass-volume ratio of the carrying capacity, one can make maximum use of a vehicle's payload capacity.

If the payload mass capacity is 20 000 kg and the volume of the payload space is 40 m^3, the mass-space relationship is 500 kg per m^3. Should the load have a density of 500 kg per m^3, both the loading space and the payload mass capacity can be fully utilised. The payload is not fully utilised if the density of the goods is greater or smaller than 500 kg per m^3.

The example above implies that the form, size, and shape of the goods permit full utilisation of the available load space. However, space between packages and between small partial load lots might be inevitable – or indeed required – in order to avoid contact, for ventilation, temperature control or easy access. Even when transporting liquids, one must allow space for changes in volume due to temperature changes. With loose or bulk commodities (e.g. grain) the loss of payload space is limited to the voids caused by the irregular shape of the particles. The loss of payload space increases when transporting goods with bigger and more irregular shapes (e.g. iron ore and coal). Indivisible articles that are not rectangular or cubic (e.g. cylinders and casks) and odd-shaped items (e.g. unpacked machinery and animals) occupy a relatively large proportion of unused space.

The practical density of goods, expressed as a ratio, is the stowage factor. It is calculated by dividing the consignment mass of the goods by the vehicle payload space required for transporting the goods. The stowage factor is representative of the vehicle utilisation or payload space required for the goods. Where additional space is required to stow the goods appropriately, the additional allowance is added to the payload space for the calculation.

15.4.4 Size and divisibility

The size of individual items may be measured in their cubic dimensions (length, width and height); volume (for liquids, e.g. litres); or mass (e.g. kilograms). Cubic size is important for matching handling and carrying capacities with the size of the articles. The permissible size of articles may be limited by handling equipment and the cubic carrying capacity available (i.e. space). It is often more economical to assemble articles such as power generators and electrical transformers at the place where they are manufactured, rather than at the destination where the ability and facilities for proper assembly might be lacking.

15.4.5 Stowage ability and ease of handling

The form and shape of goods and the method used to pack them affect their stowage ability and ease of handling. Stowage ability and ease of handling are reflected in the cost of securing against movement and handling a consignment. Items that are difficult to handle cost more to transport – even more so when a consignment is subject to transhipment. In this respect, goods can be divided into two broad classes: loose or bulk commodities and packed commodities.

15.4.5.1 Loose or bulk commodities

The natural properties of some goods permit them to be transported in bulk (i.e. without any wrapping or packaging). These commodities may be resistant to damage and may be transported in sufficiently large quantities to permit handling equipment and vehicles to be specially constructed for their conveyance. Examples are crude oil, petroleum products, timber, grain, ores, minerals and coal.

15.4.5.2 Packed commodities

The features of many commodities necessitate their wrapping and packaging. The packaging should allow for ease of handling and safe and secure carriage. Packaging consolidates materials into bigger lots that can be marketed and handled conveniently. It also protects the goods from damage. In the case of dangerous goods, packaging protects people and animals from injury, and equipment, other goods and property from damage. When making decisions about packaging, the cost of packaging should be compared with savings in transport costs resulting from the packaging.

15.4.6 Liability

Four factors are important when considering the impact of liability on the choice of transport:
- The value of the goods determines how high the transport costs can be. The transport costs should be compared with the value of the particular commodities.
- The packaging of fragile items needs to be robust enough to withstand vibration or impact with other goods. Special packaging arrangements may assume importance when it becomes necessary to determine liability for loss or damage in transit. For example, carriers sometimes require packaging to be of a specific standard due to known vehicle vibration during travel and jerking during marshalling (shunting) in a rail marshalling yard.
- Robust and non-transparent protection may be necessary to secure valuable items against loss through theft and pilferage, which adds to their transport costs.
- Liability may stem from the risk-bearing characteristics of dangerous goods. This requires additional insurance coverage against liability for fatality, injury, illness, damage etc. necessitated by dangerous goods.

15.5 Freight transport service providers

15.5.1 Background

Any transport system fulfils two principal functions: to provide accessibility and to provide mobility.

> Accessibility is the availability of a transport system close to users and potential users, and reflects the ease with which destinations can be reached.

Accessibility is dependent on the supply or availability of transport infrastructure and services. Infrastructure includes fixed facilities, for example, railway lines, pipelines, roads, airports, seaports and road transport terminals. With the exception of road transport terminals, virtually all other types of transport infrastructure have traditionally either been provided by authorities or supplied by the private sector through government mediation, or through government concession.

> Mobility is the frequency of transport activities, or the intensity with which users make use of a transport system or service.

Mobility is measured through actual transport demand, i.e. the volume of passengers and freight transported between places on the infrastructure network.

An important part of the business logistics process is identifying the providers of transport, and being aware of their role in the supply chain. Two groups of transport service providers can be distinguished: transport operators and non-operating transport service providers.

- Transport operators can be classified as private transport operators (firms with an in-house transport function) and professional carriers (operators whose core business is to provide transport services to clients).
- Non-operating transport service providers can be classified as freight forwarders (also known as freight consolidators) and freight brokers (so-called freight agents).

15.5.2 Private transport operators

> Private transport refers to a firm that operates its own leased or hired vehicles for ancillary purposes as a secondary business function in support of its primary (i.e. core) business, rather than making use of a professional carrier.

Private or ancillary operators, known as first-party operators, provide carriage to their customers (the buyers of their products), the latter being the second party. Ancillary operators not only conduct inbound movements of goods supplied by their vendors, but also intra-firm movements, namely conveyances between subsidiaries or facilities belonging to the same owner.

Private transport costs may be less than the cost of hiring professional carriers. The service advantages of control and flexibility may also be greater. The choice between private and professional carriers is not a straightforward or standard one. It is complicated and requires careful evaluation.

15.5.3 Professional carriers

> Professional carriers offer transport services for financial reward. The service that they trade is commercial transport.

Professional carriers are known as commercial carriers – or professional hauliers in the case of road transport – and they operate within all modes of transport. Professional carriers serve clients on a contractual basis. The contracts may be long term when they form part of a standing business logistics arrangement, or they may be single transactions (i.e. one-off or infrequent consignments) bound to agreed conditions. Professional carriers thereby act as third-party operators who enter into a specific carriage agreement with a consignor (the first party) who sends consignments of goods to a receiver (the second party).

Since the advent of the economic deregulation of freight transport, an increasing number of users are turning to professional road transport carriers to fulfil their transport requirements under long-term agreements or contracts. Within the framework of these agreements, carriers often customise their services to fit the needs of their clients. Contract carriers are also extending their services into a broader field of contract logistics, or so-called third-party logistics. This means that a package of integrated and coordinated logistics services is negotiated and offered to clients. This package serves to complement and enrich traditional professional transport activities, which were mostly limited to carrying goods between points of origin and points of destination.

15.5.4 Freight forwarders

> Freight forwarders undertake to have consignors' freight shipments transported. They are not carriers – they act as fourth-party service providers or transport wholesalers.

Freight forwarders are often a worthwhile service alternative for shippers in the supply chain. They acquire carriage from professional operators within any of the modes. They then collect small shipments (consignments) from shippers, and consolidate them into larger rail wagon, road truck or container loads for long-distance, inter-terminal movements. At the destination terminal, i.e. the bulk-breaking point, the separate consignments are dispersed to their destinations, with delivery transport arranged by the freight forwarder.

Freight forwarders assume full responsibility for the freight entrusted to them, from the points of origin to the points of destination. They have agreements with consignors to have the service performed; they enter into contracts with carriers to supply the required transport. Freight forwarding offers consignors comprehensive transport services. The consignor only needs a single contract and single insurance for the consignment despite the fact that the movement may require the use of the facilities of several operators.

Freight forwarding only requires consolidation and bulk-breaking terminals. They may, however, also own and control a limited number of vehicles for the purpose of collecting and delivering consignments from clients in close proximity to the consolidation and bulk-breaking terminals. By carrying out their own collections and deliveries, freight forwarders do not purport to be professional transport operators. They merely provide these services for ancillary purposes as a secondary function in support of their core business of freight forwarding.

15.5.5 Freight brokers

> Freight brokers are intermediaries who bring shippers and carriers together. As is the case with freight forwarders, brokers act as fourth-party service providers in transport transactions.

Brokers find carriers for shippers' consignments, or recruit clients for carriers. They charge a proportional fee (percentage commission) for their services. Receivers or consignees can also use the services of brokers for inbound goods. In this respect, brokers fulfil a vital role in activating and enhancing the ability of the transport system to supply quick-response services, emergency services and ad hoc services during peak demand periods or during sudden upsurges in the demand for specific products.

Since the deregulation of freight transport, the scope for transport brokerage has also broadened. For example, private operators (ancillary operators) increasingly make use of brokers to obtain loads for return trips (back hauls) that would otherwise have been made with empty vehicles. Professional carriers also use freight brokers in an attempt to maximise vehicle utilisation when their contractual obligations leave them with spare capacity on certain hauls.

The development of electronic communications and information technology, such as the Internet, have greatly improved the opportunity for consignors, carriers and consignees to meet one another in the marketplace through the mediation of freight brokers.

15.6 The freight transport user

> In the transport market, the user is the client. The user is the first party in transport transactions. Depending on the context, the transport user is also known as the sender, shipper or consignor.

Transport users are dependent on adequate access to their resources and markets. In order to maximise their revenue, transport users strive towards having their products delivered to their clients (the second party) as effectively as possible within cost constraints. The desired level of transport effectiveness, within the constraints set by efficiency, dictates whether users should conduct their own (ancillary or private) transport or seek the services of a third-party professional transport operator.

15.7 Government as stakeholder in the transport system

Throughout history, governments have involved themselves in transport. Transport has significant economic, social, political and strategic functions. Governments apply various mechanisms, deemed to be in the public interest, to intervene in transport. This is because transport is indispensable for sustaining society's welfare and economic development. Governments are to a lesser or greater extent involved in transport both as producers or providers of infrastructure, facilities and services and as regulators. A diverse range of motives have been advanced for government involvement in transport. These are outlined in the following sections.[4]

15.7.1 Control of excessive competition

Unrestrained competition may lead to prices being driven down so that total cost coverage is not possible. In reaction to this, an operator may neglect to provide for vehicle replacement; ignore the cost of invested capital; or terminate vehicle insurance payments, which can jeopardise the quality of service. Loss-making operators that desperately want to stay in the market may be inclined to avoid essential expenses or to apply dangerous tactics, such as overloading vehicles, not replacing worn tyres when necessary or not conducting routine vehicle maintenance. The more that users fail to recognise lessening standards in safety and quality of service, the more operators may be tempted to cut back even further on safety and service quality to their clients, which ultimately gives rise to instability in the transport market.

15.7.2 Coordination of transport

Owing to the general inability of vehicle operators to accurately perceive their true transport costs, oversupply of transport capacity may occur, leading to a waste of resources. On the other hand, an overestimation of transport costs could lead to an undersupply of transport services, which could unduly inhibit transport-dependent economic activities if the transport market is not coordinated through government intervention.

15.7.3 Integration of transport with economic policy

The interaction between land use and transport needs to be coordinated. For example, industrial settlement should be close to where sufficient labour is available and primary production should occur close to the point of origin of resources. This type of coordination may form part of the central government's wider macroeconomic strategies and regional authorities' spatial planning.

15.7.4 Maintenance of safety, security and order

Conventions and rules of conduct required for good transport sectoral housekeeping need to be in place. Technical regulation and safety measures are needed for safe, secure and orderly use of transport infrastructure and operation of services. Driving on a certain side of the road; not overloading freight vehicles; not driving too fast; and securing dangerous freight are areas where such regulation applies.

15.7.5 Provision of costly infrastructure

Certain infrastructure developments, which are usually a prerequisite for effective logistics service and economic growth and development (for example, seaports and airports), involve high investment costs, long periods for recouping capital costs and high levels of risk. The consequence is that such developments are provided by government.

15.7.6 Provision of public goods

Certain types of infrastructure cannot be supplied by the private sector in the absence of government intervention at an acceptable profit; or an effective means for collecting income from users is not readily available to private investors. Examples are the road network and lighthouses, which that benefit coastal shipping and sea traffic at ports.

15.7.7 Recovery of the true resource cost of transport inputs

The market mechanism may fail to reflect the scarcity value of exhaustible resources, such as petroleum. Governments may, therefore, steer transport decision makers away from over-utilisation of such resources through pricing tactics. One example of such tactics is indirect taxes built into the price of certain fuels.

15.7.8 Regulation of harmful conduct and externalities

Transport activities may impose costs and hardship on others not party to the transport activity. Examples are pollution caused by freight vehicles; traffic congestion; and third-party and public liability caused by accidents (such as pain, suffering and loss of income). These social costs are often excluded in transport decision making. The need arises, therefore, for governments to apply social justice and 'internalise' these externalities through legislative measures.

15.7.9 Restraint of monopoly power

Measures to prevent transport monopolies were previously particularly related to rail transport and were applied to reduce the potential for exploitation. In industrialised countries, technical advances within other modes of transport and the economic deregulation of the freight transport industry have reduced the potential for monopolistic exploitation. Nowadays, more pertinent is the potential for cartel formation, the process by which a small number of operators (i.e. an oligopoly) dominate a market segment through collusion.

15.7.10 Social support

Social criteria may be needed to guide transport resource allocation in order to afford all spheres of society mobility and access to economic activities. Corrective measures may be necessary when groups in society are too indigent to afford participation in transport or lack adequate transport infrastructure and/or services.

15.8 Conclusion

Freight transport adds value in the business logistics process by creating place and time utility. The goods carried in freight transport can be classified as raw materials, semi-finished goods, or finished goods.

There are five modes of transport: air, road, rail, pipeline, and water. All transport systems fulfil two principal functions: to provide accessibility and mobility. Accessibility refers to the ease with which users can participate in the transport process between chosen locations. Mobility refers to the measure of transport activity taking place.

Transport operators and non-operating transport service providers provide the mobility of goods. Transport operators can be classified as private operators or professional carriers. Non-operating transport service providers act as freight forwarders or freight brokers. The user, also known as the shipper or consignor, seeks access to resources and to the market, and requires optimal mobility to serve customers.

Governments are involved in transport as providers of infrastructure and services and as regulators.

Key terms

- Accessibility
- Air transport
- Density
- Divisibility
- Ease of handling
- Freight broker
- Freight forwarder
- Goods
- In-transit care
- Liability
- Mobility
- Pipeline transport
- Place utility
- Private transport
- Professional transport
- Rail transport
- Road transport
- Sea transport
- Stowage ability
- Terminal
- Time utility

Case study

Province X lies in the interior of South Africa. The province's capital is centrally located in the province, 1 000 km from the closest seaport and 200 km from the closest international airport. A Transnet Freight Rail railway line runs through Province X, with its only freight terminal within the province located in the outskirts of the capital. However, this line is not linked – through branch lines and private sidings – with the four large industrial growth points that the provincial government intends to develop in partnership with the private sector. The locations of the planned industrial growth points are between 60 km and 80 km from the railway line. They are close to sufficient semi-skilled labour, water and raw material resources. The industrial parks are all located between 100 km and 120 km from the capital and from one another. Satisfactory road links exist between the various industrial areas and the capital. The products manufactured in the planned industrial parks will be destined for all other provinces in South Africa, as well the international market.

The premier of Province X, whom you serve as transport and business logistics advisor, has to appoint a new MEC for Transport and Public Works to lead the province's industrial and transport development policy formulation. The premier wants you to brief her on:

(a) the various roles that freight transport can fulfil in Province X;
(b) which mode(s) of transport the province should help promote, and how this can be done;
(c) the types of utility that are created by transport in the value chain of products; and
(d) the meaning of the concepts accessibility and mobility, including why all of the concepts in points (a) to (d) are important in transport policy formulation.

1. Make your own assumptions regarding the type and volume of products that will be manufactured.
2. Write a briefing of not more than 1 000 words for the premier.

Case study

With a mounting fuel supply crisis resulting from capacity constraints of existing petroleum pipelines and refineries, petroleum marketers in several countries are compelled to import petroleum products and transport them by rail and road to their markets. Against the background of (a) the substantial increase in the international price of crude oil, (b) the apparent inability to stabilise the political and economic climate in certain of the largest oil-producing regions and (c) the growing demand for petroleum products in large, emerging, industrial countries (for example, China and India) and in large, developed, industrial countries (for example, the USA and Japan), it is imperative that the logistical aspects of petroleum product supply chains be arranged as safely, efficiently and effectively as possible.

During a discussion in late 2007 between the chief executive officer of Transnet Pipelines and the head of a leading university logistics department, the following statement was made: 'Pipeline transport of crude oil and petroleum products should, subject to economic assessment, be considered the preferred mode of transport between all ports of entry, refineries and the major downstream tank farms at wholesale depots.' You are a teaching and research assistant in the department of logistics at the university, and were present at the discussion.

You are tasked to draft a memorandum to the Minister of Transport on the likely effects that acceptance of the abovementioned statement will have on:

1. The country's transport system
2. Consumers of fuel products in general
3. Road and rail traffic conditions on main corridors

Questions

1. Why is transport imperative in the business logistics process?
2. Discuss your understanding of accessibility; mobility; place utility; time utility; transport modes; and transport nodes.
3. Discuss the five modes of transport by comparing each of the following: operational overview; typical strengths and limitations; freight characteristics.
4. What are terminals and what functions do they fulfil?
5. Discuss the stages of processing and the characteristics of goods, and explain how the characteristics of goods influence their transport requirements.
6. Why would a business make use of a freight forwarder and a freight transport broker?
7. There may be four parties involved in a transport transaction. Who are they and what is the role of each?
8. Identify and briefly describe the two types of transport operators and the two types of non-operating service providers.
9. Discuss the various reasons why governments involve themselves in transport.
10. Briefly describe the reasons why governments act as producers or providers of elements of the transport system.

Consult the web

Air transport
British Airways World Cargo:
 www.baworldcargo.com
International Air Transport Association (IATA):
 www.iata.org
International Civil Aviation Organization (ICAO):
 www.icao.org
KLM: klmcargo.com
Lufthansa Air Cargo: www.lhcargo.com
South African Airways (SAA): www.flysaa.com

Road transport
Cargo Carriers: www.cargocarriers.co.za
Cross Roads Distribution (Pty) Ltd:
 www.crossroads.co.za
International Road Transport Union (IRU):
 www.iru.org
Road Freight Association (RFA): www.rfa.za
Unitrans: www.unitrans.co.za

Rail transport
Association of American Railroads: www.aar.org
International Union of Railways (UIC):
 www.uic.asso.fr
Transnet Freight Rail:
 www.transnet.co.za/FreightRail.aspx

Pipeline transport
American Pipeline Association:
 www.api.org/industry/pipelines/pbasic.htm
Petroline: www.petroline.co.za
Transnet Pipelines:
 www.transnet.co.za/Pipelines.aspx

Sea transport and ports
Grindrod: www.grindrod.co.za
International Maritime Organization (IMO):
 www.imo.org
Maersk Sealand: www.maersksealand.com
Ports Operations:
 www.transnet.co.za/PortTerminals.aspx
Safmarine: www.safmarine.com
Transnet National Ports Authority:
 www.transnetnationalportsauthority.net

Government-related sites
National
Air Traffic and Navigation Services Company Ltd:
 www.atns.co.za
Airports Company of South Africa:
 www.airports.co.za
Civil Aviation Authority: www.caa.co.za
Department of Public Enterprises:
 www.dpe.gov.za
Department of Transport: www.transport.gov.za
South African Maritime Safety Authority:
 www.samsa.org.za
South African National Roads Agency Ltd:
 www.nra.co.za

Provincial

Eastern Cape: www.ecprov.gov.za
Free State: http://www.freetrans.gov.za/
Gauteng:
  www.transportandpublicworks.gpg.gov.za
KwaZulu-Natal: www.kzntransport.gov.za
Limpopo: www.limpopo.gov.za
Mpumalanga: www.mpumalanga.gov.za
North West Province: www.nwpg.gov.za
Northern Cape: www.northern-cape.gov.za
Western Cape: www.capegateway.gov.za

Consult the books

Bowersox, D. J., Closs, D. J., and Cooper, M. B. 2007. *Supply Chain Logistics Management*, 2nd edition. New York: McGraw-Hill.

Button, K. J. 1993. *Transport Economies*, 2nd edition. Aldershot: Edward Elgar.

Schumer, L. A. 1974. *Elements of Transport*, 3rd edition. Sydney: Butterworths.

Wells, A. T. 1999. *Air Transportation: A Management Perspective*, 4th edition. Belmont: Wadsworth.

Notes

1 Wells, A. T. 1999: 375.
2 Schumer, L. A. 1974: Chapter 3.
3 Bowersox et al. 2007: 192; 193.
4 Button, K. J. 1993: 244–5.

16 Transport cost structures and pricing principles

W.J. Pienaar

Learning outcomes

After studying this chapter, you should be able to:
- explain what efficiency in transport means;
- discuss how economy can be achieved in transport;
- describe the cost structure of each mode of transport;
- explain cost trade-offs in transport;
- outline why profit planning and control are crucial at operational, tactical and strategic management levels; and
- discuss how the financial integrity of a professional transport carrier can be supported by making use of total-cost, marginal-cost and value-of-service pricing tactics.

16.1 Introduction

We have seen that the emphasis in business logistics should not be simply on the cheapest or fastest transport or on reducing inventories, but rather on achieving an integrated and coordinated systems approach to the logistics process. The acceptance of the total-cost logistics concept has led firstly to logistics cost trade-offs between the various transport services provided and secondly to the operations at facilities assuming greater importance.

This chapter concerns itself with:
- aspects of efficiency in the supply of the transport function within business logistics practice;
- cost trade-offs in transport; and
- transport pricing tactics that link the aspects of service efficiency and effectiveness within transport supply and demand.

16.2 Efficiency in transport

Transport is not demanded in its own right: it is a means to an end, namely moving goods. At the basis of any analysis of the demand for transport is the fact that this demand is a function of other activities. Freight transport is an inescapable cost in the supply function of consignors and consignees and they seek to minimise it whenever possible.

The efficiency with which one uses and organises inputs to achieve set goals has a direct effect on the competitiveness of a business. The lower the cost per unit of output (without sacrificing service quality) in relation to the value or price of the delivered product, the greater the efficiency of the logistics process. Technically, efficiency refers to the combination of the best and most up-to-date production, marketing and logistics techniques; prudent management; a highly skilled workforce; and organisation of the business (including its logistics function) so that it operates at a scale or size at which maximum economy is derived.

> Economy is the optimum use of resources so that the maximum benefit is gained from any given input of resources.

16.3 Economies of scale

Economies of scale are achieved when an expanded level of output results in reductions in the total unit cost of transport (per ton-kilometre).

The prerequisite for economies of scale is a cost structure that is characterised by a high ratio of fixed to total cost, so that with increasing output, the fixed cost per unit of output declines faster than the variable cost increases per additional unit of output. The three transport management strategies discussed next can contribute to attaining economies of scale in transport:

- **Increasing vehicle sizes and maximising use of their capacity**

    The capacity utilised in a vehicle is proportional to the volume of the load, while the costs are proportional to the area the load occupies. Thus, the capacity can increase at a greater rate than the costs of transporting the increased capacity. This relationship accounts for the trend towards very large bulk-cargo vessels; wide-body aircraft; long-haul road vehicles whose length, width and height are the maximum that road-traffic legislation allows; and pipelines with a large diameter.

    The fundamental relationships involved depend upon the principles of geometry concerning the relation between the surface of a carrying unit (either box-shaped or cylindrical) and its volume. Consider a circular cross-section of a pipe or a cylindrical tank wagon or road trailer. Because the area of a circle is πr^2, its area increases with the square of the radius. The circumference increases only in proportion to the radius, since the circumference is $2\pi r$. For example, the friction that must be overcome to move a liquid commodity through a pipeline is the friction between the liquid and the wall of the pipe. Therefore, increasing the diameter of a pipe will increase the quantity of liquid in the pipe faster than it will increase the area of the wall of the pipe in contact with the liquid. Consequently, there are gains in economies in the propulsion power required to pump the same quantity of commodity by increasing the diameter of the pipe. There are also economies in the cost of the pipe or cylindrical container itself. For larger pipes or containers, the quantity of body steel per unit of vehicle carrying capacity is less than for smaller vehicles.

    The same kind of relationship between the area of the surface of a container and the volume of its contents applies to other modes of transport. It applies, for example, to road trailers, rail wagons and aircraft. Yet the scale of rail wagons is limited by the gauge of the railway line and by overhead clearances along the right of way. In the case of rail transport, efficiency requires that the same gauge be used throughout the system. Air, road and water transport also face limitations on the size of the vehicles. Technological capability permitting, pipelines can be built to whatever size is required – the only effective limit on their size comes from the demand side of the market. There is no sense in building pipelines of larger capacity than will be required.

- **Increasing fleet size and maximising use of its capacity**

    Overhead charges generally increase at a much slower rate than the revenue generated by an increased fleet size that is well utilised. Larger fleets can also obtain larger discounts with, for example, bulk purchasing rebates on fuel, finance costs with vehicle acquisition, spare parts, and group short-term insurance. The business also benefits from the improved utilisation of its own workshop and consolidation facility, while standardisation results in lower spare-part inventories.

- **Intensifying the use of indivisible facilities and infrastructure**

    When indivisible facilities and infrastructure are used to their maximum capacity, the result is a lower fixed unit cost for these facilities. The unit cost decreases as long as there is no congestion. For example, when increasing the utilisation of a rail network, the fixed unit cost decreases until the level of traffic starts to cause delays due to congestion.

Whenever congestion endures and forecasting indicates that demand will grow even further, one should contemplate capacity expansion. Whenever demand growth can be sustained, incremental expansion of infrastructure may result in substantial returns of scale.

With rail transport, the move from a single-track to a double-track system may quadruple the capacity of the line by eliminating directional conflict, and a quadruple track should increase capacity even more, as it permits segregation by speed.[1]

Engineers involved with petroleum refining and pipeline transport capacity extension use the so-called two-thirds rule: the capacity of any facility can be doubled at only a two-thirds increase in cost.

In the case of terminal buildings, the reduced cost associated with size increase can be explained by simple arithmetic. A single-truck square-shaped garage with an area of 36 m^2 requires an enclosing wall of 24 linear metres. A square-shaped garage that is 100 times bigger, i.e. 3 600 m^2, requires an enclosing wall of only ten times the length, i.e. 240 linear metres.

16.3.1 Subgroups of economies

Economies of scale in transport depend on the attainment of one or more of three subgroups of economies: economies of density, economies of scope and economies of distance.

16.3.1.1 Economies of density

A quantity of goods can often be transported at a lower unit cost when moved together in one consignment or load, or in one uninterrupted flow, rather than in different consignments or loads. This type of economy stems from the fact that one can serve the largest possible portion of a market with the same technology. The same volume of throughput occurs, but the movement is concentrated into one process, permitting more intensive use of the capital involved.

To achieve economies of density, one usually needs specialised technology to handle large volumes of a specific or homogeneous type of goods. The inherent danger of this is the empty return trip. To reap the optimum rewards of specialisation, handling equipment at terminals should allow for rapid loading and unloading of freight in order to maximise the number of full vehicle load-kilometres per unit of time. Economies of density necessitate the maximum utilisation of large, durable equipment over as long a period as possible.

16.3.1.2 Economies of scope

When the cost of producing two or more products together, in either a joint or a common process, is less than the cost of producing them separately, then economies of scope can be achieved.

Joint products (also called by-products) are the inevitable and inseparable consequence of a single production process. For example, an outbound journey automatically gives rise to an inbound journey. This implies that if a full vehicle load has to be hauled from home depot A to point B, carriage of a back haul from point B to home depot A would be cheaper than carriage from just A to B, as the vehicle inevitably has to return to its home depot. Failure to solicit available back haul business is a foregone revenue opportunity (i.e. a waste), and therefore implies failure to deal with joint costs profitably.

Common production (also called shared production) occurs when different products are deliberately produced together in a common process. In this case, the similarities of the production processes permit the use of the same technology. The cost that arises in this instance is common and therefore shared among the commonly produced products. For example, when the same vehicle can be used for passengers and freight transport, and when fleet capacity exceeds the demands set by seasonally fluctuating contractual agreements, the spare capacity can be filled with spot-market shipments solicited through reduced tariffs.

Achieving economies of scope usually requires standardised, or at least compatible, technology that can accommodate product diversification. This implies that one must be able to share the technology between two or more users, and spare capacity should be available to accommodate product diversification.

16.3.1.3 Economies of distance

Economies of distance (also known as long-haul economies) are attained when the total transport cost per ton-kilometre decreases as the trip distance increases.

Economies of distance arise when there are trip-specific fixed costs that are not affected by the distance of the journey. Examples are terminal costs, such as aircraft landing fees and seaport charges; trip documentation; and loading, stowing, and unloading costs. As one has to pay these costs regardless of the distance, doubling the length of a haul does not result in doubling the costs.

Note that economies of distance are not synonymous with increasing the number of full vehicle-load kilometres – this is an economy of density. For example, ten trips of 12 kilometres each is more costly than one trip of 120 kilometres. The lower cost of the latter reflects an economy of distance. However, economies of density can be achieved in both cases if all the work is done with existing fleet capacity.

16.4 Competition within modes of transport

Competition within modes of transport – also known as intramodal competition – is largely related to cost structure, distance of haul, and the diversity and physical characteristics of the goods carried. The various modes are, therefore, characterised in terms of forms of competition and cost economies.

16.4.1 Air transport

Since the economic deregulation of airfreight transport markets, there has been a trend towards an oligopolistic market structure. (An oligopoly is a market in which relatively few sellers supply many buyers.)

In air transport, there is a technical limit to the economies of scale that one can achieve with increasing the fleet size. Making use of a large aircraft fleet requires frequent and large operations, but this is feasible only if there is continuous high demand for the big number and large sizes of aircraft. It also requires effective loading procedures and equipment to load and unload aircraft quickly.

Although increasing fleet and aircraft size does not necessarily result in significant economies of density, larger but mixed operations may result in significant economies of scope. It may be more economical for one carrier to undertake both scheduled and charter flights than for separate carriers to specialise in one of the two types of service. In seasonal or peak-oriented markets, operating aircraft with flexible cargo-passenger combinations may result in increased loads and thus increased economies of scope.

On condition that intermediate landing is not necessary and that the crew does not need to change, longer route lengths give rise to significant economies of distance. With no intermediate landings, large time savings are achieved, as well as savings with each of the eight variable cost items explained in Section 16.5.2.2. For example, the fuel consumption rate of a Boeing 737-200(F) between Johannesburg and Cape Town carrying a payload of 20 tons over the route length of 1 271 km is 330 litres per ton payload. The comparative fuel consumption with the same aircraft and payload for the 502 km route between Johannesburg and Durban is 170 litres per ton payload carried. The fuel consumption rate per ton freight on the latter route is 52 per cent of the former, while the route length of the latter is only 40 per cent of the former. This is because the aircraft consumes between 1 200 and 1 300 litres of fuel extra to reach its cruising altitude, whereafter it cruises at 4,24 ℓ/km.

16.4.2 Road transport

Road freight transport competition ranges from open to oligopolistic. Fleet sizes in this market vary between one and more than a thousand vehicles. The fixed costs of single-vehicle hauliers that do not own any terminal facilities are very low, and this market sector is very competitive.

Specialised carriers and carriers of part-loads and parcels generally require terminal facilities, which increases their fixed costs. Their unit costs decrease with increased traffic volume (economies of density) and distance of haulage (long-haul economies). Generally, owing to the high ratio of variable (i.e. running) costs to total costs of individual vehicles, and the relatively small terminal facilities, road transport does not enjoy significant economies of distance.

Increased vehicle sizes and fleet sizes, coupled with productive utilisation of this greater capacity result in increased economies of scale. Infrastructure, such as terminals – particularly for specialised carriers – provides further opportunities for economies of scale. Other potential sources of economies of scale are specialised vehicles; a workshop owned by the business for vehicle maintenance and repairs; specialisation in terminals; and management efficiency. However, none of these potential advantages preclude competition from smaller operators.

Road transport carriers can achieve considerable economies of scope by consolidating consignments effectively.

16.4.3 Rail transport

Since the 1990s in Europe and Australia, ownership of rail infrastructure and of train operations have been organisationally divorced. With this arrangement, any prospective rail transport operator may gain open access to existing rail infrastructure and tracks under certain prescribed conditions. The advocates of this new rail transport agreement argue that it limits monopolies, making the rail transport market more competitive, thus functioning more efficiently and effectively.

When analysing rail transport, one should distinguish between unit costs (for example, the cost per ton-kilometre) decreasing due to economies of density and due to economies of distance. Through economies of density and distance, a rail transport operation may enjoy a natural monopoly on a particular route. On the condition that the utilisation of train carrying capacity is high the former economy stems from its cost structure, which is characterised by a very high ratio of fixed cost to total cost (the second-highest fixed-cost ratio of all modes of transport after pipeline transport). In view of the fact that rail transport has relatively high terminal costs it enjoys substantial economies of distance as trip length increases.

The combination of long-distance haulage, double-track operation with increased frequency of trains and capacity loads (also on back hauls) on long trains may lead to significant unit cost advantages, all related to economies of distance and density.

16.4.4 Pipeline transport

Because the fixed costs of pipeline transport are proportionately much higher than variable costs – the highest of all modes – and continuous pumping may take place with no need for any return flow and no materials handling takes place, economies of scale do prevail in pipeline transport. Because of the high capital costs of a pipeline, the financial barrier to entering the market is high.

In terms of the number of market participants, the supply of pipeline transport is the most highly concentrated of all transport modes. The absolute number of firms is low, but the significant measure of concentration is the number of participants in a specific transport market segment or transport corridor. With a few exceptions, there is but one crude oil, one products and one natural gas pipeline connecting producing areas or refineries and areas of consumption. This high degree of monopoly power results from declining unit costs with increases in capacity, so that the lowest costs are achieved by a concentration of output in a single pipeline. A high degree of concentration is efficient, and changes towards a more competitive market structure through economic regulation would entail high losses in efficiency. Therefore, pipeline operations that can fulfil entire market demand are natural monopolies.

Where the distance between supply points (such as geographically separated oilfields or ports of entry) is high in relation to the delivery distance to the market area, such an area's fuel demand can often be most efficiently fulfilled by two or more different pipeline operations. For example, from 2010 onwards, the province of Mpumalanga in South Africa will receive petroleum products via the Transnet products pipeline from refineries close to the Port of Durban and the Petroline products pipeline from the Port of Maputo in Mozambique. In the latter case, a pipeline transport oligopoly (in this case, more specifically a duopoly) will exist.

In view of the abovementioned considerations, financial stakeholders in pipeline operations tend to consolidate and start with a large initial investment, which tends to yield higher returns, partly because of economies of scale and partly because of inherent performance characteristics (for example, a 30 cm pipe operating at capacity transports three times the quantity carried by a 20 cm pipe).[2] The gains from scale are substantial. For example, the lowest cost for a throughput of

100 000 barrels of crude oil per day in a 45 cm pipeline would be approximately double the cost per barrel when compared to carrying 400 000 barrels per day in an 80 cm pipeline over the same distance.

The implications for the industry are important. It would be extremely wasteful, for example, for four competing refineries in a consuming area in which each used crude oil from the same area of origin to build four pipelines. If, for example, each required 100 000 barrels per day, then building four parallel 45 cm pipelines instead of a single 80 cm pipeline would double the cost per barrel for transport. Efficiency dictates a common system for use of the same pipeline in such circumstances. It also follows that costs for carrying petroleum on a route that has a large pipeline will be much lower than on other routes not thus provided. There will be external economies in locating large refining capacity in the same area.

On the principle of economies of density, an increase in pipe diameter can result in a lower unit cost. An uninterrupted and prolonged throughput of a large volume of homogeneous product increases economies of density. Should such continuous pumping with a specific product not be sustainable, common production can make petroleum pipelines more cost-effective, since a variety of petroleum products can be pumped consecutively, thereby enhancing the achievement of economies of scale through economies of scope.

Longer pipelines do not give rise to significant economies of distance, as additional pump stations are required for longer distances.

16.4.5 Sea transport

Seaborne trade can be classified into two main categories – bulk cargo and general cargo. Both the bulk and general cargo trades make use of ships that are supplied partly from fleets owned by the bulk and liner industries, supplemented by vessels obtained from the charter market. Ocean shipping competition ranges from open competition, as in the case of bulk (tramp) shipping and the charter market (individual ships seeking cargo), to oligopolistic cartels, as in the case of liner shipping conferences.

> A liner shipping conference is an association between a number of shipowners that offer their services on a given sea route according to conditions agreed by the members.

In exchange for the right to operate as legal cartels the participating operators usually assume common-carrier obligations within the market they serve. Common-carrier obligations include: (a) operating according to published route plans (i.e. predetermined ports of call), time schedules (although this is difficult to adhere to in sea transport) and tariffs (freight rates); and (b) acting in a non-discriminatory way towards users.

As opposed to the services offered by liner shipping conferences, charter ships do not operate according to a fixed route or published schedule. Instead, a shipper charters, or leases, a ship for a particular voyage (or voyages) or a given time, called a voyage charter or a time charter. A charter agreement can either be a gross charter or bareboat charter. A gross charter is a charter agreement by which the shipowner furnishes crew and equipment and incurs other expenses, such as port costs. A bareboat charter is a charter agreement under which a shipper charters a vessel without a crew, assumes full possession and control of the vessel, and is generally invested with temporary ownership powers.

Like most forms of transport, shipping benefits from economies of scale associated with operating larger ships. Larger ships result in lower costs per ton (in the case of bulk shipping) and lower costs per standard container (in the case of container shipping). However, larger ships may result in problems for other areas of the maritime industry, mostly at the ports. Bigger ships require wider entrance channels, deeper draughts, larger cranes and other loading and unloading equipment, as well as sufficient storage space to hold the commodities before or after loading and unloading the ships. In view of the fact that sea transport is subject to high terminal costs (various types of port-related charges and relatively large loading and unloading costs), it enjoys substantial economies of distance as voyage lengths increase.

As is the case with air transport, economies of scale are possible with large individual vessels and not necessarily with large fleet operations. Single-ship operators or operators owning a few ships – for example, owners of charter ships – are often able to compete with larger scheduled conference liners.

Should shippers making use of liner operations judge that the rates charged by conferences are too high they may turn to a charter operator in an effort to obtain more competitive rates. The presence of charter operators can inhibit conference liners from charging excessively high tariffs, which works in favour of shippers. However, the main operational benefit of charter operators is that they are often able to supply service in peak periods, thereby helping to bring the demand for and supply of ship capacity into balance. The market for ship chartering is a fluid supply-and-demand situation: varying from peak-season to low-season demand, the charter phenomenon is said to be one of feast or famine for shipowners.[3]

16.5 Cost structures of the different transport modes

16.5.1 Overview

> Cost structure refers to the relationship between the fixed and variable components of total cost.

Total transport cost is traditionally divided into vehicle operating and overhead costs. Vehicle operating cost is subdivided into standing costs and variable costs. Overhead and standing costs jointly represent the fixed cost of transport supply.

Overhead costs are not directly related to vehicle operation, but represent the costs involved in general management, administration, overall support services, land, buildings and other facilities. Overhead costs, therefore, are common to all vehicles.

Standing costs are period-bound costs inherently associated with vehicles. These costs include depreciation, vehicle leasing, fixed crew cost, licences and vehicle insurance.

Standing costs usually occur on an annual basis. Many individual journeys may take place within a financial period under different conditions. The standing cost responsibility for each journey is, therefore, not directly traceable. The common standing costs are proportionately allocated for each journey.

Variable costs fluctuate proportionately to variations in transport output. Whether a trip takes place or not, fixed costs cannot be avoided. Variable costs are avoided if a trip is not undertaken. This cost is readily determinable, even in the case of very short trips. It is, therefore, a direct cost at any level of vehicle performance. Figure 16.1 illustrates the proportional increase in variable, fixed and total transport costs when one increases the trip distance.

The marginal cost of carrying one additional ton of freight usually includes the additional storage, handling and stowage costs; minor additional fuel costs; and sometimes additional terminal charges.

In the case of a full consignment on a return trip (i.e. when the trip must take place whether a consignment is available or not), an operator will seek to recover:

- all variable costs;
- an appropriate time apportionment with respect to fixed costs for including the consignment; and
- a mark-up for profit.

Figure 16.1 Proportionate increase in transport costs

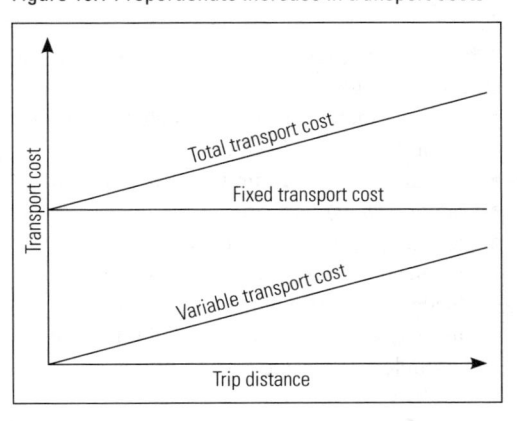

16.5.2 Air transport cost structure

Air transport, as is the case with sea transport, does not need a supplied right of way. Besides the high initial cost of acquiring aircraft, the vast majority of other cost commitments are of a variable or semi-variable nature. The limited carrying capacity and high capital and operating costs of aircraft lead to high unit costs of mostly small consignments.

16.5.2.1 Fixed costs
Fixed costs are those not affected by fluctuating levels of air transport activities. They include:

Overhead costs
- Acquisition and maintenance of buildings, equipment and facilities
- Insurance of assets other than aircraft
- Management, administration and supervision
- Training costs

Standing costs
- Depreciation, interest and aircraft insurance
- Aircraft operating permits and licences
- Salaries
- Routine maintenance

16.5.2.2 Variable costs
The variable cost items relating to air transport include:
- fuel;
- engine and component overhaul and replacement costs; and
- flight crew expenditures.

A few operating cost items vary according to the number of flights. These include:
- airframe maintenance necessitated by number of landings (e.g. wheel fittings; tyres);
- charges for traffic control and navigation;
- landing charges;
- terminal services (such as cleaning; power connection; charges for cargo handling, loading and unloading; parking); and
- insurance against individual flight risks, for example, crew, cargo and other property.

16.5.3 Road transport cost structure

Of all forms of transport, road transport has the highest proportion of variable costs to total costs. Among the factors leading to this are the following:

- The road infrastructure is publicly owned. Governments typically recover road-user cost responsibility through levies included in the price of fuel and toll tariffs, thereby converting a fixed cost responsibility into variable transport expenditure.
- Terminal facilities are less capital-intensive than the terminal facilities of other forms of transport.
- The fuel consumption of road transport vehicles is relatively high, making fuel cost a proportionally large variable-cost component.

16.5.3.1 Fixed costs
The following paragraphs summarise the fixed-cost items relating to road transport.

Overhead costs
- Land and buildings (premises, offices and warehouses)
- Terminal facilities (vehicle depots, parking areas, garages, fixed loading facilities and equipment)
- Managerial and administrative expenditure and other support functions

Standing costs
A business has to invest capital when purchasing a vehicle or make a commitment when leasing or renting a vehicle. The standing cost can be either the cost of the lease (or rental), or the depreciation plus the interest burden on the investment. It also includes all time-bound, vehicle-specific coss.

Depreciation
The depreciation of a vehicle amounts to the difference between the purchase price of the vehicle, excluding tyres (since tyre wear is a separate running-cost item) and its resale price.

Interest on capital (opportunity cost)
Interest is not an autonomous cost item, but rather an inseparable and unavoidable part of the cost of capital employed. The interest cost arises from the opportunity cost associated at all times with money or capital invested in the purchase of the vehicles.

Licences
This item represents a compulsory levy for the right to use public roads. It is a fixed cost because it involves the annual payment of a given amount.

Insurance

There are various types of insurance relating to transport operations. These range from comprehensive fleet insurance to separate insurance for individual vehicles against a variety of risks. Insurance is generally taken out against:
- the damage to and loss of a firm's own vehicles and damage to the vehicles of other parties;
- the damage to and loss of payload and crew;
- damage caused to other property; and
- public and private liability.

Comprehensive insurance packages also provide cover against theft, fire and other damage to vehicles and property occurring when the vehicle is off the road. If one insures each vehicle separately, the annual premium is merely allocated to each vehicle. If the fleet is insured as a whole, apportionment of the annual premium becomes more intricate. It can either be divided equally among the total number of vehicles, or it can be allocated according to the type, size, capacity, accident record, operating area and distance covered by each vehicle.

Crew costs

If vehicle crews (drivers and drivers' assistants) are appointed permanently, they are paid even when a vehicle is not in service. Their basic remuneration package is a standing-cost item. Costs incurred for overtime and sundry allowances are part of the trip cost and therefore vary. If the overtime assumes a fixed pattern (for example, shifts), it becomes a standing cost.

16.5.3.2 Variable costs

Running-cost items for road transport comprise fuel consumption, tyre wear, engine oil consumption and maintenance.

Fuel consumption

Fuel consumption constitutes the largest single running-cost item and, in the case of the majority of road transport modes, the biggest component of the total transport cost. It amounts to between 25 and 35 per cent of the total transport cost of the various types of road transport vehicles.

Tyre usage

The cost of tyre usage can be ascribed to three factors: tread wear, punctures and casing damage. Tyre cost is expressed in terms of cents per kilometre. It is calculated by dividing the purchase price of the tyres by the expected amount of kilometres they should cover.

Engine oil consumption

Engine oil consumption is increased through impurities – which necessitate oil replacement – and through loss from leakage, combustion and evaporation – which necessitate oil replenishment. Engine oil consumption constitutes the smallest running-cost item and, although its cost is expressed in c/km, physical consumption is usually expressed as litres (or fractions of a litre) per 1 000 km.

Maintenance

Maintenance cost is generally the second-largest running-cost item. Maintenance cost is the cost involved in keeping a vehicle:
- in good mechanical and electrical working order;
- roadworthy in terms of legal regulations; and
- in an appropriate condition for the purpose for which it is intended.

It includes the cost of servicing and lubrication (excluding engine oil, which is a separate running-cost item); examination and adjustments of parts; and the overhaul, repair and/or replacement of defective parts.

Trip-specific operating costs

A few trip-specific operating cost items occur on certain journeys. These are:
- toll fees payable where road sections are tolled;
- permit fees, in the case of trips into neighbouring countries;
- escort fees, when certain abnormal loads are carried;
- accommodation allowances for vehicle crews; and
- handling costs at trip ends when consignors and consignees are unable to provide handling equipment.

16.5.4 Rail transport cost structure

Due to the high capital investment in rail infrastructure (railway lines and terminal facilities, such as large administrative buildings, stations, marshalling and classification yards, sheds, goods depots and workshops) and the longevity of rolling stock, such as freight wagons, the ratio of fixed costs to total costs is very high.

Because the unit cost decreases when output increases, rail transport can gain the benefits of economies of scale when utilisation increases – and even more so in the case of a double-track operation with long trains. As a result, rail transport possesses a cost advantage over road transport with respect to bulk loads that are conveyed over long distances.

Total rail transport costs can be classified in a continuum of fixed to variable costs. The first two items in this list are fixed costs, while the rest are predominantly variable costs:
- Depreciation
- Administration and management overheads
- Maintenance of facilities, rail tracks and rolling stock
- Traffic expenditure
- Running costs
- General costs

Depreciation and overheads are not affected by traffic fluctuations. Maintenance of railway tracks, and especially of rolling stock, varies according to the volume of traffic. Maintenance of facilities keeps pace with traffic fluctuations to an extent. Traffic expenditure, running costs and general costs are directly dependent on the volume of traffic.

The allocation of cost to transport units is very difficult, because direct and indirect costs are almost indiscernible, and because joint and common costs occur. These problems have prompted rail carriers to find other criteria for identifying and allocating costs. The following five main cost groups, where the allocation of the costs is based on performance criteria, are indicative of one method of recording rail transport costs:
- Terminal costs (expressed in cost per ton of freight)
- Track costs (expressed in train kilometres)
- Traction power cost (expressed in locomotive kilometres)
- Train operating costs (expressed in train kilometres)
- Marshalling costs (expressed in shunting hours)

The ratio of fixed cost to total cost of rail transport is substantially higher than that of road transport. For this reason it is usually cheaper to use road transport than rail for short distances, and to use rail transport for long hauls. Point A in Figure 16.2 represents the distance where road and rail transport costs per ton of freight are equal. For distances shorter than A, road is the cheaper mode; for distances longer than A, rail is the cheaper mode. The equal cost distance for the carriage of standard intermodal containers by road and rail is approximately 520 km, with minor variances for different economies.

Figure 16.2 Comparative road and rail cost per freight ton over distance

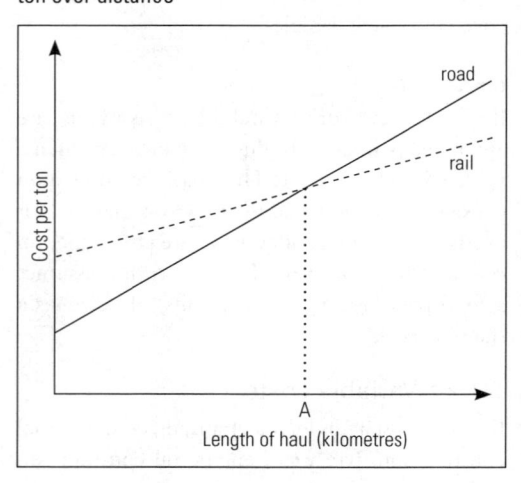

16.5.5 Pipeline transport cost structure

As with rail transport, pipelines provide their own right of way. Since the pipe component, the pumps and the tank and plant facilities are highly specialised and durable, fixed cost constitutes a high portion of the total cost – the highest of all modes. Pipeline transport is highly efficient when the utilisation of capacity remains consistently high. Transport cost per unit handled rises rapidly if actual usage falls below capacity, because of the high ratio of fixed cost to total operating cost.

The fixed costs of pipeline transport can be classified in a sequence from almost permanent through to items that are fixed for a one-month period, and include:
- pipeline right of way;
- pipes;
- storage facilities;
- terminal buildings;
- pumps;
- management and administration overheads;
- routine maintenance of facilities, pipes and pumps; and
- monthly charge for a continuous minimum availability of electricity supply.

In the construction of the long-run cost function, the three principal fixed-cost components are those that change with pipe diameter, those that change with pumping power and those that change with pipeline length.

Fixed costs that change with pipe diameter include the interest and depreciation on the pipeline itself; the costs associated with constructing and laying the pipeline; the costs of steel, pipe coating, valves and corrosion protection; and the scheduled maintenance costs of the pipeline. Although these costs rise as pipe diameter increases, the rise in costs is less than proportional to the increase in diameter for various reasons. The width of the pipeline right of way (i.e. the cost of the servitude) remains the same regardless of pipeline diameter. In most cases, the width of the trench in which the pipe is laid remains the same (or increases very little). Whenever wall thickness remains the same, or increases to a lesser extent than the increase in the diameter, proportionally less steel is needed as the inside diameter of the pipe increases. And finally, the routine inspection, monitoring and general management costs for a large pipeline are only fractionally more than for a small pipeline of the same length.

Fixed costs that change with pumping power include the interest and depreciation on the investment in pumping stations and the outlays for electric power, plus the unavoidable labour used in the routine maintenance and the operation of pumping stations.

Fixed costs that change with pipeline length rise in direct proportion to increases in distance. These costs include the initial surveying and obtaining the right of way for the pipe; additional pumps; tankage; trenching and laying the pipe; backfilling the trench and restoring the surface; making good damages to terrain crossed; and scheduled (preventive) maintenance and operation of a communications system. Hence, longer pipelines do not give rise to significant economies of distance, as directly proportional longer items (or more of these items) are required for longer haulage distances. Furthermore, the terminal costs are relatively small. Thus the cost per ton-kilometre is sensitive to the regularity of flow, but not to the length of the pipe. Consequently, there is no distinct taper in the tariffs charged per ton-kilometre as the length of haul increases.

The only discernible variable costs (where variable costs refer to cost items with a commitment period of less than one month) in pipeline transport are the electricity (or other energy) consumed during pumping over and above the volume that is paid under the fixed availability charge; overtime wages paid to maintenance staff to repair faulty components; and the actual repair costs over and above routine or preventive maintenance.

There is one operating-cost item that varies according to the number of slugs that are pumped. (A slug is an uninterrupted throughput of a single commodity, for example 50 million litres of unleaded petrol, transported in one batch.) This is the cost of recycling the intermix that develops between consecutive slugs. Whenever a petroleum product arriving at a pump station starts to contain 2 per cent or more per volume of the following slug, the diluted fuel is diverted to an intermix tank until the following slug is at least 98 per cent pure. The intermix is then mixed into the second slug at such a rate that its purity does not drop below 98 per cent per volume. In view of the fact that the intermix only occurs where two slugs meet, the unit cost thereof will decline with increasing slug volume or length. For example, in exactly the same pipe section and at the same pumping rate, the same volume of intermix will develop between two slugs of petrol and diesel of 10 million litres each as will between two slugs of petrol and diesel of 20 million litres each. When only one commodity is pumped continuously there is no intermix.

16.5.6 Sea transport cost structure

The cost structure of sea transport is similar to that of air transport. It is characterised by a high proportion of variable costs due to the fact that the means of transport involved, namely the sea, does not require investment and seaports are not owned or supplied by shipping firms. Expenses in ports can be as high as 40 per cent of sea transport costs. However, these obligations only arise when a port is visited.

16.5.6.1 Fixed costs

Overhead costs
- General overheads (management, administration and office commitments)
- Marketing costs (advertising, sales costs and agents' commission)
- Marine costs (land administration directly involved in shipping activities)

Standing costs
- Maintenance and repairs
- Vessel inspection and check-ups (usually every four years)
- Insurance
- Depreciation
- Fixed crew costs (unless contracted for individual voyages)
- Radio and communication dues
- Auxiliary stores aboard

16.5.6.2 Variable costs

Variable costs of shipping are voyage-specific and include:
- fuel;
- crew costs (when contracted for individual voyages);
- port and other terminal costs;
- insurance to cover risks on the water;
- maintenance relating to motion;
- freight (all costs associated with freight storage, loading, stowing and unloading); and
- miscellaneous sailing costs.

Table 16.1 provides a comparative summary of the most salient economic features of the five modes of freight transport.

16.6 Cost trade-offs in transport

An objective in logistics management is to be efficient across the entire product supply chain. This objective can be achieved by minimising system-wide costs, from goods flow (i.e. transport and materials handling on the one hand) to warehousing and keeping inventory of raw material, semi-finished goods and finished goods on the other hand. Therefore, the emphasis is not on simply the cheapest or fastest transport, or on reducing inventories, but rather on an integrated and coordinated logistics approach. The acceptance of the total-cost concept has changed the relative importance of the different logistics activities and has led to cost trade-offs between transport/goods flow services and the operation of warehouse and production facilities assuming greater importance. For example, traditional wisdom is that materials can be carried and handled most efficiently by using maximum-size vehicles and handling equipment to reduce the number of trips needed for a given amount of material. While reducing the number of trips required is a good objective, the drawback of this approach is that it tends to encourage the acceptance of big production lots, huge vehicles, high-volume handling equipment and large storage space requirements. Small unit loads necessitate continuous goods flow processes, but allow for more flexible, responsive and less expensive goods flow systems.

The concept of total cost for the overall logistics system is illustrated in Figure 16.3 (page 354). The minimum point on the total annual transport cost curve is at four storage facilities. With one warehouse only the combined cost of warehousing and inventory keeping is at a minimum. However, transport cost is high because

Table 16.1 Comparison of salient economic features of transport modes

Economic characteristics	Air	Road	Rail	Pipeline	Sea
Cost	High	High/moderate	Moderate	Low	Lowest
Cost structure (fixed-cost to total-cost ratio)	Balanced	Lowest	High	Highest	Balanced
Predominant intramodal market type	Oligopoly	Open to oligopoly	Natural monopoly; duopoly when access is open	Natural monopoly	Open (charters) to oligopoly (liner operators)
Predominant intermodal competition	Road: small shipments; sea: trans-oceanic	Rail: breakbulk and containers; air: small shipments with route lengths > 1 000 km	Road: breakbulk and containers; coastal shipping	Rail when pipeline operates close to capacity	Road and rail: inter-port services; air: trans-oceanic, small, high-value shipments
Market coverage	Terminal-to-terminal	Point-to-point	Terminal-to-terminal (with private sidings: yard-to-yard)	Terminal-to-terminal	Terminal-to-terminal
Economies of fleet size	Low	Moderate	Moderate	Lowest (referring to number of pipes)	Low
Economies of vehicle size	High	Moderate	Moderate	Highest (referring to pipe diameter)	High
Economies of distance	High	Low	Highest	Lowest (almost non-existent)	High

all deliveries take place from a single point to many customer destinations. This implies long trip turnaround times and a high ratio of empty running, because firstly, deliveries are unloaded outbound from the warehouse until the furthest customer is reached, and secondly, vehicles return empty. As Figure 16.3 shows, the total annual transport cost initially decreases as the number of storage facilities increases. As the initial number of warehouses increases, empty vehicle running can be reduced and overall fleet utilisation increases. As the number of storage facilities further increase the opportunity to achieve economy of density through load consolidation and the achievement of long-haul economy decline. These economies eventually vanish so that the total annual transport cost reaches a minimum (shown in Figure 16.3 at four warehouses) and immediately starts to rise as transport inefficiencies take further effect with a sustained addition of storage facilities. This rise takes place at a progressive growth rate per additional storage facility. The main reasons for the progressively rising transport cost are that:

- the number of trips increase;
- the trips become shorter and therefore more inefficient;
- vehicle loading and unloading times relative to travel time increase;

- more vehicles are required to maintain service levels; and
- although the number of storage facilities increase, their individual capacity decreases so that the proportion of transit stock increases at the cost of the transport function.

The total annual inventory-related cost increases with each additional warehouse. Figure 16.3 shows that to serve the same market with two storage facilities rather than with one would less than double the total annual inventory cost. Similarly, by increasing the number of facilities from two to three, with total storage capacity remaining constant, the total annual inventory cost would increase by less than half. With all subsequent increases in the number of storage facilities, the total annual inventory-related cost will increase less than proportionally to the increase in number of storage facilities. The point of lowest inventory cost is with a single store or warehouse.

As the number of warehouses increases, the economies of scale related to size of warehouse and large inventory levels decline, but less than proportionally to the increase in the number of warehouses (because the market size does not increase). A second reason for this trend is the problem of setting the safety stock level for inventories. Increasing the overall level of inventories will increase the inventory-carrying cost.

For the overall system, the lowest total annual cost is achieved with three storage locations. The identification of the least cost network of three storage locations in Figure 16.3 illustrates the trade-off relationship. The minimum total annual cost point for the system is not at the point of least cost for either transport or inventory.

In practice, the identification and measurement of total logistics cost is a complex matter. Many assumptions are required to perform logistics network analysis. The trade-off analysis, as illustrated in Figure 16.3, does not encompass the full complexity of total cost integration. First, inventory cost as a function of the number of warehouses is directly related to the desired level of inventory availability. If no safety stock is maintained in the system, total inventory requirement is limited to base and transit stock.

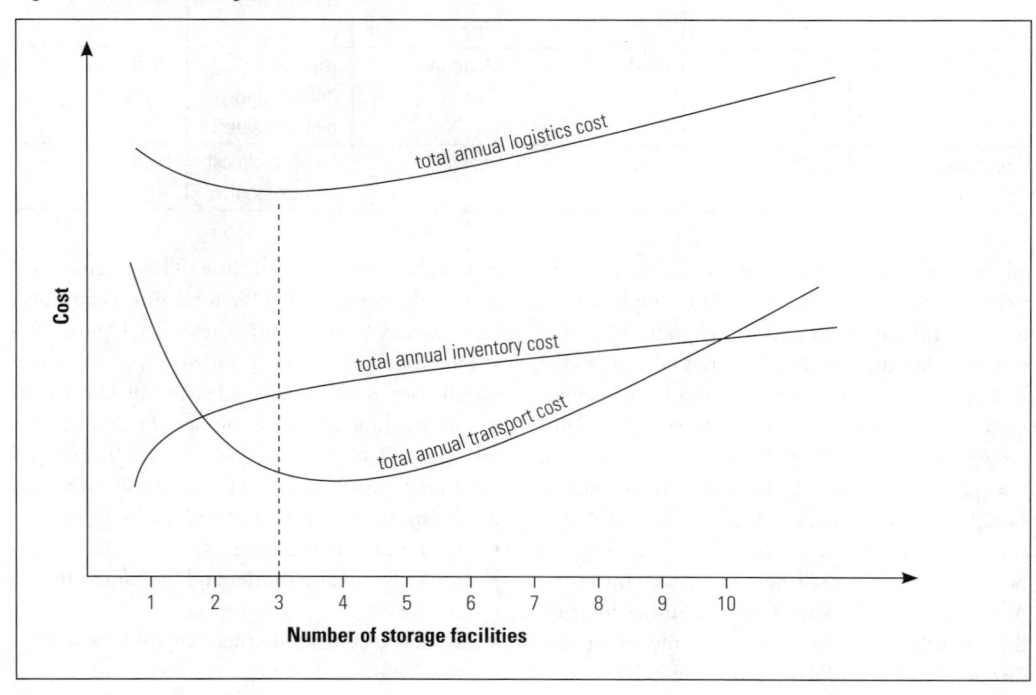

Figure 16.3 Least cost logistics network

In a no safety stock situation, the overall lowest cost for the system would be at or near the point of least transport cost. Therefore, a reliable forecast of the desired inventory availability and fill rate is a prerequisite for trade-off analysis and the minimum total cost solution.[4] Second, cost minimisation ought to be confined only to eliminating waste and not pruning costs at the expense of greater revenue. Reducing logistics costs makes sense only if the foregone profits are smaller than the cost reduction. Similarly, the acceptance of additional costs, such as an airfreight delivery instead of delivery with a cheaper, but slower, mode of transport, but which is not offset by lower warehousing, materials handling, inventory-carrying cost or other logistics cost savings is justified only if net revenue increases as a result (for example, through increased sales and customer retention).

In the absence of an integrated and coordinated logistics approach, transport decision makers may concentrate on a low-cost transport mode. The use of low-cost transport services may reduce total transport costs, but does not guarantee minimum total logistics costs. Low-cost transport is usually associated with slow and inflexible service, which means higher warehousing and inventory costs and lower customer satisfaction.

Whenever the transport function is treated as a cost centre, rather than as a profit centre, performance is measured upon transport costs incurred. The decision to use a high-cost transport mode or service is not desirable from the viewpoint of a transport-operating budget. In the absence of an integrated approach, the switch to any other high-cost, but more effective, transport service would not be made unless an incentive mechanism is in place whereby demand for additional expenditure by the transport function in favour of greater revenue for the firm as a whole is rewarded.

Pruning transport costs at the expense of greater revenue, or reluctance to incur additional transport expenditure in favour of more profit, means lost sales. Such foregone or sacrificed revenue opportunities represent a cost. This is known as opportunity cost. In view of the fact that the aim of the firm is to maximise profit, opportunity cost needs to be incorporated as a third variable in the cost trade-off process. However, opportunity cost does not represent a tangible cash flow; neither is it reflected in a business's accounts.

If a curve representing opportunity cost (i.e. the cost of lost sales) appeared in Figure 16.3, it would slope down to the right. As the number of warehouses increases, the opportunity for better order fulfilment and more effective customer services increases. The extreme case would be where each retail outlet (or another type of business customer) is served by its own dedicated warehouse with ample safety stock and that each such retail outlet is within walking distance from its customers. This would be very service-effective (no lost sales), but extremely cost-inefficient. The optimum level of logistics performance occurs where the aggregate of all three cost groups forms a minimum. These cost groups are:

- transport-related cost;
- inventory-related cost; and
- opportunity cost.

Including the latter cost into Figure 16.3 would move the overall minimum cost point to the right.[5]

16.7 Profit planning and control

Profit planning and control are crucial to carriers at operational, tactical and strategic management levels.

16.7.1 Tactical and operational aspects

Since profit results are sometimes not available until as late as 18 months after the beginning of a financial year, these results have little value for tactical and operational transport management. A faster method of controlling transport cost is needed to monitor daily activities.

When rendering a transport service, one apportions inputs, such as labour, vehicles and fuel, in a certain ratio. Each cost item comprises a quantity component and a price component, which, when multiplied, represent the cost per item. Costs for fuel, lubricants, maintenance, direct labour and so on are, therefore, easy to determine.

It is more difficult to calculate the item cost of overheads such as managerial and administrative costs, since one must first determine realistic criteria for apportioning each of the respective services to specific journeys.

Other cost items that are difficult to calculate and, therefore, often erroneously omitted, are durable means of production, such as vehicles and handling equipment, and non-durable, but slow-wearing inputs, such as tyres and vehicle parts. The result is often that the cost is not apportioned to certain transport outputs or services, simply because actual cost and perceived trip cost do not correlate.

The difference between actual trip cost and perceived trip expenses can be illustrated with the following example. A certain vehicle is capable of doing 40 000 km with the same set of tyres. If the vehicle covers on average 2 000 km per week, then the weekly cost of tyres will amount to one-twentieth of their purchase price. The same problem arises with the costs of interest and of depreciation.

Only by continuously monitoring the accrual of all the costs during the transport process is it possible to calculate the approximate profit generated by each journey and for the carrier to institute remedial measures when necessary.

16.7.2 Strategic aspects

To show an acceptable rate of return at the end of a financial period, a carrier must have a sound profit policy. The ideal is to add a sufficient profit margin to transport costs, subject to market constraints, to meet or exceed the desired return on capital invested.

The rate of return required by a carrier can be expressed through two values.

The first value is the cost of capital for the business. This value includes the opportunity cost of the capital needed to fund investments, as well as factors such as the risk of the market and the sector in which the business operates and the competitive position of the business.

The second value is the current return earned by the firm. This return needs to be above the former for the company to sustain its current profitability in the long run.

Any investment should exceed the cost of capital. If it does not, the firm loses value as the capital could be utilised more profitably elsewhere. It is important to preserve or enhance the current return to maintain current profitability.

The profit margins of the various segments of the business are not identical. Carriers need to divide the activities into categories and calculate specific returns for each category. Take care not to make substantial investments in lower return categories without realising that this will reduce the overall returns.

16.8 Tariff quoting

16.8.1 General overview

To attain business logistics objectives, such as maximum long-term profit, it is essential to cover total costs plus a sufficient surplus. The nature of transport activities, however, precludes total cost coverage on all individual link services at all times. Consequently, market factors relating to demand as well as supply will have a decisive impact on tariff policy. In some cases, say where fleet capacity is not fully utilised, marginal cost pricing may be justified. Services operating at a loss have to be cross-subsidised in the short term by services that generate surplus revenue. Carriers must, therefore, keep track continuously (i.e. with each trip) of the full extent of the costs involved in their services.

Broadly speaking, transport services may be priced using any of three tactics:
- The price (tariff) covers transport cost and makes provision for a profit. This is also known as total cost coverage or individual cost coverage.
- The carrier may, because of tactical business considerations, decide for limited periods to accept consignments at a tariff that does not fully cover the total costs, but covers all the direct costs caused by undertaking the service. This is known as marginal cost coverage.
- The carrier may charge higher tariffs that yield supernormal profits when an unparalleled and superior customer service is supplied. This method of maximum-limit, ceiling or

premium tariff quoting is based on the value-of-service principle, or how much users are willing to pay.

Total-cost coverage and marginal-cost coverage are supply-side pricing tactics. The floor, or minimum price, using these tactics, depends on how efficiently the transport function is being conducted. Value-of-service pricing is demand-oriented. The maximum price, using this tactic, depends on how effectively customers are served.

16.8.2 Total-cost pricing

Overhead costs are usually associated with the strategic aspects of transport supply; standing costs usually relate to the tactical aspects; and variable costs result from operational activities.

16.8.2.1 Overhead costs

Overheads can only be apportioned, and not allocated according to determinable cost criteria, to transport activities. One should select a method of apportionment that adequately reflects overheads for each trip. The most common bases for apportioning overhead costs are:
- the number of vehicles;
- the payload carried by vehicles;
- the distance travelled by vehicles;
- a combination of the previous two, expressed as ton-kilometres; and
- a surcharge on operating cost.

A one-ton truck may bear the same amount of overhead costs as a combination vehicle with a carrying capacity of 30 tons, thereby imposing an intolerable tariff load on parcels or small consignments carried with the one-ton truck. Therefore, ton-kilometres travelled per period (in other words, the fourth option above) is commonly regarded as an equitable method of apportioning costs, although it may place an excessive tariff load on heavy commodities with a low value, such as raw materials. In these circumstances, the carrier may decide to apportion overhead costs in proportion to the value of the commodities transported.

The apportioning method depends on the type of business and loads carried. Carriers need to find the most appropriate method to ensure that each sector of their operations bears the overall costs and hence delivers the desired profits.

16.8.2.2 Standing costs

Standing costs are period-bound obligations that are inherently coupled with a vehicle. They include depreciation, interest, licences, insurance and drivers' wages. Because standing cost has a direct bearing on a particular vehicle and does not relate to other vehicles, it is apportioned to individual trips for the period of use.

The apportionment of standing costs is generally effected as follows. The total time that the vehicle is used for each trip is expressed as a fraction of the time it can be realistically utilised over a certain period. This fraction is then multiplied with the total standing cost per period.

16.8.2.3 Running costs

Running costs vary with vehicle output and are assigned according to the distance travelled. For example, the cost of fuel, oil and tyres would be equal to the price of the quantity of fuel and oil consumed and the tyre tread wear over the distance.

In order to realise a return on each service, the tariff quoted should cover all of the above-mentioned overheads, standing and running costs plus a margin for profit. Transport services that are characterised by effective competition and few opportunities for cross-subsidisation are typically priced at levels that cover full costs, including a profit that equals the opportunity cost of capital.

16.8.3 Marginal-cost pricing

The variable cost items of transport represent marginal trip costs. Overhead costs represent indirect fixed-cost inputs that are common to all carrier activities and vehicles. There is not a causal relationship between individual trips or services that take place and overhead costs.

A direct causal relationship exists between standing cost and the use of vehicles during given financial periods. However, it is not possible to link standing costs directly to particular trips. Consequently, these costs are divided among the total number of trips simply on a proportional basis – often in relation to time consumed. This implies that the shorter the accounting period, the more fixed the costs tend to be. Conversely, the longer the accounting period, the greater the tendency of the fixed costs towards variability. Wages, which are a fixed item in the short term, will be the first to display signs of variability. The more intensively a vehicle is used, the more variable are the items that are fixed for the short term. When a vehicle is put to such intensive use that its lifespan is reduced so that the length of the accounting period exceeds the actual life of the vehicle, even depreciation assumes a purely variable character.

Direct-cost responsibility, therefore, can readily be allocated to a service or particular performance. In effect, it may be regarded as the incremental cost associated with actual performance. The direct cost of using a vehicle includes the variable vehicle cost and the specific fixed (i.e. standing) costs that are automatically coupled with the vehicle.

When applying the marginal-cost principle in tariff decision making, it is essential to ensure that the minimum cost recovered is equal to the costs that might be avoided by cancelling a service (the direct cost). The avoidable costs form the 'floor' in marginal cost pricing.

Carriers will undertake to carry loads at marginal cost for tactical reasons, provided they are able to cross-subsidise their total deficit – either from other remunerative services during the same period or from the same service during a period of surplus recovery. The latter method of recovering deficits attributable to marginal-cost pricing may also be applied in highly competitive conditions. If a tariff war develops or a market intruder makes its appearance, the carrier could lower its tariffs to the marginal-cost level until the market stabilises. At this stage, it can increase its tariffs to generate a surplus from which it can recover the earlier loss.

16.8.4 Value-of-service pricing

Whereas the minimum, or floor, tariff that can be charged for a transport service is determined by marginal cost, the maximum tariff is determined by the value that users attach to it. Value-of-service is also known as effectiveness pricing.

The value that a customer attaches to a transport service is determined by:
- the place and time utility obtained in getting a certain commodity to a specified destination at a certain time; and
- the reliability of the service (i.e. the consistency with which this level of service is achieved).

The level of utility is determined by the extent to which a carrier satisfies the needs of the user by supplying the desired level of service quality through offering acceptable goods security, transit time, reliability and flexibility of service.

It is only feasible to charge this type of tariff where a superior service, which cannot be matched by a competitor, is offered. If the use of this tariff is taken to extremes, a competitor will emulate the service or the user will resort to private transport.

16.9 Conclusion

The efficiency and economy with which inputs are organised to achieve set goals have a direct effect on the competitiveness of a business. Economy refers to the optimum use of resources so that the maximum benefit is gained from any given output. Economies of scale in transport are dependent on the attainment of any or all of three subgroups of economies. These are economies of density, economies of scope and economies of distance. The extent to which any of these economies may be achieved within each transport mode is determined largely by its physical characteristics and cost structure.

The acceptance of the total-cost concept has changed the relative importance of the different logistics activities and has led to cost trade-offs between them. The optimum level of logistics performance occurs where the aggregate of transport-related cost, inventory-related cost and the cost of lost sales (opportunity cost) forms a minimum.

Profit planning and control are crucial to the carrier at operational, tactical and strategic management levels. Broadly speaking, transport services may be priced using any of three tactics: total-cost coverage; marginal-cost coverage; and value-of-service (premium) tariff.

Key terms

Air transport
Common costs
Cost structure
Cost trade-off
Economy of density
Economy of distance
Fixed cost
Joint cost
Marginal cost
Operating cost
Overhead cost (OC)
Pipeline transport
Rail transport
Road transport
Running cost (RC)
Sea transport
Standing cost (SC)
Total cost
Total-cost concept
Variable cost

Case study

Alpha Carriers operates a fleet of 30 combination vehicles. One of these is a four-axle combination vehicle consisting of a truck tractor and a semi-trailer, covering 110 000 km per annum. This vehicle combination can carry (a) a 20-ton load of bulk goods, or (b) 14 pallets of merchandise (single layer), or (c) two 6 m goods containers. The April 2008 costs of this vehicle are shown in Table 16.2.

RC + SC + OC = TVC (total vehicle cost)
TVC per annum at 110 000 km   = R1 016 171
Vehicle cost per kilometre at 110 000 km = R   9,238

You are requested to determine the following in April 2008 terms:

1. What will TVC per annum be at an annual travel distance of 80 000 km and 120 000 km respectively? Assume that driver cost remains the same (i.e. no overtime wages are incurred and driver wages are still paid on days when no driving takes place).

2. Assuming that there are 225 working days per annum and that the driver is permanently employed, what amount of vehicle cost will be avoided if four days of work (at 400 km/day) in the year are cancelled?

3. Business is hard to find and Alpha Carriers cannot find work that covers TVC plus a mark-up for profit. It is expected that business will pick up in a month's time. Alpha Carriers decides to revert to marginal cost pricing, which enables them to find work during the slack month, entailing 8 000 km of travel. This is conditional on Alpha Carriers charging avoidable cost plus 20 per cent to make a contribution to unavoidable cost. What should the tariff be per kilometre?

4. The 110 000 km that the vehicle covers per annum comprise 1 100 return trips of 100 km each. On each trip (a) 20 tons of bulk goods are delivered and empty packaging material is brought back; or (b) 14 pallets of merchandise are delivered and 14 loose pallets are returned; or (c) two 6 m goods containers are delivered and two empty containers are returned. Loading and unloading are undertaken by the shippers and receivers of the goods. Alpha Carriers charges a tariff equal to TVC plus 15 per cent. How much do they charge to deliver (a) a ton of bulk goods; (b) a pallet of merchandise, and (c) a 6 m goods container?

Table 16.2 Alpha Carriers' vehicle costs (2008)

Overhead cost per annum (OC)	R87 524
Standing vehicle costs per annum (SC)	R257 867
Cost of capital	R158 782
Licences (Gauteng)	R9 357
Insurance	R46 500
Crew costs (driver only)	R43 228
Running costs (RC) (c/km)	609,8c
	(= R670 780 p.a.)
Fuel consumption (47,0 ℓ/100 km @ 946,7 c/ℓ)	445,0c
Tyre usage	53,7c
Engine oil consumption	11,1c
Maintenance cost	100,0c

Case study

Newly formed Electron Gimicks and Optics (EGO) has obtained the sole right to market the products of Electrajap Electronic and Optical Products in South Africa. EGO has signed a contract with a third-party physical distribution service provider to distribute its products and spare parts during the first five years of business. EGO judges that the volume of products and spare parts to distribute will reach a plateau at the end of the fifth year of distribution, and that the initial buyers of these products will by then either start replacing their original purchases, or start buying spare parts to repair and/or upgrade their products.

EGO intends to conduct its own physical distribution from the beginning of the sixth year of business. EGO foresees that it will have at least three fierce competitors which will distribute products of approximately the same quality. This implies that any less-than-excellent logistics service provision will lead to a loss of sales.

EGO has to determine how many warehouses it should have in order to service the South African market from the beginning of the sixth year of business. The total annual inventory-related cost with one warehouse serving the entire market will amount to R48 million.

EGO's logistician has determined that the total annual inventory-related cost (TIC) to service the South African market can be determined by the following formula:

TIC = R34,83 million + $13{,}17 \times W$

where

W = number of warehouses to service the entire South African market.

With only one warehouse, EGO's total annual transport cost will amount to R96 million. As the number of warehouses increases from one warehouse, the total annual cost of transport will decrease by 15 per cent. For example, with two warehouses the total annual transport cost will amount to R81,6 million. This rate of cost decline will continue up to the point where the whole country is served by five warehouses. With five warehouses, total annual transport cost will be at its minimum. As the number of warehouses increases above five, the total annual transport-related costs increase by 8,5 per cent for each additional warehouse, with the percentage increase calculated using total annual transport cost with the last warehouse as base. EGO's logistician and marketing expert have estimated that all customers' orders can be perfectly fulfilled if they are served by 20 or more well-placed warehouses (i.e. the cost of lost sales would be zero). As the number of warehouses decreases (below 20) the total annual cost of lost sales will increase. This cost will be R0,5 million for 19 warehouses. A further decrease in warehouses from 19 downwards will result in a 34 per cent accumulative increase in the total annual cost of lost sales per warehouse below 19. The total annual cost of lost sales will reach a maximum of R97,02 million if the entire country is served from one warehouse only.

You are requested to determine and explain the following:

1 The number of warehouses that will result in the minimum-cost distribution outcome, ignoring the cost of lost sales.
2 The number of warehouses that will result in the minimum-cost distribution outcome by taking the cost of lost sales into consideration.
3 Which of (1) or (2) would you recommend that EGO implements, assuming that all forecasts are correct?
4 Give reasons for the trend in TIC that will occur as the number of warehouses increases.
5 Give reasons for the trend in total transport cost that will occur as the number of warehouses increases.
6 Explain why cost of lost sales will decline with an increase in the number of warehouses.

Questions

1 Explain what efficiency in transport means and discuss whether it is possible to operate efficiently when customers need to be served effectively.
2 Define economies of scale and mention three aspects (with supporting examples) that can help to attain economies of scale in transport.
3 Discuss the three subgroups of economies on which economies of scale depend.
4 Outline the cost structure of each mode of transport and identify the cost items that appear on the strategic, tactical and operational levels.

5 Indicate the marginal cost and avoidable costs of:
   a) Adding or withdrawing a single consignment, consisting of a small parcel, to or from a large vehicle load.
   b) Scheduling one additional trip or cancelling a trip.
   c) Adding or withdrawing a specific haulage service, involving four vehicles, to or from an existing transport operation engaging 40 vehicles.
6 Explain what is meant by a cost trade-off and identify the cost groups between which cost trade-offs within the logistics process can be made.
7 Discuss and explain through the use of a graph how a total-cost analysis is performed in the logistics process.
8 Outline why profit planning and control are crucial at operational, tactical and strategic transport management levels.
9 Discuss how the financial integrity of a professional transport carrier can be supported by making use of total-cost, marginal-cost and value-of-service pricing tactics.

Consult the web

Activity-based costing – the ABC Authority: www.abctech.com

Consult the books

Bardi, E. J., Coyle, J. J. and Novack, R. A. 2006. *Management of Transportation*. Mason: Thomson.

Bowersox, D. J., Closs, D. J. and Cooper, M. B. 2007. *Supply Chain Logistics Management*, 2nd edition. New York: McGraw-Hill.

Button, K. J. 1993. *Transport Economics*, 2nd edition. Aldershot: Edward Elgar.

Papacostas, C. S. and Prevedouros, P. D. 2001. *Transportation Engineering and Planning*, 3rd edition. Englewood Cliffs: Prentice Hall.

Pienaar, W. J. 2005. 'Operations research: An indispensable toolkit for the logistician', *Orion* 21(1): 77–91.

Notes

1 Button, K. J. 1993: 72.
2 Papacostas, C. S. and Prevedouros, P. D. 2001: 240.
3 Bardi et al. 2006: 249.
4 Bowersox et al. 2007: 311.
5 Pienaar, W. J. 2005: 15.

17 Transport management

W.J. Pienaar

> **Learning outcomes**
>
> After you have studied this chapter, you should be able to:
> - explain what is understood by strategic, tactical and operational transport management;
> - describe the policy instruments that governments use to influence the performance of the freight transport industry;
> - discuss the considerations of efficiency and effectiveness when choosing ancillary transport and professional carriers;
> - discuss the features of transport service effectiveness and the ways of selecting a professional carrier;
> - discuss traffic consolidation;
> - supply guidelines for the efficient routing and scheduling of long-distance trips and of collection and delivery trips; and
> - explain how incoming traffic can be coordinated in order to enhance effectiveness.

17.1 Introduction

The conveyance of goods from one place to another within supply chains is a key activity and the largest cost component of business logistics. This places exceptional challenges on the management of the transport function.

First, prudent transport management can be instrumental in gaining competitive advantage. It must help to ensure that the right goods are delivered at the designated place and time, in the required condition and quantity and at an acceptable cost or price. This objective requires that the transport function should be managed as effectively as is necessary to conform optimally to the requirements of clients and customers.

Second, the sheer magnitude of freight transport activities (which, in South Africa, constitute 57 per cent of all business logistics expenses – see page 3) requires that transport should be utilised as sparingly as possible, whilst still adhering to the effectiveness requirements alluded to above. Considering that freight transport in South Africa amounted to R157 billion in 2006, or 9 per cent of the country's GDP, it is obvious that efficient management of the transport function within product supply chains should be afforded a high priority. Often, it may be the case that it is easier to save one rand through more efficient transport than it is to gain one more rand in revenue through more effective transport.

The optimal trade-off between transport efficiency and transport effectiveness – as well as managing transport optimally alongside other functional activities within the broader context and objectives of the entire product supply chain – requires that the transport activity should be managed holistically. This means that management of the transport function should be led by the strategic business objectives that transport serves. The strategic objectives within transport management in turn give guidance to tactical decision making. The latter eventually dictates how transport operations will be performed.

This chapter focuses on the following areas:
- Management of the transport function on the strategic, tactical and operational levels
- The ways in which governments can affect the performance of the freight transport sector through its strategic influence

- The prerequisites for efficient and effective transport service provision
- The organisation of efficient goods flow, and the successful management of transport operations
- The coordination of incoming traffic (see note below)

(Note that transport is a broader concept than traffic. While freight transport refers to the conveyance of goods from one place to another, traffic refers to the movement, or presence, of vehicles along routes.)

17.2 Strategic transport management

17.2.1 Policy instruments of governments that affect the performance of the freight transport sector

We have seen that governments around the world find reasons deemed to be in the public interest to intervene in transport. In an attempt to pursue certain economic, social, political and strategic goals, governments to a lesser or greater extent apply policy instruments that affect the availability and performance of transport. Transport and logistics managers need to be mindful of these instruments because, although the freight transport industry has been economically deregulated in the vast majority of countries internationally, government intervention in the industry still influences strategic transport management decision making, which, in turn, affects performance on tactical and operational levels.

A set of nine instruments can be identified that governments apply to influence the performance of the freight transport industry (elaborated in the following sections):
- Legislation
- Direct supply
- Fiscal measures
- Monetary measures
- Moral appeal and persuasion
- Policies relating to strategic commodities
- Procurement policy
- Provision of information
- Research and development

17.2.1.1 Legislation

Governments exert statutory control over transport on three levels.[1] First, in the broadest sense, this covers the laws that govern the conduct of all legal subjects (for example, human behaviour and the activities of business). From this point of view, all business is regulated, since it is subject to the rules of conduct prescribed by the state.

Second, governments impose a) general industrial and business legislation in order to deal with market imperfection and failure (governing aspects such as restrictive and unfair business practices and mergers); and b) consumer-protection legislation (including areas like advertising). These embrace all forms of activity in the economy and not just transport.[2]

Third, legislation may be aimed specifically at the freight transport sector in order to control and direct the activities of both transport suppliers and users. This level of transport legislation includes economic and technical regulation.

Economic regulation is aimed at manipulating the supply of and demand for transport by controlling the quantity and price of transport (for example, market entry; place of operation; service volume; maximum and minimum tariff levels; and profit margins). From the late 1970s through to the early 1990s, governments of industrialised states liberalised the freight transport industry in their countries from these measures. The newly created free-market conditions in this sector enhanced the pursuit of more innovative and dynamic business logistics and supply chain initiatives and practices.

Technical regulation addresses a) qualitative issues (for example, traffic safety; the carriage of abnormal loads and dangerous goods; vehicle dimensions; gross vehicle and axle mass; and vehicle roadworthiness); and b) social matters (for example, external costs, such as vehicle emissions and noise, and the maximum number of driving hours per shift). Governments promulgate technical regulations and enforce them by law. The avenue through which they enforce these

regulations is by granting conditional permissions and then policing and monitoring the way in which use is made of the permissions. Examples of these are:
- toll road concessioning;
- vehicle roadworthiness certification and annual vehicle licensing;
- licensing vehicle drivers and granting professional driver permits;
- a permit system to carry hazardous or dangerous goods and abnormally sized loads; and
- area licensing (e.g. a quota system to limit the number of vehicles entering congested areas during hours of business).

Although these measures are technical and social, they also significantly impact on the business performance of the freight transport industry.

17.2.1.2 Direct supply
Different tiers of government and state corporations are providers of a wide range of transport services (for example, rail and air transport operations). They are also responsible for supplying transport infrastructure (for example, railway tracks, roads, seaports and airports) and support services (for example, navigation and traffic control).

17.2.1.3 Fiscal measures
Governments may use their fiscal powers either to increase or reduce the costs of different modes of transport or services in certain areas or over certain routes by imposing taxation or granting subsidies. They also may influence the factor costs of transport inputs through import duties, customs and excise levies.

17.2.1.4 Monetary measures
Governments may use their monetary powers to influence the quantity of money supply by manipulating the interest rate and applying credit control. The latter may include direct control over credit arrangements (for example, determining minimum deposit requirements and maximum payback periods when vehicles and other durable transport equipment are procured through hire-purchase and lease agreements).

17.2.1.5 Moral appeal and persuasion
This is usually a weak policy instrument, often involving educational messages, or rendering advice on issues like safety (for example, publicising the advantages of not overloading vehicles, or not speeding). It may, however, be effective when the alternative to accepting advice is the exercise by government of its powers, such as the refusal of a permit or licence, or the withdrawal of a subsidy.

17.2.1.6 Policies relating to strategic commodities
The freight transport sector is a major user of energy, especially petroleum products, and a wide spectrum of other raw materials and intermediate goods. Government policies relating to these matters can have a significant influence on transport, even more so when these commodities or goods are imported or when international conflict prevails.

17.2.1.7 Procurement policy
Most government activities require the use of transport services. Therefore, through their position as large consumers/users, governments may exert a degree of countervailing power over transport operators and input suppliers. A government body might, for example, require that a successful tenderer provide in-house training to a number of junior public officials, or that a portion of the provider's income must be invested in a project that promotes government policy. Governments may also wish to demonstrate social responsibility by preferring to procure inputs from groups that may be judged to come from disadvantaged backgrounds.

17.2.1.8 Provision of information
Through various agent bodies governments provide technical advice to transport operators (for example, navigation services for aviation and weather services for shipping) and provide general information to improve decision making within transport (for example, information on international trade arrangements).

17.2.1.9 Research and development
Governments may promote innovation within, and the development of, transport through their own research activities, or by supporting and

commissioning outside research, such as research development projects conducted by academic institutions. These are usually conducted or financed in the public interest by governments, as transport operators/providers might not have the capacity to conduct such research.

17.2.2 Selecting transport services

17.2.2.1 Overview

Carrier selection is a strategic transport management decision. Selecting carriers (and by implication also the choice of transport technology) necessary to offer service at the level demanded by customers is critical for achieving the business's goals.

A business may decide to invest exclusively in private (ancillary) transport; to outsource the transport function comprehensively to professional carriers; or to make use of a combination of the two types of operations.

Productivity can be improved through cost savings and increased returns. Cost savings are achieved by conducting the transport function more efficiently. Increases in return may stem from the selection of a transport-operating arrangement that leads to greater output by conforming more effectively to customer service requirements.

The economic deregulation of land freight transport allows more opportunity for users to negotiate rates and services with carriers. There are now more road and airfreight carriers and, therefore, more open competition. This makes customers more important to the carrier, which increases customer negotiating power. Users exert more control and pressure on carriers than in the past, so that freight tariffs have been reduced and tariff increases kept to a minimum.

The spectrum of ownership of transport services ranges from exclusively private to exclusively outsourced. The position of the transport function of a business on this spectrum depends on considerations of efficiency and effectiveness.

17.2.2.2 Efficiency considerations in service selection

Various efficiency considerations influence whether use is made of third-party (i.e. professional) transport service providers or not.

First, the volume of traffic, especially on line-haul movements, might be insufficient for private (ancillary) transport to achieve the economies enjoyed by professional carriers. The latter generally operate at an output level more conducive to economies of scale.

Second, it may be difficult for ancillary operators to obtain back hauls. This contributes to wastage and therefore to lower levels of vehicle utilisation than those achievable by professional carriers.

Third, professional carriers often have greater opportunity for labour specialisation. They are geared towards training, occupying, monitoring, administering and utilising staff employed as drivers, loaders, packers and mechanical and other technical staff.

Fourth, the adoption of an ancillary transport function entails new and additional issues that need to be dealt with within the management and administration of the business. Examples include additional trade unions; separate traffic and trade legislation; and fleet vehicle management matters that are not in line with the core management focus of the firm.

Fifth, private transport involves large capital investment. The capital that the firm invests in the transport fleet has alternative uses (foregone opportunities). This capital must, therefore, provide a return that at least equals the return yielded by the firm's primary investment opportunities. However, the current deregulated environment has produced substantially lower professional carrier rates, occasionally making ancillary transport more costly.

Regardless of the five considerations discussed above, one can sometimes manage to conduct private transport just as efficiently as professional operators do. If the same levels of efficiency and fleet utilisation are possible, theoretically private transport should cost less, since the business does not pay for the profit of the professional carrier.

17.2.2.3 Effectiveness considerations in service selection

If the transport decision makers are frustrated with inconsistent service performance, it might be necessary to move away from professional transport to private transport. Private transport gives a business greater control and flexibility in responding to buyer and facility requirements. This increased control and flexibility may result in lower inventory levels, better client service and satisfaction and greater efficiency at the loading and unloading docks. The business can also use private vehicles as an advertising medium. This can be especially effective when the vehicles are attractively designed and have courteous drivers, leaving a positive impression with potential customers.

The most pertinent service-performance determinants are suitability, accessibility, goods security, transit time, reliability and flexibility. Suitability and accessibility determine whether a carrier is capable of physically performing the desired services. Goods security, shorter and more reliable transit times and greater service flexibility are sources of competitive advantage.

Suitability

> Suitability is the technical ability of a carrier to provide the equipment and facilities required for transporting a particular commodity.

Appropriate technology and handling equipment are needed for a mode of transport (or vehicle types within a mode) to accommodate the conveyance of goods according to:
- their physical characteristics and stage of processing;
- their size (in terms of both mass and volume);
- the distance of conveyance; and
- the natural element on or in which they have to be moved (air, land, sea or water).

These four factors are usually interrelated so that they determine, in combination, the technical (physical) suitability of a mode or intermodal combination to conduct the required service.

For example, a small consignment of finished goods destined for another continent will most likely be transported by air. A full container load of semi-finished goods destined for another continent will probably be moved by ship. A bulk load of raw material that has to be moved over a long distance within a country will most likely be transported by rail. A small shipment of finished goods that has to be conveyed between two neighbouring cities will probably be transported by road. The ability to provide controlled temperatures or humidity and special handling facilities are examples of suitability factors.

Accessibility

> Accessibility is the ability of a carrier to provide service across a particular link and to physically gain access to facilities. More specifically, it is the ability to move goods from a designated point of origin to a desired point of use or consumption.

Accessibility (also known as market coverage) lies at the heart of the attainment of place utility. Within the supply chain of a product, the linkage of nodes where form utility is created (i.e. where raw materials and semi-finished goods are processed) constitutes the inbound, or supply, part of the chain. The distribution of finished goods (i.e. tangible products) to places where they are relatively scarce constitutes the outbound, or distribution, part of the supply chain. The method and tempo of processing and the marketing requirements during distribution greatly influence how close to the actual point of processing or storage the goods need to be delivered or collected.

Air and sea transport provide terminal-to-terminal service only.

Rail transport can at best provide a yard-to-yard service if both the origin and destination have a private siding at their disposal. Other origin–destination combinations for rail transport are yard to terminal; terminal to yard; and terminal to terminal.

Pipeline transport (in the case of petroleum commodities) can provide a tank farm to tank farm service only. Tank farms are situated at oil wells, refineries, seaports, pipeline terminals and wholesale depots. In theory, therefore, pipeline transport can provide a fully accessible service upstream between wholesale depots and a petroleum refinery. Downstream from depots, pipelines supply zero accessibility. Consequently, the distribution of petroleum products from the depot to the customer is conducted almost without exception by road transport.

Road transport provides the greatest accessibility of all modes of transport. Although constrained in its ability to provide a high-volume service over long distances, its unparalleled accessibility to facilities makes road transport the best mode of transport for the collection and delivery of almost all types of goods.

Goods security

Goods should arrive in the same physical condition and quantity as when tendered to the carrier. Insecure links in the service result in opportunity costs of foregone profits or productivity because the goods are not available for sale or use, or have to be sold at a lower price than intended.

Transit time

> Transit time is the total time that elapses between collection and delivery.

Of specific importance from a time-management perspective is the total time lapse between a consignment's prearranged collection time and the moment of its delivery. It is often assumed that the higher the speed, the higher the transport cost. In logistical terms, speed means short replenishment and delivery cycles and consequently less stock within the system.

The following high-value goods tend to be transported more effectively with the faster modes:
- Goods in which a relatively large amount of capital is tied up
- Goods that can realise high profits and must, therefore, reach the market quickly
- Goods that are susceptible to theft and, therefore, bear high insurance costs while in transit

Such goods are usually called supply-time-sensitive freight. Other types of freight that tend towards the faster modes are those with their own product-specific time sensitivity. Their intrinsic properties necessitate special in-transit care. Examples are highly perishable commodities; highly obsolescent items; fragile products; and live animals.

Some goods need to be transported in the shortest possible time due to demand-time sensitivity. This occurs when the demand is unpredictable, infrequent, seasonal or when goods are needed urgently or at short notice.

In summary, faster modes should be used whenever the premium paid for utilising them is less than the value added by transporting the goods faster than is possible with the next-fastest mode of transport.

Reliability

> Reliability refers to the consistency of the transit time provided by a carrier.

Generally, reliability is the most important service criterion.[3] It reflects the record or reputation for consistently maintaining punctual performance in terms of prearranged collection and delivery times of goods in the same condition and quantity as when tendered to the carrier. Reliability encapsulates both consistency in terms of time and physical security.

Certain modes, such as pipeline transport, are associated with reliability by virtue of their physical characteristics. However, operators of all modes have to demonstrate ability, readiness, and willingness – and need to build a sound track record – before the customer will regard them and their mode of transport as reliable.

Reliability lies at the heart of the attainment of time utility. Business logistics developments have led to large inventory reductions, so that the consequences of uncertain collections and deliveries have become serious. For example, with short production runs and within a system where there is only enough stock for a day's production, delayed supply delivery may stop the entire production process owing to lack of stock.

Reliable transit time impacts on inventory and stockout cost and customer service. Consistency of service is generally more important than transit time. It is the cornerstone on which customers base their scheduling and planning. Therefore, if a carrier provides a shorter transit time, but is inconsistent in delivering that level of service, customers will more likely choose a carrier with a longer transit time, but greater consistency of service.

Many benefits may result from providing a consistently punctual and secure service. These include improved customer goodwill; marketing and sales advantages; ability to plan more precisely; fewer stockouts; inventory cost savings; and improved efficiency resulting from increased opportunity to adhere to production schedules.

Flexibility

> Flexibility is the proven ability, readiness and willingness to effectively handle variations in load volumes, load mass and collection and delivery times and locations without any significant loss in overall efficiency.

Flexibility supports reliability when the transport operator is able to accommodate supply disruptions; schedule deviations; expedite the progress of a consignment; and alter collections and deliveries.

In order to be able to respond effectively to customer requests for flexibility, carriers need to have effective, user-friendly information services in place. Successful information and communication services presuppose the ability to:
- transfer promptly complete and accurate information about the movement of specific consignments at different points along the logistics channel; and
- notice quickly as soon as anything goes wrong.

Transit time, reliability and flexibility affect the nodal costs of inventory and stockouts. Shorter transit times, higher reliability and greater flexibility lead to lower inventory levels and stockout costs.

The transport mode employed depends on the needs of (a) the consignor, or shipper, (b) the service characteristics of the mode, (c) the nature of the commodity and (d) the needs of the receiver or consignee. A general service comparison of the five modes of freight transport is given in Table 17.1.

17.2.2.4 Carrier selection criteria

The potential carriers are limited to those that have the technical capability to perform the desired service. Technical capability refers to the suitability and accessibility of the carrier.

From the available technically capable carriers, a business selects those which offer services that promise to provide the greatest operational capability at an acceptable price. Operational capability refers to a carrier's ability, willingness and readiness to provide a secure service at desired transit times in a reliable and flexible fashion. The measure of success that the carrier achieves in providing a technically and operationally effective service determines the willingness (or not) of the business to pay for the carrier's efforts. When the carrier and the business agree on the price, the service and the standards, the selection process has been completed.

17.3 Tactical transport management

17.3.1 Consignments

A consignment consists of a specific lot of goods tendered together by a consignor at a point of origin for conveyance to a consignee at a single

Table 17.1 Approximate service comparison of transport modes

Service characteristics	Relative performance in general terms				
	High	High/moderate	Moderate	Moderate/low	Low
Suitability	Water	Rail	Road	Air	Pipeline
Accessibility	Road	Rail	Air	Water	Pipeline
Goods security	Pipeline	Air	Road	Water	Rail
Journey speed	Air	Road	Rail	Water	Pipeline
Reliability	Pipeline	Air	Road	Rail	Water
Flexibility	Road	Rail	Air	Water	Pipeline

point of destination. Consignments are also known as shipments, even if they are carried in vehicles other than ships.

Consignments may vary in size (mass, volume and number of items) and may consist of bulk or packed goods stowed together.
- The mass of individual consignments varies from less than a kilogram to many thousands of tons. The upper limit is constrained by the carrying capacity of vehicles, which varies according to the mode of transport. The range extends from as small as a one-ton truck (in the case of a road transport parcel service) to a long heavy-haul train or a bulk ocean carrier, capable of carrying more than a quarter of a million tons of iron ore.
- The state in which goods are best carried and the maximum quantity that can be carried in a single trip affect the volume of consignments. The term 'state of carriage' refers to the bulk or packed condition of the goods. The optimum size of the package depends on the handling requirements between origin and destination, and on the protection required against the standard hazards associated with carriage.
- The quantity of goods that constitutes a consignment is affected by the methods applied for marketing the particular commodity, convenience in transport and trip frequency.

The best way to achieve efficiency is to carry large mass, volumes and quantities. When the size of individual consignments is less than the carrying capacity of vehicles, the shipments should be consolidated so that every vehicle trip may constitute a full load, or as close to one as possible. When there is a mixture of small and large consignments as a result of marketing efforts, freight carriers consolidate them into single vehicle loads whenever it is economically viable.

17.3.2 Methods of consolidation

Broadly, there are three methods for consolidating traffic:[4]
- Transferring goods from small to large vehicles for the part of a journey that is common to all vehicles. For example, one can make use of consolidated line-haul or through-movements between consolidation and bulk breaking terminals.
- Pooling and redistributing traffic to reduce the total distance travelled.
- Reducing trip frequency.

17.3.2.1 Consolidated through-movements

To illustrate this method, let us assume that a number of consignments originate at separate points and are intended either for a common destination or for various destinations. A part of the route, however, is common to all the consignments.

If there is a single destination, the consignments are consolidated at a terminal, from where through-movement takes place on a common vehicle or combination of vehicles. The consignments are unloaded at the common destination.

Should the consignments have different destinations, the common vehicle takes them to a conveniently located bulk breaking facility. There they are dispersed into other vehicles that carry them to their various destinations. These methods are illustrated in Figure 17.1 (page 370).

17.3.2.2 Traffic pooling and distribution

In addition to changing the size of the load or the number of vehicles, as illustrated in Figure 17.1, consolidation may be directed towards preventing any overlap of movement.

Traffic from each point of origin may carry a full vehicle load comprising a number of consignments for separate destinations. Each vehicle may travel directly to all the various facilities of the consignees.

Alternatively, all consignments may be moved to a concentration point located close to all points of origin. At the concentration point, all the consignments are unloaded, sorted according to destination and transferred to other vehicles, so that one vehicle carries all consignments for a particular consignee or destination. This reduces the total overall distance travelled.

17.3.2.3 Reducing trip frequency

If a particular volume of goods needs to be conveyed every day, the consignments may be insufficient to fully engage the capacity of the vehicles. In such a case, one can reduce the frequency of trips. If the frequency is thus reduced, consignments must be stored until the time scheduled for vehicle departure. This implies a trade-off between transport costs and storage costs. It is important that this does not reduce the service level to below what is required by the customers.

17.3.2.4 Other methods of consolidation

The origins and destinations of consignments may be spread along a route, making it necessary to interrupt line-haul trips at each collection or delivery point on the route. An alternative is to nominate a number of points as the only places where consignments will be collected and delivered, necessitating some local collection and

Figure 17.1 Consolidation of traffic to eliminate separate trips along a common route

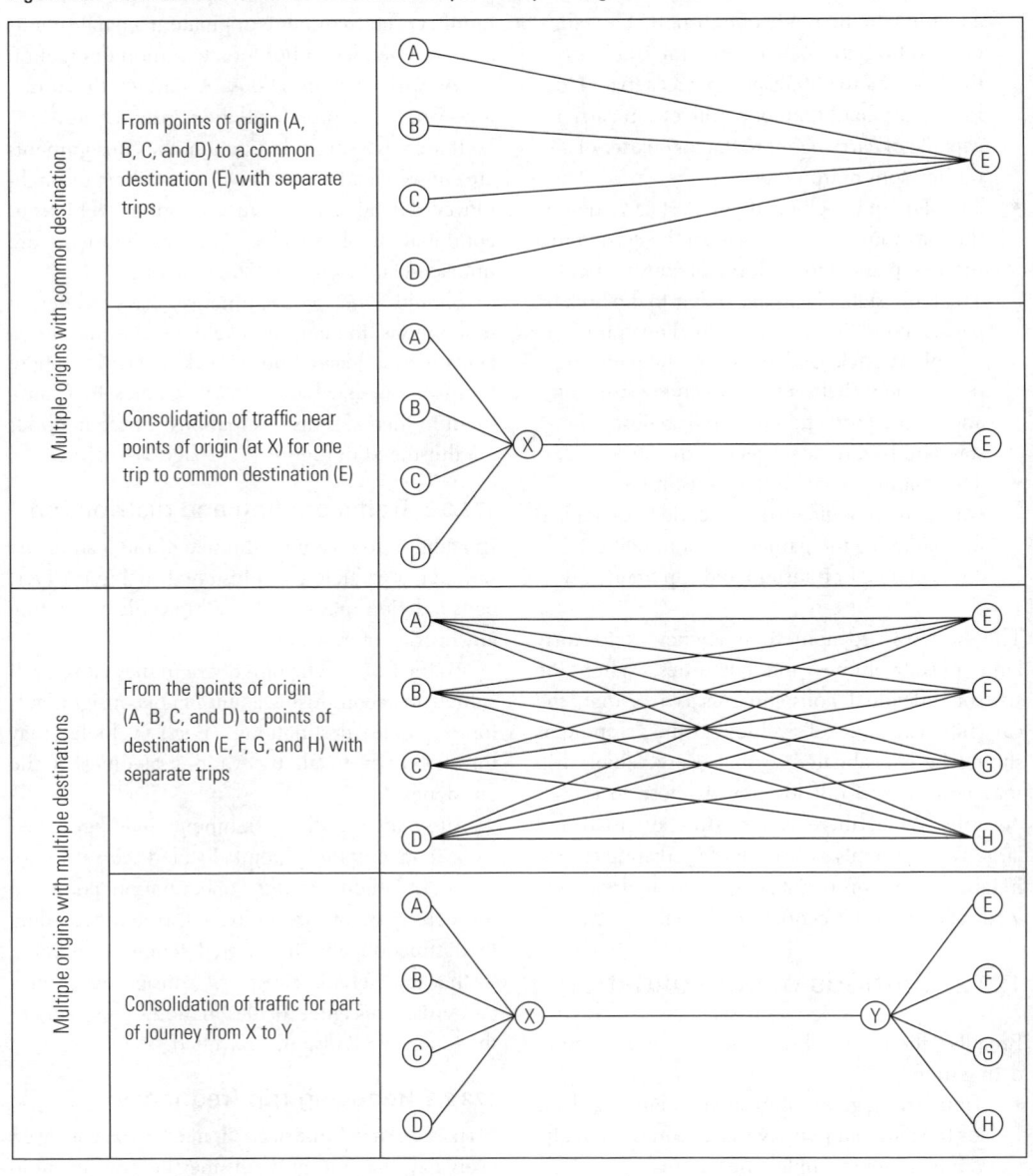

Multiple origins with common destination	From points of origin (A, B, C, and D) to a common destination (E) with separate trips	A, B, C, D → E
	Consolidation of traffic near points of origin (at X) for one trip to common destination (E)	A, B, C, D → X → E
Multiple origins with multiple destinations	From the points of origin (A, B, C, and D) to points of destination (E, F, G, and H) with separate trips	A, B, C, D → E, F, G, H
	Consolidation of traffic for part of journey from X to Y	A, B, C, D → X → Y → E, F, G, H

delivery to and from these stops. The location of each stop depends on the volume of traffic and the availability of local transport. This shortens the duration of a line-haul trip and consolidates loading and unloading. However, it has no effect on the volume of goods carried in any one trip. Unless consignors are prepared to bear the cost of operating partially loaded vehicles, carriers should always consider consolidation to increase vehicle utilisation.

Where traffic movement is continuous as, for example, with a pipeline system (or a conveyor belt, in the case of materials handling), capacity can be measured as the quantity throughput during a certain period. Consignments or batches of such commodities can be handled by the facilities in succession. Where compatible products are transported successively through the pipeline, the segregation between the batches can be reduced. Where the products are identical, no segregation is necessary.

With rail transport, traffic can be managed by consolidating:
- partial wagon loads into full wagon loads; and
- wagon loads into train sets.

Where carriage is provided by single road vehicles, consolidation is limited to loading two or more consignments into rigid vehicle units.

17.3.3 Unit loads and containers

> A unit load is a collection of items grouped together by being bound as a package, stacked securely on a portable platform (for example, a pallet) or packed into a container.

The greater the number of items transported in the unit load, the smaller the transport cost per item. Grouping goods into units has the following advantages:
- Efficiency. Storing, handling and carrying items in unit loads is more efficient, as repetitive and costly manual handling of individual items is eliminated.
- Goods identification and consignment tracing. Goods are more readily identifiable when stored in unit loads. Tracing and tracking items while they are in transit is also less problematic.
- Goods security. Unit loads can be handled with mechanical equipment. Mechanised handling requires orderly operational methods and is therefore more secure (and safe for staff) than manual handling. Unit loads are less susceptible to damage and theft than loose items.
- Space utilisation. Unitised loads can be stacked, stored, handled and stowed more efficiently than individual items, reducing the investment in storage facilities and vehicles.
- Transit time. Unit loads can be handled and stowed in less time, thereby providing better vehicle utilisation.

> Containers are rectangular, box-like devices used to consolidate, store, protect and handle a number of items as a freight unit.[5]

Once in the container, the goods are not handled again until unpacked from the container at the final destination. The container can be transferred from carrier to carrier – by road, rail, sea or aircraft – when transhipped from mode to mode.

Shipments of less than a vehicle load vary substantially in size. Therefore, there is a need for a preliminary consolidation into standard containers capable of enclosing a number of small shipments. A vehicle load can consist of one or more such containers, as Figure 17.2 (page 372) illustrates.

Using containers may enhance efficiency, as they reduce:[6]
- goods-handling cost at trip ends and transfer points by eliminating the handling of individual packages;
- the turnaround time of vehicles, as loading and unloading speed is increased;
- theft and damage while in transit by providing protection and security; and
- labour requirements, as containers are too large and heavy to be handled manually.

Containers have the following disadvantages:
- They cannot be handled in every port, which limits the number of shipping routes available.

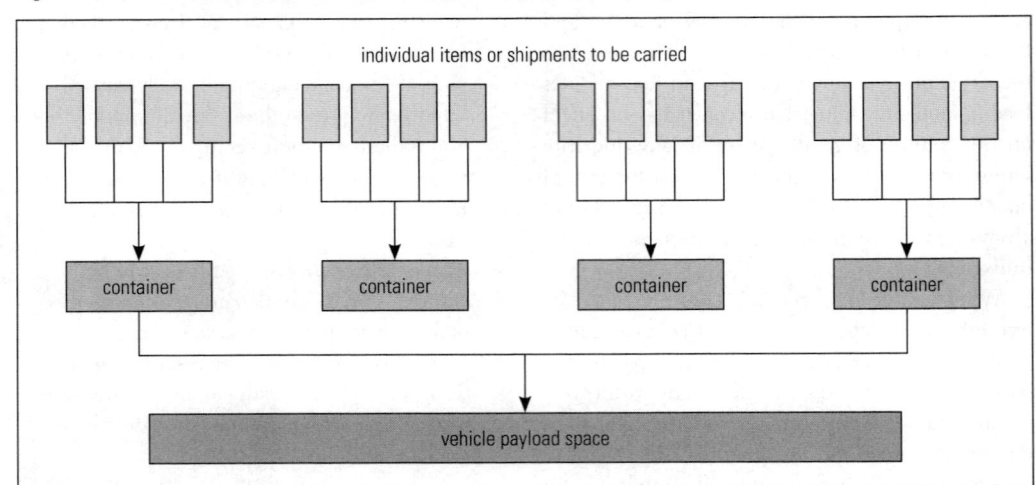

Figure 17.2 Use of containers to facilitate loading, carriage and unloading

```
individual items or shipments to be carried
           │              │              │              │
      [container]    [container]    [container]    [container]
                                    │
                         [vehicle payload space]
```

- The difficulty of finding freight for return trips leads to the transportation of empty containers.

The size (external dimensions and gross mass) of containers that can be used effectively in each mode is constrained by:
- the linear and cubic dimensions of the payload space and mass-carrying capacity of vehicles;
- the capacity of handling facilities at transfer points; and
- lateral and overhead obstructions on the routes.

These three factors vary between modes. With intermodal movement, the handling facilities at some transfer points may be inferior to others, or obstructions on the routes may vary in degree. The size of the containers is then governed by the most unfavourable conditions. Alternatively, the freight can be reloaded from one container to another at a transfer point, or the use of containers can be limited to a part of the trip only.

17.3.4 Intermodal transport

Intermodal transport is a logistically linked movement using two or more modes of transport on the line-haul part of the route.[7]

Intermodal transport typically (but not always) involves the interchange of freight between containers or loaded road trailers among different transport modes. The containers and road trailers are of standard sizes and have common handling characteristics. This allows for efficient transhipment of containers between modes.

A logistically linked origin-to-destination movement (sometimes referred to as seamless transport) is one where the consignor contracts a single service provider to coordinate or organise the entire movement. The service provider may be:
- a non-operating (or fourth-party) service provider that facilitates the service;
- a multimodal operator that physically conducts the entire movement; or
- a unimodal carrier that subcontracts carriers within other modes in order to complete the movement.

Because it is a single transaction, all the risks and service obligations associated with the transaction are vested in the service provider, and the consignor only needs to make payments to the service provider.

The basic reason for using intermodal services is the differing operational characteristics and costs of the various modes. By complementing modes in a coordinated fashion, the logistics manager can overcome the disadvantages of a mode, while benefiting from its advantages. Intermodal services maximise the primary advantages inherent in the combined modes and avoid their operationally weak characteristics.

Because road transport is so accessible, road carriers frequently participate in intermodal services. However, the combination of modes in intermodal service depends on the cooperation of the carriers concerned. Despite the fact that the economic deregulation of freight transportation has made intermodal freight operation possible, the reluctance of carriers to participate in intermodal combinations has inhibited the introduction of such services.

It is important to note that a line-haul movement refers to the part of a trip that takes place between:
- a point of origin and a bulk breaking terminal;
- a consolidation terminal and a point of destination;
- a consolidation terminal and a bulk breaking terminal; or
- an origin and a destination, i.e. a direct, consolidated movement. (Carrying consolidated long-distance freight directly from origin to destination is known as trunking.)

Therefore, if the line-haul part of a movement and the local collection and delivery movements are conducted by different modes, such a service is not regarded as being intermodal. In practice, a line-haul trip usually includes an intercity or port movement.

17.4 Principles of efficient operational transport management

17.4.1 Guidelines for routing and scheduling long-distance trips

A set of nine principles act as guidelines for promoting efficient freight transport operations:[8]
- Continuous flow
- Maximum unit size
- Maximum vehicle size
- Maximum mass-carrying capacity in relation to total vehicle mass
- Adaptation of vehicle unit to volume and nature of traffic
- Standardisation
- Compatible unit load equipment
- Long-haul freight consolidation
- Maximum utilisation of inputs

Carriers should endeavour to implement as many of these principles as is practically feasible. Although some of them may appear to contradict each other, they can be carefully traded off to complement one another in an efficiently integrated transport function. When professional carriers and third-party logistics providers provide line-haul transport services, the efficiency preferences of the carriers must be carefully balanced with the effectiveness requirements of their clients. These principles are discussed in the following sections.

17.4.1.1 Continuous flow

Continuous flow enhances both service reliability and cost effectiveness. The objectives of minimum transport cost and in-transit time require that:
- reverse, out-of-line and unduly delayed or slow movements are avoided; and
- the handling and transfer of goods are minimised.

This principle links with the principle of maximum utilisation of inputs.

17.4.1.2 Maximum unit size

The optimum size unit of freight is the largest size that all vehicles can carry and that the equipment can handle securely. Within the capabilities of standard vehicles and freight-handling equipment, the cost per ton-kilometre of handling freight tends to vary inversely with the size of the unit of shipment. This is because as the size of units increases, a less than proportional increase in time and effort is needed to handle, transfer, load and stow them. For example, the costs of handling or stowing a quarter-size, half-size and full-size container are almost the same.

17.4.1.3 Maximum vehicle size

As the carrying capacity of vehicles increases, vehicle-specific costs increase less than proportionally. Vehicle-specific costs are running costs, such as fuel consumption, maintenance, and tyre wear. The costs of handling, dispatching, drivers and load documentation tend to remain the same regardless of load or shipment size.

17.4.1.4 Maximum mass-carrying capacity in relation to total vehicle mass

The vehicle running costs are related to the total (i.e. gross) mass of the vehicle, whereas revenue is only related to the payload. The larger the vehicle, the higher the ratio of payload mass capacity to gross vehicle mass. Given that all vehicles have a maximum registered gross vehicle mass that may not be exceeded, the challenge exists to exchange vehicle mass (cost) for payload mass (revenue). A tactic in this respect may, firstly, make maximum use of trailers before scheduling additional vehicles. For example, a truck with a carrying capacity of 8 tons, drawing a 4-ton trailer will be more efficient than using two 6-ton trucks. Secondly, lightweight materials and design can help to minimise the tare (i.e. empty) mass of containers and vehicles.

17.4.1.5 Adaptation of vehicle to traffic

The traffic volume handled by a carrier may vary from hour to hour, day to day, week to week and season to season. The size of the vehicle, or combination of vehicles, should be adapted to match these fluctuations in traffic volume. For example, a small vehicle can be assigned to carry a small load when time constraints prohibit consolidation of loads. Multiple units of rail wagons or road trailers can be combined so that the capacity of the train or combination exactly matches the volume of traffic.

Specialised vehicles can also be introduced to maximise the potential for economies of density. Examples are rack trailers for the delivery of new passenger cars, and double- and triple-deck trailers for conveying livestock.

17.4.1.6 Standardisation

One should standardise vehicles, equipment and facilities whenever feasible in order to maximise the potential for economies of scope. Specialised vehicles and equipment are often necessary to carry certain goods efficiently (see the principle 'Adaptation of vehicle to traffic' in the previous section). However, general-purpose vehicles can be used to:
- transport a broad scope or variety of goods;
- top up vehicle loads with one-off shipments when fleet capacity exceeds standing contractual obligations; and
- obtain back hauls to avoid empty return runs.

Examples of such vehicles are standard rail wagons, road trailers, cargo ships and intermodal containers.

The use of standardised containers also increases the opportunity for intermodal freight movements and minimises handling of freight during transfer between collection, line-haul and delivery movements. Standardised manufacturing of vehicles and other mechanical equipment may reduce both maintenance costs and the required levels of spare-part stock.

17.4.1.7 Compatible unit load equipment

This principle is an extension of the principle of standardisation. Freight-handling equipment fitted onto vehicles should not occupy any space that could accommodate payload. Unitised packages, pallets and containers should be of dimensions that readily fit into the payload space to maximise volume utilisation. For example, if the payload space is designed to accommodate a 12 m × 2,5 m × 2,5 m container, then shorter containers (with the same width and height) should have lengths of 6 m, 3 m and even 1,5 m to allow for a multitude of ways in which the 12 m-long payload space can be filled to capacity. In addition, equipment and packages or containers should be positioned to minimise damage to freight and reduce load shift during carriage.

17.4.1.8 Long-haul freight consolidation

Identify the areas within the entire region of operation where traffic generation and attraction are concentrated. Consolidate traffic into line-haul freight movements to and from the locus, or hub, of each area of concentration. Optimal long-haul freight consolidation relies heavily on the achievement of economies of density, scope and long haul. Utilising all three of the main transportation economies, effective consolidation promises to afford the operator a high degree of economies of scale.

17.4.1.9 Maximum utilisation of inputs

Utilisation of inputs is related to the periods when a vehicle moves with a load compared to when it remains idle or runs without a load. The effective utilisation of resources can be inhibited by seasonal variations in business activity. In addition, the imbalance of traffic between destinations induces empty vehicle movement. To reduce this imbalance, carriers may:
- solicit casual or spot consignments through low tariffs based on marginal costs during times when fleet capacity exceeds standing contractual obligations;
- offer lower back-haul rates;
- invest in rigorous promotion to gain further consignments; or
- merge or form alliances.

17.4.2 Guidelines for routing and scheduling collection and delivery trips

A set of ten principles can be used as guidelines for the efficient routing and scheduling of local collection and delivery trips.[9, 10] As is the case with line-haul trip planning, these principles are not always perfectly compatible. However, should distribution management succeed in employing all of them in a well-balanced and complementary fashion, a high level of efficiency will be achieved. These principles are as follows:
- Clustering the service points as densely as possible.
- Clustering the service points according to daily trips.
- Determining routes starting with the furthest service point.
- The sections of a route must not cross.
- Two routes must not overlap.
- Using the largest available vehicles.
- Collecting and delivering in the same trip.
- Minimising the distance the heaviest loads will travel.
- Avoiding single service points located far from a cluster.
- Avoiding narrow time windows at service points.

Collection and delivery trips are predominantly undertaken using ancillary transport, and, to a lesser extent, using line-haul transport. An important reason for this is that customer service and consumer demands play a prominent role in the marketing of the final product towards the end of a product's supply chain. As a result, end-of-chain marketers often use private transport for service effectiveness, sometimes at the cost of efficiency.

When planning collection and delivery trips, it is important not to lose sight of the abovementioned ten principles. They are discussed in the following sections.

17.4.2.1 Clustering the service points as densely as possible

Cluster the delivery and collection points so that the distances between the stops on each trip are as short as possible. This minimises total route distance and trip time. Figure 17.3 shows examples of inefficient and efficient clustering. In (a) the total distance of the two routes is longer than that in (b).

17.4.2.2 Clustering the service points according to daily trips

Whenever delivery and collection points need to be served on different days, they must be tightly

Figure 17.3 Clustering service points

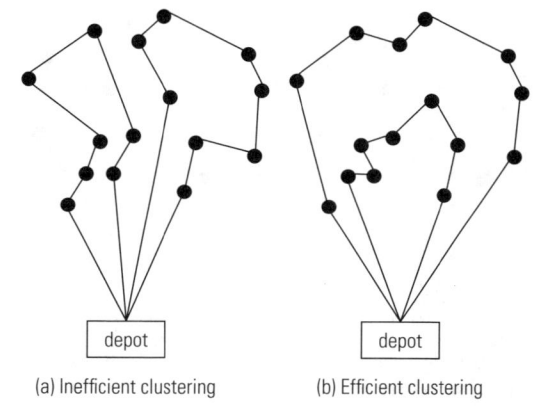

(a) Inefficient clustering   (b) Efficient clustering

clustered according to the day of visit. The clusters should not overlap geographically. (Any overlap will violate the guideline explained in Section 17.4.2.5.) Clustering points according to daily trips minimises the number of vehicles needed, the total distance travelled and the total trip time.

17.4.2.3 Start with the furthest service point when determining routes

When clustering the service points on a trip, commence with the service point furthest from the terminal. Once the furthest point from the terminal has been identified, assign the largest available vehicle and select the densest concentration and greatest number of service points that will fully occupy the vehicle's carrying capacity. Select the furthest point from among the remaining service points, and repeat the sequence until each service point is covered by a trip.

17.4.2.4 Sections of a route must not cross

The service points should be sequenced so that the path of the route is raindrop-shaped (see Figure 17.4). The introduction of time window constraints and the collection of large volumes only after completion of all the deliveries can result in sections of the route crossing.

17.4.2.5 Two routes must not overlap

Cluster service points in such a way that the paths of two separate routes do not cross. Each route should lie, therefore, within distinct contiguous service areas. When routes overlap, unnecessary distance is covered.

17.4.2.6 Using the largest vehicles

This principle links closely with the principle of determining routes starting with the furthest service point (see Section 17.4.2.3). Using the largest available vehicle minimises the total distance travelled, the total trip time and the number of vehicles required. A potential disadvantage is that service frequency is reduced. Take care that this does not reduce service levels to below those required by customers.

17.4.2.7 Collecting and delivering in the same trip

The results of collecting only after completion of all the deliveries are that route sections cross and that some service points are visited twice. Conformation to this guideline depends on the type and size of vehicle, the load volume and the extent to which new collections will obstruct the delivery of consignments that are still on board.

17.4.2.8 Minimising the travelling distance of the heaviest loads

Choose the direction of travel in such a way that the heaviest deliveries are made first, or that the heaviest collections are made last. This helps reduce fuel consumption.

17.4.2.9 Avoiding single service points located far from a cluster

A single service point located far from a cluster of service points is a candidate for a separate visit. Its size and extent of isolation dictate whether it should be incorporated into a cluster or whether it should be served separately with a small vehicle matching its delivery or collection volume.

17.4.2.10 Avoiding narrow time windows at service points

Narrow time windows can disrupt the desired sequence of visits to service points. When narrow time windows unduly distort the efficiency of delivery and collection, one should negotiate the widening of the time windows. This will allow more latitude in the routing and scheduling of trips.

Figure 17.4 Construction of routes

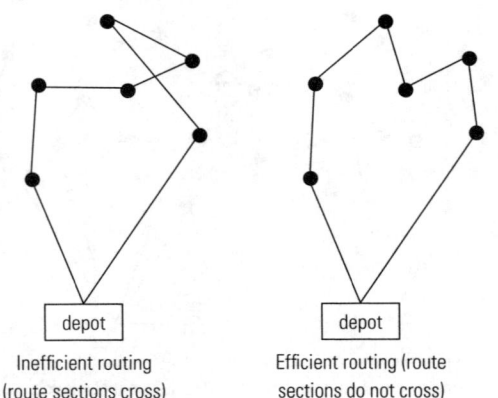

Inefficient routing (route sections cross) | Efficient routing (route sections do not cross)

17.4.3 Coordinating incoming traffic

17.4.3.1 Overview

The coordination of incoming traffic supports the procurement function of a business with a view to receiving goods from vendors or materials suppliers at the desired time and place. Goods traffic can be classified into industrial and commercial traffic. Industrial traffic is the movement of physical inputs used to manufacture products (e.g. raw materials to make an intermediary good, and the components and goods-in-process needed to assemble finished products). Commercial traffic consists of the movement of finished goods purchased for resale (e.g. products purchased by a wholesaler or a retailer).

A smooth flow of materials to the business is necessary to ensure uninterrupted operations. Serious operational bottlenecks can result from poor materials flow into receiving and storage. Some causes of bottlenecks are inadequate layout, size and location of the receiving area; inadequate materials-handling design; poor labour utilisation; inferior information systems; and poor delivery scheduling.

The physical delivery of goods can be performed by the business buying the goods, the supplier, or a third-party service provider. Suppliers are generally responsible for the control of their outbound transport function, which includes the coordination of traffic. However, if a business receives time-sensitive deliveries from many suppliers, incoming traffic should also be coordinated by the receiver to avoid congestion at the receiving point and to ensure that goods arrive at the desired time. Effective communication between the business and its suppliers is required to plan the daily delivery schedules efficiently. For this reason supply chain partners should share information to improve scheduling of deliveries. If the entire incoming transport activity is under the control of the receiving business, it is easier to coordinate traffic aspects, such as daily collections, with other activities.

Professional carriers provide certain complementary terminal and line-haul services that enhance the flexibility of their service. Logistics managers can use these services to coordinate the flow of incoming goods effectively. These additional services may include tracking and tracing; expediting; diversion and reconsignment; in-transit privileges; and demurrage and detention. Such services – outlined in the next sections – can help improve or support service reliability.

17.4.3.2 Tracking and tracing

The visibility of a consignment in the supply chain requires the ability to know where it is during carriage or where it is in a terminal or warehouse.

> Tracking comprises the actions taken by the service provider to follow the movement and progress of a vehicle or a goods consignment.

Tracking is a fleet-management activity (specifically vehicle routing and scheduling) by the service provider for his own purposes.

> Tracing refers to the actions followed to determine a consignment's location while in transit in order to keep the shipper informed of the progress of its shipment.

Tracking and tracing are often necessary to trace lost or late consignments during the course of a move. Tracing is critical in situations where on-time delivery is necessary to ensure continuous manufacturing operations. The use of information technology, such as on-line freight information systems, satellite communications and bar coding, assists in tracing a consignment after its departure and in recording its movement. Bar coding enables one to transfer information quickly and in an error-free way at intermediate points. On-line freight information systems allow consignors and consignees to link directly with the carrier's computer system in order to determine the status of a particular consignment.

Tracing is usually a free service, but should be requested only when a consignment is unreasonably late. Guaranteed delivery times are often promised, especially by courier, parcel and express-freight carriers. A sophisticated shipment tracing system helps to fulfil this objective. Delivery staff of service providers for whom reliability is an overridingly important indicator of the quality of their service carry equipment that enables them to record and report the moment each consignment is delivered.

17.4.3.3 Expediting

The need to expedite a consignment may arise because it has been delayed, the carrier has lost track of it through misfortune, or because the consignee or consignor desires delivery earlier than originally arranged. In the former case, once the shipment is traced, the expediting function attempts to accelerate shipment movement along to delivery. In the latter case, when it is crucial that a consignee receives a specific consignment by a particular date or at a certain time, the consignor or the carrier can be requested to expedite or accelerate movement of the consignment through the carrier's system. In this case, the shipper will be charged a service fee to have the delivery expedited. Ideally, the arrangements should be made before dispatching the consignment in order to afford the consignor or the carrier the greatest opportunity to speed up the movement. However, the request for expediting a consignment may be lodged at any stage before its arrival at a junction or transfer point, from where faster movement, or carriage directly towards the destination, may be arranged.

Another tactic for expediting a delivery is to arrange for a consignment to be cross-docked at a transfer point or warehouse en route. In such a situation, a consignment that arrives at an incoming dock is transferred directly to a vehicle that will tranship the consignment directly to the customer. Cross-docking is an operation used to fulfil customer orders by transhipping consignments directly from a dock regardless of the fact that there is stock at the supplier's facilities through which the order could have been fulfilled. Expediting, like tracking and tracing, is a valuable tool for the consignor, consignee and carrier because all of them can plan their operations in line with the progress and problems of a consignment.

17.4.3.4 Diversion and reconsignment

> Diversion privileges permit a consignor (often on behalf of a consignee) to notify a carrier that a shipment needs to be diverted to a new destination.

To minimise diversion charges, this must happen before the shipment's arrival at junctions or transfer points from where diversion can be arranged. Diversion is a convenient option when unexpected changes in market conditions or production requirements necessitate a change in the destination of a consignment.

> Reconsignment is when the consignor directs a shipment to another destination after it has arrived at the originally arranged destination.

Diversion and/or reconsignment are often utilised when the aggregate demand for the consigned goods in a market area is fairly predictable, but the cyclical nature or volatility of volumes demanded at specific locations are not known beforehand. It frequently happens that a central (or large) destination in the market area is proactively chosen according to forecasts or expectations by the consignor, but while the goods are in transit a new destination is nominated in quick reaction or response to a delivery order received. Examples are fashionware and perishable goods (such as fresh produce) for which demand may flare up unpredictably at locations in the general direction of travel. The consignee can gain substantially through this quick-response service in terms of flexibility in fulfilling orders in volatile market conditions at a relatively low diversion charge per vehicle load.

17.4.3.5 In-transit privileges

In-transit privileges permit the consignor (on behalf of a consignee) to unload a consignment en route, perform some processing function on the goods and reload the consignment into the waiting vehicle(s) for its final destination. In-transit privileges are based on the principle of long-haul economies. For example, a trip of 600 km is less costly than two trips of 300 km each.

A consignment would be charged a through-tariff as if it is carried directly from origin to destination, plus a relatively small additional charge for the stopping and waiting. However, this charge is less than the difference between the through-tariff between the origin and destination and the total of the through-tariffs of two uncoordinated trips from origin to stopping point and from stopping point to destination. Stopping-in-transit arrangements can reduce location disadvantages of the en route processing where stopping takes place, while the carrier also gains by capturing the consignor's business for both sections of the haul.

A variation of stopping-in-transit privileges is to make use of an additional set of rail wagons or road trailers. Instead of stopping and waiting for processing to take place, an arriving train or road vehicle might simply detach the wagons or trailers loaded with the unprocessed goods and depart with a set of wagons/trailers waiting on-site already loaded with the processed goods. A fee similar to a demurrage or detention levy will in the latter case be payable by the consignor for the wagons/trailers remaining at the processor's premises.

17.4.3.6 Demurrage and detention

Demurrage and detention can be regarded as the charges payable when consignees use transport equipment for storage beyond the periods acceptable for in-transit storage.

> Demurrage is incurred when ships or rail wagons are not moved on time. When consignees receive a rail wagon, the rail carrier allows them a specified amount of free time to unload it. When the rail wagon is retained beyond this allowed time, the rail carrier assesses and applies a demurrage charge.

The argument to justify demurrage charges is that retained rail equipment produces no revenue for the rail carrier, and therefore bears an opportunity cost when it stands idle at a customer's siding.

Demurrage charges fluctuate according to supply and demand. They may vary according to the type of rail wagon and according to the specific contract between the rail carrier and the customer.

When a road truck, trailer, or container is retained beyond the specified free loading or unloading time, road freight carriers use the term detention charges for the same concept. In the road freight industry, the allowed time, or the time window, is specified in the tariff and is generally limited to a few hours. There are no fixed or standard detention charges in the road freight industry and shippers must negotiate the free time and detention charges with each carrier.

Good coordination between the various departments can ensure the orderly flow of consignments to a business. Efficient planning and control of the inbound traffic not only minimise congestion, but also reduce demurrage and detention charges. By capitalising on a carrier's flexibility, the business does not suffer delays or interruptions in its operations.

17.5 Conclusion

Transport management is effected on strategic, tactical and operational levels. Governments apply various policy instruments to influence the performance of the freight transport industry. These policy instruments are:
- legislation;
- direct supply;
- fiscal measures;
- monetary measures;
- moral appeal and persuasion;
- policies relating to strategic commodities;
- procurement policy;
- provision of information; and
- research and development.

Efficient and effective transport helps ensure that customers receive the right goods at the designated place and time in the required condition and quantity, and at an acceptable cost or price. The most pertinent service performance determinants are suitability, accessibility, goods security, transit time, reliability and flexibility.

Goods are transported in consignments. Efficiency may be best achieved by carrying goods in large mass, volumes and quantities. In order to lower the cost of carrying and handling small consignments, carriers consolidate consignments

and create unit loads whenever feasible. A set of nine principles can act as guidelines to promote efficiency when conducting long-distance trips. These are:
- continuous flow;
- maximum unit size;
- maximum vehicle size;
- maximum mass-carrying capacity in relation to total vehicle mass;
- adaptation of vehicle unit to volume and nature of traffic;
- standardisation;
- compatible unit load equipment;
- long-haul freight consolidation; and
- maximum utilisation of inputs.

The following set of ten principles can be used as guidelines for routing and scheduling local collection and delivery trips:
- Clustering service points as densely as possible.
- Clustering service points according to daily trips.
- Determining routes starting with the furthest service point.
- The sections of a route must not cross.
- Two routes must not overlap.
- Using the largest available vehicles.
- Collecting and delivering in the same trip.
- Minimising the distance the heaviest loads will travel.
- Avoiding single service points located far from a cluster.
- Avoiding narrow time windows at service points.

Purchasers and suppliers can make use of private transport or professional carriers. In addition to the primary transport service, professional carriers also provide certain complementary terminal and line-haul services that enhance the flexibility of their service. Logistics managers can make use of these services to coordinate effectively the flow of incoming materials to the business. These additional services may include tracking and tracing; expediting (including cross-docking); diversion and reconsignment; in-transit privileges; and demurrage and detention.

Key terms

Accessibility	Policy instrument
Consignment	Reconsignment
Consolidation	Regulation
Container	Reliability
Coordination	Routing
Demurrage and detention	Scheduling
	Service selection
Diversion	Strategic transport management
Effectiveness	
Efficiency	Suitability
Expediting	Tactical transport management
Flexibility	
Goods security	Tracing
Intermodal transport	Tracking
In-transit privileges	Transit time
Legislation	Unit load
Line-haul	
Operational transport management	

Case study

Despite the fact that the carriage of standard intermodal freight containers by rail transport becomes cheaper than road transport for hauls exceeding 520 km, rail transport is losing container traffic in favour of road transport between Johannesburg and Durban – a distance of 713 km by rail. The traffic movements at issue represent a) domestic South African transport forming part of materials management (i.e. inbound logistics) and physical distribution management (i.e. outbound logistics), and b) international movements of finished products between the Port of Durban and consignors/consignees in Gauteng.

1. Give reasons for the trend mentioned above.
2. What can Transnet Freight Rail (the local rail carrier) do to counter the abovementioned trend with respect to domestic containerised freight movements?
3. What can Transnet Freight Rail do to counter the abovementioned trend with respect to international containerised freight movements?

Notes
1. State all your assumptions clearly.

2 In question 3, you should take cognisance of the fact that the Port of Durban is operated by Transnet Port Terminals (TPT). Both Transnet Freight Rail and TPT are subsidiaries of Transnet.

Case study

At a recent conference of the Council for Supply Chain Management Professionals (CSCMP), which focused on managing lean and agile supply chains, the plenary speaker's opening statement was:

> 'The world over, we have seen that in the supply of final products, and increasingly of intermediary products, supply chain systems have moved away from being organised as push-oriented, to supply or value chains being organised as pull-oriented, and lately, also push-pull-oriented. This trend has manifested itself strongly after the economic deregulation of freight transport. The two modes of transport that I see as "logistics winners" here are road and airfreight transport. I say this not only due to the logistics-friendly attributes of road and air transport, but also due to the fact that (1) road and air transport form excellent intermodal combinations; and (2) road traffic lends itself to relatively easy coordination on the incoming leg of freight movement.'

On the basis of this introduction, provide a summary of the plenary speaker's address in less than 1 800 words.

Questions

1 Discuss what is meant by strategic, tactical and operational transport management, and supply examples of transport activities that occur at each of these levels of management.
2 Identify and discuss the various policy instruments that governments may apply to influence the supply and performance of the freight transport industry.
3 Discuss the policy instruments that the government of your country applies to intervene in the freight transport industry, and point out in your view how these measures affect business logistics management and performance in the country.
4 Discuss the efficiency and effectiveness considerations involved in the decision about whether to make use of ancillary or professional transport.
5 Explain in detail what you understand by technical capability and operational capability of a professional carrier.
6 Is transport price a separate service performance criterion, or is it determined through other service performance criteria? Motivate your answer.
7 Supply guidelines for the efficient routing and scheduling of long-distance trips and collection and delivery trips.
8 Discuss how incoming traffic can be coordinated in order to enhance effectiveness.

Consult the web

Air transport

British Airways World Cargo:
    www.baworldcargo.com
KLM: www.klmcargo.com
Lufthansa Air Cargo: www.lhcargo.com
South African Airways: www.flysaa.com

Road transport

Cargo Carriers: www.cargocarriers.co.za
Cross Roads Distribution (Pty) Ltd:
    www.crossroads.co.za
Unitrans: www.unitrans.co.za

Rail transport

Transnet Freight Rail:
    www.transnet.co.za/FreightRail.aspx

Pipeline transport

Petroline: www.petroline.co.za
Transnet Pipelines:
    www.transnet.co.za/Pipelines.aspx

Sea transport

Grindrod: www.grindrod.co.za
Maersk Sealand: www.maersksealand.com
Safmarine: www.safmarine.com

Consult the books

Ballou, R. H. 2004. *Business Logistics/Supply Chain Management*, 5th edition. Upper Saddle River: Pearson Prentice Hall.

Button, K. J. 1993. *Transport Economies*, 2nd edition. Aldershot: Edward Elgar.

Fair, M. L. and Williams, E. W. 1981. *Transportation and Logistics*, 2nd edition. Plano: Business Publications.

Muller, G. 1995. *Intermodal Freight Transportation*, 3rd edition. Lansdowne: Eno Transportation Foundation.

Pegrum, D. F. 1973. *Transportation: Economics and Public Policy*, 3rd edition. Homewood: Richard D. Irwin.

Pienaar, W. J. 2003. 'Rail or road: An overview', *Civil Engineering* 11(9):18–21.

Schumer, L. A. 1974. *Elements of Transport*, 3rd edition. Sydney: Butterworths.

Visagie, S. E. 2005. *Inleiding tot operasionele navorsing: Teorie en praktyk*. Stellenbosch: Department of Logistics, University of Stellenbosch.

Notes

1. Pegrum, D. F. 1973: 243.
2. Button, K. J. 1993: 246.
3. Pienaar, W. J. 2003: 20.
4. Schumer, L. A. 1974: 38–43.
5. Muller, G. 1995: 256.
6. Schumer, L.A. 1974: 43–4.
7. Muller, G. 1995: 262.
8. Principles 1 to 7 and 9 are based on Fair and Williams, 1981: 6. Principle 8 is proposed by this author.
9. Ballou, R. H. 2004: 236–8.
10. Visagie, S. E. 2005: 107–10.

18 Managing international supply chains

W.J. Pienaar and J. Vogt

Learning outcomes

After studying this chapter, you should be able to:
- name the factors that distinguish international logistics from domestic logistics;
- describe why it is important for logistics managers involved in international distribution to acquaint themselves with marketing channels;
- supply an overview of the series of transactional activities that will take place from when an exporter tenders a goods consignment for international carriage by ocean or air to when the consignment is delivered to the importer;
- identify the intermediaries who may become involved in international marketing and describe their respective functions;
- identify the operating and non-operating service providers in international transport and describe their respective functions;
- explain what Incoterms stands for and what these terms mean;
- indicate the seller's and buyer's obligations within each of the 13 Incoterms;
- identify the various categories of international trade documents; and
- discuss the function of the most important transport documents.

18.1 Introduction

International economic developments have a serious impact on the domestic economic activities of countries. A business cannot ignore competitive situations and technological innovations in other countries. Modern economies are highly interdependent and the successful ones are those that compete effectively in international markets. In a rapidly integrating and globalising world market, therefore, efficient and effective international logistic support structures relating to international goods transactions are of particular importance. International logistics practice must accommodate all domestic logistics demands. In an international context, logistics managers have to deal with more channel partners or intermediaries; longer distances; more steps in the supply chain; greater diversity; and more statutory requirements and documentation.

This chapter focuses on those areas that distinguish international logistics practice from domestic logistics activities. These include:
- aspects pertinent to the choice of an appropriate international distribution channel;
- international goods transport;
- international trade;
- uniform rules for the interpretation of commercial terms in international goods transactions; and
- the important documents used in international goods transactions and movements.

18.2 Distribution channels

18.2.1 Choosing a distribution channel

Distribution channels in international trade are the physical routes that a product follows from the seller (exporter) to the buyer (importer).

A seller can choose an appropriate distribution channel for its product(s) once it has identified a target market. An appropriate distribution channel enhances the efficiency of the international marketing effort. Sellers and logistics managers involved in international marketing and distribution must acquaint themselves with distribution channels because they need to understand how products flow to foreign consumers.

Successful international marketing often results from partnering with a key intermediary who has access to distribution channels in a foreign market. Sellers need to appreciate the importance of the role of intermediaries in getting products to their target markets and in ensuring that they receive them at a reasonable price. Forming a business alliance with a reputable partner who can channel export products to appropriate distribution points is called the push strategy.

The longer the distribution channel, the greater the number of intermediaries, resulting in less profit accruing to the seller. Sellers can use the following criteria to determine the length of their distribution channels:[1]

- Complexity of technical requirements
- Lifespan of the product
- Price of the product
- Service requirements
- Turnover

Whenever profit within a distribution channel is not related to the amount of risk accepted and the cost of distribution functions performed, conflict may arise among the channel members. As for channel performance, the objective is to bring about cooperation and coordination within the channel and not disharmony or conflict.

Channel leaders usually earn a larger share of profits because of their initiative and innovative roles in organising and promoting the channel and providing services and credit. The seller (exporter) should assume the role of channel leader. Being a larger shareholder within the channel, the seller is most likely to be motivated to conduct more market research and to add value to its export products.

If sellers were to market their products directly to end-users by means of their own sales force, they would be the only profit-earning party. However, direct marketing in foreign countries can be very difficult and expensive, eroding profits. Exporters, therefore, have to trade off the costs and benefits of employing intermediaries against conducting their own sales. Delivering products directly to end-users, as is often the case with manufactured products, is called the pull strategy. As this is often a costly strategy, it is generally only feasible for large exporting firms.

Producers and manufacturers that enter the international market may be tempted to entrust the entire export process to an established international distributor. In doing so, sellers may not become aware of the way consumers react to their products. Furthermore, all the initiative for increasing market share rests with the distributor. This strategy of risk avoidance may cost exporters dearly in lost marketing opportunities.

Distribution channels include sole distributors; trading houses; government departments; industrial buyers; wholesalers; retailers and chain stores; and export agents. These intermediaries are discussed in the following sections.

18.2.2 Distributors

The foreign distributor acts as a principal, buying goods from the exporter and selling them for his own account to a specific type of customer, usually wholesalers. The distributor is the exporter's customer, not the end-user. The distributor sells on its own terms, but in close consultation with the exporter. Delivery to end-users is made by the distributor, who manages the local customer relationship directly. The distributor may be restricted from selling competitors' goods or services in terms of the distribution agreement. The distributor is usually trained by the exporter and easier to monitor than an export agent. A distributor is usually a better channel to market abroad than an agent in the case of technically complex finished goods that require intensive customer service, after-sales service and repair facilities.

The distributor does not pay the importer immediately. The seller has to wait for payment until the distributor has resold the consignment or a part thereof. The seller may have to invoice the distributor separately for each part of the consignment that is sold and file a separate exchange-control application for each invoice in order to receive payment.

The biggest advantage of making use of a distributor is the saving in the cost, time and trouble as a result of dealing in large consignments. Another advantage is a better profit margin because the distributor pays the seller a higher price for delaying payment until products are sold. It can also be useful to have large product inventories readily available in the foreign market.

Distributors operating on a consignment basis have to be chosen very carefully. Most of them sell the products as quickly as possible because of the opportunity costs of keeping the products in stock. However, they may be less eager to sell products that they have yet to pay for.[2]

18.2.3 Trading houses

A trading house may deal in imports and exports (i.e. two-way trade). It may buy directly from the seller, acting as an agent for the exporting seller. It may also act as an agent for an importing buyer.

Sales to trading houses are mostly single, complete transactions. Trading houses do not usually enter into a contract for exclusive rights over a period, as distributors do. Trading houses conduct their own marketing, carry the credit risk, administer all documentation and oversee the physical distribution of products to their final destination.

18.2.4 Government departments

Government departments in some countries occasionally import commodities, often on a long-term basis. For example, they may require a certain quantity of grain to be delivered at regular intervals over a number of years; they may enter into import agreements with sellers to do this.

18.2.5 Industrial buyers

Large industrial firms often purchase directly from manufacturers. For example, a ship builder may purchase steel sheeting or furnishing material directly from foreign sellers if importation constitutes the cheapest way of building ships. An aircraft manufacturer may source certain highly advanced aircraft components directly from foreign specialist component manufacturers. Multinational sourcing of specialised components may be the most affordable way for a group of nations, or even the entire international community, to obtain, for example, certain types of aircraft. The aircraft manufacturer does not need to develop the capability to manufacture the components in question at a high cost. This way, an additional market is generated for the component manufacturer. The country in which the manufacturer resides may now be in a position to import completely manufactured aircraft from the buyer of the components without having to develop and manufacture the aircraft at a higher cost.

18.2.6 Wholesalers

Some wholesalers may be direct importing purchasers, or they may obtain their supplies through an importing distributor. Wholesalers do not usually have exclusive selling rights for the products they buy. However, they may have a commanding market position with little competition.

18.2.7 Retailers

Large chain stores and franchise retail groups may also buy directly from exporters. They often negotiate exclusive selling rights. Occasionally, a number of independent stores establish a joint buying group and employ a single buyer for the group. Chain stores and supermarkets are often multiples with a central buying organisation. Multiples are becoming increasingly important as direct importing clients. They may be particularly interested in the way products are packaged and presented to be attractive on store shelves and in showrooms. They often purchase in bulk and demand that the products are packaged in their own consumer packs.

18.2.8 Export agents

An agent is an individual or legal entity authorised to transact business for and in the name of another, known as the principal. An agent's authorised actions bind the principal. In export practice, the export agent is a party which acts for the exporter, the latter being the principal. Agents work on a commission basis and do not assume risks.

An agent is generally not restricted to selling one exporter's goods only, but is restricted territorially. A territory can be a defined geographical area, or a specific market within a geographical area, such as the retail trade or mail-order houses, in the case of consumer goods. Alternatively, there may be no specific geographical limitation, but the territory may be defined by the way in which the goods or services are provided – for example, by e-commerce for books and other consumer products or services.[3]

In the territory assigned to it, an agent is responsible for:
- customer service;
- order finding;
- problem solving;
- promotion;
- research; and
- selling.

When examining the role of the export agent, it is also important to consider distributors, as their role in the international market has become increasingly significant. Exporters may market their products in certain countries through agents for a commission, but in other countries through distributors, who buy the goods for their own account and earn a profit.

Table 18.1 lists the salient points of difference between distributors and export agents.[4]

Whenever a seller decides to market products directly in a specific country, it has to consider whether to make use of an agent or appoint its own marketing staff in that country. If the seller is new to a country or region, market penetration can often be achieved most effectively by appointing an export-sales agent. The potential value of an agent in such circumstances can stem from the following:
- Remuneration is based on sales volume. Therefore, there are no sales expenses unless sales are achieved.
- The agent has local knowledge.
- An agent's experience with other products may help when introducing a new product.
- Agents are usually highly motivated because they are only paid if they succeed in selling.

18.3 Transporting goods internationally

18.3.1 Overview

All modes of transport – pipelines included – can offer international services. However, the majority of goods exchanged internationally are transported by sea and by air. By value, approximately 80 per cent of all international trade is carried by sea transport and 10 per cent by air. The remaining

Table 18.1 Differences between distributors and export agents

Export agent	Distributor
No financial involvement; works for commission	Buys for own account and sells to earn profit
Leaves importation to the buyers and passes orders to the principal	Imports the products
Paid a commission at an agreed percentage on orders secured	Marks up the supply price to cover own profit
Any service necessary is rendered by the buyer	Where necessary, undertakes responsibility for the service
Carries no stock except for showroom purposes	Usually carries stock
Unlikely to be involved in publicity except where required to give advice or report on impact	Likely to be involved in local publicity
May be authorised to engage sub-agents	Appoints sub-distributors
No control over resale prices	Controls selling prices in countries where retail price maintenance is possible
Leaves distribution to the buyers	Conducts distribution in the market

10 per cent of international trade is transported overland by road, rail and pipeline.

International pipeline services are confined to overland crude oil and natural gas, and, in limited cases, petroleum products between neighbouring countries. Although pipelines can be built under the sea, such a process is both economically and technically highly challenging, so the majority of oil at sea is transported by tank ships. All international trade of crude oil and petroleum products that involves long-distance and trans-oceanic carriage is done by ship. Despite the fact that tank ships run empty during return trips, pipeline transport can only compete with sea transport between the same origin and destination if the pipeline route is considerably shorter than the sea route, or where sea transport is subject to exceptional charges, such as heavy canal dues. An example is the 254-km Trans-Israel crude oil pipeline route between Eilat on the Red Sea and Ashkelon on the Mediterranean coast. This route is substantially shorter than the one around Africa, and cheaper than the Suez Canal.

Because transport between neighbouring countries is so similar to domestic transport, this chapter focuses on sea and air transport. Attention is also given to the transport intermediaries, which are critical components of international transport.[5]

18.3.2 Sea transport

18.3.2.1 Overview of basic commercial ocean transport practice[6]

The process of organising the logistics arrangements of ocean carriage begins when the exporter (shipper, or consignor) concludes a contract with an importer (consignee). The exporter contacts a freight forwarder to arrange the carriage. The forwarder makes enquiries to determine the dates and places of departure of suitable ships. Generally, the forwarder will do this by contacting loading brokers, the agents of shipowners (carriers), which market the available ship space.

Loading brokers handle the logistics arrangements from the carrier's (i.e. the shipowner's) side. They advertise the dates of departure, supervise loading and consult with the shipowner's cargo superintendent with regard to the loading and stowage of the goods consignment(s) in the ship's hold. In practice, a single forwarding firm often acts as both forwarding agent and loading broker, although these tasks are usually handled separately.

The forwarder usually reserves space on a specific vessel, and then completes a set of pre-printed bills of lading (a set comprises from two to four identical originals). Most shipowners print their own bills of lading and make these freely available to forwarders. The forwarder will indicate on the draft bill of lading all necessary details, including the identity of the exporter, a description of the freight, which includes shipping marks (visible identification markings on the packages) and the arrangements regarding the payment for carriage of the consignment(s).

The exporter, with the forwarder's assistance, has to ensure that the freight is either delivered alongside the ship or into the care of a port terminal, or warehouse. When the freight is delivered, the exporter will customarily receive a receipt document, such as a dock receipt (wharfinger's note) or a mate's receipt. A dock receipt is a document indicating that a given shipment has arrived on a particular date. This receipt transfers accountability from the delivering domestic carrier to the vessel owner. Since the checker at the port or wharf will note any apparent damage or shortage on the document itself, a clean dock receipt evidences good receipt. Dock receipts are normally prepared by forwarders or shippers, and are either faxed to the ship line's terminal or given to the delivering carrier to accompany the shipment.[7]

A wharfinger (also wharf inspector, wharf superintendent or dock superintendent) is in charge of receiving and registering goods in a port on behalf of the carrier. The wharfinger's signature (and note) on the dock receipt assures the shipper that it can proceed to draw up bills of lading pursuant to the terms of the note. A mate's receipt is a transport document acknowledging receipt of freight for transport issued by a responsible ship's officer after the freight has been tallied into the vessel. The mate's receipt can be taken to the master or his representative and exchanged for a bill of lading.

The ship owner will record the details of the freight received, as well as any important defects or damages, on the mate's receipt. This is important because the bill of lading is based on the details recorded on the mate's receipt. If the mate's receipt indicates damaged goods, then the ship owner will not issue a 'clean' bill of lading, which is usually necessary for the exporter to obtain payment under a letter of credit.

The ship owner compares the details of the loaded freight (as recorded by his staff) with the draft bills of lading that the forwarder or exporter has furnished. Provided the details match and the freight does not exhibit damage or defects, the ship owner will issue the completed and signed clean bills of lading. The details from the bills of lading are also recorded on a register kept on the ship, called the ship's manifest.

Once the freight has been stowed and the exporter has obtained a marine insurance policy and a bank draft, the exporter is able to assemble a set of shipping documents. These serve as the hub of many international payment and finance mechanisms. Control over the freight can be freely transferred by endorsement of the bill of lading. Endorsement is effected when the party holding the bill of lading and wishing to make the transfer signs the back of the bill of lading. The signature may also be accompanied by instructions to deliver to a specific person.

When the freight arrives at the port of destination, the ship's master delivers the freight to the first party who presents an original bill of lading. Usually, the importer presents this to the ship's agent, who then issues a delivery order. The importer then uses the delivery order to obtain release of the consignment(s).

Sometimes, consignments arrive before the bills of lading have been processed through the payment system and received by the importer. Since a delay in receiving a consignment can result in penalties or storage charges, the importer may ask its bank to issue a letter of indemnity (LOI) to the ship owner. This protects the ship owner in the event that he incurs liability for delivery to the wrong person. The ship owner will then release the consignment(s) against the letter of indemnity.

The ocean carriers involved in international transport are:
- liner operators;
- tramp ship operators; and
- private ship operators.[8]

Each type provides specific service features to the international transport user. Lighter-aboard ship operations are a feeder service, which brings cargo to a port (via a river or inland waterway), whereas a liner or tramp ship can pick up the goods for on-carriage over an ocean.

18.3.2.2 Liner ship operations

Liner ships provide service on fixed routes according to published schedules. They usually charge according to published tariffs that are either unique to the independent liner operator or fixed by several lines forming a group conference operation on a particular trade route. A shipping conference is a legal cartel, or oligopoly.

Liner services offered are either container, breakbulk, or bulk. The shipper must transport the freight to the liner's terminal at the port after making the reservation. The freight is loaded onto the ship with a machine if it is bulk or by crane if it is containerised. It is then stowed in accordance with ship mass, balance, safety rules and the shipper's requirements. In the case of a roll-on roll-off (ro-ro) ship, the cargo is driven, pushed or pulled onto and off the ship by use of a ramp.

Container ship operations

Container shipping is rapidly gaining market share over the traditional breakbulk method of ocean carriage. Containers provide much of the protection needed for goods that have to be heavily crated and packaged for breakbulk movement. It may take days to unload a breakbulk ship and load its new cargo with a small crane and human labour. An entire container ship, however, can enter, unload, load and clear a port in less than 12 hours. Such speed brings about labour savings to the users and ship operators alike. It also increases ship utilisation and, because a ship only earns revenue at sea, capital utilisation.

The container shipping service has introduced various operating and management concerns for ship operators. For one, this service requires a large investment in containers. While some containers are on board, many more are in the process of being distributed, delivered, or loaded, or are awaiting collection. For every hundred containers that a ship can carry, an investment of 200 to

300 containers is typically required to support its operation. At least two sets of containers are needed – one on board and the other on land at the different ports of call. A further concern is control over the containers. Previously, liner operators were port-to-port-oriented. With inland movement of containers, control over the land movement becomes a necessity, especially with logistically linked intermodal transport. Computerised container-tracking systems make this possible.

Roll-on roll-off ship operations

Ro-Ro ships have ramps upon which vehicles can be driven directly into their cargo holds. Ro-Ro ships are often used to transport road vehicles, trailers, construction machinery on wheels and other wheeled consignments. A Ro-Ro vessel can be more flexible than a container ship, because it can call at ports that do not have extensive container-handling equipment. However, Ro-Ro vessels also often carry conventional containers on their top deck. Although Ro-Ro ships are generally operated within liner operations, some of them are used in private (i.e. ancillary) operations.

18.3.2.3 Tramp ship operations

Tramp ships are bulk or tank ships that are hired for a voyage or a specific period.

If an exporter wants to hire a tramp ship for a voyage, it seeks a ship that will be emptied at the local port. It then hires (or charters) the ship for a one-way voyage to a foreign port. Port fees, a daily operating rate and demurrage are part of the charter contract.

Time charters are period-based agreements that allow for more than one voyage. The exporter can decide whether the ship owner should provide a crew or not. A time charter of a ship without a crew is known as a bare-boat charter. By the nature of their business, tramp ships do not operate on fixed routes or on fixed schedules. Tramp ships, and especially bare-boat charters, lend themselves to be used almost as a form of private transport.

18.3.2.4 Private ship operations

Private ships are owned or leased long-term by firms for whom transporting goods is an ancillary function. Many oil tankers and bulk-ore ships fit into this category. The advantages of this form of operation are similar to those of ancillary road truck operations. In the short term, for example during peak trade periods, private ship operations may be supplemented with tramp ships.

An interesting aspect of international shipping is ship registry. For example, a ship may be owned by a South African citizen and ply a route between Australia and Japan; but it may be registered in and fly the flag of Liberia or Panama. These countries allow so-called flag of convenience arrangements. Ship owners derive certain benefits with respect to taxes, staffing, and relaxed safety requirements by being registered in those countries rather than in, say, South Africa or Australia.

18.3.2.5 Lighter-aboard ship operations

Lighter-aboard ships (LASH) carry barges from inland rivers or waterways to the sea port by water tow. A specially designed ocean ship carries the payload and barge intact to a foreign port to be dropped off in the harbour. This system minimises port handling and enables short ship turnaround times and high utilisation. The disadvantages of the LASH ship are similar to those of the container ship in that the ocean ship also requires a high capital investment, while the presence of barges or containers reduces the stowage factor. These two factors are generally traded off against the short port turnaround time provided by these systems. LASH ships operate mostly in North America and to some extent in Europe.

18.3.3 Air transport

18.3.3.1 Background

As in the case of domestic carriage, air transport offers the international transport user short airport-to-airport transit times and reliable service. When trading time-sensitive and high-value goods between businesses located in landlocked countries or between businesses located far from a seaport but close to an international airport, the potential benefits of using air transport are obvious.

Although air transport accounts for only 1 per cent of international trade by volume, it represents approximately 10 per cent by value. Although airfreight rates are substantially higher than sea freight rates, air carriage does provide savings with respect to other costs:[9]

- Insurance premiums are usually less than half those for ocean transport, for example, 0,3 per cent of airfreight value against 0,7 per cent of ship freight value.
- Freight is charged on gross mass. This is usually lower for air consignments due to fewer packaging requirements than for sea shipments.
- Packaging is substantially lighter and cheaper for air transport.
- Inventory and warehousing costs in many cases can be reduced and even eliminated by using air transport rather than carriage by ocean transport. Inventory reduction depends on reliable and high-frequency shipment arrivals of low-unit volume, which can be a decisive cost factor in favour of air transport.
- Regarding financing costs for consignments in which the receiver's payment obligation is effected by delivery to the receiver's premises, the seller receives payment substantially sooner with air transport. Not only is sooner receipt of payment preferred to receipt of payment later, but opportunity cost (interest) tied in carrying high-value inventory is also eliminated.

Four types of air carriers are available for international freight consignors: air parcel post; express or courier; passenger; and freight aircraft.

18.3.3.2 Air parcel postal services

Air parcel postal services, designed for carrying small packages, are provided by the public mail service of a country. Mail service providers contract air transport providers to carry the parcels from one country to another. The operator's obligations are limited to carriage between airports only. There are restrictions on the size and mass of the items handled by air parcel post: the maximum mass of airmail parcels is often restricted to 30 kg, but this limit varies from country to country.

18.3.3.3 Express or courier services

Express or courier services are generally restricted to small consignments weighing less than 30 kg. The main characteristic of this service is that short transit times, and next-day or second-day delivery are standard. Courier services include collection and delivery; the service is offered on a door-to-door basis.

18.3.3.4 Passenger carriers

Regularly, scheduled international passenger flights carry freight in the cargo hold of the aircraft. These carriers focus on transporting passengers, but the excess capacity in the freight compartment also allows the carriage of freight. (So-called combi aircraft are used, where passengers and freight form a payload combination.) Freight capacity and freight size are limited by the size of each aircraft, but high-frequency flight schedules usually afford consignors the choice of many international flights between large cities.

18.3.3.5 Freight carriers

Freight (or all-cargo) aircraft have larger hatch openings, freight compartments and higher floor-bearing ratings than passenger aircraft. Many freight aircraft have mechanised materials-handling devices on board for the movement of heavy cargo inside the aircraft. Some of the larger aircraft are capable of transporting 12 m container and road vehicles. These operators accept consignments weighing considerably more than 30 kg.

18.3.4 Non-operating service providers

In addition to the basic modes, the international goods transport user can make use of non-operating service providers. These providers offer several functions that afford the user lower costs, improved service and technical expertise.

18.3.4.1 Airfreight forwarders[10]

Overview

Through the International Air Transport Association (IATA), air carriers oversee a worldwide airfreight agents' organisation, to which most airfreight forwarders adhere. Appointment as an IATA airfreight agent allows a forwarder to market airfreight services, knowing that IATA member airlines carry the freight for a fixed price and with a commission for the forwarder. IATA agents must demonstrate certain financial and freight-handling resources, and must agree to remit to the air carrier freight billings according to fixed schedules.

Air carriers often freely provide forwarders with air waybills (AWBs) that bear the airline's logo. As with other non-negotiable transport documents, an AWB is both a receipt for the goods and a contract of carriage. In most countries today, the AWB system is computerised and the air carriers only issue AWB numbers to the forwarders. The forwarder then prints out the AWB number and airline logo on a form known as a neutral AWB.

Forwarders also acting as consolidators may issue AWBs in their own name as carriers, in which case their role can be likened to that of non-vessel operating common carriers (NVOCCs) in sea transport. By consolidating, or grouping, different consignments together, forwarders are able to obtain the lower freight rates offered by carriers for large consignments. In this, the air consolidators perform a groupage function like that of container shipping terminals. Consolidators may provide warehouse services upon departure; upon arrival, they may handle the notification of the consignee by e-mail or telephone. In addition, consolidators often offer a door-to-door service, which includes customs clearance and insurance coverage.

International airfreight forwarders reserve space on an operator's aircraft and solicit freight from several consignors to fill the reserved space. An airfreight forwarder can offer the sender of small consignments a rate saving as a result of advance booking. In addition, they offer convenience to the user when more than one airline is involved or when ground transport is necessary at one or both ends of the flight. They may also assist in completing all documentation and taking care of statutory requirements.

Freight handling

Airfreight containers corresponding to the shape of an aircraft's cabin are known as unit load devices (ULDs). There are various shapes and sizes of ULDs, each designed to be stored in a different section of the aircraft. Freight is handled primarily by pushing or pulling pallets and ULDs into and out of an aircraft over roller devices. Since ULDs are usually packed in terminals at or near the airport, it is possible for freight delivered to an air terminal to be loaded on a departing flight in two hours. The actual loading or unloading can take less than one hour. Rather than going into storage at a bonded warehouse, departing and arriving air consignments are normally cross-docked or transhipped at the forwarder's terminal in order to reduce total transit time.

Guaranteed shipment time

Some airlines offer guaranteed shipment dates and times. This eliminates the risk to the exporter of freight being delayed as a result of being forced off a particular flight to make room for special high-priority shipments. Although the extent of the guarantee varies from airline to airline, it is generally useful for the exporter to request it, especially as some airlines make such guarantees at little or no extra charge.

18.3.4.2 International ship freight forwarders

These service providers arrange transport for the consignor of international shipments. They do not necessarily act as consolidators. International ship freight forwarders act as agents for users, applying their experience and expertise to facilitate through-movement. Although they concentrate on ocean transport, ship freight forwarders often also provide a forwarding service in international air transport. They represent the consignor in arranging activities like inland transport, packaging, documentation, booking and legal and government formalities, charging a percentage of the tariffs levied for these services. They fulfil an indispensable function for consignors who are not familiar with the intricacies of international ocean transport or who do not have the scale or volume to warrant the employment of such expertise.

18.3.4.3 Non-vessel operating common carriers

NVOCCs provide scheduled ocean shipping services without owning, operating or chartering ships. NVOCCs are similar to freight forwarders: they assemble and disperse partial container shipments so that these are transported as full container consignments. Instead of a consignor moving a small item by breakbulk ocean carrier or airfreight, an NVOCC consolidates it with others and gains the advantages of full-container transport. Some NVOCCs operate from inland, especially in landlocked countries, where they unload inbound containers and distribute the goods to consignees. They then solicit outbound freight, consolidate shipments and send them back to a seaport for outbound movement. Through the NVOCC solicitations, the shipping line benefits from broadened territorial traffic and additional services, and gains control over containers. Consignors and consignees gain from the shipping expertise and business practices of the NVOCC, as well as from expanded and simplified import and export operations. Foreign freight forwarders may select an NVOCC instead of an ocean liner for the ocean segment of the freight movement.

18.3.4.4 Shipbrokers

Shipbrokers act as intermediaries between tramp ship operators and chartering consignors or consignees. The brokers' extensive exposure to, contacts within and knowledge of, the tramp ship market make them valuable parties in shipping arrangements. They charge a percentage of the chartering fees.

18.3.4.5 Ship agents

Ship agents act on behalf of a liner operator, ship owner or tramp ship operator in facilitating ship arrival; clearance; loading; unloading; provision of supplies; and fee payment at the port. Liner operators appoint agents when the frequency of voyages is so irregular that it is not economical for them to invest in their own terminals or to employ staff at a specific port.

18.4 International trade

Briefly, the origins of trade are believed to lie in local communities, with people bartering goods and services between each other. As travel extended beyond the immediate community and markets became separated from the source of production, trade transactions became more complex, necessitating the movement of goods.

Since the time of the ancient Greek philosophers, there have been multiple views of trade. These have ranged from the two ends of the spectrum of free trade to protectionism. Certain theories of commerce, such as mercantilism, were based on interventionist policies, with governments regulating the commercial environment, while free trade, advocated by 18th-century economist, Adam Smith, aimed to promote specialisation and enhanced productivity with minimal state interference.

18.4.1 The World Trade Organization

A world without any accepted practice for trade between nations would mean a regression to the times when pirates ruled the seas, and marauding nations conquered others for their resources.

The World Trade Organization (WTO) helps to foster world trade in an orderly and efficient manner. The WTO is the only international organisation dealing with the global rules of trade between nations. The role of the WTO is to ensure that trade flows as smoothly, predictably and freely as possible. It does this by:
- administering trade agreements;
- acting as a forum for trade negotiations;
- settling trade disputes; and
- reviewing national trade policies.

The WTO also supports and promotes regional agreements, such as the Southern African Development Cooperation (SADC), where a simpler movement of goods and services is allowed between the partners.

The WTO has 150 members, which accounts for more than 97 per cent of the world's trade. The organisation makes decisions by consensus amongst all members. The WTO's policy and top-level decision-making body is a ministerial conference, which occurs every two years. To support this body is a general council made up of ambassadors and trade officials from the various governments. The WTO is administered by a secretariat based in Geneva, Switzerland. The secretariat supplies the administrative and technical support to enable the various councils to reach decisions.

18.4.2 Multilateral Trading System

The increase in global trade has meant that nations with different ideologies, culture and religion are trading regularly. To make this work with the least amount of setbacks caused by such different backgrounds and understandings, those engaging in global trade need to have the assurance that they are working within a set of rules and procedures that allow them to trade with confidence and efficiency, as all the parties need to understand the processes and terms used. This is known as the Multilateral Trading System. It is a series of agreements that have been negotiated to foster trade. The WTO agreements are put into place by consensus among all WTO member countries, not just a majority, and then ratified by each country's government. These then flow into binding agreements between nations that govern the trade between them and other nations.

World trade has grown substantially and continues to grow. In nearly 50 years, world trade has grown annually at a rate of approximately 6 per cent. The growth in merchandise trade, shown in Table 18.2 and Figure 18.1, represents an even greater increase in the international movement of goods.

18.4.3 Benefits of WTO trading agreements

The smooth flow of trade achieves a number of advantages for partners in trade. It helps to remove trade disputes that, historically, have flared into political conflict or wars and promotes prosperity for the trading partners.

Table 18.2 World merchandise trade in current $US with a 1950 base

Flow	1950	1955	1960	1965	1970	1975	1980	1985	1990	1995	2000	2005
Exports	62 000	95 000	130 000	190 000	317 000	877 000	2 034 000	1 954 000	3 449 000	5 164 000	6 454 000	10 482 000
Imports	64 000	99 000	137 000	199 000	329 000	912 000	2 075 000	2 015 000	3 550 000	5 284 000	6 726 000	10 853 000
Total	126 000	194 000	267 000	389,000	646 000	1 789 000	4 109 000	3 969 000	6 999 000	10 448 000	13 180 000	21 335 000
Growth ratio	1,0	1,5	2,1	3,1	5,1	14,2	32,6	31,5	55,5	82,9	104,6	169,3

Source: WTO Statistics. Time Series on International Trade: http://stat.wto.org. Reprinted by permission of the WTO.

Figure 18.1 World merchandise trade growth ratio by year

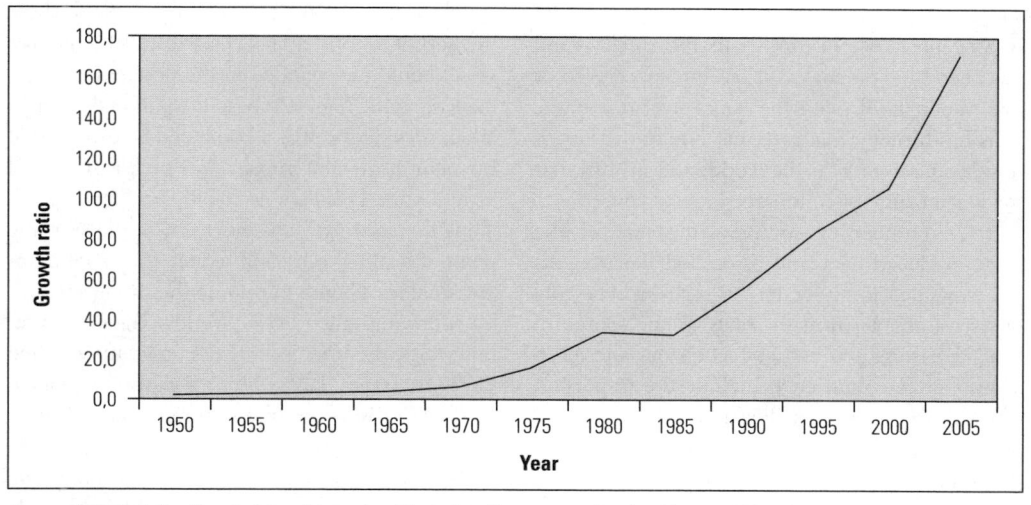

Source: WTO Statistics. Time Series on International Trade: http://stat.wto.org. Reprinted by permission of the WTO.

Protectionism in trade increases costs. An example is the cost of agricultural protectionism in the European Union. This protectionism is estimated to cost in the order of $1 500 for a family of four per year.

From these issues come ten benefits from the WTO:
- The system helps to keep the peace.
- Disputes are handled constructively.
- Rules make the lives of trading partners easier.
- Freer trade reduces the cost of living.
- The system provides more choice of products and quality levels.
- Trade raises incomes.
- Trade stimulates economic growth.
- Basic principles of free trade make life more efficient.
- Governments are shielded from lobbying.
- The system encourages good government.

18.5 Customs departments

The customs department arose from governments' desire to levy fees for imported goods. While the argument for free trade with no tariffs is valid, almost all countries have customs departments so that tariffs can be applied or at least records maintained of movements of goods into and out of a country. Countries have created customs or other departments to administer these tariffs and this statistical information. One of the most successful developments of this latter type of model is Singapore, where growth in the small island has been phenomenal as it has embraced zero or low import tariffs with the concept of free trade. This has turned Singapore into one of the largest transhipment ports in the world, and in turn, has made it a centre of commerce in its region.

In a number of countries the role of the customs department and associated departments has expanded to also cater for security. The role of a customs department solely as the source of tariff determination and collection has altered in a number of countries to include the inspection of goods to ensure that illegal and, in particular, explosive materials are not imported. Security is discussed further in Section 18.6.

18.6 Security issues

The importance of security in the supply chain to support international trade is not a new phenomenon. Historically, the emphasis has been on theft and piracy, which has plagued international movements for most of history. However, with the 9/11 attack in New York and other terrorist attacks around the world before and after that date, the risk of terrorist impact on the supply chain has risen to the forefront. Security has taken on a whole new dimension.

Terrorism has changed the world of international trade. Previously, the customs department was focused on determining tariffs, the collection of revenue from these tariffs and the provision of import and export data. The last decade or more of terrorism has seen a wider focus from many nations beyond tariffs and data. Terrorism is no longer a domestic threat, but a problem where political pressure can be exerted on countries using equipment imported across borders.

The ability to search each container or movement of goods across a border and still allow trade to be cost-effective is virtually impossible. The flow of goods is so large and the points of entry into and out of countries so numerous that there is no nation currently that can do this effectively. Terrorist attacks all over the world have led to another form of security – that of the entire chain of movement.

The entire chain is a problem in a world where this sort of terrorist attack is feasible. A bomb on a vessel could be exploded in the port where it was loaded, on the high seas or in the port of discharge. What is evident is that a bomb can be exploded at the point of greatest impact once on board a vessel or in a port. This logic is equally true for airports. Thus the security focus has been to move to the point of loading to try and reduce the exposure or potential for a bomb to get into the supply chain.

Following the 9/11 World Trade Center bombings, the USA instituted a programme called Customs-Trade Partnership Against Terrorism (C-TPAT). Run by the Customs and Border Protection Agency, this came into effect in late 2001 – a remarkable feat in such a short time. The programme is aimed at ensuring all the supply

chain is physically secured, and that bombs or radiation sources are not moved into the USA. The emphasis is on a partnership between the US customs and the members engaged in international trade. C-TPAT focuses on assessments of good security practice in:
- procedural security;
- physical security;
- access control to facilities supplying, handling and storing goods;
- personnel security/screenings;
- manifest accuracy; and
- total supply chain security for each leg.

Only C-TPAT members' freight will move during the next USA national security attack or threat. Therefore, there is a reduced number of inspections from customs; customs account managers are appointed to each company to facilitate their goods' movement; and the company will be eligible for account-based processes, allowing each company to operate their own account.

There are diverse views of the C-TPAT programme, but the principles are correctly focused on the supply chain. The issue is not complex: the security of goods cannot be achieved in international trade by an inspection at the inbound country's border. In today's world, the port – air or ocean – is part of the lifeblood of international trade. A ship exploding with radioactive fallout will close that port potentially for decades, and it is immaterial whether that explosion takes place in the entrance to the port or at a quay. Such an explosion can occur before the border or customs inspection, so the traditional security methods are ineffectual. The realisation that the entire chain must contribute to the security was novel, but very necessary with certain types of terrorist activity.

Today, the C-TPAT programme is voluntary. And it is only an inbound programme to try to prevent the movement of bombs or hazardous materials into the USA. The new World Customs Organization (WCO) framework extends this concept into a much broader view of safety and security, as is discussed later.

International trade focuses on trying to reduce the impact of terrorism, piracy and theft. To achieve this there are multiple models for security.

In essence, security in the supply chain focuses on a number of issues:
- Security adherence and credentials of the participants in the supply chain
- Screening and validation of the goods to be shipped by the loading entity or owner
- Advanced notice of goods being shipped to a recipient and the receiving country
- In-transit cargo security by all parties in the supply chain, including tamper-proof seals and locks
- Inspection of cargo at the port of entry

The recognition of this problem of life and goods security at sea was first addressed at the International Convention for the Safety of Life at Sea (SOLAS) of the International Maritime Organization (IMO). This convention gave rise to the International Ship and Port Facility Security (ISPS) code to cater for special measures to enhance maritime security. There is one part that is mandatory and one part that is recommended, which deals with how to comply with the mandatory section. Some of the mandatory issues are as follows:
- The requirement that administrations of contracting governments set security levels and provide security information to vessels that fly the administration's flag. Ships will comply with the contracting government's requirement for security while entering or while in a port.
- The master of the vessel is required to maintain the security of his ship without external influence from company, country or person.
- Ships must be provided with a security-alert system to reflect a security situation to an authorised agency on shore.
- Contracting governments must have port security facilities and assessments in place.

In addition to these, other security initiatives are being developed. Chief amongst these is the WCO's new security programme, entitled SAFE Framework of Standards, which the WCO adopted in June 2005. This initiative is a comprehensive set of global supply chain security standards.

It covers arrangements between customs-to-customs organisations and customs-to-business. The concept is progressive implementation by customs administrations and trade communities alike worldwide. The SAFE framework is a broad approach to supply chain security, meant to be consistent between countries, and organisations, thereby ensuring trade between mutually trusted traders in a safe and secure manner. As the WCO comprises 170 member countries representing approximately 99 per cent of global trade, this is a major global initiative.

Directly resulting from the SAFE framework, the European Union has developed and adopted the Authorised Economic Operator (AEO) programme. This came into effect on 1 January 2008 and incorporates all 27 member states of the EU. It is at present a voluntary programme, and is based on the SAFE framework. It has a large measure of the same principles as the C-TPAT programme. However, it is a wider review of the companies that are involved in the movement of goods. It embraces five sections of review:

- Company information. This is a detailed view of the company including its structure, ownership and its demonstrated capability and knowledge to comply with customs procedures.
- Compliance record. The record of customs compliance must be demonstrated.
- Company's accounting and logistical systems. The presence of adequate systems and controls within the IT system for both finance and logistics portions of the business must be proven.
- Financial solvency. Proof that the company has at least the last three years of solvency and good financial standing must be supplied.
- Safety and security requirements. A comprehensive plan to identify and manage the safety and security risks is required. The company must also demonstrate that it has adequate physical security for cargo and premises.

It is evident that the name of AEO, which the EU has chosen correctly, describes the programme. It is not merely a programme for physical security, as is evident in the US C-TPAT programme. It is a review of the company for its economic stability, systems capability, political propensity (from shareholding and structure) and physical security. This is a significant level above the C-TPAT programme, but as it comes six years later and is still in its infancy, one can see that this is the way the world will be required to adapt in order to maintain free-trade movements without major inspections and delays at every port and transition point.

Some of the other programmes around the world aimed at improving safety and security in international trade are:
- Australia's Frontline programme;
- Jordan's Customs Department Golden List Programme (GLP);
- New Zealand's Secure Export Scheme (SES);
- Singapore's Secure Trade Partnership (STP); and
- Sweden's StairSec programme.

As can be seen, international trade security is not an isolated, single-country initiative, but a worldwide programme that is gaining momentum.

18.7 Free-trade agreements and free-trade zones

18.7.1 Free-trade agreements

Free-trade agreements are allowed under the WTO agreements (from the GATT period). They are an agreement by two or more nations to allow trade between their countries with lower or reduced tariffs than are applied to the other nations with which they trade. They are also known as regional trade agreements. These agreements foster trade between the nations within the agreements. Some examples of these agreements are as follows:
- The EU has the European Free Trade Association (EFTA).
- The USA has the North American Free Trade Agreement (NAFTA), which is an agreement between the USA, Canada and Mexico.
- The Southern African Customs Union (SACU) agreement with Botswana, Lesotho, Namibia, South Africa and Swaziland.

There is some concern about these agreements, as they allow preferential trade between countries that are party to the agreements. This moves away from the ideal that all nations should be allowed free trade at common tariffs. However, the enhanced movement of goods within a region allows the regional economy to be stimulated and from this point of view, free-trade agreements are of value to international trade. The value is that some regions may become an entity with enhanced movement of goods and, as in the case of the EU, this leads to new economic unions.

18.7.2 Free-trade zones

A free-trade zone (FTZ) is an area that is considered by a country to be outside of its customs territory. This allows importers to move goods into the zone without clearing customs or paying duties. This usually also excludes taxes on the goods. The goods are then exported without customs duties, as long as they are sent out of the country. This type of agreement fosters the growth of business in a low-cost environment and brings jobs and hence labour skills to these zones. FTZs are often augmented by incentives to promote investment in manufacturing facilities in the zone and, therefore, in the skills of the country.

While an FTZ is considered to be outside of the country's customs zone, the goods entering and leaving are carefully documented and the information managed. Any goods that have entered the FTZ and need to be moved into the country attract a duty and require special documentation.

18.8 International trade information requirements

As Section 18.4 of this chapter explained, trade has grown more complex since the days of direct bartering between two parties. Today, the movement of goods requires the correct information and documentation. The information to move goods internationally must allow all the parties in the movement to perform their activities in an efficient manner, so it must be correct, clear and intelligible to multiple parties. To move goods internationally, the following parties must have a clear understanding and records to refer to:
- Exporter
- Importer
- Shipping company (ocean or air)
- Freight forwarder
- Land transport (truck or rail)
- Banks
- Exporting country's regulatory agencies
- Importing country's regulatory agencies
- Regulatory agencies of intermediate countries' (i.e. through which goods pass)

The data that is required is set internationally, largely by the WTO and WCO. A number of these are standardised coding of the goods, so that customs officials can apply tariffs and check that licences are appropriate without detailed knowledge of the products. This is essential, as the normal customs official can hardly be expected to understand and recognise all the varied products that pass through their review. Thus, classification systems enable them to recognise categories of products and perform their reviews on the types of products.

18.8.1 Harmonised Schedule or Tariff Code number

All products moved internationally are allocated a Harmonised Schedule, or Tariff Code, number. Every item can be classified by a set of numbers that allows similar material to be given a standardised number in this schedule. These categories are designated by a series of numbers that start with the broadest category and become more specific. This is administered as part of the WTO. This grouping allows items to be classified according to an international standard method for movement globally.

An example to illustrate this would be to assign all mugs that one drinks out of in the following way:
- Highest level
    Liquid receptacle
- Next level
    Drinking purposes
- Next level
    Personal use
- Next level
    Mug

The system allows all mugs for drinking coffee, for example, irrespective of shape or colour, to be classified with the same number. Customs authorities use HS numbers to allocate duties, as each number attracts a standard duty. This facilitates trade, as the customs official does not need to identify each item. The HS codes have been assigned to each item, and all the items with the same HS code will be declared as a group and attract the same duty.

The import tariff rate that is applied to goods with a particular HS code is often modified by the source of the goods or the country of origin. This allows countries to control imports from certain countries and make it more attractive to source those goods from alternative countries by means of differential tariffs based on country of origin. Thus, regional trade agreements result in lower tariffs for goods from the member countries, and countries can raise tariffs if a country is exporting subsidised goods.

18.8.2 Export Control Classification Number

The Export Control Classification Number (ECCN) is a five-digit alpha-numeric code that identifies the technology level and the capabilities of an item, and, in combination with the country of destination, customer and the intended application, then determines if an export licence is required for a specific transaction or whether an item can be exported without a licence. The ECCN must be determined prior to shipment. This is merely a grouping of all products into specific categories as defined by the above requirements so that all items in the category are given the same licensing requirements. The specific licence must also be recorded if one is required.

18.8.3 Licences

A number of goods in each country require a licence either to be exported, or imported as the case may be. The requirements for these licences will be based on the HS code and the country of origin or the country of ultimate destination. In addition, there are cases for specific companies to be precluded from trade for categories of goods defined by the HS code. This varies from country to country and may alter as trade restrictions are applied. One aspect that is internationally applied is the movement of products that are sources of radiation, where export and import licences are given for individual sources only, and for specific periods.

18.8.4 Country of origin

The country of origin is required in an international shipment because a large number of the customs duties are dependent on the HS number and the country of origin. For example, countries that sell goods at below realistic market value (known as dumping) are given very high customs tariffs for the goods to prevent unrealistic amounts from being imported. It is not uncommon in these sorts of market conditions to have the tariff for one country of origin at, say, 50 per cent, while the commodities from other countries may have tariffs at just 5 per cent.

Some countries require the country of origin documentation to be on official paperwork from an organisation such as a chamber of commerce or council. Documents may also be certified by an appointed official. These requirements detract from electronic data exchange, as the documents have to be sent to the importing country in original format. Fortunately, the number of countries that require this is small. Most developed countries do not require this, as they deliberately foster ease of trade.

18.9 International trade documentation

There is a large number of service providers and agencies involved in the movement of goods. Documentation forms an integral part of all international goods transactions. Sellers and buyers need documents for bookkeeping; invoicing; cost accounting; taxation; export and import formalities; and payment. The aim of all the documentation is to facilitate the movement of goods from exporter to importer. To achieve this, the documentation must be present, correct and comprehensive. Documentation falls into four major categories:

- Export documents, which enable goods to move legally and correctly out of the country.
- Import documents, which enable goods to legally enter the country of receipt with duties paid.
- Transport documents, which assign tasks to each party in the supply chain for the movement of goods.
- Financial documents, which are associated with the financing of and payments for the transaction. These range from letters of credit from a bank to cashing a cheque for payment and insurance for the goods.

18.9.1 Documents required

Documentation for international trade is a complex subject, and the rules and requirements change frequently. Many of these documents are not well known. The principles that underlie the process are discussed in this section to give an understanding of the details required and to shed light on what can be a complex area.

The previous sections have shown that there are multiple service providers in the movement of goods internationally. Instructions for their duties and performance need to be recorded in written format. There are also numerous types of special documents needed, for example, for hazardous goods. A set of documents is required for all the following stages of a transaction:
- Supplier receives an order from the buyer
- Issues an invoice to the buyer
- Obtains the licences to move the goods
- Packs the goods and produces a packing list
- Produces the documentation to advise that the goods are:
  - hazardous (Material Safety Data Sheet, or MSDS); and/or
  - inspected with a certificate of inspection;
  - have complied with sanitation requirements (phytosanitary certificate)
- Gives country of origin where required
- Produces a shipping letter of instruction (SLI)
- Produces a commercial invoice
- Performs an export declaration
- Obtains banking documents
- Books the move with the shipping service provider (carrier or forwarder)
- Obtains dock receipt and master's receipt
- Provides the information to the importer for submission to the import country's customs to pay duties and clear the goods for import
- Goods receipt on delivery is acknowledged by the buyer
- Funds are transferred for the purchase in terms of the agreement between buyer and seller

18.9.2 Types of documents in international trade

This section provides examples of the most common documents used in international goods transactions and transportation. These documents can be divided into several categories.

18.9.2.1 Transaction documents

The key transaction document is the commercial invoice. All parties to the transaction use this document for invoicing, cost accounting and bookkeeping purposes. It is also required for export and import formalities and for most banking and payment procedures.

18.9.2.2 Export documents

These are documents required by the customs or export authority of the country of export. Export documents include licences; permits; export declarations; inspection certificates; commercial invoices; and sometimes transport documents.

18.9.2.3 Inspection documents

These documents are usually issued by (third-party) inspection firms acting on behalf of the buyer to certify the physical condition and quantities of the content of a consignment. Inspection documents are also issued to meet export and import requirements and health and safety regulations. In certain countries and for certain commodities, the health and safety inspection certificate must be issued by an appropriate government entity or by a government-accredited inspection body.

18.9.2.4 Insurance documents

These documents describe the exact insurance coverage of a consignment and can be in the form of an insurance policy contract or certificate.

18.9.2.5 Financial documents

These include banking and payment documents, such as letters of credit, amendments to letters of credit and financial advice pertaining to a transaction. To conclude the financial aspects of an international goods transaction, virtually all the other documents used in international trade (e.g. bill of lading, commercial invoice, insurance documents and inspection certificate) must be available.

18.9.2.6 Import documents

These are documents required by the customs authority of the country of import. The minimum requirement is an entry form and a commercial invoice. Additional documents may be required if:
- the imported merchandise is sensitive (e.g. live animals, dangerous goods, drugs, foodstuff);
- the importer is requesting special tariff treatment under an import programme; or
- the goods are imported from certain countries.

18.9.2.7 Transport documents

These documents – issued by the transport operator or non-operating service provider – detail the terms of transport. The key transport document is the bill of lading. A packing list often supplements the bill of lading.

18.9.3 Common documents in international trade

18.9.3.1 Customs declaration or commercial invoice

A commercial invoice is a document issued to reflect the sale of goods to a buyer and contains all the information required for the customs department of both the seller's and buyer's country as a record of goods that move internationally. A commercial invoice contains the information shown in Section 18.10.1. Additional accompanying documents may be required if the goods being moved warrant them, such as a dangerous goods certificate. When the commercial invoice is produced, almost always a shipper letter of instruction (SLI) is produced as well to facilitate the movement.

To move goods internationally they must be declared to customs or another designated department of the country from which the goods are exported and to the customs or other designated department of the country into which they are moved. The declaration to customs for export is primarily to ensure that only goods that are permitted may leave the country (hence the need for licences for certain goods), and to gain information as to what is leaving the country in the form of statistics.

The customs department for the importing country may well have a different view. That country's authorities need to know what is imported in order to levy the appropriate duties for the class or category of goods defined by the HS number. Of course, they are also focused on ensuring that only goods with licences or those that do not require licences are imported.

The principle that needs to be understood is that the declaration to the exporting country defines the category of goods to be exported to the country to which they are moving. Some countries require a declaration that the goods will not be diverted to another country. Once this information is declared, the goods must be moved to that country, and the same information that is put on the export documentation must be put on the import documentation. As computer systems become more integrated between trading partners, this is becoming increasingly important, as it will cause problems if there are discrepancies.

A sample of the information that needs to be included in a commercial invoice is shown in Appendix 18.1 (page 420).

18.9.3.2 Packing list

This document, prepared by the consignor, lists the types and quantities of merchandise in a particular consignment. A copy of the packing list is often attached to the consignment and another copy is sent directly to the consignee to assist in checking the shipment when it is delivered. The packing list includes the following elements:
- name and address of seller;

- name and address of buyer;
- date of issue;
- invoice number;
- order or contract number;
- quantity and description of the goods;
- shipping details, including mass of the goods, number of packages and shipping marks and numbers;
- quantity and description of the contents of each package, carton, crate or container; and
- any other information required in the sales contract or documentary credit (e.g. country of origin).

18.9.3.3 Shipper's letter of instruction

The consignor of the goods needs to appoint forwarders or service providers to perform the moves and prepare the goods for movement or receipt in the total logistics chain. These service providers also require an instruction that gives them the authority to actually perform these services. The combined document that achieves this is the SLI.

The consignor issues the document, which then gives specific and detailed instructions to the service provider or providers to perform functions such as:
- arranging transport;
- booking ships;
- delivering goods to a customs broker in the receiving country;
- crating the goods; and
- adding marks to the crates (see following paragraphs).

The SLI must be clear and precise. The service providers cannot have ambiguity otherwise there will be an overlap in the service and extra charges will be incurred, plus confusions – or even worse, there may be a gap in the required service and the goods do not move because a step in the movement for export is not complete. In the above list of actions, the one step that is missing is who files the export declaration to the country of export's customs department. Without this, the goods will not move legally from the country.

When goods are prepared for movement, each box or pallet has some form of identification that makes sense to the sending company. This may just be a simple number that the sending company's computer system records, or it may be some additional information on a label. However, when these are delivered to a logistics service provider, to them this is just one of multiple crates that they receive for onward movement. This is exacerbated when the goods are crated into plywood boxes for movement by breakbulk modes. To remove confusion a summary of the delivery information is placed on the crate so that it can be identified and, in the absence of paperwork, the ultimate consignee can be determined. In short, the marks show the name and address of the receiving company, any special handling needs and any information required by the service providers to correctly move the crate. These marks are usually repeated in the SLI so the logistics service provider can take this paperwork and identify each individual item.

While not that common, one additional part of the SLI needs to be considered. There is the right to specify the way the goods must be placed in the ship. This is predominantly for breakbulk ships, and can be done in the SLI or in a separate document, called the stowage instructions. Goods that require extra protection may be specified to be in the hold, not under hatch locations, for example. The addition of these instructions places extra responsibility on the forwarder and the shipping line, and may incur additional costs or delays until the ship can find the space to allow these conditions to be met. This should be used with care.

18.9.3.4 Bill of lading or loading

The bill of lading (BOL) is a document issued by a carrier to a consignor and signed by the carrier or agent in charge of the means of transport. It furnishes written evidence of the receipt of the freight, the contractual conditions and the engagement to deliver a consignment at a prescribed destination to the legitimate holder of the bill of lading.

A completed bill of lading contains at least the following elements:
- The name of the carrier or multimodal transport operator, together with the signature of one of the following persons: the carrier, multimodal transport operator, ship's master, person in charge of the transport if not a ship, or agent.

- An indication that the consignment has been 'dispatched', 'taken in charge', 'loaded on board', or 'loaded on deck', along with the date.
- An indication of the place of departure, which may be different from the place of loading.
- An indication of the place of delivery, which may be different from the place of discharge.
- An original copy or, if multiple originals are issued, the full set of originals.
- The terms and conditions of carriage or a reference to the terms and conditions of carriage in another source or document.

A BOL is both a receipt for merchandise and a contract to deliver a consignment. There are various types of BOLS.

Non-negotiable bill of lading

A non-negotiable BOL indicates that the consignor will deliver a consignment to the consignee only. Possession of the document itself does not entitle anyone to the goods (hence non-negotiable), so the consignee needs some form of identification to claim the goods. A non-negotiable BOL is often used when the buyer has paid in advance or when goods are shipped on open account. A non-negotiable BOL cannot be transferred by endorsement. It is also known as a straight BOL.

Negotiable bill of lading

A negotiable BOL is a title document to the goods. It is issued 'to the order of' a party, usually the consignor, whose endorsement is required to effect its negotiation. Because it is negotiable, it can be bought, sold or traded while goods are in transit. The buyer needs an original as proof of ownership in order to take possession of the goods.

Air waybill

An air waybill is a BOL used for air transport. It is not negotiable.

Ocean bill of lading

An ocean BOL – also known as a marine or port-to-port BOL – is a document covering port-to-port consignments carried solely by sea transport. An ocean BOL must contain a notation that the goods were loaded on board or on deck.

An on-board notation means that the goods were loaded on board or carried onto a ship. The carrier, the carrier's agent, the master of the ship, or the ship's agent may make this notation. The transport document issued by the carrier must reflect that the consignment is on board in order for the seller to obtain payment under a documentary credit.

An on-deck notation means that the goods were secured on the deck of a ship, rather than in its hold, and are, therefore, subject to the elements. Such a notation is generally not acceptable in documentary credit transactions unless specifically authorised. If the transport document shows that the goods are loaded on deck, the enclosed insurance documents must show cover against on-deck risks. Live animals, dangerous goods (including certain chemicals), and odd-sized items are often carried on deck.

Clean bill of lading

A clean BOL is one on which the carrier notes that the merchandise has been received in apparent secure and good condition. Most transaction contracts require a clean BOL in order for the seller to obtain payment.

Claused bill of lading

A claused BOL – also called an unclean BOL – is the opposite of a clean BOL. It serves to confirm that a consignment was not delivered securely. It contains notations that specify a shortfall in quantity or deficient condition of the goods or packaging.

18.9.3.5 Dangerous goods certificate

The consignor has a responsibility and duty to advise if the goods are hazardous in any way. To do this in a consistent manner, the consignor issues a dangerous goods certificate (DGC). This is a document that specifies the nature of the hazard or hazards, what people must wear and know in order to handle the products and what people must do if the product is spilled. A DGC summarises the risks to people of dangerous goods, and how they must be handled to ensure safety of the goods and people.

DGCs are issued for a multitude of hazards: corrosiveness; irritation (for example, vapour harming eyes, nose and skin); flammability;

radioactivity; explosives; and any other dangers or problems. If the product requires a DGC, the packaging must have the appropriate international warning placards, which include the familiar diamond symbols for hazards.

18.9.3.6 Dock and master receipt

As goods are moved onwards for carriage, each party must acknowledge that the goods are received and in the care and custody of the company doing the movements. As goods are moved to a dock, the company receiving the goods or containers issues a dock receipt acknowledging the goods were received and the company loads them into the ship. Once on board, the master of the ship issues a master's receipt for the goods.

If goods are delivered damaged at any stage of the supply chain, the receipt may contain an endorsement which specifies the visible damage, or in more extreme cases, the goods may be rejected for movement.

18.10 Data to be submitted for international movement

18.10.1 Data required for exports

The following data is required essentially for all exports:
- Name and address of seller
- Name and address of buyer
- Date of issue

Then for each group of products under an HS number:
- HS number
- Material number
- Category description
- Quantity
- Value of the goods in the material number and totalled by HS number
- Weight of the goods
- ECCN and licence details

A number of countries require that a statement be added that requires goods to be delivered to the address, without diversion and an authorised signature for the shipper of record, which is the entity actually responsible for the exported goods.

18.10.2 Enhancements of data for transactions

As part of US customs and security, the submission of the data for movements to enter that country is now prescribed. As other security initiatives expand their scope, it is to be expected that these will become standard requirements so any company moving goods internationally must be prepared to produce this information for all shipments.

The following are the ten items of information that must be provided in the customs declaration:
1. Seller information. The name and address of the entity that is selling the goods via an export trade. This is the shipper of record entity that takes the formal and legal responsibility for the goods that are exported and is the responsible party for the declaration of these goods to the exporting country's customs or other designated department.
2. Buyer information. The name and address of the buyer of the goods and the address to which the goods are consigned. The goods must move to the country of the address given in this part of the information, as the entire licensing process ties categories of goods to the end destination. The address must be the final delivery point for the goods, and hence must be a physical address.
3. Importer of record number/foreign trade zone applicant identification number. The number assigned to the importer for tax or trade purposes that uniquely identifies the company.
4. Consignee number(s). The number that uniquely identifies the company to which the goods are consigned.
5. Supplier or manufacturer information. The name and address of the supplier of the goods that are to be exported. This may be the final manufacturer, assembler, supplier or producer of the goods.
6. Ship to party. The name and address of the first party that will physically receive the goods once they are released from customs. This is the notification party to ensure onward movement to the end destination.

7. Country of origin. This is the country from which the goods are deemed to be sourced. There is a complex set of rules that determine the country of origin. Where goods are assembled from items originating in different countries care must be taken to correctly specify the origin country, as it may not be the country of final assembly.
8. Commodity Harmonized Tariff Schedule number of the United States (HTSUS). This is the classification of the goods which determines the percentage charge that customs authorities levy to calculate the duties payable on entry into a country.
9. Container-stuffing location. The name and address of the physical location where the container was loaded. Where the shipments are breakbulk, this would be the physical location where the goods were crated.
10. Consolidator information. The name and address of the entity where the goods were consolidated for the shipment. In the case of the container, this might be the company arranging the loading of the container. The definition is the location where the goods were made ship ready.

Two new data fields are being added to assist with security:

Vessel stow plan
Under proposed regulations, the vessel stow plan must include standard information relating to the vessel and each container and unit of breakbulk cargo laden on the vessel. The vessel stow plan must include the following standard information. With regard to the vessel:
- Vessel name (including IMO number)
- Vessel operator
- Voyage number

With regard to each container or unit of breakbulk cargo:
- Container operator if containerised
- Equipment number if containerised
- Equipment size and type if containerised
- Stow position
- Hazmat-UN code
- Port of lading
- Port of discharge

Container status messages (CSM)
A notice of proposed rulemaking lists the proposed requirements for carriers to submit daily CSMs based on certain events. For each CSM submitted, the following information must be included:
- Event code reported, as defined in the ANSI X.12 or UN EDIFACT standards
- Container number
- Date and time of the event being reported
- Status of the container (empty or full)
- Location where the event took place
- Vessel identification associated with the message

18.11 International commercial terms

> International commercial terms (Incoterms) are the worldwide standard for the interpretation of trade terms.

The International Chamber of Commerce (ICC) developed these terms to serve as a set of uniform rules for the interpretation of commercial terms defining the costs, risks and obligations of sellers and buyers in international goods transactions. Note: in this chapter, 'seller' means seller, manufacturer or exporter; 'buyer' means buyer or importer. First published in 1936, Incoterms have been periodically revised to account for technological developments and changing modes of transport and document delivery. The current version is called Incoterms 2000.[11] Incoterms do not deal with title or point of payment. These must be defined specifically in the contract of sale.

18.11.1 Use of Incoterms

Incoterms are a set of contractual instruments facilitating the sale and transport of goods in international transactions. However, Incoterms are not implied by default in an international sales contract. If a contractor wants to use them,

they must be specifically included in the contract. The contract should expressly refer to the rules of interpretation as defined in the latest revision of Incoterms – Incoterms 2000. Additional contract provisions should ensure proper application of the terms. Incoterms are not laws, but precise definitions of the costs, risks and obligations of both parties in a contract. In the case of a dispute, courts and arbitrators will look at:
- the sales contract;
- who has possession of the goods; and
- what payment, if any, has been made.

Incoterms 2000 may be included in a contract of sale if the parties want to:
- complete a sale of goods;
- indicate each contracting party's costs, risks and obligations with regard to delivery of the goods; and
- establish basic terms of transport and delivery in a short format.

The costs, risks and obligations in the second part of the list above may be specified with respect to the following:
- The conditions that constitute completion of delivery
- How a party ensures that the other party has met the required conditions
- Which party must comply with requisite licence requirements and/or government-imposed formalities
- The mode(s) and terms of carriage
- The delivery terms and requirements for proof of delivery
- The stage when the risk of loss will transfer from the seller to the buyer
- How transport costs will be divided between the parties
- The notices that the parties are required to give to each other regarding the transport and transfer of the goods

Incoterms can be very useful, but if they are used incorrectly, contracts may be ambiguous, if not impossible to execute. It is, therefore, important to understand the scope and purpose of Incoterms – when and why they might be used – before relying on them to define such important terms as transport mode of delivery, customs clearance, passage of title and transfer of risk.

18.11.2 Organisation of Incoterms 2000

Incoterms 2000 are grouped into four categories, which are explained in the following sections.[12]

18.11.2.1 The E term (EXW)

This is the only instance where the seller makes the goods available to the buyer at the seller's own premises (see Figure 18.2).

Figure 18.2 Division of risks and costs between seller and buyer: EXW

Seller/ exporter premises	Export documents formalities	Delivery at named place of shipment: frontier/terminal/ quay	Loading port of shipment	On board ship's rail		On board ship's rail	Discharging port of arrival	Delivery at named place of destination: frontier/terminal/ quay	Import documents formalities	Buyer/ importer premises
Seller's risk									Buyer's risk	
Seller's costs									Buyer's costs	

Figure 18.3 Division of risks and costs between seller and buyer: F terms

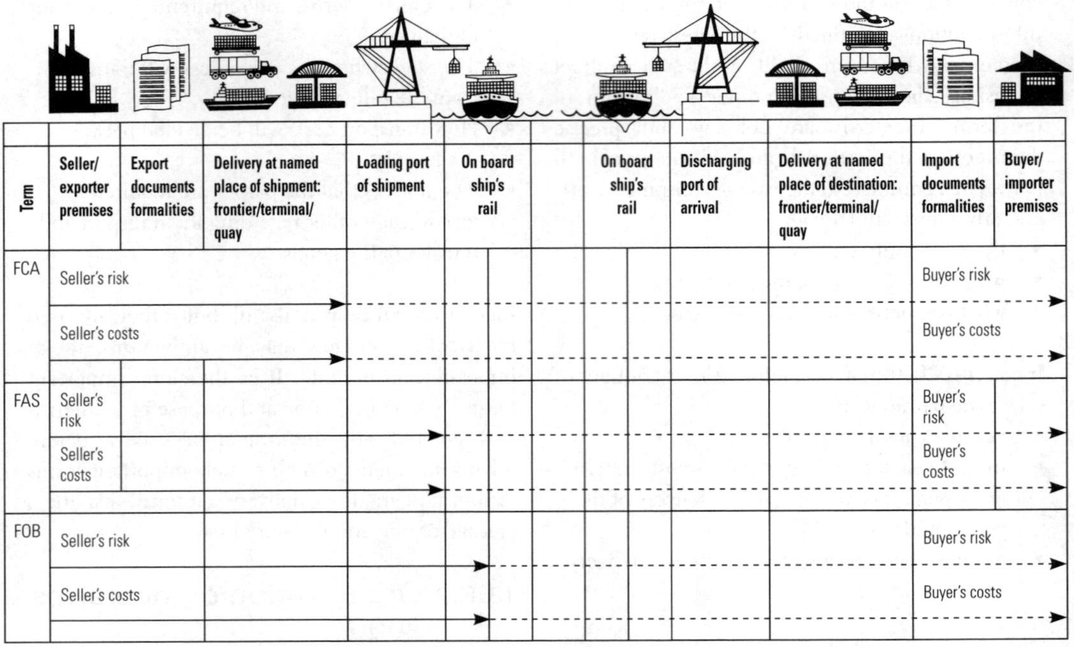

Term	Seller/exporter premises	Export documents formalities	Delivery at named place of shipment: frontier/terminal/quay	Loading port of shipment	On board ship's rail	On board ship's rail	Discharging port of arrival	Delivery at named place of destination: frontier/terminal/quay	Import documents formalities	Buyer/importer premises
FCA	Seller's risk								Buyer's risk	
	Seller's costs								Buyer's costs	
FAS	Seller's risk								Buyer's risk	
	Seller's costs								Buyer's costs	
FOB	Seller's risk								Buyer's risk	
	Seller's costs								Buyer's costs	

18.11.2.2 The F terms (FCA, FAS and FOB)

These terms indicate that the seller is responsible to deliver the goods to a carrier named by the buyer (see Figure 18.3).

18.11.2.3 The C terms (CFR, CIF, CPT and CIP)

According to these terms, the seller is responsible for contracting and paying for carriage, but not for additional costs or for risk of loss or damage once the goods have been shipped. C terms are appropriate for departure or shipment – as opposed to arrival – contracts (see Figure 18.4).

18.11.2.4 The D terms (DAF, DES, DEQ, DDU and DDP)

These terms indicate that the seller is responsible for all costs and risks associated with transporting the goods to the destination. D terms are appropriate for arrival contracts (see Figure 18.5, page 408).

Table 18.3 (page 409) sets out the four categories. Not all Incoterms are appropriate for all modes of transport. Some terms are applicable to carriage by ship, while others are applicable to any mode of transport. Table 18.4 (page 409) sets out which terms are appropriate for each mode of transport.

18.11.3 Description of Incoterms 2000

18.11.3.1 EXW – ex works (named place)

EXW means that the seller has completed delivery when it places the goods at the disposal of the buyer. This must be done at the seller's premises or another named place (for example, at point of production, factory or warehouse) before the goods are cleared for export and loaded onto a collection vehicle (see Figure 18.2).

This trade term places the greatest responsibility on the buyer and minimum obligations on the seller. The seller does not clear the goods for export and does not load the goods onto a means of transport at the named place of departure. The parties to the transaction may, however, decide that the seller should be responsible for the costs and risks of loading the goods onto a

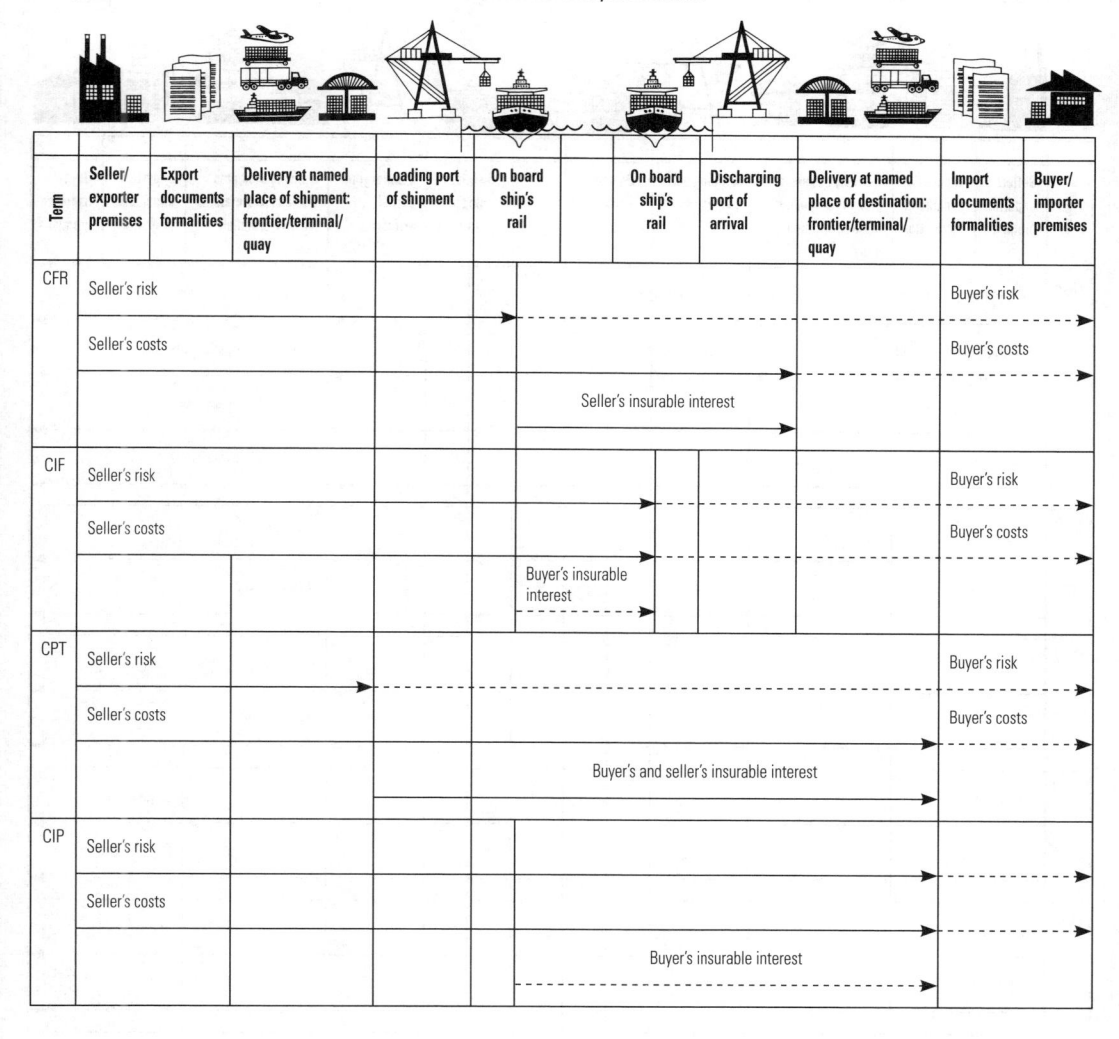

Figure 18.4 Division of risks and costs between seller and buyer: C terms

Term	Seller/exporter premises	Export documents formalities	Delivery at named place of shipment: frontier/terminal/quay	Loading port of shipment	On board ship's rail		On board ship's rail	Discharging port of arrival	Delivery at named place of destination: frontier/terminal/quay	Import documents formalities	Buyer/importer premises
CFR	Seller's risk				→					Buyer's risk	→
	Seller's costs					→				Buyer's costs	→
						Seller's insurable interest →					
CIF	Seller's risk				→					Buyer's risk	→
	Seller's costs					→				Buyer's costs	→
					Buyer's insurable interest →						
CPT	Seller's risk			→						Buyer's risk	→
	Seller's costs				→					Buyer's costs	→
					Buyer's and seller's insurable interest →						
CIP	Seller's risk								→		→
	Seller's costs								→		→
						Buyer's insurable interest →					

vehicle. Such a stipulation must be made in the contract of sale. If the buyer cannot handle export formalities, the EXW term should not be used. In such a case, free carrier (FCA) is recommended (see Figure 18.3).

The EXW term is often used when making an initial quotation for the sale of goods. It represents the cost of the goods without any other costs included. Payment terms for EXW transactions are generally cash in advance and open account. An open account is a credit and invoicing arrangement whereby the seller invoices the buyer periodically and payments are made over a specific period.

Examples
- EXW KWV Winery, Paarl, South Africa
- EXW XYZ Printing Plant, Heidelberg, Germany

18.11.3.2 FCA – free carrier (named place)

FCA means that the seller delivers the goods at the named place, cleared for export, to the carrier nominated by the buyer. The 'named place' in FCA and all other F terms is domestic to the seller. If the named place is the seller's place of business, the seller is responsible for loading the goods onto the

Figure 18.5 Division of risks and costs between seller and buyer: D terms

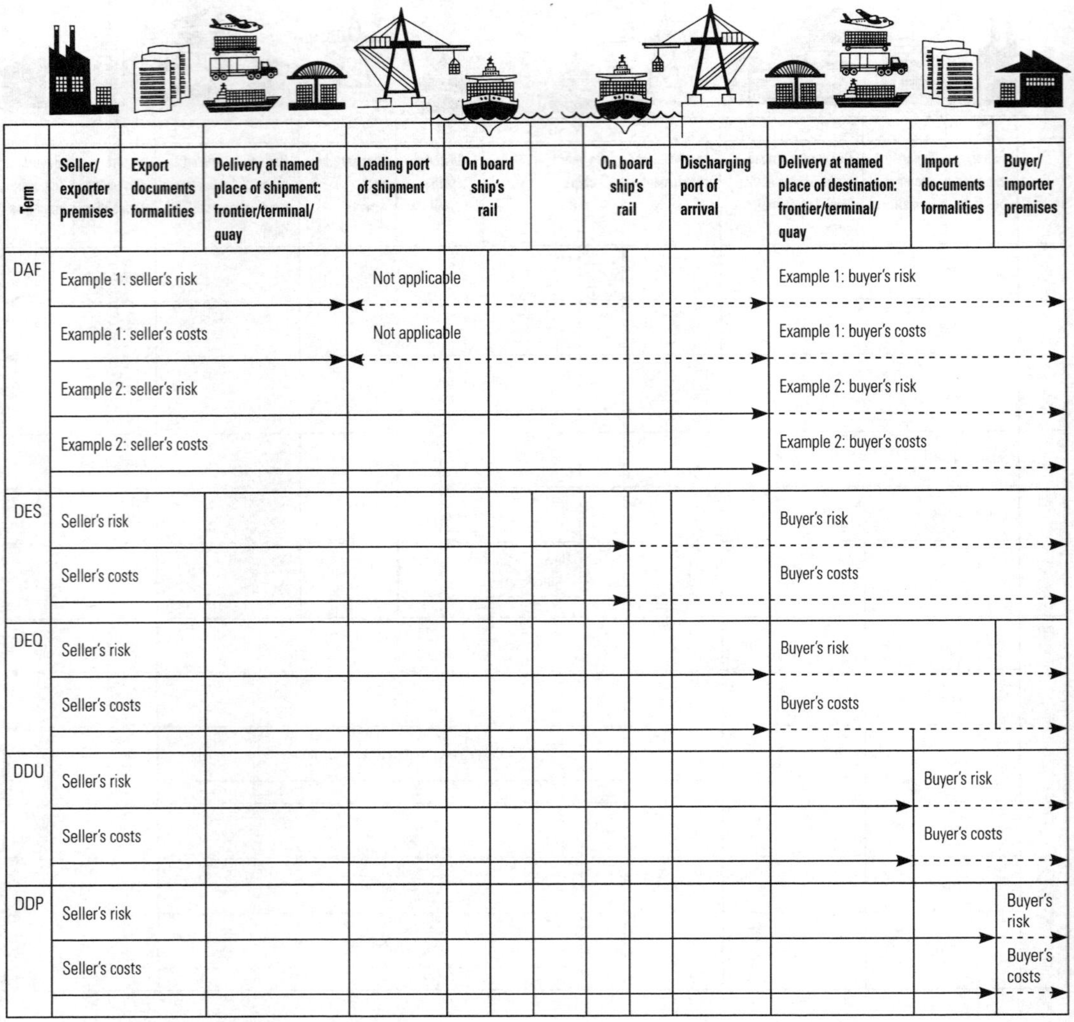

Term	Seller/ exporter premises	Export documents formalities	Delivery at named place of shipment: frontier/terminal/ quay	Loading port of shipment	On board ship's rail		On board ship's rail	Discharging port of arrival	Delivery at named place of destination: frontier/terminal/ quay	Import documents formalities	Buyer/ importer premises
DAF	Example 1: seller's risk			Not applicable					Example 1: buyer's risk		
	Example 1: seller's costs			Not applicable					Example 1: buyer's costs		
	Example 2: seller's risk								Example 2: buyer's risk		
	Example 2: seller's costs								Example 2: buyer's costs		
DES	Seller's risk								Buyer's risk		
	Seller's costs								Buyer's costs		
DEQ	Seller's risk								Buyer's risk		
	Seller's costs								Buyer's costs		
DDU	Seller's risk										Buyer's risk
	Seller's costs										Buyer's costs
DDP	Seller's risk										Buyer's risk
	Seller's costs										Buyer's costs

vehicle. If the named place is any other location, such as the loading dock of the carrier, the seller is not responsible for loading the goods onto the vehicle (see Figure 18.3).

The FCA term may be used for any mode of transport, including multimodal. The term 'carrier' has a somewhat broad meaning. A carrier can be a shipping line, airline, road freight operator or a rail transport operator. The carrier can also be a non-operating service provider that undertakes to procure carriage within any of the above modes of transport, including multimodal. In such a case, the buyer names the carrier that is to receive the goods.

The FCA term, like the EXW term, is often used when making an initial quotation for the sale of goods. Payment terms for FCA transactions are generally cash in advance and open account.

Examples
- FCA ABC Shipping Lines, Athens, Greece
- FCA South African Airways, Johannesburg International Airport, South Africa
- FCA AZ Freight Forwarders, Sydney, Australia

Table 18.3 Categories of Incoterms

Group	Code	Name of term
Group E Departure	EXW	Ex works (named place)
Group F Main carriage unpaid	FCA	Free carrier (named place)
	FAS	Free alongside ship (named port of shipment)
	FOB	Free on board (named port of shipment)
Group C Main carriage paid	CFR	Cost and freight (named port of destination)
	CIF	Cost, insurance and freight (named port of destination)
	CPT	Carriage paid to (named place of destination)
	CIP	Carriage and insurance paid to (named place of destination)
Group D Arrival	DAF	Delivered at frontier (named place)
	DES	Delivered ex ship (named port of destination)
	DEQ	Delivered ex quay (named port of destination)
	DDU	Delivered duty unpaid (named place of destination)
	DDP	Delivered duty paid (named place of destination)

Table 18.4 Modes of transport and appropriate Incoterms 2000

Mode of transport	Geographical point designation	Code	Term
Any mode of transport, including multimodal	Named place	EXW	Ex works
		FCA	Free carrier
		DAF	Delivered at frontier
	Named place of destination	CPT	Carriage paid to
		CIP	Carriage and insurance paid to
		DDU	Delivered duty unpaid
		DDP	Delivered duty paid
Sea and inland waterway transport only (ship)	Named port of shipment	FAS	Free alongside ship
		FOB	Free on board
	Named port of destination	CFR	Cost and freight
		CIF	Cost, insurance, and freight
		DES	Delivered ex ship
		DEQ	Delivered ex quay

18.11.3.3 FAS – free alongside ship (named port of shipment)

FAS means that the seller has completed delivery when the goods are placed alongside the vessel at the named port of shipment. The buyer has to bear all costs and risks of loss of or damage to the goods from that moment. The FAS term requires the seller to clear the goods for export. (This requirement is a new provision to Incoterms 2000.) The parties to the transaction may, however, stipulate in their contract of sale that the buyer will clear the goods for export. The named port in FAS – and all F terms – is domestic to the seller (see Figure 18.3).

The FAS term is used only for ocean or inland waterway transport. The term is commonly used in the sale of bulk goods, such as oil, grain and ore.

Payment terms for FAS transactions are generally cash in advance and open account, but letters of credit are also used. A letter of credit is a document issued by a bank stating its commitment to pay the seller a stated amount of money on behalf of the buyer, providing the seller meets very specific terms and conditions.

Examples
- FAS Buenos Aires, Argentina
- FAS Le Havre, France

18.11.3.4 FOB – free on board (named port of shipment)

This means that the seller has completed delivery when the goods pass the ship's rail (or ramp, in the case of a ro-ro ship) at the named port of shipment. The buyer has to bear all costs and risks of loss of or damage to the goods from that point. The FOB term requires the seller to clear the goods for export (see Figure 18.3).

The FOB term is used only for ocean or inland waterway transport. Payment terms for FOB transactions include cash in advance, open account and letters of credit.

The FOB term is commonly used in the sale of bulk goods, such as oil, grain and ore, where it is important to deliver the goods on board the ship. It is also used for shipping container loads.

The key document in FOB transactions is the on board bill of lading.

Examples
- FOB 'Vessel ABC' Dar es Salaam, Tanzania
- FOB 'Vessel XYZ' Auckland, New Zealand

18.11.3.5 CFR – cost and freight (named port of destination)

CFR means that the seller clears the goods for export and has completed delivery when the goods pass the ship's rail (or ramp, in the case of a ro-ro ship) at the port of departure (not destination). The named port of destination in CFR – and all C terms – is domestic to the buyer (see Figure 18.4).

The seller clears the goods for export and is also responsible for paying for the costs associated with transporting the goods to the named port of destination. Once the goods pass the ship's rail or ramp at the port of departure, the buyer assumes responsibility for risk of loss or damage as well as any additional transport costs. The seller may, however, have 'insurable interest' during the voyage. Prudence may dictate procurement of additional insurance coverage.

The CFR term is used only for ocean or inland waterway transport. It is commonly used in the sale of indivisible large or heavy items that do not fit into a container or which exceed the mass limitations of containers. The term is also used for LCL (less than container load) consignments. Payment terms for CFR transactions include cash in advance, open account and letters of credit.

Examples
- CFR Casablanca, Morocco
- CFR Antwerp, Belgium

18.11.3.6 CIF – cost, insurance and freight (named port of destination)

CIF means that the seller has completed delivery when the goods pass the ship's rail (or ramp, in the case of a ro-ro ship) in the port of departure (not destination). The named port of destination in CIF – and all C terms – is domestic to the buyer (see Figure 18.4).

The seller clears the goods for export and is responsible for paying for the costs associated with transporting the goods to the named port of destination. The seller is also responsible for procuring and paying for marine insurance in the buyer's name. Once the goods pass the ship's rail or ramp at the port of departure, the buyer assumes responsibility for risk of loss or damage and any additional transport costs. The buyer may exercise prudence and acquire additional insurance coverage.

The CIF term is used only for ocean or inland waterway transport.

Payment terms for CIF transactions include cash in advance, open account and letters of credit.

Examples
- CIF Walvis Bay, Namibia
- CIF Seward, Alaska, USA

18.11.3.7 CPT – carriage paid to (named place of destination)

CPT means that the seller nominates a carrier and delivers the goods to the nominated carrier. The named place of destination in CPT – and all C terms – is domestic to the buyer, but does not necessarily refer to the final delivery point (see Figure 18.4).

The seller clears the goods for export and pays the cost of carriage to the named destination. The seller is also responsible for the costs of unloading, customs clearance, duties and other costs of carriage. Once the seller delivers the goods to the carrier, the buyer becomes responsible for all additional costs. If subsequent carriers are used for carriage to the agreed destination, the risk is passed on when the goods are delivered to the first carrier. While neither the carrier nor the buyer is obligated to provide insurance during the main voyage, both may have an insurable interest. Prudence may indicate the acquisition of insurance coverage.

The CPT term is valid for any mode of transport, including multimodal.

A 'carrier' can be a shipping line, airline, road freight operator, rail transport operator or a non-operating service provider that undertakes to procure carriage from a transport operator.

The CPT term is often used in sales where the carriage is by airfreight or containerised ocean freight as well as for courier consignments of small parcels and ro-ro shipments of road vehicles.

18.11.3.8 CIP – carriage and insurance paid to (named place of destination)

CIP means that the seller nominates a carrier and delivers the goods to the nominated carrier (see Figure 18.4).

The seller must pay the cost of carriage to the named destination. The buyer bears all risks and any additional costs occurring after the goods have been delivered at this destination. However, in CIP the seller has to procure and pay for insurance against the buyer's risk of loss or damage during carriage. If subsequent carriers are used for the carriage to the agreed destination, the risk is passed on when the goods are delivered to the first carrier. Although the seller has to provide insurance coverage during the main voyage, the buyer may have additional insurable interest. Prudence may dictate the acquisition of additional insurance coverage.

The seller is also responsible for the costs of unloading, customs clearance, duties and other costs included in the cost of carriage.

The CIP term is valid for any mode of transport, including multimodal.

The CIP term is often used in sales where the carriage is by airfreight, containerised ocean freight, or courier, or where road vehicles are transported with ro-ro ships. A 'carrier' can be a shipping line, airline, road freight operator, rail transport operator or a non-operating provider that undertakes to procure carriage within any of the above modes of transport, including multimodal.

Examples
- CIP Frankfurt, Germany
- CIP Cairo, Egypt

18.11.3.9 DAF – delivered at frontier (named place)

DAF means that the seller has completed delivery when the goods are placed at the disposal of the buyer on the arriving vehicle, not unloaded. The seller has to clear the goods for export at the named point and place at the frontier, but not for import. However, goods have to be cleared for import before the customs border of the adjoining country. The term frontier may relate to the country of export or import (see Figure 18.5).

When using the DAF term, it is very important to name the precise place and time of delivery at the frontier, as the buyer must arrange to unload and secure the goods in time. The seller is not responsible for procuring and paying for insurance.

The DAF term is valid for any mode of transport – providing the final carriage, to the named place at the frontier, is by land.

Examples
- DAF Beit Bridge, Limpopo Province, South Africa. The consignment is transported by road truck from the premises of the seller in South Africa to the frontier at Beit Bridge. Here, the buyer takes possession and carries the goods by road truck to its premises in Zimbabwe. (See Figure 18.5.)
- DAF Basel, Switzerland. The seller arranges for the consignment to be transported from Manchester in England via truck and ferry

to the Netherlands, and then by truck to the border of Switzerland. The buyer takes possession of and arranges carriage for the consignment from this point onwards to the final destination in Bern (see Figure 18.5).

18.11.3.10 DES – delivered ex ship (named port of destination)

DES means that the seller has achieved delivery when the goods are placed at the disposal of the buyer on board the ship, but not cleared for import at the named port of destination. The seller is responsible for all costs related to transporting the goods to the named port of destination prior to unloading (see Figure 18.5).

The DES term is used only for shipment by ocean or inland waterway, or by multimodal transport where the final delivery is made on a vessel at the named port of destination.

All forms of payment are used in DES transactions.

Examples
- DES Port of Marseilles, France
- DES Port of Genoa, Italy

18.11.3.11 DEQ – delivered ex quay (named port of destination)

DEQ means that the seller has completed delivery when the goods are placed at the disposal of the buyer on the wharf at the named port of destination. The seller clears the goods for export but not for import. The buyer assumes all responsibilities for import clearance, duties and other costs related to import, as well as for transport to the final destination. (This is a new provision for Incoterms 2000.)

The DEQ term is used only when shipments arrive at the port of destination by ocean or by inland waterway transport (see Figure 18.5).

All forms of payment are used in DEQ transactions.

Examples
- DEQ Alexandria, Egypt
- DEQ Dublin, Ireland

18.11.3.12 DDU – delivered duty unpaid (named destination)

DDU means that the seller is responsible for making the goods available to the buyer at the named destination, but not for unloading the goods from the arriving means of transport. The seller clears the goods only for export. The seller assumes all responsibilities for delivering the goods to the named destination. The buyer assumes all responsibility for import clearance, duties, administrative costs and any other costs related to import. The buyer is also responsible for transport to the final destination.

The DDU term can be used for any mode of transport. However, if the seller and buyer prefer the goods to be delivered on board a sea vessel or on a wharf, the DES or DEQ terms are recommended. The DDU term is used when the named destination is beyond the seaport or airport of entry.

All forms of payment are used in DDU transactions.

Examples
- DDU Rome, Italy
- DDU Nairobi, Kenya

18.11.3.13 DDP – delivered duty paid (named destination)

DDP means that the seller is responsible for making the goods available to the buyer at the named destination, but not for unloading the goods from the arriving vehicle. The seller clears the goods for export and import and, therefore, assumes all responsibilities for delivering the goods to the named destination – including import clearance, duties and other costs payable upon import (see Figure 18.5).
- The DDP term can be used for any mode of transport. It is often used when the named destination (point of delivery) is beyond the seaport or airport of entry.
- All forms of payment are used in DDP transactions.

Examples
- DDP Xian, China
- DDP VAT unpaid, Paris, France

18.11.4 Notes on Incoterms 2000

18.11.4.1 Added wording

It is possible, and in many cases desirable, for the seller and buyer to add additional wording to an Incoterm. For example, if the seller agrees to DDP terms and is willing to pay for customs formalities and import duties, but not for VAT, the term 'DDP (VAT unpaid)' may be used.

18.11.4.2 Appropriate contract

Incoterms were designed to be used within the context of a written contract for the cross-border (international) sale of goods. Incoterms therefore refer to the contract of sale, rather than the contract of carriage. Buyers and sellers should specify that their contract is governed by Incoterms 2000.

18.11.4.3 Customs of the port or trade

Incoterms are an attempt to standardise trade terms for all nations and all trades. However, different ports and different trades have their own customs and practices. It is best to specify customs and practices in the sales contract.

18.11.4.4 Electronic data interchange

It is increasingly common for sellers to prepare and transmit documents electronically. Incoterms provide for electronic data interchange (EDI), provided that buyers and sellers agree on its use in the sales contract.

18.11.4.5 Export and import customs clearance[13]

International freight movements involve at least two customs clearances: one upon export and one upon import. Upon export, an export licence may or may not be required. Export licences are generally required in the case of exporting politically or strategically sensitive goods, for example, firearms, armaments, chemicals or high-technology goods.

Upon import, customs and excise duties, taxes and port charges will be payable. The choice of Incoterm will determine who between exporter or importer has the responsibility of export or import clearance.

It is usually desirable that the seller handles export customs formalities and the buyer handles import customs formalities. However, some trade terms require that the buyer handles export formalities and others require that the seller handles import formalities. In each case, both the buyer and seller have to assume risk arising from export and import restrictions and prohibitions. In some cases, foreign exporters may not be able to obtain import licences in the country of import. This should be researched before accepting the final terms.

Exporters and importers normally use customs brokers (also known as customs-house brokers) to clear their consignments through customs. Brokers act as the agents of traders in their dealings with customs authorities. It is important, therefore, that traders carefully instruct their brokers as to the nature and the value of the goods and the taxes and duties they expect (and are willing) to pay. Traders often require that the broker contact them for assistance whenever difficulties arise during clearance, for the trader will usually be more able to answer questions or resolve disputes concerning the technical details, quality or value of the consignment.

18.11.4.6 EXW and FCA

When goods are bought EXW or FCA, the buyer needs to arrange for the contract of carriage. Since the shipper does not receive a BOL, it is not possible to use a letter of credit requiring a BOL.

18.11.4.7 Inspection

The original contract should include the terms of inspection. The following conventions often apply:
- The seller is responsible for the costs of inspecting whether the quantity and quality of the shipment conform to the sales contract.
- The party responsible for export formalities needs to take care of pre-shipment inspections as required by the export authority.
- The party responsible for import formalities needs to take care of pre-shipment inspections as required by the import authority.
- Third-party inspections for independent verification of quality and quantity (if required) are generally the responsibility of the buyer. The buyer may require such an inspection and inspection document as a condition of payment.

18.11.4.8 Insurable interest

In many cases, either the buyer or the seller is obligated to provide insurance. Sometimes neither party is obligated to provide insurance. Prudence often dictates purchasing insurance coverage. In some cases, however, neither buyer nor seller may have provided insurance coverage and are at risk for the portion of the trip specified in the Incoterms in the contract.

18.11.4.9 Packaging

It is the responsibility of the seller to provide packaging, unless the goods are customarily shipped in bulk (e.g. ore, oil, or grain). The buyer and seller should preferably agree in the sales contract on the type and extent of packaging required. If the type or duration of transport is not known beforehand, the seller is only responsible for providing safe and appropriate packaging to withstand the circumstances that the buyer has made known beforehand.

If the seller is responsible for sending goods in an ocean or airfreight container, it is also the seller's responsibility to see that the container is packed to withstand shipment.

18.11.4.10 Passing of risks and costs

The general rule is that risks and costs pass from the seller to the buyer once the seller has delivered the goods to the point named in the trade terms. These points are illustrated in Figures 18.2 to 18.5.

18.11.4.11 Precise point of delivery

If the buyer is unable to name the precise point of delivery in the contract in time, the seller has the option to deliver at a range of points that fall within the terms of the contract. For example, the original terms of sale may state CFR Port of Rotterdam. The Port of Rotterdam is very large and the buyer may favour a particular point within the port. The buyer should state this point in the sales contract and in the trade terms. The buyer becomes liable for the goods once they arrive and may be responsible for unloading costs, storage and other charges once the goods arrive at the named point.

Delivery may take place at a bonded warehouse at or close to the port of arrival. A bonded warehouse is authorised to store imported goods without payment of duties and taxes during the period of storage. The warehouse owner has to provide a bond to the customs authorities in order to cover any potential liability for duties and taxes. A benefit of a bonded warehouse is that the importer or his customers may inspect the goods before paying the duty. In the event of the goods being defective, the importer can either reject them, or if he already owns the goods, seek to have them sold or re-exported to another party. Another benefit of a bonded warehouse is that for goods assessed as having high duties (for example, tobacco and alcohol products), payment of the duty can be delayed, thereby enabling the importer to save the interest on the amount of the duty and taxes during the period of storage.[14]

Before the introduction of Incoterms 2000, many exporters quoted FOB Airport prices for air consignments. This often caused misunderstandings with respect to airport handling charges and extent of insurance coverage. The FOB term was developed in ocean transport, where the ship's rail is the traditional point for the division of costs and risks. Obviously, an aircraft does not have a ship's rail, and goods are not delivered alongside an aircraft. Therefore, the application of FOB principles derived from ocean transport is not appropriate. Consequently, the ICC discontinued the FOB Airport term in its 2000 revision of Incoterms. The ICC recommends that shippers use the FCA Incoterm instead, with the specified point of delivery being the named airfreight or consolidator's terminal.[15]

18.12 Conclusion

In a rapidly integrating and globalising world market, efficient and effective logistics support structures relating to international goods transactions are indispensable. Logistics managers involved in international distribution must acquaint themselves with distribution channels because they need to understand how products flow to foreign consumers. The longer the channel, the greater the number of intermediaries. International goods transport is provided by all modes. However, the vast majority of goods are moved by sea and air transport.

The required information and documents for international trade have been described in this chapter and the most common defined. These documents and the data required to complete them must be correct and supplied to the relevant service providers, government agencies and financial agencies that are party to the trade in order to allow goods to flow unhindered. Documentation forms an integral part of all international goods transactions. Sellers and buyers need transaction documents for bookkeeping, invoicing, cost accounting, taxation export and import formalities, as well as for making payments.

Incoterms are the worldwide standards for the interpretation of international trade terms. Incoterms are a set of contractual instruments facilitating the sale and transport of goods in international transactions.

Key terms

- Air parcel postal service
- Air transport
- Air waybill
- Airfreight forwarder
- Bill of lading (BOL)
- Bonded warehouse
- Commercial invoice
- Container ship
- Courier service
- Dangerous goods certificate (DGC)
- Distribution channel
- Distributor
- Dock receipt
- Export agent
- Free trade agreement
- Free trade zone (FTZ)
- Freight forwarder
- Harmonised Schedule number (HS number)
- Incoterms:
  - Carriage and insurance paid to (CIP)
  - Carriage paid to (CPT)
  - Cost and freight (CFR)
  - Cost, insurance and freight (CIF)
  - Delivered at frontier (DAF)
  - Delivered duty paid (DDP)
  - Delivered duty unpaid (DDU)
- Delivered ex quay (DEQ)
- Delivered ex ship (DES)
- Ex works (EXW)
- Free alongside ship (FAS)
- Free carrier (FCA)
- Free on board (FOB)
- Industrial buyer
- Lighter-aboard ship (LASH)
- Liner ship
- Master's receipt
- Non-operating service provider
- Non-vessel operating common carrier (NVOCC)
- Ocean transport
- Packing list
- Pipeline transport
- Point of delivery
- Ro-ro ship
- Ship agent
- Shipbroker
- Shipper's letter of instruction (SLI)
- Trading house
- Tramp ship
- Wholesaler
- World Trade Organization

Case study

The Austrian Treasury, Vienna, has awarded the contract to mint and print Euro coins and banknotes during the following five years to two subsidiaries of the South African Reserve Bank, namely, the South African Mint and South African Banknote Factory, both near Pretoria. The Austrian Treasury requires that consignments should be delivered to any customs facility in Austria. Each consignment will consist, firstly, of coins that require 24 m^3 of loading space (the outside measurements of the mint containers are 50 cm x 50 cm x 20 cm) and have a gross mass of 40 tons, and, secondly, banknotes, which will require exactly the same loading space as the coins, but which will weigh 10 tons. (1 ton = 1 000 kg.)

You are contracted to advise the South African Reserve Bank on the following:

1. The modes of transport that should be employed to move the coins and banknotes once a month from Pretoria to Vienna (or the Austrian border), indicating the origin and destination of each route section covered by each mode of transport.
2. The appropriate Incoterm(s) to use.

Include your reasons with your answers.

Notes

1. You might find the website addresses cited in Chapters 11, 13 and 18 (and that of Austrian Airlines) helpful.
2. State all your assumptions clearly.

Case study

A company's sales staff have sent a note to the logistics department advising them of a new contract. The sales staff have negotiated a deal to supply goods from a manufacturing plant in the USA and a manufacturing plant in South Africa to Nigeria. The Incoterm was DDP and the customs clearance was to be done by the customer in Nigeria, because the customer could get a special development reduction in the duties to 50 per cent of the normal duties. The sales staff have placed a logistics cost of R2 500 on each container move.

Describe the major issues that this contract would create for the supply chain and in particular the logistics group. If you feel that the DDP term is not the most suitable, then explain why you would not choose an E, F or C term and which specific term or terms you would choose, and why.

Case study

Country X is contemplating two trade agreements. The first is with two countries on its western border. Both of these countries are mineral-rich and have growing economies that are somewhat similar in size and robustness in GDP to country X. The other trade agreement proposed is with two countries to its east; these are poor countries whose economies are struggling. They have significantly less infrastructure than country X.

Which of these trade agreements should country X seriously consider and which should it not?

Questions

1. Which factors distinguish international logistics from domestic logistics?
2. Identify the various intermediaries which may become involved in international marketing and describe their respective functions.
3. Identify the salient points of difference between a selling agent and a distributor.
4. Identify the various transport operators and non-operating transport service providers involved in international logistics and describe the functions of each.
5. Give an account of the series of transactional activities that will take place and the role of the various service providers from the moment when an international shipment is tendered by the exporter for carriage by air or ocean transport until it is delivered to the importer in another country.
6. What are Incoterms and what are they used for?
7. Describe the four Incoterms groupings.
8. Identify the 13 Incoterms and detail the seller's obligations within each term.
9. What is a bonded warehouse and what are the potential benefits of using one?
10. Identify the categories of international trade documents and briefly describe the purpose of each.
11. What is a bill of lading and for what purpose are the various types of bills of lading used?
12. What is a packing list and what information does it include?
13. What is the value of a Free Trade Zone to an economy?
14. What happens if a company does not have an HS number for its goods?
15. With world trade increasing consistently, what is the impact for all infrastructure, including ports, road and rail links for countries if this growth rate is maintained for another 12 years?

16 Describe the data required in a customs declaration?
17 What is the benefit for the WTO to have its agreements approved by all members?
18 While some countries have adopted security measures, do you feel all members need to adopt these same measures for economic reasons?
19 Why is a Harmonised Schedule (HS) utilised and what are its benefits to customs departments as well as for the importation of goods?
20 Are the same HS numbers used for the same goods in every country?
21 Which is correct: most customs departments are/are not primarily focused on ensuring all tariffs are paid correctly?

Consult the web

International Air Transport Association (IATA): www.iata.org
International Cargo Handling Coordination Association (ICHCA): www.ichca.org.uk
International Chamber of Commerce (ICC): www.iccwbo.org
International Civil Aviation Organization (ICAO): www.icao.org
International Federation of Freight Forwarders Association (FIATA): www.fiata.com
International Maritime Organization (IMO): www.imo.org
International Road Transport Union (IRU): www.iru.org
International Union of Railways (UIC): www.uic.asso.fr
World Customs Organization (WCO): www.wcoomd.org
World Trade Organization (WTO): www.wto.org

Consult the books

Branch, A. E. 1994. *Export Practice and Management*, 3rd edition. London: Chapman & Hall.
Council for Supply Chain Management Professionals. 2008. 'CSCMP explores', *Supply Chain Security* 5, spring 2008.
Council for Supply Chain Management Professionals. 2008. Comment: 'Trade security across the pond'. Jan/Feb 2008.
Coyle, J. J., Bardi, E. J. and Novack, R. A. 2000. *Transportation*, 5th edition. Cincinnati: South-Western College Publishing.
Hinkelman, E. G. 2000. *Dictionary of International Trade: Handbook of the Global Trade Community*, 4th edition. Novato: World Trade Press.
International Chamber of Commerce (ICC). 2003. *Guide to Export-Import Basics*, 2nd edition. Paris: International Chamber of Commerce.
Ramberg, J., Rapatout, P., Reynolds, F. and Debattista, C. 2000. *Incoterms 2000: A Forum of Experts*. Paris: International Chamber of Commerce (ICC Publication Number 617).
Reuvid, J. 2001. *A Handbook of World Trade: A Strategic Guide to Trading Internationally*. London: Kogan Page.
Reynolds, F. 2002. *A to Z of International Trade*. Paris: International Chamber of Commerce.
Van Vuuren, J. P. 1996. *Effective Exporting: A South African Guide*. Pretoria: Institute for International Marketing.
Wood, D. F. and Johnson, J. C. 1996. *Contemporary Transportation*, 5th edition. Upper Saddle River: Prentice Hall.

Notes

1 Van Vuuren, J. P. 1996: 74.
2 Reuvid, J. 2001: 327.
3 Ibid.: 326.
4 Branch, A. E. 1994: 372.
5 Coyle et al. 2000: 241–4.
6 ICC. 2003: 251–3.
7 Reynolds, F. 2002: 64; 131–2.
8 Wood, D. F. and Johnson, J. C. 1996: 356–551.
9 ICC. 2003: 260.
10 Ibid.: 261; 262.
11 Hinkelman, E. G. 2000: 275–303.
12 Ramberg et al. 2000: 96–103.
13 ICC. 2003: 269; 270.
14 Ibid.: 272.
15 Ibid.: 261.

418 BUSINESS LOGISTICS MANAGEMENT

Incoterms 2000: a visual guide

Division of risks and costs between seller and buyer: EXW

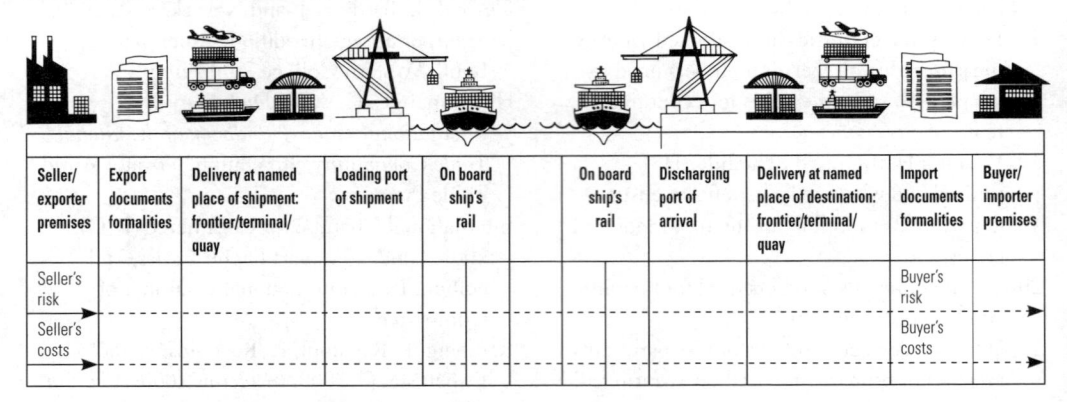

Seller/exporter premises	Export documents formalities	Delivery at named place of shipment: frontier/terminal/quay	Loading port of shipment	On board ship's rail		On board ship's rail	Discharging port of arrival	Delivery at named place of destination: frontier/terminal/quay	Import documents formalities	Buyer/importer premises
Seller's risk									Buyer's risk	
Seller's costs									Buyer's costs	

Division of risks and costs between seller and buyer: C terms

Term	Seller/exporter premises	Export documents formalities	Delivery at named place of shipment: frontier/terminal/quay	Loading port of shipment	On board ship's rail		On board ship's rail	Discharging port of arrival	Delivery at named place of destination: frontier/terminal/quay	Import documents formalities	Buyer/importer premises
CFR	Seller's risk									Buyer's risk	
	Seller's costs									Buyer's costs	
						Seller's insurable interest					
CIF	Seller's risk									Buyer's risk	
	Seller's costs									Buyer's costs	
					Buyer's insurable interest						
CPT	Seller's risk									Buyer's risk	
	Seller's costs									Buyer's costs	
						Buyer's and seller's insurable interest					
CIP	Seller's risk									Buyer's risk	
	Seller's costs									Buyer's costs	
						Buyer's insurable interest					

Division of risks and costs between seller and buyer: F terms

Term	Seller/exporter premises	Export documents formalities	Delivery at named place of shipment: frontier/terminal/quay	Loading port of shipment	On board ship's rail	On board ship's rail	Discharging port of arrival	Delivery at named place of destination: frontier/terminal/quay	Import documents formalities	Buyer/importer premises
FCA	Seller's risk		→							Buyer's risk →
	Seller's costs		→							Buyer's costs →
FAS	Seller's risk			→						Buyer's risk →
	Seller's costs			→						Buyer's costs →
FOB	Seller's risk				→					Buyer's risk →
	Seller's costs				→					Buyer's costs →

Division of risks and costs between seller and buyer: D terms

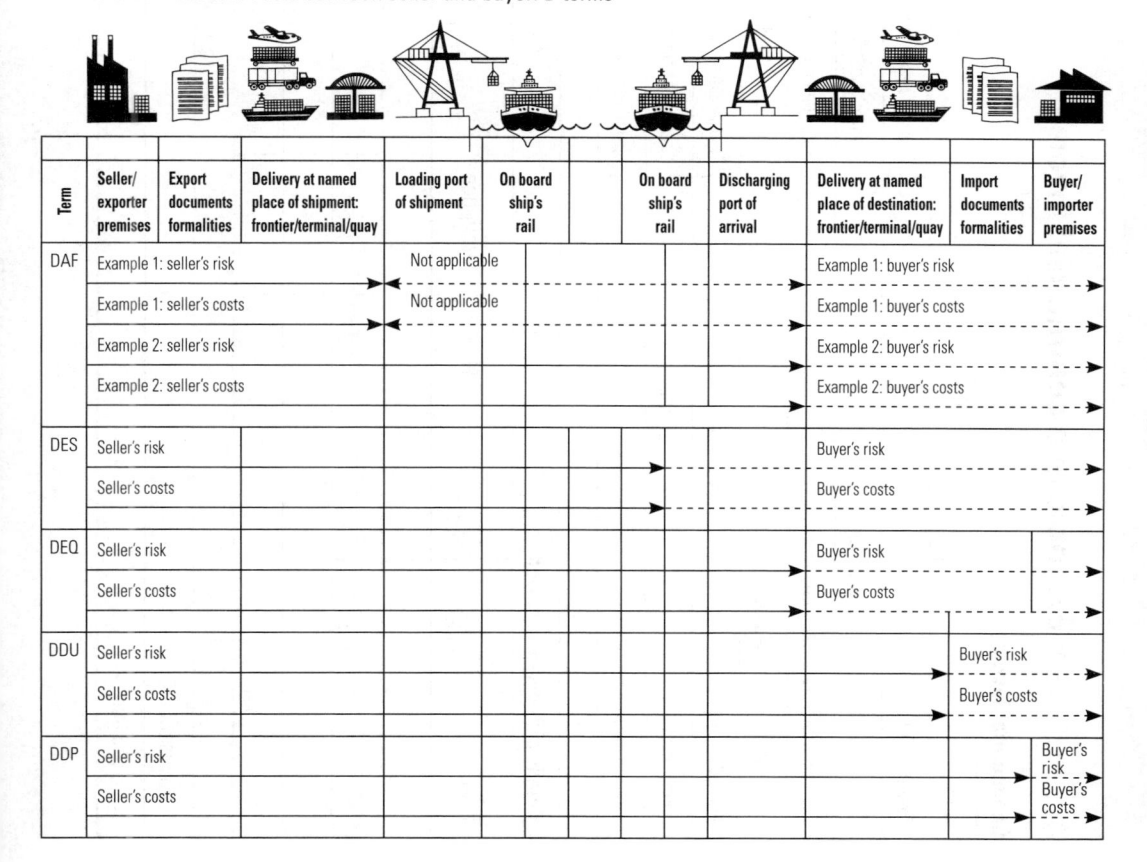

Term	Seller/exporter premises	Export documents formalities	Delivery at named place of shipment: frontier/terminal/quay	Loading port of shipment	On board ship's rail	On board ship's rail	Discharging port of arrival	Delivery at named place of destination: frontier/terminal/quay	Import documents formalities	Buyer/importer premises
DAF	Example 1: seller's risk		→	Not applicable				Example 1: buyer's risk		→
	Example 1: seller's costs		→	Not applicable				Example 1: buyer's costs		→
	Example 2: seller's risk							Example 2: buyer's risk		→
	Example 2: seller's costs							Example 2: buyer's costs		→
DES	Seller's risk						→	Buyer's risk		→
	Seller's costs						→	Buyer's costs		→
DEQ	Seller's risk							→Buyer's risk		→
	Seller's costs							→Buyer's costs		→
DDU	Seller's risk								→Buyer's risk	→
	Seller's costs								→Buyer's costs	→
DDP	Seller's risk									→Buyer's risk →
	Seller's costs									→Buyer's costs →

Appendix 18.1 Example of a commercial invoice

Commercial Invoice

Date			
Exporter/seller name and address		Shipper name and address	
Company or tax number of exporter		Invoice number	Ship date
Consolidator/forwarder name and address		Ship to name and address	
International consignee name and address		Buyer name and address	
Port of export	Country of export	Carrier name and address	
Terms of sale	Applicable Incoterm	County of origin	Ultimate destination
Method of transportation		Gross weight	Letter of credit reference

Details of items to be moved

Item	HS number	Licence number	ECCN	Description	SKU number	COO	Quantity	Unit price	Net weight	Total value

Authorisation

Name and title   Signature

19 Product returns and reverse logistics management

U. Kussing and W.J. Pienaar

Learning outcomes

After you have studied this chapter, you should be able to:
- define the returns management process and reverse logistics;
- give an account of the role of reverse logistics within the returns management process;
- understand why finished products and other items are returned;
- explain the difference between product recovery and waste management;
- understand the difference between managing forward and reverse logistics;
- explain the financial impacts of reverse logistics;
- describe the stages of what takes place when products are returned to a warehouse;
- briefly discuss environmentally sound supply chain management;
- explain how ISO 14000 works; and
- understand the concept of closed-loop supply chains.

19.1 Introduction

Traditionally, logistics systems were designed to handle product flows in one direction, namely towards the final customer or consumer. Large manufacturers focused on optimising forward logistics and on the best way to push products into the market as efficiently as possible. Manufacturers believed in their products and did not expect them to fail or to receive them back from their customers.

Despite this belief, manufacturers and retailers are frequently on the receiving end of product or part returns. They also find that the processes of returning these items to source and replacing or repairing them are often more expensive than the delivery of the item to the marketplace. Reverse logistics is generally more important in industries where the products have high values or where there are high volumes of product returns.

19.2 The role of reverse logistics within the product returns management process

From a business logistics perspective, reverse logistics refers to the supportive role of logistics in product returns; source reduction; recycling; materials substitution; reuse of materials; waste disposal; and refurbishing, repairing and remanufacturing.[1] Similarly, as logistics management is a subset of supply chain management, reverse logistics is a part of the broader returns management process.

The supportive role of logistics in the returns management process can be regarded as being, firstly, physical (i.e. the movement and positioning of returned or disposed goods), and, secondly, analytical (i.e. logistical analysis to enhance efficiency and effectiveness).

The returns management process includes the planning, implementation and execution (including control) of avoidance, gatekeeping and the product disposition process.

Avoidance refers to analysing returns, determining the causes of product returns and implementing programmes that minimise the number of return requests. These may include changes to product design; more stringent manufacturing quality control; changes to promotional activities, including better instructions supplied with the product; changes to product warranty conditions; and more suitable physical logistics arrangements, such as using a more suitable mode of transport, a more capable carrier and securer packaging.

Gatekeeping refers to the screening of return requests and the returned products at the earliest point in the reverse flow. It is likely that multiple gatekeeping points are required across the supply chain. Logistics should help design the gatekeeping guidelines in order to make the reverse flow efficient, and may be involved in the execution of the gatekeeping activities.

Disposition options are manifold, including recycling, remanufacturing, refurbishing and removing products to waste sites or landfills. These options need to be carefully evaluated because products should flow as quickly as possible to the desired destination to minimise their lost value in the reverse flow.[2] Logistics managers provide cost data to evaluate disposition options. Often, management requires certain items to be returned, for example, reusable containers and pallets. Returnable containers should be considered a corporate asset, rather than an expense. Logistics managers help assess the flow and holding of reusable containers and determine the investment required.

All the activities covered in the Council of Supply Chain Management Professionals' (CSCMP) definition of logistics management (see Chapter 1, Section 1.6, page 11) are also found in reverse logistics. However, the forward and reverse logistics systems may not be the same. In modified form, reverse logistics can be defined as follows:

> Reverse logistics is that part of returns management that plans, implements and controls the efficient, effective flow of goods and related information between the point of consumption and the point of origin in order to recapture value or properly dispose of the goods.

An amplification of this definition is in order. First, the term 'goods' covers raw materials; in-process inventory; finished goods; containers and packaging material; and waste material (the latter being a 'bad' rather than a 'good').

Second, the flow of goods takes place in an upstream (reverse) direction within a supply chain, while the flow of waste takes place laterally, or away from the supply chain.

Third, the flow can be between any intermediate point in a supply chain, including, for example, manufacturing returns of surplus raw materials to the primary producer; distribution returns of defective products from retailers and wholesalers to a manufacturer; and consumer returns of defective products under a warranty agreement.

19.3 Product returns management: scope and activities

Product returns management mainly consists of the management of product returns and waste disposal. Product returns management has to take place because parts, materials and products sometimes have to be returned to source, either from the consumer to the retailer or from the manufacturer to the supplier. Waste is an inevitable by-product of any manufacturing and consumption activity. This waste has to be processed, reused, recycled or disposed of in an effective and responsible way. Waste management presents many opportunities for businesses to become more environmentally friendly through recycling, reusing and reducing the amount of materials used during the manufacturing and distribution of their products.

Returns management covers a wide array of activities, such as:
- customer service and help-desk enquiries;
- the collection, sorting, screening, grading and processing of returned products and parts;
- gatekeeping (managing the insertion of products into the reverse chain);
- the trade-off between the cost of conducting quality control of manufactured products against the cost of warranty management;
- depot repair services;

- the management of recycling programmes;
- the management of hazardous material programmes;
- asset recovery and dispositioning of obsolete equipment;
- measuring vendor performance in terms of product failures;
- the management of returns policies and procedures;
- the repair, remanufacturing, refurbishment and upgrading of products;
- accounting and reconciliation practices related to returned products;
- the contracting of third-party service providers to handle various reverse logistics activities;
- service logistics (including field service, supporting spare-parts management and supporting replacement management); and
- all the physical logistics activities involved in the movement and positioning of returned/disposed material, and supportive logistics analysis.

The activities involved in reverse logistics should not be confused with those of so-called green or environmental logistics management. For example, while the redesign of packaging for the purpose of using less material and reducing pollution is an important activity, it does not directly involve goods or materials being sent 'backwards' and, therefore, does not strictly fall under reverse logistics. The fields of reverse logistics and green logistics are, however, closely related and sometimes have overlapping goals, especially with regard to the issues of reuse, recycling and waste disposal.

19.3.1 Management of product returns

In product supply chains the primary flow of goods takes place from the resources' points of origin to the points of consumption. At various intermediate points along the supply chain value addition takes place until desired products are consumed by consumers or used by end-customers. Sometimes, at any of these points the holding and/or onward (downstream) movement of goods (raw materials, in-process goods, finished goods and containers and packaging material) become undesirable and these goods are then sent upstream to intermediate points towards the resources' origins for the purpose of recapturing value, while waste is moved away from the supply chain to waste sites and landfills for proper disposal.

Product returns can occur at three general stages of a product's movement through the supply chain:
- Manufacturing returns, which include the return of surplus raw materials, returns due to failed quality controls and production scrap.
- Distribution returns, which include product recalls, returns due to inventory adjustments, commercial returns and returns due to redistribution of products.
- Customer returns, which include warranty returns, service returns and the return of products that have reached their end of use.

Products can be returned to an upstream point in the supply chain for various reasons. The most common causes are:
- refusal of items upon delivery or items that are undeliverable;
- excess or wrongly delivered items;
- damaged, malfunctioning or defective items;
- items that reach the end-of-marketing period while still unsold;
- consumer returns of unwanted products due to buyers' dissatisfaction;
- product recalls and warranty returns;
- reusable containers and packaging materials; and
- scrap material (for example, glass and metal) that can be recovered and reutilised as raw materials in further manufacturing.

The way in which a business handles these returns depends to a large extent on how downstream and upstream partners handle reverse logistics.

Avoidance and gatekeeping are key to the successful management of returns. Through avoidance, an organisation will try to minimise the number of items that *need* to enter the return flow of products. This can be achieved by ensuring that the quality of the product and its user-friendliness are at the highest possible levels before the product is sold and shipped. It can be seen as a pre-emptive strategy that aims to reduce the possibility of customers returning a product. Gatekeeping aims to limit the number of items that are *allowed* to enter the return flow of products. Products will be screened before a decision is made regarding their specific disposition (i.e. if the products should be returned and if so, where to). This process reduces the cost of products being returned to inappropriate destinations.

Returned products and materials can move along one of the following paths:
- Returned to vendor for refund
- Sold as new if not used or opened
- Repackaged and sold as new
- Sold via outlet or auction
- Remanufactured or refurbished
- Sold to broker
- Donated to charity
- Recycled
- Disposed of in a landfill

The first choice will always be to obtain a full refund for the product from the vendor, or to sell the product at the full market price. If these are not possible, the product can be sold at a reduced price at an auction or outlet store. Sometimes remanufacturing or refurbishment is necessary in order to repair or improve the product to such an extent that the whole or part thereof can be returned to a customer, or sold elsewhere. Failing this, the product can be sold to a broker who can sell the product in a secondary market. This option is seldom considered, however, for premium-brand products, as this might be seen to reduce the brand value of the product. The last resort is to donate the product to charity, or to dispose of it through recycling or in a landfill.

Return goods handling is complex due to the small quantities involved and the ad hoc nature of returns, which make it difficult to predict when and in what quantities they will take place. The cost of handling these returns tends to be high, thereby forcing organisations to give more attention to the issues surrounding them. Effective returns management and processing can also reduce a business's waste-disposal cost and increase its environmental compliance.

Efficient returns management can help reduce the cost of obsolescence. If products are selling at a lower rate than forecasted, they should be returned to manufacturers and wholesalers in a timely manner so that an alternative sales channel can be explored before the only option is to write off and then dispose of the products. This is especially critical in the case of seasonal products, and those with a short life cycle and at the end of their life cycle. The formulation and implementation of channel-cleaning policies with dealers and retailers to manage the quantity and timing of returned products can provide opportunities to reuse inventory before it becomes obsolete.

The way in which claims, complaints and returns are handled have a cost and customer-service impact on an organisation. If these processes do not run smoothly, they can lead to dissatisfied customers that struggle to get their money back for unwanted or defective products. On the other hand, unconditional returns and replacements can lead to extra expenses for the organisation.

An organisation should have policies in place that specify how claims, complaints and returns are to be handled. The organisation should also maintain data on claims, complaints and returns in order to provide feedback to engineering, manufacturing, logistics and other departments. This data can also be used to identify 'problem' clients or products for further investigation.

19.3.2 Product recovery and waste management

Reverse logistics is also involved with the removal and disposal of waste generated during production, distribution and packaging processes. This waste can be stored temporarily before being transported to sorting, disposal, reuse, reprocessing or recycling facilities. The recycling and reuse of packaging materials has received particular attention in Europe, where very strict regulations regarding the removal of packaging materials exist.

The waste hierarchy ranks waste-disposal options in terms of environmental impact (see Figure 19.1). In general, there are four categories of waste-disposal options: cleaner processes; recycling; treatment; and disposal.

Figure 19.1 The waste hierarchy

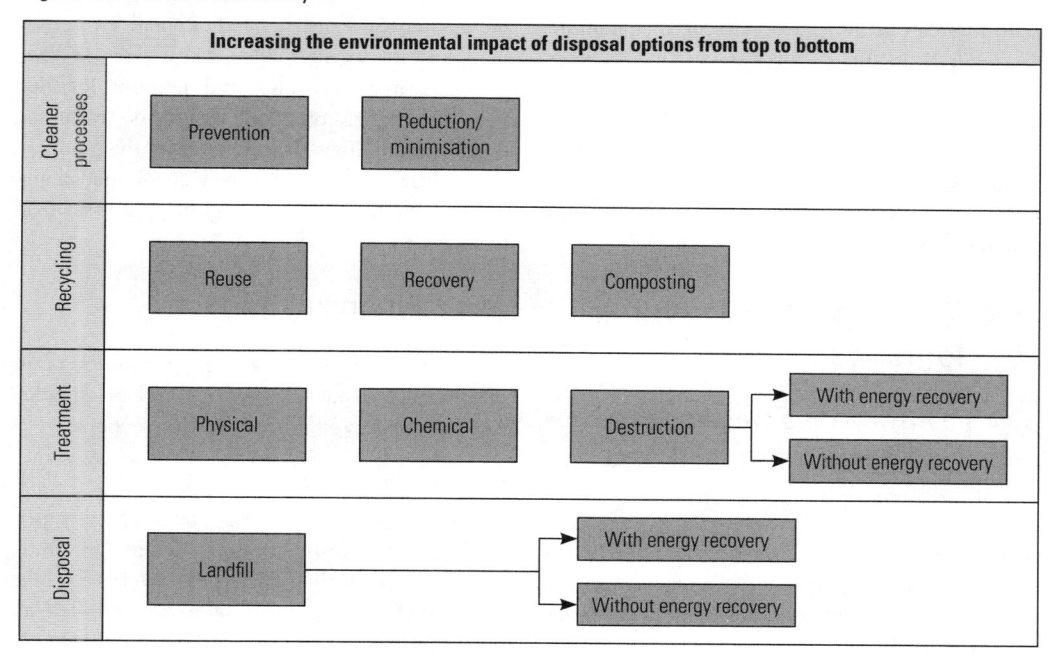

	Increasing the environmental impact of disposal options from top to bottom
Cleaner processes	Prevention — Reduction/minimisation
Recycling	Reuse — Recovery — Composting
Treatment	Physical — Chemical — Destruction → With energy recovery / Without energy recovery
Disposal	Landfill → With energy recovery / Without energy recovery

The best option is to avoid producing waste in the first place, or otherwise to reduce or minimise the waste that is produced. For example, the current level of packaging could be re-evaluated to determine whether current product packaging contains excessive protection. Electronic annual reports could be sent out instead of paper copies to save paper.

If waste cannot be avoided, the aim should be to maximise the reuse of products and materials. Returnable packaging can, for example, be used to deliver parts to a manufacturer or bottles to a supermarket. Printer cartridges can be sourced from a supplier that has a returns policy. Paper from misprints can be reused as scrap paper in the office. Alternatively, parts can be recovered from a product that has reached the end of its useful life. Parts of a wooden pallet, for example, can be salvaged and used to manufacture new pallets. Organic matter can be recycled through composting. A hotel kitchen can, for example, use its organic waste to generate compost for its gardens.

If materials cannot be reused or recycled, they can be transformed through physical or chemical treatment to metals or minerals that can be reused elsewhere. Paper waste, for example, can be shredded and bleached before being included in the manufacturing of hand towels or toilet paper. In some markets, the recyclability of packaging material even influences the purchasing decision of consumers. Some consumers would rather buy a product packaged in an easily recyclable carton than one which contains materials that are more difficult to recycle. The last treatment option would be to destroy the materials through incineration. Ideally, a process of energy recovery should take place during incineration.

The least environmentally friendly option is to dispose of the waste in a landfill. Some landfills offer the option of limited energy recovery, but in most cases, the landfill is a dumping site. Hazardous waste is seldom recycled, but most often disposed of in approved dump sites or destroyed under controlled conditions. Nuclear and biomedical wastes are good examples of these.

Traditionally, used products were most often disposed of as mixed waste, both by consumers and in industrial sectors. This practice is not very conducive to recycling, with mixed waste most often ending up in landfills or being incinerated.

In these cases no reuse of resources takes place, with limited energy recovery during incineration. In contrast to this, source separation enables recycling by segregating waste by material, such as paper, cans, glass, biological and hazardous. Source separation is a legislative requirement in some countries, where segregated waste is often collected from households and organisations in different coloured containers or bags.

19.4 The impacts of reverse logistics

19.4.1 Differences between managing forward and reverse logistics

The environment in which reverse logistics has to be managed is vastly different from the forward logistics environment. Forward logistics works off sales and marketing forecasts to plan the optimal distribution of a limited number of products from one or more manufacturing or warehousing points to multiple distribution or retail points. Mostly, the destination and routing of the products is known beforehand and distribution planning can take place accordingly. The forward distribution process is normally highly visible through advanced shipping notices (ASNs); distribution costs are known, or can be accurately estimated, before shipping takes place.

By contrast, reverse logistics is much more reactive, with product flows that are much less visible. Organisations can only react and respond to actions by consumers or downstream channel members. In reverse logistics there is normally no clear forecasting plan for the volume of reverse logistics activities that can be expected. Even if bathtub curves are used to predict the failure rate of a product, this does not tell you in which geographical point the failure will occur. Nor does it tell you which part of the product is likely to fail and will have to be repaired or replaced. Instead of having a typical one-to-many distribution pattern of forward logistics, reverse logistics has to deal with a many-to-one distribution network. This makes it difficult to pre-define routing and to gain visibility into the reverse logistics processes and costs. Even though reverse logistics handles smaller volumes than forward logistics, the reverse processes are generally more complex and per-unit logistics costs higher. Every effort should be made to design forward logistics processes and the products themselves in a way that will accommodate or simplify the future reverse logistics processes that may occur.

19.4.2 Financial impacts

The costs of reverse logistics differ from the costs of forward logistics both in type and magnitude. These are discussed in the following sections.

19.4.2.1 Transport

Reverse logistics has greater transport costs per product than during forward logistics, as there are generally smaller quantities that have to be transported from a variety of locations (often at uncertain times) to a centralised depot. Little or no advantage can thus be taken of full truck load or bulk transport rates, and efficient fleet scheduling and route planning are often not possible.

19.4.2.2 Inventory-holding costs

Reverse logistics has little or no inventory-holding costs, as products are normally moved quite quickly through the reverse chain to a point where they can be reused, repaired, remanufactured, refurbished, recycled, disassembled or disposed of. Due to the reduced value of this type of inventory, the cost of capital is mostly insignificant.

19.4.2.3 Shrinkage (theft)

Losses due to shrinkage are normally much lower in reverse logistics. This is due to several factors. First, as the product value is generally below market value, the loss per unit that disappears is lower. Second, returned products are often kept in a caged area for processing and are therefore under a higher level of control and less likely to disappear. Third, products returned because of defects are not as attractive to potential criminal elements, and fourth, shrinkages are naturally lower due to the lower volume of products moving through the reverse chain.

19.4.2.4 Obsolescence

These costs may be higher, as products that are already in the reverse chain are less likely to be sold at full market value and more likely to have to be scrapped.

19.4.2.5 Collection

Collection costs are much higher, as collections are less standardised and normally take place by special arrangement. In the case of Internet sales, the cost of returning the items is normally carried by the vendor if the products were delivered in a damaged condition or if defects were identified while the product was still under warranty.

19.4.2.6 Sorting

Sorting costs are much higher in reverse logistics, as each product has to be inspected closely before one can decide on possible destinations for the product.

19.4.2.7 Handling

Handling costs per unit of product are also much higher in reverse logistics, as products are most often handled in units of one and not in unitised loads of boxes or pallets.

19.4.2.8 Refurbishment and repackaging

Refurbishment and repackaging costs are largely non-existent for forward logistics and are incurred for returned products that have to be made ready to be returned to the marketplace.

19.4.2.9 Change in book value

The book values of products in the forward supply chain are not likely to decrease, except in the case where obsolescence occurs. Returned, refurbished and repackaged products cannot normally be sold at the full market value of a new product.

Reverse logistics, however, should not just be seen as a cost-draining environment in which every effort is made to minimise costs. Although the objective should indeed be to minimise the cost of moving products back towards their source, reverse logistics also frequently presents opportunities to recapture and create value in the supply chain. For example, the parts that are reclaimed from old or defective products can sometimes be reutilised in the forward supply chain at a lower cost than that of a new part. Even if a level of refurbishment is required, the manufacturer does not have to procure raw materials anew or totally transform them again in order to gain additional revenue. This practice is common in the appliance and electronic goods industry. Firms that lease office equipment often have comprehensive asset-recovery initiatives to reclaim end-of-lease products, as many of these products or their parts still have useful life that can be offered to other customers at little extra cost.

19.4.3 Information management challenges

Forward logistics activities and processes can be supported by a variety of information management systems, such as enterprise resource planning (ERP), warehouse management and transport management systems. Reverse logistics has special information management requirements, which often cannot be handled by these types of systems. In the past, there was little focus from management on reverse logistics and so even less focus on developing information systems to support the various processes and activities.

Ideally, an end-to-end information systems solution for reverse logistics should be able to support the following:[3]
- Warranty and return management
- Recall management
- Critical inventory/parts management
- Disposition management
- Depot repair management
- Asset recovery and disposal management
- Liquidation management
- Regulatory compliance management
- Transport and logistics management
- Business analytics and reporting

Consider, for example, the information support of Internet vendors' reverse logistics processes. Internet sales are estimated to account for more than 10 per cent of worldwide sales.[4] When a product is bought on the Internet it cannot be returned to a physical store, but normally has to be returned via mail. The management of this returns process cannot take place without an information system that keeps track of orders, returns and credits. When customers receive their orders, they will often already include instructions for possible product returns. Customers can indicate online when they want to return a product or if the product has to be repaired or replaced. The Internet vendor will use one information system to track inbound and outbound shipments, including the return of orders and, if necessary, the repair or replacement of a product. This system will also have to be linked to their financial system in order to process possible credits owing to the customer.

19.4.4 Life-cycle assessment

> Life-cycle assessment (LCA) is the quantitative determination of the resource and energy use and environmental burdens of a given product or process over its entire life cycle.[5]

LCA evaluates products and materials from a cradle-to-grave perspective, starting at the acquisition of the raw material and ending at the final disposal of the product or its remnants. An LCA is generally comparative in nature, typically comparing one or more products or processes that provide the same functional use or result. It considers the product throughout its lifespan, starting at the development of the product and ending at its ultimate disposal in the solid waste stream. LCA takes into consideration source reduction, recycling, substitution and disposal.

In each phase of a product's life cycle, the total impact of the product on the environment can be taken into account to make the total life of the product more sustainable, with less of an impact on the environment. Table 19.1 provides an example of how this can be achieved.

The same process can be followed when comparing distribution strategies from an environmental perspective. The choice of suppliers, distribution channels, transport modes, transport equipment, handling equipment, energy sources and logistics service providers should all be made from a total life-cycle perspective. The supply chain strategy with the lowest total impact on the environment should be given the highest consideration. In such an environment, the potentially lower cost of off-shoring production to countries such as China and India would not carry as much weight, since off-shoring increases the burning of fossil fuels for transport purposes.

Table 19.1 Sustainability efforts in a product's life cycle

Life-cycle phase	Sustainability efforts
Design	Incorporate materials into the product that can be recycled and try to include materials that have low energy requirements during their manufacturing process.
Source	Source parts and materials from suppliers that comply with environmental regulations. Source as much as possible locally on an ex-works basis, thereby reducing transport requirements.
Manufacture	Implement an effective environmental management system and try to reduce energy consumption at the manufacturing plant. Make sure that waste products from the manufacturing process are collected, reused and/or recycled.
Distribute	Reduce the use of packaging during distribution; consolidate loads where possible and measure the carbon footprint of your logistics decision.
Service	Try to repair products instead of always replacing them. Provide feedback to design and manufacturing on defects so that they can try to limit the possibility of defects.
Return/recycle	Sell returned products into secondary markets. Implement remanufacturing and recycling programmes.

19.5 Product returns and reverse logistics processes

A large portion of the physical work related to reverse logistics is conducted at warehouses. A major problem in the product returns process is the unpredictability of when returns will actually arrive at the warehouse. Usually, the returns processing facility does not know what and how much product will be returned on any given day. The vast majority of all returns are unplanned and are therefore unpredictable to a large extent. Consequently, problems arise when trying to conduct proper route planning or to schedule staff, vehicles, equipment and other resources when demand for those resources is unknown or variable.

19.5.1 Stages in the reverse logistics process[6]

The following five stages are typical of what takes place when products are returned to a warehouse: receipt; sort and stage; returns processing; returns analysis; and support operations. These stages are discussed in turn.

Stage 1: Receipt
The delivery of returned goods from retail outlets back to warehouses can be by a variety of transport operators, including overnight express operations; part-load breakbulk carriers; or own vehicles that have picked up returns when making deliveries to stores or customer locations. Goods returns are received at dedicated or combination receiving doors in the warehouse.

In certain cases, when firms handle returns in the same warehouse where finished goods distribution occurs, dedicated doors will be used to receive product returns. In other cases, the same doors used for outbound shipments are also used for returns, sometimes at different times during the day (utilising carrier appointments or scheduled deliveries during time windows), or else randomly (whenever the carrier calls at the facility).

Receiving doors, which may be dedicated to product returns, are usually located near the returns processing area of the warehouse. The primary reason for the proximity of the returns processing area – or the handling equipment that will move the returned items to this area – is that the cost per unit to move individual items is greater than moving larger quantities of items. It is beneficial to minimise the handling and moving distances between goods receiving and initial sorting and staging. In many cases, if the items being returned are fairly standardised in terms of size and mass, belt conveyor systems will be used to move the products from the receiving area to other parts of the warehouse.

Full pallets, packages or containers of returns are usually the easiest to process because their handling is similar to that of finished goods being shipped to customers. However, most items being returned do not occur in the same product mix as the originally distributed products. Returned items may include a wide assortment and variety of products, some still in their original packaging. Other items may come back from final consumers in containers or packages that must be handled differently from when the items were originally shipped out to customers.

Stage 2: Sort and stage
Once returned products are received, they are sorted and staged for initial returns processing. This sort could be based on how the goods have been returned (for example, in pallets, boxes or packets); the type of return (which can be identified from the address on the item, the colour of the label, or another kind of easily identifiable feature); the size and/or number of the items being returned; or a method that would balance the workload for staff involved in the initial processing activity in stage 3 (below).

Stage 3: Returns processing
During this stage, returned items are sub-sorted according to their stock-keeping unit (SKU) number, while the sortation of vendor returns is based on the specific vendor name. Items move from the sort and stage area to the processing station(s) where the items can be processed in order of their receipt (first in first out – FIFO); by the type of product; by customer type or location; by

the physical size of the items; or by a combination of these factors. Staff who process returns are instructed (often by supervisors) to take items from various packages or from the same package as long as they are not the simplest or quickest items to process. This eliminates the tendency for employees to select the easiest and/or quickest items to process and leave the more complicated or slower items for later. Handling a mixture of items smooths out the workflow and makes it easier to monitor and measure the rate of processing.

Most of the necessary information about the returned item should be captured during this initial processing activity. Some of the information entered into the system includes: company name; ID of the person processing the return; date and time; SKU number; description of the item; number of items processed; location of item in inventory; package code; description of condition; reason for the return; and other information that may pertain to an item's processing and final disposition. Increasingly, businesses utilise computer terminals and scanners to enter information necessary to process the return and to assist employees later in the process where refurbishing or restoration takes place. The paperwork that accompanied the return is separated from the item and usually placed into slots above or to the side of the processing station. These documents are sent to the administrative area for comparison with the electronic records and to check for discrepancies.

Many businesses perform audits of the returns. Realising that there are controllable and non-controllable returns, managers will usually examine the summary reports of so-called reason codes to determine what can be done to eliminate the cause of or need for returns. For example, if items are being damaged through improper handling somewhere in the forward logistics process, measures can be taken to reduce or eliminate the handling mistakes. Leading-edge businesses tend to minimise their controllable returns in order to reduce costs and increase customer goodwill. Fewer returns also enable a business to process the returns that do occur more expeditiously. Businesses that would be considered to have excellent returns-management programmes utilise a very detailed list of reason codes for returns.

Stage 4: Returns analysis

A large number of products will have been processed at the analysis stage of the returns process. However, this is dependent on the industry, firm and types of products that are returned. For analysis of returns, staff must be highly trained since it is here that the most important disposition decisions are taken. For this reason information related to processing efficiency and effectiveness should be available.

Repackaged or refurbished items usually result in higher revenues than items being sold as scrap. In turn, products that can be repackaged for resale will return greater financial reward than items that have to be refurbished or remanufactured prior to sale. The value of the returned item varies depending on the product disposition strategy adopted. Therefore, staff involved in this stage must be very knowledgeable about the products; repairing or refurbishing opportunities; allowable versus non-allowable returns; and the financial benefits associated with each disposition choice.

The returns analysis stage is only completed after the business has entered all of the recordable information about the product, customer, vendor etc., which is available before product disposition.

Stage 5: Support operations

During this stage, returned items are distributed according to where they should go. If they are back-to-stock or back-to-stores items, they are moved back into inventory – either existing inventory, or a special area of the warehouse that stocks returned items ready for resale. The items are then picked from inventory as orders come in.

Whenever repair/refurbishment and repackaging are required, appropriate evaluation, repairs and assembly/disassembly operations are performed in order to get the items into a saleable condition. Repair and/or refurbishment are not activities performed by all businesses, since some products are not candidates for this activity (for example, food, pharmaceutical, chemical products), but for those who can perform these tasks it is very important that product restoration is evaluated well from both a cost (efficiency) and service (effectiveness) viewpoint.

In relation to costs, the amount of repair or refurbishing that occurs should be in line with the potential value of the product once it has been restored. Because recovery rates for repaired/refurbished products can be high, often exceeding other disposition options, performing repair and/or refurbishment efficiently at low cost is important to a business's return on investment. Similarly, by restoring products into a saleable condition promptly usually also reduces inventory-carrying costs. From a service perspective, promptly restored products are ready for resale to customers, while carrying defective products bears an opportunity cost. This is important when there is high demand for the products and regular inventories are unavailable.

Whenever products are to be returned to vendors, staff determine the appropriate quantities and/or time windows acceptable to vendors receiving the returns and ship them back accordingly. These returns must be performed swiftly, as vendor return time windows can be very short, especially when the time to get products back from customers or stores is taken into consideration.

Restored products can either be sold to downstream customers or serve as replacements for warranty repairs. Returned items are sometimes donated to charities or welfare organisations. Whenever returned items are not saleable, they will often be sold to a scrap dealer, which will purchase the items for the value of their components. Whenever products have to be destroyed – which is often the case with food, chemical and cosmetic products, and goods that are classified as hazardous materials – arrangements are made to dispose of or destroy the items properly, either by the business itself or by a third party that provides such a service.

19.6 Logistics and the environment

Logistics activities consume materials during their various functions and also require energy for the operation of various types of equipment. The way in which the activities consume these materials and the amount of energy that they require have a direct impact on the environment within which the logistics activities take place. Logistics managers must now take into account environmental issues, such as recycling, energy conservation and carbon footprints. This is not just necessary from the perspective of social responsibility, but it is frequently a requirement placed on them by prospective clients and supply chain partners. Legislation and government initiatives sometimes also force logistics managers to 'green' their supply chains (see Chapter 12, Sections 12.5.6 and 12.5.7, pages 275–6).

19.6.1 Environmentally sound supply chain management

Businesses face increasing pressure to take responsibility for their environmental performance. Consumers are starting to expect products that will not harm the environment, and legislation places restrictions on resource use and conversion processes. These pressures not only apply to the physical products themselves, but also to how a supply chain is managed and which resources are used to get the product to market. Supply chain managers needs to expand their perspective upwards and downwards in the supply chain if they want to ensure that they are part of an environmentally sound supply chain.

The term environmentally sound refers to the degree to which activities in the supply chain comply with the composite framework of requirements that an organisation identifies on the part of its stakeholders. Stakeholders can be anything from government and corporate shareholders to customers and the communities in which organisations operate. The understanding of stakeholders' perspectives is therefore central to the development of each organisation's own definition of environmentally sound supply chain management.

Environmental supply chain projects sometimes need to be conducted because of legislative pressures – in which case they will not necessarily lead to cost savings. Sound environmental practices, however, have the potential to generate financial benefits. In some operational areas it is relatively easy to measure environmental performance; such measures include:

- kilometres per litre of fuel used;

- percentage of vehicle fleet utilising environmentally-friendly fuel;
- CO_2 emissions;
- average kilometre-lifetime of tyres;
- percentage of tyres retreaded;
- percentage use of vehicle load capacity;
- number of times packaging material is reused; and
- weight of packaging waste recycled.

Within a supply chain, environmental performance can be easily addressed in the areas of reverse logistics, packaging, transport and facility location. Reverse logistics should focus on recovering as much value as possible from returned products and try to move up the waste hierarchy as far as possible. Packaging should be designed for reuse and recycled where possible. Transport can conserve resources through better training of drivers; sticking to speed restrictions; preventive maintenance programmes; on-board monitoring technology; and optimised routing and scheduling. Facilities should be located in a way that minimises transport requirements during both inbound and outbound transportation.

Businesses in different stages of the supply chain will experience different types of environmental pressures, depending on the priorities of their stakeholders. Supply chain partners must inform each other of their respective environments and requirements. Internal collaboration within and between divisions of an organisation is just as important. Dialogue is important so that materials and techniques can be chosen that will have the least impact on the environment. The manufacturer of any part or product in the supply chain must be aware of the restrictions of materials used for the production process, as well as their impact on the rest of the supply and recycling chain.

Product-related environmental information required for compliance and procurement purposes often relies on large amounts of data and complex analysis. This data has to be collected from various stakeholders. Without collaboration between supply chain partners, this kind of data would not be available to support green procurement programmes and to allow customers to make objective comparisons of products.

19.6.2 ISO 14000

The International Organization for Standardization (ISO) is the world's largest developer of standards. The best-known management systems developed by them are the ISO 9000 and ISO 14000 families of standards. ISO 14000 addresses environmental management in terms of what an organisation does to:
- minimise harmful effects on the environment caused by its activities; and
- achieve continual improvement of its environmental performance.[7]

The ISO 14001:2004 and ISO 14004:2004 standards deal with the requirements of and guidelines for an environmental management system (EMS). Meeting the requirements set out in the standards will enable an organisation firstly to identify and control the potential environmental impact of all its activities and products; secondly, continuously improve its environmental performance; thirdly, provide a systematic approach for setting environmental objectives and targets, and, fourthly, allow it to demonstrate whether these objectives and targets have been achieved.

A variety of benefits can be achieved from the implementation of an ISO 14000 system:
- It functions as a framework for the capturing and communication of best practices.
- The formalised procedures lead to greater consistency in terms of actions and outcomes.
- Environmental quality is seen as an important management issue, rather than an inspection activity.
- Environmental audits provide objective information on environmental performance.
- A common language of quality is used that can be communicated between parties in a supply chain.
- There is a reduced cost of waste management.
- There is a reduction in the use of energy and materials.
- External stakeholders (i.e. customers, communities and government) can be assured that a proper EMS is in place.

- Environmental certification is often required from potential clients and compliance can therefore support sales and revenue generation.

Care should be taken, however, that the implementation of ISO 14000 is not just seen as a way of achieving minimal certification, instead of performance. A lack of process thinking and analysis can also lead to fragmented procedures, with conflicting interests and little or no focus on customers. Third-party certifiers have an important role to play in judging whether environmental performance is compliant to ISO standards or not.

19.6.3 Carbon footprint

The impact of human activities on the environment in terms of greenhouse gases produced can be measured in units of carbon dioxide (CO_2). The amount of CO_2 emitted by an activity or accumulated over the life cycle of a product is referred to as the carbon footprint of that activity or product. Carbon footprints have to be calculated by all countries that signed the Kyoto Protocol, but can also be calculated for individual companies, regions or households.

Organisations, households and even individuals should aim to reduce their carbon footprint if they want to reduce their negative impact on the environment. For an individual or household this is relatively easy. They can simply buy a car than consumes less petrol or make use of bicycles to travel short distances. For large organisations, reducing their carbon footprint is not as easy. In a supply chain the largest emissions of CO_2 arise from fossil fuel combustion during manufacturing, transportation, storage, disposal and recycling of products.

The following are some of the strategies that can be followed by an organisation to achieve carbon footprint reduction:

- Determine the current carbon footprint of all products and services through LCA.
- Actively try to reduce the carbon footprint by redesigning products or reconfiguring the way services are provided.
- Try to use renewable sources of energy, such as wind turbines, solar panels or hydroelectric power.
- Make sure that energy is recovered during any incineration processes.
- Invest in projects that aim to reduce CO_2 emissions, such as tree-planting initiatives.
- Encourage employees to switch off all air conditioners, lights and computers when nobody is in the office over weekends, holidays and at night.
- Design new office buildings and manufacturing plants to make optimal use of natural light and natural cooling techniques.
- Optimise the layout of manufacturing and storage facilities to minimise the distance that forklifts have to travel.
- Optimise the distribution network to minimise the distance that trucks have to travel to make deliveries.
- Try to source as many products as possible from local manufacturers and suppliers.

In order to reduce their emissions, organisations need to be able to collate, view and analyse their environmental impact. Technology is already available that can help organisations to capture, analyse and optimise CO_2 emission data across the supply chain (see CarbonView in Consult the web, page 436). This technology also enables organisations to evaluate how different carbon management strategies are likely to impact on the environment and on their financial results.

19.7 Closed-loop supply chains

Closed-loop supply chains (CLSCs) are essentially formed when forward and reverse supply chain activities are combined into a single system in order to integrate returned products back into the production or distribution network. In essence, it is a zero-waste supply chain in which all materials are reused, recycled or composted. The term is also often used to refer to corporate take-back programmes, where products are returned to the manufacturer at the end of their useful life. The manufacturer is then responsible for disposal of the product, preferably in an environmentally-friendly manner.

The concept of CLSCs can be illustrated by looking at the life cycle of a glass bottle in which soft drinks are sold (see Figure 19.2, page 434). The bottle is manufactured and filled with the drink at the bottling plant. The bottle is transported to a supermarket where a customer buys it. In a CLSC, the bottle will be returned to the supermarket after the content has been consumed. The supermarket will return the bottle to the bottling plant, where the bottle will be inspected for damage. If the bottle can be used again, it will be cleaned and filled again for distribution to a supermarket. If the bottle cannot be used again, the glass will be recycled to manufacture another glass bottle. The transportation and environmental costs of transporting bottles to and from the bottling plant would need to be reasonable in order for this CLSC to be viable. The closer the links in the supply chain are to each other physically, the more likely that a CLSC will be viable.

Not all CLSCs are as simple to set up as in this example. An automotive manufacturer would, for example, have to initiate complex processes in order to make their supply chain a closed-loop in which they take back their cars from customers after the cars have reached the end of their lives. Stakeholder pressure, environmental regulations, increasing pressure on the capacities of landfills and incineration facilities, increasing product returns from dissatisfied customers and business opportunities related to the residual value of end-of-life products are forcing and encouraging manufacturers to explore opportunities for the implementation of CLSCs.

19.8 Conclusion

Reverse logistics is part of the broader returns management process. The role of logistics in the returns management process can be regarded as being, firstly, physical (that of movement and positioning of returned or disposed goods) and, secondly, analytical (that of logistical analysis to enhance efficiency and effectiveness). The returns management process includes the planning, implementation and execution (including control) of avoidance, gatekeeping and the product

Figure 19.2 Closed-loop supply chain of a glass bottle

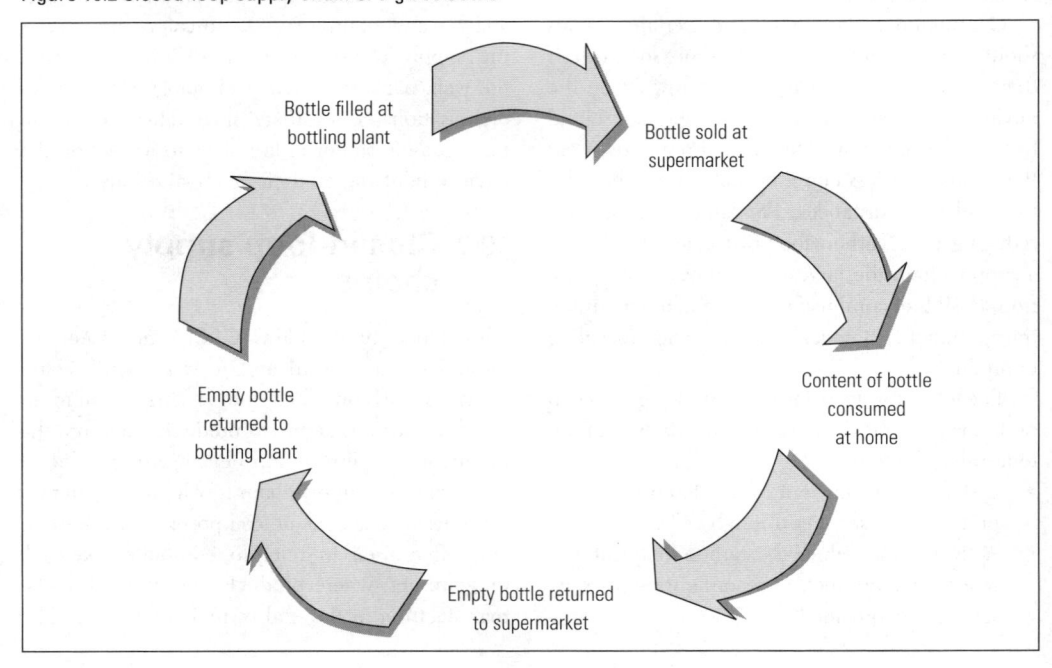

disposition process. Reverse logistics is the part of returns management that plans, implements and controls the efficient, effective flow of goods and related information between the point of consumption and the point of origin in order to recapture value or properly dispose of goods.

Products may be returned to an upstream point in the supply chain for various reasons. The most common are: refusal of items upon delivery or items that are undeliverable; excess or wrongly delivered items; damaged, malfunctioning or defective items; items that reach the end-of-marketing period while still unsold; consumer returns when products become unwanted owing to buyers' remorse and buyers changing their minds; product recalls and warranty returns; reusable containers and packaging materials; and scrap materials (for example, glass and metal) that can be recovered and utilised as raw materials in other manufacturing.

A major problem in the product returns process is the unpredictability of when returns will actually arrive at the warehouse. Usually, the returns processing facility does not know what and how much product will be returned on any given day. The vast majority of all returns are unplanned and, therefore, unpredictable to a large extent. Consequently, problems arise with trying to conduct proper route planning or to schedule staff, vehicles, equipment and other resources when demand for those resources is unknown or variable.

The environmental impact of products and the supply chains through which they reach their markets should also be taken into consideration when managing both forward and reverse logistics. ISO 14000 standards can be followed to ensure that organisations implement sound environmental management systems that will help them limit their environmental impact. Wherever possible, supply chain partners should work towards the establishment of closed-loop supply chains in which all materials are reused or recycled.

Key terms

Avoidance
Carbon footprint
Closed-loop supply chain (CLSC)
Disposal
Disposition
Environmental management system (EMS)
Environmentally sound supply chain management
Gatekeeping
ISO 14000
Life-cycle assessment (LCA)
Product returns
Recycling
Refurbishing
Remanufacturing
Returns analysis
Returns management
Returns processing
Reverse logistics
Sort and stage
Stock-keeping unit (SKU)
Support operations
Waste hierarchy

Case study

Imagine that you have been appointed as environmental officer for Tutti-Frutti Drinks, a Durban-based South African manufacturer of fruit juices and carbonated beverages. Tutti-Frutti currently sells its products in KwaZulu-Natal, Gauteng and the Free State, but wants to expand its market into the rest of South Africa and the African continent. Currently, Tutti-Frutti sells its fruit juices in 1-litre plastic sachets in the local market, and the carbonated beverages in 340 ml clear-glass bottles. The non-returnable glass bottles are packed in wooden crates with limited stackability for distribution to spaza stores, supermarkets and restaurants. The plastic sachets are placed in stackable plastics crates for distribution. Tutti-Frutti has a fleet of eight- to ten-year-old trucks for deliveries.

Tutti-Frutti realises that it will have to re-evaluate its supply chain if it wants to become more environmentally-friendly. You have been asked to provide input as to the logistics and environmental requirements that the new supply chain will have to meet.

1. How can Tutti-Frutti redesign its packaging in order to move up the waste hierarchy?
2. What can Tutti-Frutti do to make its distribution process more environmentally-friendly?

Case study

Automotive manufacturer Subaru's manufacturing plant in Indiana is the first zero landfill auto plant in the world.[8] Subaru's campaign has been to reduce, reuse and recycle. For example, the manufacturer has managed to reduce the use of solvents by 79 per cent and oil by 40 per cent. The investment in some of the recovery processes was high, with payback periods of seven to ten years on the solvent recovery system. Each piece of refuse is looked at and a decision is made to use it either in its original form or in a secondary form. All of this has helped Subaru achieve a 99 per cent recycling rate.

1. Do all the initiatives by Subaru mean that it has an environmentally sound supply chain?
2. Will the Subaru cars manufactured at the Indiana plant have a lower carbon footprint than cars manufactured elsewhere?

Questions

1. Describe the differences between forward and reverse logistics. Do these differences present different challenges to the management of forward and reverse logistics?
2. What is the role of reverse logistics within the returns management process?
3. Describe the five stages of reverse logistics that take place in a warehouse when products are returned to the facility.
4. What are the main groups of activities that have to be managed in the product returns management process and in reverse logistics?
5. What should retailers do with products that are returned to them by consumers?
6. What practical steps can be taken to reduce the carbon footprint of a product?
7. What is a closed-loop supply chain and how is it formed?

Consult the web

Carbon Disclosure Project:
    www.cdproject.net
CarbonView (carbon management model):
    www.carbon-view.com
Cradle to Grave:
    www.howproductsimpact.net
International Standards Organization:
    www.iso.org
LCA Frame: www.life-cycle.org
Reverse Logistics Association:
    www.rltinc.com
Reverse Logistics Magazine:
    www.rlmagazine.com
Waste Online: www.wasteonline.org.uk

Consult the books

Blumberg, M. R. 2008. 'Strategic evaluation of the market for reverse logistics management software'. *Reverse Logistics Magazine*, July/August 2008: 18–21.

Brody, A. L. and Marsh, K. S. (eds.) 1997. *The Wiley Encyclopedia of Packaging Technology*, 2nd edition. New York: John Wiley & Sons.

Guide, V. D. R., Harrison, T. P. and Van Wassenhove, L. N. 2003. 'The challenge of closed-loop supply chains'. *Interfaces* 33(6): 3–6.

Lambert, D. M., Garcia-Dastugue, S. J. and Croxton, K. L. 2008. 'The role of logistics managers in the cross-functional implementation of supply chain management'. *Journal of Business Logistics* 29(1): 113–32.

Rogers, D. S. and Tibben-Lembke, R. S. 1998. *Going Backwards: Reverse Logistics Trends and Practices*. Reverse Logistics Executive Council.

Stock, J. R. 1998. *Development and Implementation of Reverse Logistics Programs*. Oak Brook: Council of Logistics Management.

Stock, J. R. 2004. *Product Returns/Reverse Logistics in Warehousing: Strategies, Policies and Programs*. Oak Brook: Warehousing Education and Research Council.

Talbot, S., Lefebvre, E. and Lefebvre, L-A. 2007. 'Closed-loop supply chain activities and derived benefits in manufacturing SMEs'. *Journal of Manufacturing Technology Management* 18(6): 627–58.

Tibben-Lembke, R. S. and Rogers, D. S. 2002. 'Differences between forward and reverse logistics in a retail environment'. *Supply Chain Management: An International Journal* 7(5): 271–82.

Weers, J. 2008. 'Integration of forward and reverse value chains'. *Reverse Logistics Magazine*, July/August 2008: 36–7.

Notes

1 Stock, J. R. 1998: 10.
2 Lambert, D. M. et al. 2008: 126.
3 Blumberg, M. R. 2008: 18.
4 Weers, J. 2008: 37.
5 Franklin, W. E., Boguski, T. K. and Fry, P. In Brody, A. L. and Marsh, K. S. (eds.) 1997: 563.
6 Section 19.5.1 is based on Stock, J. R. 2004: 7–17.
7 http://www.iso.org/iso/iso_catalogue/management_standards/iso_9000_iso_14000.htm (accessed 30 November 2008).
8 http://www.subaruwest.com/press_release.cfm (accessed 15 July 2008).

20 Controlling logistics performance

U. Kussing

Learning outcomes

After you have studied this chapter, you should be able to:
- understand why the planning and control of logistics activities is a cyclical process and not a once-off event;
- identify the ISO standards that are of importance in logistics management;
- differentiate between the different types of performance measures, and provide examples of performance measures that can be used to track processes in various functional areas of logistics;
- describe the steps involved in a benchmarking exercise;
- identify the supply-chain operations reference (SCOR) processes involved in any supply chain; and
- understand the important role that business intelligence can play in supply chain management.

20.1 Introduction

A sprinter measures the time it takes him to run 100 metres in order to see whether training has led to improved performance, and to see whether he has a chance of competing successfully in his next race. His chances of success will depend on his own performance and on that of his competitors. In the same way, an organisation has to measure and control its business performance to see whether investment in training and technology has improved the overall performance of the organisation and whether this improvement is enough to maintain or improve its competitive position in the market. The organisation also needs to measure whether it is on track to meet its strategic objectives over time.

The following definition of logistics management offered by the Council of Supply Chain Management Professionals (CSCMP) emphasises not only planning and implementation, but also control of the flow of goods, services and information.

> Logistics management . . . plans, implements, and controls the efficient, effective forward and reverse flow and storage of goods, services and related information between the point of origin and the point of consumption in order to meet customers' requirements.[1]

Monitoring and controlling logistics performance should mainly focus on two things:
- Ensuring that resources in the logistics processes are used efficiently, namely, to produce the required output with the minimum input.
- Monitoring the expenses incurred by logistics activities to ensure that money is spent prudently and that budgets are not exceeded, while also giving financial information feedback to other functional areas for future use in planning, costing and budgeting.

Traditionally, businesses have largely focused on controlling logistics costs, while less attention has been given to the elimination of inefficiencies in the supply chain. This chapter focuses on non-financial systems that can be used for measuring and controlling logistics performance.

20.2 The process of control

20.2.1 Definition of control

> Control is a continuous, dynamic process of management in order to achieve a business's goals and objectives, involving all levels of management throughout the organisation. Within a logistics context, the process of control has the goal of maximising profit over the long term while ensuring that customer-service requirements are met, subject to other organisational objectives.

The process of control is greatly influenced by various factors, the most important being:[2]
- the stability of the social, political, economic and technological environments in which the business functions;
- the degree of uncertainty present in the operating environment;
- the level of focus – wide or narrow – that is required;
- the impact cycle of decisions affecting the goals and objectives of a business; and
- the extent of the impact of decisions on the business.

Organisational objectives, for example, have to be achieved in a globally competitive environment, which increases the complexity of decision making. The task of formulating and achieving the objectives should take a broad focus. All the factors contributing towards instability and uncertainty in the global environment should be taken into account. On the other hand, technical standards have to be achieved in a stable and predictable environment, which makes the decision-making process less complex and easier. Achieving technical standards focuses on a particular process and the limited number of inputs that are associated with it.

20.2.2 The planning and control cycle

The planning and control of logistics activities is a cyclical process aimed at continually reviewing and revising plans, policies and operations. Information is an important ingredient in this cycle, and care should be taken that data is collected and made available at the right time and in the right form to the right decision makers. Figure 20.1 shows a typical framework for the planning and control cycle.

Figure 20.1 The logistics planning and control cycle

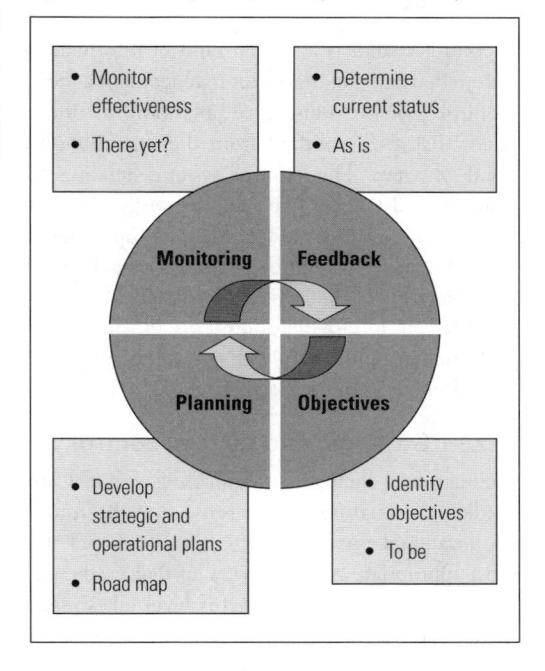

- Monitor effectiveness
- There yet?

- Determine current status
- As is

Monitoring | Feedback
Planning | Objectives

- Develop strategic and operational plans
- Road map

- Identify objectives
- To be

The planning and control cycle first investigates the current status of the organisation's logistics operations. Information feedback or logistics audits can be used for this purpose. Next, the objectives of logistics have to be identified, for example in terms of customer-service or cost objectives. This means that the organisation must decide where it wants to be in the future in terms of market share and positioning. The third stage in the cycle is the planning process in which strategic and operational plans are developed to achieve the previously stated objectives. This stage will describe how the organisation plans to get to where it wants to be. During the final stage of planning and control the effectiveness of logistics operations has to be compared against the plans. This way, the organisation checks to see whether it has arrived at the desired destination. Once this cycle has turned full circle, the process starts over again.

Continual review and revision of objectives, plans, policies and operations help an organisation ensure continuity and progress.

20.2.3 Characteristics of the control process and system

A control system is a special kind of information system that acts as a trigger for management action. Control systems must give attention to those issues that are important from the organisation's point of view. The control systems relating to strategic and tactical planning are vastly different from those relating to technical or operational control. Strategic control is aimed at achieving the objectives of the organisation; tactical control is aimed at improving short-term organisational performance; and technical control is aimed at performing according to standards.

20.2.3.1 Strategic and tactical control

Strategic and tactical, or budgeting, control are predictive in nature, in the sense that the future organisational environment is predicted and the most appropriate action in view of that prediction is initiated. Management at this level takes place in an open environment, where the interaction between a large number of variables has to be anticipated and considered. Consideration should also be given to future changes in cause-and-effect relationships, and the effect that these will have on the achievement of the organisation's objectives.

The control system should attempt to forecast organisational results at a future date. These forecasts should take into account anticipated changes in the environment. When these forecasts are compared to organisational objectives, they should give an indication of whether the objectives will be met or not, or whether an unfavourable trend is developing, thus serving as a trigger to re-planning and corrective management action. Strategic control is long-term in nature, with reviews of objectives only taking place every 6 to 12 or even 18 months.

Predicted results should be quantified to enable higher levels of management to evaluate the feasibility of proposed plans of action, as well as the assumptions underlying them. Strategic control systems trigger entrepreneurial plans, with managers being held responsible for developing innovative plans aimed at achieving the organisational objectives. The development of these plans has a virtually unlimited scope within which to search for opportunities for improvement.

In the case of budgetary control, costs must be controlled by agreeing on a budget and seeing to it that budgeted expenses are not exceeded. In the case of real or anticipated overspending, corrective action will involve re-planning and re-allocation of resources. If overspending takes place on one cost item, this must be recouped from another cost item or category. Budgetary control is medium term in nature, as review and re-planning can take place every three to six months, depending on how often financial data becomes available.

20.2.3.2 Technical control

Technical, or operational, control makes use of feedback regarding actual current performance. This feedback indicates the current state of operations and whether corrective action has to be initiated. Variances from pre-set standards at a technical level will always result in corrective action aimed at the elimination of future variances. This type of control serves to ensure that specific tasks and activities are performed well, giving it a short-term focus, with measurement taking place daily or on a continuous basis.

The management of technical aspects has a narrow focus due to the relative stability of the environment in which it takes place. Most often, the situation itself will dictate a solution to the problem, although a number of alternatives could in many cases be generated. Unfavourable variances are often due to input-process-output malfunctioning, so that the source of malfunction can be easily identified and corrected.

20.2.4 Technical control systems

Technical control is a dynamic process that aims to ensure that specific tasks are carried out efficiently. The purpose of technical control is to achieve efficiency standards at supervisory levels of management. It deals, therefore, with the resource conversion process, specifically with the quantity and quality of a product that is manufactured or a service that is rendered within a specific time period. Technical control monitors actual output of the physical process, with variances from expected or standard performance targets serving as triggers for corrective action.

The aspects that need to be incorporated in a technical control system are covered in the following sections.

20.2.4.1 Yardsticks

Yardsticks are of a statistical nature in that they specify a unit of quantity, rather than value; a unit of labour, rather than cost; and some unit of asset utilisation, rather than the cost associated with it. In general, yardsticks have to be chosen to measure quantity, quality and time. The type and spectrum of yardsticks chosen depends on the underlying resource conversion structure. For example, for a once-off event, where only one unit is produced or a single service rendered, time and quality have to be measured by checking whether milestones have been met and by comparing projected to actual results. On the other hand, yardsticks for batch-type resource conversion processes measure quantity in volume or number of units per person of machine hour, quality in terms of waste or number of rejects per batch and time by looking at lost and productive time at each workstation.

20.2.4.2 Standards

A standard is a measure of satisfactory performance. Standards have to be set for the yardsticks determined during the first stage of technical control. This can be done by an experienced individual applying his or her judgement and experience of similar or related situations. Analytical standards can be used when a precedent exists for some of the process activities, for example, when components of a unique product or service are manufactured by a process that has previously been undertaken. Scientific standards can be established through various work measurement techniques. Historical standards can be used in cases where a historical precedent for an activity exists. In general, the most appropriate method for establishing standards depends on the type of resource conversion process for which the standards are being established.

20.2.4.3 Range of satisfactory performance

Even in closed and stable environments, single-value standards show some variation. For example, a worker will never take exactly the same time to pick an order line, but the time will vary around an average value. Therefore, once a standard has been established, a range reflecting acceptable performance levels also has to be established. The range can either be set arbitrarily or

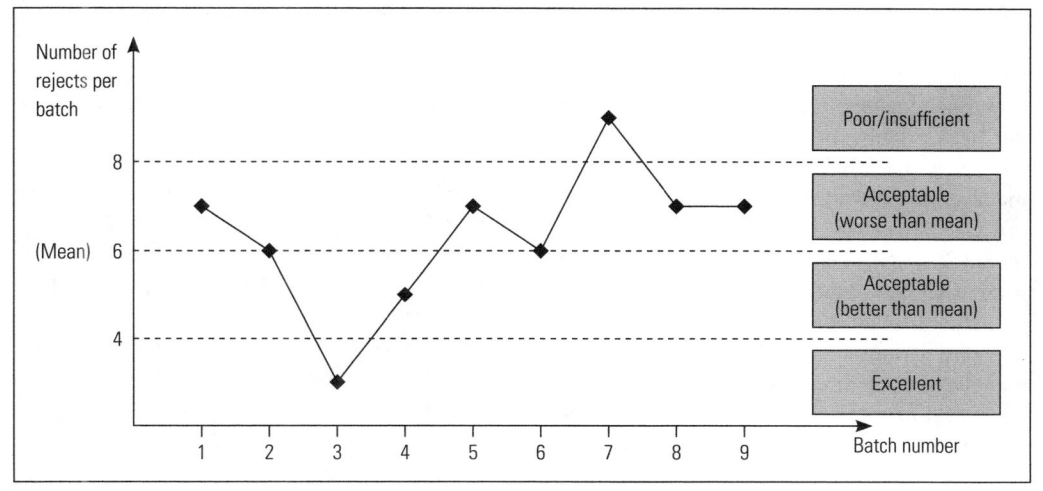

Figure 20.2 Ranges of performance

calculated by assuming a normal distribution and using the principle of standard deviation. Ranges can be set for poor, acceptable (below mean), acceptable (above mean) and excellent performance. An example of this is given in Figure 20.2. Observations that fall outside the range will require the attention of and action from higher levels of management. In Figure 20.2, batch no. 3 shows excellent performance, while batch no. 7 has performed poorly. Management will have to investigate the reasons for excellent performance, so that they can be duplicated, as well as the reasons for poor performance, so that they can be avoided in future.

20.2.4.4 Frequency of measurement

The physical activity that is being controlled has to be completed before performance can be measured. In the case of once-off events, performance will be measured in terms of completed activities according to milestones specified in a project plan. In the case of a batch process, quantity can only be measured at the end of the production run, but quality can be measured continuously. For standardised activities, such as order picking, measurement will have to take place continually on a daily or weekly basis. In general, measurement has to be frequent enough to enable corrective action to be taken before the end product or service has been delivered.

20.2.4.5 Reporting system

Most of the time, performance will be recorded and presented to management in aggregate form on a weekly or monthly basis as long as performance falls within an acceptable range. When variance exceeds this range, reports have to be generated for higher levels of management. In general, the larger the problem, the higher the level of management that should be notified, so that they can take corrective action. At the lowest level of reporting, graphs can be kept at shop-floor level where they are visible to everyone. This enables the workforce to compare their performance to previous performance or to pre-set targets. Car manufacturers, for example, utilise graphs at shop-floor level of the number of units manufactured during the week or month to date, as well as accident-free work days or hours.

20.3 The concept of quality

Quality is a concept that is very closely related to the goal of achieving optimal customer service in logistics. Price[3] says that quality is:

'Giving the customer what he wants today,
at a price he is pleased to pay,
at a cost we can contain,
again, and again, and again,
and giving him something even better tomorrow.'

Logistics is involved in making sure that the customer is satisfied by delivering goods and services when wanted at a cost that still leaves room for the business to make a profit or at least cover its costs. Customers generally do not want to be surprised by products of varying quality, nor do they want to have anything to do with their supplier's quality problems. The management of quality is, therefore, largely an unseen process, of which the results have an impact on customer satisfaction.

Quality is the result of a well-organised system, in which processes are managed in a systematic and formalised way. The two systems of quality control that are often used in logistics are total quality management (TQM) (see also Chapter 8) and ISO 9000. Six sigma is another methodology that is aimed at improving a company's operational performance by eliminating defects in manufacturing and service-related processes. This methodology is not, however, discussed in this chapter.[4]

20.3.1 Total quality management

> TQM is a philosophy and a set of principles used to achieve continuous improvement in an organisation. The principles are general in nature and can be applied to any business process or activity. TQM regards continuous improvement as a cyclic, iterative and never-ending process that focuses on the proactive identification and solving of current and potential problems.

The quality principles on which TQM is based are as follows:[5]

- Customer focus and customer involvement: Customers should be known and understood so that their needs can be integrated in the activities. Changing customer needs should lead to improvements, while complaints should be prevented instead of only reacting to them.
- Involvement of all employees: Teamwork is used to leverage knowledge and provide synergy. Open communication, respect and trust are important.
- Process-oriented: The means of work accomplishment should be addressed – not only the outcomes. Processes are documented and, if successful, converted into standard working procedures. Suppliers are long-term partners who help to reduce process variation.
- Consistency of purpose: An inspiring mission and vision should be developed and communicated to all levels of employees. SMART goals should also be formulated. (SMART stands for specific, measurable, achievable, realistic, time-specific.) The commitment of top management is crucial to success.
- Act according to facts: Data analysis is used to identify the causes and consequences of problems. Quality costs should be analysed and data collected to measure whether quality goals have been reached.
- Focus on continuous improvement: Problems are regarded as opportunities for process improvement. Improvements are realised through a cross-functional, structured and holistic approach applied by multi-disciplinary teams. Continuous documentation of improvements is performed.

The problem-solving discipline (PSD) contained in TQM is shown in Figure 20.3. This is a methodology for the systematic, gradual and team-based solving of problems. This approach starts off by defining the problem present in a process. The problem should be identified in terms of its characteristics; the effect it has; the difference between how it is supposed to be and how it is now; and an overall measurement of the problem (frequency, degree and time). Questions that should typically be asked about the problem are: When? How? Where? What? Who? and Why?

Figure 20.3 The problem-solving discipline of TQM

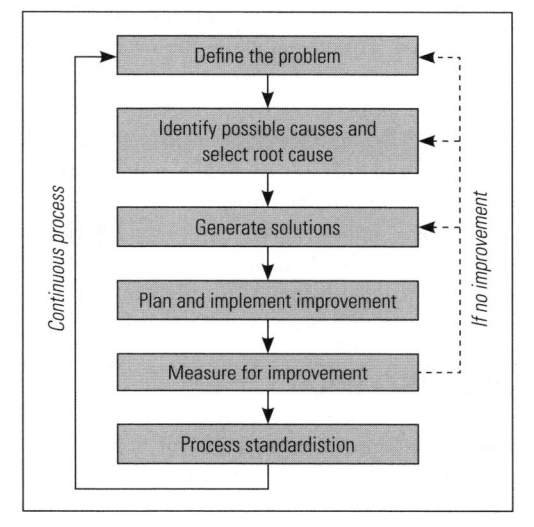

Source: Adapted from Rampersad, H. K. 2000. Total Quality Management: An Executive Guide to Continuous Improvement. *Berlin: Springer: 12. Reprinted with kind permission of Springer Science and Business Media.*

The second step of the PSD is aimed at identifying as many possible causes of the problem as possible and selecting the most logical root cause from amongst them. During the third step, as many possible solutions to the root cause as possible are generated through brainstorming. All solutions should be evaluated and the one with the best chance of success and highest suitability should be chosen.

The planning and implementation of proposed improvements take place during step four of the PSD. The consequences of implementation, potential barriers to implementation and resource requirements should be considered. Communication with all stakeholders regarding the proposed solution is vital in order to ensure that stakeholders will take ownership of the solution.

The fifth step of the PSD is concerned with measuring whether the problem has been solved or reduced by the implemented solution. If the customers' requirements are still not being met, the problem definition, identification of root cause and generation of a solution should be investigated and checked for errors.

If the implementation of a new process has led to quality improvements, the sixth step of the PSD requires that the process should be standardised. This encompasses the establishment or documentation of process executions in standard procedures, which should then be incorporated into the daily routine of the organisation. The solution could then also be implemented in other sectors within the organisation.

The most important techniques used during a successful PSD include brainstorming, fishbone diagrams, flow charts, line graphs, histograms, Pareto diagrams, scatter diagrams and control charts.

20.3.2 ISO 9000

The International Organization for Standardization (ISO), a network of national standards institutes of 148 countries, is the world's largest developer of standards. National delegations, representative of various economic stakeholders, gather at the ISO to 'agree on specifications and criteria to be applied consistently in the classification of materials, in the manufacture and supply of products, in testing and analysis, in terminology and in the provision of services'.[6] International standards provide a reference framework or common technological language between suppliers and their customers, which facilitates trade and the transfer of technology.

The benefit of widespread adoption of ISO standards means that suppliers can base the development of their products and services on specifications that have general acceptance in their respective sectors, enabling them to freely compete in many markets around the world. Conformity of products and services to international standards gives consumers assurance about quality, safety and reliability.

ISO 9000 and ISO 14000 are among ISO's most widely known and used standards. ISO 9000 is an international reference for quality requirements in business-to-business dealings, while ISO 14000 helps organisations to meet their environmental challenges. Both of the above are generic management-system standards in that they can be applied to any organisation, with any product, in any sector of activity and are used by organisations to manage their processes or activities. (For more on ISO 14000, see Chapter 19, page 432.)

ISO 9001:2000 is part of the ISO 9000 family of standards and is used for the purpose of conformity assessment. The objective of ISO 9001:2000 is to provide organisations with a set of requirements that, if they are met by their suppliers, will provide them with confidence that their suppliers can consistently provide goods and services that meet their needs and requirements, and that comply with applicable regulations. The requirements cover various topics, including, amongst others, top management's commitment to quality; adequacy of resources; process management; product design; processes to resolve customer complaints; and monitoring of customer perceptions about the quality of goods and services provided by the supplier.

20.4 Performance measurement

Every company has some kind of measurement system that keeps track of various financial and operational performance measures (often referred to as metrics). Traditionally, measurement systems were dominated by financial performance measures, as this information was easily available from accounting systems. With the development of logistics information systems and automatic data capturing, data relating to the operational aspects of a company has become more readily available so that non-financial performance measures have, in recent times, gained in importance. The SCOR model, discussed in Section 20.6, is one such model that rests heavily on non-financial performance measures.

If one uses the analogy once again of the sprinter, measuring his performance by just looking at the time it takes him to run 100 metres will not suffice in the modern sporting arena. The performance factors that influence the time it takes him to run the 100 metres will also have to be kept track of, for example, level of fitness, strength, endurance, nutrition etc. In the same way, a business cannot only measure business performance by looking at profit: it must also measure the performance of those activities and processes that enable it to perform competitively.

20.4.1 Definition, objectives and purpose of performance measurement

The term business performance refers to the efficiency, effectiveness and adaptability of a business. Effectiveness refers to the extent to which requirements from the environment are met, while efficiency refers to how economically the resources of the business are utilised.

> Performance measurement is a process of quantifying strategic, tactical and operational actions. A performance measurement system is the set of performance measures used to quantify actions.

A performance measurement system must be designed in such a way that it is able to accomplish the three objectives of monitoring, controlling and directing operational logistics employees. Monitoring takes place through the establishment of performance measures to track system performance. This performance is then reported to management. Controlling indicates where the logistics system requires modification by establishing standards of performance relative to the established performance measures. Lastly, performance measurement has to direct employees towards higher productivity by motivating and rewarding them for good performance.

The purposes of a performance measurement system are as follows:[7]
- It should support the decision-making process by indicating where to act and how to act, and by monitoring the effect of implemented action plans.
- The system should monitor the effect of strategic plans so that corrections can be made to ensure the achievement of long-term goals and objectives.
- Performance evaluation is required for internal purposes and for satisfying requirements from various external stakeholders.
- The system should have diagnostic properties so that warning can be given in advance of decreasing business performance.
- Performance measurement is part of a continuous improvement process. For example, it plays an important role in step 5 of the TQM PSD (see Section 20.3.1).
- Measurement of progress has a motivational effect on the labour force of a business and is necessary to justify further effort in any improvement process.
- The measurement of performance is necessary for comparison and for identifying performance gaps.
- Records should be kept of all business activities so that they can be supplied on demand to, for example, customers and suppliers. A record of supplier performance can, for example, be used to give input to their improvement processes.

This list of purposes should be taken into account during the development of a measurement system.

20.4.2 Types of performance measures

Rolstadås[8] differentiates between hard and soft performance measures, between financial and non-financial performance measures and develops a model for performance measurement based on the three dimensions of performance, namely efficiency, effectiveness and adaptability.

Hard performance measures are based on facts and can be measured directly and accurately. For example, a warehouse manager can measure forklift utilisation by dividing the active time in usage of a forklift by the total time in a measurement cycle. Soft performance measures are intangible in nature and have to be measured indirectly. Customer satisfaction is an example of such a measure. The number of complaints, the number of customers gained or lost, or the fill rate can be measured, but none of these will give a clear indication of the level of satisfaction that customers experience.

Hard performance measures can be divided into financial and non-financial performance measures.

Examples of financial performance measures are:
- return on investment (ROI);
- cash-to-cash cycle;
- customer profitability;
- operating ratio; and
- net profit ratio.

Non-financial performance measures include:
- inventory turnover;
- asset utilisation;
- order cycle time;
- percentage defective; and
- percentage of demand met.

A mixture of these performance measures is needed to give a balanced view of the overall performance of a business.

An example of a performance measurement model is given in Figure 20.4. The model focuses on three types of performance measure, used to measure the three dimensions of performance.

Figure 20.4 Validity of performance measures

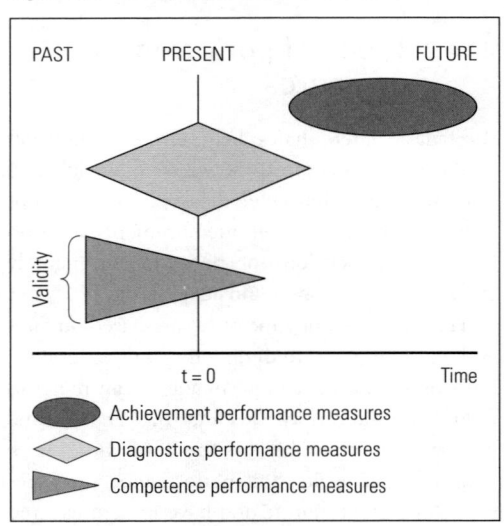

[Figure: Chart showing Validity vs Time, divided into PAST, PRESENT, and FUTURE regions at t=0. Legend:
● Achievement performance measures
◆ Diagnostics performance measures
▶ Competence performance measures]

Source: Adapted from Rolstadås, A. 1994. Performance Management: A Business Process Benchmarking Approach: 81. Springer. Reprinted with kind permission of Springer Science and Business Media.

Achievement performance measures are direct measures of business achievement based on hard facts and can be measured directly. Financial measures dominate this category. The problem with these types of performance measures is that they give no explanation or early warning of a negative trend in performance. They have limited predictive validity and mainly serve to show whether past performance has been good or bad. Unfavourable variance from last year's budget can, for example, only show how much money was overspent or by how much the profit was less than expected. It cannot give an indication of future performance.

Diagnostic performance measures are indirect measures of business achievement in that they measure critical success factors for competitiveness without looking at traditional financial achievements. Critical success factors are characteristics, conditions or variables that have an impact on customer satisfaction and consequently on business success. Diagnostics performance measures are part of an early-warning system and should be able to explain trends in achievements or suggest suitable corrective actions. They are, however, most valid at the time of measurement and have little predictive value. Examples of diagnostic performance measures are:
- delivery lead times;
- number of backorders;
- delivery flexibility; and
- product reliability.

Competence performance measures describe how well a business is prepared for the future or for new market or customer requirements. There is no acceptable range of performance for these performance measures, as they focus on how well the business is positioned to face future challenges. They are strategic in nature and show how well prepared the business is to stay competitive. Time to market of new products; investment in research and development; and the flexibility to manufacture completely new products are examples of measures that give an indication of the success of future product offerings. They are also important factors taken into consideration when suppliers and customers consider long-term relationships with a business.

A performance measurement system should contain a balanced mixture of achievement, diagnostic and competence performance measures in order to make sure that the business has a good indication of past, present and future performance.

20.4.3 Hierarchy of performance measures

Performance measures need to be aligned across all levels of the business. All measures should be applied first at the highest level of an organisation, before cascading down through the tactical and operational levels. This will go a long way towards ensuring that organisational performance and supply chain performance are closely aligned and that they will be assessed for performance and improvement in the same way.

Within a supply chain, performance measures form a hierarchy. For example, in order to measure supply chain reliability, an organisation could choose to measure what is known as perfect order fulfilment. This is the percentage of orders that

Figure 20.5 Hierarchy of perfect order fulfilment

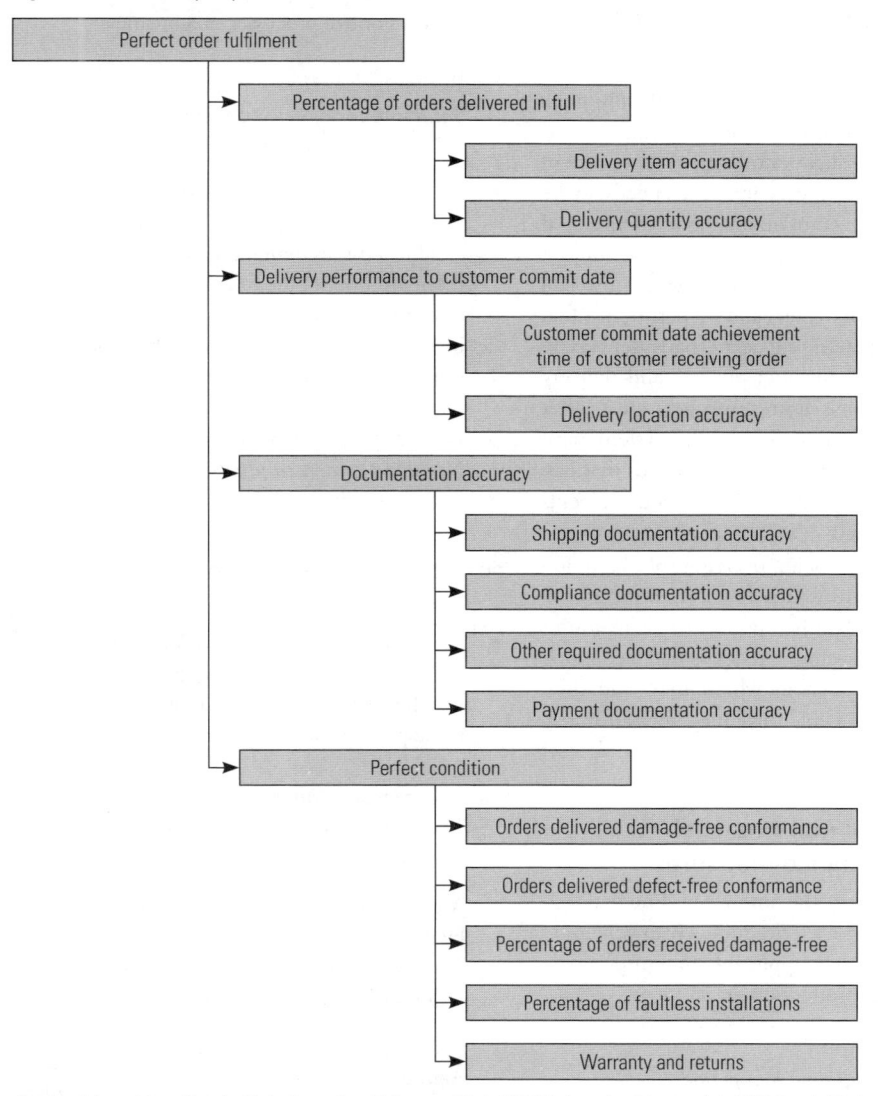

- Perfect order fulfilment
  - Percentage of orders delivered in full
    - Delivery item accuracy
    - Delivery quantity accuracy
  - Delivery performance to customer commit date
    - Customer commit date achievement time of customer receiving order
    - Delivery location accuracy
  - Documentation accuracy
    - Shipping documentation accuracy
    - Compliance documentation accuracy
    - Other required documentation accuracy
    - Payment documentation accuracy
  - Perfect condition
    - Orders delivered damage-free conformance
    - Orders delivered defect-free conformance
    - Percentage of orders received damage-free
    - Percentage of faultless installations
    - Warranty and returns

Source: Adapted from Supply-Chain Operations Reference Model (SCOR©) version 9.0, copyright 2008 Supply Chain Council

meet delivery performance with complete and accurate documentation and no damage during delivery. Perfect order fulfilment can only be measured if the percentage of orders delivered in full, the delivery performance to the customer commit date, the documentation accuracy and perfect condition are measured. Each of these measures, in turn, consist of other performance measures (see Figure 20.5), some of which will be measured by supply chain partners of the organisation measuring its perfect order fulfilment.

20.4.4 Logistics performance measures

Logistics performance measures specifically track certain processes within the logistics framework. The first step in logistics performance measurement is the definition of the system that needs to be measured and its components. For example, if the performance of the parts and service support function is to be measured, managers must first identify all the activities and departments that are part of this system (e.g. spare parts delivery to dealers; spare-part stocking; pick-up and delivery of defective products from customers etc.). After the functional requirements of the system have been determined, performance measures that can quantitatively measure the functional requirements have to be identified.

This section gives an overview of the main performance measures used within the logistics framework.[9] The logistics performance measures provided in this section are classified according to the functional area in which they find their main application. Generally, they measure cost, customer service, quality, productivity and asset management in logistics functions.

20.4.4.1 General non-financial performance measures

- Asset utilisation – the amount of time that assets are being used productively to generate the desired output; applicable to transport, warehousing, production etc.:

$$\text{Asset utilisation} = \frac{\text{Actual working time in a period}}{\text{Total number of hours in a period}}$$

- Total cycle time – the time from placement of an order till the time when it is received by the customer:

$\text{Total cycle time} = \text{maximum of (order processing time} + \text{manufacturing lead time} + \text{transportation time)}$ and $(\text{order processing} + \text{delivery time from warehouse})$.

- Percentage defective – measures the number of defective items shipped, thereby giving an indication of the quality of the production and quality control processes in a business:

$$\text{Percentage defective} = \frac{\text{Total number of defectives shipped}}{\text{Total number of items shipped}}$$

- Percentage of demand met – this is an indicator of the operational capability of a business, as demand cannot be met if one or more of the following areas – forecasting, production, warehousing, inventory management or distribution – are functioning poorly:

$$\text{Percentage of demand met} = \frac{\text{Number of orders fulfilled}}{\text{Total demand}}$$

20.4.4.2 Performance measures for procurement

- Price reduction quota – indicates how good the purchasing staff are at negotiating with suppliers to achieve prices that are lower than those paid in the open market:

$$\text{Price reduction quota} = \frac{\text{Realised object price reductions}}{\text{Market price (index)}}$$

- Average cost per order – this can be measured by department, product, member of staff or framework agreement, with the goal being a reduction of average costs per order:

$$\text{Average cost per order} = \frac{\text{Total cost of orders}}{\text{Total number of orders}}$$

20.4.4.3 Performance measures for supplier selection

- Delivery reliability – indicates the variability of delivery times, with lower variability and longer delivery time preferred over shorter delivery with high variability:

$$\text{Delivery reliability} = \frac{\text{Maximum delivery time} - \text{minimum delivery time}}{\text{Average delivery time}}$$

- Complete shipments – measures the percentage of orders that are delivered in full, without the customer having to wait for backorders:

$$\text{Complete shipments} = \frac{\text{Number of orders delivered in full}}{\text{Total number of orders}}$$

- Percentage good parts – measures reliability of the supplier in terms of the quality of parts delivered by the supplier:

$$\text{Percentage good parts} = \frac{\text{Total quantity supplied} - \text{number of defectives}}{\text{Total quantity supplied}}$$

20.4.4.4 Performance measures for inventory control

- Inventory turnover – measures the speed with which inventory moves through a business, and thereby also the number of times inventory is turned during the course of a year. This is also an important factor when measuring asset utilisation. The first formula is used by the majority of organisations; the second formula is used in some retail organisations:

$$\text{Inventory turnover} = \frac{\text{Cost of goods sold during a time period}}{\text{Average inventory valued at cost during the period}}$$

$$\text{Inventory turnover (retail)} = \frac{\text{Cost of goods sold during a time period}}{\text{Average inventory valued at selling price during time period}}$$

- Demand not met – looks at inventory control from the customer's perspective in terms of availability of products, with low availability leading to a large number of backorders, high stockout costs and loss of customers:

$$\text{Demand not met} = \frac{\text{Demand not met in time}}{\text{Total demand}}$$

- Inventory-carrying cost (as discussed in Chapter 10) and aggregate inventory value can also be used as measures of inventory performance.

20.4.4.5 Performance measures for warehousing

- Order picking time – refers to the time it takes to pick all items on a customer's order, including order processing time (time taken to locate the items and plan a routing sequence to pick them up) and interference time (time spent waiting for equipment and interruptions in movement due to congestion):

Order picking time = order processing time + travel time to first location + interlocation travel time + travel time from last location + pick-up time + interference time.

- Warehouse throughput – measures the number of loads a storage system can handle, which is greatly influenced by order picking time and the utilisation of the materials-handling system:

$$\text{Warehouse throughput} = \frac{\text{Number of loads received, placed in storage and retrieved}}{\text{Number of hours}}$$

- Utilisation of warehouse equipment and warehouse operating cost per unit can also be used as measures of warehousing performance.

20.4.4.6 Performance measures for transport

- Total transit time – measures the time to transfer a shipment from origin to destination:

  Total transit time = travel time + waiting time at terminals/docks + transfer time + handling time.

- Transit time variability – indicates the reliability of the transport function, with low variability in transit time enabling better planning of logistics functions:

  Transit time variability =
  $$\frac{\text{Maximum transit time} - \text{minimum transit time}}{\text{Average transit time}}$$

- Percentage of perfect shipments – measures the overall quality of the transport function by looking at the percentage of shipments that arrived at the final destination on time, complete, damage-free and with complete documentation attached:

  Perfect shipments =
  $$\frac{\text{Number of perfect shipments}}{\text{Total number of shipments}}$$

20.4.4.7 Performance measures for customer service

- Service reliability – measures how often shipments are delivered within or close to the promised delivery time:

  Service reliability =
  $$\frac{\text{Number of shipments within} \pm \text{'x' hours of promised delivery time}}{\text{Total number of shipments}}$$

- Fill rate – indicates what percentage of units is available when requested by the customer. It can be measured in a variety of ways, for example:

  Line count fill rate =
  $$\frac{\text{Number of order lines shipped on initial order}}{\text{Total number of order lines ordered}}$$

  Stock-keeping unit (SKU) fill rate =
  $$\frac{\text{Number of SKUs shipped on initial shipment}}{\text{Total number of SKUs ordered}}$$

  Case fill rate =
  $$\frac{\text{Number of cases shipped on initial order}}{\text{Total number of cases ordered}}$$

- Customer complaints – it is important to keep track of the total number of complaints during a period of fixed length. For example, if the number of complaints per week is measured, a business should monitor whether this number increases, decreases or stays the same from week to week.

20.5 Benchmarking

> Benchmarking is a form of performance measurement with which a business compares the performance of its activities against the performance of other businesses.

Benchmarking is more an exercise of performance comparison than performance measurement. If one uses the analogy of the sprinter, benchmarking means that the runner measures his own performance and compares it to that of other athletes. If his aim is to just win the next athletic championship, he will compare against the season's best times of his likely competitors in this championship. If, however, he wants to become world champion, he will have to compare his performance against the world record and against the best times run in the world during that season. If the performance of other athletes is better than his, he will investigate their training methods to see whether he can improve his own performance by using similar methods. In the same way, benchmarking compares performance at various levels and looks for ways in which best-in-class performance can be achieved.

20.5.1 Characteristics of benchmarking

Benchmarking is a process during which an organisation's strategies, systems and/or operating performance are compared with direct industry competitors or with best-in-class organisations outside the industry. Ideally, this should lead to the development of best practices within the organisation carrying out the benchmarking exercise.

While no two benchmarking exercises follow exactly the same procedure, they have the following characteristics in common:
- Benchmarking is a process. This means that it is not just a once-off activity, but rather a transformation process.
- It focuses on continuous measurement and improvement. The aim of benchmarking is not to achieve a once-off improvement, but rather to compare and improve processes within the organisation continuously.
- Products, services and business practices are compared. While the main focus of benchmarking is the comparison of business processes and operational systems, it can also be used to compare the products and services of an organisation.
- Benchmarking must take place against comparable processes. No two processes are identical to one another, but benchmarking has to compare processes that are comparable in some way, for example, comparing order processing systems of two international corporations with one another. The American Productivity and Quality Center (APQC) process classification framework is a high-level, industry-neutral model that enables benchmarking regardless of industry, size or geography by allowing organisations to see their activities from a cross-industry point of view.
- Comparison must be with leading organisations. In order to be market leaders, organisations need to have an idea of what world-class or best-in-class performance entails. Benchmarking has to take place, therefore, against the best possible example of exceptional performance that can be found.

20.5.2 Benchmarking partners

Before a benchmarking exercise can start, one needs to decide whom to benchmark against. The main options available are:
- internal colleagues;
- industry competitors; and
- non-competitive organisations.

Benchmarking against internal colleagues is the easiest form of benchmarking, as data should be readily available. Different divisions or branches of the same organisation can be compared easily. For example, Volkswagen South Africa could benchmark its performance against Volkswagen Brazil. As both companies are part of the same parent company, access to data should not be a problem. However, if performance within the company is poor, benchmarking against internal colleagues will lead to little or no improvement.

Industry benchmarking entails benchmarking against competitors within the same industry. The main problem with this type of benchmarking is that it is often very difficult to convince a competitor to share business information. Even if a direct competitor provides information, it should be treated carefully, as information may be incomplete, outdated or incorrect. Industry statistics provided by trade associations are of little use in industry benchmarking, as they are normally based on averages. Comparison with such statistics will only indicate whether the organisation is above or below average, and not whether they are leaders in their field.

Other activities that can take the place of a formal benchmarking exercise with a benchmarking partner include the following:
- Computerised databases. Databases of benchmarking information are available on the Internet. There is, however, no way of knowing how up-to-date and valid this information is, as sources of information are often not revealed. The APQC initiated an Open Standards Benchmarking Collaborative (OSBC) in 2004. Any company can enter its performance data through a survey on the APQC website,[10] where it then gets added to the OSBC database and provides the company with feedback on how its performance compares to the database median and to top performers.
- Reverse engineering. Competitors' products can be bought, tested and dismantled to see whether they have technical aspects that make them superior to one's own products.
- Press articles and conferences. Publications on competitors and addresses delivered at

trade conferences can give information on new processes and technology used within an industry, as well as anticipated future developments.
- Gleaning information from customers. An organisation's customers are often the best source of information – after all, they are the ones who buy the product or services. By asking one's customers about their perceptions of one's own and competitors' products/services, it is possible to glean information about competitors' performance.
- Recruitment from competitors. A less ethical way of getting information on a competitor's business practices is by luring their employees in order to gain insider information from them.

These are all ways in which information can be gathered on competitors' performance, without needing the cooperation of internal colleagues, industry competitors or non-competitive organisations.

20.5.3 Conducting a benchmarking exercise

Each organisation that goes through a benchmarking exercise has to ensure that it is tailor-made to the organisation's particular requirements. However, successful benchmarking exercises generally follow the pattern set out in the following steps.

Step 1: Ensure management support and set objectives

A benchmarking exercise normally takes quite a long time to complete and requires various human and other resources. Before starting out on such an exercise, management must be convinced of the importance of such a project, and preferably a senior manager should be identified who can serve as champion for the project. Management support is necessary to ensure that resources are made available to the benchmarking team when needed, and that the results of the benchmarking exercise are accepted and implemented in the organisation.

At this stage, objectives also need to be set for the benchmarking exercise. As it is impossible to benchmark all the activities of an organisation, only a few specific activities or processes should be identified for benchmarking. The focus of the exercise will be influenced by the mission and vision of the organisation as well as its customers and their needs.

Step 2: Find a benchmarking partner

In order for benchmarking to take place, an organisation needs to have access to comparable business data from world-class or best-in-class organisations. This type of data is seldom freely available. Therefore, the organisation has to find a benchmarking partner willing to share often highly confidential business information. This partner should be convinced that it also has something to gain from benchmarking. As described in the previous section, there are various choices regarding whom to benchmark against.

Step 3: Assemble a benchmarking team

A decision has to be made regarding the size and composition of the benchmarking team. This entails identifying what disciplines are needed in the team. Obviously, one member of the team must have detailed knowledge of the process to be benchmarked. It is, however, equally important that there is a 'neutral' member on the team, who is not aligned to the process under review, but who knows the business, its products and strategic objectives.

Step 4: Measure and understand one's own performance

Before an organisation can compare its own performance against that of another, it needs to have detailed knowledge of its current state of performance. This process of baselining[11] consists of:
- establishing the current state of logistics strategies, systems and operational performance;
- mapping the flow of goods and materials between supply and production, and to distribution points in the network;

- mapping information systems and the flow of information that corresponds to the physical flow above; and
- profiling current management practices.

It is essential that any available information is identified and located. Often the information will have to be processed before it can be used for the purposes of comparison. Key performance measures can also be calculated at this stage.

Step 5: Measure and understand benchmarking partner's performance

Information received from the benchmarking partner has to be analysed. Some of the information will be available in a usable format, but the rest may have to be gathered through site visits, tours of facilities and meetings between the respective benchmarking teams. The exchange of information is an iterative process, in which teams return to their organisation to analyse the information they have received. Further questions will arise from this analysis, which will be attended to during the next meeting of the teams.

Step 6: Compare performance

At this stage the organisations' strategies, systems and/or operating performance have to be compared. Current performance gaps have to be identified and projections made of future performance levels. Reasons for the performance gaps will give an indication of which practices should be adopted in order to improve performance. Even if there are no significant performance gaps, the benchmarking partners will have gained a better understanding of their own systems and processes.

Step 7: Develop best practices

If better ways of doing business have been identified through benchmarking, plans should be made to close the previously identified gaps and meet future needs. These plans could include the repositioning of internal assets and the use of new practices and/or new technology. Third- or fourth-party logistics service providers can be used to help with the implementation of these plans if there is insufficient internal capacity. Management must ensure that all employees are informed of pending major changes. The results of the changes should show up in the relevant performance measures. Performance improvements should also be widely communicated within the organisation.

Step 8: Continue the benchmarking process

The last step of the benchmarking exercise is optional, but advisable. In large organisations staff can be allocated on a permanent basis to engage in continuous benchmarking activities with long-term benchmarking partners. In an ever-changing global environment, organisations have to ensure that they keep up to date with the latest developments and best practices.

20.6 The SCOR model

The supply-chain operations reference model (SCOR) is a process reference model that integrates the 'concepts of business process re-engineering, benchmarking, and process measurement into a cross-functional framework'.[12] The first version of SCOR was developed by the Supply-Chain Council (SCC), with SCOR Version 1.0 launched in November 1996.[13] The SCC was established in 1996 with the goal of developing cross-industry standards for supply chain management. The latest version of SCOR, Version 9.0, was released in 2008 and included risk management and GreenSCOR for the first time.

SCOR is a standard methodology to:
- describe supply chains in a common language;
- identify a supply chain's performance requirements;
- measure performance through common metrics;
- set performance targets through benchmarking;
- systematically identify improvement opportunities within the supply chain; and
- identify best practices and provide a platform for shared learning.

SCOR starts off by capturing the current (i.e. as is) state of a process and deriving the desired future (i.e. to be) state. After this, the operational performance has to be quantified and compared to similar companies in order to establish internal targets based on best-in-class results. Finally, best-practice analysis has to be performed, in which management practices and software solutions are identified that can result in best-in-class performance. The main goal of SCOR is the description, measurement and analysis of supply chain configurations.

The SCOR model defines supply chain management as an integration of five types of level-1 processes that take place within the supply chain: plan, source, make, deliver and return. The scope of these processes is as follows:

- Plan – matching resources to requirements
  The planning and management of demand and supply aims to balance resources with requirements and communicates these plans to the whole supply chain. It is also involved in the management of supply chain performance, data collection, inventory, transport, legal requirements and compliance.
- Source – connection to suppliers
  This process sources stocked, make-to-order and engineer-to-order products or materials. Supply sources are identified; supplier payment is authorised; and deliveries must be scheduled, received and verified.
- Make – transforming materials
  This covers make-to-stock, make-to-order and engineer-to-order production. Some of the activities that fall under this process are scheduling of production activities; product manufacturing and testing; management of production rules; and final engineering for engineer-to-order products.
- Deliver – connection to customers
  Delivery processes manage all order steps, from processing customer inquiries and quotes to routing shipments and selecting carriers. Warehouse and transport management; customer invoicing; and the management of finished product inventories are also covered.
- Return – returning to suppliers/returns from customers
  This function covers the return of raw materials to suppliers and the receipt of returns of finished goods from customers, including defective products, maintenance, repair and operations (MRO) products and excess products.

Each of these five process types is further broken down into process categories (level 2). For example, a make process can be either make-to-stock (M1), make-to-order (M2) or engineer-to-order (M3). Level 3 defines an organisation's ability to compete successfully by decomposing the process categories further into process elements. A further fourth implementation level is identified by the SCC, but this is not currently in the scope of SCOR. Figure 20.6 illustrates the three main levels of SCOR in terms of process types, process categories and process elements.

SCOR recognises that there are five main areas within which supply chains compete. These are referred to as performance attributes. At the start of a SCOR exercise, an organisation should decide which of the following performance attributes is most important to it, as it is seldom advisable to focus on all at the same time:

- Supply chain reliability – correct product, correct place, correct time, correct condition and packaging, correct quantity, correct documentation, correct customer
- Supply chain responsiveness – speed with which customer gets products
- Supply chain agility – responsiveness to market changes
- Supply chain cost – cost to operate supply chain
- Supply chain asset management – effective management of fixed and working capital

A few hundred performance measures have been developed by the SCC to measure the achievement of goals relating to performance attributes within an organisation. Guidelines are also given for each process category and element that provides the following:
- A process definition
- Performance attributes
- Performance measures (metrics)
- Best practices
- Features of the above best practices

SCOR suggests the use of supply-chain thread diagrams to illustrate how SCOR configurations can be done. Each thread consists of linked plan, source, make, deliver and return processes and

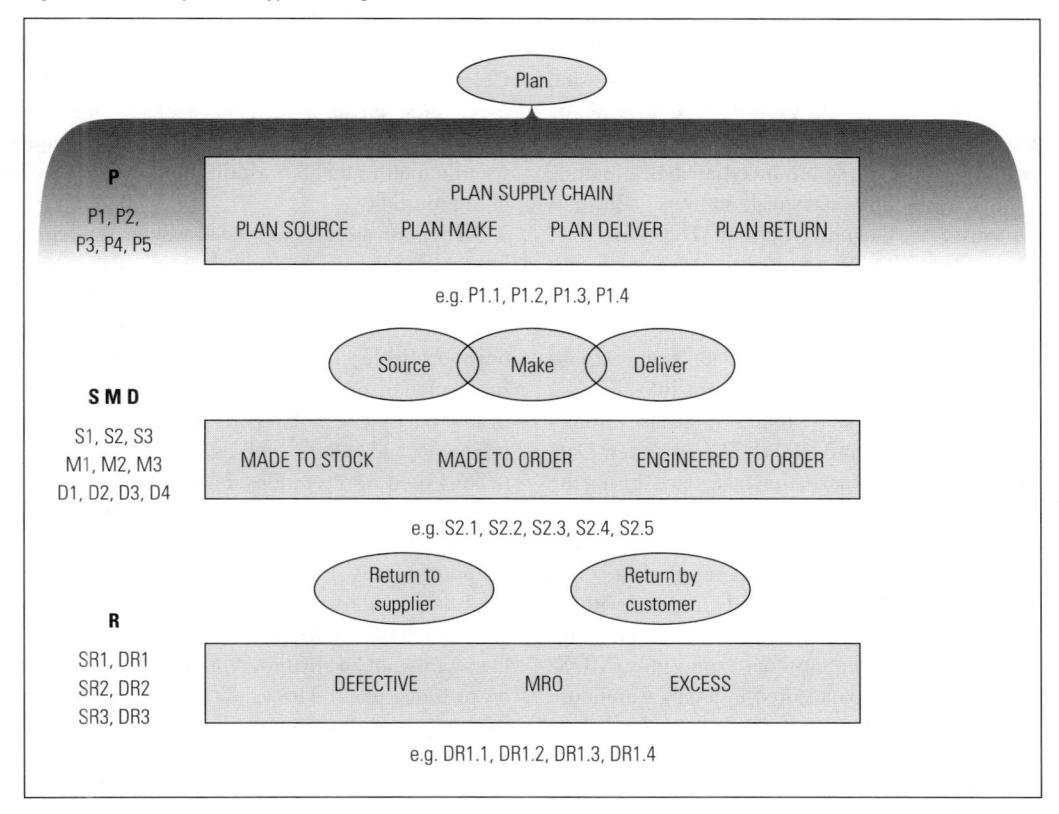

Figure 20.6 SCOR process types, categories and elements

```
                                    Plan

P
P1, P2,                    PLAN SUPPLY CHAIN
P3, P4, P5        PLAN SOURCE   PLAN MAKE   PLAN DELIVER   PLAN RETURN

                          e.g. P1.1, P1.2, P1.3, P1.4

                        Source    Make    Deliver
 S M D
S1, S2, S3
M1, M2, M3        MADE TO STOCK   MADE TO ORDER   ENGINEERED TO ORDER
D1, D2, D3, D4

                          e.g. S2.1, S2.2, S2.3, S2.4, S2.5

                     Return to              Return by
   R                 supplier               customer

SR1, DR1
SR2, DR2             DEFECTIVE       MRO        EXCESS
SR3, DR3

                          e.g. DR1.1, DR1.2, DR1.3, DR1.4
```

is used to describe, measure and evaluate supply chain configurations. This is done in the following stages:[14]

- Select the business entity or process to be modelled.
- The physical location of production facilities (make), distribution activities (deliver) and sourcing activities (source) must be illustrated.
- Primary point-to-point material flows must be shown on the above illustration.
- Appropriate level-2 execution process categories must be identified to describe activities at each location.
- Each distinct supply-chain thread must be described. A supply-chain thread is the set of source-make-deliver processes that a given product group flows through. Each thread should be developed separately in order to understand common and distinctive execution and return process categories.
- Planning process categories have to be linked with execution processes in the illustration.

The execution of these steps should provide the organisation with a SCOR process map that can be used for evaluating and understanding its supply chain. SCOR thus provides a framework and a common language within which organisations can describe their supply chain, and measure the performance of various supply chain activities. It plays an important role in assisting organisations to gain insight into the working of their supply chain.

20.7 Business intelligence

Business intelligence (BI) is the utilisation of software programs to collect, integrate, analyse and present business information from various sources with the purpose of supporting better decision making.

Originally, BI tools were used mainly for data query, reporting and analysis (QRA), but this has expanded to the use of advanced analytics for forecasting, optimisation and other decision support techniques. QRA software includes ad hoc query analysis tools, dashboards and production reporting tools, while advanced analytics include data mining and statistical software. Business Objects, SAS, Cognos, Microsoft, Hyperion, SAP, Oracle and SPSS are some of the leading vendors of BI tools.[15]

BI solutions have a data warehouse, or data marts, as their foundation. Data from various operational data sources is brought into the data warehouse at pre-determined intervals through extract, transform and load (ETL) processes. Data cleansing and summarisation take place during the ETL process. Online analytical processing (OLAP) cubes provide access to data in the data warehouse through data structures that aggregate data across multiple dimensions and provide the user with an analytical environment. Structured query language (SQL) and multi-dimensional expressions (MDX) are used to query data stored in a data warehouse or OLAP cube. A query interrogates records in a database of cubes and thereby aims to find a list of records that match certain search criteria, while allowing counting of items and summing of amounts.

Within a supply chain context an organisation has access, for example, to supply chain data in its enterprise resource planning (ERP) system, warehouse management system, order-processing system, and the tracking systems of its transport providers. BI enables an organisation to sift through the information contained in these systems to measure operational performance and to find relationships that explain events and possibly even predict future ones. BI reports can be pre-built to draw customised information on key performance indicators focused on supporting the decisions made by various managers in the supply chain. A transportation manager will see a report totally differently from the report seen by a procurement manager, as their management objectives and areas of responsibility differ greatly.

Dashboards are reporting tools that consolidate, aggregate and arrange performance measures, indices, charts, graphs and sometimes even maps on a single screen so that the information contained in them can be monitored at a glance. Colour-coded indicators are often used to draw the user's attention to areas in need of management attention. Dashboards are tailored to monitor specific metrics that fall within the recipient's area of responsibility.

BI reports are an automated way of rendering information requested from existing data, with some level of formatting and added calculations. Previously, this information would only have been available through manual extraction and manipulation of data, usually in MS Excel or a similar package. These reports were highly labour-intensive and often took weeks to complete, making their results outdated and not really useful for daily decision making. By contrast, BI reports can be delivered though the Internet, to portals, cellphones and PDAs and virtually any other electronic medium. Depending on the frequency with which data in the data warehouse is updated, the reports can be anything from real-time to based on historical data. The validity and usefulness of these reports will always depend, however, on the quality and availability of supply chain data. Data needs to be accurate, consistent, complete and valid in order for it to be usable.

20.8 Conclusion

In order to remain competitive, an organisation has to ensure that all its resources are used as efficiently and effectively as possible. The monitoring and controlling of logistics performance focuses on ensuring that resources are used in the best way possible and that logistics-related costs are kept under control. The management of quality in the supply chain aims to reduce variability through standardisation of processes. This is done to ensure that customers receive no nasty surprises through defective products or varying lead times. Monitoring and controlling also involve comparing an organisation's own performance with that of its main competitors.

Various controlling and measurement activities that can be used for the above purposes have been described in this chapter. Controlling can take place at a strategic and tactical level, or at an operational, day-to-day level.

The management of quality in the supply chain can take place through TQM or various ISO standards.

Benchmarking is an important tool for the comparison of an organisation's business performance against the performance of best-in-class or world-class organisations. This comparison of performance gives an organisation an indication of its competitiveness and indicates areas and methods for improvement.

The SCOR model, one of the newest developments in the field of logistics control, enables organisations to map their supply chains before measuring the performance of the various process activities.

Key terms

- Benchmarking
- Business intelligence (BI)
- Control
- Dashboard
- ISO 9000
- Performance attribute
- Performance measure
- Planning and control cycle
- Problem-solving discipline (PSD)
- Quality
- Reporting system
- Standard
- Strategic control
- Supply-chain operations reference (SCOR) model
- Tactical control
- Technical control
- Total quality management (TQM)
- Yardstick

Case study

Imagine that you have been appointed as a business analyst in the procurement and logistics department of GoFar, a local developer and manufacturer of hybrid vehicles. The technology that was developed for the hybrid vehicle is best-in-class and has the potential to be highly competitive in the international market. Currently, the vehicles are mainly distributed to local dealers, with some exports to the USA, Germany and Spain. GoFar has its own small exports team that handles the marketing and logistics for all exports. The export process seldom runs smoothly and lead times are highly variable. This leads to dissatisfied customers and cancelled orders.

1. Do you think that GoFar could benefit from a benchmarking exercise? Motivate your answer.
2. How would you convince your manager to allow you to initiate a benchmarking exercise?
3. What should be the focus of the benchmarking exercise?
4. Describe what steps you would take to conduct a successful benchmarking exercise. Provide as much detail as possible for each step.

Case study

Chris Hani Baragwanath Hospital (CHBH) is situated on the southern extremity of Soweto, South Africa, and provides curative services to approximately 3,5 million people from the southern and western parts of Gauteng. It grew from a 1 544-bed military hospital, commissioned by the British War Office in 1940, to one of the largest hospitals in the world. In 1997, it held the record for the largest hospital in the world. Annually, approximately 150 000 patients are admitted to the hospital and another 500 000 outpatients are treated.[16]

As with any other hospital, CHBH is committed to improving the health of its patients. Logistics can play an important role in supporting this commitment by ensuring that all resources (e.g. medical supplies, nurses, doctors, medicines etc.) necessary for the treatment of patients are available in the right place at the right time. Hospital logistics cover areas such as patient logistics; drug management; laboratory logistics; document and information management; disposal of hazardous waste; food management; mail service and management of beds.

In the past, CHBH has faced great challenges in terms of service delivery, as infrastructure was often old and not well maintained and there were frequent shortages of skilled staff. In 2004, the Gauteng Department of Health kicked off an extensive revitalisation programme at CHBH.

1. Do you think that SCOR can add value to the revitalisation process?
2. Which performance attribute would be important for each of the areas of hospital logistics mentioned above? Briefly motivate your answer.
3. Which level-1 SCOR metrics would you use to measure whether the revitalisation programme has led to improvements in hospital logistics?
   Note: You can download the SCOR Reference Guide from the website of the SCC to assist you in answering this question.

Questions

1. Explain why the planning and control of logistics activities is a cyclical process.
2. Which of the following in your opinion offers a higher quality of service if you wish to travel to your nearest airport: (a) a limousine-service that picks you up from home; (b) a municipal bus service that leaves four times a day from your local shopping centre, or (c) a high-speed train service that leaves every 15 minutes from your local train station.
3. What are the potential benefits of dealing with an ISO 9001 certified supplier?
4. Why is it necessary for an organisation to implement and use a logistics performance measurement system?
5. What are the advantages and disadvantages of using (a) internal colleagues, and (b) industry competitors as partners in a benchmarking exercise?
6. SCOR defines supply chain management as an integration of five types of basic processes that take place within a supply chain. Identify and describe these five processes.

Consult the web

APQC (American Productivity and Quality Centre): www.apqc.org
International Organization for Standardization: www.iso.org
ISixSigma: www.isixsigma.com
Supply-Chain Council (SCC): www.supply-chain.org
Supply Chain Metrics: www.supplychainmetric.com

Consult the books

Bolstorff, P. and Rosenbaum, R. 2003. *Supply Chain Excellence: A Handbook For Dramatic Improvement Using the SCOR Model*. New York: AMACOM.

Bowersox, D. J., Closs, D. J. and Cooper, M. B. 2002. *Supply Chain Logistics Management*. New York: McGraw-Hill/Irwin.

Boyson, S., Dresner, M. E., Harrington, L., Corsi, T. M. and Rabinovich, E. 1999. *Logistics and the Extended Enterprise: Benchmarks and Best Practices for the Manufacturing Professional*. New York: John Wiley & Sons.

IDC. 2007. Worldwide Business Intelligence Tools 2006 Vendor Share (excerpt from IDC #207422). Framingham: IDC.

Kasilingam, R. G. 1998. *Logistics and Transportation: Design and Planning*. Dordrecht: Kluwer Academic.

Niedereichholz, J. 'Information technology II'. University of Mannheim. Available from: http://www.steigele.ch/itcontrollingniedereichholz.pdf (accessed on 5 March 2009).

Price, F. 2003. 'The quality concept and objectives'. In Seaver, M. (ed.), *The Gower Handbook of Quality Management*, 3rd edition. Aldershot: Gower.

Rampersad, H. K. 2000. *Total Quality Management: An Executive Guide to Continuous Improvement*. Berlin: Springer.

Rolstadås, A. 1994. *Performance Management: A Business Process Benchmarking Approach*. Berlin: Springer.

Rushton, A., Oxley, J. and Croucher, P. 2000. *The Handbook of Logistics and Distribution Management*, 2nd edition. London: Kogan Page.

Schutte, F. G. 2000. *Integrated Management Systems: Strategy Formulation and Implementation*, 2nd edition. Sandown: Heinemann.

Supply-Chain Council. 2003. 'Supply-chain operations reference model: overview of SCOR Version 6.0'. Anaheim: Supply-Chain Council.

Taras, J. 2005. Supply Chain Metric.com. Available from: http://www.supplychainmetric.com/fillrate.htm (accessed on 5 March 2009).

Notes

1. www.cscmp.org/Website/AboutCSCMP/Definitions/Definitions.asp
2. Schutte, F.G. 2000: 99–101.
3. Price, F. 2003: 5.
4. See the six sigma Internet resource for more information (www.isixsigma.com)
5. Rampersad, H. K. 2000: 6–7.
6. International Organization for Standardization. 2005.
7. Rolstadås, A. 1995: 172–3.
8. Ibid.: 176–82.
9. Kasilingam, R. G. 1998: 218–29.
10. www.apqc.org/OSBCdatabase
11. Boyson et al. 1999: 151.
12. Supply-Chain Council. 2003: 1.
13. Niedereichholz, J.
14. Supply-Chain Council. 2003: 17–19.
15. IDC. 2007.
16. www.chrishanibaragwanathhospital.co.za/bara/article.jsp?id=161

Index

Page numbers in **bold** refer to figures and tables.

A

ABC classification 240–243
   A class **241**, 241, **242**, **243**, **244**, 244, 246
   annual turnover and percentage 242, **242**
   B class **241**, 241, **242**, **243**, **244**, 244, 246
   C class **241**, 241, **242**, **243**, **244**, 244, 246
   cumulative percentage of turnover 242, **242**
   customer service levels 242, **243**
   D class 242
   policy and control based on 242, **243**
   ranking 242, **242**
accessibility 325, 326, 333, **333**, 334, 337, 366–367, **366**, **368**, 369
accrual-based accounting 77
accuracy **181**
action plan **38**, 38, 49, 50, **51**
activity-based costing (ABC) 84–85, **84**, 152, 240–243, 246
   causes 84
   classification 240–243
   (*see also* ABC classification)
   cost drivers 84
   cost pools 84
   delivery costing **85**
   Pareto analysis and Principle (*see* the main entry for Pareto analysis)
   worked example 95–96
air transport 270, 324–325, 344, 347–348, 389–390
   air parcel postal services 390
   assessment of freight charges 270
   effective loading procedures and equipment 344
   express/courier services 390
   fixed costs 348
   freight carriers 390
   freight characteristics 325
   impact of atmospheric changes 270
   oligopolistic market structure 344
   operational overview 324
   overhead costs 348
   passenger carriers 390
   savings with respect to other costs 390
   seasonal/peak-oriented markets 344
   standing costs 348
   time- and handling-sensitive goods 270
   typical limitations 325
   typical strengths 324–325

unit load device (ULD) (*see* the main entry for unit load device (ULD))
   variable costs 348
air waybills (AWBs) 391
Al Enns (Motts North America) 104
alternative solutions, generation of 7, **9**
American Productivity and Quality Centre (APQC) 451
analysis with simulation 7
Annual Business Logistics Forum 6
applied marketing **12**, 12, 23
approximate modelling methods 160, **160**
assemble to order **64**, 64–65, **67**, 73
   demand forecasting 65
   key components 64
   main challenge 65
   major risks 65
   mass customisation 65
assessment stage of supply chain design 149–152, **149**
   business orientation 150
   capital cost and operational cost 152
   corporate governance issues 151
   key elements 150
   key stakeholders 150
   key supply chain participants 152
   performance indicators 152
   potential commercial risks 151
   product and marketing information 150
   steering committee 150
   supply chain cost drivers 152
   supply chain network alternatives 150–151, **151**
Authorised Economic Operator (AEO) programme 396
   company information 396
   company's accounting and logistical systems 396
   compliance record 396
   financial solvency 396
   safety and security requirements 396
availability 27, **27**, 215, 216, 217, 218–219, **218**, 244, 246
   fill rate 27–28, **27**, 218–19
   orders shipped complete 28, 219
   stockout frequency 23, 26, 27, **27**, 28, 29, 32, 218–219
average inventory 219–220, **219**, 244
   calculation 220
   cycle stock 219
   inventory-carrying costs 219
   safety stock 219
   transit inventory stock 219

B

balanced scorecard **38**, 39, **40**, 44, 47, 48, 49, 52
balancing supply and demand 214–215
ban cards (requisition cards) 238

barcodes 279–280
   European Article Number (EAN) 280
   main benefits **280**
   matrix 279, 280
   one-dimensional (1D) 279
   stacked 279, **280**
   two-dimensional (2D) 279, **280**
   Universal Product Code (UPC) 280
benchmarking 157, 450–453, **450**
   characteristics 450–451
   conducting an exercise 452–453
   Open Standards Benchmarking Collaborative (OSBC) 451
   partners 451–452
bills of lading (BOL) 401–402
bins 287, **287**
block stacking 290, **293**
breakeven point 90–91, **91**, 99
bulk-packaging systems 274–275
business competition 40
   factors involved 40
business complexity, developments affecting 34
business context, understanding of 157, 158
business intelligence (BI) 455–456, **455**
   BI reports 456
   dashboards 456
   data query, reporting and analysis (QRA) 456
   data warehouse 456
   enterprise resource planning (ERP) 456
   extract, transform and load (ETL) processes 456
   multi-dimensional expressions (MDX) 456
   online analytical processing (OLAP) 456
   structured query language (SQL) 456
business logistics **6**, 6, **11**
   activities 11–12
   introduction 1–18
   macroeconomic perspective 2–5
business logistics systems, management of 1
business objectives 38, 39, 40, **40**
   key success criteria 38
business response 66
   assessment of service level 66
business strategy 34, 35, 37, 39, 40, 42, 43, 49, 51, 52, 53
   assessment 39
   concerns 35
   design 35
   key objectives and goals 39
   key strategies 39
   mission statement 39
   strategic action plans 39
   vision 39

INDEX | 461

business success indicators 4
business-to-business (B2B) goods 198, 208, 209, 210
business unit 36, 37, 52, 53
business unit strategy 36, **36**, 37
   objectives 37

C

capability indices **4**, 5
   logistics effectiveness 4
   manufacturing flexibility 4
   product innovation 4
   supply chain reliability 4, 5
   time to market 4
capacity planning 171–173, **171**
   changing demand 171
   lag strategy 172, **172**
   lead strategy 172, **172**
   long-term perspective 173
   match strategy 172, **172**
   medium-term perspective 173
   process 173
   production capabilities 171
   production capacity 171
   short-term perspective 173
capital asset pricing model 78, 94
carbon footprint 433
carousels 288–289, **288**
cash-to-cash cycle 31, 446
change management strategy 38, 50, **51**, **149**
closed-loop supply chains (CLSCs) 433–434, **434**, 435
collaborative inventory initiatives 239–240
collaborative planning, forecasting and replenishment (CPFR) 239, 246
   profile replenishment (PR) 240, 246
   quick response (QR) 239–240, 246
   vendor-managed inventory (VMI) 240, 246
combining areas 261–262
   computer-aided design (CAD) 261
   design principles 262
   manual design 262
common market 6
competitive advantage 68, 144, 362
   aspects of 29–30
   definition 29
   obtained by logistics 19–33
   role of logistics management in creation 29–30
competitive environment **36**
competitive requirements 40
competitive strategy 40
competitiveness 25, **29**, 30
complexity indices **4**, 5
conceptual supply chain flow design 152–154
   buffer locations 152
   dynamic simulation model 153
   first-order functional and operational requirements 152
   flow dynamics 153
   functional logistics requirements 153
   geographical and product flow diagrams **145**, **148**, 152
   geographical spread 152

infrastructure 152
insourcing and outsourcing approach 153
internal and external costs 154
inventory flow 152
potential markets 152
risk assessment studies 153
supply risks 153
concurrent engineering 174, **174**
   environmental friendliness 174
   manufacturability 174
   procurement 174
   storage and transport 174
consumer packaged goods (CPG) 52
consumer surplus 21, 23–24
consumer value 24
containerisation 267–284, **276**, **277**
   improvements in handling efficiency 277
   ISO containers (see the main entry for ISO containers)
   multi-technology integration 281
   smart containers (see the main entry for smart containers)
   role in supply chain 267
   unit load devices (ULDs) (see the main entry for unit load devices (ULDs))
contribution approach to CVP analysis 90–92
   breakeven graph 92, **92**
   breakeven point 90–91, **91**, 99
   margin of safety 91, 99
   sales to achieve target profit 91–92
coordination of incoming traffic 377–379
   demurrage and detention 379, **379**
   diversion 378, **378**
   expediting 378–379
   in-transit privileges 3
   reconsignment 378, **378**
   tracking and tracing 377–378, **377**
corporate strategy 36
   corporate directives 36
   mission statement 36
cost accounting and calculations for decision-making purposes 86–93
   activity-based costing 84–85
   cost-volume-profit (CVP) analysis 90–93
   logistics costing 84
   marginal costing 86–90
cost advantage 24
cost and freight (C&F) 151
cost-benefit trade-offs 35, 45, 146
cost effectiveness **20**, 22, 24, **24**
costs involved in site selection 13
cost leadership 24, 25, 40, 41
cost of equity 76, 77–78, **77**, 79, 94
   beta factor 77, 78
   capital asset pricing model 78, 94
   equation 77
   government bonds 77
   market risk premium 77
   risk-free rate 77
cost of goods sold (COGS) 41
cost of quality 178, 179–180, **179**, **180**
   appraisal cost 179
   external failure cost 179

internal failure cost 179
   prevention cost 179
cost per freight ton over distance **350**
cost structures of different modes of transport 347–352, **347**
   (see also alphabetical entries for various modes of transport)
cost trade-offs in transport 352–355
   integrated and coordinated logistics approach 352
   inventory-related cost 355, 358
   opportunity cost (cost of lost sales) 355, 358
   total cost for overall logistics system 11, 20, 351, 352, **353**, **354**, 357, 358
   total annual inventory-related cost 354, **354**
   total annual transport cost 353, **354**
   trade-off analysis 354, **354**
   transport cost mode 355
   transport-related cost 355, 358
   minimising system-wide costs 352
cost-volume-profit (CVP) analysis 90–93
   contribution approach (see contribution approach to CVP analysis)
   in decision-making (see decision-making using CVP analysis)
   relevance to logistics 90
Council of Supply Chain Management Professionals (CSCMP) 8, 10, 20, 422, 438
cross-dock operations 305–308, **306**, 378, 380, 391
   cross-dock-managed load (CML) 306, 307
   factors influencing utilisation 306
   joint-managed load, 306, 307
   processes 307–308
   supplier-managed load 306, 307
   supply chain criteria 306
customer feedback 30
   critical measures 30
customer order decoupling points 61, **64**, **67**
   assemble to order **64**, 64–65
   engineer to order **64**, 66
   make to order **64**, 65, **65**
   make to stock **64**, 64
   pick/assemble and ship to stock **64**, 64
   purchase and make to order **64**, 65–66, **66**
customer satisfaction 30, 57
customer service 8, 11, **12**, 13, 14, 15, 16, 25–26, 31, 183
   after-sale service 15
   pre-transaction component 20, 25–26, 29, 32
   post-transaction component 26, 32
   process 25
   transaction component 26, 32
customer service components 26
customer value 24
   differing perceptions 30
Customs and Border Protection Agency 394

Customs Department Golden List
  Programme (GLP) (Jordan) 396
Customs-Trade Partnership Against
  Terrorism (C-TPAT) 394, 395, 396
cycle stock 182, 217, 219, 223–226
  planning 245
  review level (reorder point (ROP))
    system 223–226
  (see also economic order quantity
    (EOQ); reorder point (ROP))
  target stock level (TSL) system
    226, 245

D
data collection and analysis **9**
data to be submitted for international
  movement 403–404
  ANSI X.12 standard 404
  buyer information 403
  Commodity Harmonized Tariff Schedule
    number (HTSUS) 404
  consignee number(s) 403
  consolidator information 404
  container status messages (CSM) 404
  container stuffing location 404
  country of origin 404
  foreign trade zone applicant
    identification number 403
  importer of record number 403
  seller information 403
  ship to party 403
  supplier or manufacturer
    information 403
  UN EDIFACT standard 404
  vessel stow plan 404
decision-making using CVP analysis 92–93
  change in fixed cost **92**, 93
  change in selling price 93
  change in variable cost 93
  logistics management policies 92
  worked example: change in fixed
    cost 100
  worked example: change in selling
    price 100
  worked example: change in variable
    cost 100
decisions 167–168
  capacity 168
  inventory 168
  quality 168
decoupling 214
  economies of scale 214
  inventory of WIP 214
  production economies 214
  reduction in purchasing cost 214
  transport economies 214
delivered duty paid (DDP) 151
demand **36**
  average daily **229**, 230
  forecasting 12, 14, 16, 64, 65,
    104–142
  management 64
  uncertainties 42, **42**, 62, **62**, 217,
    228–229
demand uncertainty 42, **42**, 62, **62**, 217,
  228–229, 230
  deviation from mean **229**

deviation squared **229**
equation 228
equation when combined with lead
  time uncertainty 230
mean **228**
standard deviation 228, **229**
stockout protection for variability in
  demand 228, **228**
demand/pull strategy 53
Deming 178
Deming Prize 178
density of goods 332
  high-density goods 332
  loose/bulk commodities 332, 333
  low-density goods 332
  mass-to-volume ratio 332
  packed commodities 333
  payload mass limit 332
  payload space 332
  practical density of goods 332
  stowage ability/ease of handling
    333
  stowage factor 332
design
  manufacturing process 9
  plant and factory 9
  product 9
  storage and handling facilities (see the
    main entry directly below)
design of storage and handling
  facilities 250–266
  combining areas (see the main entry
    for combining areas)
  dispatch 253, 257–258, 261, 262
  external areas 261, **261**
  fire 262–263
  flows (see the main entry for flows)
  growth forecast 251, 252
  lighting (see the main entry for lighting)
  loading doors 260
  movement zones 258, 261, 262
  pick area (order picking) (see the main
    entry for pick area (order picking))
  purpose 251–252
  process 253–262
  product process category (PPC) 251,
    251, 252, 254, 262
  receiving 253, 256–257
  restrictions 251
  security 263
  sources of potential inefficiency 251
  storage 253, 254–256
  warehouse sizing 252–253
design stages of supply chain design **149**,
  152–155
  conceptual flow design 152–154
  functional design 154–155
  implementation 155–157
  operation 157
desktop purchasing 208
differentiation 41, 52
discontinuation of a department or
  product 87
  marginal cost in total 87
  total sales income of product 87
  worked example 97–98
dispatch 253, 257–258, 261, 262

distribution channels 383–386, **383**, 44
  channel leader 384
  determination of length 384
  distributors 384–385, **386**
  export agents 385–386, **386**
  government departments 385
  industrial buyers 385
  retailers 385
  territory 386
  trading houses 385
  wholesalers 385
distribution requirements planning
  (DRP) 233, 234, **234**, 237, 245
  independent demand (demand for final
    product) 234
Dr Eliyahu Goldratt 185
drive-in and drive-through racks 291–292,
  291, **293**
drivers of wealth creation 30–31, 32
  fixed capital efficiency 31, 32
  operating cost reductions 31, 32
  revenue growth 30–31, 32
  working capital efficiency 31, 32

E
economic features of transport modes **353**
economic order quantity (EOQ) 223,
  224, 245
  adjustment for quantity discounts
    225, **225**
  adjustment for volume transport
    rates 225, **225**
  adjustments: other 225
  equation 223
economic value added (EVA) 78–79, **78**
  CCE 79
  equation 79
  market value added (MVA) 79
  negative 79
  NOPAT 79
economies of density 343, 344, 345, 346,
  358
economies of distance 343–344, 345, 346,
  353, **353**, 358
  long-haul economies 343, 344
  trip-specific fixed costs 343–344
economies of scale 25, 62, **62**, 267, 341–
  343, 344, 345, 346, 347, 350, 354, 358
  capacity expansion 342
  high ratio of fixed to total cost 342
  increasing fleet size and maximising
    use 342
  increasing vehicle sizes and
    maximising use 342
  intensifying use of indivisible facilities
    and infrastructure 342
  lowering fixed unit costs 342
  overhead charges 342
  returns of scale 342
  two-thirds rule 343
economies of scope 343, 344, 345, 346,
  358
  common production (shared
    production) 343
  joint products (by-products) 343
  product diversification 343
  standardised technology 343

INDEX | 463

economy 25, **341**
effectiveness 20–21, **20**, 27, 36, 365, 373, 379, 430
  accessibility (market coverage) 366–367, **366**, **368**, 369
  flexibility 368, **368**, 369
  goods security 367, **368**, 369
  reliability 367–368, **367**, **368**, 369
  suitability 366, **366**, **368**, 369
  transit time 367, **367**, **368**, 369
efficiency 20–21, **20**, 25, 27, 36, 430
  (*see also* cost-effectiveness)
  cost minimization 21
  direct effect on business competitiveness 341
  in transport 341, 346, 365, 366, **368**, 369
electronic procurement (e-procurement) 207–209
  benefits 207, **207**
  electronic auctions 207–208
  electronic catalogues 207
  electronic exchanges 207
  functional marketplaces 209
  horizontal marketplaces **208**, 209
  types of transactions 209
  vertical marketplaces 208–209, **208**
enablement strategies 36
engineer to order **64**, 66, **66**, **67**, 73
  accurate assessment of job 66
  cost and lead times 66
  fully integrated system 66
  raw material supplier 66
enterprise resource planning (ERP) 427
environmental concerns with regard to packaging 276
  direct take-back obligation 276
  European Parliament directive of 1994 276
  life-cycle assessment (LCA) 276
  paper bag legislation 276
  recycling 276
environmental performance measurement 431–432
environmental supply chain operations 431
equipment used in facilities 285–301
  accelerator belts 296–297
  angled roller belt (ARB) 298
  block sorter 297, **298**
  containers 298–300, **298**, **299**
  conveyors: belt and roller bed 296, **296**
  cranes 295
  diverters 297–298, **298**
  forklift (counter-balance) truck 294, **294**
  hanging rail systems 293–294
  in-line barcode scanners and RFIDs 297
  in-line weighing and measuring 297
  manual and powered pallet trucks 294, **294**
  merge systems 297, **297**
  narrow aisle trucks 295
  pallets, storage 289–293
  pop-up sorter 297, **298**
  quayside container cranes 300, **300**
  reach stackers **290**, 299, **299**

reach trucks **290**, 295, **295**
risks involved in purchasing 286
  selection 285–286
  spreaders 299
  stacker crane 290
  storage methods for small items 286–289
  straddle carriers and straddle cranes 300, **300**
  tilt-tray diverter 298
  turret trucks 295, **295**
  twistlocks 299, **299**
European Community (EC) 6
evaluation 7, **9**
exponential smoothing models 111, **111**, 116–120, **117**, **118**
  (*see also* Holt-Winter; Holt's method)
  Holt 111, **111**, 120–121
  simple 111, **111**
  smoothing parameters 120
ex works (EXW) 151

F
facility location 7, 13, 146, 147
facility site selection and design 11, 13, 16
fast-moving consumer goods (FMCG)
  market 64, 239
feasibility analysis 7
fill rate 230–236
  equation 231
  f(K) (magnitude factor) 231, **232**
  K (safety factor) 231, **232**
  order quantity (EOQ) 230, **231**
financial impacts of reverse logistics 426–427
  change in book value 427
  collection 426
  handling 427
  inventory-holding costs 426
  obsolescence 427
  refurbishment and repackaging 427, 430, 431
  shrinkage (theft) 426
  sorting 427
  transport 426
financial management decision-making 76–84
  cost of equity 77–78
  economic value added 78–79
  free cash flow 78
  return on investment 82–84
  shareholder value 76–77
  value drivers 79–82
financial performance measures 49
  drivers 49
finished goods 20, 323, 324, 325, 331, 337
first in, first out (FIFO) 292, 429
flexibility 151, 153, 154, 155, 368, **368**, 369
flows 258–260
  challenges 259
  charting of flow of good 258
  design principle 260
  diagrammatic representation 259
  operational design: good **259**
  operational design: poor **260**
  prevention of cross-flows 258–259
  visibility at intersections 258

wide turning areas 258
forecasting 5, 7, 11, 104–143
  examples 128–133
  features 105–106
  long-, medium- and short-term 107
  models **111**, 111–112
  process 107–108
  qualitative 106
  quantitative 106
  seasonality 125–128
  selection of appropriate techniques 108–111
  types 106–107
forecasting models/techniques 108–111, **111**, 111–112
  creation of line graphs with Excel 109, **109**
  exponential smoothing models **111**, 116–120
  graphical plotting 108, **108**
  moving averages **111**, 113–116
  naïve **111**, 112–113
  regression-based models **111**
  time series data 108
  validation of 111–112
Forrester Research 35
forty-foot equivalent unit (FEU) 277
free cash flow 78, **78**
  calculation 78
  time value of money 78, **78**
free on board (FOB) 406, **406**, **409**, 410, 414
free-trade agreements 396–397
  European Free Trade Association (EFTA) 396
  North American Free Trade Agreement (NAFTA) 396
  regional trade agreements 396
  Southern African Customs Union (SACU) agreement 396
freight transport 2, 323
  classification 324–330
  efficiency of long-haul transport 4
  typologies **3**
freight transport service providers 333–335
  contract carriers 334
  freight brokers 335, **335**, 337
  freight forwarders 335, 337
  private operators 334, **334**, 337
  professional (commercial) carriers (hauliers) 334–335, **334**, 337
  third-party operators 334
French Academy 5, 6
Frontline programme (Australia) 396
function 167
functional design stage of supply chain flow design 154–155
  determination of final requirements 154
  focus 154
  functional/operational design outcomes 154
  identified commercial risks 155
  identified operational risks 155
  operating philosophy 154
  performance indicators 154
  refinement and finalisation 154

scheduling heuristics 154
shortlist of suppliers 154
sourcing and inventory strategies 154
total cost evaluation 155

G
GDP
   logistics costs 3
   physical components 2, **2**
geographical specialisation through inventory control 215
general pallet storage racks 290
goods and services 19
goods flow 68
   delivery **57**
   direction **71**
   management 57–59, **57**
   master production schedule (MPS) **57**, 58, **59**
   material planning **57**
   material requirements planning (MRP) **57**, 58, **59**
   production planning **57**, 58
   purchase order (PO) **57**, 58
   purchasing **57**
goods 331–333
   factors influencing transport cost 331
   size and divisibility 333
government as stakeholder in transport system 336–337
   control of excessive competition 336
   coordination of transport 36
   integration of transport with economic policy 336
   loss-making operators 336
   maintenance of safety, security and order 336
   provision of costly infrastructure 336
   provision of public goods 337
   recovery of true resource cost of transport inputs 337
   regulation of harmful conduct and externalities 337
   restraint of monopoly power 337
   social support 337
gross margin 79–80

H
hanging rails 293, **293**
Harrington
   process involvement approach 71–72
Henri, Antoine, Baron of Jomini 5
   logistique 5
   Précis de l'art de la guerre 5
heuristics models 161–162
   centre of gravity method 161–162, **162**
Holt-Winter
   additive model 111, **111**, 138–140, **138**, **139**, **140**
   basic equations 141
   multiplicative model 111, **111**, **138**, 141–143, **142**, **143**
   seasonality 111, **111**, 138–143
   smoothing equations 138
Holt's method (double exponential smoothing) 111, **111**, 120–121, **120**, **121**, 121, 125, 128, **131**, **133**, 133

forecasting function 120
smoothing parameters 120
trend/growth factor 120

I
implementation 5, 7, **9**, 10
implementation stage of supply chain flow design 155–157
   commencement of new operation 156–157
   communication 155
   documentation 156
   drafting of agreements 156
   finalisation of sales and marketing plans 155
   inbound and outbound logistics channels 155
   infrastructure establishment and construction 155–156
   inventory policy 157
   potential deviation analyses 156
   pre-operation audit 156–157
   replenishment controls 157
   total supply chain operational cost estimates 156
in-transit care 331
   animation 331
   classes of dangerous goods **332**
   destructibility 331
   form 331
   fragility 331
   natural physical deterioration 331
   obsolescence 331
   perishability 331
   potential danger 331
   wetness 331
inbound logistics **6**, 11, **11**, **12**, 13, 80, **149**, 155
Incoterms 404–414, **404**, 415
Incoterms 2000 405, 406, **409**, 412, 413–414
   added wording 413
   appropriate content 413
   C terms (CFR, CIF, CIP, CPT) 406, **407**, **409**, 410–411, **418**
   customs of the port or trade 413
   D terms (DAF, DDP, DDU, DEQ, DES) 406, **408**, **409**, 411–412, **419**
   E term (EXW) 405, **405**, 406–407, 409, 413, **418**
   electronic data interchange (EDI) 413
   export and import customs clearance 413
   EXW and FCA 413
   F terms (FAS, FCA, FOB) 406, **406**, **407**–410, **409**, 413, 414, **419**
   inspection 413
   insurable interest 414
   packaging 414
   passing of risks and costs 414
   precise point of delivery 414
ineffectiveness 60
inefficiency 60
information flow **57**
information management challenges in reverse logistics 427–428

asset recovery and disposal management 427
business analytics and reporting 427
critical inventory/parts management 427
depot repair management 427
disposition management 427
liquidation management 427
recall management 427
regulatory compliance management 427
transport and logistics management 427
warranty and return management 427
information requirements (demand) 7
information technology 28
   electronic data interchange (EDI) 28, 69
   outdated 69
infrastructural decisions 170
   human resources 170
   new product development 170
   performance measurement 170
   planning and control 170
   quality 170
infrastructure 144, 145, 146, **146**, **149**, 151, 152, 153, 154, 155–156, 158, 159, 163,
initiatives and strategic actions 49–50, **50**
integer programming 7
integration 320
interdependencies with related supply chains 15, 158
   common elements 158
   economies of scale 158
International Air Transport Association (IATA) 270, 390
international business expansion drivers 40–41
International Chamber of Commerce (ICC) 404, 414
International Convention for the Safety of Life at Sea (SOLAS) 395
International Financial Reporting Standards (IFRS) 77
International Maritime Organization (IMO) 395, 404
International Ship and Prot Facility Security (ISPS) code 395
International Standards Organization (ISO) 178, 414
   benefits 432–433
   ISO 9000 179, 442, 444
   ISO 9001:2000 444
   ISO 14000 46, 179, 432, 435, 444
   ISO 14001:2004 432
   ISO 14004:204 432
international supply chain
   management 383–420
   customs departments 394
   data required 403–404
   distribution channels 383–386
   domestic logistics 383
   free trade agreements 396–397
   free trade zones (FTZs) 397
   international commercial terms (Incoterms) 404–414, **404**

INDEX | 465

(*see also* Incoterms)
international logistics 383
international trade 392–394
international trade
  documentation 398–403
international trade information
  agreements 397–398
security issues 394–396
transport of goods 386–392
international trade documentation
  398–403, 415
  bills of lading or loading (BOL)
    401–402
  commercial invoice 399, 400
  customs declaration 400
  dangerous good certificate (DGC)
    402–403
  dock receipt 387, 399, 403
  export declaration 399
  export documents 399
  financial documents 399, 400
  import documents 399, 400
  inspection documents 399
  insurance documents 400
  master's receipt 399, 403
  Material Safety Data Sheet
    (MSDS) 399
  packing list 400–401
  shipping letter of instruction (SLI) 399,
    400, 401
  transaction documents 399
  transport documents 399, 400
international trade information
  agreements 397–398
  country of origin 398
  Export Control Classification Number
    (ECCN) 398, 403, **420**
  Harmonized Schedule number
    397–398, 400, 403, **420**
  licences 398, **420**
  Tariff Code number 397–398
intramodal competition 344–347
inventory 182–184, **182**, 187
  anticipation 182
  average (*see* the main entry for
    average inventory)
  buffer/safety 182, 217, 219, 227–233
  classification based on position in
    supply chain 216
  classification based on purpose
    216–218
  costs 220–223
  cycle 182, 217, 219, 223–226
  dead 218
  finished goods 182, 216
  important concepts 218–220
  packaging material 216
  pipeline 182
  raw materials 182, 216
  speculative 218
  transit 217, 219
  turnover 220, 244
  work-in-process (WIP) 182, 216
inventory control 240–244
  ABC analysis (Pareto analysis)
    240–243
  (*see also* activity-based-costing (ABC))

  main objectives 240
  setting stock targets based on
    ABC 244
  stock balance 243, 246
  stock cover 243–244, **244**
  stock cover ratios 244
inventory costs 220–223
  carrying 220–223
  ordering 220, 245
  purchasing 245
  storage 221, **222**
inventory management 2, 7, 8, 10, 11, **12**,
  13, 14, 16, 28, 182–184, 213–249
  accurate forecasting 213
  customer service 183
  importance 213
  inventory costs 183
  operating costs 183
  purpose 183–184, 214–216
inventory modelling 7
inventory planning 223–240, 245
  collaborative initiatives 239–240
  distinction between dependent and
    independent demand 223
  reliable and accurate forecasts 223
inventory-carrying cost percentage
  222–223, **222**
  impact on financial records 222
  impact on logistics decisions and
    strategies 222–223
inventory-carrying costs 220–223
  annual percentage 245
  capital cost 221, **222**
  categorisation 220
  damage 221, **222**
  hurdle rate 221
  insurance 221, **222**
  obsolescence 221, **222**
  risk costs 221
  shrinkage 221, **222**
ISO containers 277–278
  collapsible 278
  dry cargo 278
  flat rack 278
  insulated 278
  ISO recommendations 277
  open top 278
  platform 278
  reefer 278
  ventilated 278

J
JSE Limited 202
Juran 178
just-in-time (JIT) 184–185, 204, 206, 210,
  237–239, 245, 326
  application possibilities 238
  benefits 239
  contrast between JIT and conventional
    systems 238, **238**
  general approach 237–238
  ideal environment 184
  identification of waste in production
    process 184–185
  key elements 184
  main features 238
  requirements 238

  scheduling 204
  typical features of the ideal company
    for JIT application 238

K
Kaizen 187
Kanban 184, 237, 314
kan cards (production cards) 237
Kaplan 38
key business considerations 52
key performance indicators (KPIs) **38**, **40**,
  44, 45, 46, 47, 49, **50**, 51, 73
Kyoto Protocol 433

L
lag indicators 49
  drivers 49
last in, first out (LIFO) 291
lead-time 58, 59, 66, **67**, 68–73, 230
  duration 217
  reduction **207**
  uncertainty 215, 217, 229–230
  variability 217, 245
lead time uncertainty 215, 217, 229–230
  equation when combined with demand
    uncertainty 230
  deviation **230**
  deviation squared **230**
  frequency **230**
  standard deviation **230**, 230
lean systems 185, 320–321
  5S 321
  continuous improvement 185
  eliminating waste 185
  key improvements 185
  team-based approach (involving
    everyone) 185
legislation and transport
  management 363–364, 369
  conditional permissions 364
  economic regulation 363
  qualitative 363
  social 363
  statutory control 363
  technical regulation 363
legislative considerations in
  packaging 275–276
  customs regulations 275
  environmental regulations regarding
    recycling 275
  food-contact laws 275
  hazardous waste and hazardous
    product laws 275
  local and international standards
    275
  paper bags 276
  special labelling laws 275
liability 333
  impact of liability on choice of
    transport 333
life-cycle assessment (LCA) 276, 428, **428**
  design 428, **428**
  distribute 428, **428**
  manufacture 428, **428**
  return/recycle 428, **428**
  service 428, **428**
  source 428, **428**

lighting 264, **264**
   amount of light 264
   chart of lighting intensity 264
   colour rendition of light 264
   comparison **264**
   replacement intervals 264
limiting factors on choice of products 88–90
   calculation of profit-maximising production mix 89–90
   contribution per limiting factor 88, 89
   contribution per unit 88, **88**, 89, 90
   fixed and variable costs 88, 89
   limiting-factor decisions 88–90
   ranking of products 89
   worked example 98–99
linear programming (LP) 7, 161
linear regression 111, **111**, 122–125
   dependent variable 122
   independent variable 122
   linear trend line 122, 123, **124**, 125, **126, 127**
   regression coefficients **123**
   regression function **125**
line-haul 365, 369, 370, 372, 373, 374, 375, 377
live storage or case flow racks 287, **287**
live storage or pallet flow racks 292, **293**
location decisions 159
   factors affecting 159, **159**
logistical decisions
   operational level 10, 11, **12**
   strategic level 10, 11, **12**
   tactical level 10, 11, **12**
logistical service programme 28
logistical supply capability 203
logistics
   and the environment 431–433
   approach 1
   business context 5–8
   definition 5
   drivers 41
   evolution of concept 5
   systems 1
logistics analysis 6–8
logistics communications 11, 14, 16
logistics costing 84
   financial reporting 84
   management accounting 84
logistics infrastructure 159
   country-specific 159
logistics management 2, 4, 8, **9**, 10, 11, **11, 12**, 12, 14, 15, 16, **24**, 104, 105, **438**
   control 10
   definition 19, 20
   environmental/green 423
   execution 10
   financial aspects 76–100
   planning and preparation 10
   objectives 10–11
   organisation and implementation 10
   role in creation of competitive advantage 29–30
logistics network **354**
logistics performance control 438–459
   control process influences 439, **439**
   planning and control cycle 439–440, **439**

   strategic and tactical control 440
   technical control 440
logistics performance measures 448–450
   asset utilisation 448
   average cost per order 448
   complete shipments 449
   customer complaints 450
   customer service 450
   delivery reliability 449
   demand not met 449
   fill rate 450
   inventory-carrying cost 449
   inventory control 449
   inventory turnover 449
   non-financial 448
   order picking time 449
   percentage defective 448
   percentage good parts 449
   percentage of demand met 448
   percentage of perfect shipments 450
   price reduction data 448
   procurement 448
   service reliability 450
   supplier selection 449
   total cycle time 448
   total transit time 450
   transit time variability 450
   transport 450
   warehouse throughput 449
   warehousing 449
logistics requirements planning (LRP) 233–237, **234**, 245
   definition and scope 233–234
   independent and dependent demand 234
   integration with distribution requirements planning (DRP) and material requirements planning (MRP) 233–234
   practical application 235–237, **235, 236, 237**
   process 234–235
logistics strategy 35, 36, 39, 40, 44, **48**, 49, 50, 51, 56
   development 39–48
   implementation 48–50
   map 47
   planning 34–55
long-term objectives 36
lower limit control (LLC) **180**, 181

M
maintenance, repairs and operating (MRO) supplies 208
make to order **64**, 65, **65, 67**, 73
   component and sub-assembly manufacturing point 65
   inventory forecasting 65
   major logistical challenge 65
   trigger 65
make to stock **64**, 64, **67**, 73
   finished goods store 64
   main challenge: demand forecasting 64
   main risk: inventory levels 64
Malcolm Baldrige National Quality Award 178

manufacturing 2, **2**, 6, 11, **12**, 14, 15
   operations 4, 8, 9, 13, 16
   schedules 12
margin of safety 91, 99
marginal costing (relevant costing) 86–90, 356, 357–358
   choice of products where a limiting factor exists 88–90
   direct-cost responsibility 358
   discontinuation of a department or product 87
   non-financial factors 90
   replacement of equipment 87–88
   special-order decisions 86–87
market share advantage 25
market value of shares 76
   drivers 79–82
   (*see also* value drivers)
   maximization 76
   worked example: valuation of shares using discounted cash-flow method 94
marketing 13, 271–272
   final cost 271
   image 271
   logistics 271
   place 271
   point-of-purchase (POP) packaging 272
   price 271
   primary packaging 272
   product 271
   promotion 271
   right place, right condition 271
marketing and sales strategy 40
Massachusetts Institute of Technology (MIT) 43
master agreements within an organisation 158
master production schedule (MPS) **57**, 58, **59**
   customer order volumes 58
   forecasts 58
   opening inventory 58
material requirements planning (MRP) **57**, 58, **59**, 107, 233, 234, **234**, 237, 245
   bill of materials (BOM) 58
   dependent demand 234
   inputs 58
   lead times 58, **59**
   outputs 58
materials handling 10, 11, **12**, 13, 16
materials management 11, **12**
   (*see also* inbound logistics)
mathematical optimization models 160–161
   facilities and functional operations 160
   linear programming (LP) methods 161
   materials/inventory management 161
   mixed integer programming (MIP) models 161
   total logistics costs (TLC) 161
   transport alternatives 161
maximum net profit 76
McGregor reports 202

INDEX | 467

measures of accuracy, qualitative 111
    mean absolute deviation (MAD) 111,
        114, 115, 118, 128, **130**, **131**,
        132, **133**
    mean absolute percentage error
        (MAPE) 111, **114**, 115, 118, 128,
        130, **131**, **132**, **133**
    mean square error (MSE) 111, **114**,
        115, 118, **119**, **120**, 122, **122**, 128,
        130, **131**, **132**, **133**, **135**, 140, **140**,
        142, 143, **143**
military logistics 5
mission (purpose) 36, 37, **37**, 38, 49, 42–43
mixed integer programming (MIP) 161
mobile racks 292, **292**, **293**
mobile shelving 288, **288**
mobility 330, 333, **334**, 334, 337
modelling approaches to network
    integration 159–162
    approximate methods 160
    heuristics 160, 161–162
    mathematical optimization 160–161
    simulation 160, 161
money flow **57**
monitoring and review 8, **9**, 10
movement zones 258, 261, 262
Multilateral Trading System 393, **393**

N
narrow-aisle racks 290–291, **291**, **293**
    man-up version 290
net profit 80
    firm infrastructure 80
    human-resource management 80
    inbound logistics 80
    marketing and sales 80
    operations 80
    outbound logistics 80
    primary and support activities 80
    procurement 80
    service 80
    technology development 80
network integration 144–166
    and supply chain design 145–147
    (see also supply chain design)
    focal business 144, **145**
    goal 147
    integration of suppliers and
        customers 144, **145**
    modelling approaches 159–162
    movement 144
    outsourcing 144
    storage 144
    supply chain (see supply chain
        integration)
    transformation 144
non-operating service providers 390–392
    airfreight forwarders 390–391
    freight handling 391
    guaranteed shipment time 391
    international ship freight
        forwarders 391
    non-vessel operating common carriers
        (NVOCCs) 391–392
    ship agents 392
    shipbrokers 392
Norton 38

O
Occupational Health and Safety Act 321
operating costs 79–80, 183, 187
    gross margin 79–80
    net profit 80
operation stage of supply chain flow
    design 157
    benchmarking 157
    customer-satisfaction surveys 157
    post-implementation evaluation 157
    supplier evaluation 157
operational performance 28, 29, 32
    accessibility/market coverage 28
    flexibility 28, 29
    goods security 28, 32
    reliability 28, 29, 31, 32
    suitability 28, 32
    transaction time 28, 29, 32
operational procurement management 197
    monitoring and control 197
    objectives 197
operational transport management 373–
    379
    coordinating incoming traffic 377–379
    routing and scheduling of collection
        and delivery trips 375–376
    routing and scheduling of long-distance
        trips 373–375
operational strategy 37
operations management 9, 11, 13, 16,
    167–192
    as transformation process 168–170,
        168
    current approaches and
        philosophies 184–188
    decision 167
    decision-making activity 167–168
    definition 167, **167**
    function 167
    in the service sector 188–189, **188**
    process 167
operations research 6–8
    competencies 7
    principles 7
    techniques 7
order lead time 58, 59, 66, **67**, 68–73
order processing 11, **12**, 14, 16
order quantity 217
organisational change 34
organisational context 40–41
organisational strategy 36–37, **36**
organisational structure 26
Organisation for Economic Co-operation
    and Development (OECD) 188
origin-to-destination movement (seamless
    transport) 372
outbound logistics 11, **11**, 12, 13, 80,
    149, 155
owner-drivers 31

P
packaging 11, **12**, 13, 14, 16, 267–284
    benefits 269
    definitions and functions 267–269, **267**
    distribution packaging 268
    economies of scale through long
        production runs 267

logistics 13, **267**
marketing 13, 271–272
multi-technology integration 281
physical form and nature of
    product 268
point-of-purchase (POP) packaging 272
primary packaging 268, **268**, 272
protection and preservation 268
role in communication 268
role in logistics 269–271, **271**
role in supply chain 267
secondary packaging 268, **268**
supply chain perspective 281–282
trade-offs 271, **271**
transport 270–271
unitisation 268
unit load 268, **268**
warehousing and materials
    handling 269–270
packaging, benefits 269
    consumer convenience 269
    containing of costs 269
    facilitation of distribution 269
    hygiene and safety 269
    information and instruction 269
    innovation 269
    preservation 269
    protection 269
    risk elimination 269
    silent salesperson 269
    waste minimisation 269
packaging design 272
    consumer requirements 272
    dimensions 272
    physical form and nature of
        product 272
    size and shape should optimise area
        utilisation 272
    susceptibility to damage 272
    systems approach 272
packaging materials 272–273
packaging solutions 272–276
    bulk-packaging systems 274–275
    cost trade-offs 275
    environmental concerns 276
    factors influencing package design 272
    legislative considerations 275–276
    materials 272–273
    palletisation (see pallets (skids))
Palgrave 8
pallets (skids) 273–274, 289–290, **289**
Pareto analysis 240–242
    80/20 principle (Pareto Principle) 240,
        241, 246
    ABC analysis using 240–242, **241**
Pareto, Villefredo 240
performance measurement 444–450, **444**
    achievement performance
        measures 446, **446**
    business performance 445
    competence performance
        measures 446, **446**
    diagnostic performance measures
        446, **446**
    financial performance measures 444,
        445, 446
    hard performance measures 445

hierarchy 447, **447**
logistics measures 448–450
non-financial performance
  measures 444, 445, 446
purposes 445
soft performance measures 445
validity of **446**
physical distribution management 11, **12**
  (*see also* outbound logistics)
physical products, quality 199–200
  aesthetics 199
  conformance 199
  durability 199
  features 199
  performance 199
  reliability 199
  serviceability 199–200
  total quality 200
pick area (order picking) 253, 257
  aisles 257
  handover zone 257
  pick face 253, 257, **285**, 292, **293**, **303**,
    312–313, **313**, 314, 316, 318, 319
  reach truck 257
  storage or reserve stock 257
pick/assemble and ship to stock **64**, 64,
  67, 73
  distribution centre 64
  main challenge: demand
    forecasting 64
  main risk: inventory levels 64
picking **285**
pipeline transport 328–329, 355–346,
  350–352
  external economies 346
  fixed costs 351
  freight characteristics 329
  high degree of concentration 345
  high degree of monopoly 345
  operational overview 328
  typical limitations 328
  typical strengths 328
  variable costs 351
place utility **323**, 323, 337, 358
'plan-do-review' cycle 49–50
planning and control of transformation
  process 176–177, **177**
  activity scheduling 177, **177**
  aggregate planning 177, **177**
  expediting 177, **177**
  master production schedule
    (MPS) 177, **177**
  resources 177
  strategic operations planning 177, **177**
planning and preparation 10
Plowman 5
post-transaction elements 26
  availability of spares 26
  call-out time 26
  customer complaints and claims 26
  product tracing/warranty 26
precision **181**
pre-transaction elements 26
  accessibility 26
  organisational structure 26
  system flexibility 26
  written customer service policy 26

Price 442
primary producer 21, **22**
principles of design 250, 259, 262–264
problem identification 7, 8, **9**
process 167
process involvement approach 71–72
  development and implementation
    of recommendations for
    reduction 72–73
  identification of opportunities for
    reduction and improvement 71, 72
  implementation of continuous
    improvement efforts 72, 73
  measure performance 72, 73
  time management team (TMT) 71, 72
  understanding of processes 71, 72
procurement 4, 8, 11, **12**, 13, 14, 16, **48**
  electronic 207–209
procurement, strategic role 195–196
  access to external markets 195
  finance entity 196
  five-step procurement process 195
  human-resources entity 196
  internal entities 195
  intra-firm management relations
    195–196
  manufacturing entity 196
  procurement entity 195, 196
  user entity 195
procurement cost management 205–206
  expenditure-reduction
    programmes 205
  forward buying 206
  price-change management 206
  speculative buying 205–206
  stockless purchasing 206
  volume contracts 206
procurement management 193–212
  coordination of incoming traffic
    205, 210
  objectives 193–194
  tiers 196–197
  total cost of ownership (TCO) 194
  strategic role within a business
    195–196
producer surplus 21
product **36**
  physical form and nature 267
product design 173–175
  concurrent engineering 174
  criteria 173
  objectives 173
  quality function deployment
    (QFD) 174–175
product differentiation 25
product process category (PPC) 251, **251**,
  252, 254, 262
product recovery and waste
  management 424–426
  cleaner processes 424, **425**
  disposal 424, **425**
  landfill **425**, 425
  recycling 424, **425**
  treatment 424, **425**
  waste hierarchy 424, **425**
product returns 421–437
  channel-cleaning policies 424

customer returns 423
distribution returns 423
downstream movement 423, 426, 431
manufacturing returns 423
path 424
process 428–431
unpredictability 429, 435
upstream movement 422, 423, 435
product supply chain 1, **12**
product supply chain processes 59–66
  pull-based 60–61, 62, 63
  push-based 59–60, 62, 63
  push-pull-based 61
product-development strategy 40
production 6
production and order lead time, causes of
  long 68–70
  ambiguous goals and objectives 68
  batching 68
  excessive controls 68
  lack of information 68
  lack of proper training 69
  lack of synchronization in materials
    movement 68–69
  limited cooperation 69
  limited coordination 69
  non-value-added activities 69
  outdated information technology 69
  poor communication 69
  poorly designed procedures and
    forms 69
  repeating process activities 69
  serial versus parallel operations 69–70
  waiting 70
production and order lead time,
  opportunities for reduction 70–73
  buying activity 70
  determination of limiting factors 71
  end of make activity 70
  Harrington 71–73
  logistics resources 70–71
  minimizing time for order fulfilment 70
  move activity 70
  process involvement approach 71–72
  real-time scheduling 70, **71**
  sell activity 70
  store activity 70
production cycle time 66, 68–73
production management 7, 9, 11, **12**, 12,
  167–192
productive capacity (supply) 7
progress-in-action plan 49
profit margin 82, 83, **83**
  calculation of net profit 83
  gross profit 83
  management of expenses 83
  net profit to sales ratio 83
profit planning and control 355–356
  operational 355–356
  strategic 355, 356
  tactical 355–356
project management **11**, 11, 16, **149**
proof-of-delivery (POD) documentation
  30, 156
property, plant and equipment 82
  cost of borrowing 82
  costs of financing assets 82

INDEX

efficient deployment and utilization 82
 generation of income 82
 partial outsourcing 82
pull portion of supply chain **63**
pull-based supply systems 60–61, 62, 63, **67**, 73, 237
 advantages over push-based system 60
purchase and make to order **64**, 65–66, **66**, **67**, 73
 bill of materials (BOM) 66
 job-shop process 65
 major challenge: inventory forecasting 65
 order lead time 66
 production cycle time 66
 raw material store 65
purchased products, variety 197–198
 business-to-business (B2B) goods 198
 finished goods – final 198
 finished goods – intermediate 198
 raw materials 198
 semi-finished goods (goods-in-process) 198
 services 198
push portion of supply chain **63**
push-based supply systems 59–60, 62, 63, **67**, 73, 237
push-pull-based supply systems 61, **67**, 73
 customer order decoupling point 61, **64**
 postponement (delayed differentiation) 61
 push-pull boundary 61
Pycraft 179

Q

qualitative forecasting models 106–107
 consumer market survey 107
 Delphi method 106
 jury of executive option 107
 sales force composite 107
quality management 9, 178–181
 accuracy **181**
 balancing the cost 179–180
 concepts and principles 178–179
 precision **181**
quality concepts and principles 178–179, 442–444
 assurance 178
 continuous improvement 178
 control 178
 cost-of-quality 178, **179**
 fit-to-use 178
 inspection 178
 total quality management (TQM) 178
quality management system (QMS) 178
quantitative forecasting models 106
 explanatory 106
 regression 106
 time series 106
queuing theory
 application of 7

R

rack comparison 292–293, **293**
radio frequency identification (RFID) 278, 280–281, 297, 318, 319
 active tags 280, 319
 antenna 280
 chipless 280
 closed-loop system 281
 GPS technology 281
 integrated circuit or microchip 280
 open-loop system 281
 passive tags 280, 319
 unique return signal 280
rail transport 270, 326–328, 345, 350
 administration and management overheads 350
 back hauls 345
 depreciation 350
 double-track operation 345
 fixed costs 350
 freight characteristics 327–328
 general costs 350
 high ratio of fixed cost to total cost 345
 maintenance 350
 marshalling costs 350
 operational overview 326–327
 possible damage due to acceleration/deceleration and during shunting operations 270
 running costs 350
 secure and stable packaging 270
 terminal costs 350
 track costs 350
 traction power cost 350
 traffic expenditure 350
 train operating costs 350
 typical limitations 327
 typical strengths 327
 variable costs 350
rate of change
 developments affecting 34
rational decision-making 7, 14, 16
raw materials 20, 23, 323, 327, 330, 331, 337
receiving 253, 256–257, 261, 262
 aisle area 257
 aisles 256
 design principle 257
 identification of quantity and quality of goods 256
 layout 256, **256**
 pallet area 257
 recording receipt of goods 256
regression-based models **111**
 causal/cross-sectional data **111**
 time series data **111**
reliability 26, 28, 29, 31, 32, 151, 153, 154, 155, 358, 367–368, **367**, **368**, 369
reorder point (ROP) 223–226, 235, 243, 245
responsiveness 31
return on investment (ROI) 82–84, **83**, 446
 asset turnover 82, 83–84
 assets to equity ratio 82
 equation 82
 profit margin 82, 83, **83**
 return on assets 82
 worked example 94–95
returns management 421, 422–426, **422**
 activities covered 422–423
 avoidance 422, 434
 disposition 422, 434–435
 gatekeeping 422, 434
 waste management 422
revenue 79, 90, 91. 92
 customer retention 79
 sales volume 79
reverse logistics 11, **11**, **12**, 15, 16, 45–46, 421–437, **422**
 impacts 426–428
 return goods handling 15
 stages 429–431
 waste disposal 15
risk-management strategies 36, 46
road transport 2, 270, 325–326, 344–345, 348–359
 balanced, stackable distribution packaging 270
 bedding and strapping 270
 crew costs 349
 depreciation 348
 effective consolidation of consignments 345
 fixed costs 344, 348
 freight characteristics 326
 fuel and engine oil consumption 349
 infrastructure 344–345
 insurance 349
 interest on capital (opportunity lost) 348
 licences 348
 maintenance 348
 operational overview 325–326
 overhead costs 348
 possible damage to goods due to vibration and weather conditions 270
 standing costs 348
 terminal facilities 344
 trip-specific operating costs 349
 typical limitations 326
 typical strengths 326
 tyre usage 348
 variable costs 349
Rolstadås 445
route planning 7
routing and scheduling 373–379, 380
 adaptation of vehicle to traffic 374, 380
 avoidance of narrow time windows at service points 376, 380
 avoidance of single service points away from a cluster 376, 380
 clustering of service points 375–376, **375**, 380
 collecting and delivering in same trip 376, 380
 compatible unit load equipment 374, 380
 construction of routes 376, **376**, 380
 continuous flow 373, 380
 long-haul freight consolidation 374–375, 380
 maximum mass-carrying capacity 374, 380
 maximum unit size 373, 380
 maximum utilisation of inputs 375, 380
 maximum vehicle size 373–374, 376, 380

minimizing travelling distance of
heaviest loads 376, 380
standardisation 374, 380
Ruppenthal 6

S

SAFE Framework of Standards 395
safety/buffer stock 182, 217, 219,
227–233, **227**, **231**
   normal distribution theory 227, **227**
   probability theory 227
   standard deviation 227
sales and operations planning process
(S&OP) 47, 156
scheduling 7, 9, 10, 12, 14
Schroeder 167–168
sea transport 270, 329–330, 346–347,
352, 387–389
   basic commercial practice 387–388
   bulk cargo 346
   bulk carriers 329
   bulk shipping 346
   charter agreements 346
   common-carrier obligations 346
   competition, types of 346
   containerisation 270
   container ships 329, 388–389
   fixed costs 352
   fluid supply-and-demand situation 347
   freight characteristics 330
   general cargo 346
   letter of indemnity (LOI) 388
   lighter-aboard ships (LASH) 389
   liner ships 388–369
   liner shipping conference 346, **346**
   oil-bulk-ore (OBO) vessels 329
   operational overview 329
   overhead costs 352
   packages exposed to damp
conditions 270
   packages exposed to erratic movement
patterns 270
   private ships 389
   roll-on/roll-off (Ro-Ro) ships 329, 389
   ship registry 389
   ship's manifest 388, 395
   standing costs 352
   tankers 329
   tramp ships 346, 389
   typical limitations 329
   typical strengths 329
   variable costs 352
   wharfinger 387
seasonality 108, **111**, 125–128, **126**, **127**,
132, **133**, 214–215
   calculations 125
   natural factors 122
   other factors 122
Secure Export Scheme (SES) (New
Zealand) 396
Secure Trade Partnership (STP)
(Singapore) 396
security 263
   alarms (passive) 263
   fencing 263
   guards (physical) 263
   perimeter beams 263

   video cameras (hidden areas) 263
security issues in international supply chain
management 394–396
   terrorism 394
semi-finished goods 20, 323, 325, 327,
331, 337
service delivery 6
service effectiveness 22, 24
   importance of 27
service level 73
   policy 217
service level agreement (SLA) 153
service performance control 27–29
service quality 29, 200
   attributes 29
   benefits of 29
   key to superior 29
shareholder value 76–77, 79, 84
   cost of equity 76
   earnings per share 77
shelving 286, **286**
short-term objectives 36
simulation models 161
   deterministic 161
   stochastic 161
site selection 12–13
   costs involved 13
six sigma 320, 442
   DMAIC: define, measure, analyse,
implement, control 320
smart containers 278
   cellular communication 278
   detection of breaches 278
   determination of location 278
   radio frequency identification
(RFID) 278
   satellite communication 278
Southern African Development Corporation
(SADC) 392
special-order decisions 86–87
   worked example 96–97
stages in reverse logistics process
429–431
   receipt 429
   returns analysis 430
   returns processing 429–430
   sort and stage 429
   support operations 430
StairSec programme (Sweden) 396
static storage racks 290, **290**
stationary time series data 108, **111**,
112–119
   exponential smoothing 116–120
   naïve 112–113, **112**, **113**, **130**
   simple moving average 113–116,
114, **115**
statistical process control (SPC) 180–181
stock turnover 243–244
stock-keeping unit (SKU) 41, 224, 234, 246,
420, 429
stockout 215–216, 227, 228, 230, 231,
232, 233, 245
stockout prevention through inventory
control 215–216
   cost of backorders 215
   cost of lost customers 215
   cost of lost sales 215

   optimum inventory planning 216
   unavailability 215
storage 253, 254–256, 261, 262
storage cabinets 289, **289**
strategic focus areas 38, 39, **40**, 44–45,
47, **48**, 49, **50**, 51, 52
   information management 45, **48**
   inventory optimization 45, **48**
   network integration 45, **48**
   operational efficiency and
effectiveness 45, **48**
   organisational and people
capability 45, 47, **48**
   procurement management 45, 46–47,
48
   relationship management 45, 47, **48**
   reverse logistics 45–46
   risk management 45, 46, **48**
   strategy map 47–48, **48**
   supply chain planning 45, 47, **48**
strategic management 35–36
   definition 35
   key aspects and issues 36
   strategy evaluation 36
   strategy formulation 36
   strategy implementation 36
strategic objectives 43–44
strategic plan 34
   reasons for failure 49
strategic planning 37
   evaluation 37, 38
   execution 38
   formulation 37
   implementation 37, 38
strategic procurement management
196–197
   long-term planning 196
   objectives 196–197
   operational level 196
   tactical level 196
strategic response 34
strategic review 39, **40**
strategic transport management 362,
363–368
   direct supply 364, 369
   fiscal measures 364, 369
   legislation 363–364, 379
   monetary measures 364, 369
   moral appeal and persuasion 364, 369
   policies relating to strategic
commodities 364, 369
   procurement policy 364, 369
   provision of information 364, 369
   research and development 364–365,
369
   selecting transport services 365–368
strategy, definition 35, **35**
strategy and operations 170
strategy and performance objectives
170–171
strategy map 38, **38**, 39, 47, 48, **48**, 49
strategy-formulation process 37–39, **37**
structural decisions 170
supplier relationships 204
supplier selection
   choice 201, 203–204
   corporate standing 201, 202–203

dual (horizontally split) sourcing 203
  investigation and assessment 200, 201–203
  logistical supply capability 203
  specific production capability 201, 202
  survey 200–201
  vertically split sourcing 203
supply 36
  uncertainties 42, **42**
supply chain **21**, 21, 22, **22**, 24, **24**, 29, 30, 32, 35, **42**
  drivers 41
  focus 35
  foresight report 4
  identification of 41
  identification of correct approach 61–63
  implementation 63
  macro-factors 43
  management 4, 5, 8, 9, 10, 11, **12**, 12, 16, 19, **24**, 25
  network integration 45
  objectives 44
  planning 45, 47
  point of consumption 19
  point of origin 19
  response to customer demands **67**
  reverse system 10
  security 394–396
  supply-oriented 21
  time management 66–73
  vision and purpose 42
supply chain configuration 147–148, **148**, 175
  discrete-event simulation modelling tools 148–149
  establishment of operating rules (policies) 149
  evaluation of supply chain alternatives 148
  network operation 147
  network optimization 147, 148, **148**
  network optimization models 147
  policy formulations and optimization 147
  risk assessment and contingency planning 149
  robustness (preparedness for risk) 147
Supply Chain Council 169, 453
supply chain design 145–147
  applicable sources of supply 147
  attributes determining complexity 146
  business changes 144, **146**
  capacity utilisation 146
  configuration and functional requirements 147–148
  cost-benefit trade-off analysis 146
  design and redesign cycle 145, **146**
  facility location 147
  facility planning 147
  factors to take into account 157–159
  inventory turnover 146
  key determinants 146
  network integration 145–147
  stages in design and implementation 149–157, **149**

strategic planning issues 147
supply changes 144, **146**
throughput 146
transport 147
supply chain design and implementation 149–157, **149**
  assessment stage 149–152, **149**
  design stages **149**, 152–155
  implementation stage **149**, 155–157
  operation stage **149**, 157
supply chain drivers 41, 42
  asset optimization 41
  availability 41
  flexibility 41
  lowest delivery cost 41
  reliability 41
  responsiveness 41
supply chain integration 56–75, 144–166, **145**, **146**, **149**, **151**
  infrastructure 144
  overall capacity levels 144
supply chain management 76–100
  financial aspects 76–100
  goal 149
supply chain requirements, forecasting of 104–143
  buyer's perspective: decision-making 104
  logistics management forecasts 104, 105
  manufacturing schedules 104
  operations-generated forecasts 104
  seller's perspective: forecasting 104
supply chain strategy 34, 35, 36, **36**, 37, 39, **40**, 40, 41, 42, **42**, 43, 45, 47, 48, **48**, 49, 50, 51, 52, 53
  design 35, 42
  development 39–48, **40**
  elements 40–48, **40**
  implementation **40**, 48–50
  long-term 39
  map 47
  planning 34–55
  steps involved 39
supply effectiveness **24**
supply efficiency **24**
supply-chain operations reference model (SCOR) 45, 169–170, **169**, 444, 453–455
  delivery 169, **169**, 454, **455**
  GreenSCOR 453
  making 169, **169**, 454, **455**
  planning 169, **169**, 454, **455**
  relevant performance attributes 454
  return 169, **169**, 454, **455**
  sourcing 169, **169**, 454, **455**
  Version 9.0 453
supply/push strategy 53
surplus-oriented capitalist economies 21
SWOT analysis **40**, **43**, 43, **44**, 203
systems analysis 5, 7, 8, **9**, 11
  principles 7
  process 7–8
system selection 7, **9**
systems modelling 7, **9**

T
tactical logistics management 56–75
  activities 56–57
  aim 56
  objectives 57, 73
tactical procurement management 197
  objectives 197
tactical transport management 368–373
  consignments 368–369
  consolidation of through-movements 369, **370**
  containers 371–372, **371**, **372**
  increase vehicle utilisation 371
  intermodal transport 372–373
  reducing trip frequency 369–370
  segregation 371
  traffic pooling and distribution 369, **370**
  unit loads 371, **371**
target stock level (TSL) system 226, 245
tax 80
  after-tax payment 80
  fuel 80
  government 80
  on dividends declared 80
  on profits 80
  property 80
  value-added 80
technical control systems 440–442, **441**
terminals 330, **330**
theory of constraints (TOC) 185–187
  bottlenecks 186, 187
  critical-chain concept 186
  drum-buffer-rope concept 186, **186**
  Five Focusing Steps 186
  inventory 187
  operating expenses 187
  throughput 187
throughput 146, 152, 153, 187
time management in supply chains 66–73
  cycle time 68
  importance 66–68
  manufacturing quality 68
time series data 106, 108, 109, **110**, **111**, 111, 112–119, 120–125, 128, 134
  alpha values **117**, 118, **118**, 119, **119**, **120**, **122**, **123**, **131**, **139**, **140**, **142**, **143**
  beta values **120**, **122**, **123**, **131**, **139**, **140**, **142**, **143**
  cycles 108
  gamma values **139**, **140**, **142**, **143**
  level/horizontal/stationary 108, **111**
  linear/non-linear **111**, 122–125
  (see also linear regression)
  random variation 109
  seasonality 108, **111**, 125–128
  trend/non-stationary 108, **111**, 120–125
time series models 109
time utility 323, **323**, 337, 358
total-cost concept 11, 20, 351, 352, **353**, **354**, 357, 358
total cost of ownership (TCO) 46
total cost pricing 356, 357, 358
total logistics costs (TLC) 161

total quality management (TQM) 178, 180, **180**, 187–188, 442–444, **442**
   problem-solving discipline (PSD) 443–444, **443**, 445
   quality principle 443
   SMART goals 443
transaction elements 26
transformation process 168–170, **168**
   design 175–176
   inputs and outputs 168, **168**
   planning and control 176–177
   supply-chain operations reference (SCOR) model 169–170, **169**
   transformed resources 168, **168**
   transforming resources 168, **168**
transformation process design 175–176
   batch processes 176
   continuous-flow processes 176
   customer involvement 175
   flexibility 175
   job shop processes 175
   repetitive processes 176
   supply chain configuration 175
   technology 175
transit time 367, **367**, 368, **368**, 371, 373, 379
   total time lapse 367
transport **3**, 9, 10, 11, **12**, 13, 14, 16, 261, 262, 270–271
   air 270
   costs **347**
   hazards and constraints 270
   ocean 270
   rail 270
   regulation of 2
   road 2, 270
   transportation and handling cycle 270
   transhipment 2
transport cost structures and pricing principles 341–361
transport management 362–382, 427
   holistic 362
   operational 362
   strategic 362
   tactical 362
transport risk assessment (TRA) 156
transport services 365–368
   carrier selection 365, 368
   efficiency considerations 365
   effectiveness considerations 365–368
transport system 323–340
   freight transport 323
   freight transport service providers 333–335
   freight transport user 335
   goods carried 331–333
   government as stakeholder 336–337
   terminals 330
transportation modelling 7
trend-based time series data 120–125
   Holt's method 120–122
Treaty of Rome 6
trolleys **293**, 294
twenty-foot equivalent units (TEU) 277

U
uncertainty 215
   buffering through inventory control 215
   in supply 215
   lead-time 215
   of future demand 215
unit load device (ULD) 270, 278–279, **279**, 391
   better utilisation of volumetric carrying capacity 279
   enables faster offloading 279
   house airway bill (HAWB) 279
   master airway bill (MAWB) 279
   reduces handling of cargo 279
upper limit control (ULC) **180**, 181
utility 22–23, **23**

V
value advantage **24**
value analysis 204–205, 210
   'ten tests for value' 205
value chain 8, **9**, **12**, **21**, 21, 22, **22**, 32, 37
   demand-oriented 21
   logistics linked with 19
value creation 21–22
value drivers 79–82
   operating costs 79–80
   property, plant and equipment 82
   revenue 79
   tax 80
   working capital 80–82
value-of-service pricing 357, 358
   effectiveness pricing 358
   level of utility 358
   place and time utility 358
   reliability 358
vision 34, 36, 37, **37**, 39, **40**, 42, 44, 47, **48**, **51**, 51

W
warehouse management 11, 13, 16
warehouse management systems (WMS) 253, 256, 257, 261, **303**, 305, 310, 311, 312, 314, 316, 318, 319, 320, 321, 427
   picking capability 253
   receiving of goods 253
   stock management 302, **303**, 304
   use and control of equipment 253
warehouse operations 302–322
   drivers 320
   efficiency principles 308–309
   errors 304
   managing continuous change 319–320
   safety 321
   types of warehouses and facilities 305
warehouse processes 302–304, **303**, 309–316
   barcoding and scanning 317–319
   bond storage 302
   delivery **303**, 309, 315
   dispatching 302, **303**, 305, 309, 315
   delivery transport operations **303**, 317

   identification of loads **303**, 309–310
   inbound transport arrival **303**, 309–310
   order processing **303**, 309, 313–314
   pick-face replenishment and letdown **303**, 309, 312, **312**, **313**
   POD and billing **303**, 309, 315
   receiving 302, **303**, 305
   receiving bay **303**, 309, 310–311, **311**
   return of unwanted goods **303**, 309, 315–316
   stock count **303**, 309, 316
   stock picking **303**, 309, 312–313, **313**
   stock purchasing **303**, 309
   storing 302
   transfer of stock into storage **303**, 309, 311–312
   write-off stock **303**, 309, 316
warehouse sizing 252–253
   access to roads and other areas 252
   cost-effectiveness in supply chain 252
   factors affecting size 252
   possibility of growth 252
   transport area 252
warehouses and facilities 305
   cross-docks 305
   distribution centre (DC) 305, 306, 307, 320
   terminals 305
warehousing and materials management 269–270
   decisions to be coordinated with warehousing and materials handling 270
   packaging impact on stacking height of products 269
   packaging impact on utilisation of space and costs 269
   protective packaging during storage 269
   size of package affects type of storage 270
   size of package affects type of materials-handling equipment used 270
wealth, long-term 19, 32
wealth creation 30–31
weighted-factor rating method 160, **160**
Wild 238
work-in-process (WIP) 182
working capital 80–82
   accounts receivable/payable 81–82
   cash 81
   cash-flow cycle 81, **81**
   inventories 82
   profitability 82
   shortening the working-capital cash-flow cycle 81, **81**
World Customs Organization (WCO) 395, 396, 397
World Trade Organization (WTO) 392, 393, 394, 396, 397
   benefits of trading agreements 393–394
   protectionism 394